EAST ESSEX
STREET ATLAS

Ordnance Survey

EAST ESSEX
STREET ATLAS

▶ 3½ INCHES TO 1 MILE ◀

EAST ESSEX STREET ATLAS

First Edition published 1990 by

Ordnance Survey   and   George Philip Ltd
Romsey Road   59 Grosvenor Street
Maybush   London W1X 9DA
Southampton SO9 4DH

ISBN 0 319 00217 9 (Ordnance Survey)
ISBN 0 540 05590 5 (George Philip)

To the best of the Publishers' knowledge, the information in this atlas was correct at
the time of going to press. No responsibility can be accepted for any errors or their
consequences.

The representation in this atlas of a road, track or path is no evidence of the existence of
a right of way.

Printed in Great Britain by
Butler & Tanner Ltd, Frome and London

Contents

Key map   vi-vii

Administrative map   viii

Street maps   1-203

Index explanation and abbreviations   204

List of towns, villages and rural localities   205

Index   206

key to map symbols

≷ British Rail Station

⊖ London Transport Station

🚂 Private Railway Station

🚌 Bus or Coach Station

◆ Police Station
(may not be open 24hrs)

✚ Hospital with Casualty Facilities
(may not be open 24hrs)

☐ Post Office

✛ Place of Worship

■ Important Building

P Parking

⌐120⌐ Adjoining page indicator

═══ Motorway and Dual Carriageway

─── Main or through road

A 27(T) Road numbers (Dept of Transport)

┤ Gate and obstruction to traffic
(restrictions may not apply at all times and to all vehicles)

- - - - Footpath   The representation in this atlas of a road,
track or path is no evidence of the existence
— — Bridleway   of a right of way.

Amb Sta   Ambulance Station

Coll   College

FB   Foot Bridge

F Sta   Fire Station

LC   Level Crossing

Liby   Library

Mus   Museum

Sch   School

TH   Town Hall

The large letters and numbers around the edge of the maps are the referencing system.
An explanation of how to use the system for locating the position of street names appears on page 206

The small numbers identify the 1 kilometre National Grid lines.

```
0          ¼          ½          ¾        1 Mile
|----------|----------|----------|----------|
0     250m      500m      750m    1 Kilometre
```

Scale of Maps is 3½ inches to 1 mile (1:18103)

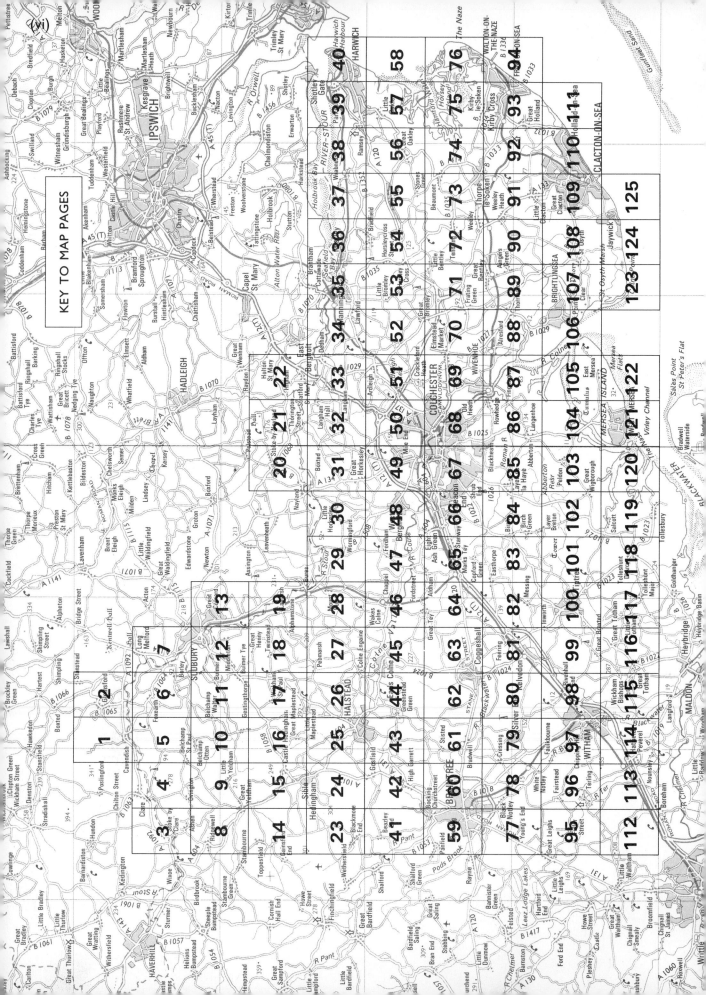

KEY TO MAP PAGES

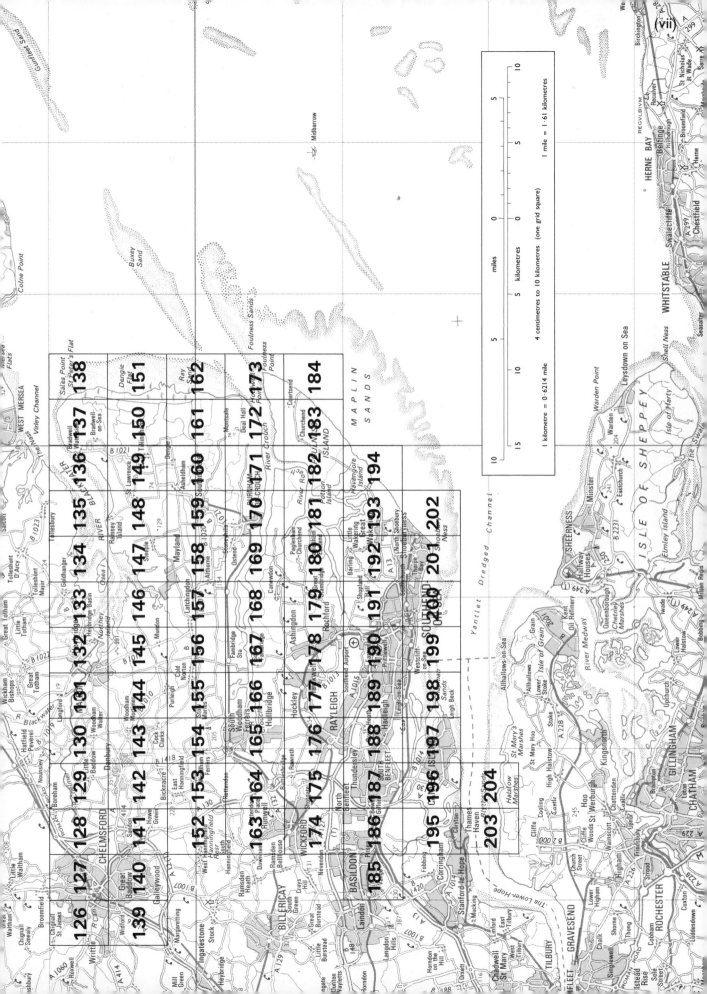

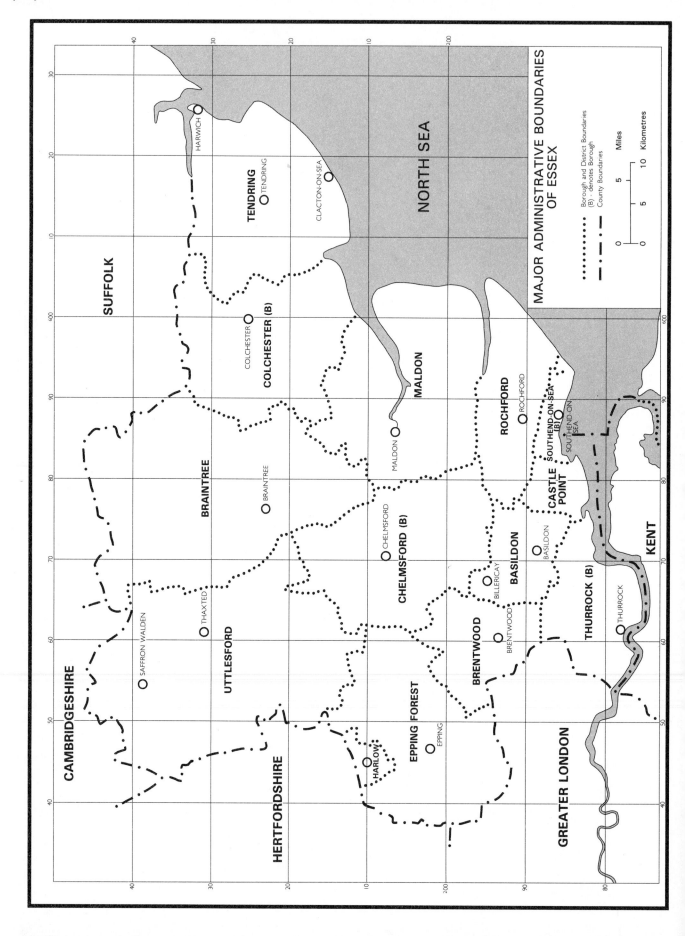

MAJOR ADMINISTRATIVE BOUNDARIES OF ESSEX

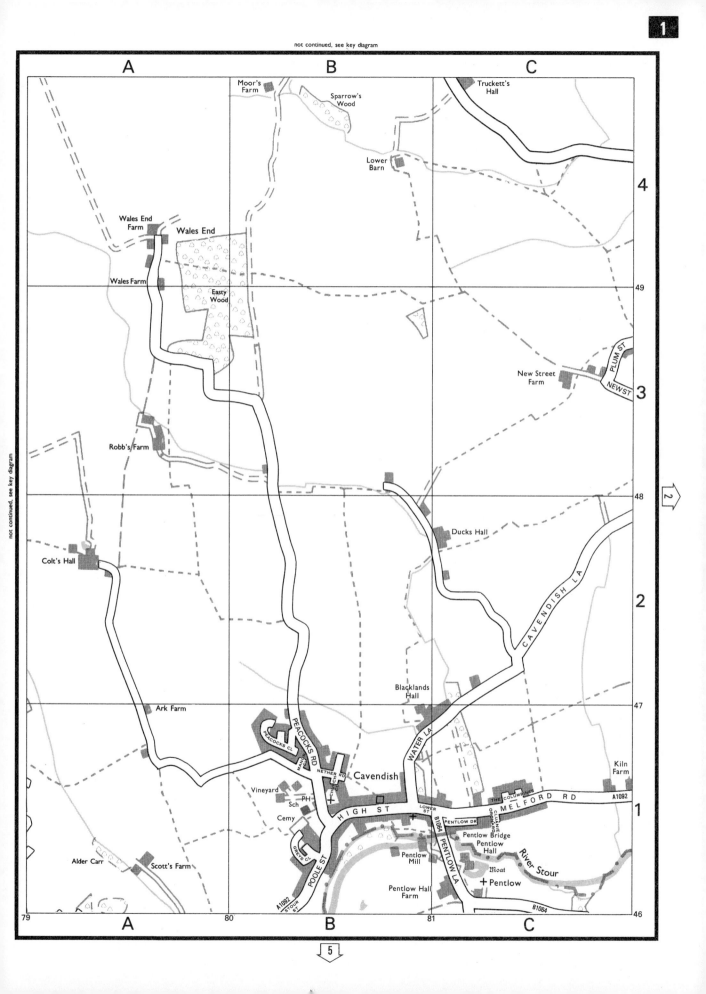

Moor's
Farm

Sparrow's
Wood

Truckett's
Hall

Lower
Barn

4

Wales End
Farm

Wales End

Wales Farm

Easty
Wood

49

PLUM ST

New Street
Farm

NEW ST

3

Robb's Farm

48

Ducks Hall

Colt's Hall

2

CAVENDISH LA

Blacklands
Hall

Ark Farm

47

Kiln
Farm

PEACOCKS CL

PEACOCKS RD

NETHER RD

Cavendish

WATER LA

THE COLUMBINES

MELFORD RD

A1092

Vineyard

Sch

PH

CHURCH CL

HIGH ST

LOWER
ST

Pentlow DR

1

Cemy

B1064

LANE ORCHARD

Pentlow Bridge

Pentlow
Hall

Alder Carr

GREYS CL

POOLE ST

Pentlow
Mill

PENTLOW LA

Pentlow Hall
Farm

Moat

Pentlow

River Stour

Scott's Farm

A1092

STOUR ST

B1064

79

80

81

46

2

5

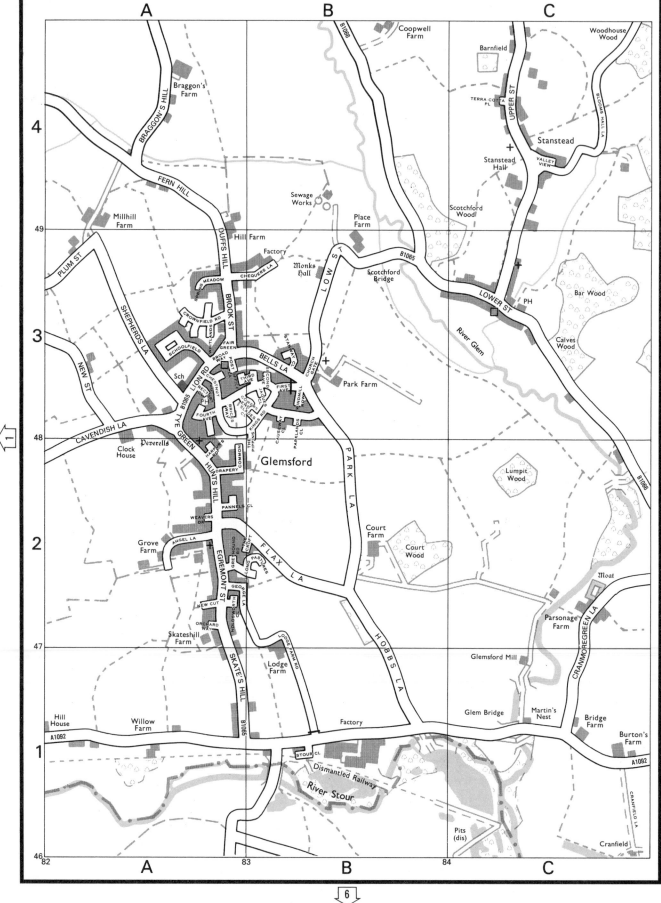

A B C

4

49

3

48

2

47

1

46

82 A 83 B 84 C

Coopwell Farm

Barnfield

Woodhouse Wood

TERRA COTTA PL

UPPER ST

Stanstead

BLOOMS HALL LA

B1066

Stanstead Hall

VALLEY VIEW

Scotchford Wood

Bar Wood

B1065

LOWER ST

PH

Braggon's Farm

BRAGGON'S HILL

FERN HILL

DUFFS HILL

Sewage Works

Place Farm

Scotchford Bridge

River Glem

Calves Wood

Millhill Farm

PLUM ST

Hill Farm

Factory

CHEQUERS LA

Monks Hall

LOW ST

SHEPHERDS LA

SPRING MEADOW

BROOK ST

CROWNFIELD RD

WHITEHANDS RD

FAIR GREEN

BROAD WAY

BELLS LA

ST ANNA'S CL

CHURCH GATE

Park Farm

NEW ST

Sch

SCHOOLFIELD

LION RD

THIRD AVE

CHESTNUT CL

SECOND AVE

FIRST AVE

WINDMILL ROW

B1065

RECTORY RD

PH

CROSS

FOURTH AVE

BRIGG'S WAY

KINGS RD

CAUSEWAY CL

PARKLANDS CL

TYE GREEN

CAVENDISH LA

Peverells

HARPER'S

THE PIPPINS

Glemsford

PARK LA

Lumpit Wood

B1066

Clock House

HUNTS HILL

DRAPERY

COMMON

PANNELS CL

WEAVERS DR

Court Farm

Court Wood

Grove Farm

ANGEL LA

EGREMONT ST

GREENWOOD

LONG CROFT

PASTURES

FLAX LA

Moat

GEORGE LA

H JACKSON RD

Parsonage Farm

CRANMOREGREEN LA

New Cut

ORCHARD WAY

Skateshill Farm

SKATE'S HILL

B1065

LODGE FARM RD

Lodge Farm

HOBBS LA

Glemsford Mill

Hill House

Willow Farm

Factory

Glem Bridge

Martin's Nest

Bridge Farm

Burton's Farm

A1092

STOUR CL

Dismantled Railway

River Stour

A1092

Pits (dis)

CRANFIELD LA

Cranfield

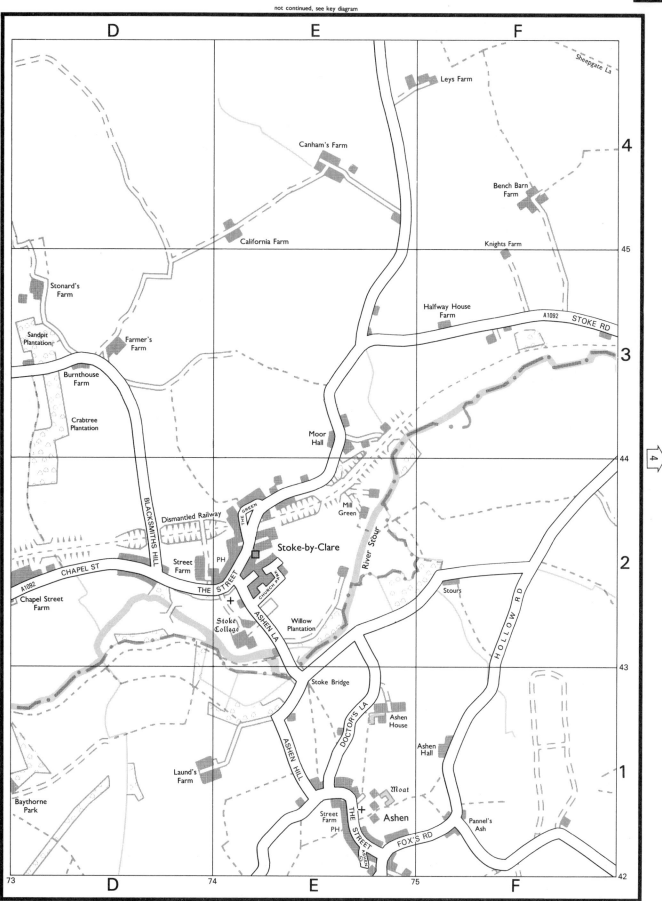

D   E   F

Sheepgate La

Leys Farm

Canham's Farm

4

Bench Barn
Farm

California Farm

Knights Farm

45

Stonard's
Farm

Halfway House
Farm

A1092   STOKE RD

Sandpit
Plantation

Farmer's
Farm

3

Burnthouse
Farm

Crabtree
Plantation

Moor
Hall

44   4

BLACKSMITHS HILL

Dismantled Railway

THE GREEN

Mill
Green

River Stour

Stoke-by-Clare

2

Street
Farm

PH

CHAPEL ST

A1092

CHURCH PATH

THE STREET

ASHEN LA

Stours

HOLLOW RD

Chapel Street
Farm

Stoke
College

Willow
Plantation

43

Stoke Bridge

DOCTOR'S LA

Baythorne
Park

Laund's
Farm

ASHEN HILL

Ashen
House

Ashen
Hall

1

Moat

Street
Farm

THE STREET

Ashen

Pannel's
Ash

PH

ASHEN

FOX'S RD

73   D   74   E   75   F   42

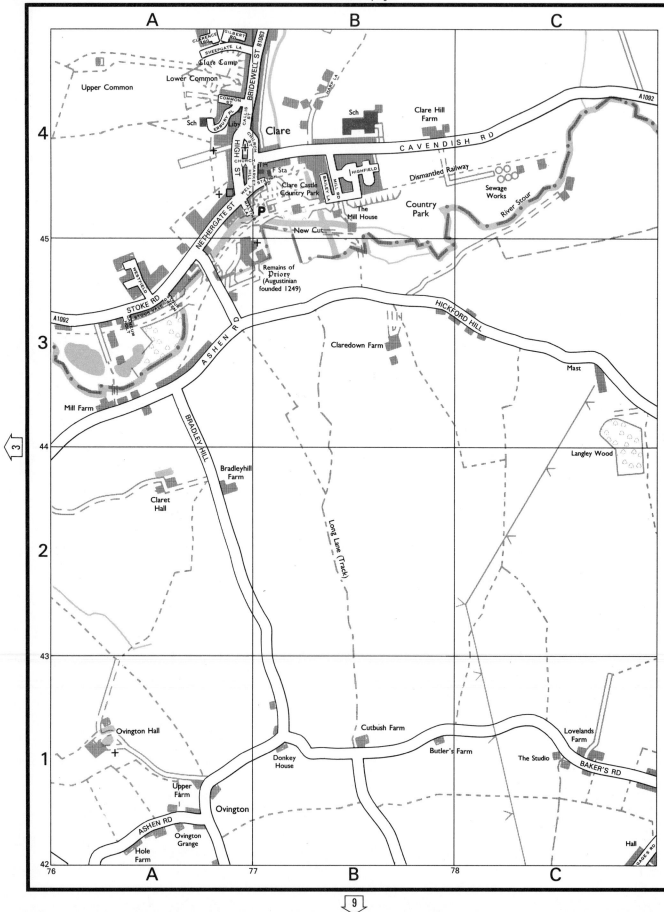

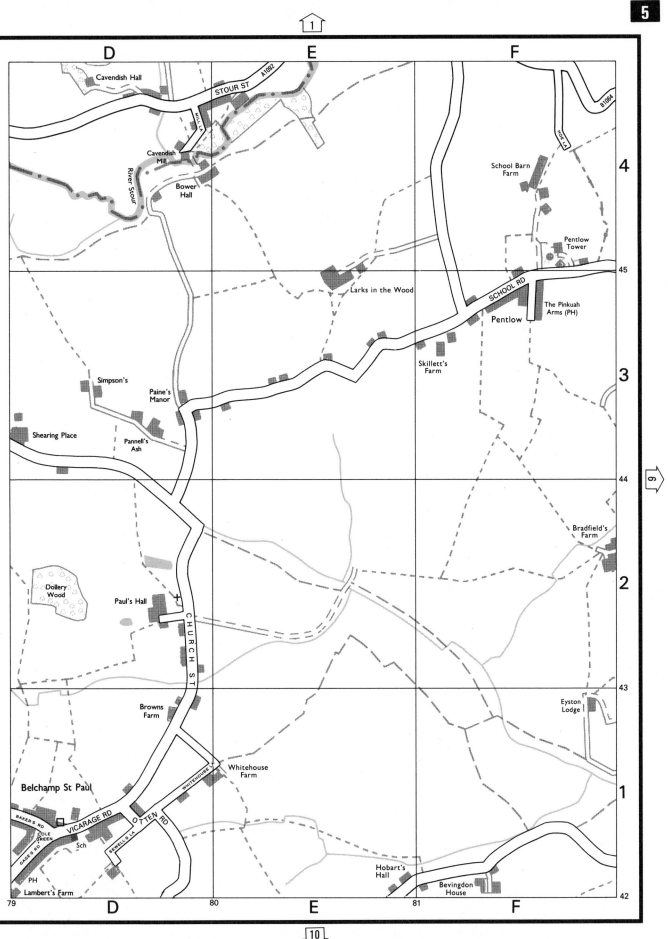

D
E
F

Cavendish Hall

STOUR ST
A1092

MILL LA

Cavendish Mill

River Stour

Bower Hall

B1064

HOE LA

School Barn Farm

Pentlow Tower

4

45

SCHOOL RD

Larks in the Wood

Pentlow

The Pinkuah Arms (PH)

Skillett's Farm

3

Simpson's

Paine's Manor

Shearing Place

Pannell's Ash

Bradfield's Farm

44

2

Dollery Wood

Paul's Hall

CHURCH ST

Eyston Lodge

43

Browns Farm

Whitehouse Farm

WHITEHOUSE LA

Belchamp St Paul

1

BAKER'S RD

COLE GREEN

VICARAGE RD

OTTEN RD

SEWELL'S LA

GAGE'S RD

Sch

PH

Lambert's Farm

Hobart's Hall

Bevingdon House

42

79
D
80
E
81
F

6

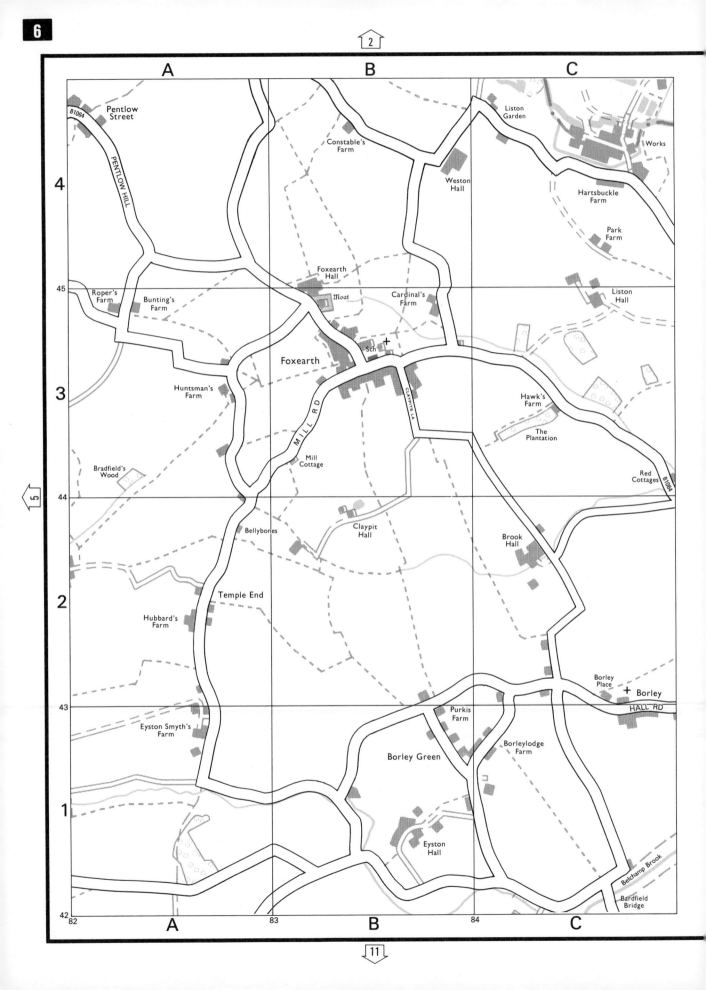

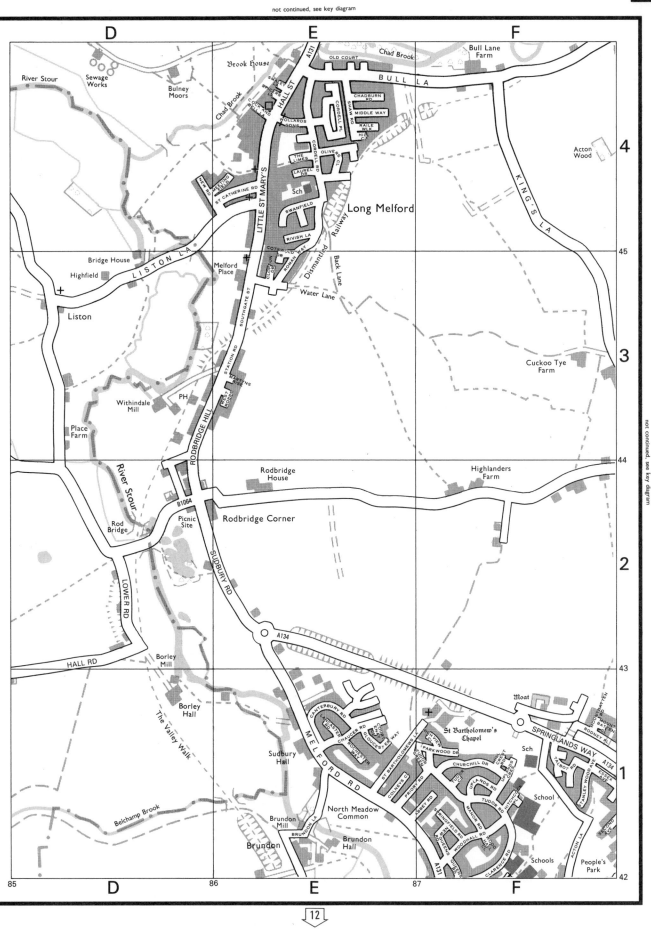

D   E   F

River Stour

Sewage Works

Bulney Moors

Brook House

OLD COURT

Chad Brook

BULL LA

Bull Lane Farm

CHADBURN RD

MIDDLE WAY

Acton Wood

4

Chad Brook

HALL ST

CORDELL PL

SHAW RD

RAILE WLK

HILL CLT

WOLLARDS GDNS

THE LIMES

OLIVER'S CL

Long Melford

KING'S LA

CORDELL RD

LAUREL DR

Sch

LITTLE ST MARY'S

SWANFIELD

NEW RD

ST CATHERINE RD

MEETING FIELD

Bridge House

Highfield

LISTON LA

Melford Place

RIVISH LA

COTSWOLD WAY

ROMAN WAY

CLOPTON RD

45

Liston

Water Lane

Back Lane

Dismantled Railway

3

Cuckoo Tye Farm

RODBRIDGE HILL

STATION RD

SOUTHGATE ST

MARTENS

WELLS RD

Withindale Mill

PH

Place Farm

44

River Stour

Rodbridge House

Highlanders Farm

B1064

Rod Bridge

Picnic Site

Rodbridge Corner

2

LOWER RD

SUDBURY RD

A134

HALL RD

Borley Mill

Borley Hall

Moat

SPRINGLANDS WAY

MOUNT BATTEN

MOUNT

RODNEY PL

43

The Valley Walk

MELFORD RD

CANTERBURY RD

LANCASTER RD

CHAUCER RD

GLOUCESTER WAY

ROWLEY

St Bartholomew's Chapel

HIGH VIEW

PARKWOOD DR

CHURCHILL DR

Sch

TALBOT RD

STANLEY WOOD AVE

ESSEX AVE

A134

1

Sudbury Hall

ST BARTHOLOMEW'S LA

COLNE'S CL

PRIORY RD

UPLANDS RD

TUDOR RD

School

Belchamp Brook

Brundon Mill

North Meadow Common

ABBEY RD

SPRINGFIELD RD

MANOR RD

WOODHALL RD

Schools

People's Park

SECOND AVE

Brundon

BRUNDON LA

Brundon Hall

QUEENS RD

CLARENCE RD

A131

ACTON LA

42

85   D   86   E   87   F

not continued, see key diagram

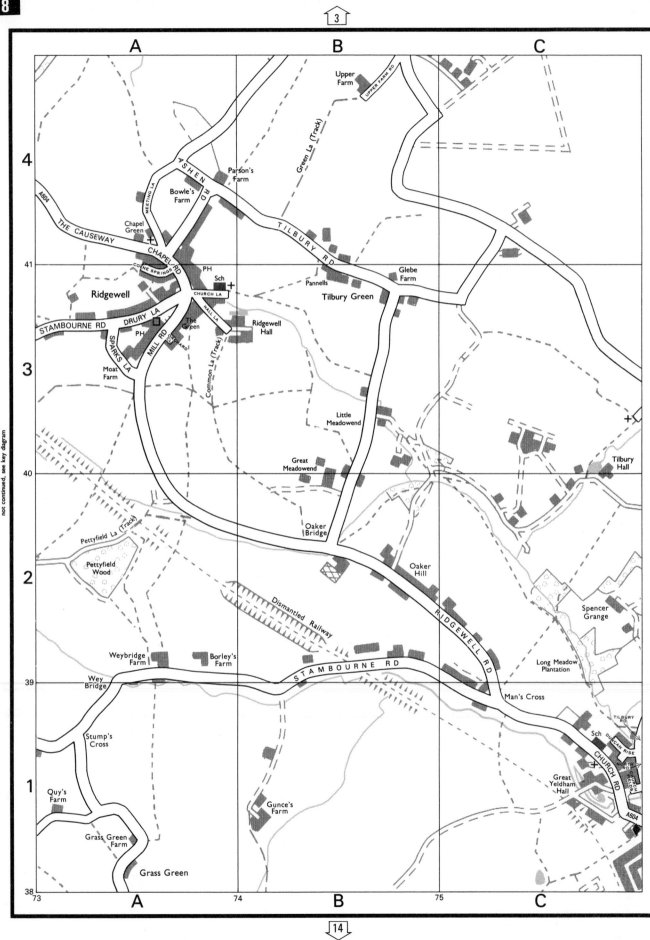

D   E   F

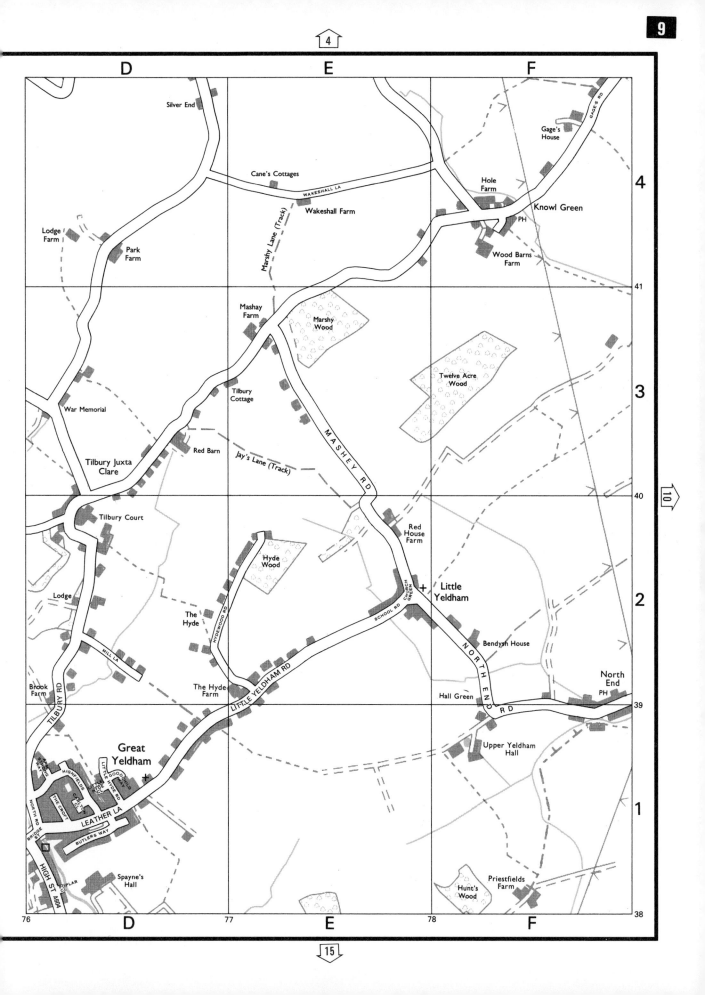

Silver End

GAGE'S RD

Gage's House

Cane's Cottages

WAKESHALL LA

Hole Farm

Wakeshall Farm

Knowl Green

4

PH

Lodge Farm

Park Farm

Wood Barns Farm

41

Mashay Farm

Marshy Wood

Marshy Lane (Track)

Twelve Acre Wood

Tilbury Cottage

MASHEY RD

3

War Memorial

Red Barn

Jay's Lane (Track)

Tilbury Juxta Clare

40

10

Tilbury Court

Red House Farm

Hyde Wood

CHURCH GREEN

Little Yeldham

2

Lodge

The Hyde

HYDEWOOD RD

SCHOOL RD

Bendysh House

NORTH END

MILL LA

North End

Brook Farm

TILBURY RD

The Hyde Farm

LITTLE YELDHAM RD

Hall Green

PH

RD

39

Great Yeldham

Upper Yeldham Hall

HIGHFIELDS

LITTLE HYDE RD

GOODCHILD WAY

ARDING WAY

LEATHER LA

CHURCH RD

THE CROFT

NORTH RD

BUTLERS WAY

BRIDGE ST

1

HIGH ST A604

POPLAR COL

Spayne's Hall

Hunt's Wood

Priestfields Farm

76   D   77   E   78   F   38

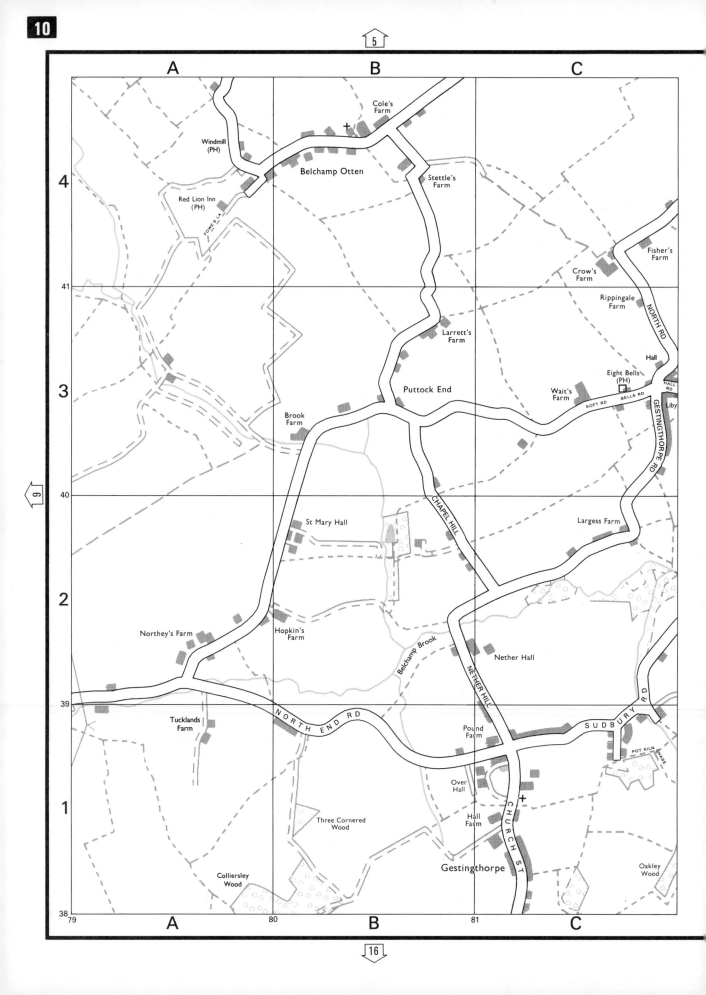

A   B   C

Windmill (PH)

Cole's Farm

Belchamp Otten

Stettle's Farm

Red Lion Inn (PH)

FOWES LA

Fisher's Farm

Crow's Farm

Rippingale Farm

4

41

Larrett's Farm

Puttock End

Hall

Eight Bells (PH)

Wait's Farm

SOFT RD

BELLS RD

Liby

NORTH RD

GESTINGTHORPE RD

HALL RD

Brook Farm

3

40

St Mary Hall

CHAPEL HILL

Largess Farm

2

Northey's Farm

Hopkin's Farm

Belchamp Brook

Nether Hall

NETHER HILL

39

Tucklands Farm

NORTH END RD

Pound Farm

SUDBURY RD

POT KILN CHASE

Over Hall

CHURCH ST

Hall Farm

1

Three Cornered Wood

Gestingthorpe

Oakley Wood

Colliersley Wood

38

79   A   80   B   81   C

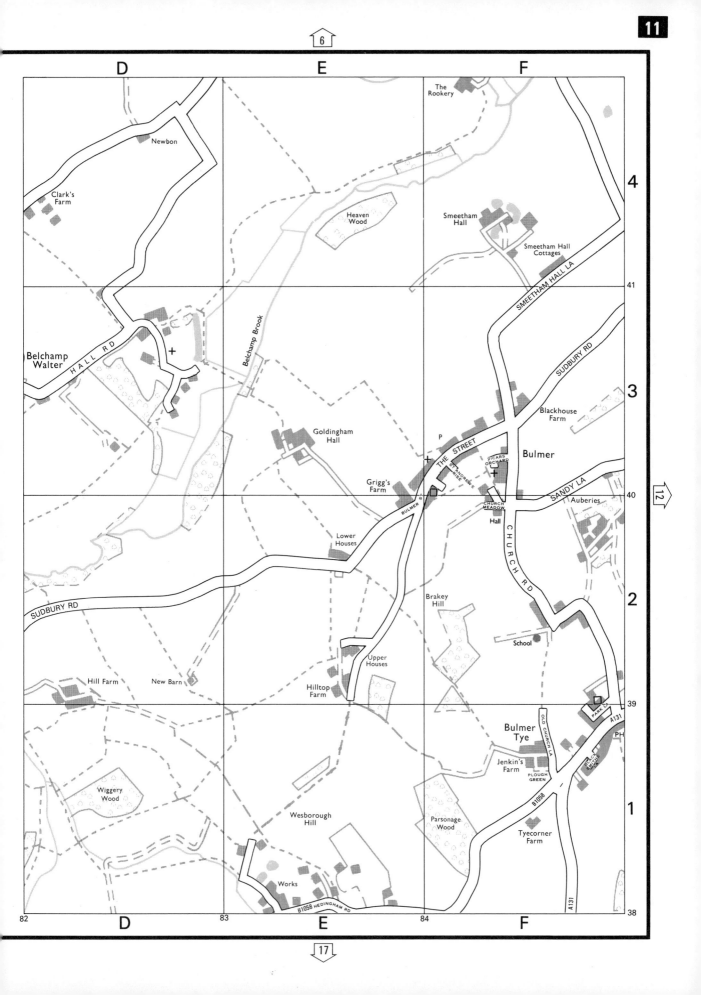

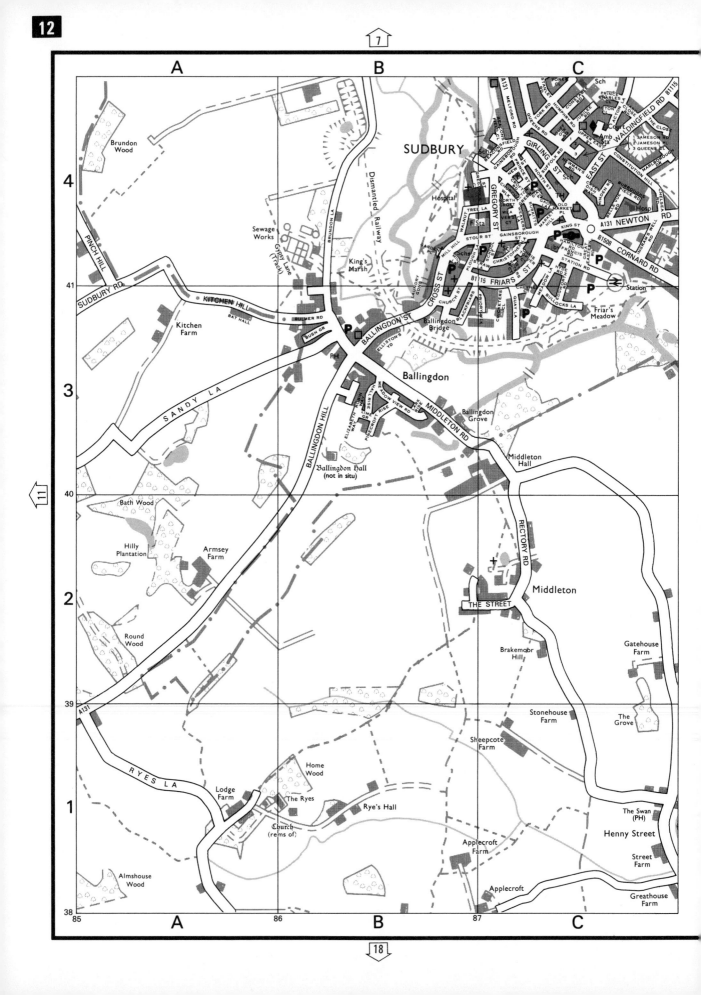

A B C

4

SUDBURY

Brundon
Wood

PINCH HILL

SUDBURY RD

41

Dismantled Railway

Sewage
Works

Grey Lane
(Track)

King's
Marsh

King's Marsh

Hospital

MELFORD RD

YORK RD

A131

GIRLING ST

EAST ST

WALDINGFIELD RD

B1115

Sch

CONSTITUTION HILL

CHELSEA RD

Amb
Sta

A131 NEWTON RD

B1508 CORNARD RD

B1115

Station

Friar's
Meadow

KITCHEN HILL

BAT HALL

Kitchen
Farm

BULMER RD

BUSH GR

P

PH

BALLINGDON'S
YD

BALLINGDON ST

Ballingdon
Bridge

CROSS ST

FRIARS ST

Ballingdon

BALLINGDON HILL

MIDDLETON RD

Ballingdon
Grove

SANDY LA

3

Ballingdon Hall
(not in situ)

ELIZABETH WAY

PIPECROFT RISE

MEADOW VIEW RD

Middleton
Hall

40

Bath Wood

Hilly
Plantation

Armsey
Farm

RECTORY RD

Middleton

THE STREET

2

Round
Wood

Brakemoor
Hill

Gatehouse
Farm

39

A131

RYES LA

Stonehouse
Farm

The
Grove

Sheepcote
Farm

Home
Wood

Lodge
Farm

The Ryes

Rye's Hall

Church
(rems of)

Applecroft
Farm

The Swan
(PH)

Henny Street

Street
Farm

1

Almshouse
Wood

Applecroft

Greathouse
Farm

38

85 A 86 B 87 C

11

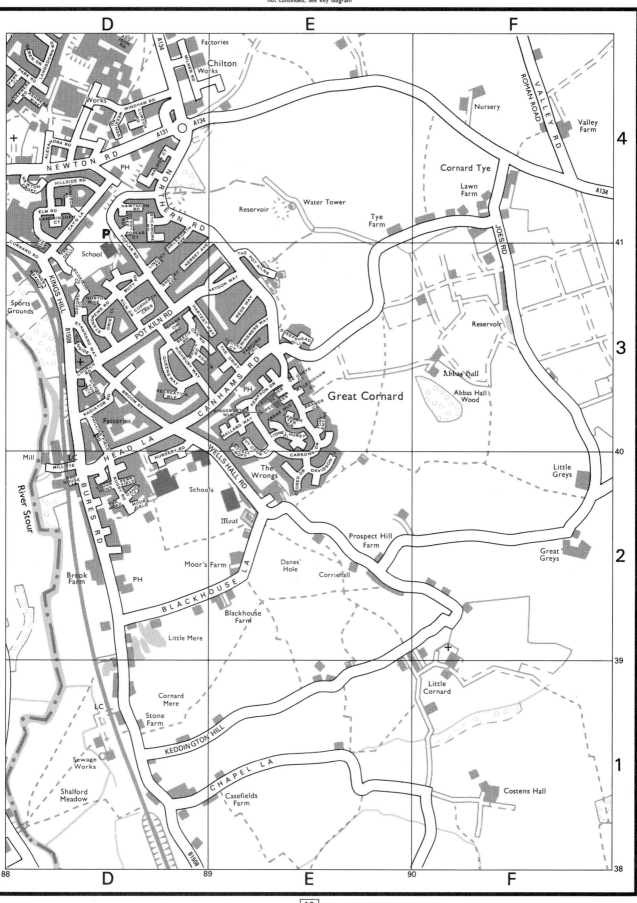

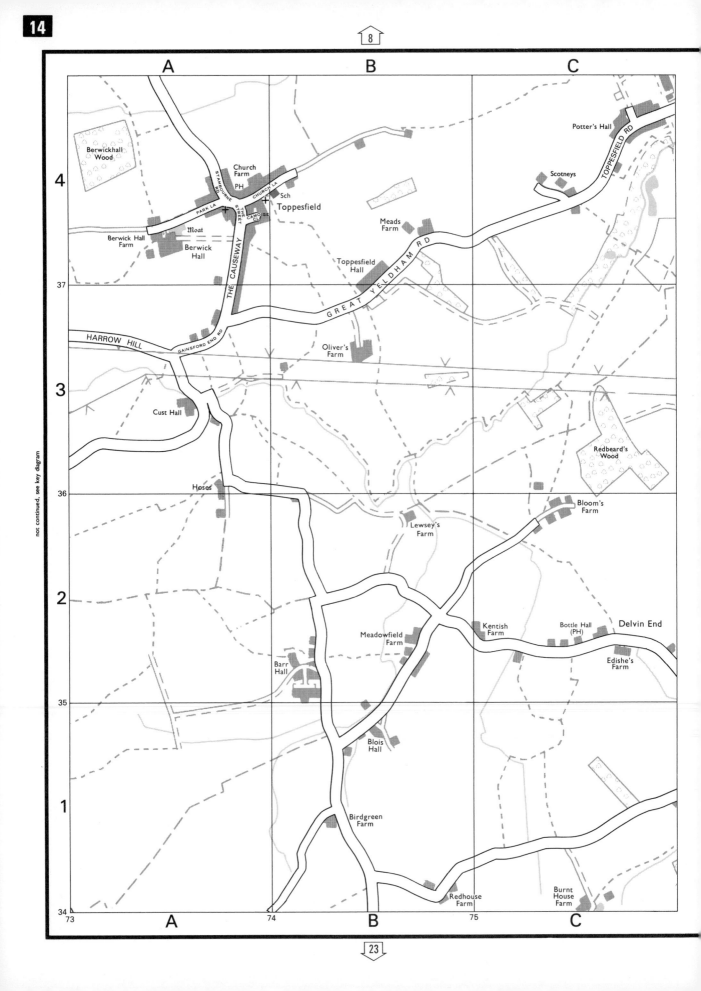

not continued, see key diagram

A   **B**   **C**

Berwickhall Wood

Potter's Hall

TOPPESFIELD RD

Scotneys

Church Farm

PH

Sch

STANBOURNE RD

CHURCH LA

Toppesfield

CAMOISE CL

PARK LA

THE STREET

Berwick Hall Farm

Moat

Berwick Hall

THE CAUSEWAY

Meads Farm

Toppesfield Hall

GREAT YELDHAM RD

37

HARROW HILL

GAINSFORD END RD

Oliver's Farm

3

Cust Hall

Redbeard's Wood

Hoses

36

Bloom's Farm

Lewsey's Farm

2

Kentish Farm

Bottle Hall (PH)

Delvin End

Meadowfield Farm

Barr Hall

Edishe's Farm

35

Blois Hall

1

Birdgreen Farm

Redhouse Farm

Burnt House Farm

34
73   **A**   74   **B**   75   **C**

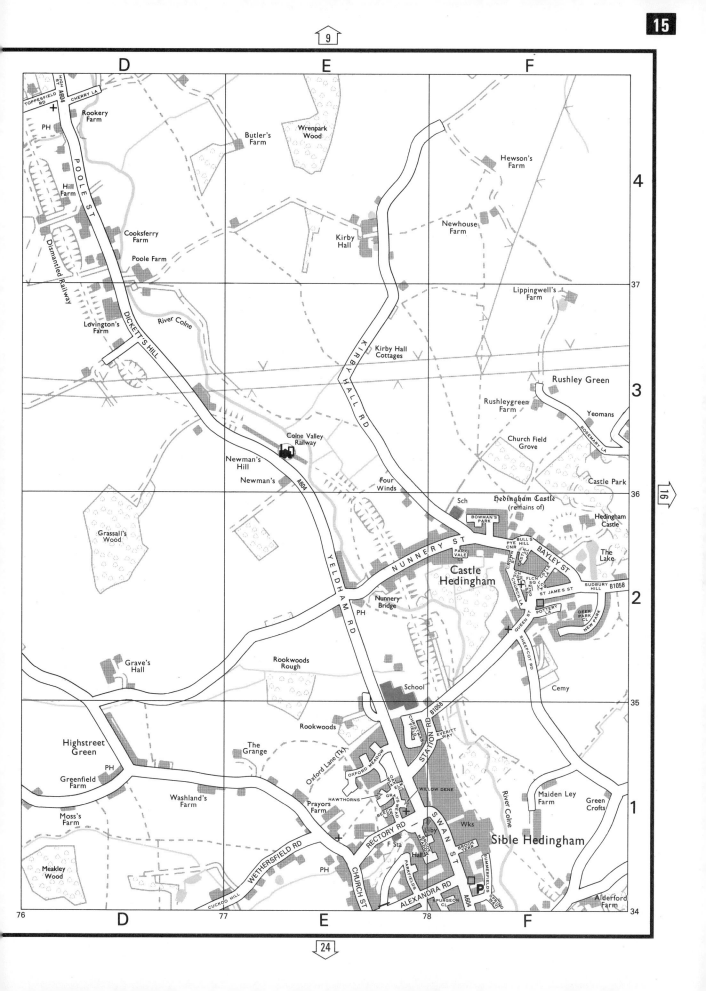

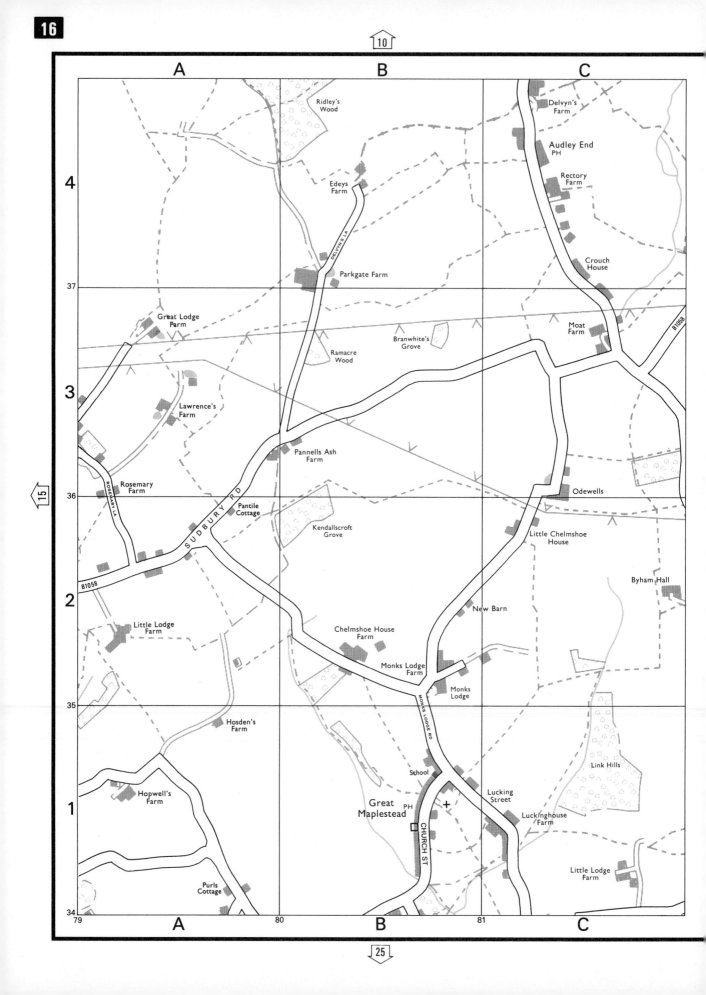

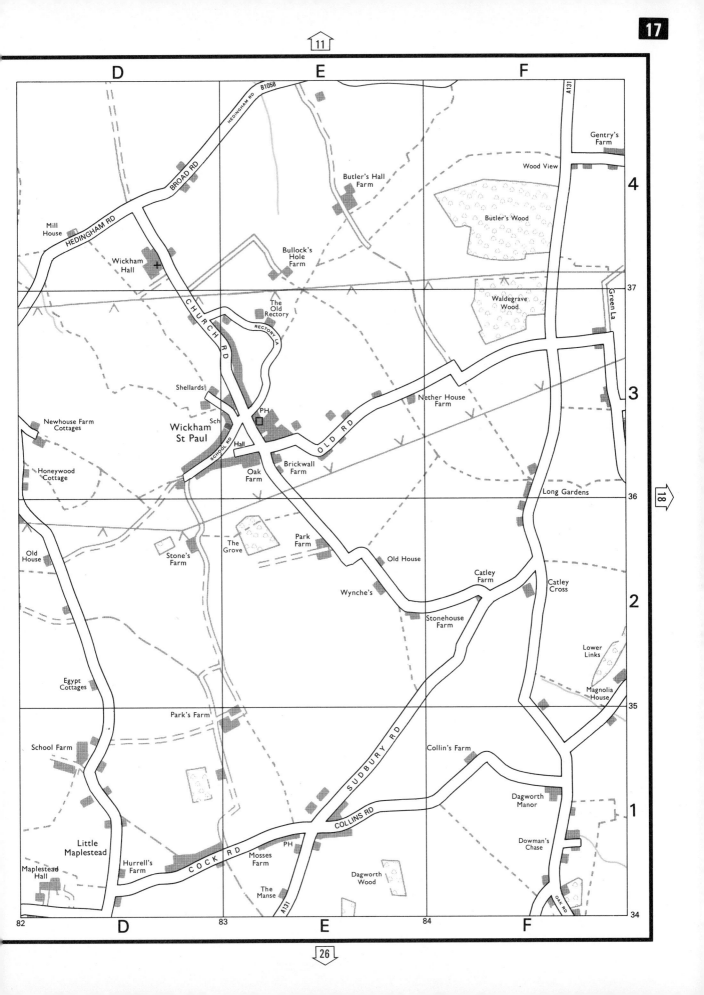

D   E   F

B1058
HEDINGHAM RD
BROAD RD
HEDINGHAM RD
Mill House
Wickham Hall
CHURCH RD
RECTORY LA
The Old Rectory
Bullock's Hole Farm
Butler's Hall Farm
Gentry's Farm
Wood View
Butler's Wood
Waldegrave Wood
A131
Green La

4

37

Shellards
PH
Sch
Wickham St Paul
Hall
School RD
Newhouse Farm Cottages
Honeywood Cottage
Oak Farm
Brickwall Farm
OLD RD
Nether House Farm
Long Gardens

3

36

Old House
Stone's Farm
The Grove
Park Farm
Old House
Wynche's
Catley Farm
Stonehouse Farm
Catley Cross
Lower Links
Magnolia House

2

Egypt Cottages
Park's Farm
School Farm
SUDBURY RD
Collin's Farm
Dagworth Manor
Dowman's Chase

35

1

Little Maplestead
Maplestead Hall
Hurrell's Farm
COCK RD
Mosses Farm
PH
A131
The Manse
COLLINS RD
Dagworth Wood
OAK RD

34

82   D   83   E   84   F

18

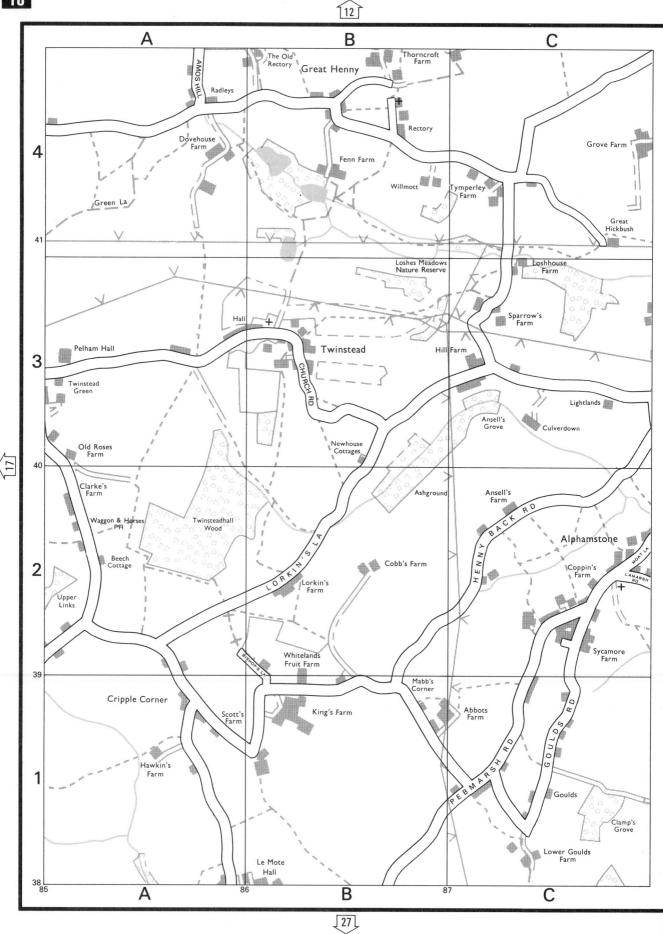

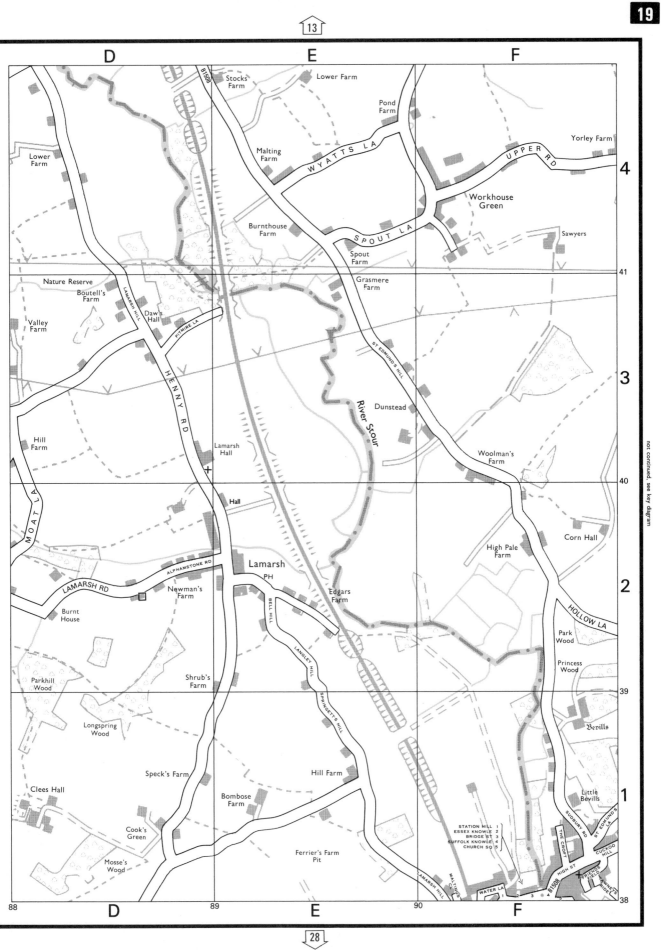

| D | E | F |

4

Lower Farm

Stocks Farm

Lower Farm

Pond Farm

Yorley Farm

Malting Farm

WYATTS LA

UPPER RD

Workhouse Green

Burnthouse Farm

SPOUT LA

Sawyers

Spout Farm

41

Nature Reserve

Grasmere Farm

Boutell's Farm

Lamarsh Hill

Daw's Hall

ST EDMUND'S HILL

Valley Farm

PITMIRE LA

3

River Stour

Dunstead

HENNY RD

Hill Farm

Lamarsh Hall

Woolman's Farm

not continued, see key diagram

40

MOAT LA

Hall

ALPHAMSTONE RD

Corn Hall

High Pale Farm

Lamarsh

LAMARSH RD

Newman's Farm

PH

Edgars Farm

HOLLOW LA

2

Burnt House

BELL HILL

Park Wood

Parkhill Wood

Shrub's Farm

LANGLEY HILL

Princess Wood

39

Longspring Wood

SPRINGETT'S HILL

Bevills

Speck's Farm

Hill Farm

Clees Hall

Little Bevills

Bombose Farm

1

Cook's Green

Mosse's Wood

Ferrier's Farm Pit

STATION HILL 1
ESSEX KNOWLE 2
BRIDGE ST 3
SUFFOLK KNOWLE 4
CHURCH SQ 5

SUDBURY RD

ST EDMUND'S LA

THE CROFT

CUCKOO HILL

LAMARSH HILL

MALTINGS

HIGH ST

WATER LA

FRIENDS FIELDS

B1508

GWYNNE'S WIDE

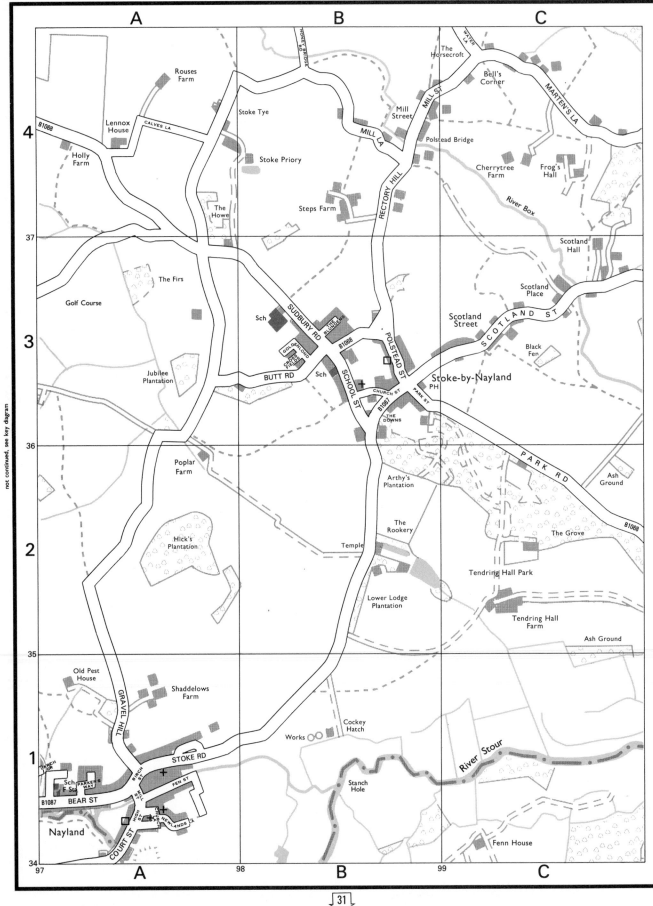

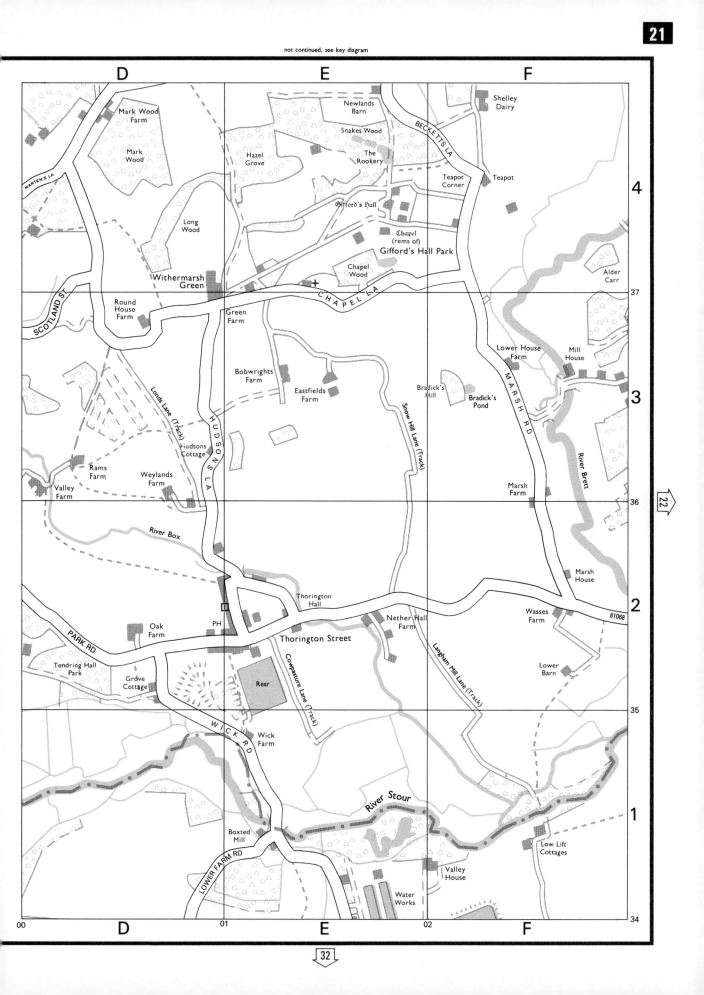

D   E   F

Mark Wood Farm

Mark Wood

MARTEN'S LA

Newlands Barn

Snakes Wood

BECKETTS LA

Shelley Dairy

Hazel Grove

The Rookery

Teapot Corner

Teapot

4

Gifford's Hall

Long Wood

Chapel (rems of)

Gifford's Hall Park

Alder Carr

Chapel Wood

Withermarsh Green

CHAPEL LA

37

SCOTLAND ST

Round House Farm

Green Farm

Lower House Farm

Mill House

Londs Lane (Track)

Bobwrights Farm

Eastfields Farm

Bradick's Hill

Bradick's Pond

MARSH RD

River Brett

3

Hudsons Cottage

HUDSONS LA

Snow Hill Lane (Track)

Rams Farm

Weylands Farm

22

Valley Farm

Marsh Farm

36

River Box

Marsh House

Thorington Hall

Nether Hall Farm

Wasses Farm

B1068

2

PARK RD

Oak Farm

PH

Thorington Street

Compasture Lane (Track)

Langham Mill Lane (Track)

Lower Barn

Tendring Hall Park

Grove Cottage

Resr

35

WICK RD

Wick Farm

Boxted Mill

River Stour

Low Lift Cottages

1

LOWER FARM RD

Valley House

Water Works

34

D   E   F

00   01   02

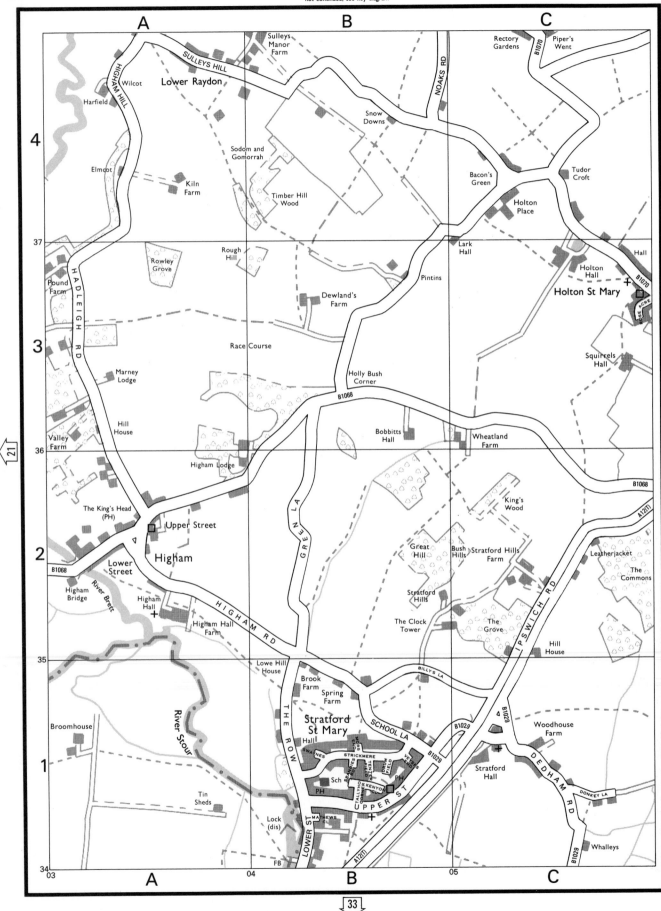

21

not continued, see key diagram

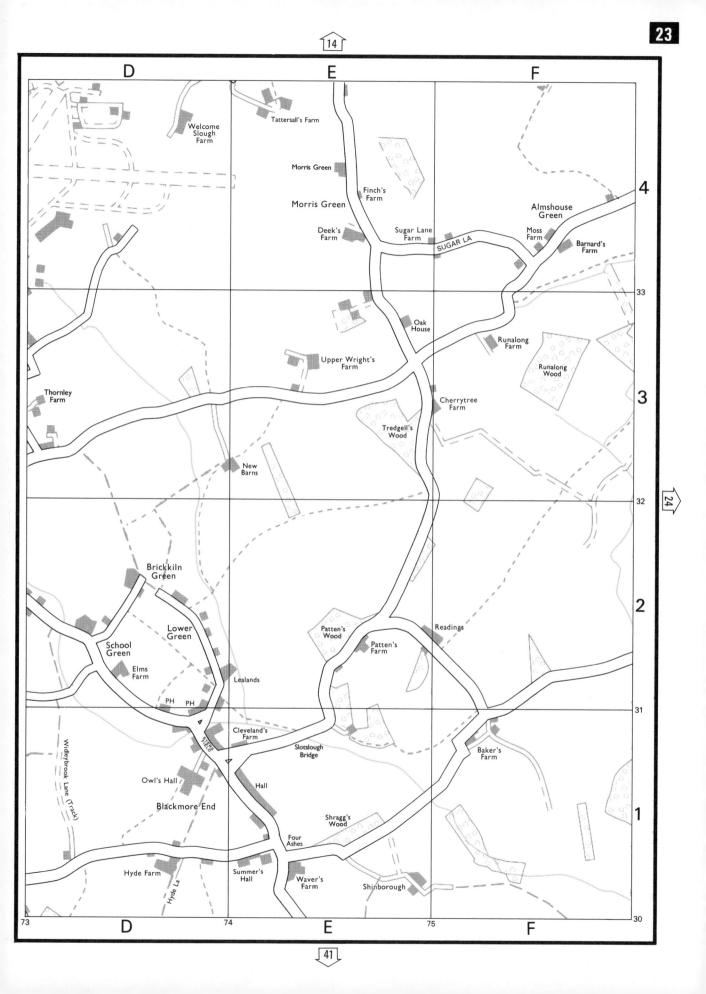

D

E

F

Welcome
Slough
Farm

Tattersall's Farm

Morris Green

Morris Green

Finch's
Farm

4

Almshouse
Green

Deek's
Farm

Sugar Lane
Farm

SUGAR LA

Moss
Farm

Barnard's
Farm

33

Oak
House

Runalong
Farm

Upper Wright's
Farm

Runalong
Wood

Thornley
Farm

Cherrytree
Farm

3

Tredgell's
Wood

New
Barns

32

Brickkiln
Green

Readings

2

Lower
Green

Patten's
Wood

School
Green

Patten's
Farm

Elms
Farm

Lealands

PH   PH

31

Cleveland's
Farm

Slotslough
Bridge

Baker's
Farm

Owl's Hall

Hall

Blackmore End

Shragg's
Wood

1

Four
Ashes

Hyde Farm

Summer's
Hall

Waver's
Farm

Shinborough

30

Widleybrook Lane (Track)

Hyde La

D

E

F

73

74

75

24

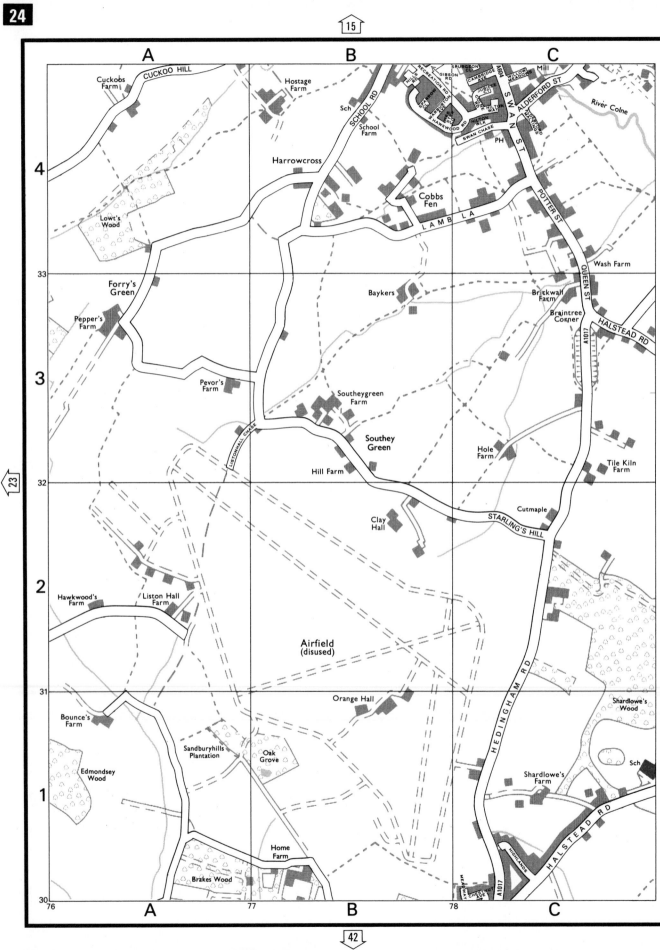

23

A   **B**   **C**

Cuckobs Farm

CUCKOO HILL

Hostage Farm

Sch

School Farm

SCHOOL RD

Harrowcross

Lowt's Wood

Cobbs Fen

LAMB LA

RECREATION RD
GIBSON RD
STURGEON CL
CAMBRIDGE AVE
SWAN ST
ALDERFORD ST
Mill

SPARROW RD
HAWKWOOD RD
HILTON RD
JUSTICE CL
COLNE CLO
HILTON WLK
SWAN WAY
SWAN CHASE
HITCHINGS

River Colne

PH

POTTER ST

Wash Farm

Forry's Green

Pepper's Farm

Baykers

Brickwall Farm

Braintree Corner

QUEEN ST

A1017

HALSTEAD RD

Pevor's Farm

LISTONHALL CHASE

Southeygreen Farm

Southey Green

Hole Farm

Tile Kiln Farm

Hill Farm

Clay Hall

Cutmaple

STARLING'S HILL

Hawkwood's Farm

Liston Hall Farm

Airfield (disused)

HEDINGHAM RD

Bounce's Farm

Orange Hall

Shardlowe's Wood

Sandburyhills Plantation

Oak Grove

Sch

Edmondsey Wood

Shardlowe's Farm

Home Farm

Brakes Wood

HALSTEAD RD

HIGHLANDS

MEADWAY

CHESTNUT AVE

A1017

76   **A**   77   **B**   78   **C**

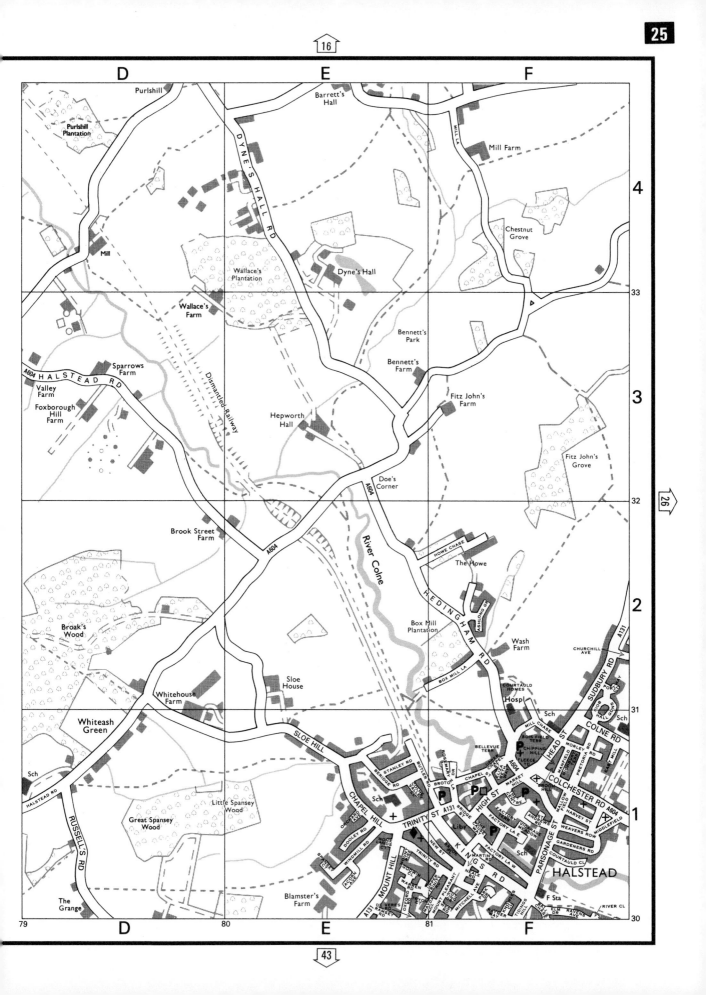

26

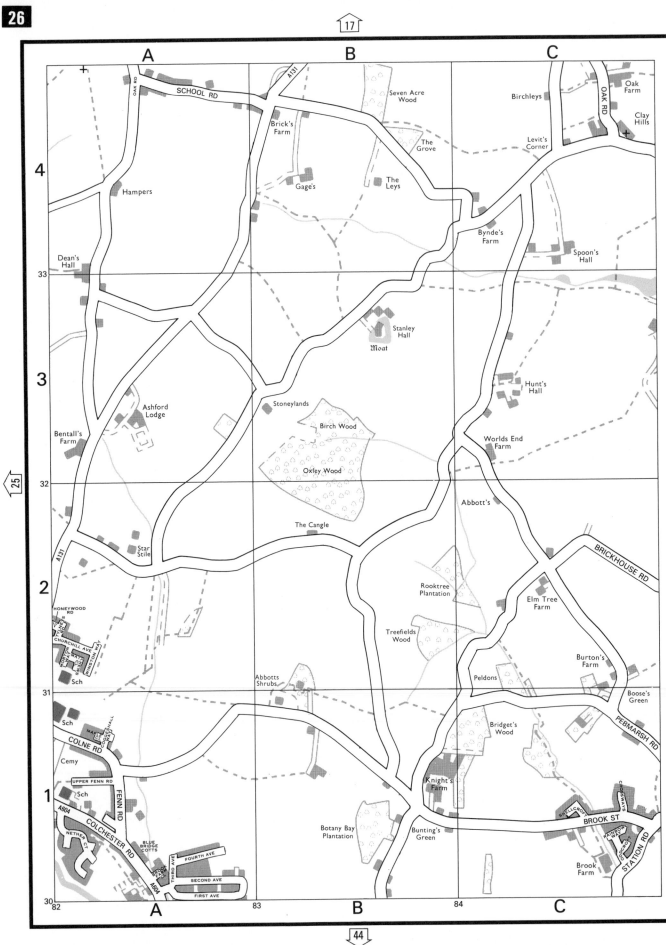

A B C

4

33

3

32

2

31

1

30

82 83 84

A B C

OAK RD
SCHOOL RD
A131
Seven Acre Wood
Birchleys
Oak Farm
Clay Hills
Brick's Farm
The Grove
Levit's Corner
OAK RD
Hampers
Gage's
The Leys
Bynde's Farm
Spoon's Hall
Dean's Hall
Stanley Hall
Moat
Hunt's Hall
Ashford Lodge
Stoneylands
Birch Wood
Worlds End Farm
Bentall's Farm
Oxley Wood
A131
The Cangle
Abbott's
BRICKHOUSE RD
Star Stile
Rooktree Plantation
Elm Tree Farm
HONEYWOOD RD
CHURCHILL AVE
WINSTON WAY
Sch
Treefields Wood
Burton's Farm
Peldons
Boose's Green
Abbotts Shrubs
PEBMARSH RD
Sch
MARKET CAUSEWAY
COLNE RD
Cemy
Bridget's Wood
UPPER FENN RD
Sch
FENN RD
Knight's Farm
SHELLCROFT
BROOK ST
CROSSWAYS
A604
COLCHESTER RD
NETHER CT
BLUE BRIDGE COTTS
STOCK PARK
THIRD AVE
FOURTH AVE
SECOND AVE
FIRST AVE
A604
Botany Bay Plantation
Bunting's Green
RAINBOW WAY
Brook Farm
STATION RD

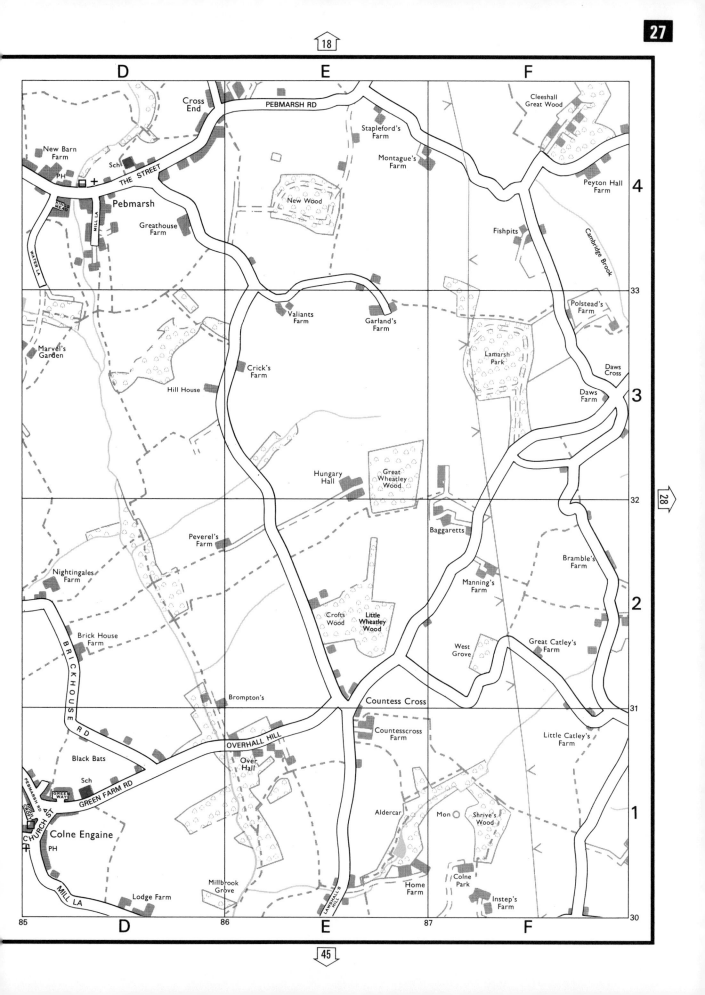

Cross End

PEBMARSH RD

Stapleford's Farm

Cleeshall Great Wood

New Barn Farm

PH

Sch

+

THE STREET

Montague's Farm

Peyton Hall Farm

4

HORSE HEAD

MILL LA

Pebmarsh

New Wood

Fishpits

Greathouse Farm

WATER LA

Cambridge Brook

33

Valiants Farm

Garland's Farm

Polstead's Farm

Marvel's Garden

Crick's Farm

Lamarsh Park

Daws Cross

Hill House

Daws Farm

3

Hungary Hall

Great Wheatley Wood

Peverel's Farm

Baggaretts

Bramble's Farm

Nightingales Farm

Manning's Farm

BRICKHOUSE RD

Brick House Farm

Crofts Wood

Little Wheatley Wood

West Grove

Great Catley's Farm

2

Brompton's

Countess Cross

31

OVERHALL HILL

Countesscross Farm

Little Catley's Farm

Black Bats

Sch

Over Hall

GREEN FARM RD

PEBMARSH RD

GREEN WAY

CHURCH ST

Colne Engaine

Aldercar

Mon ○

Shrive's Wood

1

+

PH

Home Farm

Colne Park

MILL LA

Lodge Farm

Millbrook Grove

LAMBHALL'S HILL

Instep's Farm

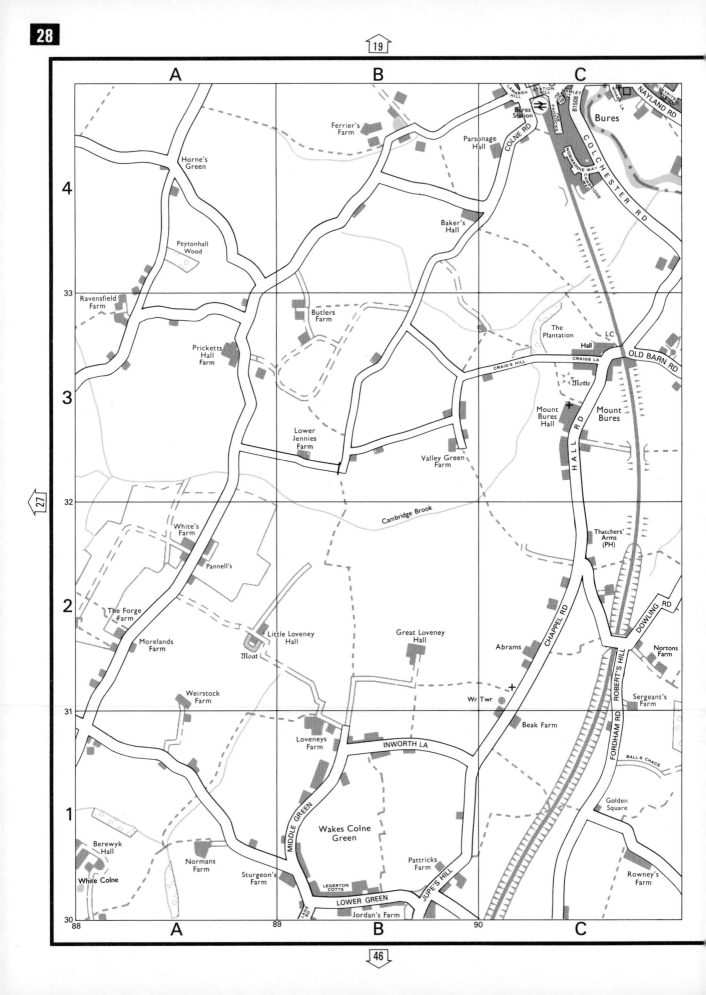

A

B

C

4

Horne's Green

Ferrier's Farm

Parsonage Hall

COLNE RD

Bures Station

LAMARSH HILL
STATION HILL
HAMLET
PADDOCKS
NORMANDIE WAY
CAMBRIDGE
B1508
Bures

NAYLAND RD

CHAPEL RISE
WHARF LA

COLCHESTER RD

Peytonhall Wood

Baker's Hall

33

Ravensfield Farm

Butlers Farm

The Plantation

Hall

LC

OLD BARN RD

Pricketts Hall Farm

CRAIG'S HILL
CRAIGS LA

Motte

3

Lower Jennies Farm

Valley Green Farm

Mount Bures Hall

Mount Bures

HALL RD

27

32

Cambridge Brook

Thatchers' Arms (PH)

White's Farm

Pannell's

CHAPPEL RD

2

The Forge Farm

Little Loveney Hall

Great Loveney Hall

Abrams

Nortons Farm

DOWLING RD

Morelands Farm

Moat

Sergeant's Farm

31

Weirstock Farm

Wr Twr

Beak Farm

ROBERT'S HILL

FORDHAM RD

BALL'S CHACE

Loveneys Farm

INWORTH LA

MIDDLE GREEN

Golden Square

1

Berewyk Hall

White Colne

Normans Farm

Sturgeon's Farm

Wakes Colne Green

LEGERTON COTTS

LOWER GREEN

Pattricks Farm

JUPE'S HILL

Jordan's Farm

Rowney's Farm

GATE RD

30

88

A

89

B

90

C

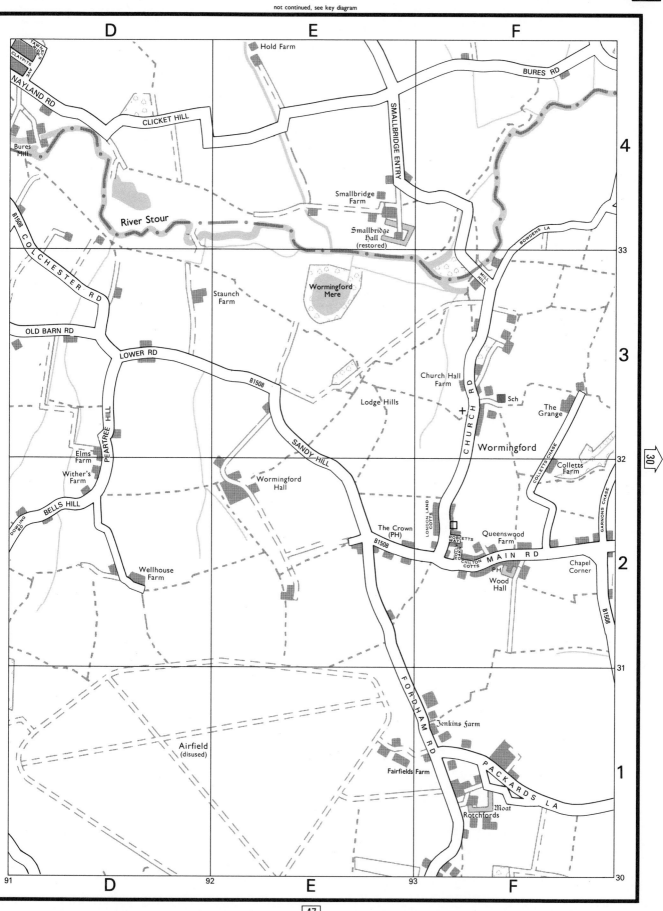

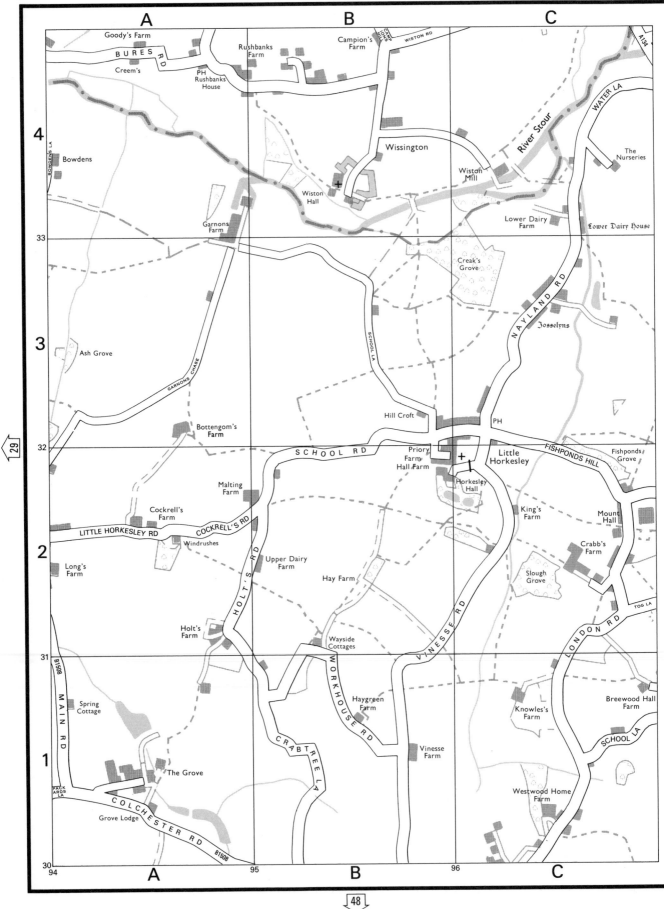

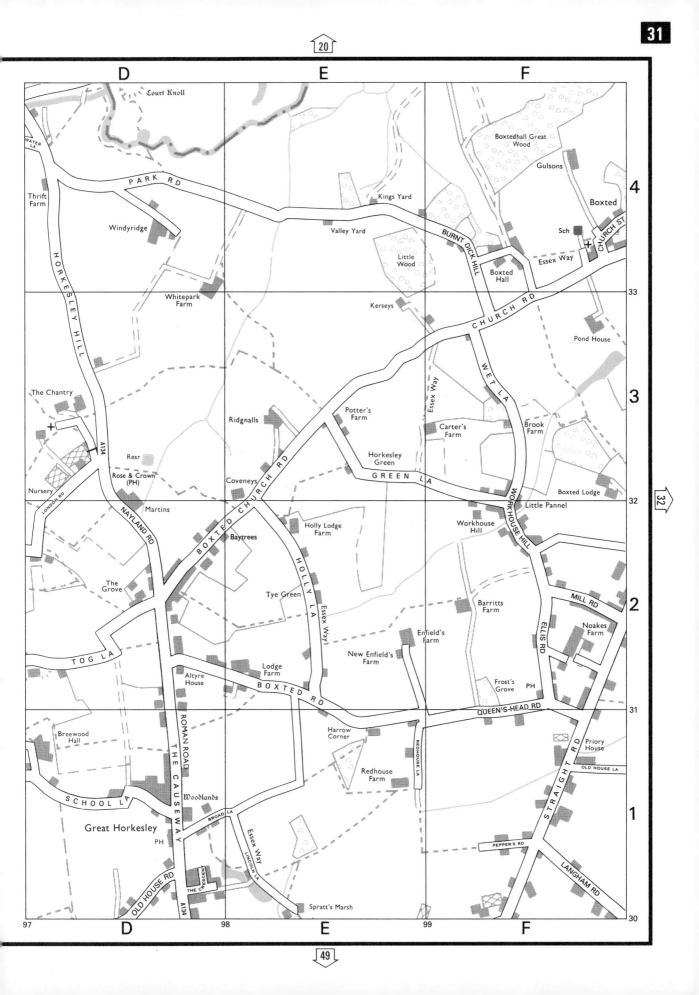

D   E   F

Court Knoll

WATER LA

Thrift
Farm

PARK RD

Windyridge

HORKESLEY HILL

Whitepark
Farm

Kings Yard

Valley Yard

Little
Wood

Kerseys

BURNT DICK HILL

Boxtedhall Great
Wood

Gulsons

Boxted

Sch

CHURCH ST

Essex Way

Boxted
Hall

CHURCH RD

Pond House

33

The Chantry

A134

Resr

Rose & Crown
(PH)

Nursery

LONDON RD

Ridgnalls

Coveneys

Potter's
Farm

Horkesley
Green

Carter's
Farm

Essex Way

WET LA

Brook
Farm

GREEN LA

WORKHOUSE HILL

Little Pannel

Boxted Lodge

32

32

Martins

NAYLAND RD

BOXTED CHURCH RD

Baytrees

HOLLY LA

Holly Lodge
Farm

Tye Green

Essex Way

Workhouse
Hill

Barritts
Farm

MILL RD

ELLIS RD

Noakes
Farm

2

The
Grove

Enfield's
Farm

New Enfield's
Farm

Frost's
Grove

PH

TOG LA

Altyre
House

Lodge
Farm

BOXTED RD

QUEEN'S HEAD RD

31

Breewood
Hall

ROMAN ROAD

THE CAUSEWAY

Woodlands

BROAD LA

Harrow
Corner

Redhouse
Farm

REDHOUSE LA

STRAIGHT RD

Priory
House

OLD HOUSE LA

Great Horkesley

PH

SCHOOL LA

Essex Way

LINCOLN LA

Spratt's Marsh

PEPPER'S RD

LANGHAM RD

1

THE CRESCENT

OLD HOUSE RD

A134

97   D   98   E   99   F   30

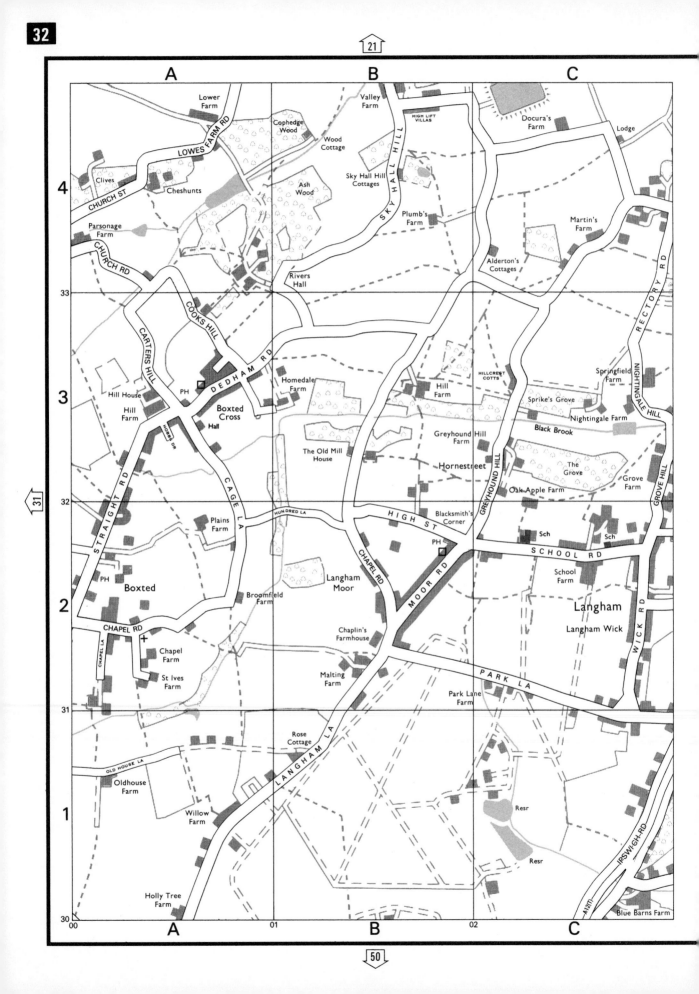

A B C

Lower Farm

LOWES FARM RD

Cophedge Wood

Wood Cottage

Valley Farm

HIGH LIFT VILLAS

SKY HALL HILL

Docura's Farm

Lodge

Clives

Cheshunts

CHURCH ST

Ash Wood

4

Sky Hall Hill Cottages

Martin's Farm

Parsonage Farm

Plumb's Farm

Alderton's Cottages

CHURCH RD

Rivers Hall

RECTORY RD

33

COOKS HILL

CARTERS HILL

DEDHAM RD

Homedale Farm

HILLCREST COTTS

Springfield Farm

NIGHTINGALE HILL

Hill House

PH

Boxted Cross

Hill Farm

Hill Farm

Sprike's Grove

Nightingale Farm

3

Hall

Black Brook

Greyhound Hill Farm

The Grove

HOMES DR

CAGE LA

The Old Mill House

Hornestreet

Oak Apple Farm

Grove Farm

GROVE HILL

32

STRAIGHT RD

Plains Farm

HUNDRED LA

HIGH ST

Blacksmith's Corner

GREYHOUND HILL

SCHOOL RD

Sch

Sch

PH

Boxted

Broomfield Farm

Langham Moor

CHAPEL RD

MOOR RD

PH

School Farm

Langham

Langham Wick

WICK RD

2

CHAPEL RD

CHAPEL LA

Chapel Farm

Chaplin's Farmhouse

St Ives Farm

Malting Farm

PARK LA

Park Lane Farm

31

Rose Cottage

OLD HOUSE LA

LANGHAM LA

Oldhouse Farm

Resr

1

Willow Farm

Resr

IPSWICH RD

Holly Tree Farm

A12(T)

Blue Barns Farm

00 A 01 B 02 C

30

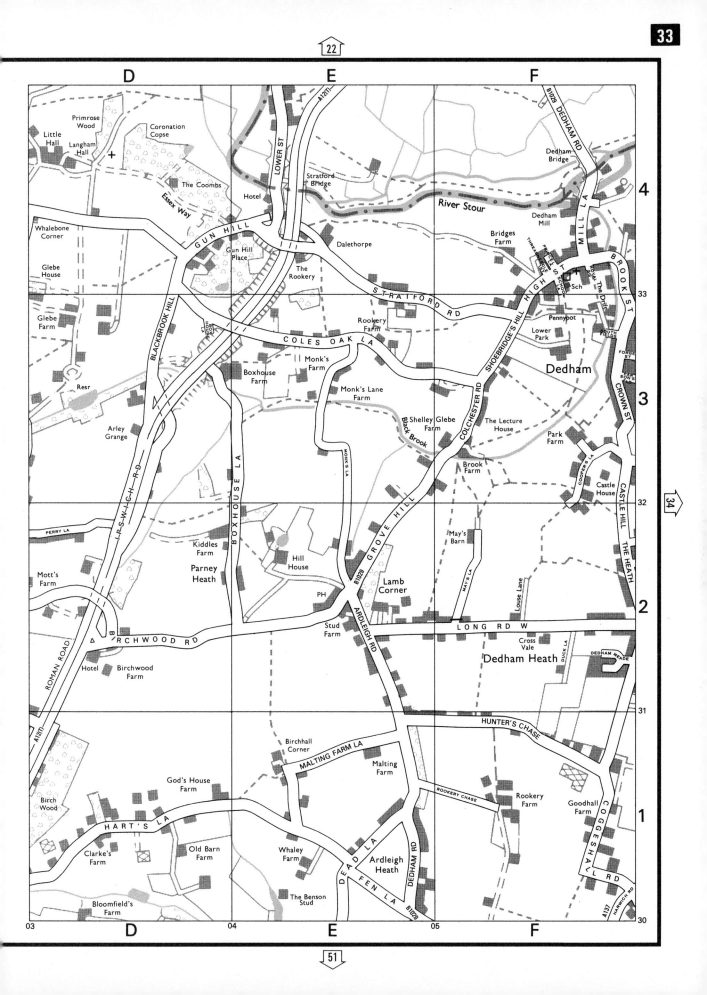

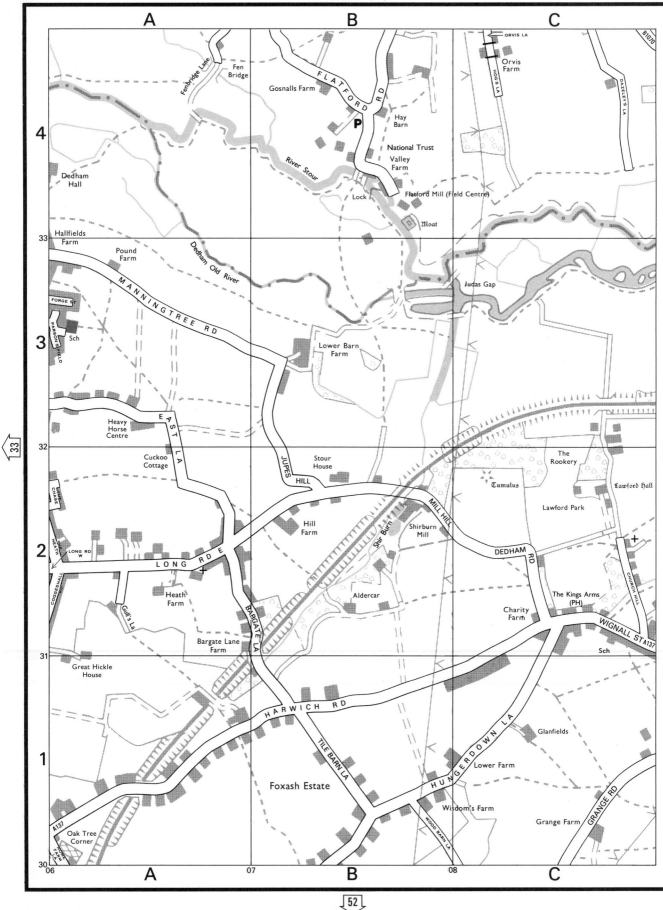

A B C

4

Fen Bridge
Fenbridge Lane
Gosnalls Farm
FLATFORD RD
P
Hay Barn
ORVIS LA
Orvis Farm
HOG'S LA
DAZELEY'S LA
B1070

National Trust Valley Farm
River Stour
Dedham Hall
Lock
Flatford Mill (Field Centre)

33

Hallfields Farm
Moat
Pound Farm
Dedham Old River
Judas Gap

3

MANNINGTREE RD
FORGE ST
PARSON'S FIELD
Sch
Lower Barn Farm

32

Heavy Horse Centre
EAST LA
Cuckoo Cottage
JUPES HILL
Stour House
The Rookery
Tumulus
Lawford Hall
Lawford Park

2

LONG RD E
LONG RD W
HEATH
COGGESHALL RD
Heath Farm
Gull's La
Hill Farm
Shir Burn
MILL HILL
Shirburn Mill
Aldercar
DEDHAM RD
The Kings Arms (PH)
Charity Farm
WIGNALL ST A137
CHURCH HILL
BARGATE LA
Bargate Lane Farm

31

Great Hickle House
Sch
HARWICH RD
TILE BARN LA
HUNGERDOWN LA
Glanfields
Lower Farm

1

Foxash Estate
Wisdom's Farm
WOOD BARN LA
Grange Farm
GRANGE RD

A137
Oak Tree Corner

30

06 A 07 B 08 C

52

33

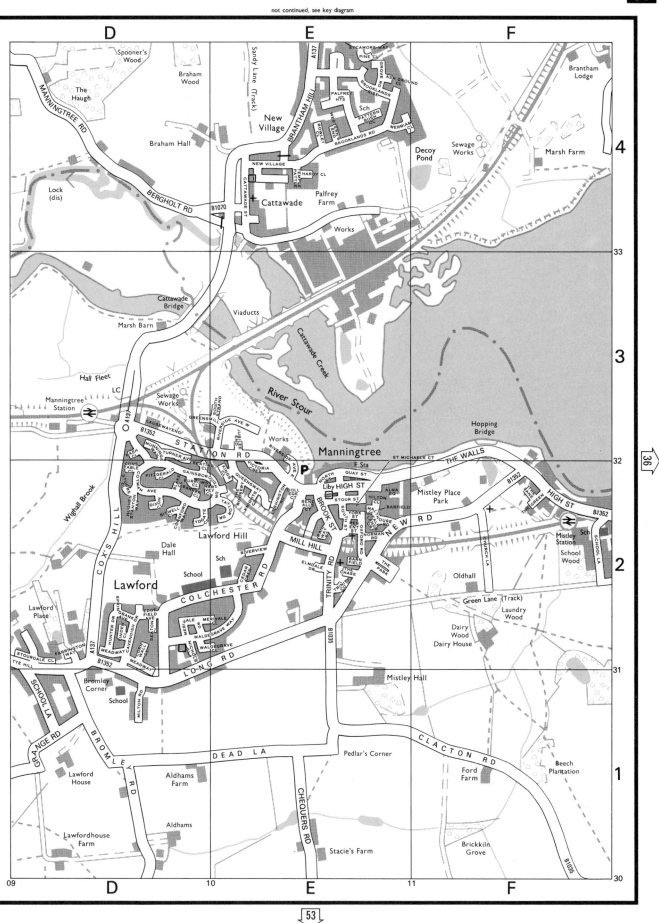

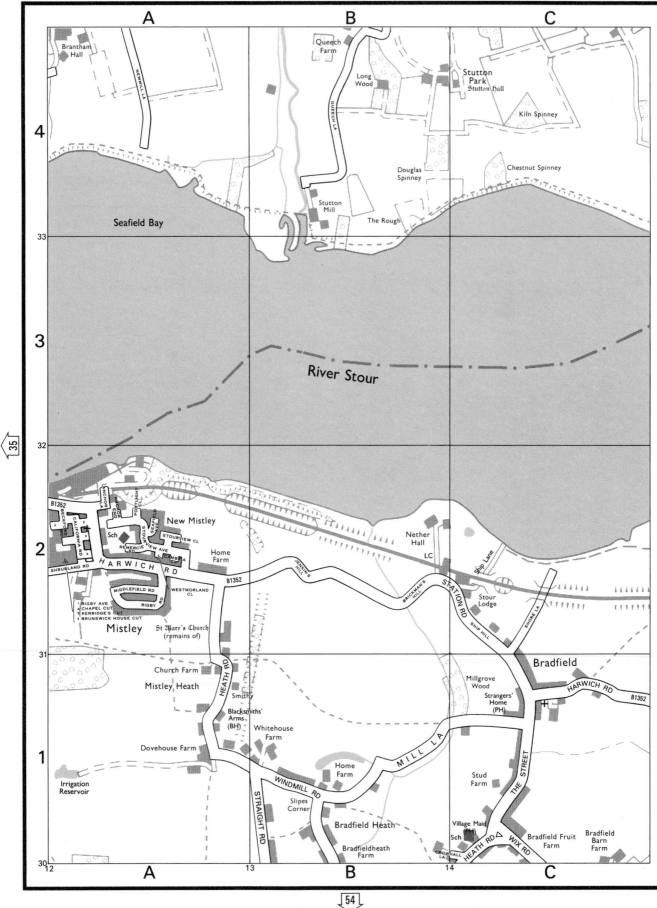

Brantham Hall

NEWMILL LA

Queech Farm

Long Wood

QUEECH LA

Stutton Park
Stutton Hall

Kiln Spinney

4

Douglas Spinney

Chestnut Spinney

Stutton Mill

The Rough

Seafield Bay

33

3

River Stour

32

B1352

ANCHOR LA

ANCHOR END

PORTLIGHT CL

STOUR ST

SEAFIELD

New Mistley

BECKFORD RD

CALIFORNIA RD

Sch

REMERCIE RD

STOURVIEW AVE

CAMBRIA CL

STOURVIEW CL

Home Farm

Nether Hall

LC

Ship Lane

2

SHRUBLAND RD

HARWICH RD

MIDDLEFIELD RD

WESTMORLAND CL

B1352

JENKIN'S HILL

BRICKMAN'S HILL

STATION RD

SHIP HILL

Stour Lodge

SHORE LA

1 RIGBY AVE
2 CHAPEL CUT
3 KERRIDGE'S CUT
4 BRUNSWICK HOUSE CUT

RIGBY RD

RIGBY

Mistley

St Mary's Church
(remains of)

31

Church Farm

Mistley Heath

HEATH RD

Smithy

Blacksmiths'
Arms
(BH)

Whitehouse Farm

Millgrove Wood

Strangers'
Home
(PH)

Bradfield

HARWICH RD

B1352

Dovehouse Farm

Home Farm

MILL LA

1

Irrigation Reservoir

WINDMILL RD

STRAIGHT RD

Slipes Corner

Stud Farm

THE STREET

Bradfield Heath

Village Maid
(PH)

Sch

Bradfield Fruit Farm

Bradfield Barn Farm

Bradfieldheath Farm

CROWHALL LA

HEATH RD

WIX RD

30

12   A   13   B   14   C

35

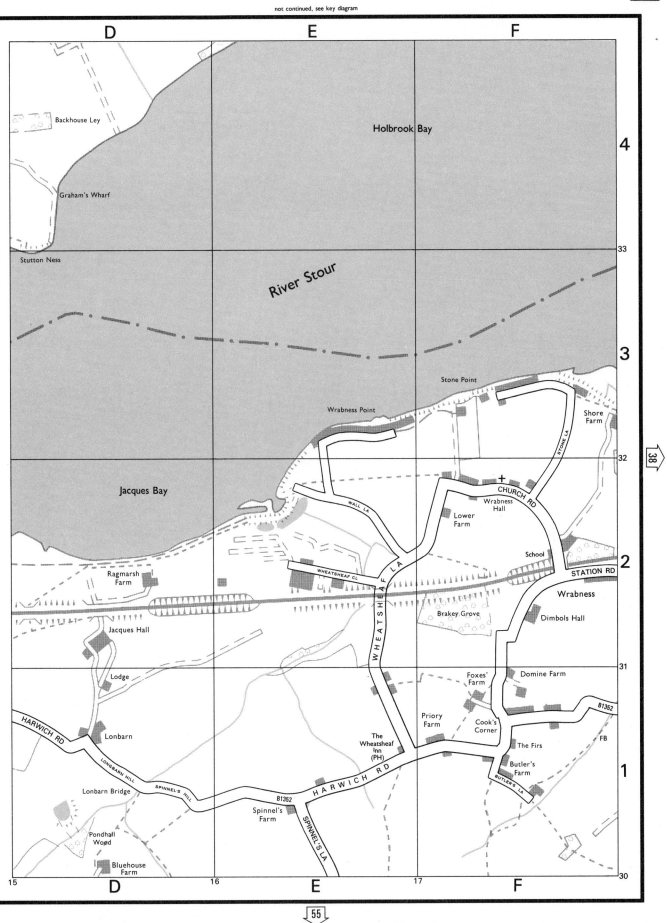

D

E

F

Backhouse Ley

Holbrook Bay

4

Graham's Wharf

Stutton Ness

33

River Stour

3

Stone Point

Wrabness Point

Shore
Farm

32

Jacques Bay

38

CHURCH RD

+

STONE LA

Wrabness
Hall

WALL LA

Lower
Farm

School

WHEATSHEAF CL

STATION RD

2

Ragmarsh
Farm

WHEATSHEAF LA

Wrabness

Brakey Grove

Dimbols Hall

Jacques Hall

31

Lodge

Foxes'
Farm

Domine Farm

HARWICH RD

Priory
Farm

Cook's
Corner

B1352

Lonbarn

The
Wheatsheaf
Inn
(PH)

The Firs

FB

LONGBARN HILL

SPINNEL'S HILL

HARWICH RD

Butler's
Farm

BUTLER'S LA

1

Lonbarn Bridge

B1352

Spinnel's
Farm

SPINNEL'S LA

Pondhall
Wood

Bluehouse
Farm

15

16

17

30

D

E

F

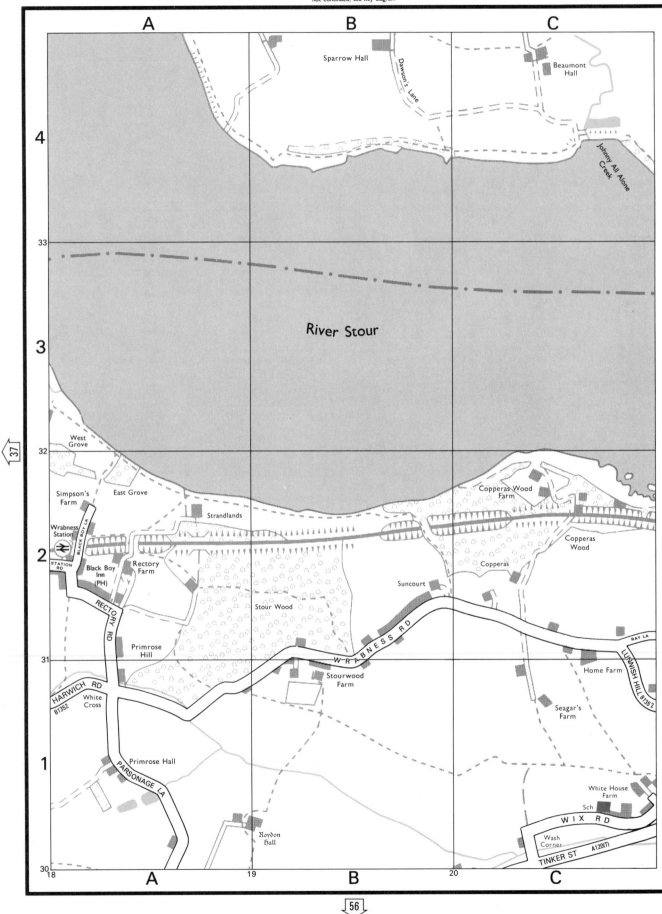

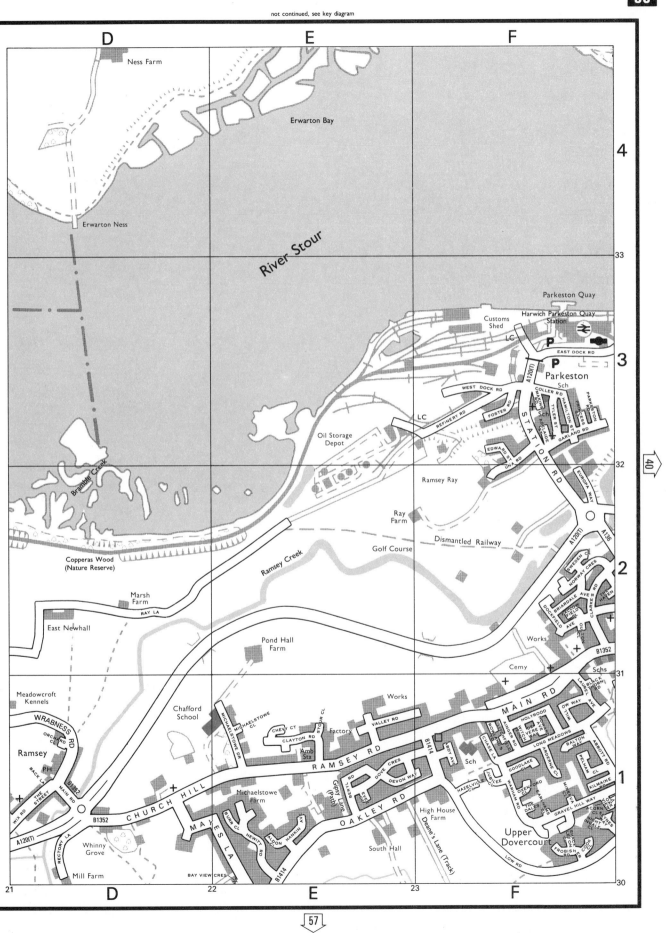

D   E   F

Ness Farm

Erwarton Bay

4

Erwarton Ness

River Stour

33

Parkeston Quay

Customs Shed

Harwich Parkeston Quay Station

LC

P

East Dock Rd

P

Parkeston

3

Sch

West Dock Rd

Coller Rd

Foster Rd

Refinery Rd

LC

Oil Storage Depot

Edward St

Una Rd

Station Rd

Hamilton St

Tyler St

Garland Rd

Princes Rd

Parkeston Rd

32

Europa Way

Ramsey Ray

Ray Farm

A120(T)

A136

Dismantled Railway

Sweden Cl

Norway Cres

2

Brantle Creek

Golf Course

Ramsey Creek

Copperas Wood (Nature Reserve)

Marsh Farm

Ray La

Briardale Ave

Harrow Field

Dockfield Ave

Clarke's Rd

Colton

Chipping Close

Works

B1352

Pond Hall Farm

East Newhall

Cemy

Schs

31

Meadowcroft Kennels

Wrabness Rd

Orchard Cl

Chafford School

Michaelstowe Cl

Michaelstowe Dr

Chew Ct

Clayton Rd

Stour Cl

Valley Rd

Factory

Works

Main Rd

Black Horn

Laurel Rd

Holyrood Rd

Ginger Rd

Ow Way

Witch Way

Vere Ave

Long Meadows

Balton Way

Abbott Rd

Ramsey

PH

Back La

B1352

The Street

Main Rd

Church Hill

Ramsey Rd

Dove Cres

Devon Way

B1414

Ardy Ave

Sch

Goodlake

Arderne Cl

Roy Rd

Chase La

Jubilee

Kilmaine Rd

Pelham Cl

Minerva Way

1

Wix Rd

A120(T)

B1352

Whinny Grove

Mayes La

Michaelstowe Farm

Hewitt Rd

Alton Cl

Hankin

Oakley Rd

Gipsy Lane (Path)

Bear La

Eye Cres

High House Farm

Deane's Lane (Track)

Low Rd

Upper Dovercourt

Frobisher Rd

Cook

Gravel Hill Way

The Dales

Oxenford

Acorn Cl

Mill Farm

Bay View Cres

B1414

South Hall

30

21   D   22   E   23   F

40

not continued, see key diagram

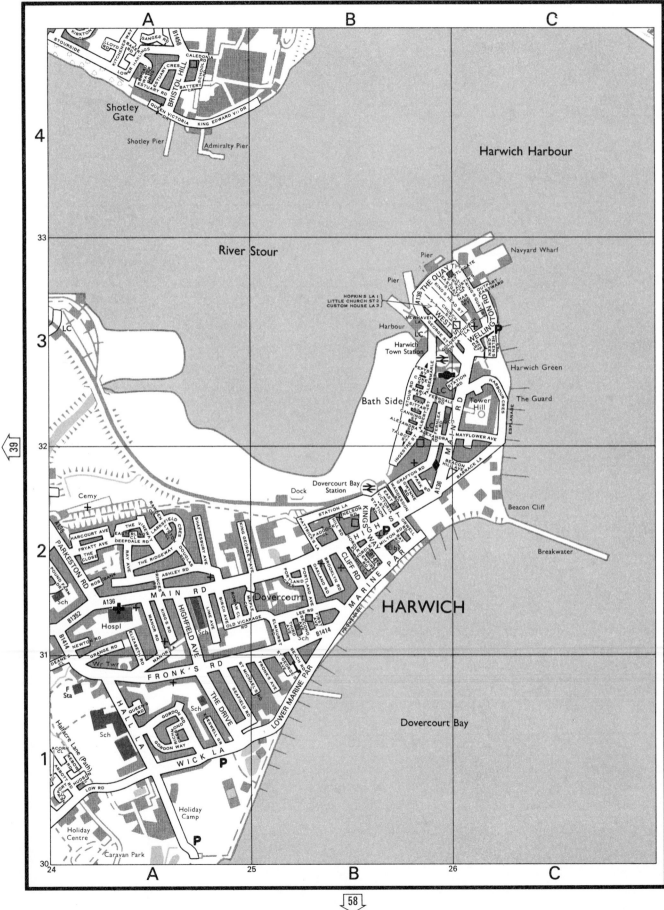

A　　　　　B　　　　　C

Harwich Harbour

Shotley
Gate

Shotley Pier

Admiralty Pier

4

River Stour

Navyard Wharf

Pier

Pier

HOPKIN'S LA 1
LITTLE CHURCH ST 2
CUSTOM HOUSE LA 3

Harbour

Harwich
Town Station

Harwich Green

The Guard

3

Bath Side

Tower
Hill

Mayflower Ave

LC

Beacon Cliff

32

Dovercourt Bay
Station

Dock

Cemy

Breakwater

Harcourt Ave

Dovercourt

HARWICH

2

MAIN RD

Sch

Hospl

Lee Rd

HIGHFIELD AVE

Sch

31

FRONK'S RD

Wr Twr

F
Sta

THE DRIVE

Sch

Sch

WICK LA

Dovercourt Bay

1

P

Holiday
Camp

Holiday
Centre

P

Caravan Park

30

24　　　　　25　　　　　26

A　　　　　B　　　　　C

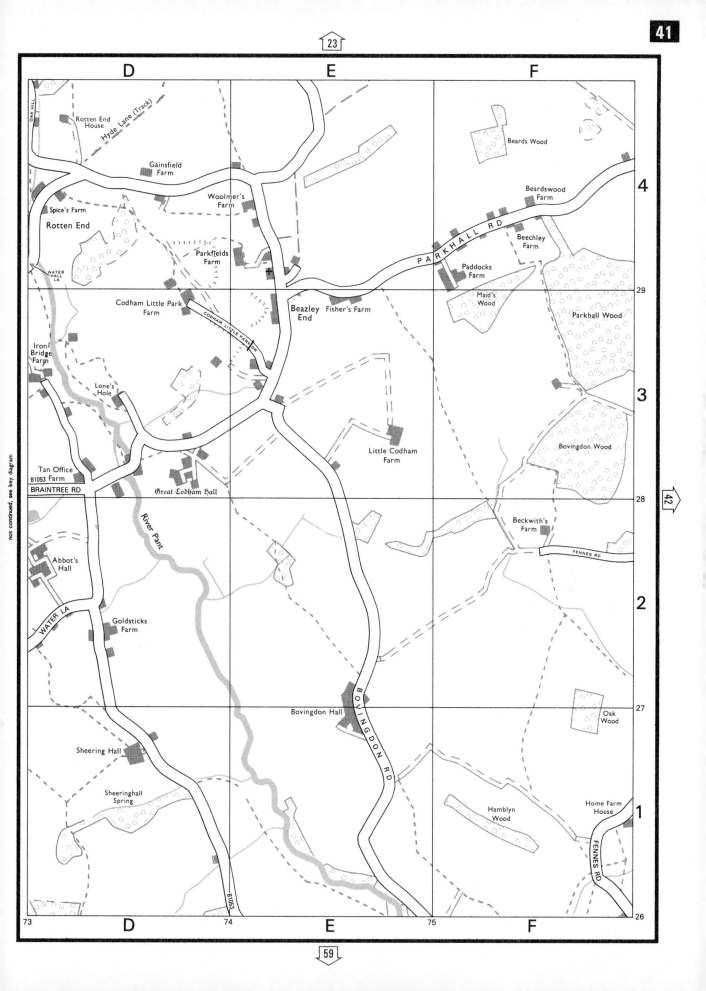

D E F

OAK HILL

Rotten End House

Hyde Lane (Track)

Gainsfield Farm

Woolmer's Farm

Spice's Farm

Rotten End

WATER HALL LA

Parkfields Farm

Codham Little Park Farm

CODHAM LITTLE PARK OR

Beazley End

Fisher's Farm

Beards Wood

Beardswood Farm

PARKHALL RD

Beechley Farm

Paddocks Farm

Maid's Wood

Parkhall Wood

4

29

Iron Bridge Farm

Lone's Hole

Little Codham Farm

Bovingdon Wood

3

Tan Office Farm
B1053

BRAINTREE RD

Great Codham Hall

River Pant

Beckwith's Farm

FENNES RD

28

Abbot's Hall

WATER LA

Goldsticks Farm

BOVINGDON RD

Bovingdon Hall

2

27

Oak Wood

Sheering Hall

Sheeringhall Spring

Hamblyn Wood

Home Farm House

FENNES RD

1

B1053

73 D 74 E 75 F **26**

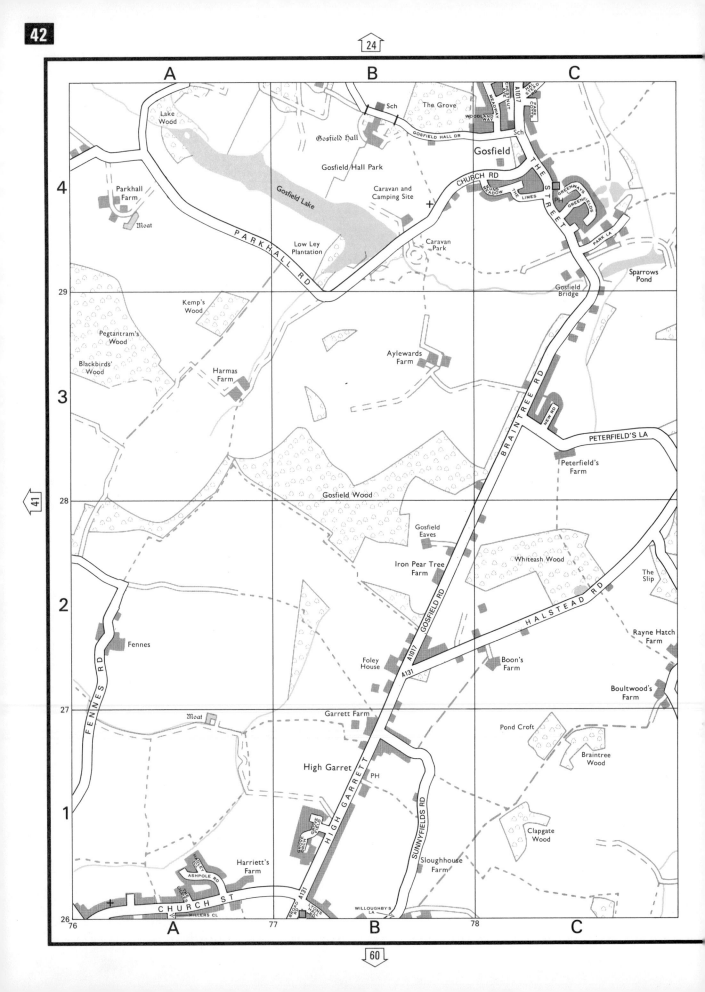

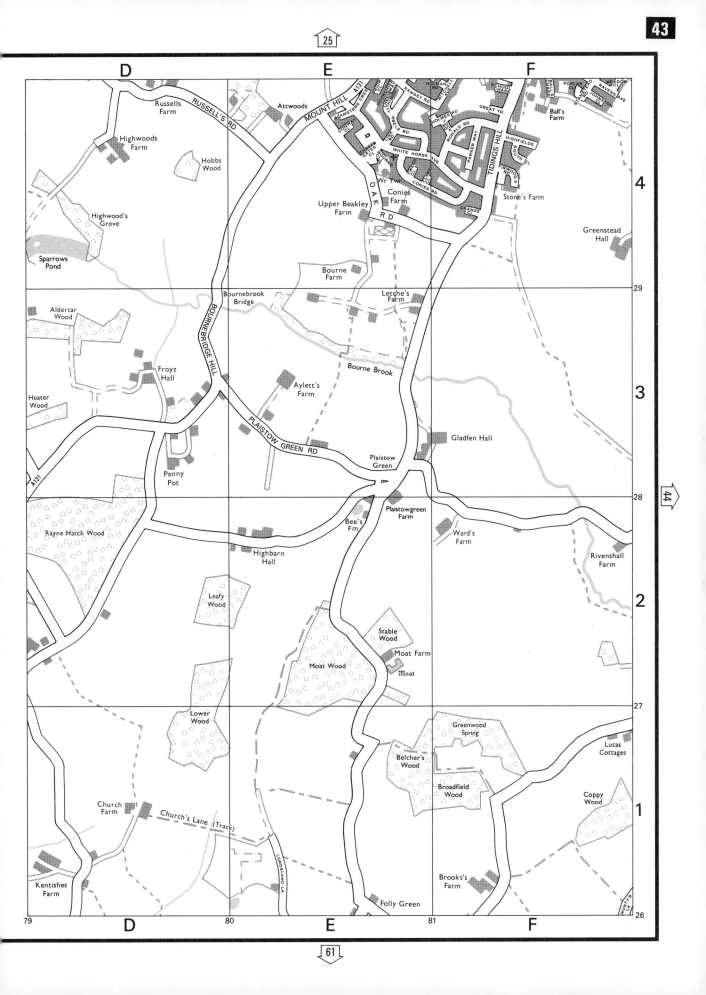

D   E   F

Russells Farm

RUSSELL'S RD

Attwoods

MOUNT HILL A131

BRAMSTEAD RD

RAMSEY RD

SCHOOL CHASE

POPLAR CL

MEADOW

RAVENS AVE

JOHNSTON

Highwoods Farm

Hobbs Wood

GREAT YD

Ball's Farm

HOLMES RD

RONALD RD

PARKER WAY

HIGHFIELDS

TIDINGS HILL

FIRWOODS

SOUTH CL

Highwood's Grove

WHITE HORSE AVE

CONIES RD

OAK RD

Stone's Farm

Sparrows Pond

Wr Twr

Conies Farm

ORANGE CL

Greenstead Hall

Upper Beakley Farm

Bourne Farm

4

Bournebrook Bridge

Letche's Farm

29

Aldercar Wood

BOURNEBRIDGE HILL

Bourne Brook

Heater Wood

Froyz Hall

Aylett's Farm

Gladfen Hall

3

A131

PLAISTOW GREEN RD

Plaistow Green

44

Penny Pot

28

Rayne Hatch Wood

Bee's Fm

Plaistowgreen Farm

Ward's Farm

Rivenshall Farm

Highbarn Hall

Leafy Wood

2

Stable Wood

Moat Farm

Moat

Moat Wood

Lower Wood

27

Greenwood Spring

Lucas Cottages

Church Farm

Church's Lane (Track)

Belcher's Wood

Broadfield Wood

Coppy Wood

1

LORDSLAND LA

Kentishes Farm

Brooks's Farm

MUNT'S LA

Folly Green

26

79   D   80   E   81   F

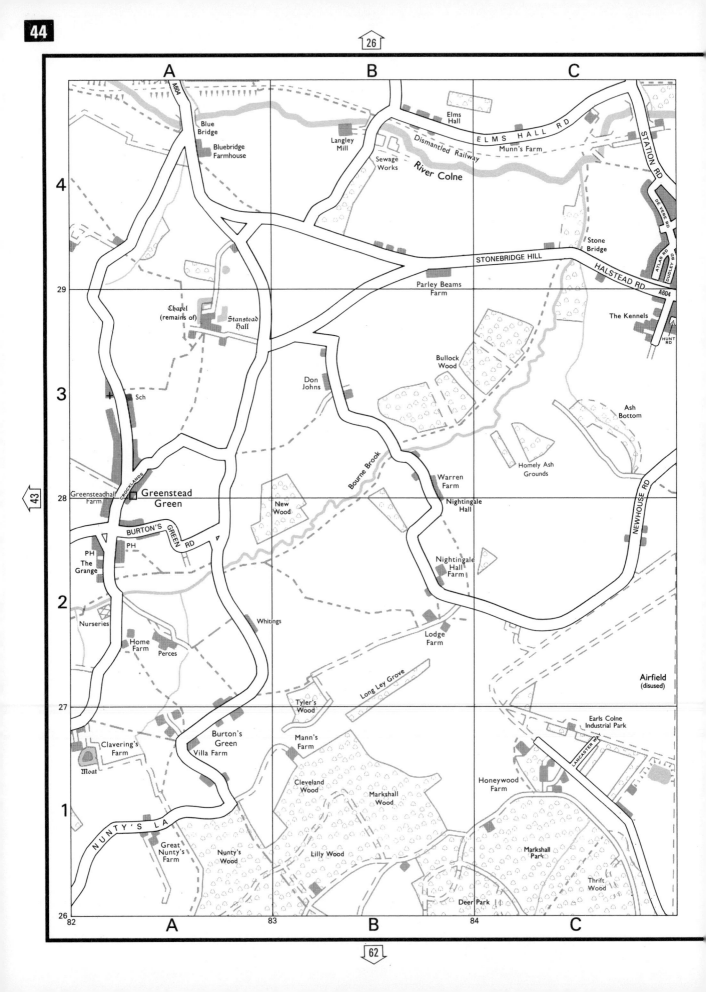

A

B

C

A604

Blue
Bridge

Bluebridge
Farmhouse

Langley
Mill

Elms
Hall

ELMS HALL RD

Munn's Farm

Dismantled Railway

River Colne

STATION RD

DE VERE RD

Sewage
Works

4

Stone
Bridge

STONEBRIDGE HILL

HALSTEAD RD

A604

29

Parley Beams
Farm

The Kennels

Chapel
(remains of)

Stanstead
Hall

HUNT
RD

Bullock
Wood

Don
Johns

Ash
Bottom

3

Sch

43

Bourne Brook

Homely Ash
Grounds

CROCKLANDS

Greensteadhall
Farm

Greenstead
Green

Warren
Farm

NEWHOUSE RD

28

New
Wood

Nightingale
Hall

BURTON'S GREEN RD

PH
The
Grange

PH

Nightingale
Hall
Farm

Nurseries

Whitings

2

Home
Farm

Perces

Lodge
Farm

Airfield
(disused)

Long Ley Grove

27

Tyler's
Wood

Earls Colne
Industrial Park

Clavering's
Farm

Burton's
Green
Villa Farm

Mann's
Farm

LANCASTER WK

Moat

Cleveland
Wood

Honeywood
Farm

NUNTY'S LA

Markshall
Wood

1

Great
Nunty's
Farm

Nunty's
Wood

Lilly Wood

Markshall
Park

Thrift
Wood

26

82

A

83

B

84

C

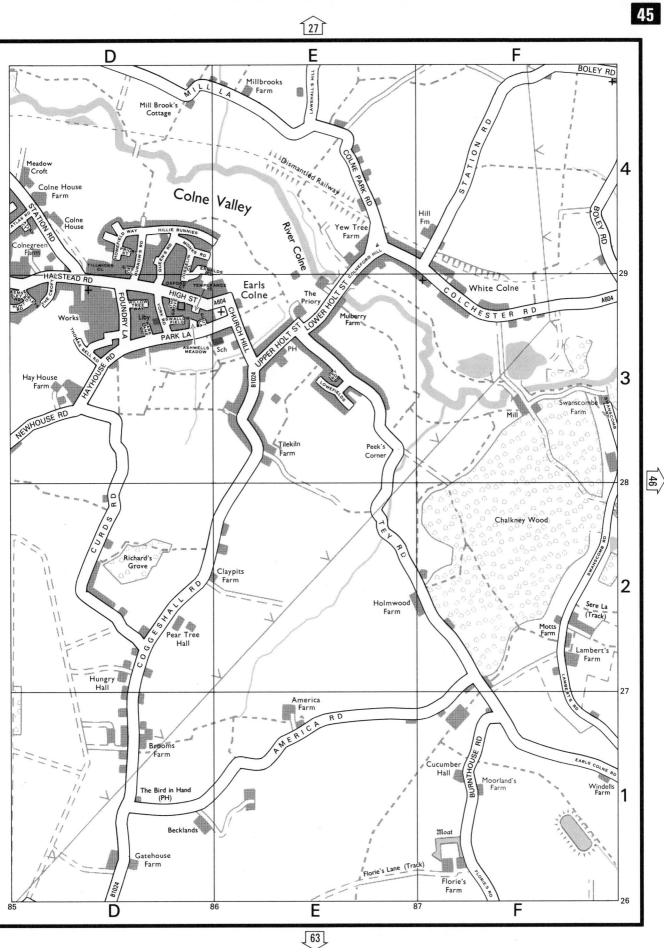

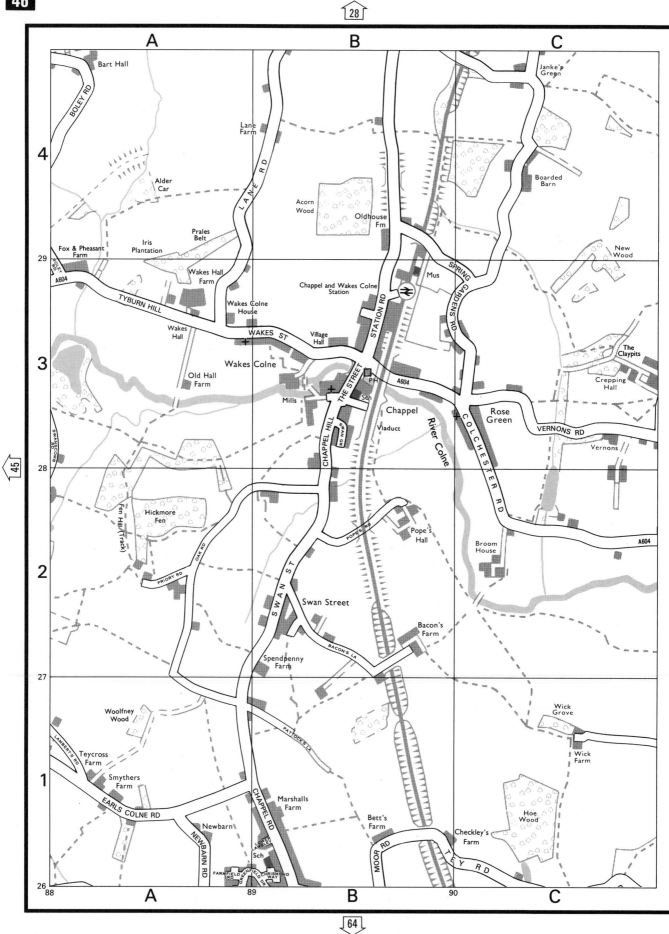

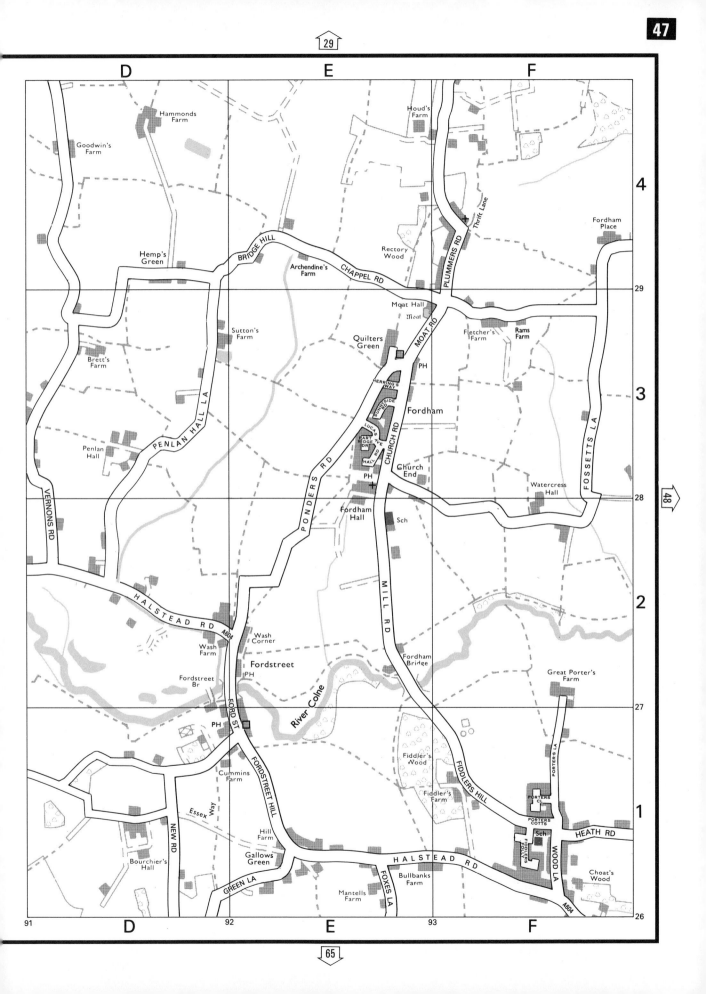

D E F

4

29

3

28

48

2

27

1

26

91 D 92 E 93 F

Hammonds Farm
Goodwin's Farm
Houd's Farm
Thrift Lane
Fordham Place
Hemp's Green
BRIDGE HILL
Archendine's Farm
CHAPPEL RD
Rectory Wood
PLUMMERS RD
Moat Hall
Moat
Fletcher's Farm
Rams Farm
Sutton's Farm
Quilters Green
PH
Brett's Farm
PENLAN HALL LA
HERRING'S WAY
SUNNYSIDE
LUCAS
PARTRIDGE DR
TYE
HALL
Fordham
CHURCH RD
MOAT RD
FOSSETTS LA
Penlan Hall
PH
Church End
Watercress Hall
VERNONS RD
Fordham Hall
Sch
HALSTEAD RD
A604
Wash Corner
MILL RD
Wash Farm
Fordstreet
PH
Fordham Bridge
Great Porter's Farm
Fordstreet Br
River Colne
PORTERS LA
FORD ST
PH
FIDDLERS HILL
Fiddler's Wood
PORTERS CL
Cummins Farm
FORDSTREET HILL
Fiddler's Farm
PORTERS COTTS
Essex Way
Sch
NEW RD
Hill Farm
WOOD LA
HEATH RD
Bourchier's Hall
Gallows Green
FIDDLERS FOLLY
Choat's Wood
GREEN LA
FOXES LA
HALSTEAD RD
Bullbanks Farm
A604
Mantells Farm

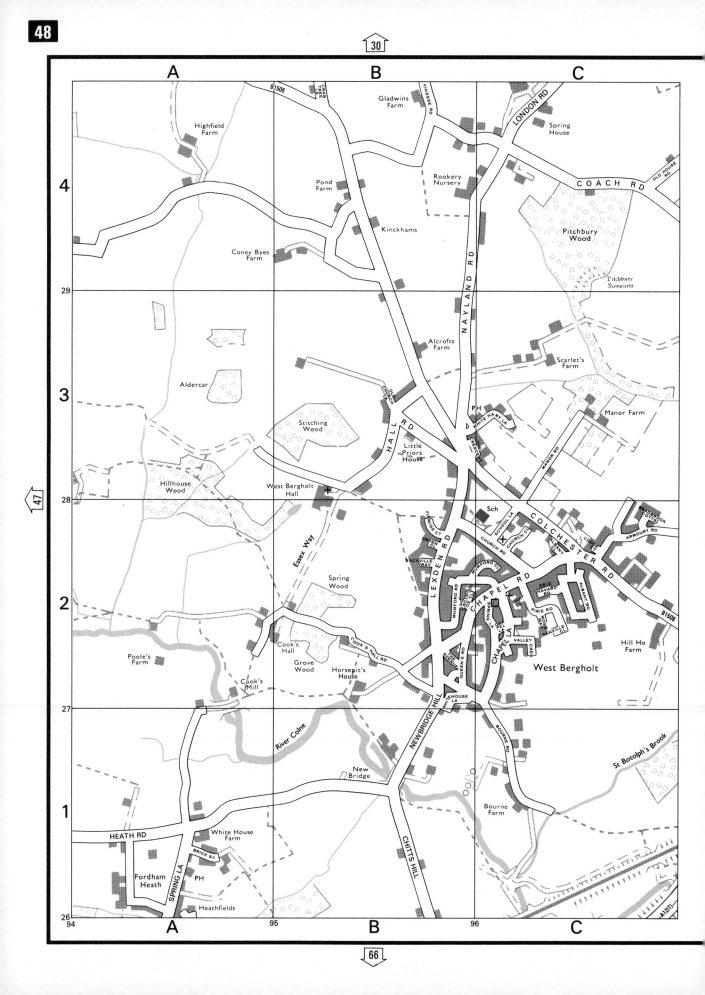

A   B   C

B1508
CRAB TREE
Gladwins Farm
VINESSE RD
LONDON RD
Spring House

Highfield Farm
Pond Farm
Rookery Nursery
COACH RD
OLD HOUSE LA

4

Kinckhams
Pitchbury Wood

Coney Byes Farm
NAYLAND RD
Pitchbury Ramparts

29

Alcrofts Farm
Scarlet's Farm

Aldercar
Stitching Wood
OLD CHURCH
PH
WHITE HART LA
Manor Farm

3

HALL RD
Little Priors House
MANOR RD

Hillhouse Wood
West Bergholt Hall
Sch
COLCHESTER RD
BRAZBROOK COTS
ARMOURY RD

28

Essex Way
SCHOOL LA
CHURCH RD
CHURCH CL
ALBANY
LODGE LA

FIRMINS CT
GREEN LA
SACKVILLE WAY
LEXDEN RD
MUMFORD CT
MUMFORD RD
CHAPEL RD
ERLE
HAVARD RD
ALBANY RD
B1508

Spring Wood
QUEEN'S RD
SPRING LA
PIRIE RD
GRANVILLE CL

2

Cook's Hall
Grove Wood
COOK'S HALL RD
Horsepit's House
CHAPEL LA
VALLEY CRES
Hill Ho Farm

Poole's Farm
Cook's Mill
AVENUE
QUEEN'S RD
West Bergholt

27

NEWBRIDGE HILL
WHITE HOUSE LA
BOURNE RD
St Botolph's Brook

River Colne
New Bridge
Bourne Farm

1

HEATH RD
White House Farm
CHITTS HILL

SPRING LA
BRICK ST
Fordham Heath
PH
Heathfields

26
94   A   95   B   96   C

A12(T)

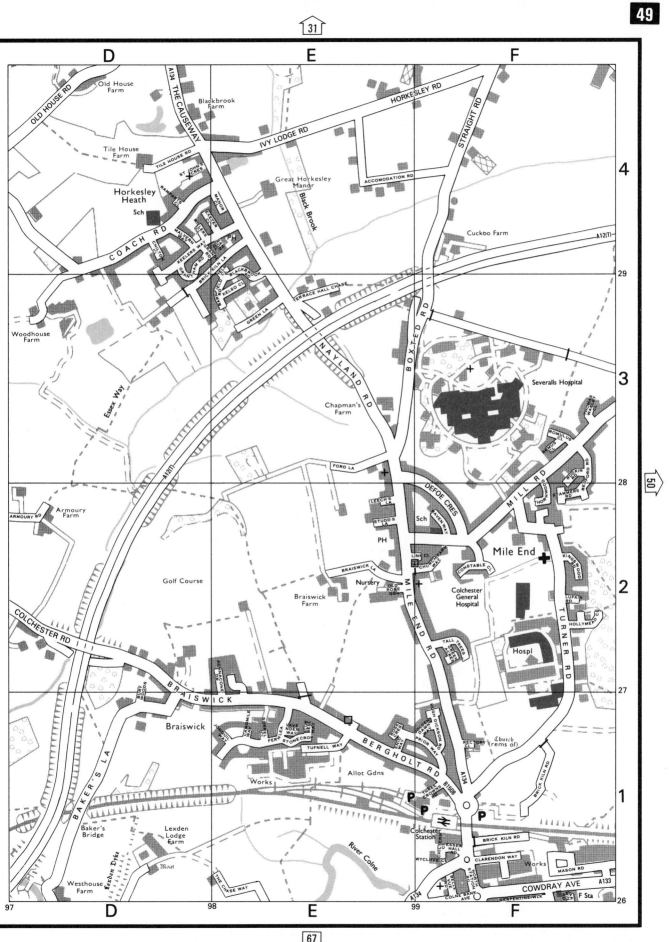

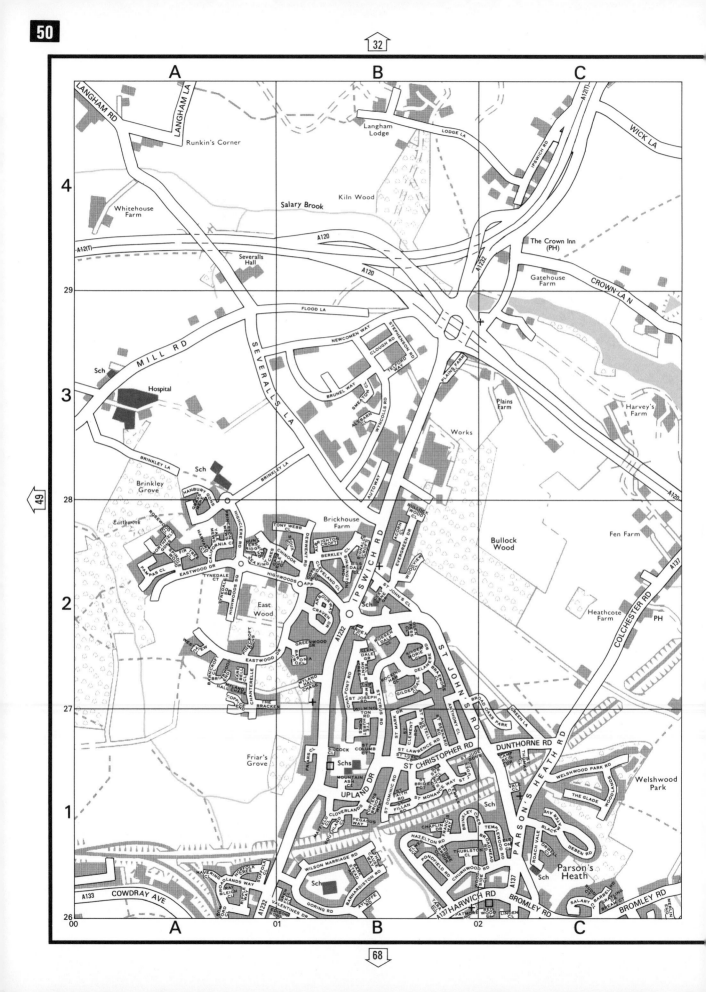

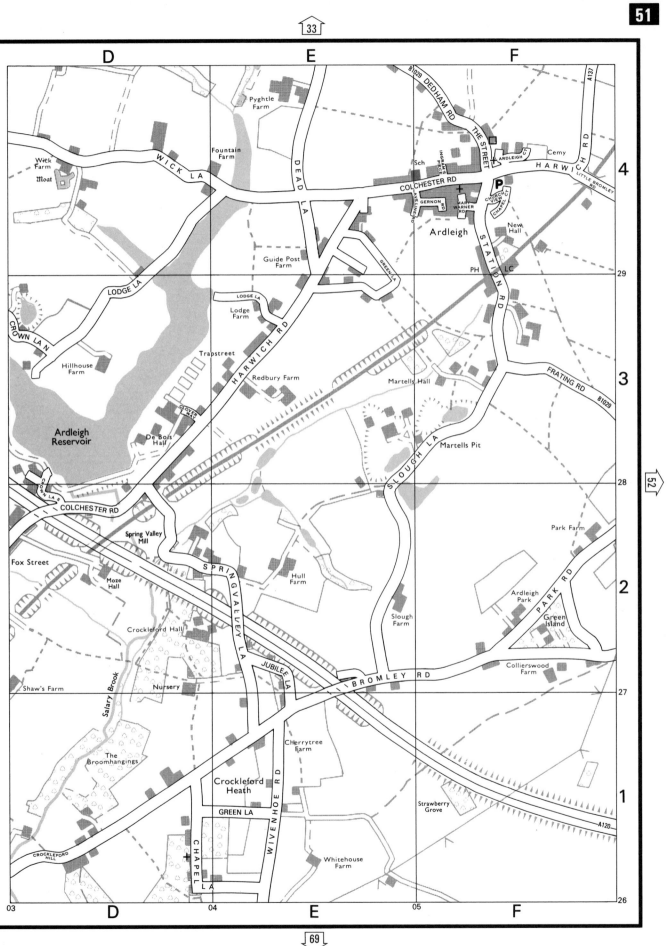

D E F

52

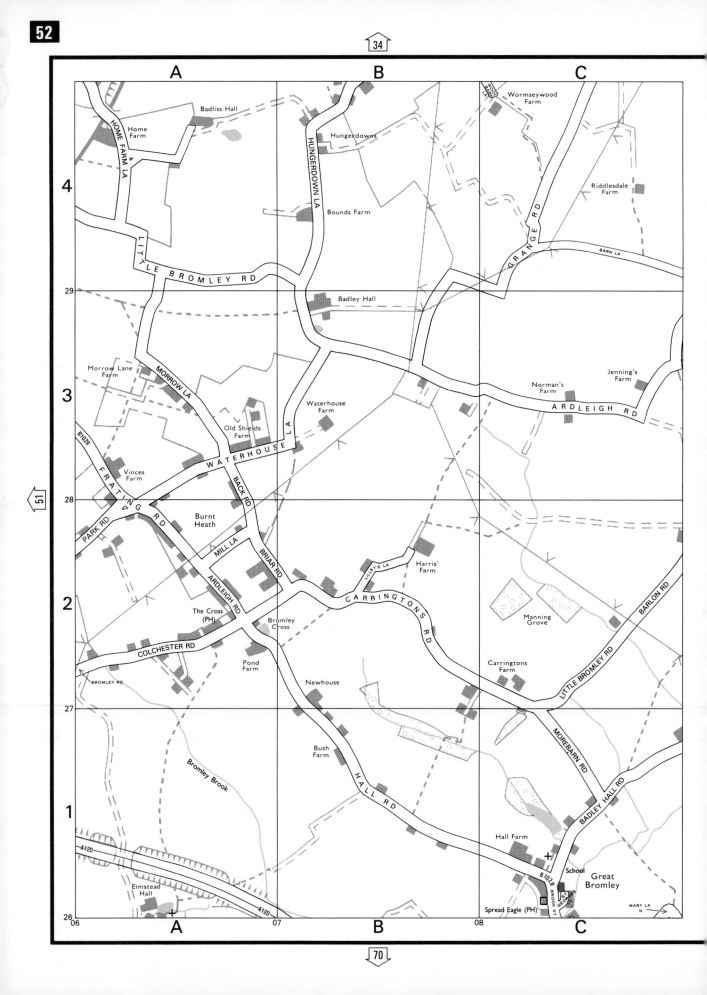

51

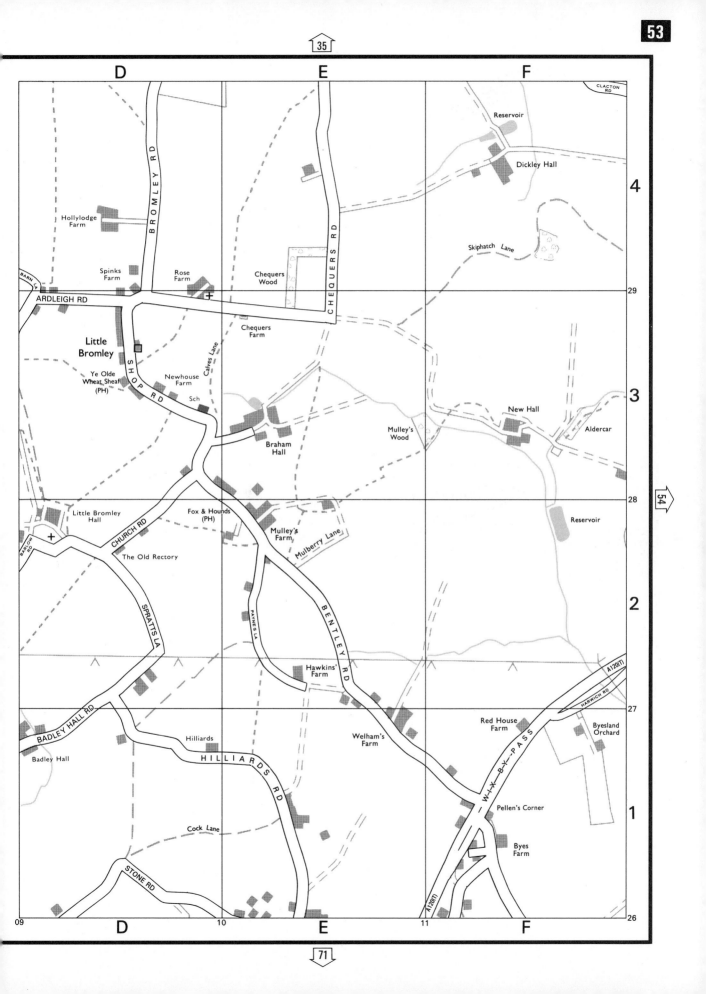

D   E   F

CLACTON RD

Reservoir

Dickley Hall

4

Skiphatch Lane

Hollylodge Farm

BROMLEY RD

BARN LA

Spinks Farm

Rose Farm

Chequers Wood

CHEQUERS RD

29

ARDLEIGH RD

Chequers Farm

Little Bromley

SHOP RD

Ye Olde Wheat Sheaf (PH)

Newhouse Farm

Calves Lane

Sch

New Hall

Aldercar

3

Mulley's Wood

Braham Hall

28

Little Bromley Hall

CHURCH RD

Fox & Hounds (PH)

Reservoir

BARLOW RD

The Old Rectory

Mulley's Farm

Mulberry Lane

54

SPRATTS LA

PAYNE'S LA

BENTLEY RD

2

A120(T)

HARWICH RD

Hawkins' Farm

27

Red House Farm

Byesland Orchard

BADLEY HALL RD

Hilliards

Welham's Farm

W—I—X—B—Y—P—A—S—S

Badley Hall

HILLIARDS RD

Pellen's Corner

1

Byes Farm

Cock Lane

STONE RD

A120(T)

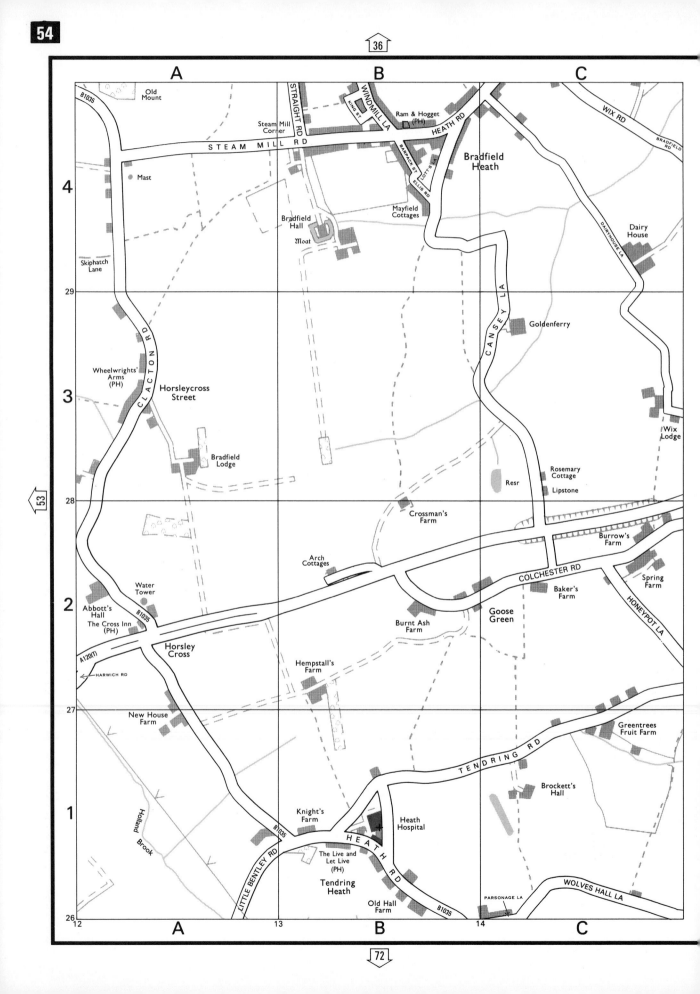

A   B   C

B1035

Old Mount

Mast

Steam Mill Corner

STRAIGHT RD

WINDMILL LA

KING ST

Ram & Hogget (PH)

HEATH RD

WIX RD

BRADFIELD RD

S T E A M   M I L L   R D

BARPACK ST

ELLIS RD

LOTT'S LA

Bradfield Heath

4

Bradfield Hall

Moat

Mayfield Cottages

Dairy House

DAIRYHOUSE LA

Skiphatch Lane

29

CLACTON RD

Wheelwrights' Arms (PH)

Horsleycross Street

CANSEY LA

Goldenferry

3

Bradfield Lodge

Wix Lodge

Rosemary Cottage

Resr

Lipstone

53

28

Crossman's Farm

Burrow's Farm

COLCHESTER RD

Spring Farm

Arch Cottages

Water Tower

B1035

Baker's Farm

Goose Green

HONEYPOT LA

2

Abbott's Hall

The Cross Inn (PH)

Horsley Cross

Burnt Ash Farm

A120(T)

HARWICH RD

Hempstall's Farm

27

New House Farm

TENDRING RD

Greentrees Fruit Farm

Brockett's Hall

Holland Brook

Knight's Farm

B1035

Heath Hospital

1

LITTLE BENTLEY RD

H E A T H   R D

The Live and Let Live (PH)

Tendring Heath

Old Hall Farm

B1035

PARSONAGE LA

WOLVES HALL LA

26

12   A   13   B   14   C

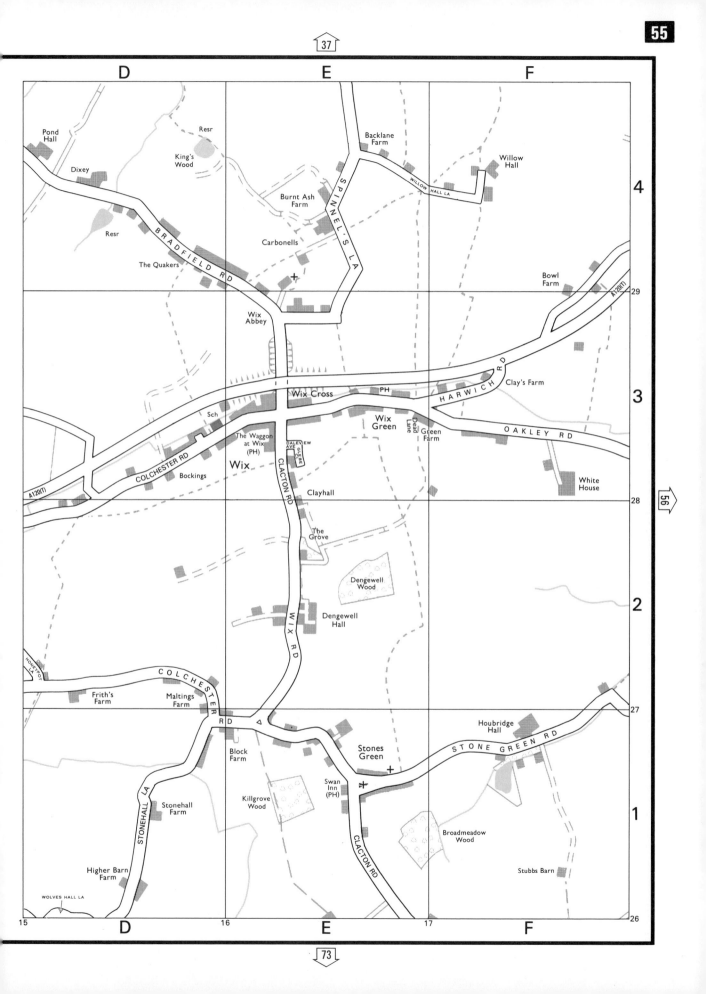

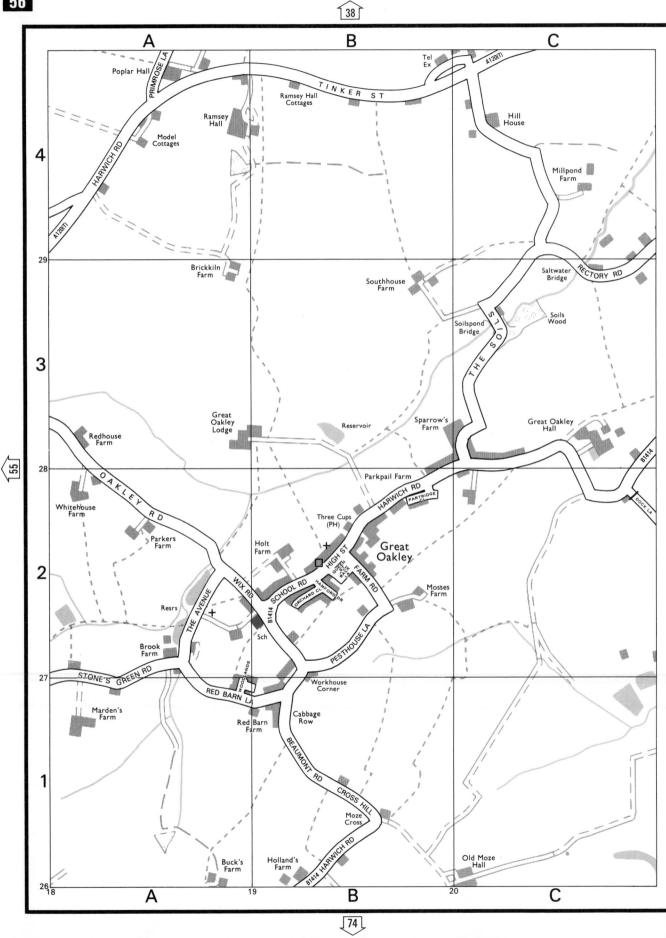

A   B   C

Poplar Hall
PRIMROSE LA
Ramsey Hall Cottages
TINKER ST
Tel Ex
A120(T)
Hill House
4
HARWICH RD
Model Cottages
Ramsey Hall
Millpond Farm
A120(T)
29
Brickkiln Farm
Southhouse Farm
Saltwater Bridge
RECTORY RD
THE SOILS
Soilspond Bridge
Soils Wood
3
Great Oakley Lodge
Reservoir
Sparrow's Farm
Great Oakley Hall
Redhouse Farm
B1414
OAKLEY RD
28
Parkpail Farm
HARWICH RD
DOCK LA
Whitehouse Farm
PARTRIDGE CL
Three Cups (PH)
Great Oakley
Parkers Farm
WIX RD
Holt Farm
HIGH ST
FARM RD
2
THE AVENUE
Resrs
SCHOOL RD
B1414
ORCHARD CL
HAMFORD DR
Mosses Farm
Brook Farm
Sch
PESTHOUSE LA
27
STONE'S GREEN RD
RED BARN LA
WOODLANDS
Workhouse Corner
Marden's Farm
Red Barn Farm
Cabbage Row
BEAUMONT RD
CROSS HILL
1
Moze Cross
Buck's Farm
Holland's Farm
B1414 HARWICH RD
Old Moze Hall
26
18   19   20

A   B   C

55

39

D   E   F

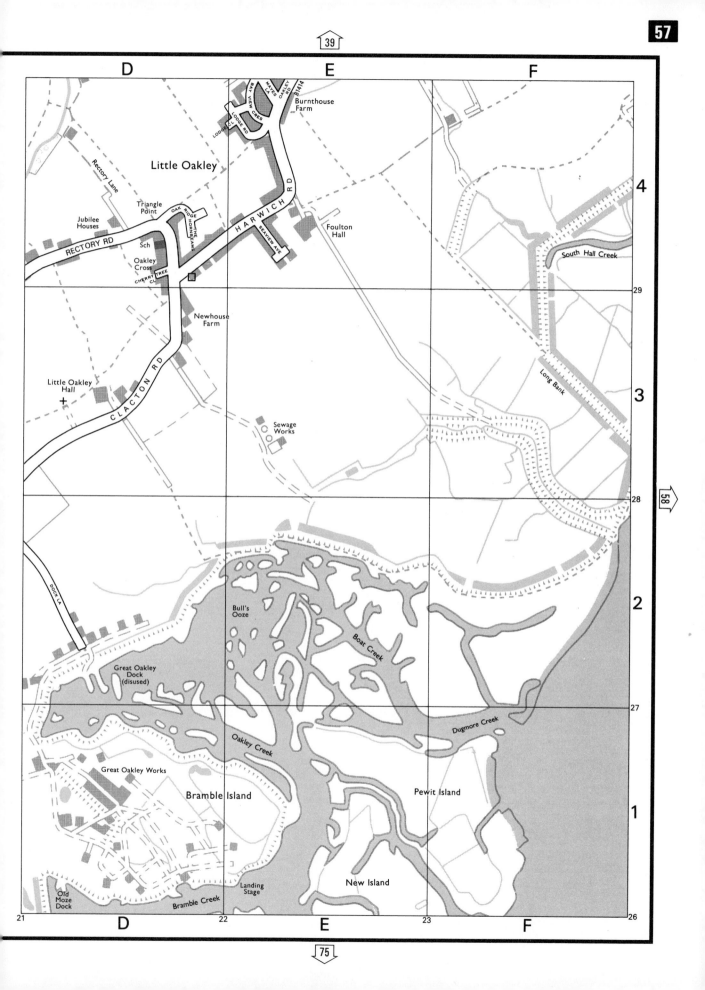

Burnthouse Farm

BAY VIEW CRES

HAYES LA

OAKLEY RD

LODGE RD

B1414

Little Oakley

Triangle Point

OAK RIDGE

THE HORNBEAMS

HARWICH RD

SEAVIEW AVE

Foulton Hall

4

Rectory Lane

Jubilee Houses

RECTORY RD

Sch

Oakley Cross

CHERRY TREE CL

South Hall Creek

29

Newhouse Farm

Long Bank

Little Oakley Hall

CLACTON RD

3

Sewage Works

28

58

DOCK LA

Bull's Ooze

Boat Creek

2

Great Oakley Dock (disused)

27

Dugmore Creek

Oakley Creek

Great Oakley Works

Bramble Island

Pewit Island

1

Old Moze Dock

Bramble Creek

Landing Stage

New Island

21   D   22   E   23   F   26

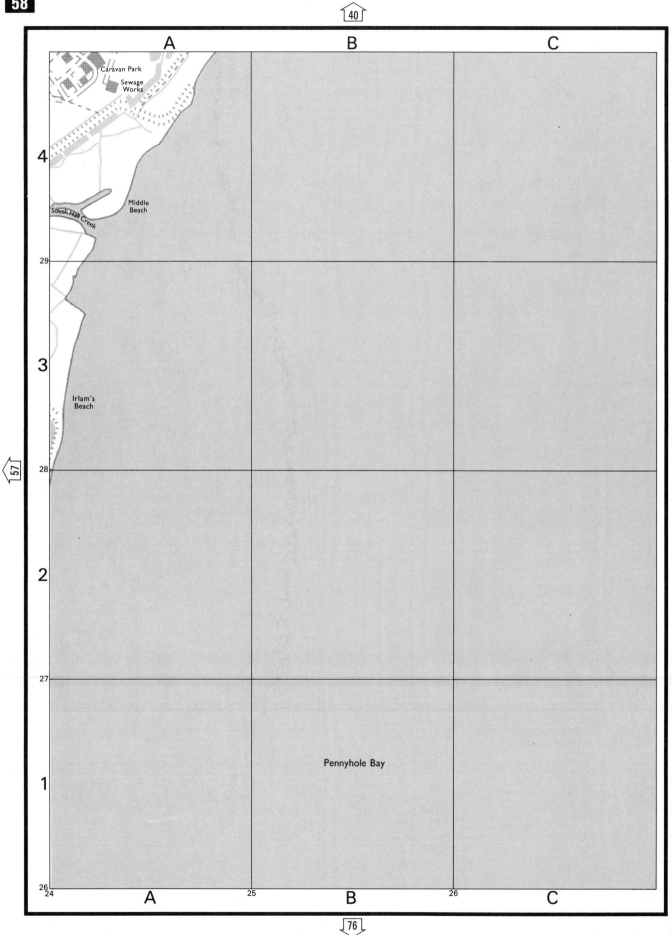

A B C

4

Caravan Park

Sewage
Works

Middle
Beach

South Hall Creek

29

3

Irlam's
Beach

28

2

27

Pennyhole Bay

1

26
24 25 26

A B C

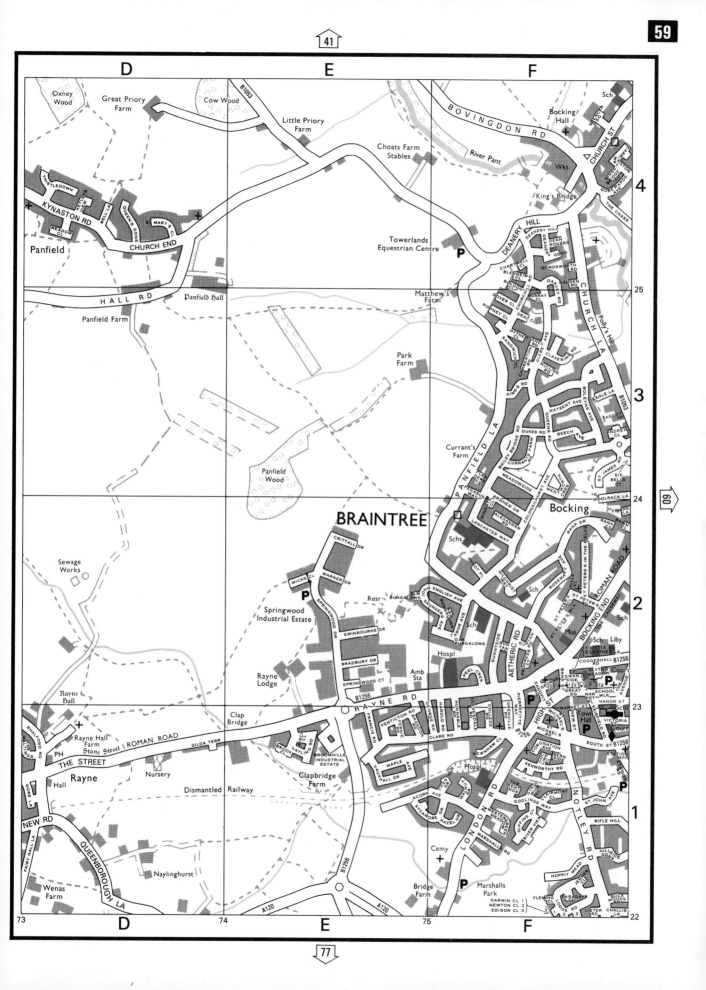

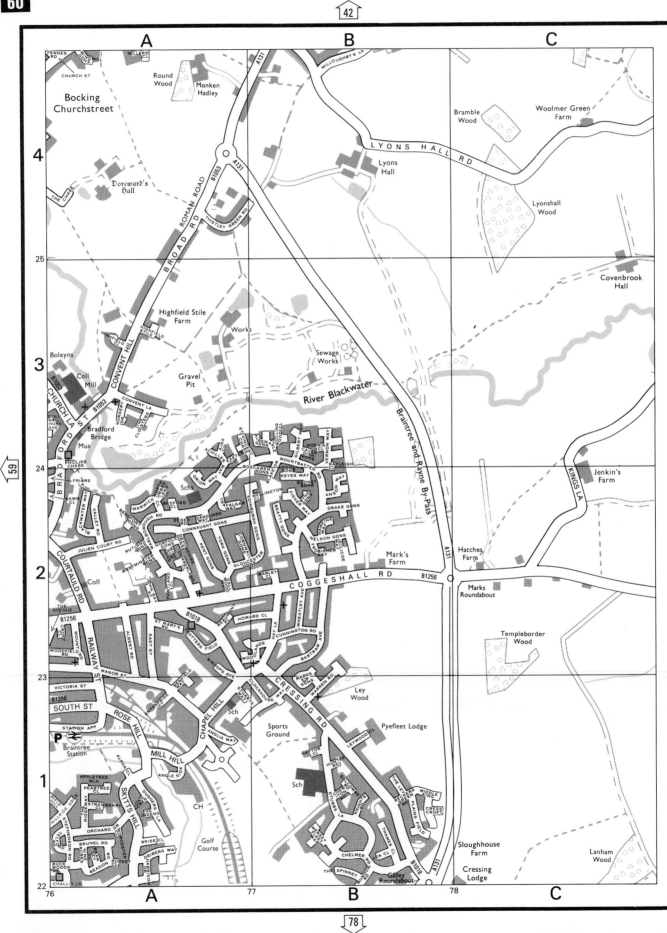

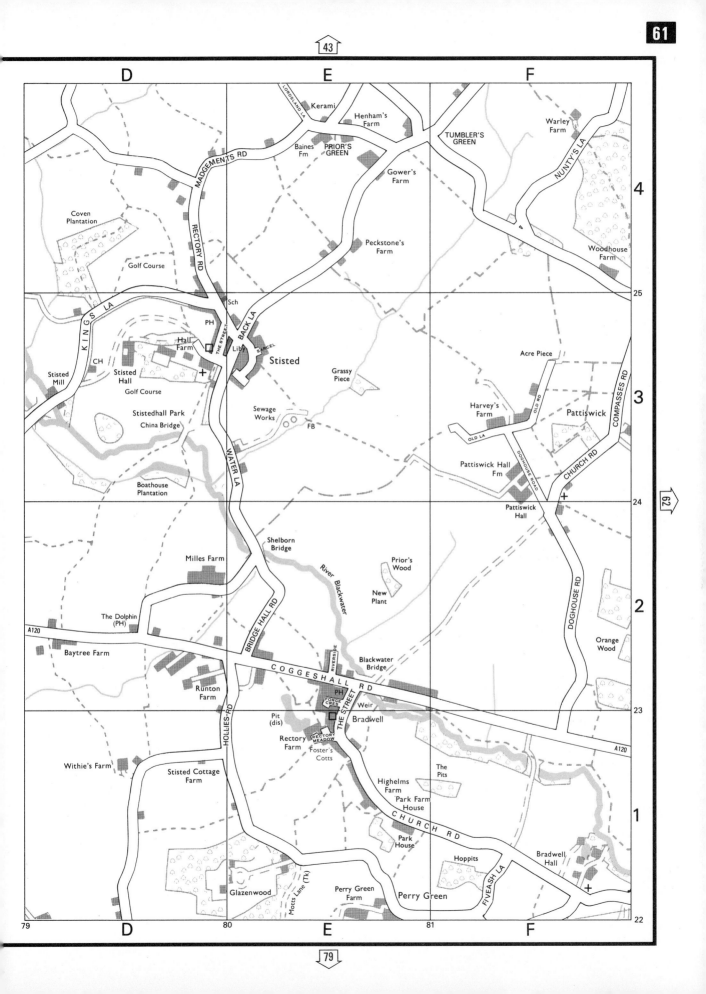

D

E

F

Kerami
LORDSLAND LA
Henham's
Farm
Baines
Fm
PRIOR'S
GREEN
TUMBLER'S
GREEN
Warley
Farm
NUNTY'S LA
MADGEMENTS RD
Gower's
Farm

4

Coven
Plantation
RECTORY RD
Peckstone's
Farm
Woodhouse
Farm

Golf Course

25

KINGS LA
Sch
BACK LA
Acre Piece
COMPASSES RD

PH
THE STREET
Libry
SARCEL
Stisted
Grassy
Piece
Harvey's
Farm
OLD RD
Pattiswick

3

CH
Hall
Farm
Stisted
Mill
Stisted
Hall
Golf Course
OLD LA
CHURCH RD

Stistedhall Park
China Bridge
Sewage
Works
FB
Pattiswick Hall
Fm
DOGHOUSE ROAD

WATER LA
Pattiswick
Hall

Boathouse
Plantation

24

Shelborn
Bridge
Milles Farm
River Blackwater
Prior's
Wood
DOGHOUSE RD

2

BRIDGE HALL RD
New
Plant
Orange
Wood

The Dolphin
(PH)
A120
Baytree Farm
Blackwater
Bridge
RIVERSIDE
COGGESHALL RD

Runton
Farm
PH
THE STREET
Weir
A120

HOLLIES RD
FORGE
CRES
Bradwell

23

Pit
(dis)
RECTORY
MEADOW
Withie's Farm
Rectory
Farm
Foster's
Cotts
Highelms
Farm
The
Pits

Stisted Cottage
Farm
Park Farm
House

CHURCH RD

1

Park
House
Hoppits
Bradwell
Hall
FIVEASH LA

Glazenwood
MOTTS LANE (Tk)
Perry Green
Farm
Perry Green

79

D

80

E

81

F

22

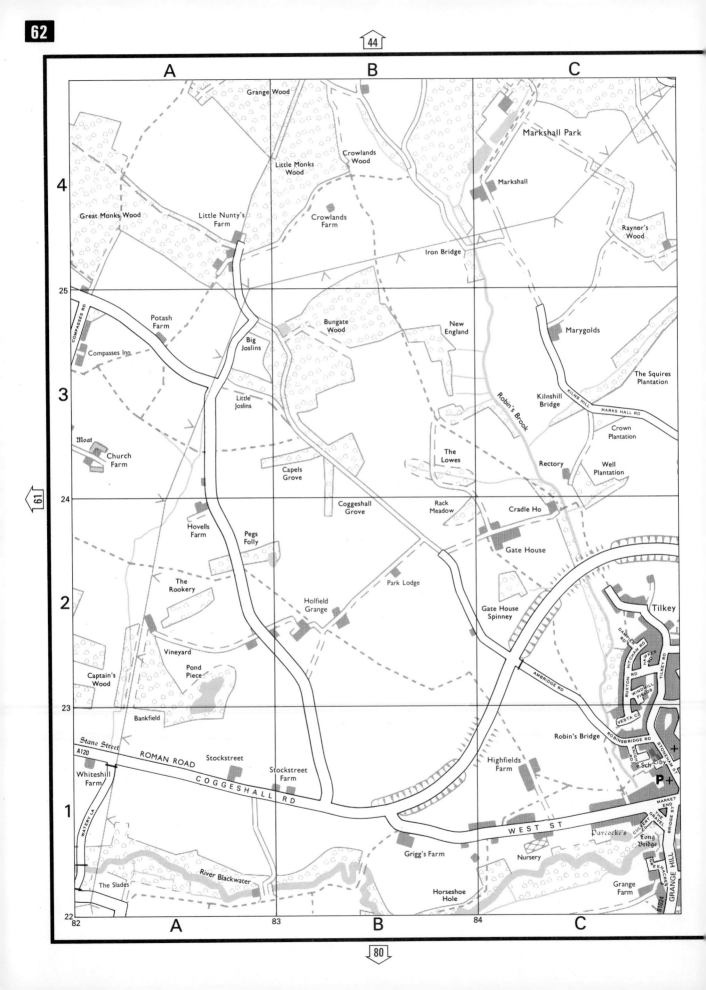

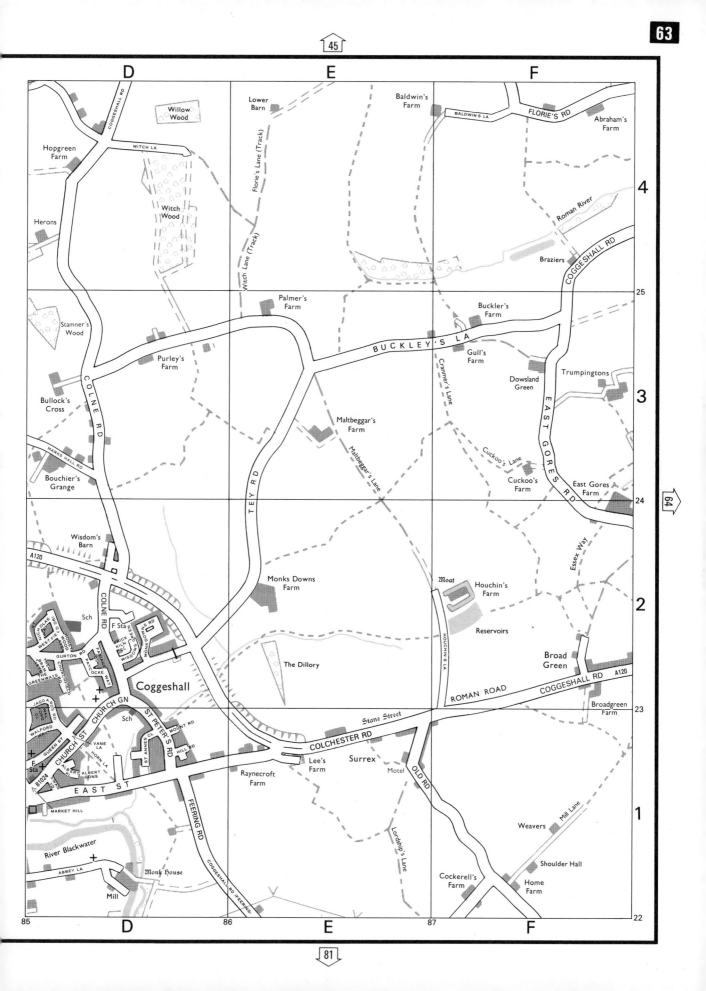

D E F

Willow Wood

Lower Barn

Baldwin's Farm

BALDWIN'S LA

FLORIE'S RD

Abraham's Farm

Hopgreen Farm

WITCH LA

COGGESHALL RD

4

Roman River

Herons

Witch Wood

Braziers

COGGESHALL RD

25

Witch Lane (Track)

Florie's Lane (Track)

Palmer's Farm

Buckler's Farm

Stamner's Wood

BUCKLEY'S LA

Gull's Farm

Dowsland Green

Trumpingtons

3

Purley's Farm

Cranmer's Lane

EAST GORES RD

COLNE RD

Bullock's Cross

Maltbeggar's Farm

Cuckoo's Lane

MARKS HALL RD

Maltbeggar's Lane

Cuckoo's Farm

East Gores Farm

24

Bouchier's Grange

TEY RD

Essex Way

Wisdom's Barn

A120

Monks Downs Farm

Moat

Houchin's Farm

2

Reservoirs

Sch

F Sta

BRICK KILN LA

MONKDOWNS RD

WISDOM'S GREEN

HOUCHIN'S LA

Broad Green

NICHOLAS RD

WEST FIE

IRED WOOD

GURTON RD

PAYCOCKE WAY

FANNING RD

Coggeshall

The Dillory

COGGESHALL RD   A120

THE BRANCH

THE GREENWAYS

CHURCHFIELD

ROMAN ROAD

Broadgreen Farm

23

JAGG ARDS RD

POWELL CL

COLNE RD

CHURCH GN

Sch

Stane Street

WALFORD WAY

QUEEN ST

CHURCH ST

ST PETER'S RD

VANE LA

ST ANNES CL

MOUNT RD

HILL RD

COLCHESTER RD

Lee's Farm

Surrex

OLD RD

F Sta

ALBERT PL

HORN LA

ALBERT GDNS

Motel

B1024

EAST ST

Raynecroft Farm

1

Weavers

Mill Lane

Market Hill

FEERING RD

Lordship's Lane

Shoulder Hall

River Blackwater

Cockerell's Farm

Home Farm

ABBEY LA

Monk House

COGGESHALL RD (FEERING)

Mill

85 D 86 E 87 F 22

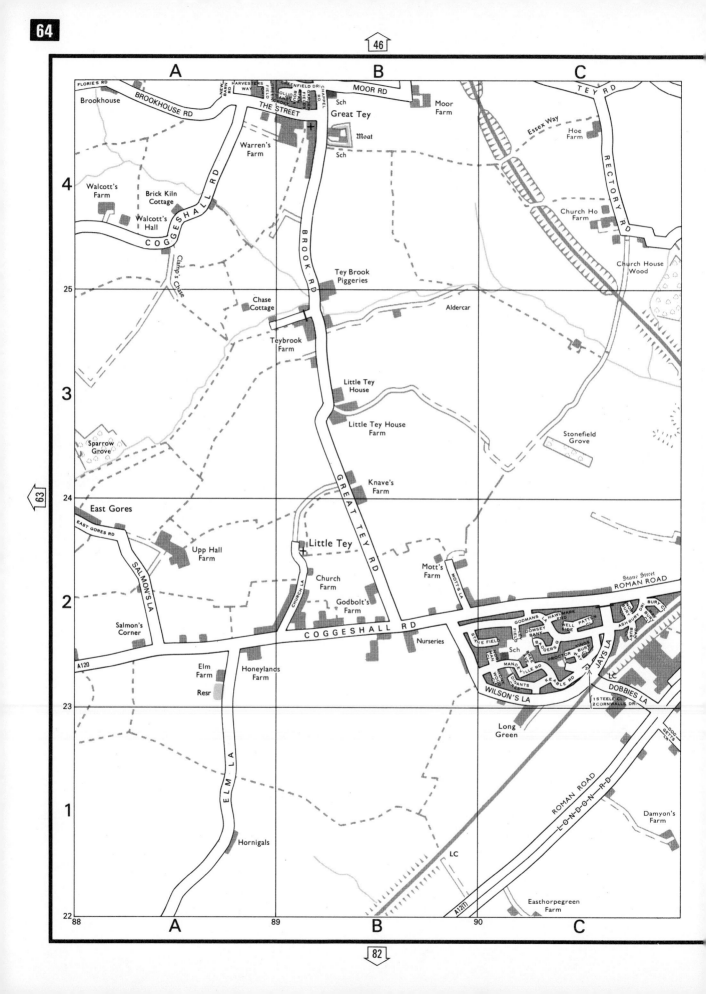

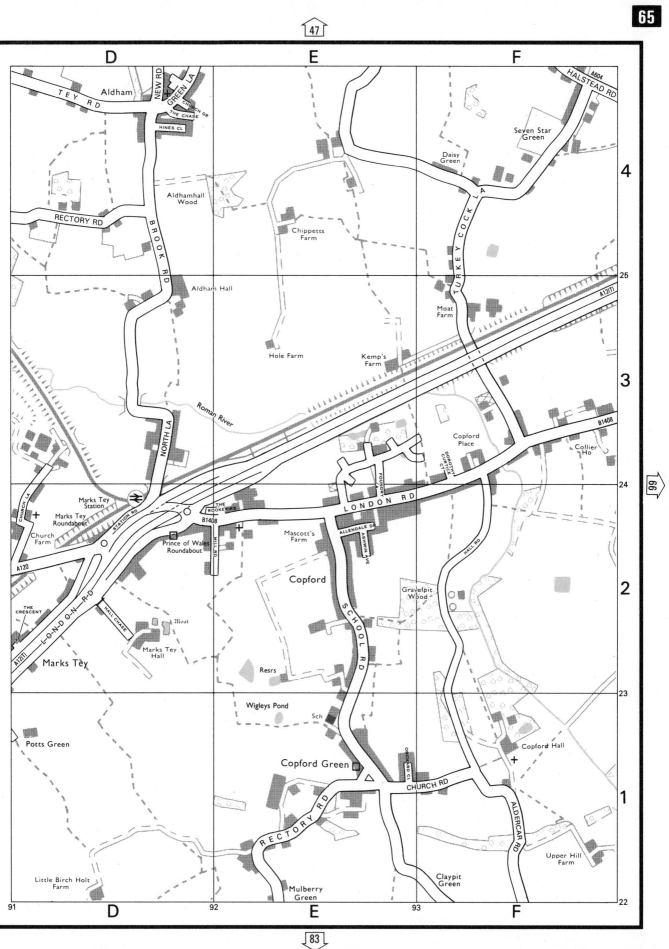

D   E   F

A604

HALSTEAD RD

NEW RD

GREEN LA

Aldham

TEY RD

CHURCH GR

THE CHASE

HINES CL

Seven Star
Green

Daisy
Green

4

Aldhamhall
Wood

BROOK RD

RECTORY RD

Chippetts
Farm

TURKEY COCK LA

25

Aldham Hall

Moat
Farm

A12(T)

Hole Farm

Kemp's
Farm

3

NORTH LA

Roman River

B1408

Copford
Place

Collier
Ho

DOROTHY CURTICE CT CE

Marks Tey
Station

LONDON RD

24

99

CHURCH LA

Marks Tey
Roundabout

STATION RD

THE
ROOKERIES

FOUNDRY LA

Church
Farm

B1408

MILL RD

Prince of Wales
Roundabout

Mascott's
Farm

ALLENDALE DR

ASHWIN AVE

HALL RD

A120

Copford

Gravelpit
Wood

2

THE
CRESCENT

L-O-N-D O-N—R-D

HALL CHASE

Moat

SCHOOL RD

A12(T)

Marks Tey
Hall

Marks Tey

Resrs

23

Wigleys Pond

Sch

Potts Green

Copford Hall

Copford Green

ORCHARD CL

CHURCH RD

1

RECTORY RD

ALDERCAR RD

Upper Hill
Farm

Little Birch Holt
Farm

Mulberry
Green

Claypit
Green

22

91   D   92   E   93   F

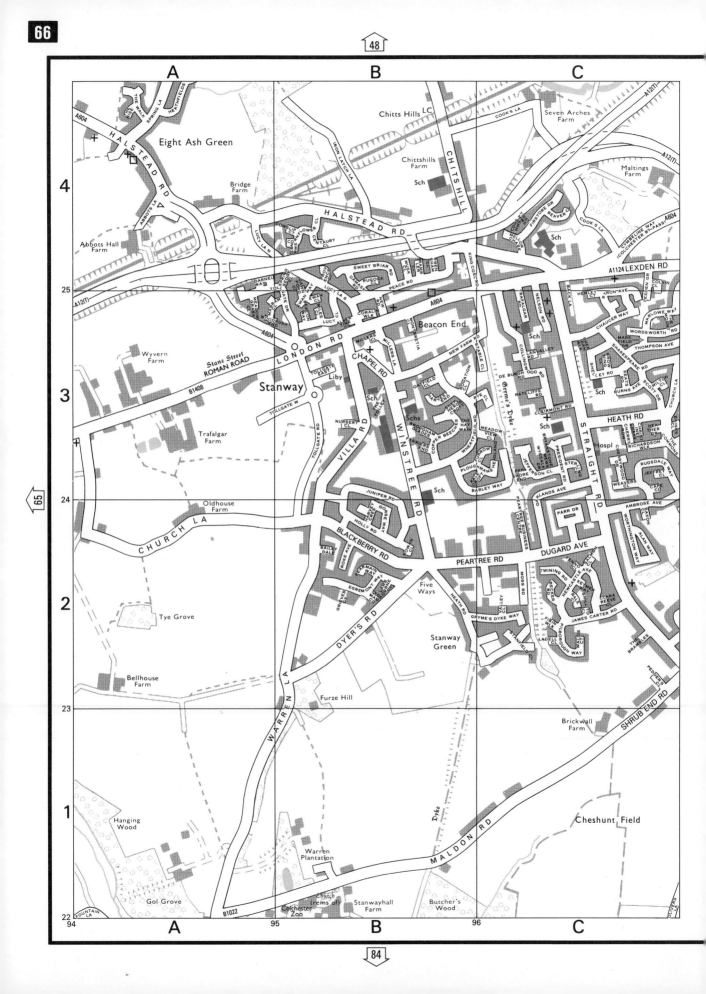

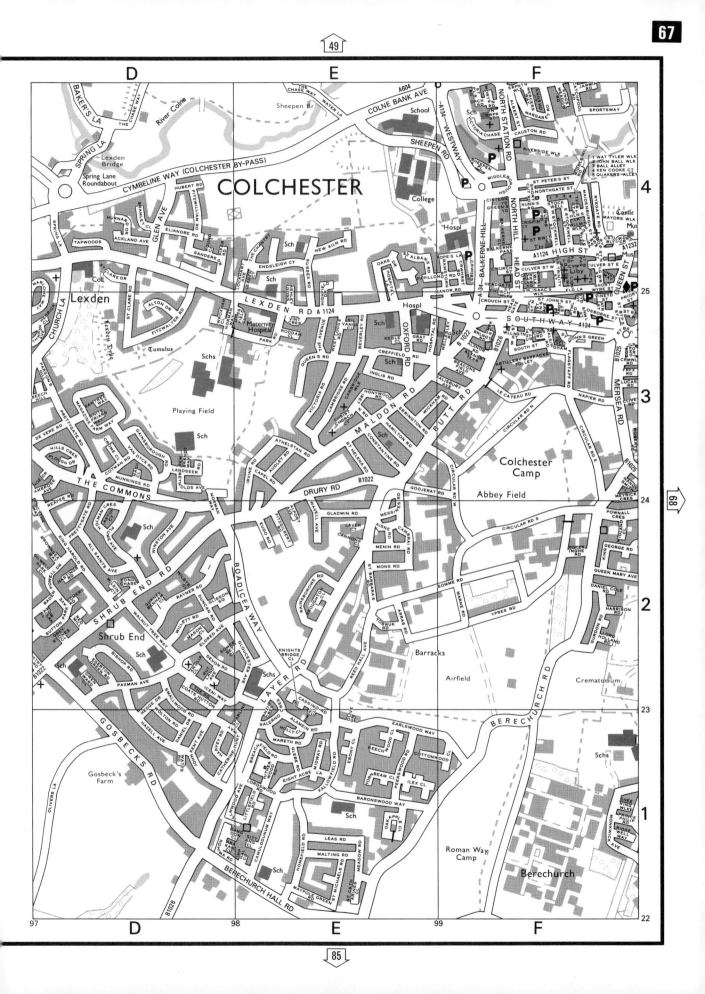

COLCHESTER

Lexden

Shrub End

Colchester Camp

Abbey Field

Barracks

Airfield

Crematorium

Berechurch

Roman Way Camp

Gosbeck's Farm

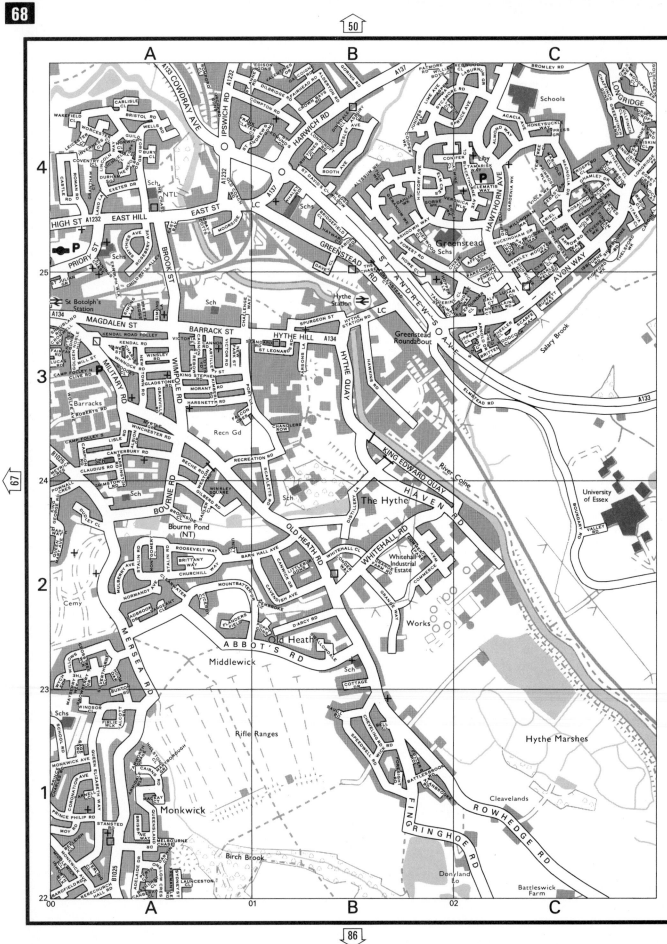

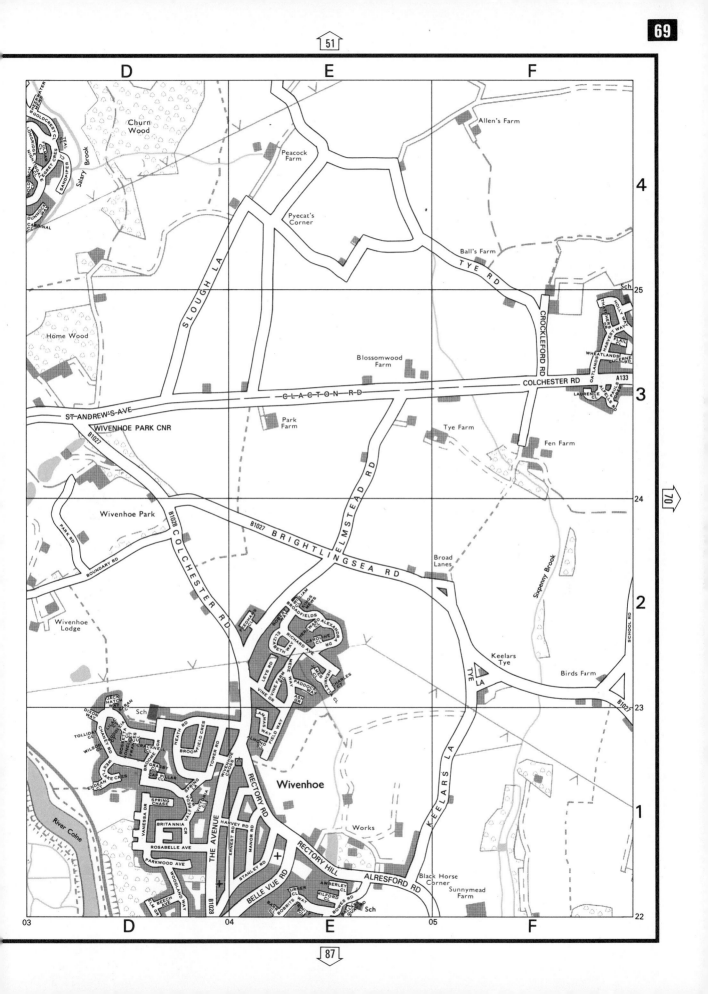

D   E   F

Churn
Wood

Allen's Farm

Peacock
Farm

Goldcrest Cl

Teal

Salary Brook

Sandpiper

Nightingale

Longridge

Egret Cres

Dunnock

Cardinal

4

Pyecat's
Corner

Ball's Farm

TYE RD

Sch.

25

SLOUGH LA

CROCKLEFORD RD

Home Wood

Blossomwood
Farm

THETHERS

HARVEST WAY

FLAIL

HOLLY WAY

WHEATLANDS

OATLANDS

LUCERNE RD

CLACTON RD

COLCHESTER RD

A133

3

ST-ANDREW'S-AVE

LAURENCE CL

ALFELS PAULS

WIVENHOE PARK CNR

Park
Farm

Tye Farm

B1027

Fen Farm

Wivenhoe Park

ELMSTEAD RD

B1028

COLCHESTER RD

Park RD

B1027 BRIGHTLINGSEA RD

Broad
Lanes

24

70

Boundary RD

Sixpenny Brook

Wivenhoe
Lodge

BROADFIELDS

ALEXANDRA DR

WILLIAM CL

ROBERT

EDWARD

CAROLINE CL

RICHARD AVE

ELIZA

MEDE WAY

PADDOCK

Keelars
Tye

Birds Farm

2

PEDHAMS

LEYS RD

VINE FARM

BETH

VINE DR

HENRIET CL

ASH GR

CHARLES

AMES

TYE LA

B1027

23

JACK HATCH

DIXON WAY

CORMORAN

Sch

TOLLIDAY CL

CHANEY RD

WILSON

ROSSETTA RD

FORD CRES

CRACKNELL

CATERPILLAR

HEATH RD

BROOM

FIELD CRES

WIVENHOE CROSS

ALMOND WAY

FIELD WAY

KEELARS LA

ENDSLAKE CRES

BROGRABBY

TOWER RD

RECTORY RD

Wivenhoe

WEST LAKE

VICE MA

SPRING

1

River Colne

SPRING
CHASE

VANESSA DR

BRITANNIA CR

HARVEY RD

Works

THE AVENUE

ERNEST RD

MANOR RD

ROSABELLE AVE

PARKWOOD AVE

STANLEY RD

RECTORY HILL

Black Horse
Corner

B1028

WOODLAND WAY

BELLE VUE RD

TURNER CL

AMBERLEY CL

ALRESFORD RD

Sunnymead
Farm

ELM

BEECH

BOBBITS WAY

MILFORD CL

BOWES RD

Sch

22

03   D   04   E   05   F

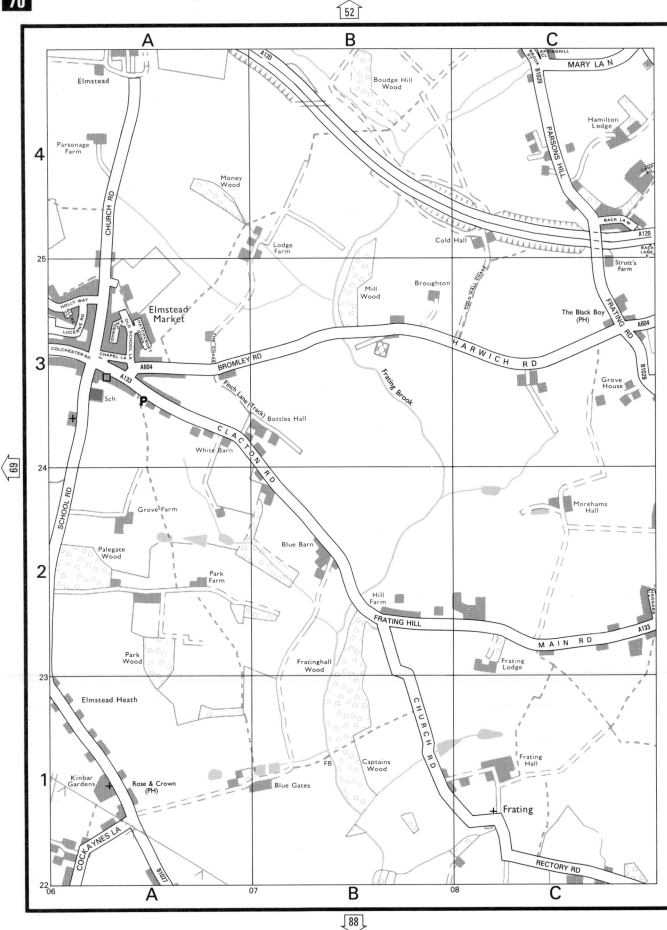

A   B   C

69

Elmstead

Parsonage Farm

4

CHURCH RD

Money Wood

Boudge Hill Wood

MARY LA N

PARSONS HILL

Hamilton Lodge

BACK LA W

A120

BACK LANE E

25

Lodge Farm

Cold Hall

Strutt's Farm

FRATING RD

HOLLY WAY

LUCERNE RD

JOHNSON'S RD

OLD SCHOOL LA

THE CROFT

CHAPEL LA

THE CHASE

Elmstead Market

Mill Wood

Broughton

COLD HALL CHASE

The Black Boy (PH)

A604

B1029

3

COLCHESTER RD

A604

A133

BROMLEY RD

HARWICH RD

Finch Lane (Track)

Bottles Hall

Frating Brook

Grove House

Sch

P

White Barn

CLACTON RD

SCHOOL RD

69

24

Grove Farm

Blue Barn

Morehams Hall

Palegate Wood

Park Farm

2

Hill Farm

FRATING HILL

MAIN RD

A133

HAGGARS

Park Wood

Fratinghall Wood

Frating Lodge

23

Elmstead Heath

CHURCH RD

Frating Hall

Kinbar Gardens

Rose & Crown (PH)

Blue Gates

FB

Captains Wood

Frating

1

COCKAYNES LA

B1027

RECTORY RD

22 06   07   08

A   B   C

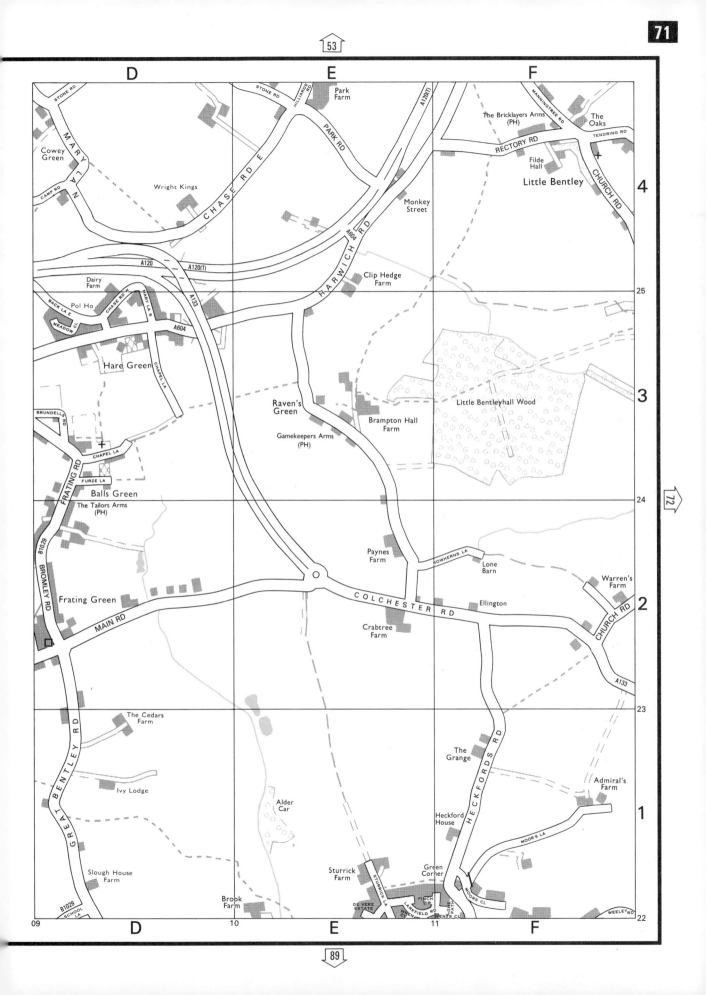

D

E

F

72

Stone Rd

Park Farm

A120(T)

The Bricklayers Arms (PH)

MANNINGTREE RD

The Oaks

TENDRING RD

Cowey Green

MARY LA N

CAMP RD

STONE RD

Wright Kings

CHASE RD E

HILLIARDS

STONE RD

PARK RD

Monkey Street

A604

HARWICH RD

RECTORY RD

Filde Hall

CHURCH RD

Little Bentley

4

A120

A120(T)

A133

Dairy Farm

Clip Hedge Farm

25

BACK LA E

Pol Ho

CHASE RO W

MARY LA S

MEADOW CL

A604

Hare Green

CHAPEL LA

Raven's Green

Brampton Hall Farm

Little Bentleyhall Wood

3

BRUNDELLS RD

FRATING RD

CHAPEL LA

FURZE LA

Gamekeepers Arms (PH)

Balls Green

The Tailors Arms (PH)

24

B1029

BROMLEY RD

Paynes Farm

NOWHERNS LA

Lone Barn

Warren's Farm

CHURCH RD

Frating Green

MAIN RD

COLCHESTER RD

Ellington

2

Crabtree Farm

A133

23

GREAT BENTLEY RD

The Cedars Farm

The Grange

HECKFORDS RD

Admiral's Farm

Ivy Lodge

Alder Car

Heckford House

MOORS LA

1

Slough House Farm

Sturrick Farm

Green Corner

MOORS CL

B1029

SCHOOL LA

Brook Farm

DE VERE ESTATE

STURRICK LA

FINCH DR

LARKFIELD RD

WRENFIELD

WENTS CL

FOOTPATH

WEELEY RD

22

09

D

10

E

11

F

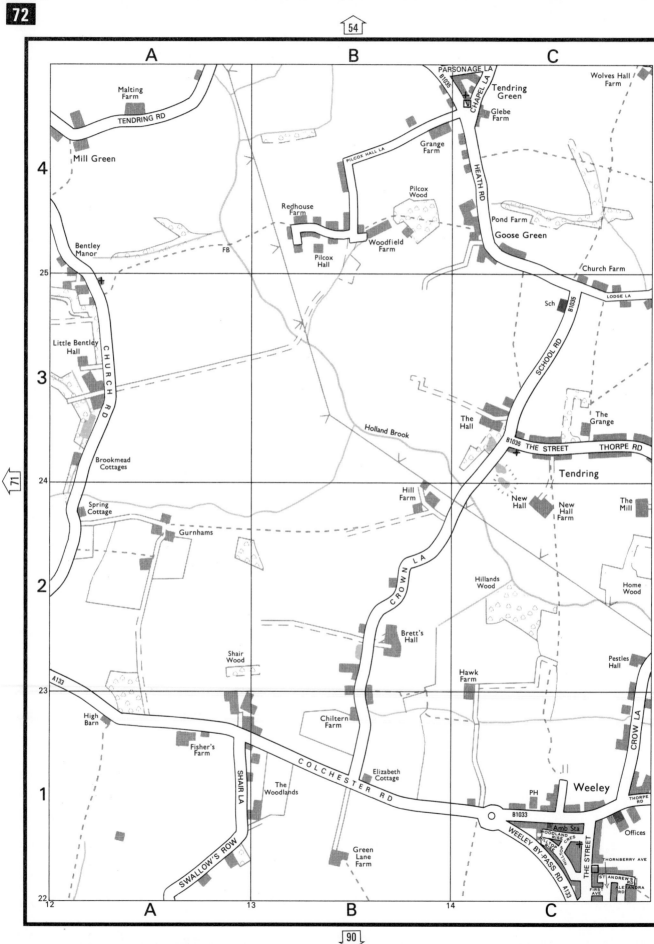

71

A   B   C

4

25

3

24

2

23

1

22

12   A   13   B   14   C

Malting Farm

TENDRING RD

Mill Green

Bentley Manor

FB

Little Bentley Hall

CHURCH RD

Brookmead Cottages

Spring Cottage

Gurnhams

Shair Wood

A133

High Barn

Fisher's Farm

SHAIR LA

The Woodlands

SWALLOW'S ROW

COLCHESTER RD

Chiltern Farm

Elizabeth Cottage

Green Lane Farm

PARSONAGE LA

B1035

Tendring Green

CHAPEL LA

Glebe Farm

PILCOX HALL LA

Grange Farm

Redhouse Farm

Pilcox Wood

Woodfield Farm

Pilcox Hall

HEATH RD

Wolves Hall Farm

Pond Farm

Goose Green

Church Farm

LODGE LA

Sch

B1035

SCHOOL RD

The Hall

The Grange

Holland Brook

B1035   THE STREET   THORPE RD

Tendring

Hill Farm

New Hall

New Hall Farm

The Mill

CROWN LA

Hillands Wood

Home Wood

Brett's Hall

Hawk Farm

Pestles Hall

CROW LA

PH   Weeley

THORPE RD

B1033

Amb Sta

Offices

WOODLAND RISE

HILLTOP RISE

CRES

Weeley BY-PASS RD   A133

THE STREET

THORNBERRY AVE

ST ANDREW'S RD

FIRS AVE   ALEXANDRA RD

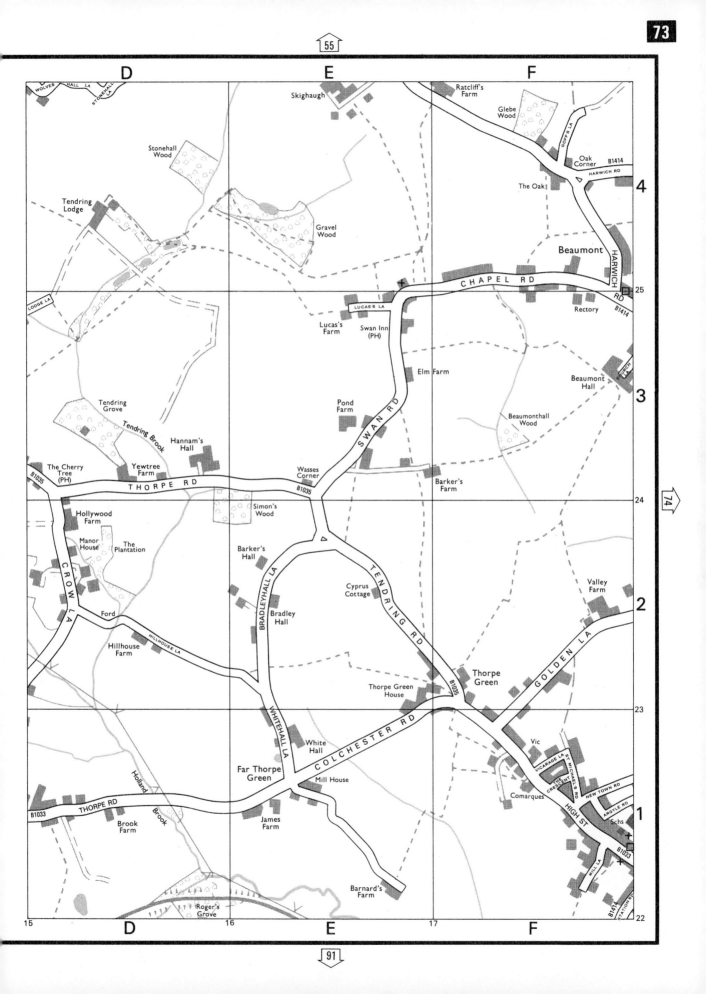

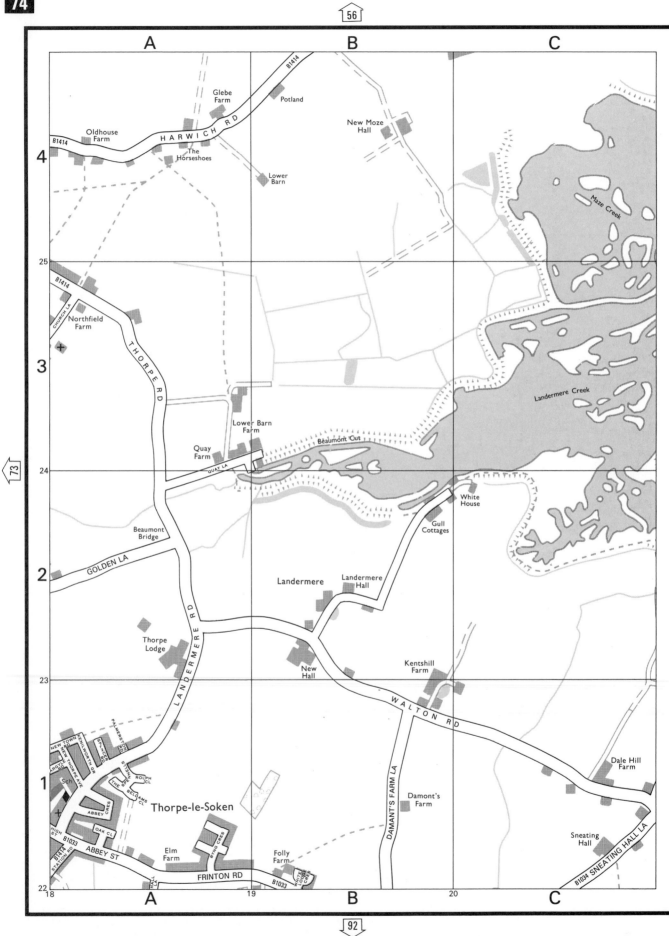

A   B   C

B1414

Glebe Farm

Potland

New Moze Hall

Oldhouse Farm

HARWICH RD

B1414

4

The Horseshoes

Lower Barn

Maze Creek

25

B1414

CHURCH LA

Northfield Farm

THORPE RD

3

Landermere Creek

Lower Barn Farm

Quay Farm

QUAY LA

Beaumont Cut

24

White House

Beaumont Bridge

Gull Cottages

GOLDEN LA

2

Landermere

Landermere Hall

LANDERMERE RD

Thorpe Lodge

New Hall

Kentshill Farm

23

WALTON RD

Dale Hill Farm

NEW TOWN RD

ARGYLL RD

KENILWORTH AVE

NEW THORPE AVE

PALMERS RD

SPENCER RD

STEINES

ROLPH CL

THE BELGANS CL

1

Sch

ABBEY CRES

DAMANT'S FARM LA

Damont's Farm

Sneating Hall

HIGH ST

OAK CL

BYNG CRES

Thorpe-le-Soken

B1033

STATION RD

B1414

ABBEY ST

Elm Farm

FRINTON RD

Folly Farm

B1033

WHITE GCRES

B1034 SNEATING HALL LA

22
18   A   19   B   20   C

D   E   F

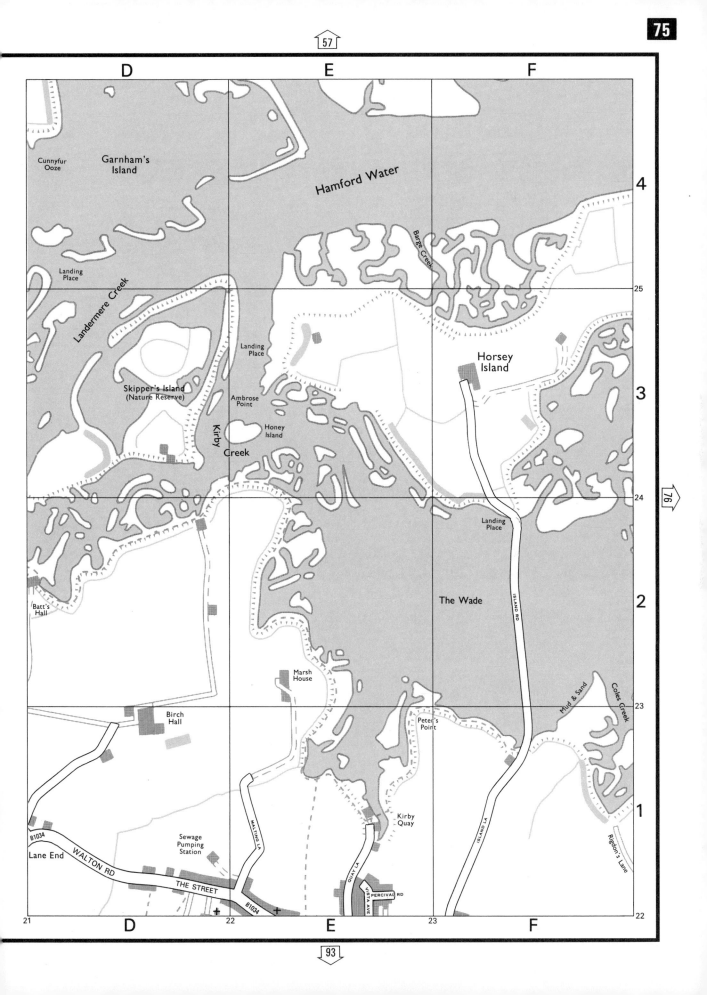

Cunnyfur Ooze

Garnham's Island

Hamford Water

Landing Place

Landermere Creek

Barge Creek

Horsey Island

Landing Place

Skipper's Island (Nature Reserve)

Ambrose Point

Kirby Creek

Honey Island

Landing Place

The Wade

ISLAND RD

Batt's Hall

Mud & Sand

Coles Creek

Marsh House

Birch Hall

Peter's Point

MALTING LA

ISLAND LA

Rigdon's Lane

B1034

Lane End

WALTON RD

Sewage Pumping Station

Kirby Quay

QUAY LA

VISTA AVE

PERCIVAL RD

THE STREET

B1034

76

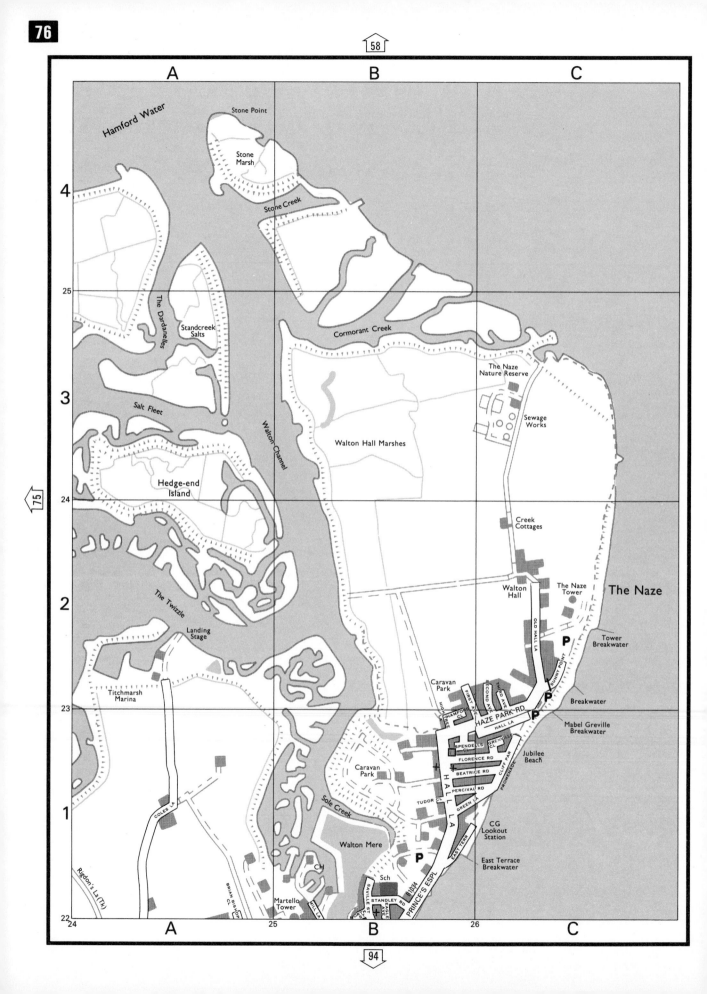

A   B   C

Hamford Water

Stone Point

Stone Marsh

Stone Creek

4

The Dardanelles

Standcreek Salts

25

Cormorant Creek

Salt Fleet

The Naze Nature Reserve

3

Walton Hall Marshes

Sewage Works

Hedge-end Island

Walton Channel

24

Creek Cottages

The Twizzle

Walton Hall

The Naze Tower

The Naze

2

Landing Stage

Tower Breakwater

Titchmarsh Marina

Caravan Park

OLD HALL LA

SUNNY POINT

P

P

23

Breakwater

FIRST AVE

SECOND AVE

THIRD AVE

HIGH TREE

HAMFORD CL

HAZE PARK RD

HALL LA

P

Mabel Greville Breakwater

SPENDELLS CL

GRENVILLE CL

FLORENCE RD

Caravan Park

BEATRICE RD

CLIFF PAR

Jubilee Beach

HALL LA

PERCIVAL RD

PROMENADE

GREEN LA

Sole Creek

TUDOR CL

CG Lookout Station

1

Walton Mere

EAST TERR

East Terrace Breakwater

Rigdon's La (Tk)

CH

P

Sch

B1034

PRINCE'S ESPL

Martello Tower

SAVILLE ST

STANDLEY AVE

BRIAN BISHOP CL

MILL LA

NORTH ST

BEAGLE RD

22

24   A   25   B   26   C

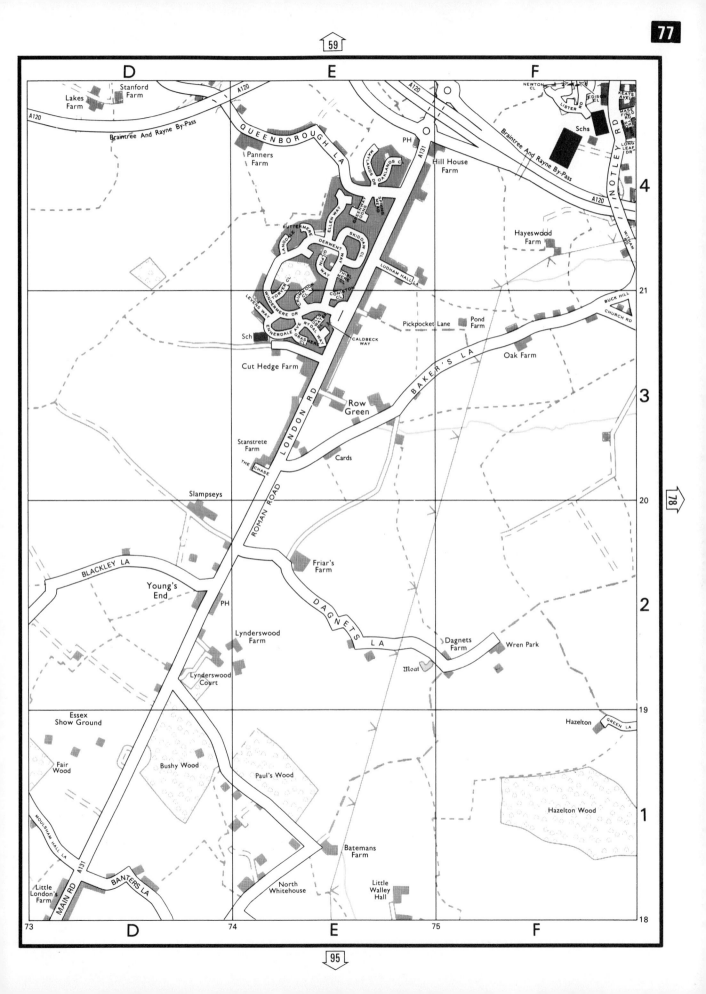

D   **E**   **F**

Stanford Farm

Lakes Farm

A120

Braintree And Rayne By-Pass

QUEENBOROUGH LA

Panners Farm

A120

PH

A131

Hill House Farm

NEWTON CL

LISTER

KEATS AVE

EDISON RD

LONG LEAF DR

Schs

Braintree And Rayne By-Pass

A120

NOTLEY RD

4

MAYLANDS DR

OAKLANDS CL

GREENWAY

SPRING MEAD

ELLEN WAY

SKIDDAW CL

Hayeswood Farm

BUTTERMERE

DERWENT WAY

LANGDALE

WINDERMERE DR

TOPVER CL

CL

ULLSWATER

WAY

THIRL MERE RD

CONISTON CL

Sch

ENNERDALE AVE

RYDAL WAY

GRASMERE

Cut Hedge Farm

LUDHAM HALL LA

Pickpocket Lane

Pond Farm

BUCK HILL

CHURCH RD

21

CALDBECK WAY

Oak Farm

LEVENS WAY

BAKER'S LA

LONDON RD

Row Green

3

Stanstrete Farm

THE CHASE

Cards

ROMAN ROAD

Slampseys

20

BLACKLEY LA

Friar's Farm

Young's End

PH

DAGNETS LA

2

Lynderswood Farm

Dagnets Farm

Wren Park

Lynderswood Court

Moat

19

Essex Show Ground

Hazelton

GREEN LA

Fair Wood

Bushy Wood

Paul's Wood

Hazelton Wood

1

MOULSHAM HALL LA

A131

Batemans Farm

Little London's Farm

MAIN RD

BANTERS LA

North Whitehouse

Little Walley Hall

18

78

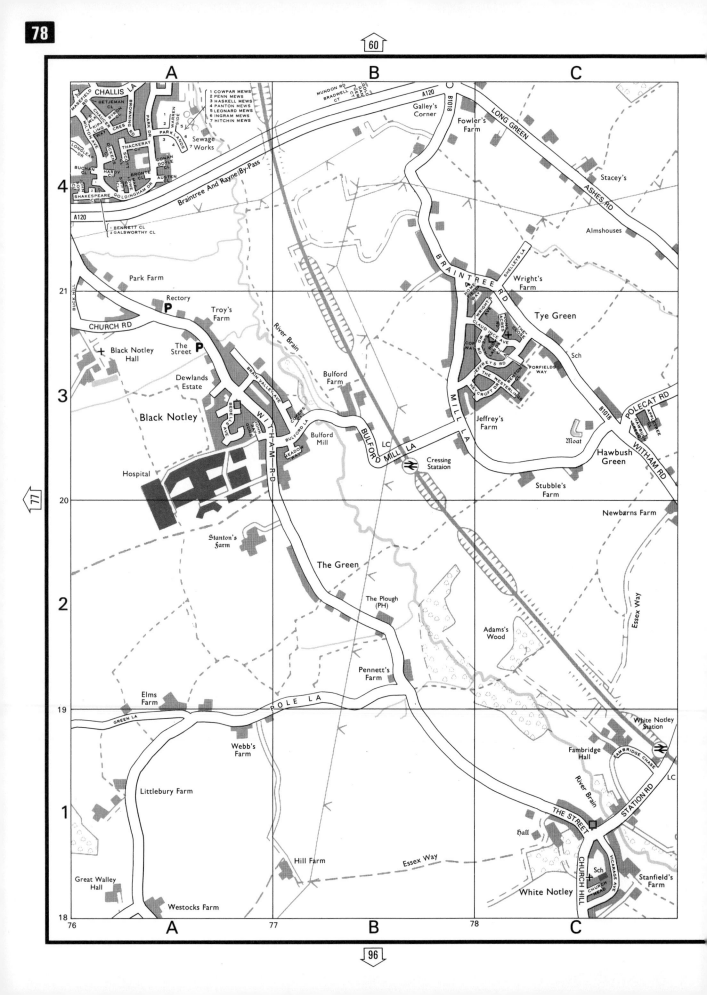

D E F

Lanham Manor
Farm

Mott's Lane (Track)

Sand and Gravel
Pit

Wr
Twr

Jubilee
Plantation

Lanham
Green

L I N K S   R D

Clapdog Green

Gosling's
Farm

4

Ashes
Farm

Link's
Wood

LANHAM GREEN RD

Schills
Farm

ASHES RD

21

THE STREET

Wright's
Farm

B O A R S   T Y E   R D

Airfield
(disused)

Cressing

Hall

Vic

POLECAT RD

Egypts
Farm

Rolphs
Farmhouse

Sheepcotes
Farm

CHURCH RD

Essex Way

SHEEPCOTES LA

3

BROOMFIELD

WEAVER
SPIELD

BROADWAY

FRANCIS
CT

RUNNACLES
ST

WALTER

Council
Houses

B1018

PETIT LA

MANORS WAY

FRANCIS WAY

Broadway

SILVER ST

Hall

RICHARD

ABRAHAM

DANIE L WAY

Silver End

20

New
House

Hotel

GROOMS LA

JOSEPH
GNS

2

80

Boat House

WITHAM RD

TEMPLE LA

VALENTINE WAY

STRETFORD

Moat
Bower Hall

Sheepcote
Wood

MAGDELENE
CRES

SCHOOL

W E S T E R N   R D

Sch

BOWERS
CL

WESTERN LA

Park
House

Sewage
Works

Rivenhall
Place

19

Cressing
Temple

Barns

Old
Court Room

Sewage
Works

1

B1018

Hungry Hall

Rivenhall Thicks

18

79 D 80 E 81 F

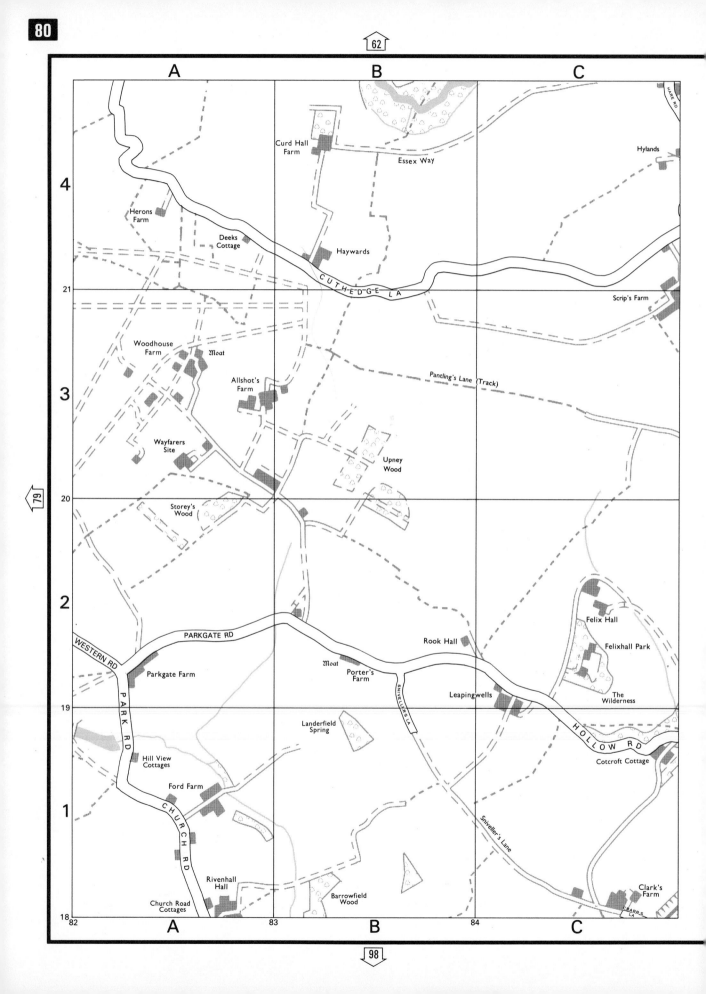

A   B   C

Curd Hall Farm

Essex Way

Hylands

Herons Farm

Deeks Cottage

Haywards

CUTH·E·D·G·E LA

21

Scrip's Farm

Woodhouse Farm

Moat

Pantling's Lane (Track)

Allshot's Farm

Wayfarers Site

Upney Wood

3

Storey's Wood

20

2

Felix Hall

Felixhall Park

PARKGATE RD

WESTERN RD

Rook Hall

The Wilderness

PARK RD

Parkgate Farm

Moat

Porter's Farm

SNIVELLER'S LA

Leapingwells

HOLLOW RD

19

Landerfield Spring

Hill View Cottages

Cotcroft Cottage

Ford Farm

CHURCH RD

Sniveller's Lane

1

Rivenhall Hall

Clark's Farm

Church Road Cottages

Barrowfield Wood

CRABB·S LA

18 82   A   83   B   84   C

HARE RD

D E F

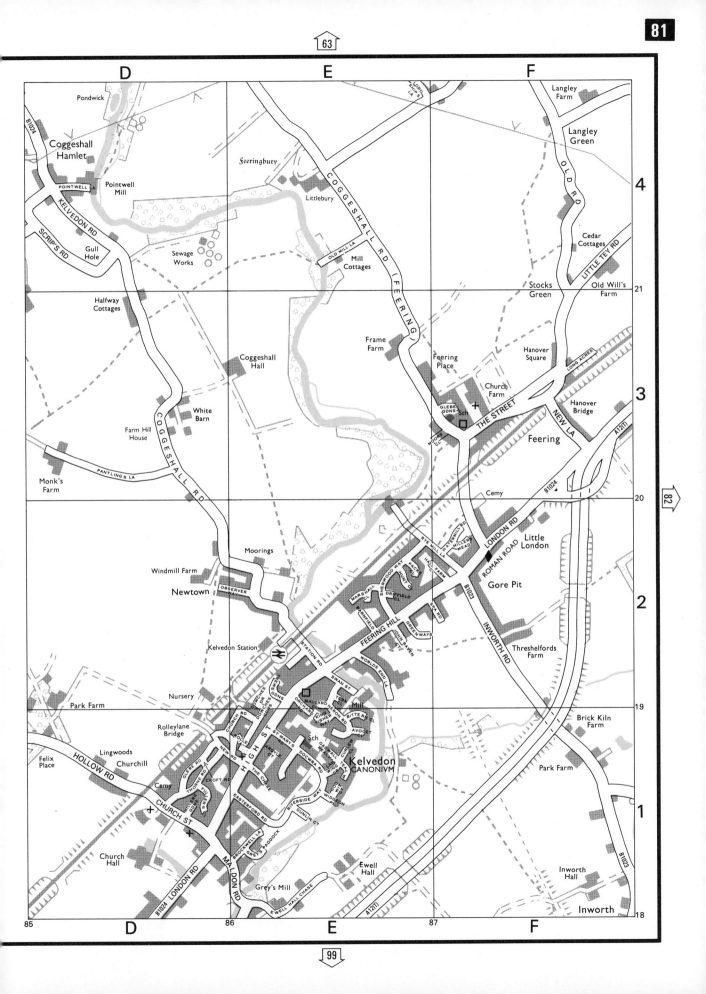

Pondwick

Coggeshall
Hamlet

B1024

POINTWELL LA

Pointwell
Mill

KELVEDON RD

SCRIP'S RD

Gull
Hole

Feeringbury

Littlebury

LOND
SLIP'S

Langley
Farm

Langley
Green

4

OLD RD

Cedar
Cottages

LITTLE TEY RD

Stocks
Green

Old Will's
Farm

21

A12(T)

Halfway
Cottages

Coggeshall
Hall

White
Barn

Farm Hill
House

COGGESHALL RD

PANTLINGS LA

Monk's
Farm

Sewage
Works

Old Mill La

Mill
Cottages

COGGESHALL RD (FEERING)

Frame
Farm

Feering
Place

GLEBE
GDNS

Sch

THE STREET

Church
Farm

MOORE
CL

Hanover
Square

LONG ACRES

Hanover
Bridge

NEW LA

Feering

3

Cemy

B1024

20

82

Monk's
Farm

Moorings

Windmill Farm

Newtown

OBSERVER
WAY

Kelvedon Station

RYE MILL LA

WATERMILL RD

MILLERS
MEAD

LONDON RD

ROMAN ROAD

Little
London

PACK CL

HALL
FARM

HUNT CL

Gore Pit

B1023

INWORTH RD

Threshelfords
Farm

2

SHERWOOD WAY

DRIFTIELD

SPA RD

MARSHALL
CL

BRANFIELD

FEERING HILL

GREENWAYS

JOHN'S
AVEN

WORLDS END LA

Park Farm

Nursery

STATION RD

SWAN ST

MILL

Rolleylane
Bridge

Lingwoods
Churchill

Felix
Place

HOLLOW RD

Cemy

CHURCH ST

HIGH ST

ST MARY'S

ARGYLE
CT

DOCWRA RD

KING ST

Sch

MALLARD
ORCHARD

HERON RD

TERN
CL

BITTERY CL

AVOCET

Kelvedon
CANONIVM

Brick Kiln
Farm

Park Farm

19

1

Church
Hall

MALDON RD

LONDON RD

B1024

EASTERFORD RD

THE CHASE

BROCKWELL LA

GRET'S PADDOCK

RIVERSIDE WAY

DUNLIN CT

WIDGEON

Grey's Mill

EWELL HALL CHASE

Ewell
Hall

A12(T)

Inworth
Hall

B1023

Inworth

18

85 D 86 E 87 F

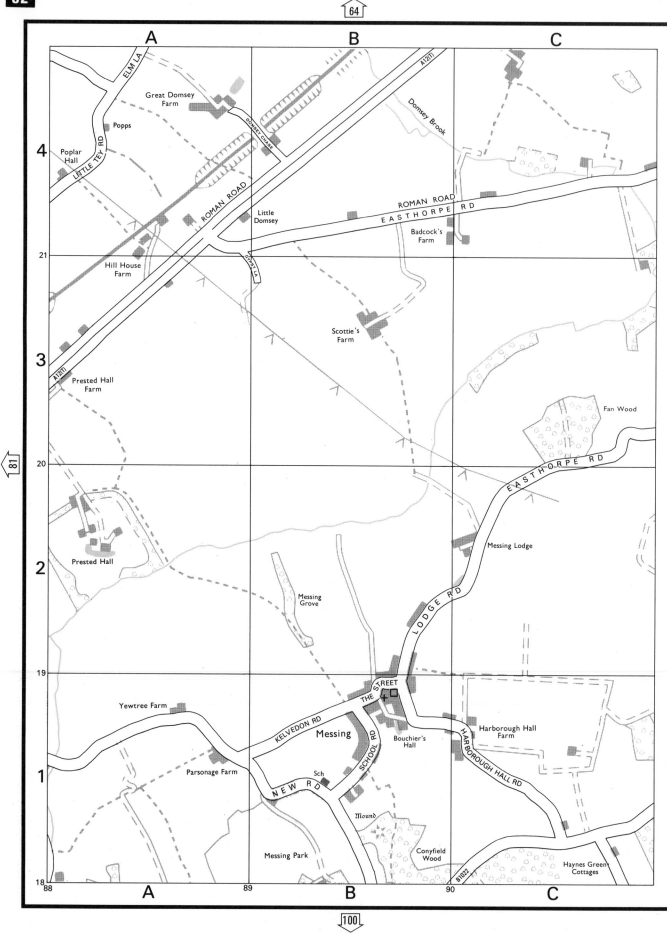

A   B   C

ELM LA.

Great Domsey
Farm

Popps

A12(T)

DOMSEY CHASE

Domsey Brook

Poplar
Hall

LITTLE TEY RD

4

ROMAN ROAD

Little
Domsey

ROMAN ROAD

EASTHORPE RD

Badcock's
Farm

21

GYPSY LA

Hill House
Farm

Scottie's
Farm

3

A12(T)

Prested Hall
Farm

Fan Wood

20

EASTHORPE RD

Messing Lodge

LODGE RD

2

Prested Hall

Messing
Grove

19

THE STREET

Yewtree Farm

KELVEDON RD

Messing

SCHOOL RD

Bouchier's
Hall

Harborough Hall
Farm

HARBOROUGH HALL RD

1

Parsonage Farm

NEW RD

Sch

Mound

Conyfield
Wood

B1022

Haynes Green
Cottages

Messing Park

18
88

A   89   B   90   C

81

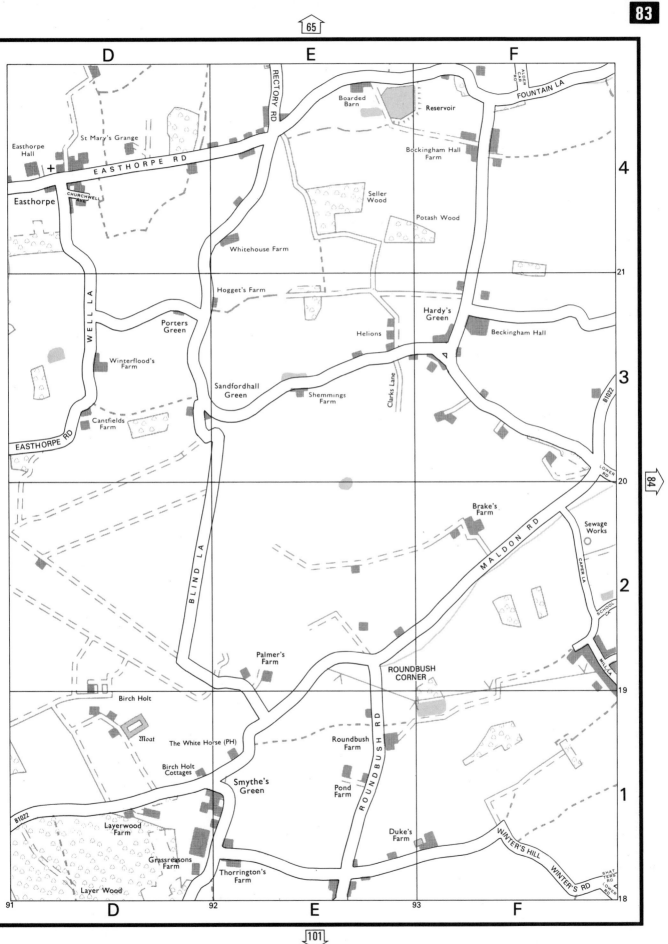

D E F

4

21

3

20

84

2

19

1

18

91 92 93

D E F

FOUNTAIN LA

ALDER CAR RD

Boarded Barn

Reservoir

Bockingham Hall Farm

St Mary's Grange

Easthorpe Hall

Easthorpe

+

CHURCHWELL AVE

EASTHORPE RD

RECTORY RD

Seller Wood

Potash Wood

Whitehouse Farm

Hogget's Farm

WELL LA

Porters Green

Winterflood's Farm

Helions

Hardy's Green

Beckingham Hall

B1022

Sandfordhall Green

Shemmings Farm

Clarks Lane

Cantfields Farm

EASTHORPE RD

LOWER RD

Brake's Farm

Sewage Works

MALDON RD

CAPER LA

BLIND LA

SCHOOL CA

Palmer's Farm

ROUNDBUSH CORNER

MILL LA

Birch Holt

Moat

The White Horse (PH)

Birch Holt Cottages

Smythe's Green

Roundbush Farm

ROUNDBUSH RD

Pond Farm

Duke's Farm

B1022

Layerwood Farm

Grassreasons Farm

Thorrington's Farm

Layer Wood

WINTER'S HILL

WINTER'S RD

SHATTERS RD

LOWER RD

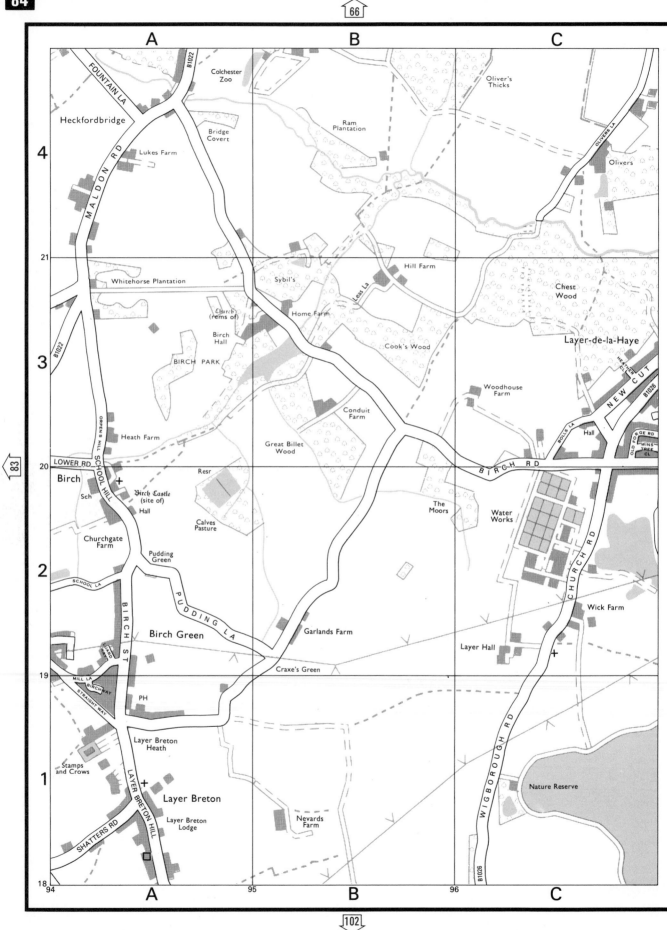

A

B

C

4

21

3

20

2

19

1

18

94

95

96

FOUNTAIN LA

B1022

Colchester Zoo

Heckfordbridge

Bridge Covert

Oliver's Thicks

Ram Plantation

MALDON RD

Lukes Farm

Olivers

OLIVERS LA

Whitehorse Plantation

Sybil's

Hill Farm

Chest Wood

B1022

Church (rems of)

Home Farm

Leas La

Layer-de-la-Haye

Birch Hall

Cook's Wood

BIRCH PARK

Woodhouse Farm

NEW CUT

HEATHER CL

B1026

ORPEN'S HILL

Heath Farm

Conduit Farm

BOLLS LA

Hall

OLD FORGE RD

WINS TREE CL

Great Billet Wood

LOWER RD

SCHOOL HILL

BIRCH RD

Birch

Resr

Sch

Birch Castle (site of)

Hall

The Moors

Water Works

Churchgate Farm

Calves Pasture

Pudding Green

SCHOOL LA

PUDDING LA

CHURCH RD

Wick Farm

Birch Green

Garlands Farm

Layer Hall

BIRCH ST

Craxe's Green

MILL LA

BIRCHWAY

STRAIGHT WAY

PH

Layer Breton Heath

WIGBOROUGH RD

Stamps and Crows

Nature Reserve

LAYER BRETON HILL

Layer Breton

SHATTERS RD

Layer Breton Lodge

Nevards Farm

B1026

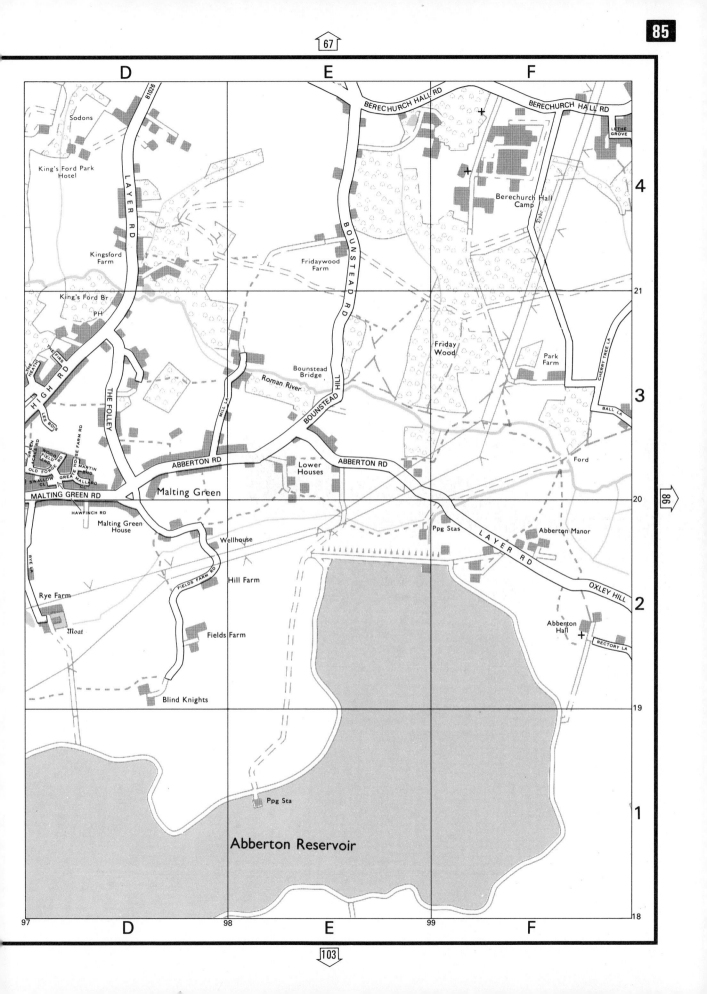

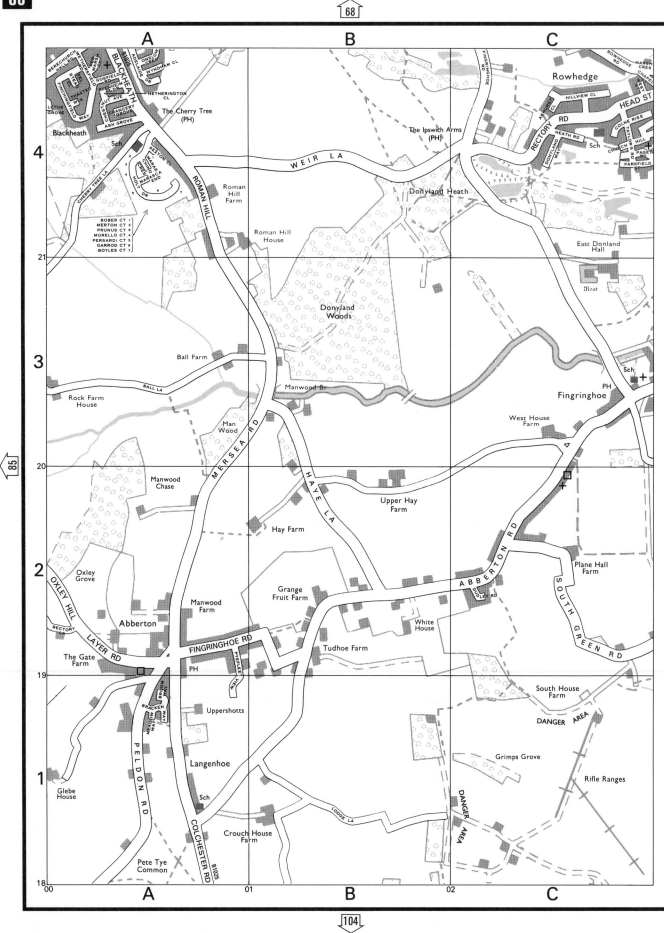

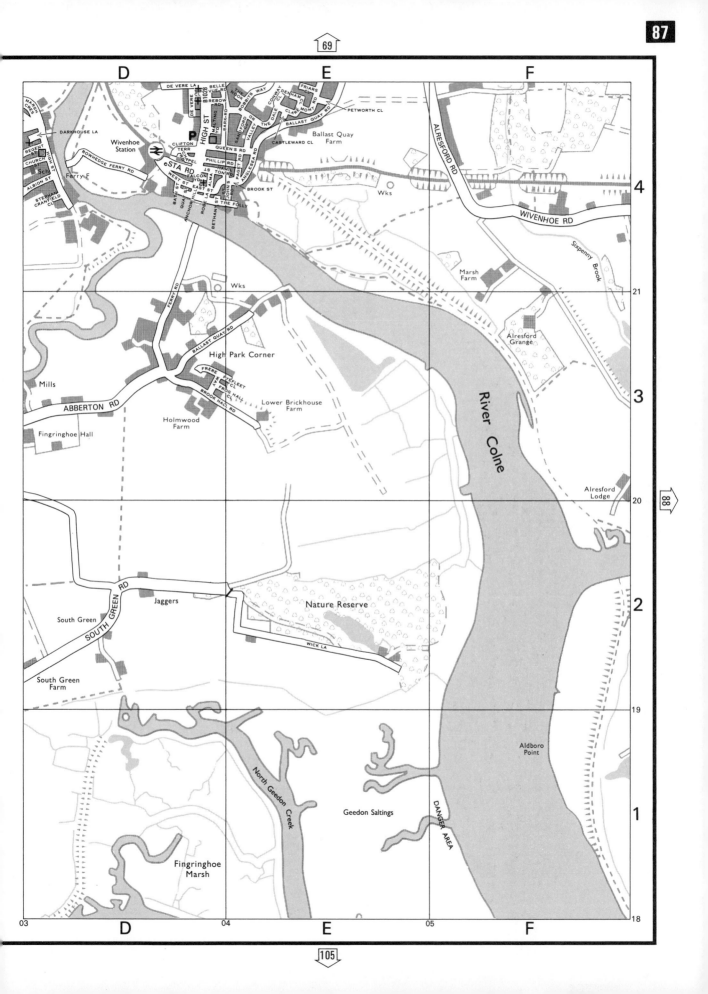

88

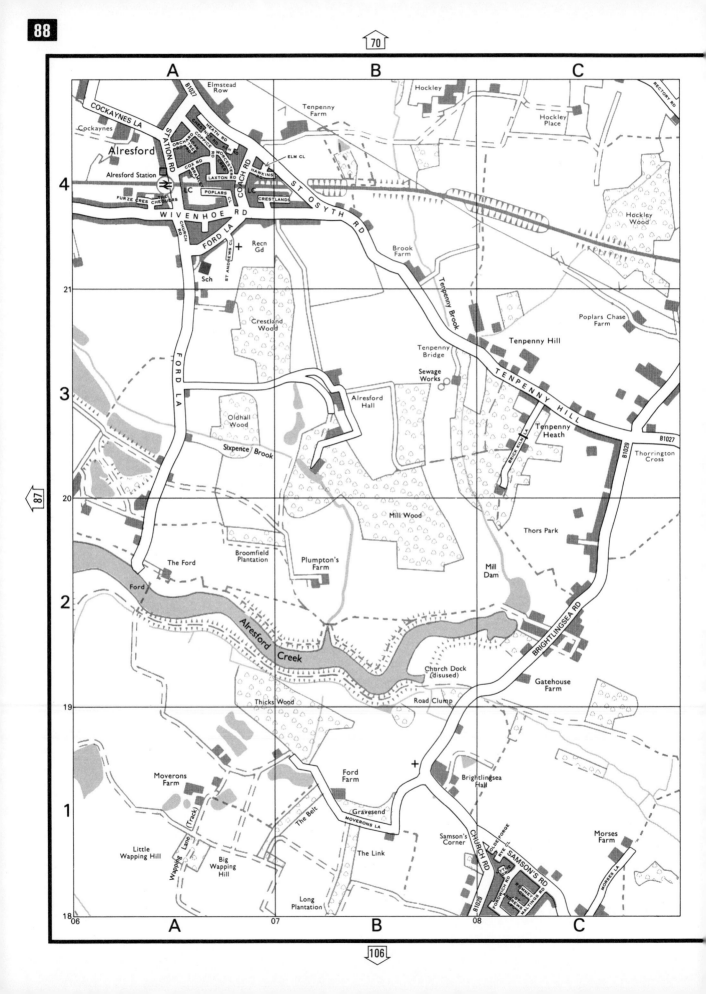

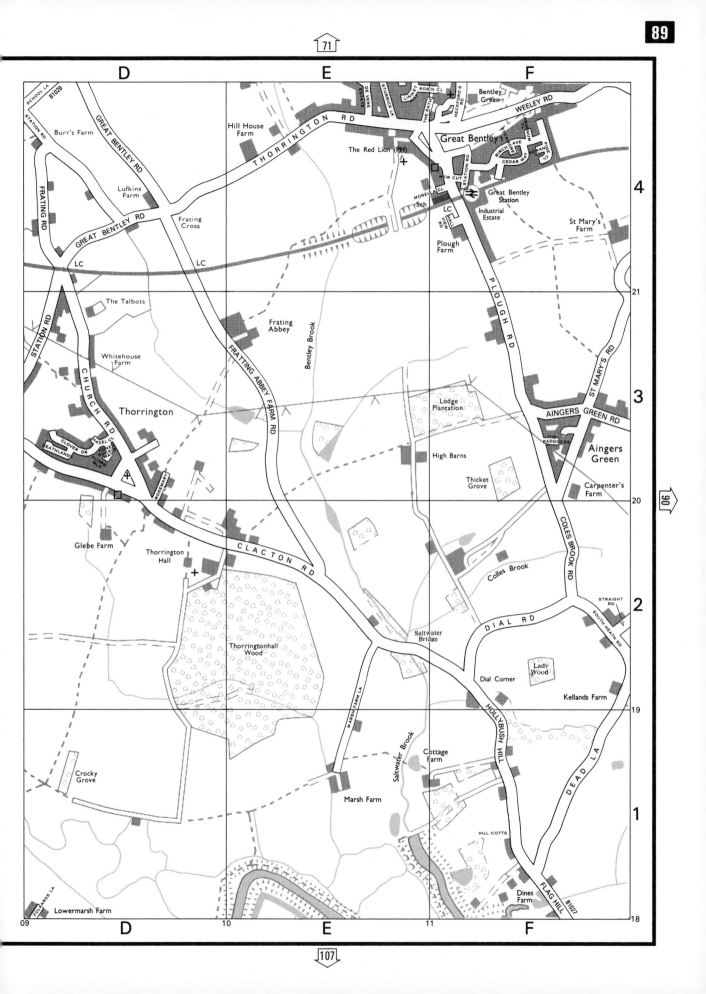

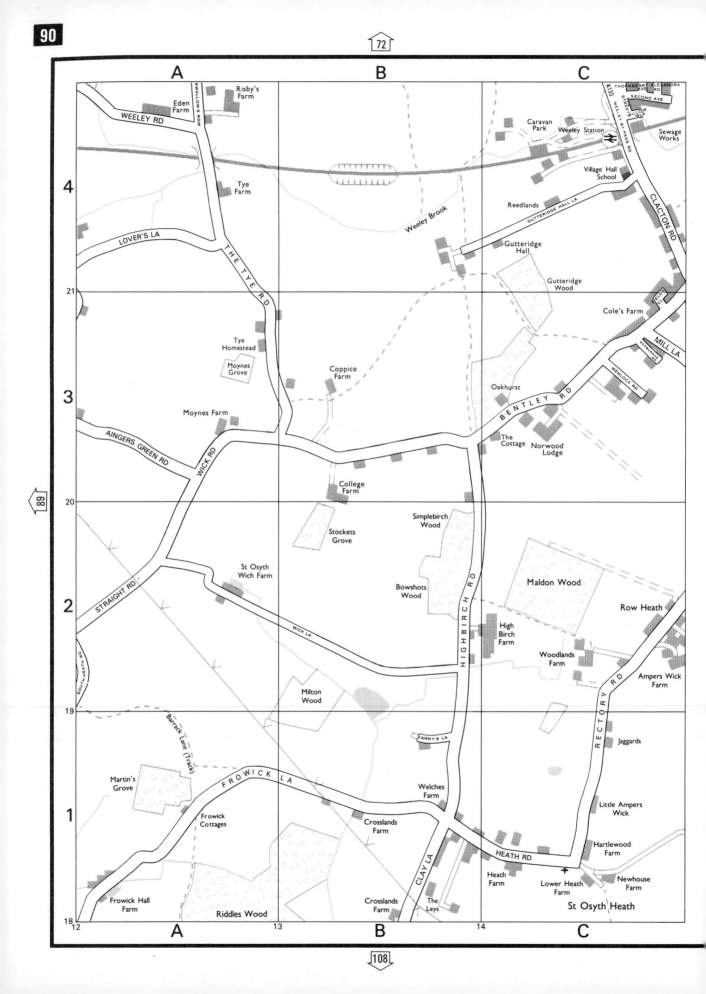

A   B   C

THORNBERRY ALEXANDRA AVE RD
A 133
SECOND AVE
WILLOW WLK
STREET
WEELEY BY PASS RD

Risby's Farm
Eden Farm
SWALLOW'S ROW
WEELEY RD

Caravan Park
Weeley Station
Sewage Works
Village Hall
School
CLACTON RD

Tye Farm
Weeley Brook
Reedlands
GUTTERIDGE HALL LA
Gutteridge Hall

4

LOVER'S LA
THE TYE RD

Gutteridge Wood
Cole's Farm
MILL LA
ELDER

21

Tye Homestead
Moynes Grove
Coppice Farm
WENLOCK RD
ROXBURGHE RD
Oakhurst
BENTLEY RD

3

Moynes Farm
AINGERS GREEN RD
WICK RD
The Cottage
Norwood Lodge

College Farm
Simplebirch Wood

20

Stockets Grove
Maldon Wood
Row Heath

2

STRAIGHT RD
St Osyth Wich Farm
WICK LA
Bowshots Wood
HIGHBIRCH RD
High Birch Farm
Woodlands Farm
Ampers Wick Farm

SOUTH HEATH RD

19

Barrack Lane (Track)
FANNYS LA
RECTORY RD
Jaggards

Martin's Grove
FROWICK LA
Welches Farm
Little Ampers Wick

1

Frowick Cottages
Crosslands Farm
Hartlewood Farm

CLAY LA
HEATH RD
Heath Farm
Lower Heath Farm
Newhouse Farm

Frowick Hall Farm
Riddles Wood
Crosslands Farm
The Leys
St Osyth Heath

18
12   A   13   B   14   C

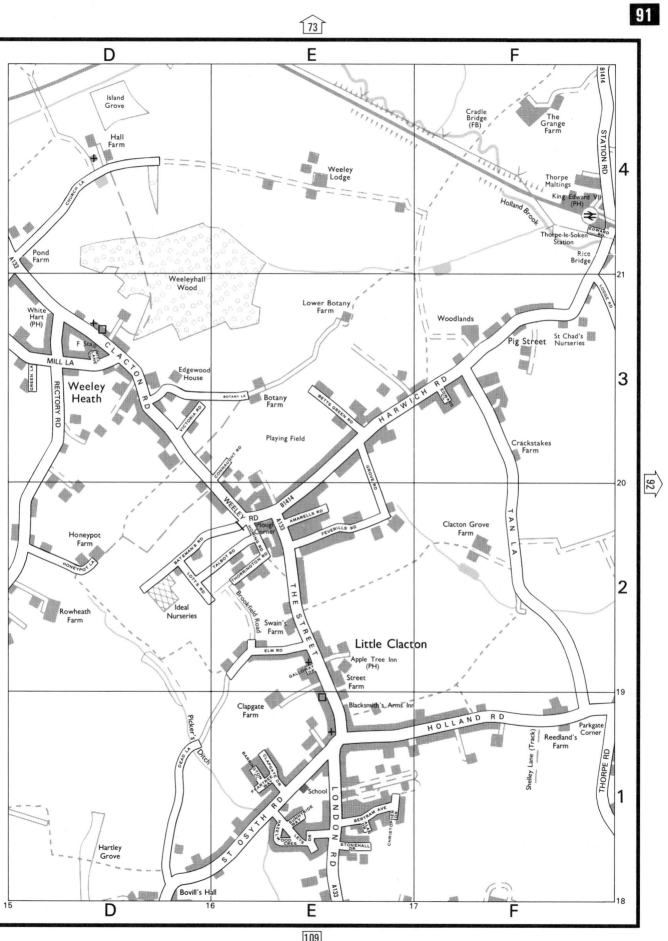

D · E · F

4

3

20 / 92

2

1

Island Grove

Hall Farm

CHURCH LA

Pond Farm

A133

White Hart (PH)

GREEN LA

MILL LA

RECTORY RD

Weeley Heath

CLACTON RD

F Sta

HELL LANE

Edgewood House

BOTANY LA

VICTORIA RD

CONNAUGHT RD

Weeleyhall Wood

Lower Botany Farm

Botany Farm

Playing Field

BETTS GREEN RD

HARWICH RD

BOYARD RD

Weeley Lodge

Cradle Bridge (FB)

The Grange Farm

B1414

STATION RD

Thorpe Maltings

King Edward VII (PH)

Holland Brook

EDWARD RD

Thorpe-le-Soken Station

Rice Bridge

LODGE RD

Woodlands

Pig Street

St Chad's Nurseries

Crackstakes Farm

Honeypot Farm

HONEYPOT LA

Rowheath Farm

WEELEY RD

Plough Corner

B1414

A133

HOLLAND RD

AMARELLS RD

FEVERILLS RD

GROVE RD

Clacton Grove Farm

TAN LA

BATEMAN'S RD

TALBOT RD

LOTT'S RD

THORRINGTON RD

Ideal Nurseries

Brookfield Road

Swain's Farm

ELM RD

THE STREET

Little Clacton

Apple Tree Inn (PH)

Street Farm

GALLOWAY

Clapgate Farm

Blacksmith's Arms Inn

Picker's Ditch

DEAD LA

Hartley Grove

ST OSYTH RD

BARRINGTON DR

CLAPGATE DR

PEARTREE DR

School

HAZELWOOD CRES

SUNNYSIDE

LETS DR

BERTRAM AVE

STONEHALL DR

CHRISTOPHER DR

LONDON RD

A133

Bovill's Hall

HOLLAND RD

Shelley Lane (Track)

Reedland's Farm

Parkgate Corner

THORPE RD

15 · D · 16 · E · 17 · F · 18

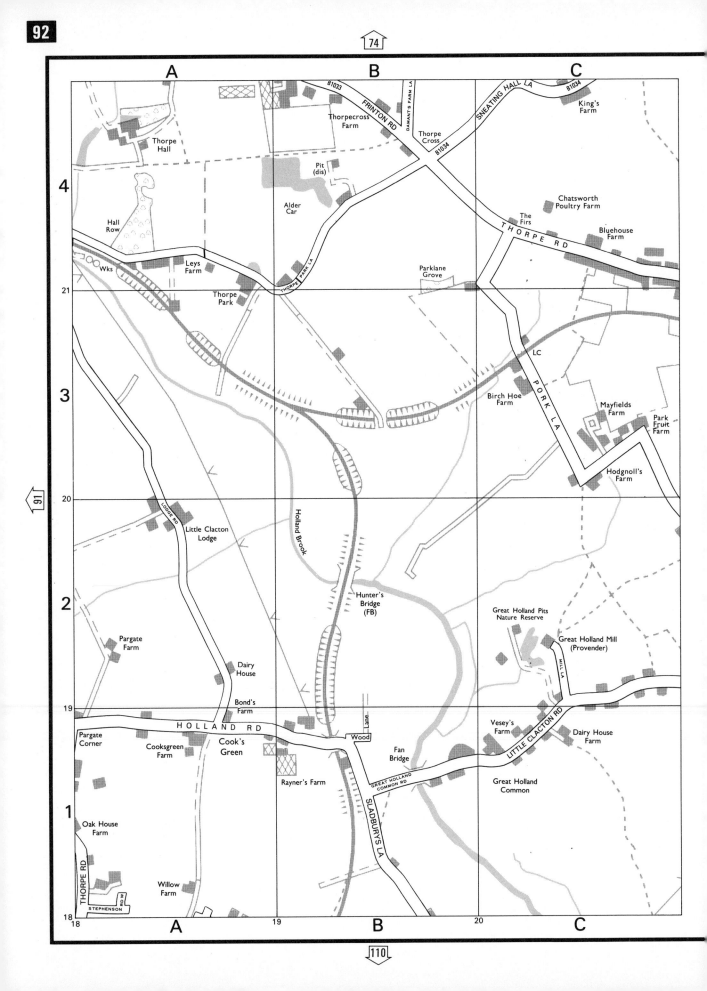

75

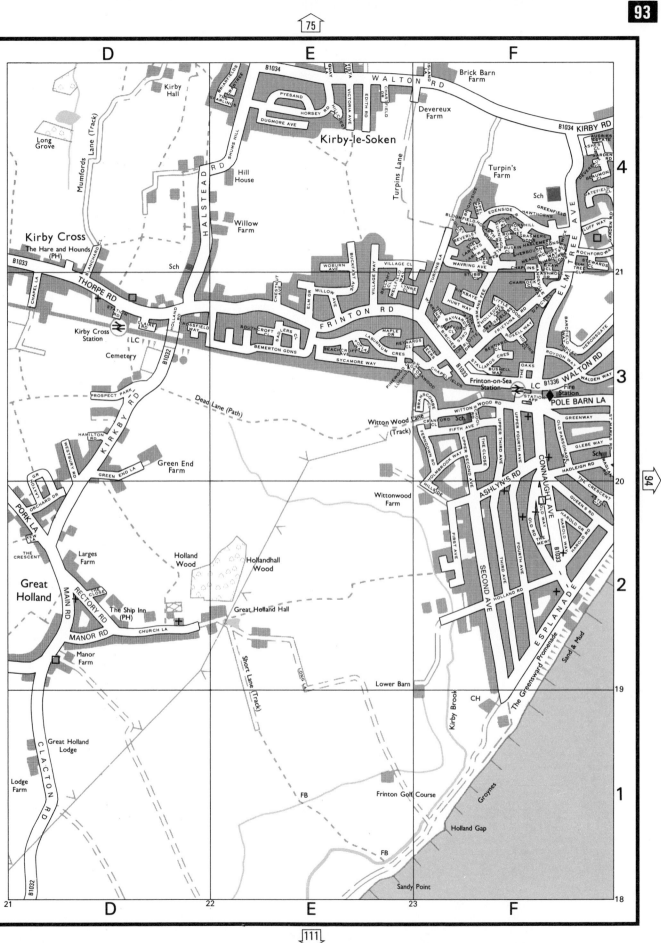

D   E   F

Kirby Hall

Long Grove

Mumfords Lane (Track)

B1034

WALTON RD

Brick Barn Farm

Devereux Farm

B1034 KIRBY RD

Kirby-le-Soken

Turpins Lane

Turpin's Farm

Sch

4

HALSTEAD RD

SHUMS HILL

Hill House

Willow Farm

Kirby Cross

The Hare and Hounds (PH)

B1033

THORPE RD

Sch

WOBURN AVE

BUCKFAST AVE

VILLAGE CL

21

CHAPEL LA

BLANCHARD'S RD

STATION RD

CLAIRE RD

HOLLAND RD

ROSSFIELD WAY

Kirby Cross Station

LC

CHESTNUT AVE

ELM GR

WILLOW AVE

FRINTON RD

MAPLE DR

Frinton-on-Sea Station

LC B1336

Fire Station

WALTON RD

3

Cemetery

B1032

KIRBY RD

SOUTHCROFT RD

SADLERS CL

BEMERTON GDNS

BEACHCROFT AVE

LABURNUM CRES

REYNARDS CL

SYCAMORE WAY

B1033

POLE BARN LA

Prospect Park

Dead Lane (Path)

Witton Wood Lane (Track)

WITTON WOOD RD

GREENWAY

GLEBE WAY

Sch

HADLEIGH RD

20

HAMILTON RD

WESTBURY RD

Green End LA

Green End Farm

Wittonwood Farm

FIFTH AVE

UPPER FOURTH AVE

THE CLOSE

HILLSIDE

ASHLYN'S RD

CONNAUGHT AVE

QUEEN'S RD

HAROLD GR

94

PORK LA

ORCHARD DR

THE CRESCENT

KEW

Larges Farm

Holland Wood

Hollandhall Wood

FIRST AVE

SECOND AVE

THIRD AVE

FOURTH AVE

HOLLAND RD

B1033

2

Great Holland

MAIN RD

RECTORY RD

THE CLOSE

The Ship Inn (PH)

CHURCH LA

Great Holland Hall

MANOR RD

Manor Farm

Short Lane (Track)

LONG LA

Lower Barn

Kirby Brook

CH

The Greensward

ESPLANADE

Promenade

Sand & Mud

19

CLACTON RD

Great Holland Lodge

FB

Frinton Golf Course

Groynes

1

Lodge Farm

Holland Gap

FB

Sandy Point

B1032

18

21   D   22   E   23   F

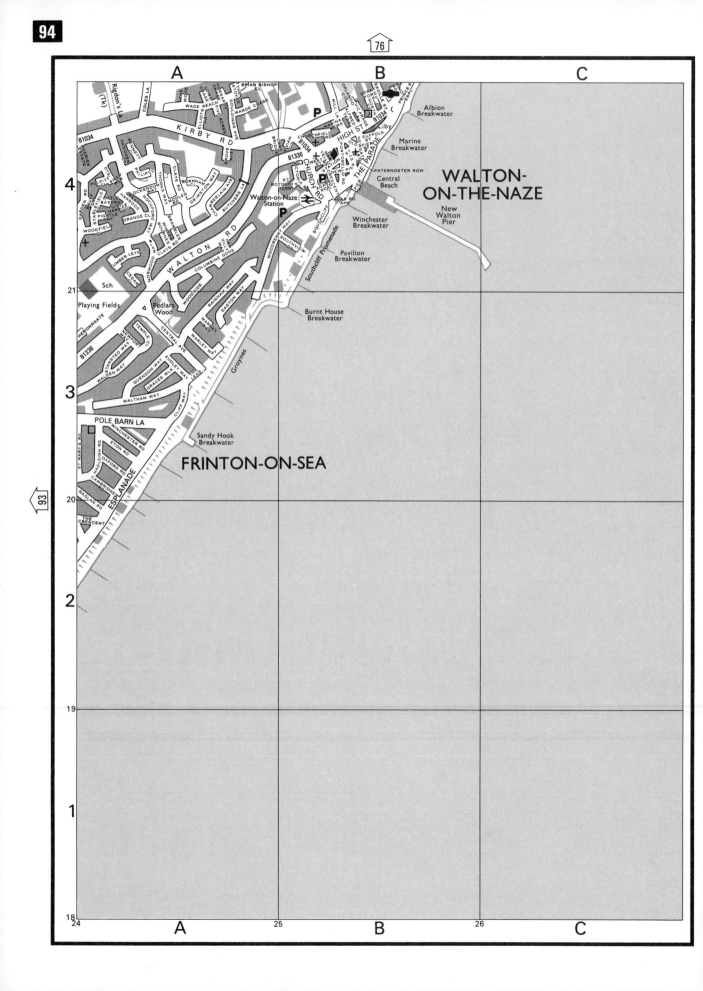

A   **B**   **C**

Rigton's La

(Tk)

COLES LA

KIRBY RD

B1034

BRIAN BISHOP CL

WADE REACH

WARDE CHASE

CLAY'S ROW

COWARD CRESCENT

GOULDINGS AVE

ELLIOTT RIDGE

RAGLAND WAY

P

HIGH ST

CHURCHFIELD

B1336

CHURCH RD

ST BOTOLPH'S TERR

B1034

WALTON-ON-THE-NAZE

Albion Breakwater

Marine Breakwater

PATERNOSTER ROW

Central Beach

THE PARADE

Walton-on-Naze Station

P

P

St Botolph's

Winchester Breakwater

New Walton Pier

4

Woodfield

WALTON WARD

Sch

Playing Fields

Pedlars Wood

Southcliff Promenade

Pavilion Breakwater

21

Burnt House Breakwater

HERONSGATE

B1336

CENTRAL AVE

Groynes

3

WALTHAM WAY

POLE BARN LA

CLIFF WAY

Sandy Hook Breakwater

FRINTON-ON-SEA

THE CRESCENT

ESPLANADE

20

2

19

1

18

24   **A**   25   **B**   26   **C**

93

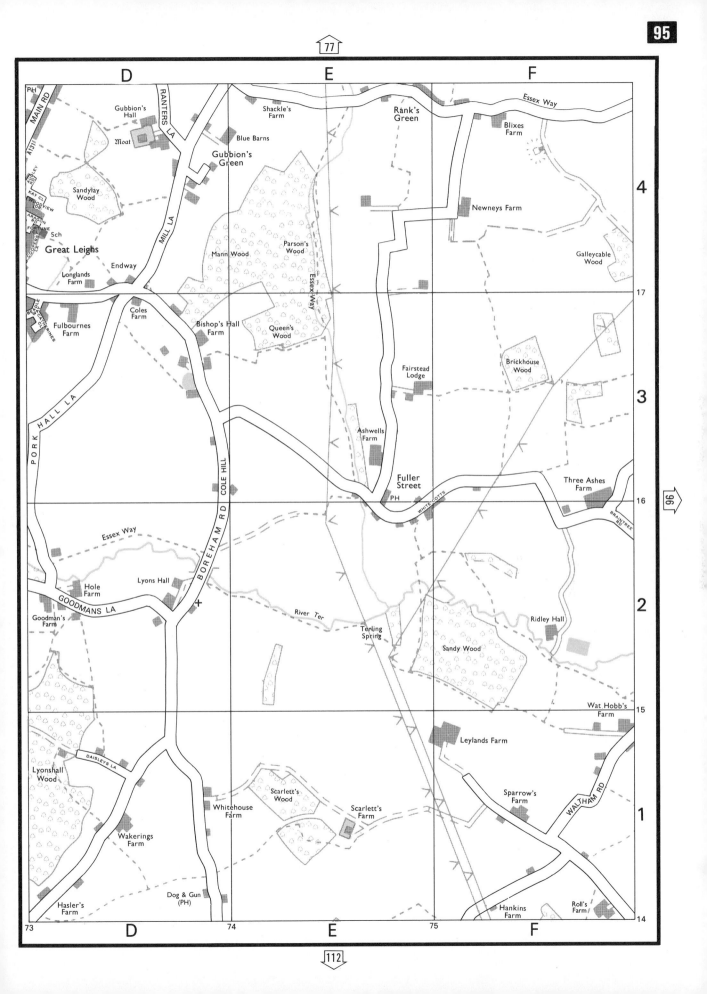

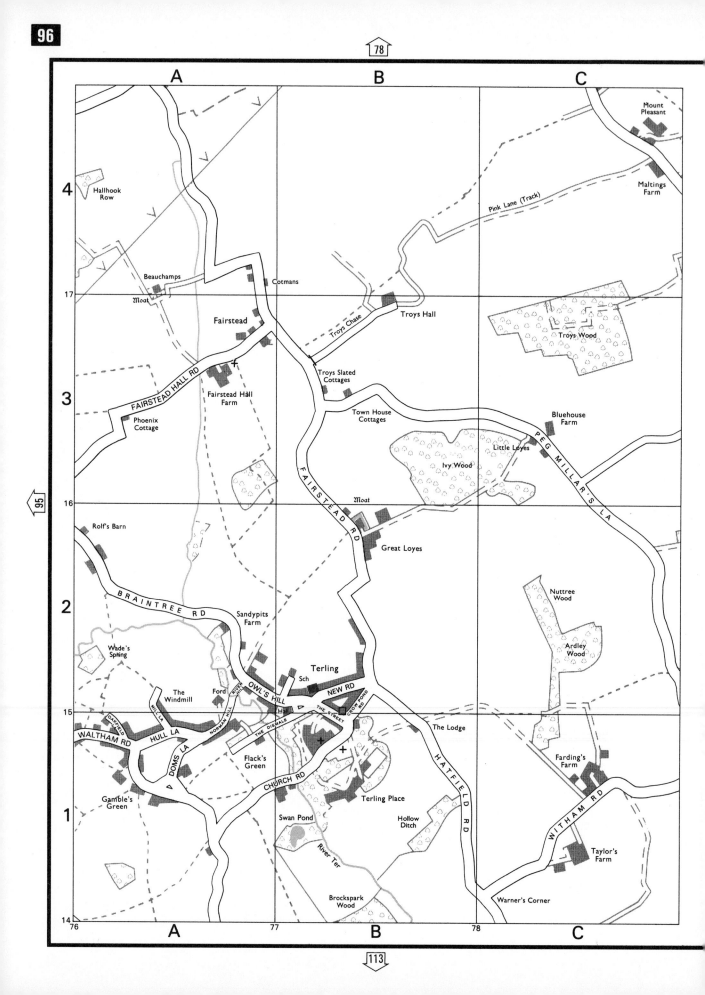

A B C

4 Hallhook Row

Mount Pleasant

Pink Lane (Track)

Maltings Farm

Beauchamps
Cotmans

17
Moat

Fairstead

Troys Chase

Troys Hall

Troys Wood

FAIRSTEAD HALL RD

Troys Slated Cottages

Fairstead Hall Farm

3 Phoenix Cottage

Town House Cottages

Bluehouse Farm

Little Loyes

PEG MILLAR'S LA

Ivy Wood

FAIRSTEAD RD

16 Moat

Great Loyes

Rolf's Barn

Nuttree Wood

BRAINTREE RD

2 Sandypits Farm

Ardley Wood

Wade's Spring

Terling

OWL'S HILL

Sch

NEW RD

The Windmill

Ford

NORMAN HILL

RIVER TER

MILL LA

The Lodge

15
HATFIELD RD

DANFIELD

THE DISWALS

THE STREET

CROW POND RD

WALTHAM RD

HULL LA

DOMS LA

CHURCH RD

Flack's Green

Farding's Farm

Terling Place

WITHAM RD

1 Gamble's Green

Swan Pond

Hollow Ditch

River Ter

Taylor's Farm

Brockspark Wood

Warner's Corner

14
76 A 77 B 78 C

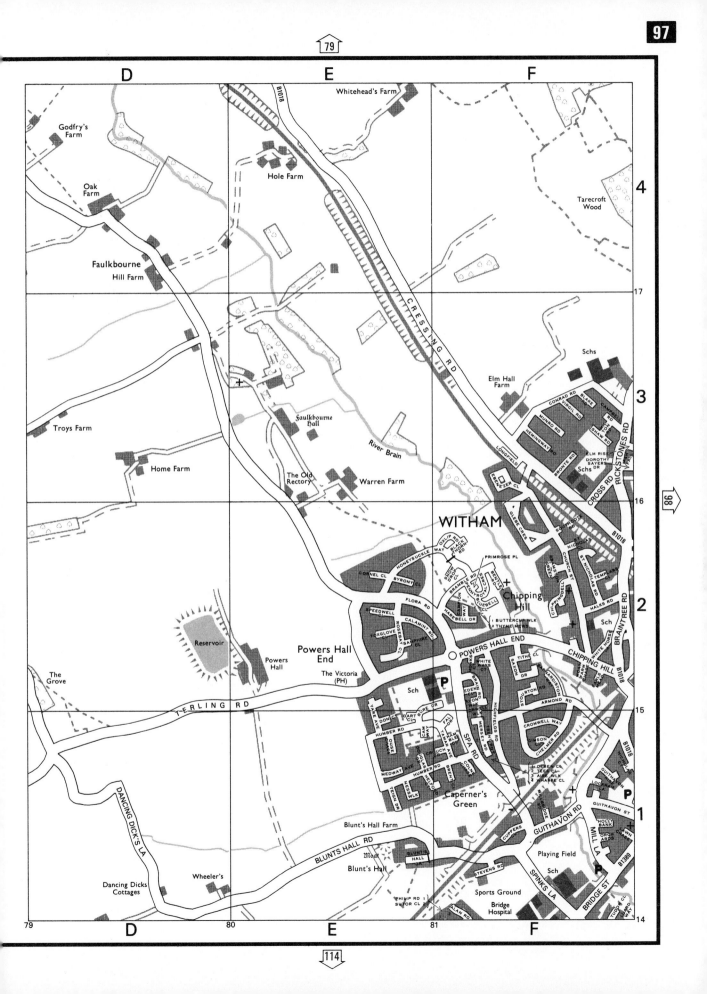

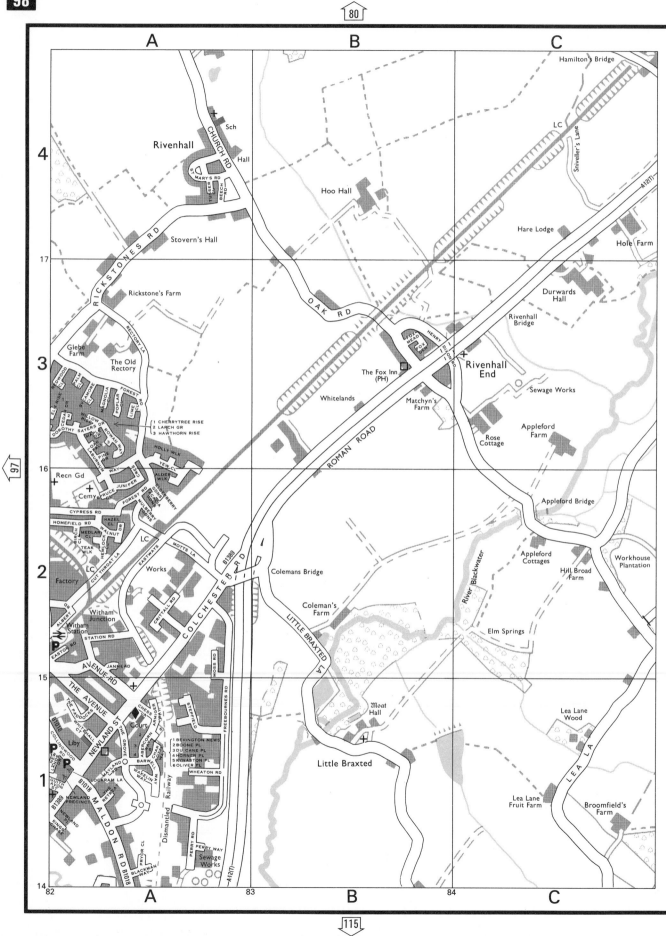

A

B

C

4

Rivenhall

Sch
Hall

CHURCH RD
ST MARY'S RD
TUSSER GR
BEECH RD

Hoo Hall

Hamilton's Bridge

LC

Sniveller's Lane

A12(T)

Stovern's Hall

Hare Lodge

Hole Farm

17

RICKSTONES RD

Rickstone's Farm

OAK RD

Durwards
Hall

Rivenhall
Bridge

3

RECTORY LA

Glebe
Farm

The Old
Rectory

FOREST RD
POPLAR RD
LIME

REDWOOD
ELM
SYCAMORE
MAGNOLIA

Whitelands

FOX
MEAD
FOX
DEN

HENRY
DIXON RD

Rivenhall
End

The Fox Inn
(PH)

Matchyn's
Farm

Sewage Works

ELM RISE
CEDAR
DOROTHY SAYERS WAY
WILLOW DR
MAPLE
ROWAN WAY

1 CHERRYTREE RISE
2 LARCH GR
3 HAWTHORN RISE

Appleford
Farm

LABURNUM
PINE
SPRUCE
OAK
HOLLY WLK

Rose
Cottage

16

Recn Gd

JUNIPER
GOOSEBERRY
ACACIA
ALDER WLK
YEW CL

Appleford Bridge

Cemy

SPRUCE
FOREST RD
MULBERRY
GNS

CYPRESS RD

HAZEL
CL
WALNUT
DR

Appleford
Cottages

Hill Broad
Farm

Workhouse
Plantation

HOMEFIELD RD
BIRCH
MEDLAR
CL
HEMLOCK DR
TEAK WLK

LC

MOTTS LA

EASTWAYS
CUT THROAT LA

LC

River Blackwater

2

Factory

Works

COLCHESTER RD
CRITTALL RD

B1389

Colemans Bridge

Elm Springs

Witham
Junction

STATION RD

Coleman's
Farm

LITTLE BRAXTED LA

Witham
Station

P

EASTON RD

JANHEAD

AVENUE RD

MOSS RD

Moat
Hall

Lea Lane
Wood

15

THE AVENUE

CHESS

ARMIGER
STEPFIELD
FREEBOURNES RD

Lea Lane
Fruit Farm

LEA LA

THE PADDOCKS
WHITEHALL
COLLINGWOOD
NEWLAND ST

ABERCORN
CHAD
BARWELL
WAKELIN WAY
THE GROVE

1 BEVINGTON MEWS
2 BOONE PL
3 DU CANE PL
4 HORNER PL
5 KYNASTON PL
6 OLIVER PL

Little Braxted

Court

P

Liby

P

MAYLAND
LOCKRAM LA

WHEATON RD

Broomfield's
Farm

1

B1018

B1389
NEWLAND
PRECINCT
NEWLAND

GRO

MALDON RD

PRYOR CL

PERRY RD
PERRY WAY

Dismantled Railway

KINGS

BLACKMAN
WAY

Sewage
Works

A12(T)

B1018

14

82

A

83

B

84

C

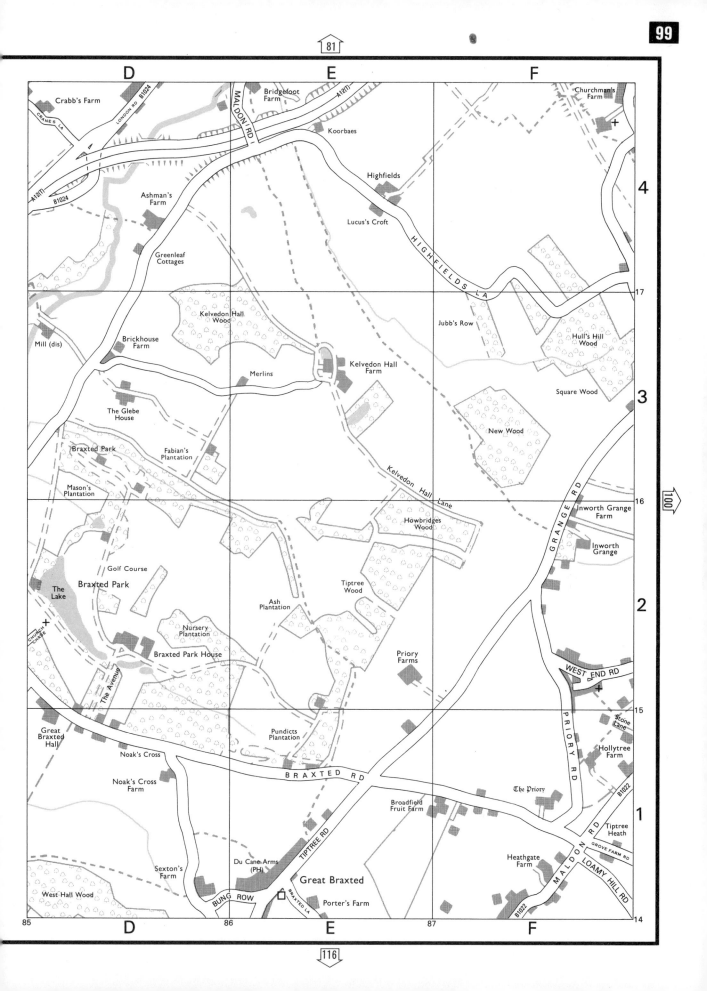

D
E
F

Crabb's Farm

CRANES LA

LONDON RD B1024

MALDON RD

Bridgefoot Farm

A12(T)

Churchman's Farm

Koorbaes

A12(T)

B1024

Ashman's Farm

Highfields

4

Lucus's Croft

Greenleaf Cottages

HIGHFIELDS LA

17

Mill (dis)

Kelvedon Hall Wood

Jubb's Row

Hull's Hill Wood

Brickhouse Farm

Merlins

Kelvedon Hall Farm

Square Wood

3

The Glebe House

New Wood

Braxted Park

Fabian's Plantation

Kelvedon Hall Lane

Mason's Plantation

GRANGE RD

Inworth Grange Farm

16

100

Howbridges Wood

Inworth Grange

Golf Course

The Lake

Braxted Park

Tiptree Wood

Ash Plantation

2

Nursery Plantation

Priory Farms

WEST END RD

Braxted Park House

CHURCH CHASE

The Avenue

PRIORY RD

15

Great Braxted Hall

Pundicts Plantation

Stone Lane

Noak's Cross

Hollytree Farm

Noak's Cross Farm

BRAXTED RD

The Priory

B1022

1

Broadfield Fruit Farm

Tiptree Heath

TIPTREE RD

GROVE FARM RD

Sexton's Farm

Du Cane Arms (PH)

Heathgate Farm

MALDON RD

LOAMY HILL RD

West Hall Wood

Great Braxted

B1022

BUNG ROW

BRAXTED LA

Porter's Farm

85
D
86
E
87
F
14

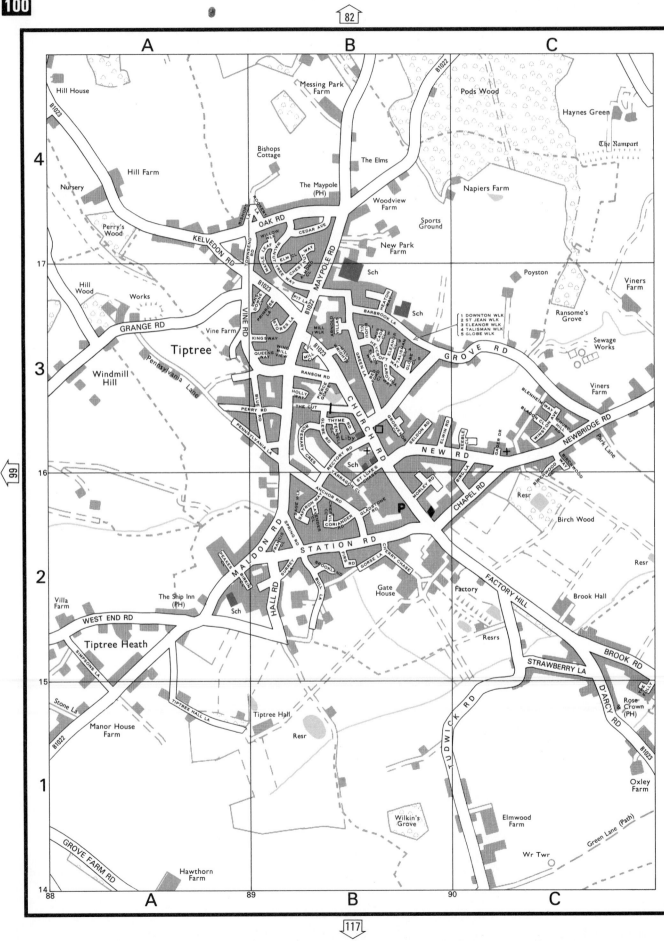

A   B   C

Hill House

B1023

Nursery

Hill Farm

Messing Park Farm

Pods Wood

Haynes Green

The Rampart

Bishops Cottage

The Elms

The Maypole (PH)

Woodview Farm

Napiers Farm

4

Perry's Wood

OAK RD

KELVEDON RD

WILLOW WLK

MAPLE LEAF

ASH WAY

ELM WAY

CEDAR AVE

CHESTNUT WAY

ACORN

TOWNSEND

BISHOPS LA

ROOKES LA

Sports Ground

New Park Farm

Sch

Poyston

Viners Farm

17

Hill Wood

Works

GRANGE RD

Vine Farm

VINE RD

B1023

DOWNSIDE

PRIMROSE LA

STORES LA

KINGSWAY

QUEENS WAY

WINDMILL VIEW

PIT LA

B1022

MILL WLK

ARNOLD

VILLAS

B1023

WRIGHTS

BARBROOK LA

HEATON

GREEN LA

CADE

ELEANOR

TALISMAN WAY

GLOBE

CAROLINA

HETHOP

BIJOU

1 DOWNTON WLK
2 ST JEAN WLK
3 ELEANOR WLK
4 TALISMAN WLK
5 GLOBE WLK

GROVE RD

Ransome's Grove

Sewage Works

Viners Farm

3

Tiptree

Windmill Hill

Pennsylvania Lane

PENNSYLVANIA LA

PERRY RD

BLUE WAY

RANSOM RD

HOLLY WAY

HEDGE ROW

THE CUT

ROSEMARY

THYME RD

FENNEL

GLEBE RD

RECTORY RD

CRES

Liby

CHURCH RD

GROSVENOR

SELDON RD

ELWIN RD

KEEBLE CL

BLADON CL

WINSLOW

BLENHEIM WAY

CHURCHILL

GLADEN DR

NEW RD

PARK LANE

NEWBRIDGE RD

16

Sch

St LUKES

TARRAGON CL

St LOMAS

MORLEY RD

BIRCH LA

CHAPEL RD

BIRCHWOOD WAY

BIRCHWOOD

Resr

Birch Wood

Resr

2

The Ship Inn (PH)

Villa Farm

WEST END RD

Tiptree Heath

MALDON RD

HALL RD

SPRING RD

SURREY CL

BIRKIN

FRANCIS

MEANS

SAFFRON WLK

LAVENDER

SAGE WLK

ANCHOR RD

CHERVIL CL

CORIANDER

GLADSTONE RD

STATION RD

BULL LA

BROOKLAND

FIRS RD

GORSE LA

CHERRY CHASE

Gate House

Factory

FACTORY HILL

Brook Hall

Resrs

Resr

Brook Hall

TUDWICK RD

STRAWBERRY LA

BROOK RD

D'ARCY RD

THE FOLLY

Rose & Crown (PH)

B1023

15

Stone La

SIMPSONS LA

B1022

Manor House Farm

TIPTREE HALL LA

Tiptree Hall

Resr

Oxley Farm

1

GROVE FARM RD

Hawthorn Farm

Wilkin's Grove

Elmwood Farm

Wr Twr

Green Lane (Path)

14

88   A   89   B   90   C

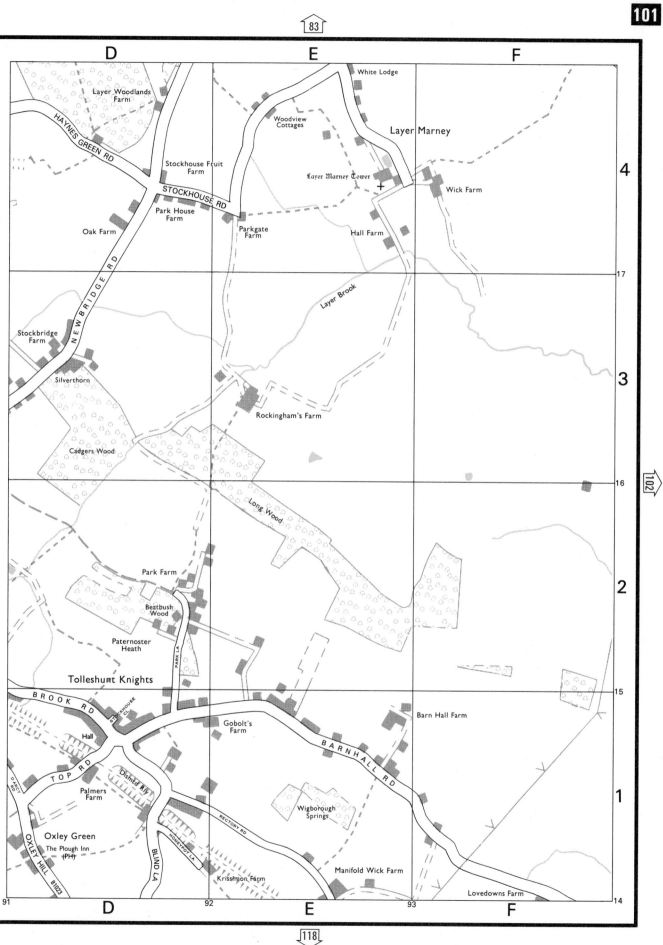

D

Layer Woodlands Farm

HAYNES GREEN RD

Stockhouse Fruit Farm

STOCKHOUSE RD

Park House Farm

Oak Farm

NEWBRIDGE RD

Parkgate Farm

E

White Lodge

Woodview Cottages

Layer Marney

Layer Marney Tower +

Wick Farm

Hall Farm

F

4

17

Stockbridge Farm

Silverthorn

Rockingham's Farm

Layer Brook

3

Cadgers Wood

16

Long Wood

102

Park Farm

Beatbush Wood

Paternoster Heath

PARK LA

2

Tolleshunt Knights

BROOK RD

Hall

STOCKHOUSE CL

Gobolt's Farm

Barn Hall Farm

BARNHALL RD

15

TOP RD

D'ARCY RD

Palmers Farm

Dismtd Rly

RECTORY RD

Wigborough Springs

1

Oxley Green

The Plough Inn (PH)

OXLEY HILL B1023

BLIND LA

HONEYPOT LA

Krissmon Farm

Manifold Wick Farm

Lovedowns Farm

14

91

D

92

E

93

F

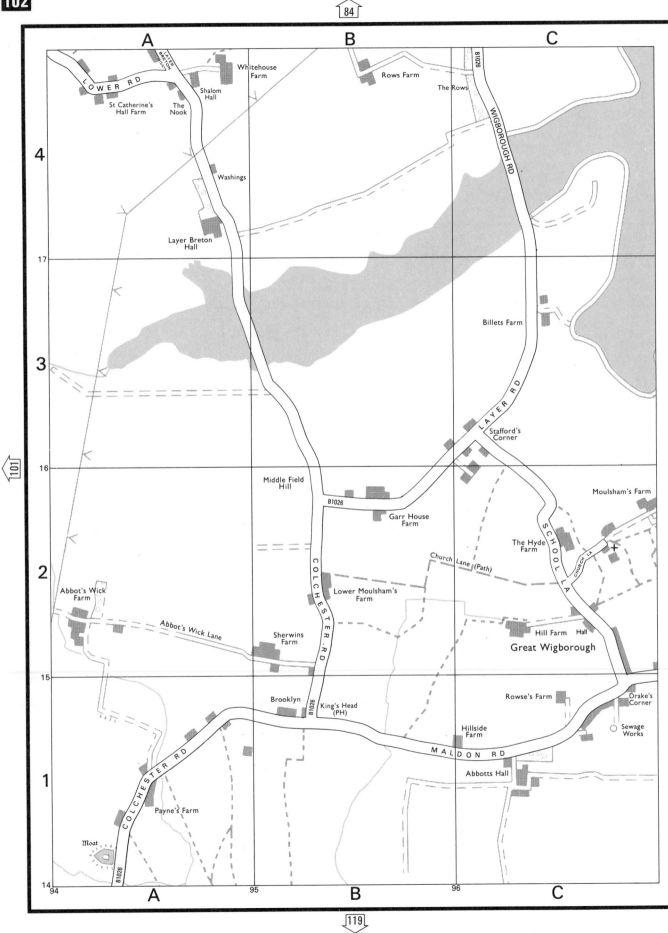

101

A · B · C

LOWER RD

LAYER BRETON (HILL?)

Whitehouse Farm

Rows Farm

The Rows

St Catherine's Hall Farm

Shalom Hall

The Nook

B1026

WIGBOROUGH RD

Washings

Layer Breton Hall

Billets Farm

LAYER RD

Stafford's Corner

Middle Field Hill

B1026

Garr House Farm

Moulsham's Farm

The Hyde Farm

SCHOOL LA

CHURCH LA

Church Lane (Path)

Abbot's Wick Farm

Lower Moulsham's Farm

COLCHESTER RD

Abbot's Wick Lane

Sherwins Farm

Hill Farm Hall

Great Wigborough

Brooklyn

B1026

King's Head (PH)

Rowse's Farm

Drake's Corner

Hillside Farm

Sewage Works

MALDON RD

COLCHESTER RD

Abbotts Hall

Payne's Farm

Moat

B1026

17 · 16 · 15 · 14

4 · 3 · 2 · 1

94 · 95 · 96

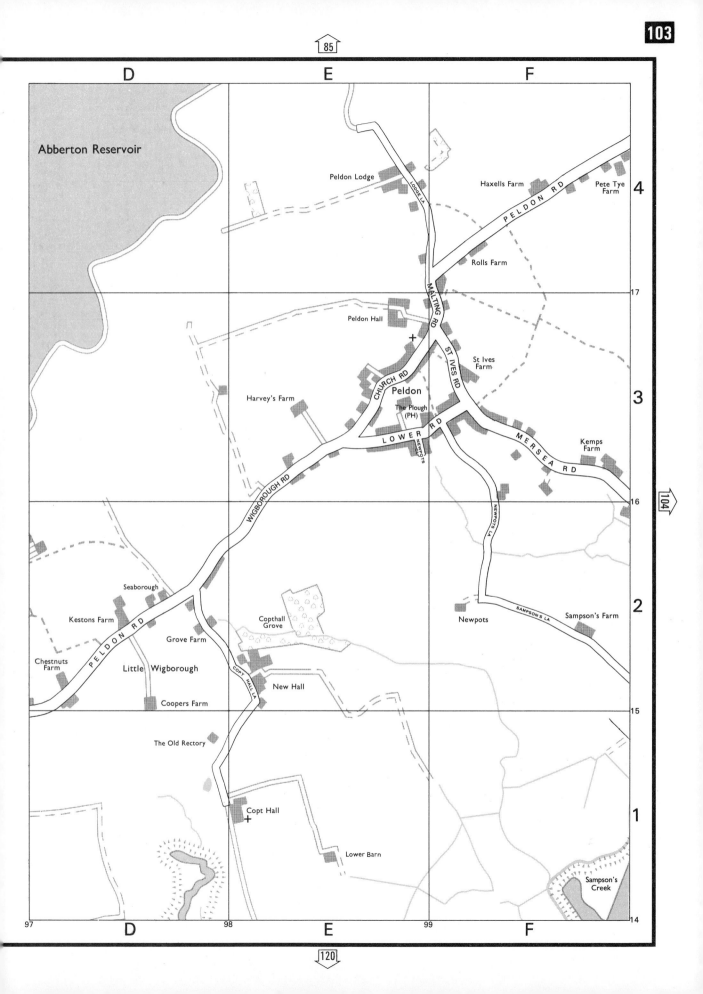

D   E   F

Abberton Reservoir

Peldon Lodge

Haxells Farm

PELDON RD

Pete Tye
Farm

4

LODGE LA

Rolls Farm

MALTING RD

17

Peldon Hall

+

St Ives
Farm

ST IVES RD

Harvey's Farm

CHURCH RD

Peldon

The Plough
(PH)

3

LOWER RD

NEWPOTS

MERSEA RD

Kemps
Farm

WIGBOROUGH RD

16

NEWPOTS LA

Seaborough

Kestons Farm

PELDON RD

Copthall
Grove

Newpots

SAMPSON S LA

Sampson's Farm

2

Grove Farm

Chestnuts
Farm

Little Wigborough

COPT HALL LA

New Hall

Coopers Farm

15

The Old Rectory

Copt Hall
+

1

Lower Barn

Sampson's
Creek

97   98   99   14

D   E   F

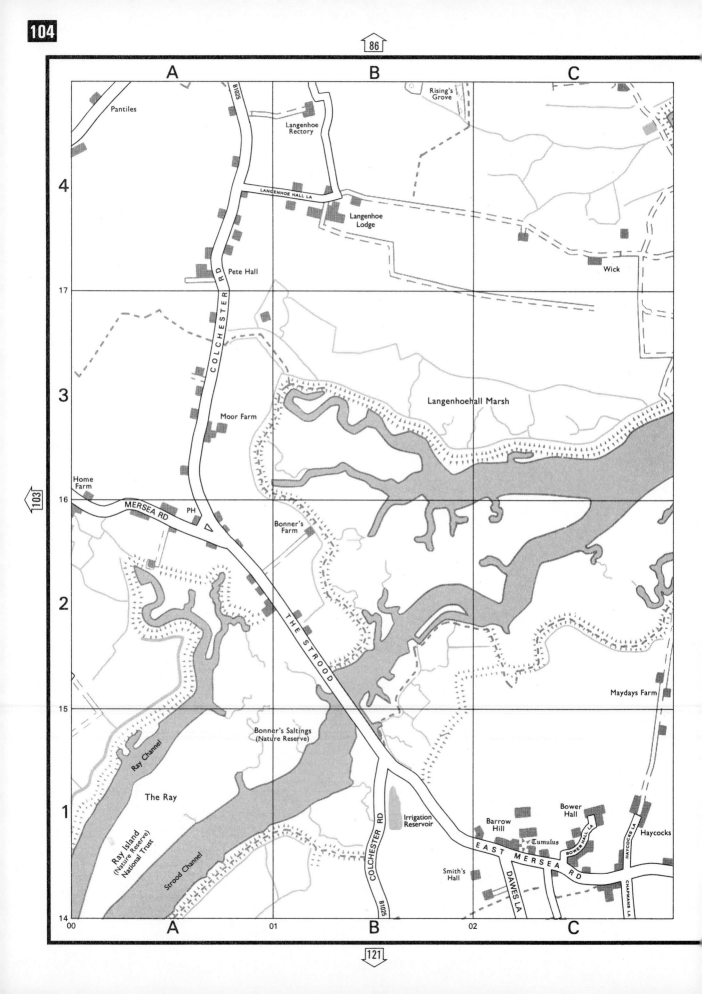

A   B   C

4

Pantiles

B1025

Rising's
Grove

Langenhoe
Rectory

LANGENHOE HALL LA

Langenhoe
Lodge

COLCHESTER RD

Pete Hall

Wick

17

3

Langenhoehall Marsh

Moor Farm

Home
Farm

16

MERSEA RD   PH

Bonner's
Farm

Bonner's
Farm

THE STROOD

2

Maydays Farm

15

Bonner's Saltings
(Nature Reserve)

Ray Channel

The Ray

COLCHESTER RD

Irrigation
Reservoir

1

Barrow
Hill

Bower
Hall

Haycocks

Ray Island
(Nature Reserve)
National Trust

Strood Channel

Tumulus

BOWER HALL LA

HAYCOCKS LA

EAST MERSEA RD

Smith's
Hall

DAWES LA

CHAPMANS LA

14

00   A   01   B   02   C

B1025

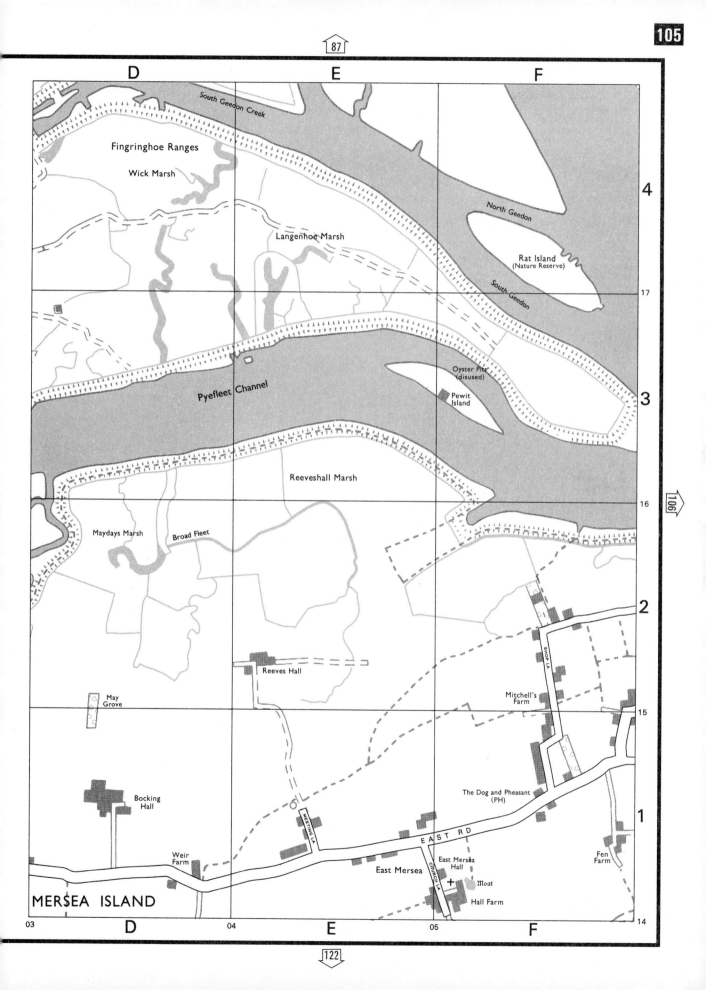

South Geedon Creek

Fingringhoe Ranges

Wick Marsh

North Geedon

Langenhoe Marsh

Rat Island
(Nature Reserve)

South Geedon

4

17

Oyster Pits
(disused)

Pewit
Island

Pyefleet Channel

3

Reeveshall Marsh

16

106

Maydays Marsh

Broad Fleet

2

SHOP LA

Reeves Hall

Mitchell's
Farm

May
Grove

15

Bocking
Hall

The Dog and Pheasant
(PH)

1

Weir
Farm

MEETING LA

EAST RD

East Mersea

CHURCH LA

East Mersea
Hall

Moat

Fen
Farm

MERSEA ISLAND

Hall Farm

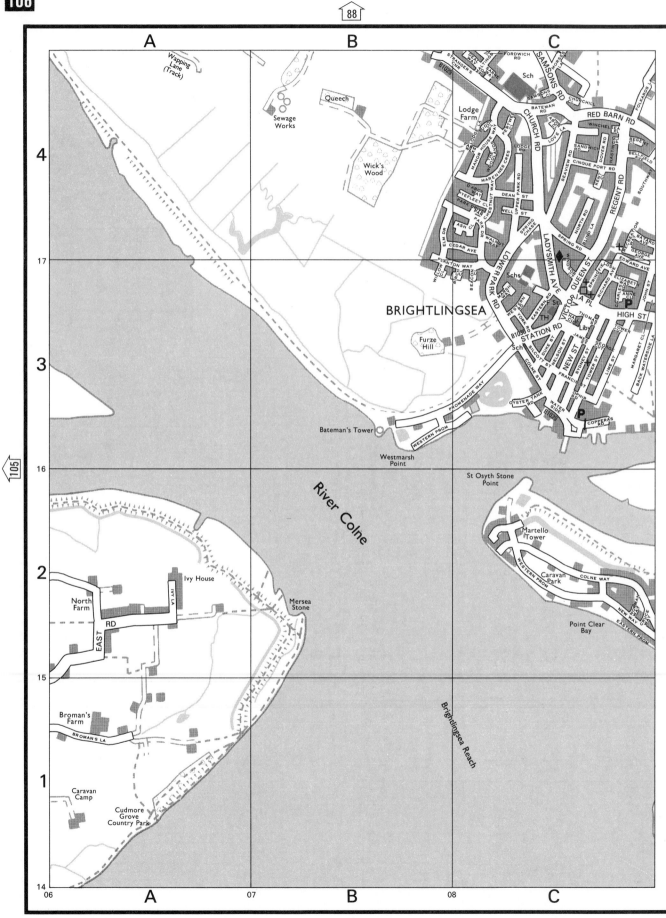

105

A

B

C

Wapping
Lane
(Track)

Sewage
Works

Queech

Wick's
Wood

4

Lodge
Farm

CHURCH RD

RED BARN RD

SAMSONS RD

Sch

BATEMAN
RD

WINCHELSEA

SANDWICH RD

SEAVIEW RD

CINQUE PORT RD

REGENT RD

BELLFIELD

NORTH RD

SPRING RD

17

BRIGHTLINGSEA

LADYSMITH AVE

VICTORIA PL

QUEEN ST

HIGH ST

Schs

LOWER PARK RD

Sch

3

Furze
Hill

Sch

STATION RD

NEW ST

PROMENADE WAY

Bateman's Tower

WESTERN PROM

OYSTER TANK
RD

COPPERAS

P

Westmarsh
Point

16

St Osyth Stone
Point

River Colne

Martello
Tower

2

Ivy House

IVY LA

North
Farm

Mersea
Stone

Caravan
Park

COLNE WAY

EAST

RD

WESTERN PROM

Point Clear
Bay

15

Brightlingsea Reach

Broman's
Farm

BROMAN'S LA

1

Caravan
Camp

Cudmore
Grove
Country Park

14

06

A

07

B

08

C

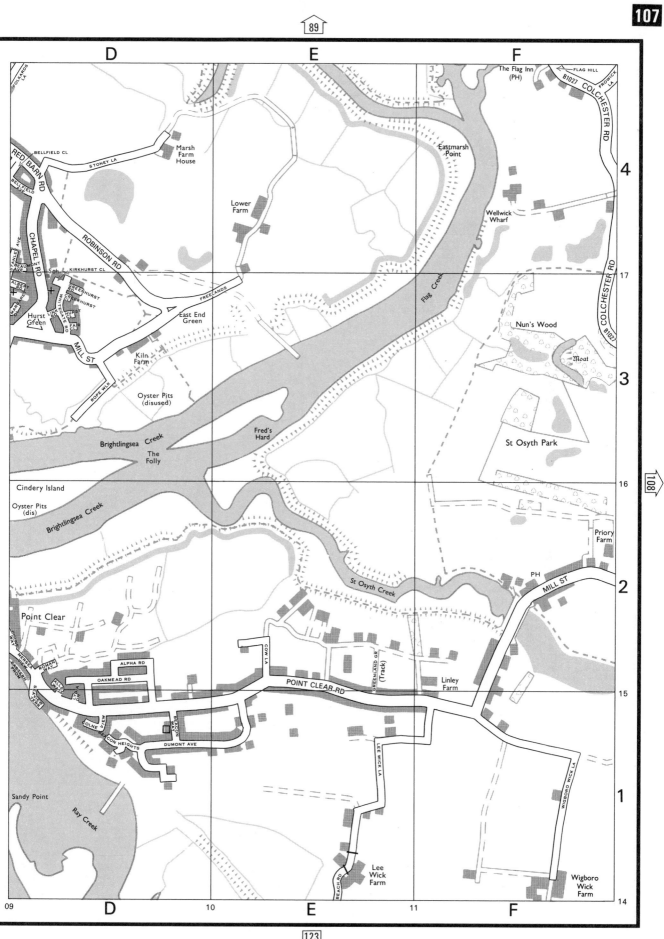

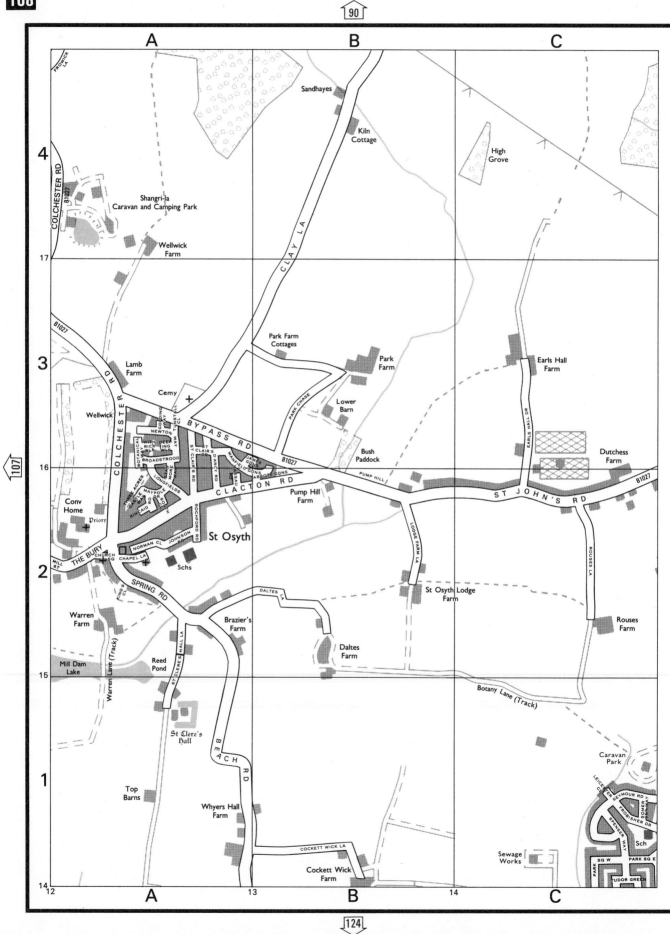

A　**B**　**C**

4

Sandhayes

Kiln Cottage

High Grove

FROWICK LA

COLCHESTER RD
B1027

Shangri-la
Caravan and Camping Park

Wellwick
Farm

CLAY LA

17

3

B1027

Lamb
Farm

Park Farm
Cottages

Park
Farm

Earls Hall
Farm

Cemy

Wellwick

BYPASS RD

PARK CHASE

Lower
Barn

EARLS HALL DR

Dutchess
Farm

COLCHESTER RD

Newton

GOODING WAY

WITH DEER

RICKLING

WALK

ROMAN

BROADSTROOD

BOTANICAL

St Clair's RD

ST CLAIR'S

DARCY RD

MANFIELD GDNS

JAMES GDNS

ABBOTS GDNS

AVIAL

HUTST CL

B1027

Bush
Paddock

16

Conv
Home

Priory

THREE ACRES

KINCAID RD

MAYPOLE RD

JOHNSON

LONGFIELDS

CLACTON RD

ROCHFORD RD

Pump Hill
Farm

PUMP HILL

St JOHN'S RD

LODGE FARM LA

ROUSES LA

B1027

St Osyth

Pump Hill
Farm

2

MILL ST

THE BURY

CHURCH
SQ

NORMAN CL

CHAPEL LA

Schs

JOHNSON RD

St Osyth Lodge
Farm

Rouses
Farm

KINGS CL

SPRING RD

DALTES LA

Warren
Farm

ST CLERES HALL LA

Brazier's
Farm

Daltes
Farm

Warren Lane (Track)

Reed
Pond

Botany Lane (Track)

15

Mill Dam
Lake

Caravan
Park

1

St Clere's
Hall

BEACH RD

Top
Barns

Whyers Hall
Farm

LEICESTER CLOSE

SEYMOUR RD

FROBISHER DR

SPENSER WAY

Sch

Sewage
Works

PARK SQ W

PARK SQ E

COCKETT WICK LA

Cockett Wick
Farm

TUDOR GREEN

14

12　**A**　**13**　**B**　**14**　**C**

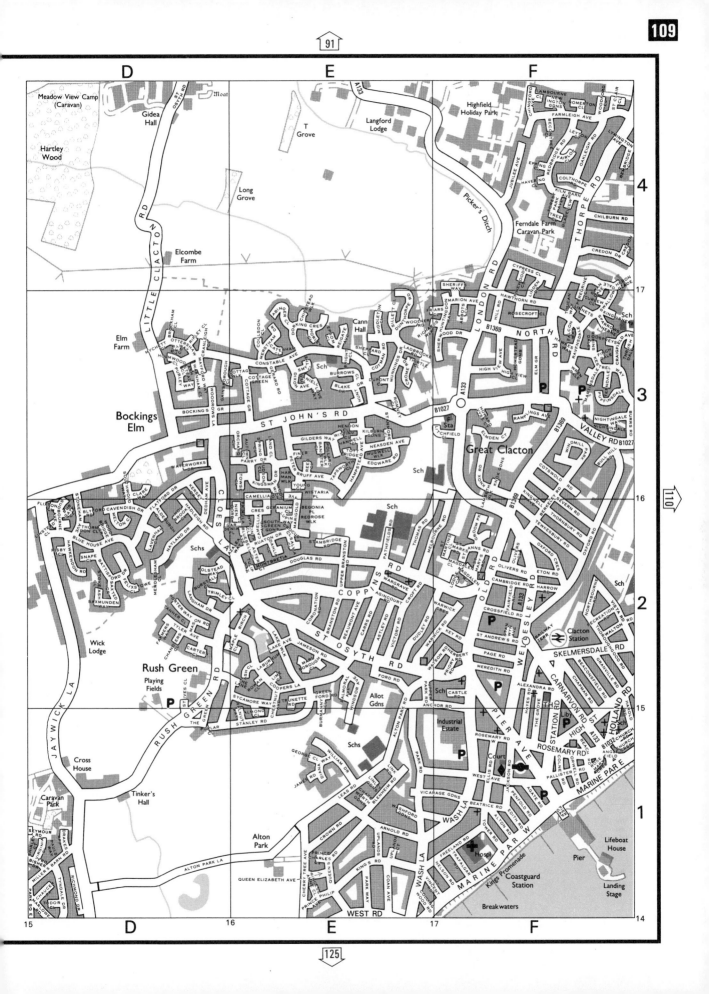

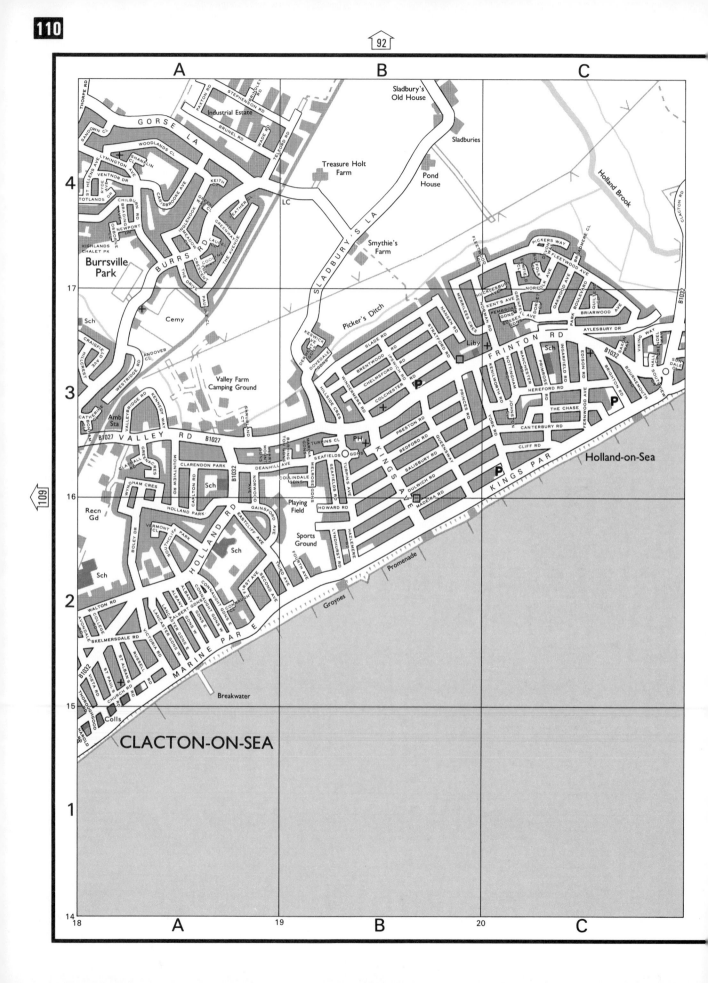

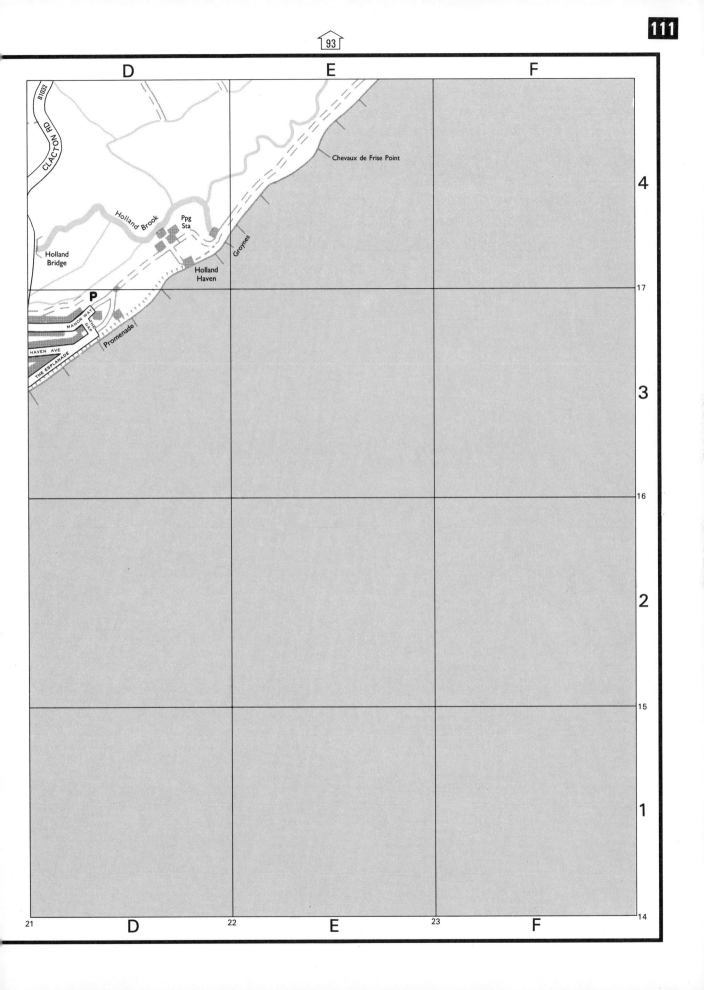

D

E

F

B1032

CLACTON RD

Holland Brook

Ppg
Sta

Holland
Bridge

Groynes

Holland
Haven

Chevaux de Frise Point

P

MANOR WAY

Promenade

HAVEN AVE

THE ESPLANADE

4

17

3

16

2

15

1

14

21

D

22

E

23

F

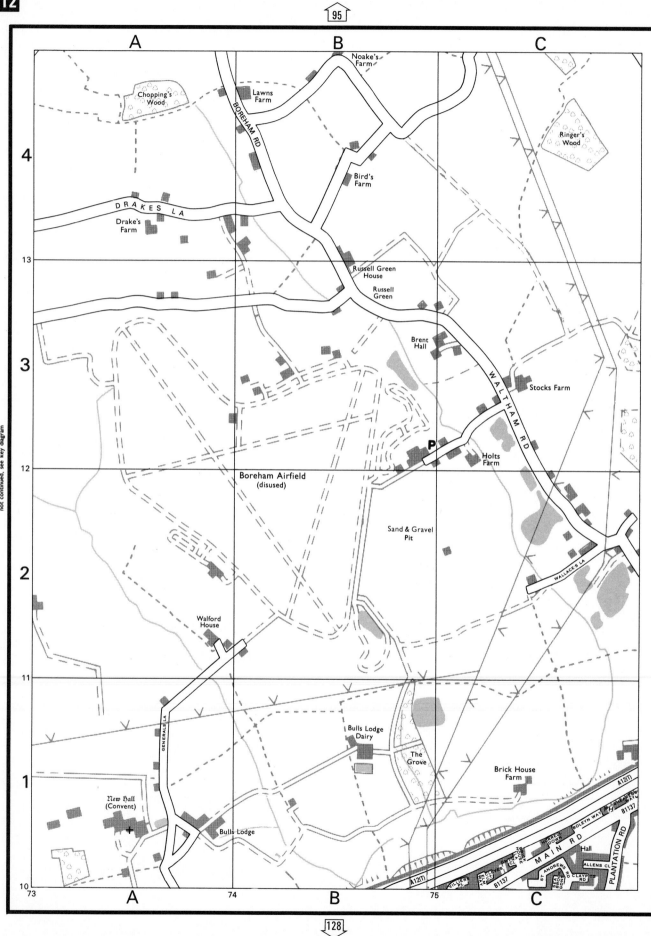

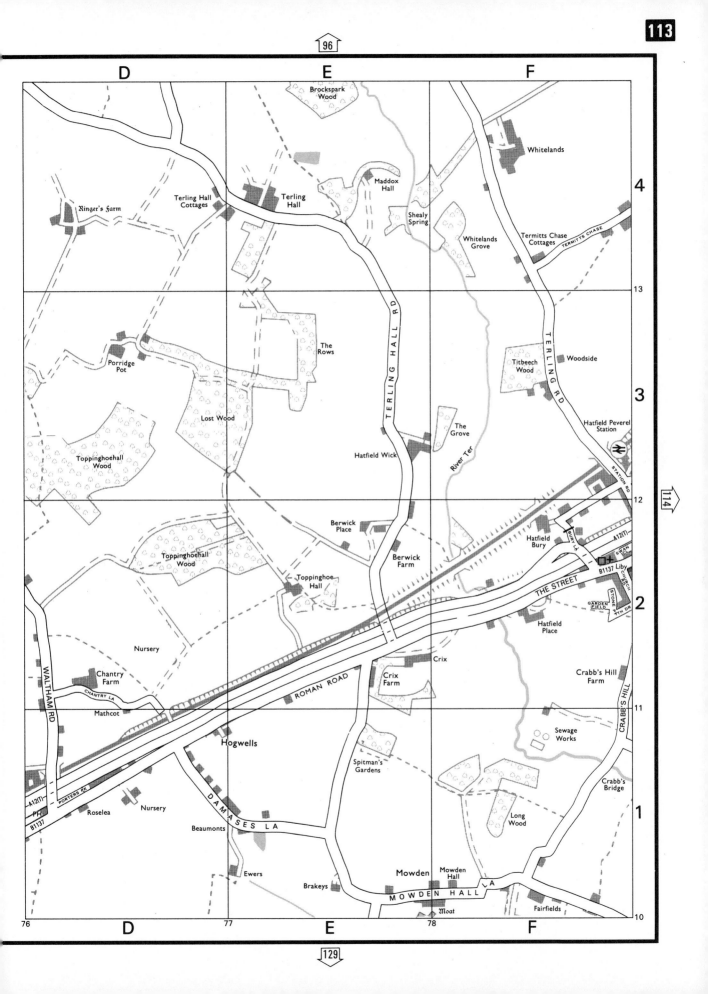

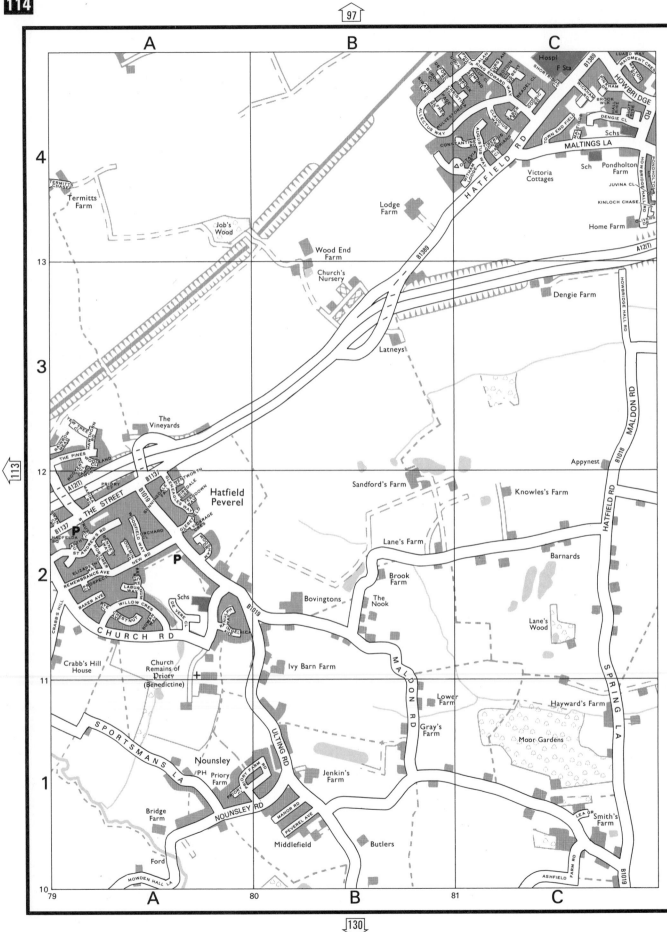

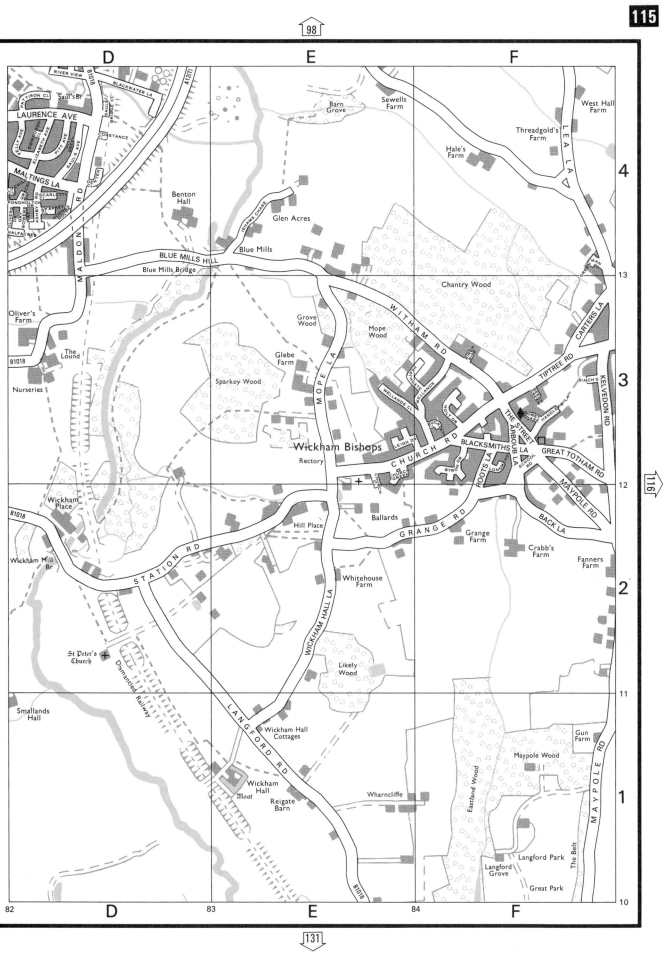

4

〈116〉

3

2

1

13

12

11

10

River View
Saul's Br
PATTISON CL
Saul's
Blackwater La
BRIDGE CL
A12(T)
B1018
LAURENCE AVE
SAULS
CONSTANCE
LILY AVE
EDINBURGH
ELIZABETH AVE
CHILES
PITT AVE
SAUL'S AVE
GREEN
MALTINGS LA
DENTEN
CL
OLIVERS
GATES
SCARLETTS
STARKEY
ASHBY RD
HODGES
PONDHOLTON
HALFACRES

MALDON RD

Benton Hall

Barn Grove

Sewells Farm

West Hall Farm

Threadgold's Farm

Hale's Farm

LEA LA

ISHAMS CHASE
Glen Acres

BLUE MILLS HILL
Blue Mills
Blue Mills Bridge

GREEN MAN

Chantry Wood

Oliver's Farm

Grove Wood

Mope Wood

WITHAM RD

CARTERS LA

B1018
The Lound

Glebe Farm

MOPE LA

TIPTREE RD

FINCH'S

KELVEDON RD

Nurseries

Sparkey Wood

HONEY CHASE
HANDLEY LA

WELLANDS CL
WELLANDS
THORNGATE
BIRCH AVE
HOLT DR
BUCK'S DR

THE STREET
ARBOUR LA

Wickham Bishops
Rectory

CHURCH RD
LEIGH DR

BLACKSMITHS LA
SCHOOL RD
GREAT TOTHAM RD

ROOTS LA
BYRON
LONG ACRES

CHURCH
CHURCH
GREEN

MAYPOLE RD

Wickham Place

BACK LA

Ballards

GRANGE RD

Grange Farm

Crabb's Farm

Fanners Farm

Hill Place

STATION RD

B1018

Wickham Mill Br

Whitehouse Farm

WICKHAM HALL LA

St Peter's Church

Dismantled Railway

Likely Wood

Smallands Hall

LANGFORD RD

Wickham Hall Cottages

Wickham Hall
Moat
Reigate Barn

Wharncliffe

Eastland Wood

Maypole Wood

Gun Farm

MAYPOLE RD

Langford Grove

Langford Park

The Belt

Great Park

B1018

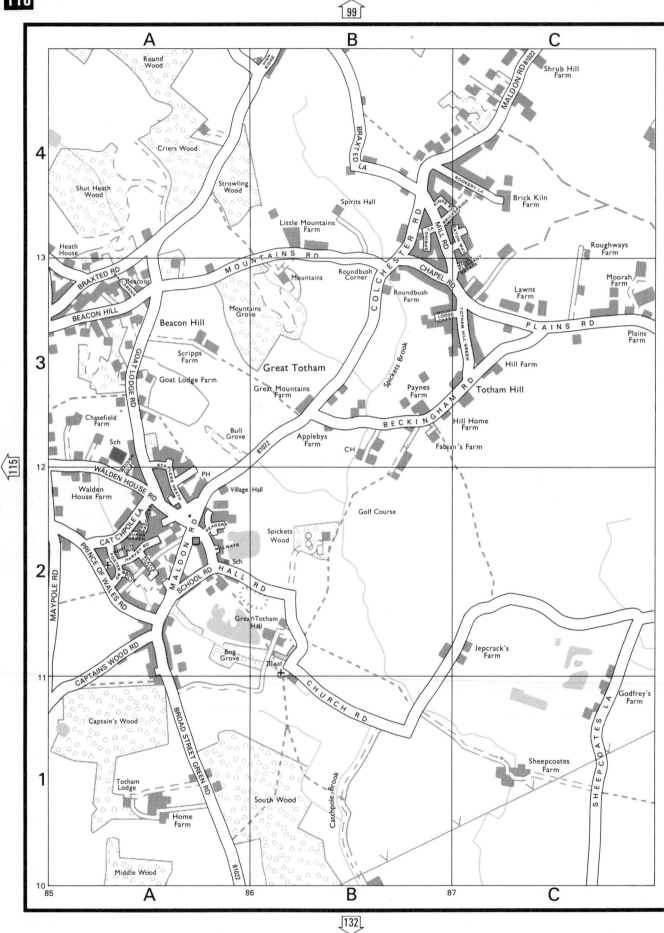

115

A   **B**   **C**

Round Wood

Criers Wood

Shut Heath Wood

Strowling Wood

HIGH RIDGE

Spirits Hall

Little Mountains Farm

Heath House

MOUNTAINS RD

Mountains

Roundbush Corner

BRAXTED LA

COLCHESTER RD

CHAPEL RD

MILL RD

ROOKERY LA

KINGS RD
SPRING LA

BRICK SPRING
TOTTAM WAY

MOUNT PLEASANT ESTATE

Shrub Hill Farm

MALDON RD B1022

Brick Kiln Farm

Roughways Farm

Moorah Farm

BRAXTED RD

Beacons

BEACON HILL

Beacon Hill

GOAT LODGE RD

Scripps Farm

Goat Lodge Farm

Mountains Grove

Great Totham

Great Mountains Farm

Roundbush Farm

Spickets Brook

Paynes Farm

MOUNS LODGE CHASE

TOTTAM HILL GREEN

Lawns Farm

PLAINS RD

Plains Farm

Totham Hill

Hill Farm

Chasefield Farm

Sch

Bull Grove

B1022

Applebys Farm

CH

BECKINGHAM RD

Fabian's Farm

Hill Home Farm

WALDEN HOUSE RD

STAPLERS HEATH

PH

Walden House Farm

CAT CHPOLE LA

MALDON RD

SEAGERS

Village Hall

Golf Course

SPOKE GREEN
BURNS GREEN

HORTON RD
HARVEY RD

FOSTERS RD

PRINCE OF WALES RD

MAYPOLE RD

Millways

Sch

SCHOOL RD

HALL RD

Spickets Wood

Great Totham Hall

Bog Grove

Moat

Jepcrack's Farm

CAPTAINS WOOD RD

CHURCH RD

Catchpole Brook

SHEEPCOATES LA

Godfrey's Farm

Captain's Wood

BROAD STREET GREEN RD

Totham Lodge

South Wood

Sheepcoates Farm

Home Farm

Middle Wood

B1022

85   **A**   86   **B**   87   **C**

D
E
F

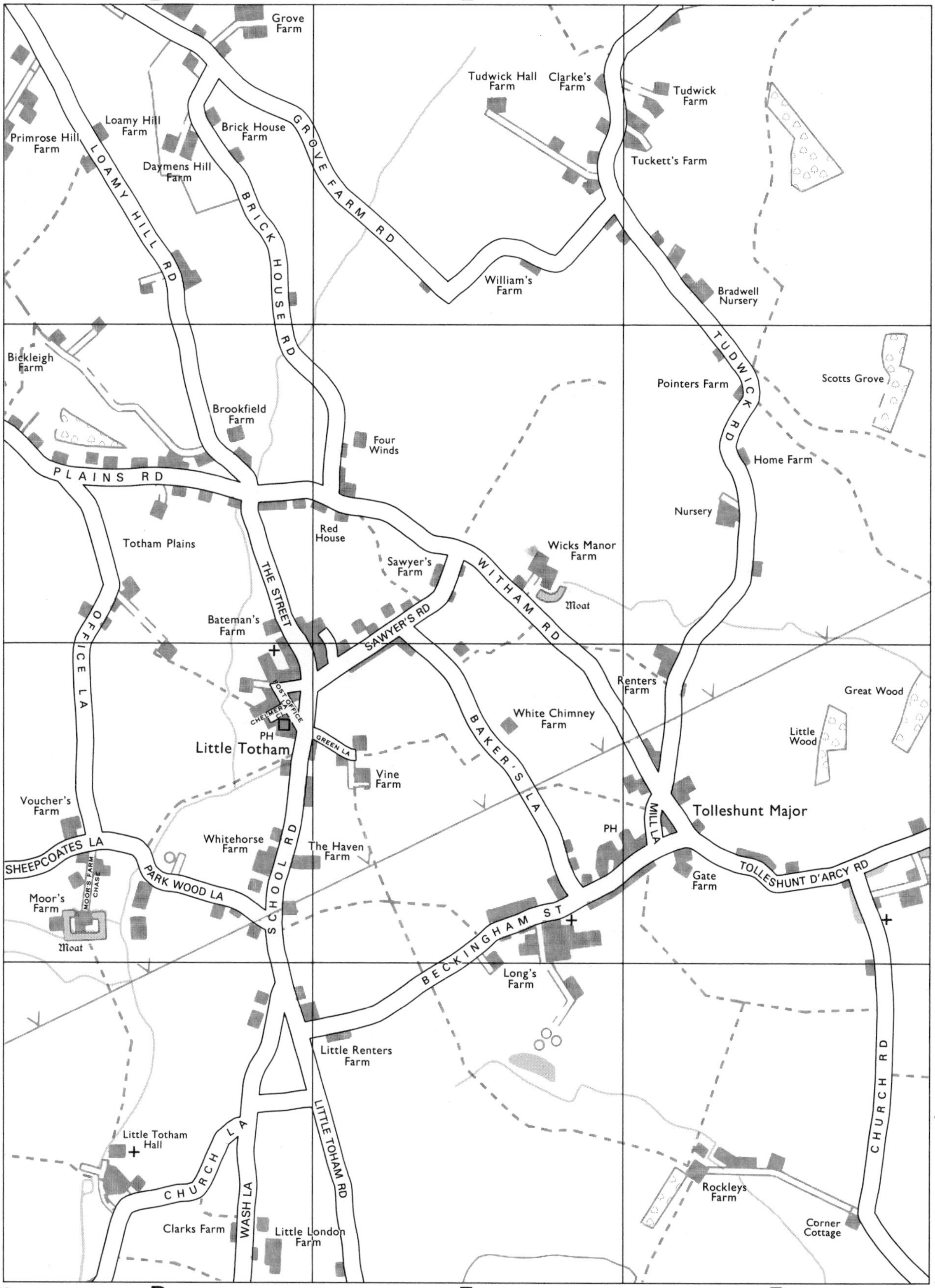

4
13
3
12
2
11
1
10

Grove Farm

Tudwick Hall Farm
Clarke's Farm
Tudwick Farm

Loamy Hill Farm
Brick House Farm
Tuckett's Farm

Primrose Hill Farm
Daymens Hill Farm

LOAMY HILL RD
BRICK HOUSE RD
GROVE FARM RD

William's Farm

Bradwell Nursery

TUDWICK RD

Bickleigh Farm

Pointers Farm
Scotts Grove

PLAINS RD
Brookfield Farm
Four Winds
Home Farm

Totham Plains
Red House
Sawyer's Farm
Wicks Manor Farm
Nursery

THE STREET
WITHAM RD
Moat

Bateman's Farm
SAWYER'S RD

OFFICE LA
Renters Farm
Great Wood

CHENNELS
POST OFFICE
White Chimney Farm
Little Wood

PH
BAKER'S LA
Little Totham
GREEN LA

Vine Farm

MILL LA
Tolleshunt Major

Voucher's Farm

SHEEPCOATES LA
Whitehorse Farm
The Haven Farm
PH

PARK WOOD LA
SCHOOL RD
Gate Farm
TOLLESHUNT D'ARCY RD

MOOR'S FARM CHASE

Moor's Farm
Moat

BECKINGHAM ST
Long's Farm

CHURCH RD

Little Renters Farm

Little Totham Hall

CHURCH LA
WASH LA
LITTLE TOHAM RD
Rockleys Farm

Clarks Farm
Little London Farm
Corner Cottage

118

D
E
F

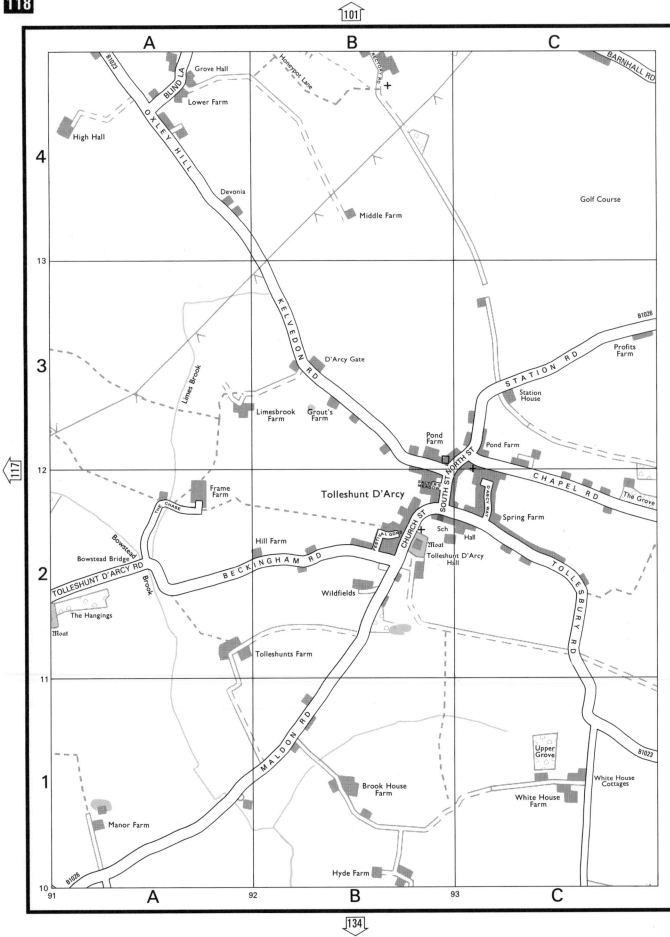

117

A · B · C

Tolleshunt D'Arcy

Grove Hall
Lower Farm
High Hall
Devonia
BLIND LA
OXLEY HILL
B1023
Honeypot Lane
RECTORY RD
BARNHALL RD
Middle Farm
Golf Course
KELVEDON RD
Limes Brook
D'Arcy Gate
Limesbrook Farm
Grout's Farm
STATION RD
B1026
Profits Farm
Station House
Pond Farm
Pond Farm
SOUTH ST · NORTH ST
CHAPEL RD
The Grove
Frame Farm
THE CHASE
SALTERS MEADOW
Spring Farm
D'ARCY WAY
Hill Farm
FESTIVAL GDNS
CHURCH ST
Sch
Hall
Moat
Tolleshunt D'Arcy Hall
Bowstead
Bowstead Bridge
Brook
TOLLESHUNT D'ARCY RD
BECKINGHAM RD
Wildfields
TOLLESBURY RD
The Hangings
Moat
Tolleshunts Farm
MALDON RD
Upper Grove
B1023
White House Cottages
White House Farm
Manor Farm
Brook House Farm
Hyde Farm
B1026

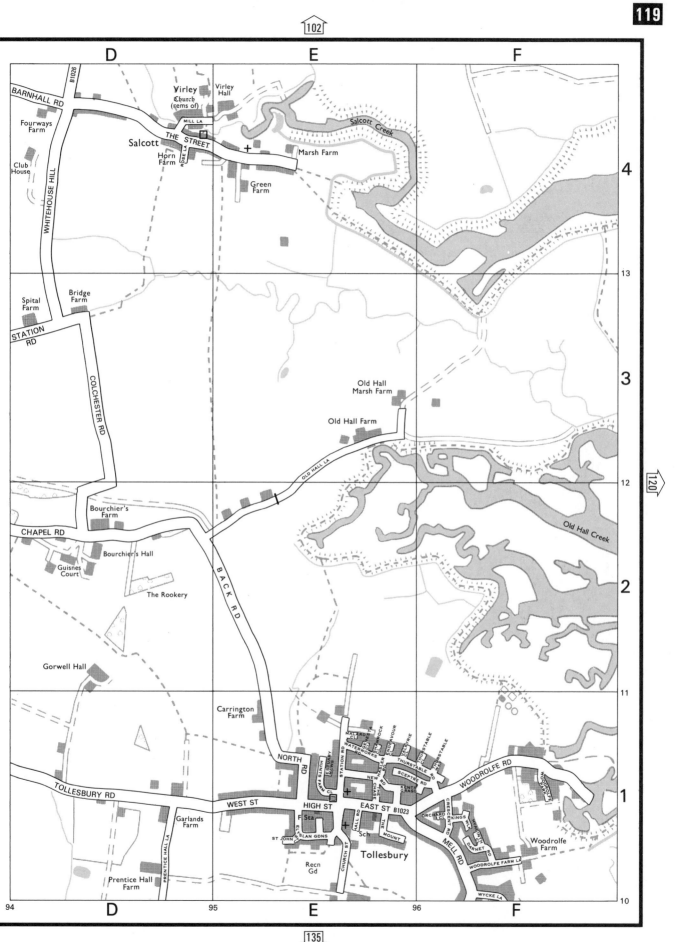

D
E
F

BARNHALL RD

B1026

Fourways
Farm

Club
House

WHITEHOUSE HILL

Salcott

Virley
Church
(rems of)

Virley
Hall

MILL LA

THE STREET

Horn
Farm

Green
Farm

Marsh Farm

Salcott Creek

4

13

Spital
Farm

Bridge
Farm

STATION
RD

COLCHESTER RD

Bourchier's
Farm

CHAPEL RD

Bourchier's Hall

Guisnes
Court

The Rookery

BACK RD

Old Hall
Marsh Farm

Old Hall Farm

OLD HALL LA

Old Hall Creek

3

12

2

Gorwell Hall

Carrington
Farm

NORTH RD

TOLLESBURY RD

Garlands
Farm

PRENTICE HALL LA

WEST ST

HIGH ST

F Sta

ST JOHN

ELYSIAN GDNS

CHURCH ST

Recn
Gd

EAST ST B1023

Sch

THE MOUNT

HALL RD

Tollesbury

Prentice Hall
Farm

MALARDS CL

HAMMOCK

ENDEAVOUR

VALKYRIE

THURSTABLE

THURSTABLE

THURSTABLE

WATERWORKS RD

STATION RD

HUNTS FARM CL

MEWS

NEW RD

HASLER RD

THE CHASE

SCEPTRE RD

KENTS GRASS

ORCHARD CL

CRESCENT RD

KINGS

WYKE

CARNET RD

WOODROLFE RD

WOODROLFE

MELL RD

WOODROLFE FARM LA

Woodrolfe
Farm

WYCKE LA

11

1

10

120

94
D
95
E
96
F

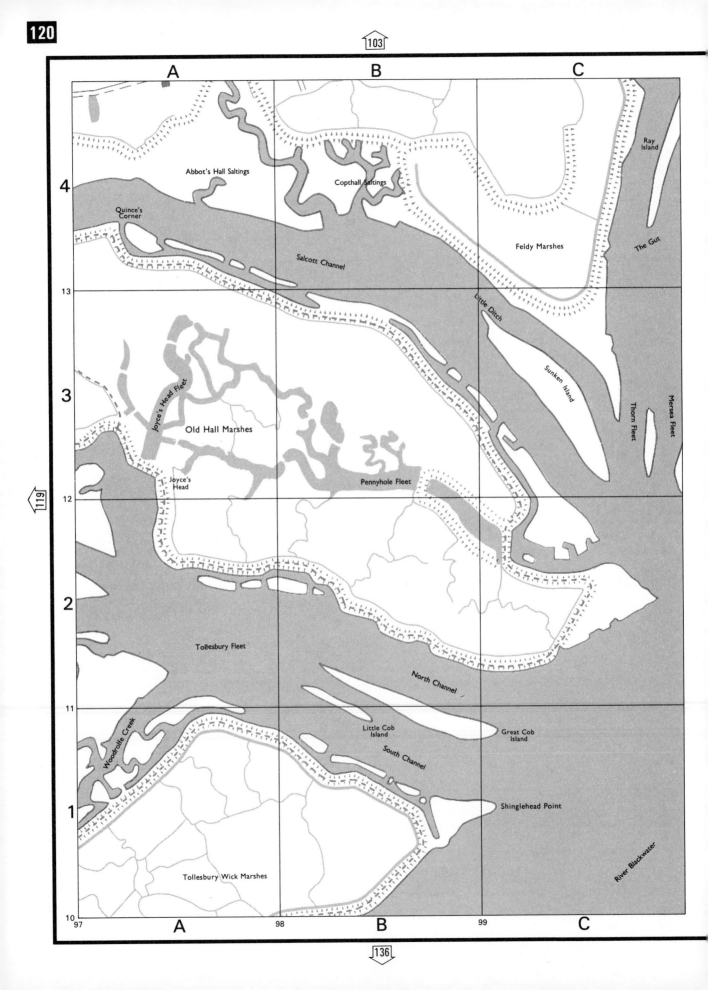

A B C

4

Abbot's Hall Saltings

Copthall Saltings

Ray Island

Quince's Corner

Feldy Marshes

The Gut

Salcott Channel

13

Little Ditch

Sunken Island

3

Joyce's Head Fleet

Old Hall Marshes

Thorn Fleet

Mersea Fleet

Joyce's Head

Pennyhole Fleet

12

2

Tollesbury Fleet

North Channel

11

Woodrolfe Creek

Little Cob Island

Great Cob Island

South Channel

Shinglehead Point

1

Tollesbury Wick Marshes

River Blackwater

10
97

A

98

B

99

C

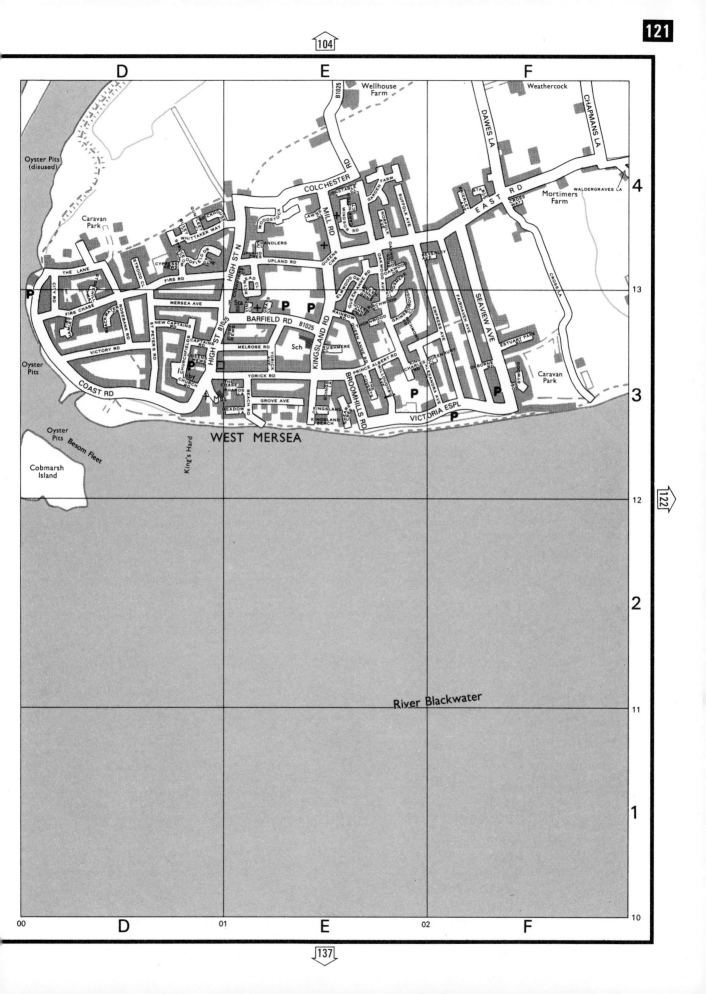

105

121

A

B

C

Chalet & Caravan Park

Rewsalls
Farm

West Barn

4

WALDEGRAVES LA

Waldegraves
Farm

Youth
Camp

13

Caravan
Site

3

12

River Blackwater

2

11

1

10
03   04   05

A   B   C

138

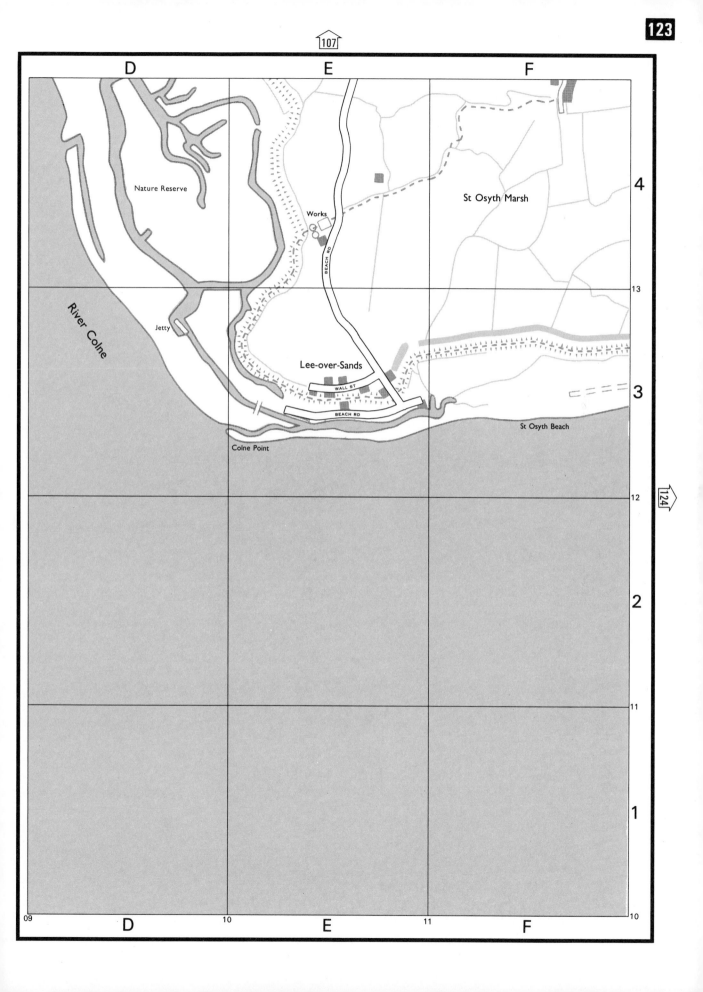

D

E

F

Nature Reserve

Works

BEACH RD

St Osyth Marsh

4

River Colne

Jetty

13

Lee-over-Sands

WALL ST

BEACH RD

St Osyth Beach

3

Colne Point

124

12

2

11

1

09

D

10

E

11

F

10

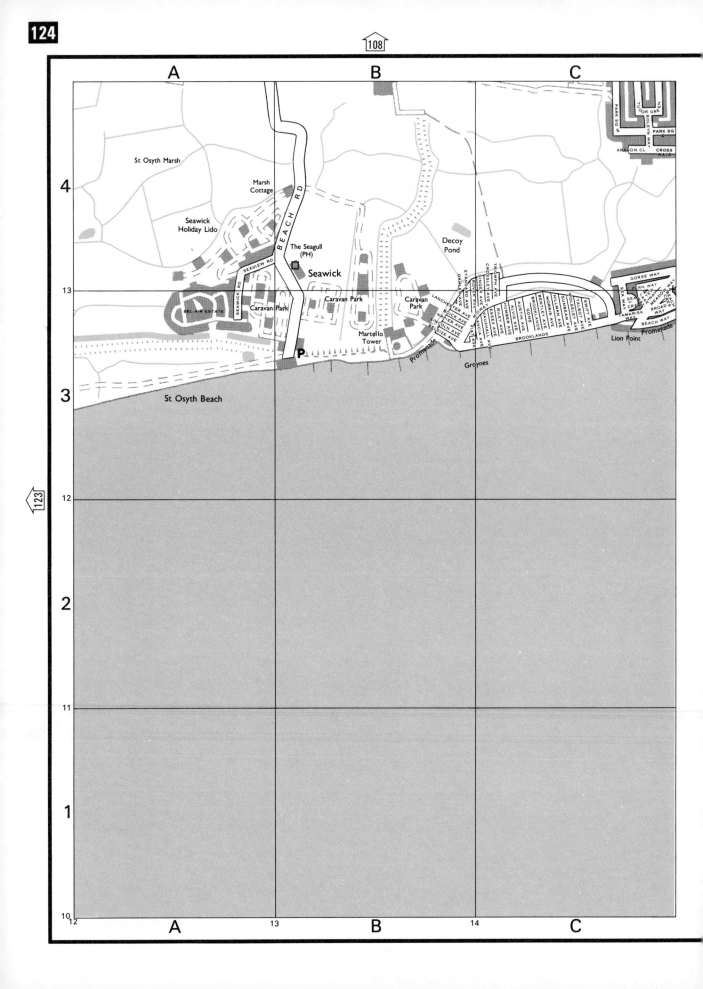

St Osyth Marsh

Marsh
Cottage

Seawick
Holiday Lido

BEACH RD

The Seagull
(PH)

Seawick

SEAVIEW RD

Decoy
Pond

PARK SQ W

TUDOR GRE

BOLEYN WAY

PARK SQ E

NA

ARAGON CL

CROSS
WAYS

13

SEAWICK RD

BEL-AIR ESTATE

Caravan Park

Caravan Park

Caravan
Park

Martello
Tower

LANCHESTER AVE

BUICK AVE

NAPIER AVE

LINCOLN AVE

BELSIZE AVE

DAIMLER AVE

STANDARD AVE

ROVER TVE

VANCIA AVE

VAUXHALL AVE

SINGER AVE

ESSEX AVE

CROSSLEY AVE

TRIUMPH AVE

HUMBER AVE

RILEY AVE

ALVIS AVE

AUSTIN AVE

MORRIS AVE

BENTLEY AVE

BROOKLANDS

ODNS

HILLMAN AVE

SUNBEAM AVE

WOLSELEY AVE

TALBOT AVE

SWIFT AVE

Brooklands

GORSE WAY

FERN WAY

SEAWICK

CRES

TAMARISK WAY

BEACH WAY

MEADOW WAY

RY WAY

BROAD RD

Promenade

Lion Point

P

Promenade

Groynes

St Osyth Beach

12

11

2

1

A 13 B 14 C

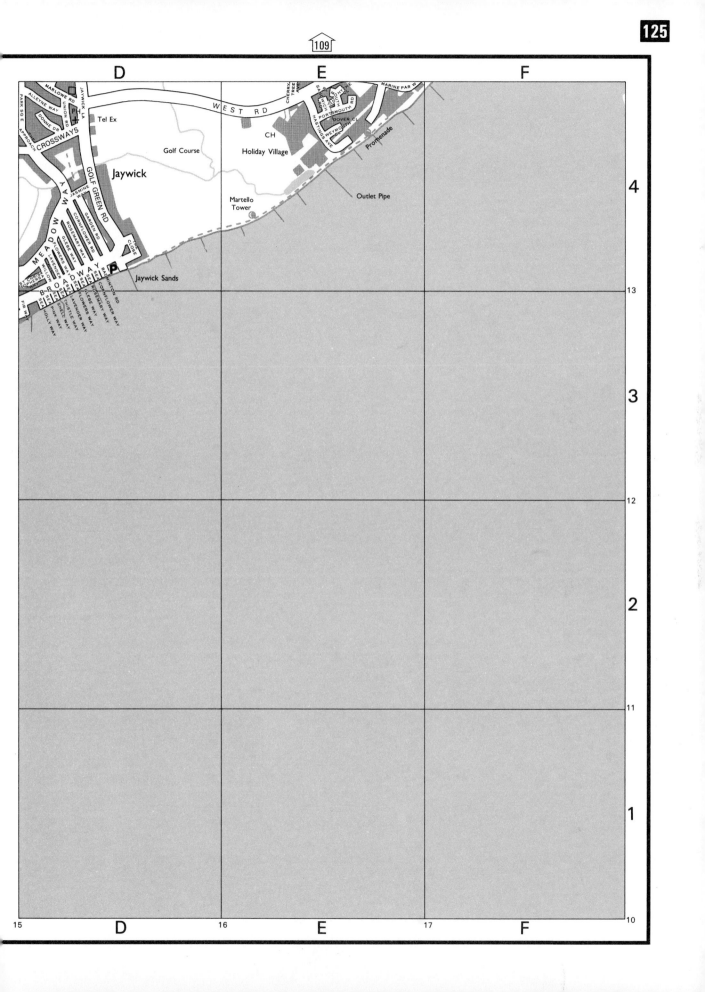

109

D

E

F

MARLOWE RD
ALLEYNE WAY
UNION RD
PARK SQ E
DONNE DR
JAYWICK LA
PL
APPROACH
CROSSWAYS

Tel Ex

WEST RD

CHERRY TREE AVE
SANDMOUTH RD
MONTH AVE
PORTSMOUTH
WICH
DOVER CL
HASTINGS AVE
WEYMOUTH
PLYMOUTH RD

MARINE PAR W

Golf Course

CH

Promenade

Holiday Village

GOLF GREEN RD

Jaywick

JASMINE WAY
GARDEN RD
CORNFLOWER RD
ROSEMARY WAY
GLEBE WAY
FLOWERS WAY

Martello
Tower

Outlet Pipe

4

MEADOW WAY
LAVENDER
WILLOW
BADMINTON RD
CLOSE

Jaywick Sands

13

BROADWAY
ST CHAD'S
DOVER'S
FIR WAY
SEA
HOLLY WAY
PINE WAY
SHELL WAY
THISTLE WAY
LAVENDER WAY
GLEBE WAY
FLOWERS WAY
ROSEMARY WAY
CORNFLOWER WAY

3

12

2

11

1

15   D   16   E   17   F   10

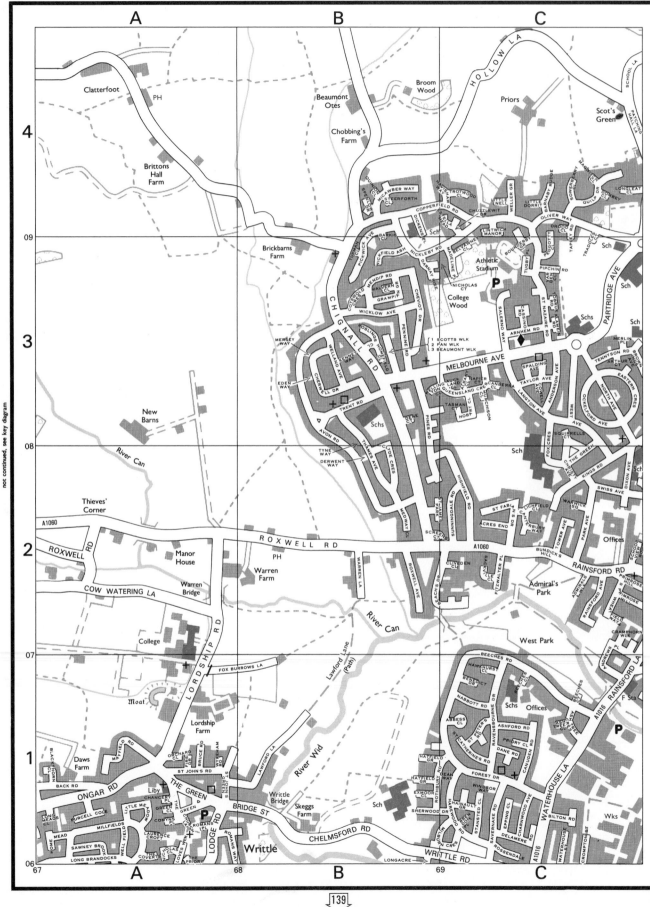

A · B · C

4

3

2

1

09

08

07

06

Clatterfoot
PH
Brittons
Hall
Farm

Beaumont
Otes
Chobbing's
Farm

Broom
Wood

Priors

Scot's
Green

HOLLOW LA

SCHOOL LA

HATCHING MALLA

Brickbarns
Farm

MICAWBER WAY
STEERFORTH
COPPERFIELD RD
CHUZZLEWIT
DICKENS
BARKIS
PICKWICK AVE
WICKFIELD ASH
NICKLEBY RD
DARNAY RISE
MADELINE
FLINTWICH
MANOR
BELVAWNEY
NICHOLAS CT
WELLER GR
LITTLE
NELL
LITTLE
DORRIT
OLIVER WAY
DROOD CT
TAPLEY CT
TRADGERS
TROTWOOD
TAPE
BARNABY RIDGE
DOWERBERRY RIDGE
QUILP GR
DOMBEY
LONGLEAT

Sch

MENDIP RD
COTSWOLD
MALVERN CL
GRAMPIT
WICKLOW AVE
PENNINE RD
CHEVIOT DR
College
Wood
Athletic
Stadium
P
BOUNDERBY
TUGBY PL
PIPCHIN RD
ST NAZARE RD
MERLIN PL
Sch

PARTRIDGE AVE

Sch

CHIGNALL RD

MERSEY
WAY
EDEN
WAY
ROSLING
HORNFIELD
ROSLING
PENNINE RD
1 SCOTTS WLK
2 FAN WLK
3 BEAUMONT WLK
ARNHEM RD
SALERNO WAY
ARNHEM RD
SPALDING
AVE
MELBOURNE AVE
TENNYSON RD
ARTHUR RD
EASTERN
CRES
BROWN

3

New
Barns

WELLAND AVE
KENNET WAY
CHERWELL DR
TRENT RD
AVON RD
TYNE
WAY
DERWENT
WAY
THAMES AVE
CLYDE CRES
Schs
THE
CT
NAPIER
LAND SCT
CANBERRA
CL
QUEENSLAND CRES
TASMAN
CL
HOBST
HOBF
PINES RD
MEDWAY
CL
Sch

TAYLOR AVE
ANDERSON RD
LANGTON AVE
SPALDING
FOX CRES
SQUIRRELLE
CT
THE GREEN
NORTH AVE
OCKELFORD AVE
KINGS RD
SWISS AVE

River Can

Thieves'
Corner
A1060
ROXWELL
Manor
House
Warren
Bridge
PH
Warren
Farm
ROXWELL RD
ROXWELL
RD
ROXWELL AVE
WARREN LA
BEACH'S DR
A1060
CLIVEDEN
CL
FITZWALTER PL
BUNDICK'S
HILL
LOWER AVE
PARK AVE
Offices
RAINSFORD RD
ST FABIA
RD
HIGHFIELD RD
SUNNINGDALE RD
SUMMERDALE RD
ACRES END
LICHFIELD
CL
CANTE
WARWICK
DR
Admiral's
Park
RAINSFORD AVE
ADMIRALS
PRIMROSE
WHELA WAY

2

COW WATERING LA

College

Moat

LORDSHIP RD

FOX BURROWS LA

Lawford Lane (Path)

River Can

West Park

BEECHES RD
HAWKHURST
BENEDICT
CL
NABBOTT RD
ARCHER
CL
Schs
Offices
BEECHES
A1016
F Sta

CRAMPHORN
WLK

07

Daws
Farm
Lordship
Farm
MAYFIELD
RD
ORCHARD
BRUCE RD
WYKEHAM RD
ST NICHOLAS
Lawford LA
River Wid
Writtle
Bridge
RAVENSBOURNE DR
ABBESS
CL
ASHFORD RD
ST CATHERINES RD
PRIORY CL RD
DANE RD
CANUDEN
HATFIELD
GR
FOREST DR
DEAN
WAY
WINDSOR
WAY
St PETER'S
Sch
ABBESS
TREES

RAINSFORD LA

1

BLACKTHORN RD
Liby
THE GREEN
CHANCERY
PL
GREEN
CL
ST JOHN'S RD
SIMONS
ONGAR RD
BACK RD
LONG
MEADS
CL
HOME MEAD
PURCELL
COLE
LITTLE ME
MEAD
WELL
FIELD
SAWNEY BROOK
MILLFIELDS
LAURENCE CROFT
LONG BRANDOCKS
COVERT
THE PRIORY
NICHOLAS
LOVES
WALK
P
LODGE RD
ROMANS PL
ROMANS WAY
THE
GREEN
BRIDGE ST
Writtle
Skeggs
Farm
CHELMSFORD RD
LONGACRE
WRITTLE RD
HATFIELD
GR
EXMOOR CL
SHERWOOD
HAINAULT
CL
HAREWOOD
FERN
SAVERNAKE RD
EPPING CL
CHARNWOOD CL
DELAMERE
ROTHBURY
ROSSENDALE
RD
STANSTED RD
CRES
AUSTIN
WATERHOUSE LA
BILTON RD
CROMPTON
A1016
Wks
P

06

67 · 68 · 69
A · B · C

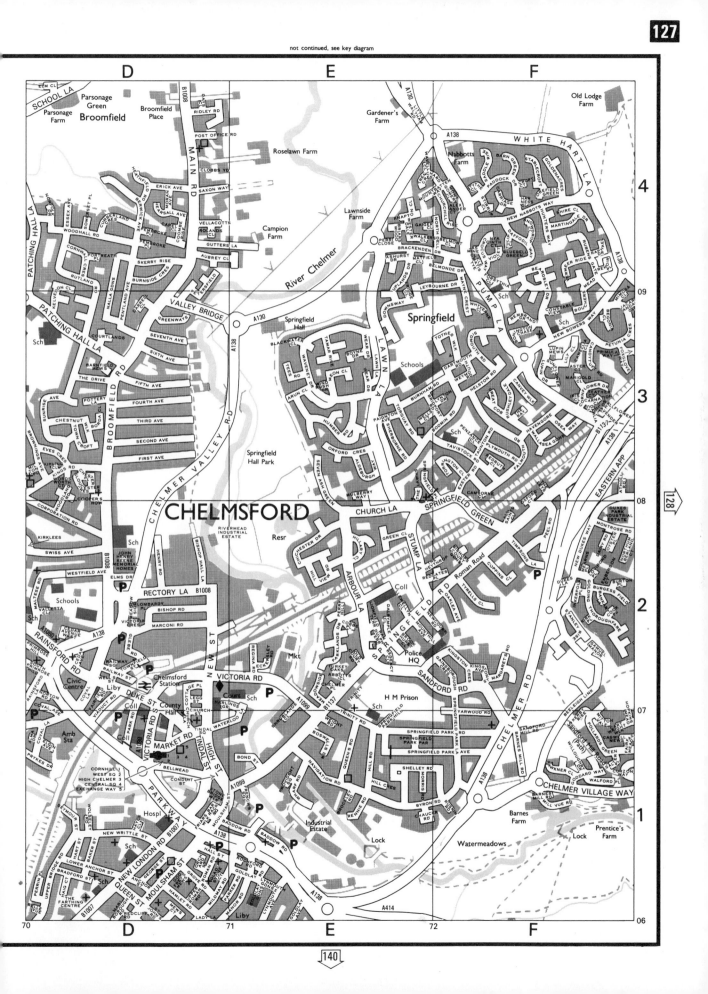

CHELMSFORD

Springfield

Broomfield

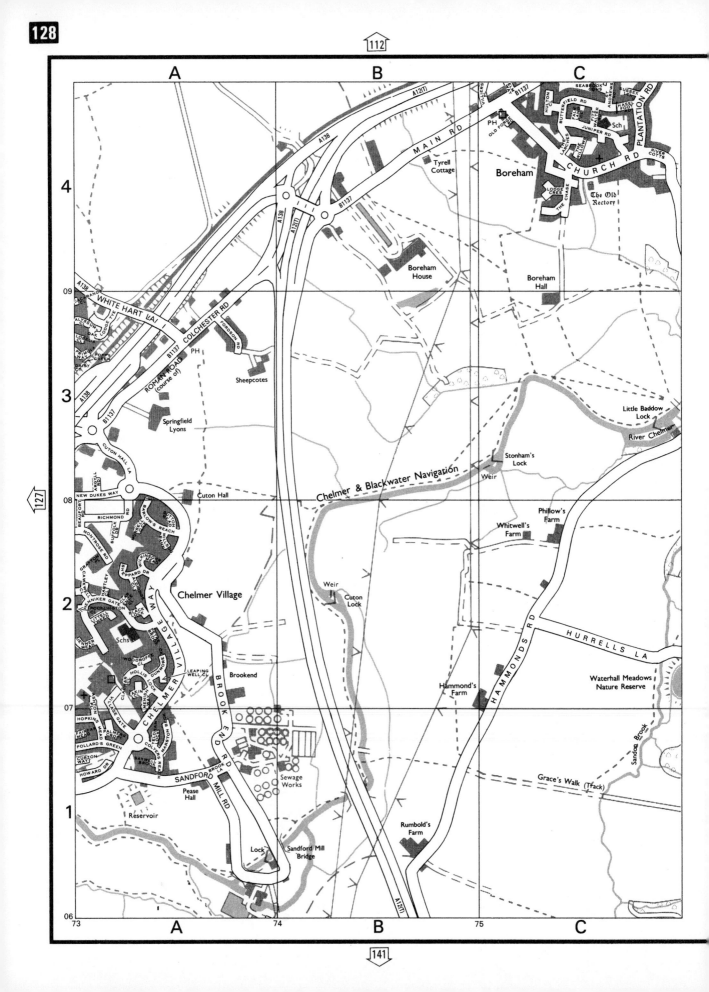

A   B   C

4

A12(T)

A138

MAIN RD

B1137

Tyrell Cottage

Boreham

CHURCH RD

Sch

PH

Old Forge

B1137

VILLIERS

BUTTERFIELD RD

SEABROOK GDNS

ST ANDREWS

HASEL FOO

SUSSEX

PLANTATION RD

HULTON

JUNIPER RD

LODGE CRES

THE CHASE

RIVER COTTS

Boreham House

Boreham Hall

The Old Rectory

A138

A12(T)

09

A138

WHITE HART LA

COLCHESTER RD

FORDSON RD

B1137

ROMAN ROAD (course of)

PH

Sheepcotes

A138

B1137

3

Springfield Lyons

Little Baddow Lock

River Chelmer

CUTON HALL LA

Stonham's Lock

Weir

08

NEW DUKES WAY

RICHMOND

Cuton Hall

Chelmer & Blackwater Navigation

Phillow's Farm

Whitwell's Farm

BARLOW'S REACH

MONTROSE RD

Chelmer Village

2

Schs

CHELMER VILLAGE WAY

LEAPING WELL CL

Brookend

Weir

Cuton Lock

HAMMONDS RD

HURRELLS LA

Waterhall Meadows Nature Reserve

WOODROFT

HOLLIS

DUNMORE

Hammond's Farm

07

HOPKINS

POLLARD'S GREEN

CURZON WAY

HOWARD DR

BROOK END RD

SANDFORD MILL RD

Pease Hall

Sewage Works

Sandford Brook

Grace's Walk (Track)

1

Reservoir

Lock

Sandford Mill Bridge

A12(T)

Rumbold's Farm

06

73   74   75

A   B   C

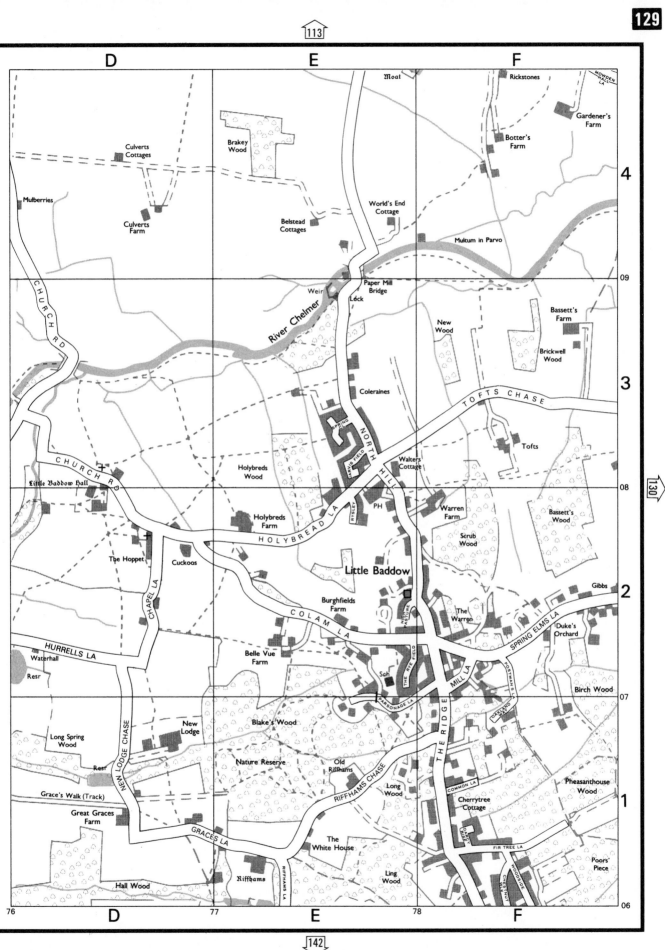

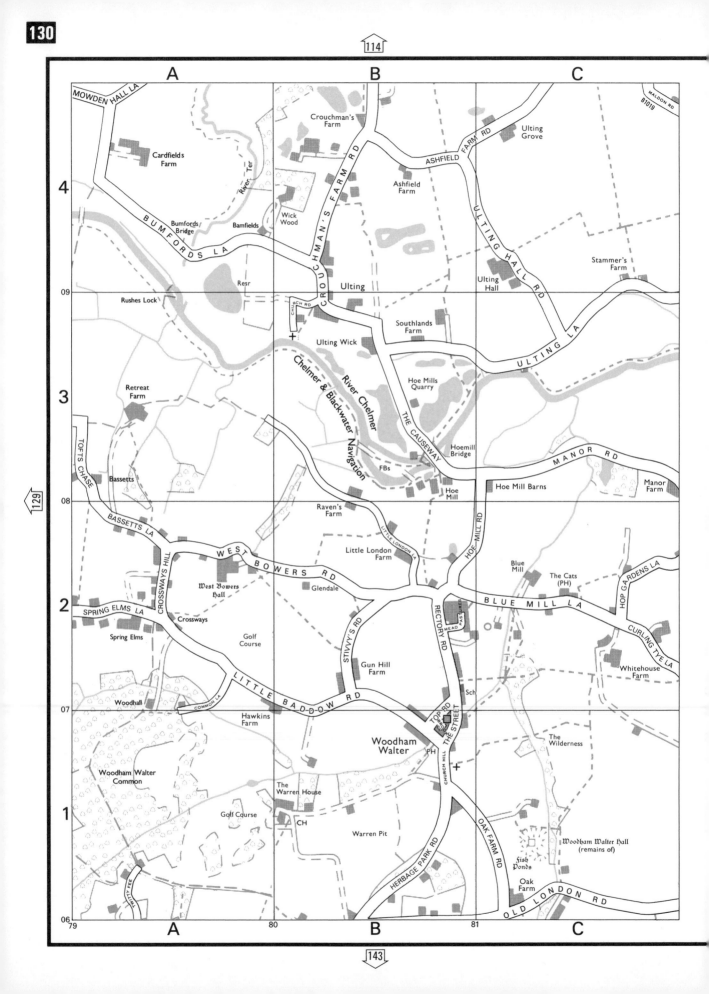

A   B   C

MOWDEN HALL LA

Cardfields
Farm

River Ter

BUMFORDS LA

Bumfords
Bridge

Bamfields

Resr

Rushes Lock

Crouchman's
Farm

CROUCHMAN'S FARM RD

Wick Wood

Ulting

Ulting Wick

River Chelmer

Chelmer & Blackwater Navigation

Retreat
Farm

TOFTS CHASE

Bassetts

BASSETTS LA

WEST BOWERS RD

West Bowers
Hall

Glendale

CROSSWAYS HILL

Crossways

SPRING ELMS LA

Spring Elms

Golf
Course

LITTLE BADDOW RD

COMMON LA

Woodhall

Hawkins
Farm

Woodham Walter
Common

Golf Course

The Warren House

CH

Warren Pit

TRINITY FEE

ASHFIELD

Ashfield
Farm

FARM RD

ULTING HALL RD

Ulting Grove

Ulting
Hall

Stammer's
Farm

Southlands
Farm

ULTING LA

MALDON RD

B1019

Hoe Mills
Quarry

THE CAUSEWAY

Hoemill
Bridge

FBs

Hoe
Mill

MANOR RD

Hoe Mill Barns

Manor
Farm

Raven's
Farm

LITTLE LONDON LA

Little London
Farm

HOE MILL RD

Blue
Mill

The Cats
(PH)

HOP GARDENS LA

STIVVY'S RD

Gun Hill
Farm

RECTORY RD

MEAD PASTURES

BLUE MILL LA

CURLING TYE LA

Whitehouse
Farm

Sch

Woodham
Walter

TOP RD
THE STREET

PH

CHURCH HILL

The
Wilderness

The remains

Woodham Walter Hall
(remains of)

Fish
Ponds

HERBAGE PARK RD

OAK FARM RD

OLD LONDON RD

Oak
Farm

A   B   C

D　　　　　　　　　E　　　　　　　　　F

The Elms

Stock Hall Farm

B1019 MALDON RD

Beavis Hall

Wks

HATFIELD RD

Fords Farm

River Blackwater

LANGFORD RD

B1018

WITHAM RD

Little Park

MAYPOLE RD

4

ULTING LA

Ppg Sta

Langford Bridge

Moat

Weir

Langford

B1019 MALDON RD

B1018

Langford Cut

09

Resrs

Lock

Langford Cut

LANGFORD RD

Dismantled Railway

B1018

HOLLOWAY RD

CRESCENT RD

BEECHES RD

3

Weir

Chelmer & Blackwater Navigation

River Chelmer

Lock

Weirs

NTL

Beeleigh Falls House

Club House

08

Guy's Farm

Woodlands

MANOR RD

HOP GARDENS LA

Beeleigh Grange Farm

BEELEIGH CHASE

Beeleigh Abbey

Golf Course

2

CUT-A-THWART LA

Northall Cottages

ABBEY TURNING RD

Great Beeleigh Farm

A414 Under Construction

CROMWELL LA

Sch

DYKES CHASE

LODGE RD

TOWER RD

BEELEIGH RD

Sch

Little Beeleigh Farm

Mound

LONDON RD

PRINCES ST

P

West Sq

Court

HIGH ST

CROMWELL

Curling Tye Green

CURLING TYE LA

Ashman's Farm

Cemy

07

Sch

WEST ST

GATE ST

A414

P

Sch

Brook Farm

BEACON HILL

HIGHLANDS DR

St GILES CRES

Sch

CHERRY GARDEN RD

Hospl

Market Hill

FRIARS

NEW ST

FAMBRIDGE RD

Bog Wood

Amb Sta

ST PETER'S RD

GRANGER AVE

Green Ways

ORCHARD RD

ORCHARD RD

Sch

Wood Corner

MALDON

SPITAL RD

NORFOLK RD

ACACIA RD

WASHINGTON RD

PLUME AVE

GLOUCESTER

Sch

1

OLD LONDON RD

Green Road (Track)

Moat

Maldon Hall

STATION RD

A414

Industrial Estate

VIKING RD

DORSET RD

82　　　D　　　　83　　　E　　　　84　　　F　　06

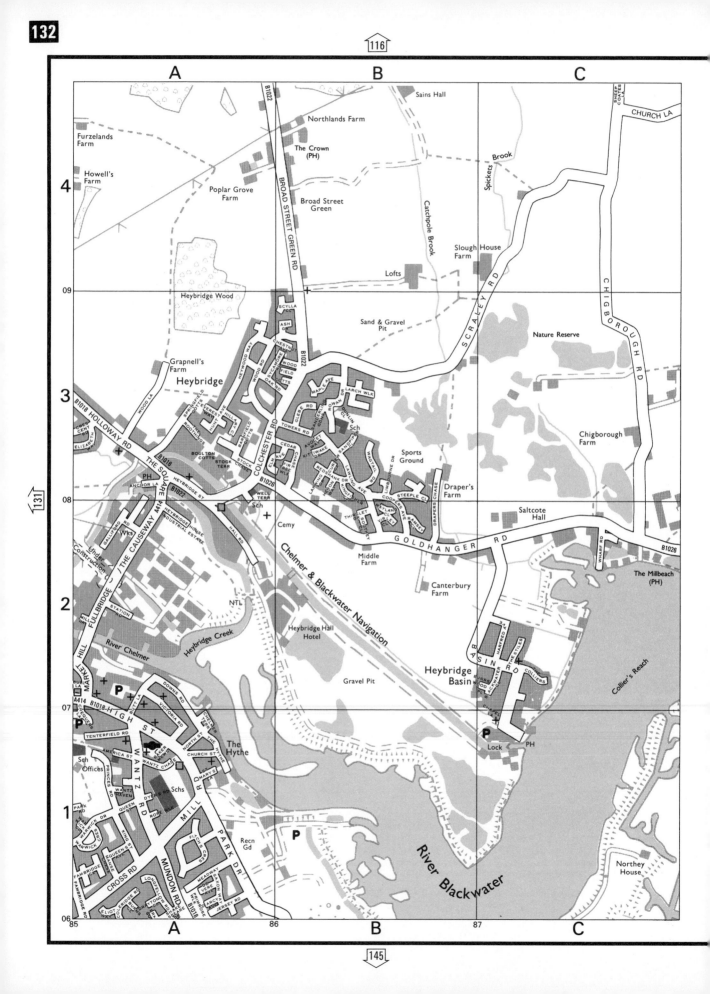

117

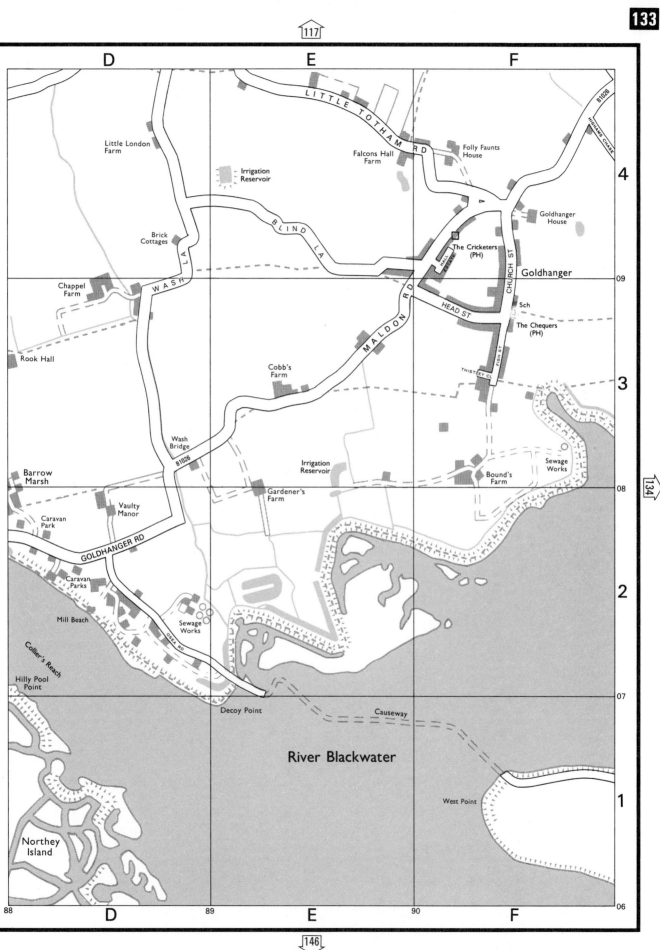

D   E   F

LITTLE TOTHAM RD

B1026

HIGHAMS CHASE

Little London Farm

Falcons Hall Farm

Folly Faunts House

Irrigation Reservoir

Goldhanger House

4

BLIND LA

Brick Cottages

The Cricketers (PH)

CHURCH ST

HALL ESTATE

Goldhanger

WASH LA

09

Chappel Farm

HEAD ST

Sch

The Chequers (PH)

MALDON RD

FISH ST

Rook Hall

Cobb's Farm

THISTLEY CL

3

Wash Bridge

B1026

Irrigation Reservoir

Sewage Works

Barrow Marsh

Gardener's Farm

Bound's Farm

08

134

Vaulty Manor

Caravan Park

GOLDHANGER RD

2

Caravan Parks

Mill Beach

Sewage Works

OSEA RD

Collier's Reach

Hilly Pool Point

07

Decoy Point

Causeway

River Blackwater

West Point

1

Northey Island

88   D   89   E   90   F   06

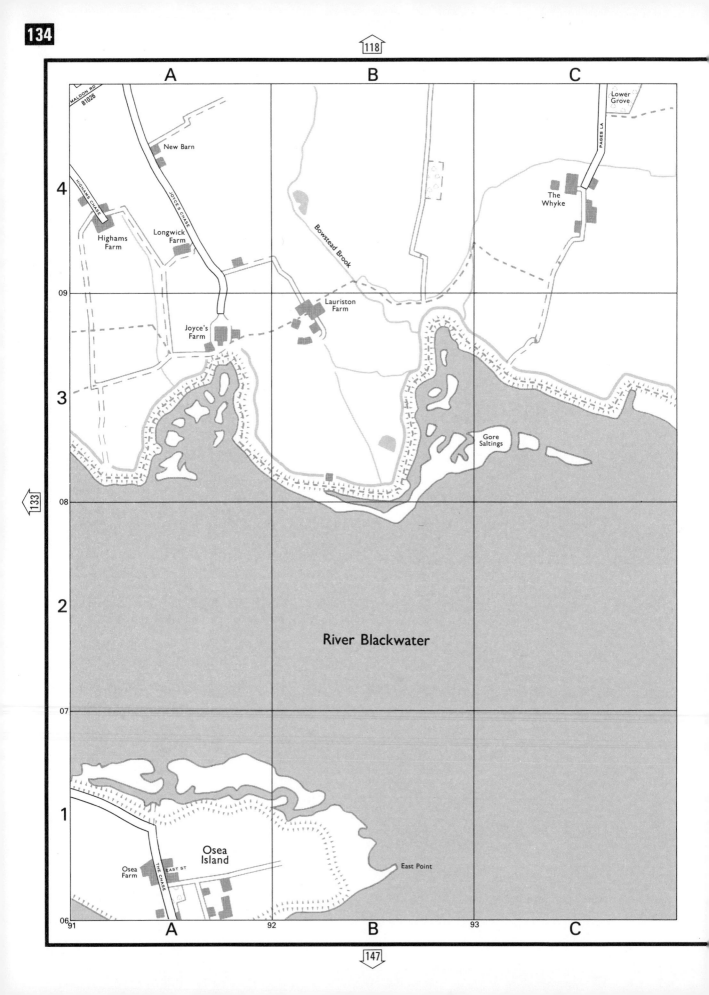

A

B

C

MALDON RD
B1026

New Barn

HIGHAMS CHASE

4

JOYCE'S CHASE

Highams
Farm

Longwick
Farm

Bowstead Brook

PAGES LA.

Lower
Grove

The
Whyke

09

Joyce's
Farm

Lauriston
Farm

3

Gore
Saltings

08

2

River Blackwater

07

1

Osea
Island

Osea
Farm

EAST ST

THE CHASE

East Point

06
91

A

92

B

93

C

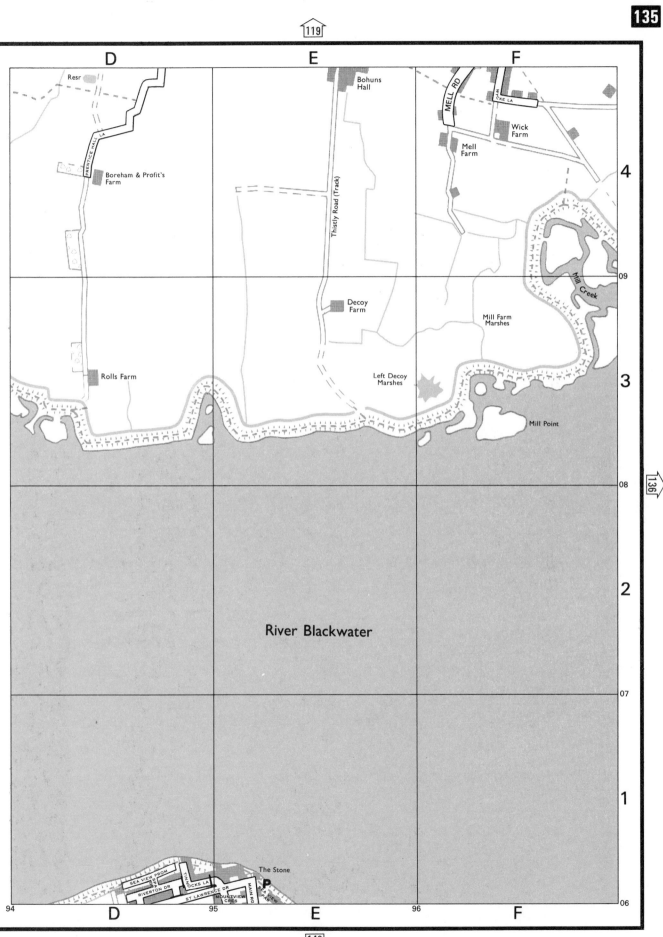

D
E
F

Resr

PRENTICE HALL LA

Boreham & Profit's
Farm

Bohuns
Hall

MELL RD

CKE LA

Wick
Farm

Mell
Farm

4

Thistly Road (Track)

09

Decoy
Farm

Mill Farm
Marshes

Mill Creek

Rolls Farm

Left Decoy
Marshes

Mill Point

3

08

136

2

River Blackwater

07

1

The Stone

SEA VIEW PROM

RIVERTON DR

ST LAWRENCE DR

TENN

OCKS LA

MOUNTVIEW
CRES

MAIN RD

BA VIEW

P

06

94

D

95

E

96

F

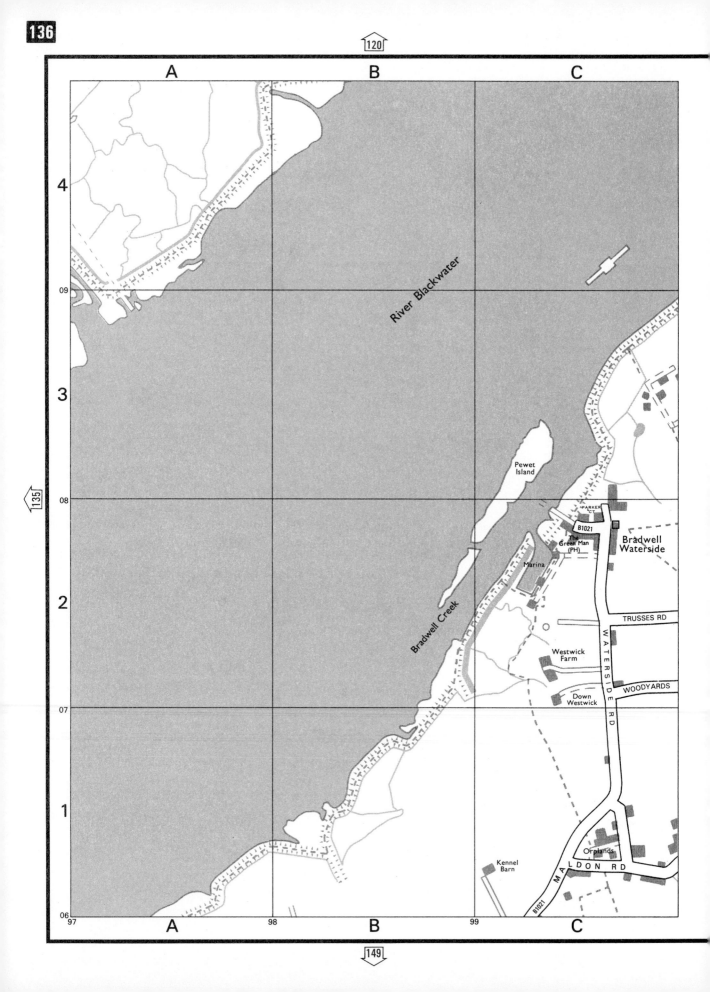

A B C

4

09

River Blackwater

3

Pewet
Island

08

PARKER
CT.

B1021

The
Green Man
(PH)

Bradwell
Waterside

Marina

2

TRUSSES RD

Bradwell Creek

Westwick
Farm

WOODYARDS

Down
Westwick

07

W
A
T
E
R
S
I
D
E

R
D

1

Orplands

Kennel
Barn

M
A
L
D
O
N   RD

B1021

97 98 99
A B C

D E F

4

3

2

1

Bradwell
Nuclear Power Station

Weymarks Farm

Electricity
Switching Station

Airfield
(disused)

Irrigation
Reservoir

Easthall
Farm

Downhall
Farm

Playing
Field

Curds
Grove

Caravan
Park

Eastlands

TRUSSES RD

Down Hall

Peveralls

The Cricketers (PH)

EASTEND RD

ROMAN ROAD

East Hall

Munkins Farm

WOODYARDS

East End

HIGH ST

Blackberry
Grove

BATES COLEY DR

Sch

The King's Head (PH)

SOUTH ST

Bradwell-on-Sea

Bradwell
Lodge

HOCKLEY CL

HOCKLEY RD

Delameres

MALDON RD

Bacons

Hockley

Bradwell Marshes

00 01 E 02 F

D E F

09

08

07

06

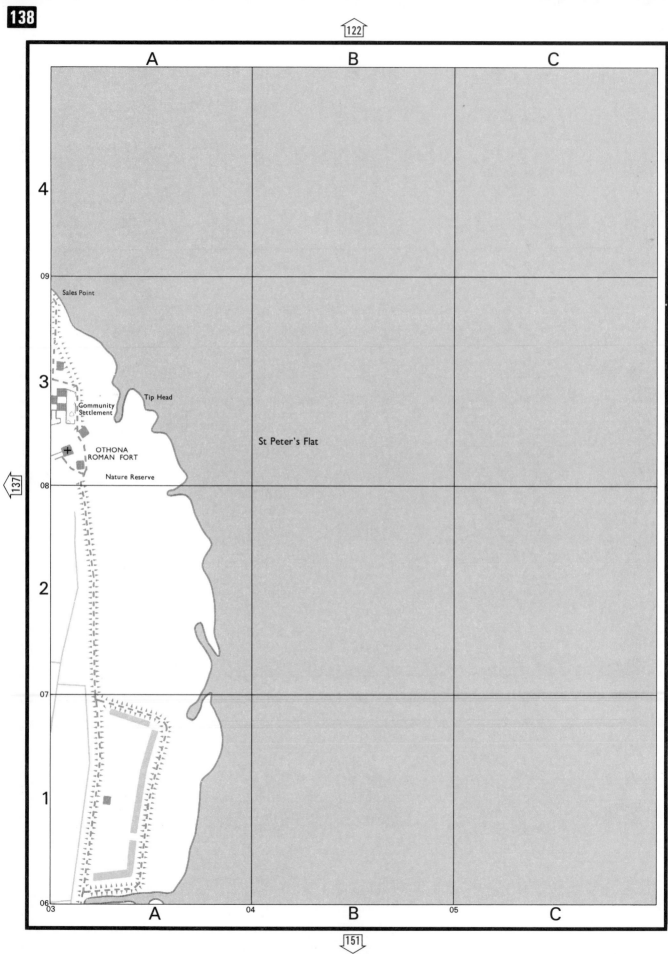

A B C

4

09

Sales Point

3

Tip Head

Community
Settlement

+ OTHONA
ROMAN FORT

Nature Reserve

St Peter's Flat

08

2

07

1

06

03 04 05

A B C

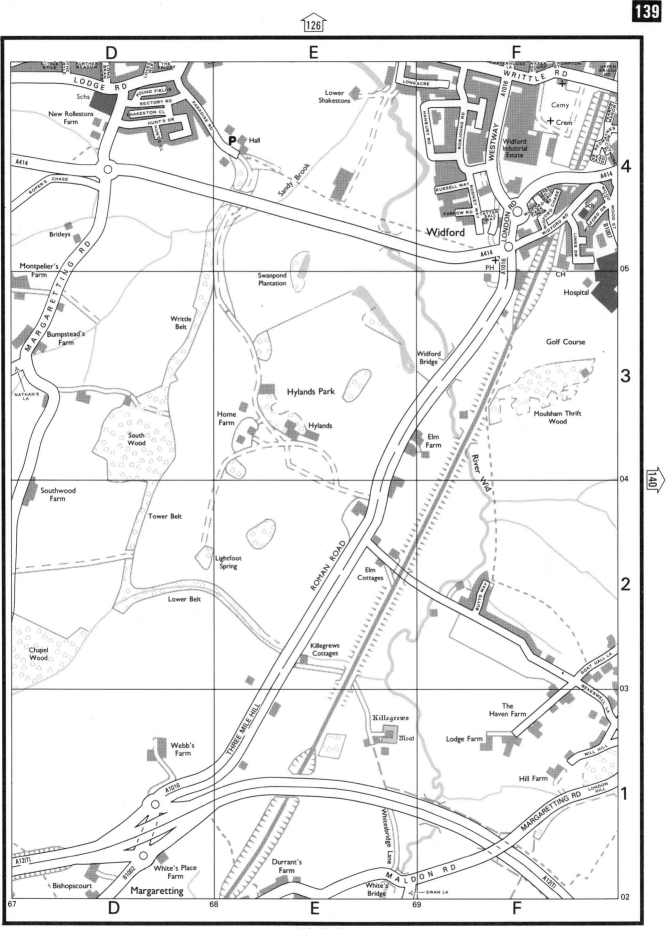

D E F

140

LITTLE STILE
FURTHERED MEADOW
THE PRIORY
LODGE RD
Schs
New Rollestons Farm
POUND FIELDS
RECTORY RD
SHAKESTON CL
HUNT'S DR
HUNT'S CL
PARADISE RD
P Hall

Lower Shakestons

LONGACRE
WATERHOUSE LA
WATER HOUSE ST
CROMPTON ST
WRITTLE RD
UPPER BRIDGE RD

Cemy
Crem

A414

A414

HANBURY RD
ROBJOHNS RD
WESTWAY
Widford Industrial Estate
A1016
PANCRAS MANOR
REDMAYNES CLYFTON
MEDD PATH

A414

ROPER'S CHASE

RUSSELL WAY
FARROW RD
RODNEY WAY
TATTER SALL

LONDON RD

Widford

A414

WIDFORD PARK
WIDFORD CHASE
WIDFORD RD
Sch
WILFORD GR
WOOD ST
B1007
WOOD ST

Britleys

A1016
PH

CH

05

Montpelier's Farm

Swanpond Plantation

Hospital

MARGARETTING RD

Bumpstead's Farm

Writtle Belt

Golf Course

NATHAN'S LA

Widford Bridge

3

South Wood

Hylands Park

Moulsham Thrift Wood

Home Farm

Hylands

Elm Farm

River Wid

Southwood Farm

04

Tower Belt

Lightfoot Spring

ROMAN ROAD

Elm Cottages

BUTTS WAY

2

GOAT HALL LA

Chapel Wood

Lower Belt

Killegrews Cottages

BEKESWELL LA

03

THREE MILE HILL

Killegrews
Moat

The Haven Farm

Webb's Farm

Lodge Farm

MILL HILL

A1016

Hill Farm

MARGARETTING RD
LONDON HILL

1

A12(T)

Whitesbridge Lane

Durrant's Farm

MALDON RD

A12(T)

B1002
White's Place Farm

Margaretting

White's Bridge
SWAN LA

02

Bishopscourt

67 D 68 E 69 F

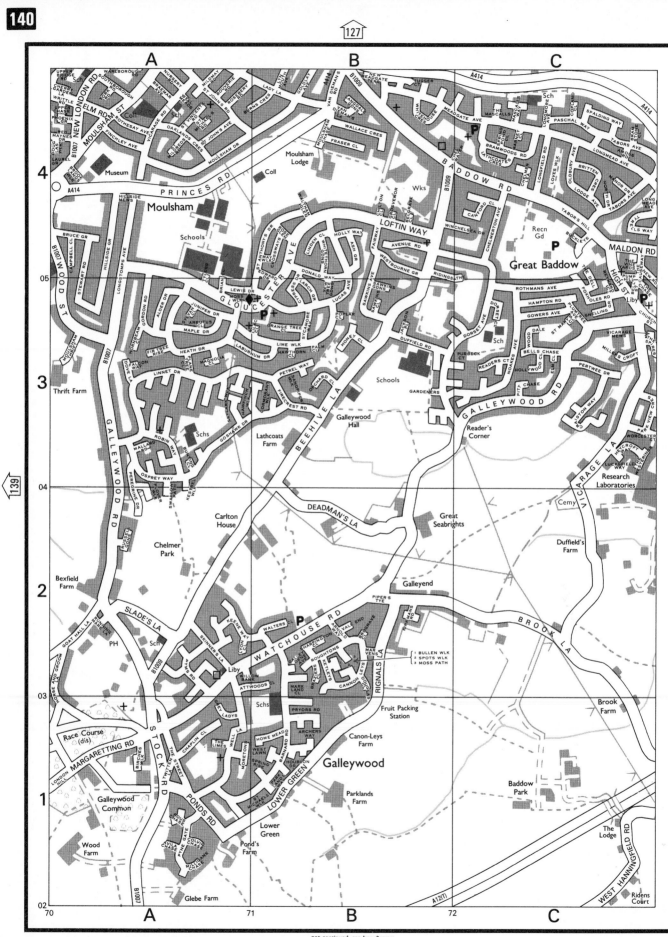

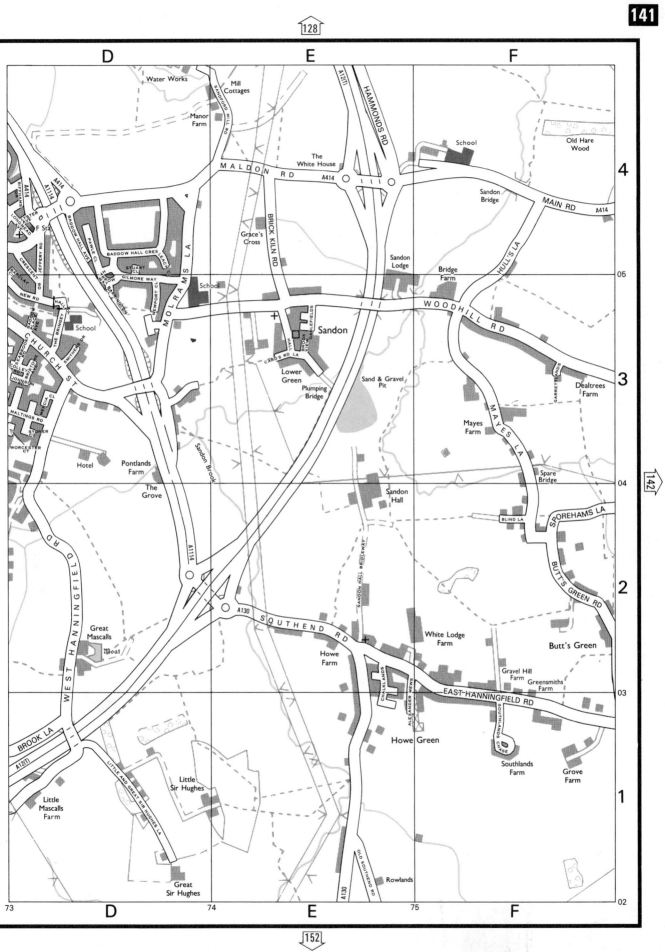

142

129

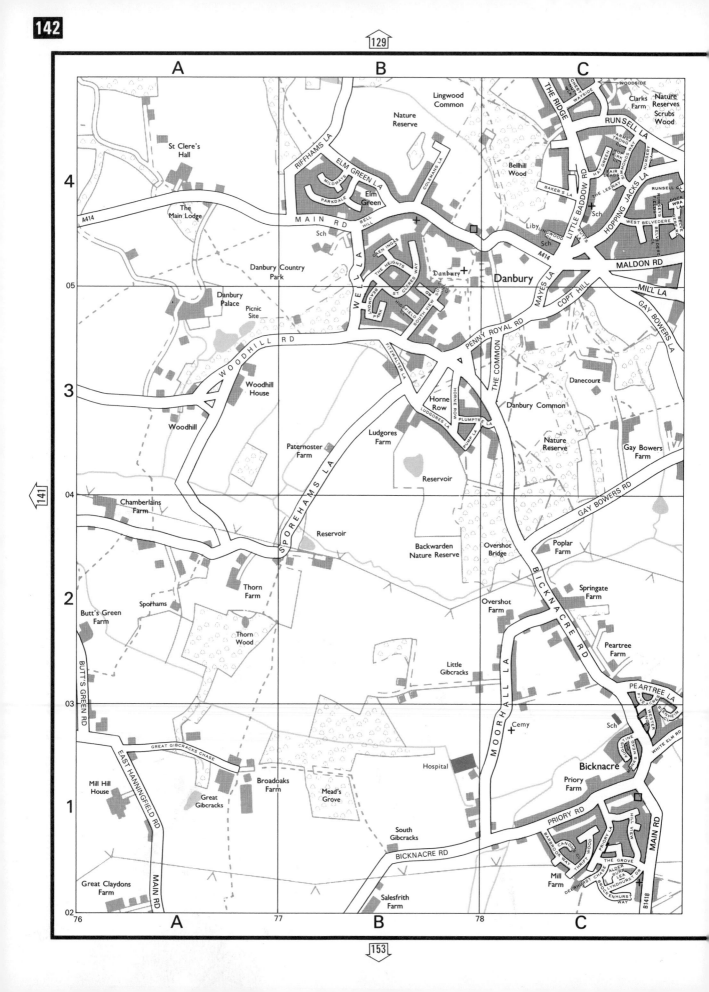

Lingwood Common

WOODSIDE

THE RIDGE

Nature Reserves Scrubs Wood

Clarks Farm

RUNSELL LA

Nature Reserve

St Clere's Hall

RIFFHAMS LA

ELM GREEN LA

COLEMANS LA

Bellhill Wood

ARMS TRONG WAY

HAY GREEN

SIMMONDS WAY

FAIR LEADS

RUNSELL CL

4

The Main Lodge

A414

MILDMAYS

PARKDALE

Elm Green

BELL HILL

Sch

MAIN RD

LITTLE BADDON RD

BAKER'S LA

THE LEEWAY

HOPPING JACKS LA

Sch

WEST BELVEDERE

WRA

Liby Lingwood Sch

A414

Danbury

MALDON RD

Danbury Country Park

WELL LA

THE HEIGHTS

St CLERE'S WAY

Danbury

Danbury

MAYES LA

COPT HILL

MILL LA

05

Danbury Palace

Picnic Site

BEAUMONT PARK

HIGHFIELD RD

SOUTH HEATH

ROAD

PENNY ROYAL RD

GAY BOWERS LA

WOODHILL RD

FITZWALTER LA

Danecourt

3

Woodhill House

HORNE ROW

THE COMMON

Danbury Common

Woodhill

Horne Row

LUDGORES LA

PLUMPTRE LA

PUMP LA

Nature Reserve

Gay Bowers Farm

Paternoster Farm

Ludgores Farm

Reservoir

SPORHAMS LA

GAY BOWERS RD

04

Chamberlains Farm

Reservoir

Backwarden Nature Reserve

Overshot Bridge

Poplar Farm

2

Sporhams

Thorn Farm

Overshot Farm

BICKNACRE RD

Springate Farm

Butt's Green Farm

Thorn Wood

Peartree Farm

Little Gibcracks

MOORHALL LA

PEARTREE LA

03

BUTT'S GREEN RD

Cemy

FIVE ACRES

WHITE ELM RD

Sch

BLENHEIM

WEBSTER

Great Gibcracks Chase

Hospital

Bicknacre

AUGUSTINE

JUKES MEAD

1

EAST HANNINGFIELD RD

Mill Hill House

Great Gibcracks

Broadoaks Farm

Mead's Grove

Priory Farm

PRIORY RD

CANON

PRIORY LA

MAY 11TH

THRIFT WOOD

THE GROVE

ALDER

BURR

LEA

South Gibcracks

Mill Farm

BARBROOK WAY

DEERHURST CHASE

BROCKENHURST WAY

LYNDHURST DR

B1418

Great Claydons Farm

MAIN RD

BICKNACRE RD

Salesfrith Farm

02

76   A   77   B   78   C

153

141

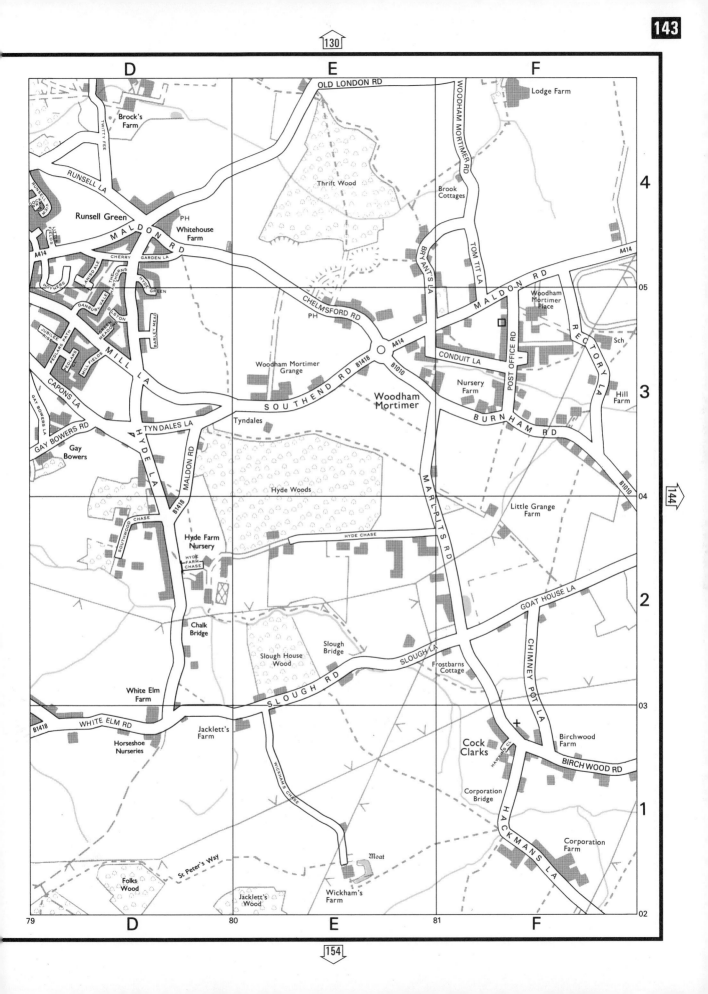

D

E

F

OLD LONDON RD

Brock's Farm

TWITTY FEE

RUNSELL LA

Thrift Wood

WOODHAM MORTIMER RD

Lodge Farm

Brook Cottages

4

Runsell Green

MALDON RD

PH

Whitehouse Farm

A414

CHERRY GARDEN LA

THE VALE

HAWTHORNS

HYDE GREEN

CHELMSFORD RD

PH

BRYANT'S LA

TOM TIT LA

MALDON RD

Woodham Mortimer Place

A414

Sch

05

HOFFERS

DANBURY VALE

OLSTON

MEADOWS

MOSLINGS

BARLEY MEAD

MILL LA

JUBILEE RISE

PEDLARS PATH

PEDLARS

MILL FIELDS

Woodham Mortimer Grange

SOUTHEND RD

B1418

A414

B1010

Woodham Mortimer

CONDUIT LA

Nursery Farm

POST OFFICE RD

RECTORY LA

Hill Farm

3

CAPONS LA

GAY BOWERS RD

GAY BOWERS LA

TYNDALES LA

HYDE LA

MALDON RD

Tyndales

BURNHAM RD

Gay Bowers

B1418

Hyde Woods

MARLPITS RD

Little Grange Farm

B1010

04

SOUTHWOOD CHASE

Hyde Farm Nursery

HYDE FARM CHASE

HYDE CHASE

GOAT HOUSE LA

2

Chalk Bridge

Slough House Wood

Slough Bridge

SLOUGH LA

Frostbarns Cottage

CHIMNEY POT LA

White Elm Farm

SLOUGH RD

03

B1418

WHITE ELM RD

Jacklett's Farm

Cock Clarks

HAWKINS CL

Birchwood Farm

Horseshoe Nurseries

BIRCHWOOD RD

WICKHAMS CHASE

Corporation Bridge

HACKMANS LA

1

St Peter's Way

Folks Wood

Jacklett's Wood

Wickham's Farm

Moat

Corporation Farm

79

D

80

E

81

F

02

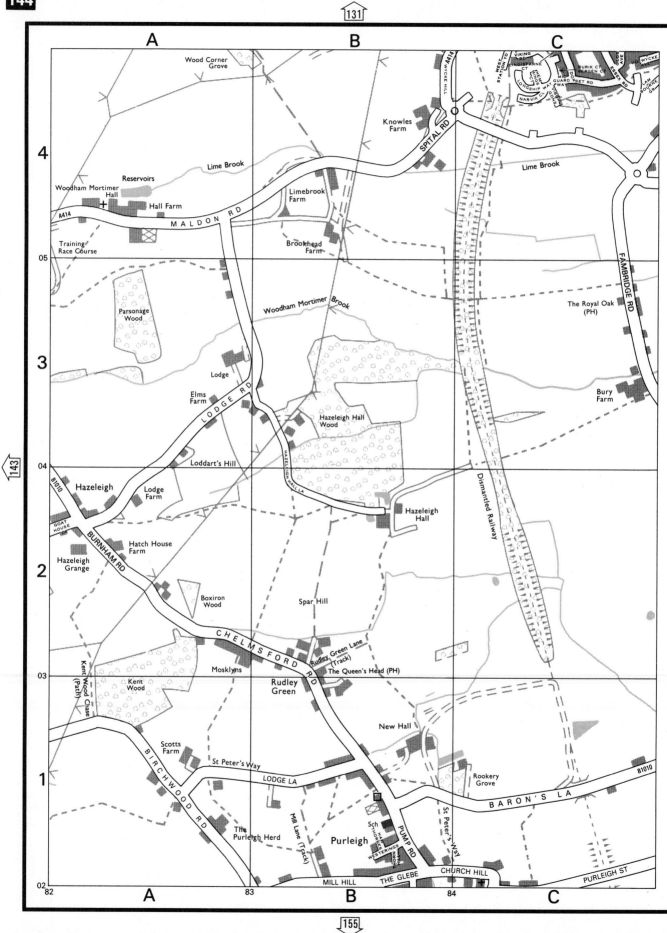

A B C

4

05

3

04

2

03

1

02

82 A 83 B 84 C

Wood Corner Grove

Knowles Farm

SPITAL RD

WYCKE HILL

WEST STATION YD
VIKING RD
LINDISFARNE
HERD CT
LONGSHIP WAY
NARVIK CL
WYCKE LANE
BURIK CT
BERGEN CT
DORSET RD
ESSEX RD
LAMBOURNE GRN

A414

Lime Brook

Lime Brook

Reservoirs

Woodham Mortimer Hall

Hall Farm

Limebrook Farm

FAMBRIDGE RD

MALDON RD

A414

Training Race Course

Brookhead Farm

The Royal Oak (PH)

Parsonage Wood

Woodham Mortimer Brook

LODGE RD

Lodge

Elms Farm

Hazeleigh Hall Wood

Bury Farm

Loddart's Hill

HAZELEIGH HALL LA

B1010

Hazeleigh

Lodge Farm

Dismantled Railway

GOAT HOUSE

BURNHAM RD

Hatch House Farm

Hazeleigh Hall

Hazeleigh Grange

Boxiron Wood

Spar Hill

CHELMSFORD RD

Kent Wood Chase (Path)

Mosklyns

Rudley Green Lane (Track)

The Queen's Head (PH)

Kent Wood

Rudley Green

New Hall

Rookery Grove

BIRCHWOOD RD

Scotts Farm

St Peter's Way

LODGE LA

BARON'S LA

B1010

St Peter's Way

PUMP RD

The Purleigh Herd

Mill Lane (Track)

Sch

NORTH WESTERINGS

Purleigh

MILL HILL

THE GLEBE

CHURCH HILL

PURLEIGH ST

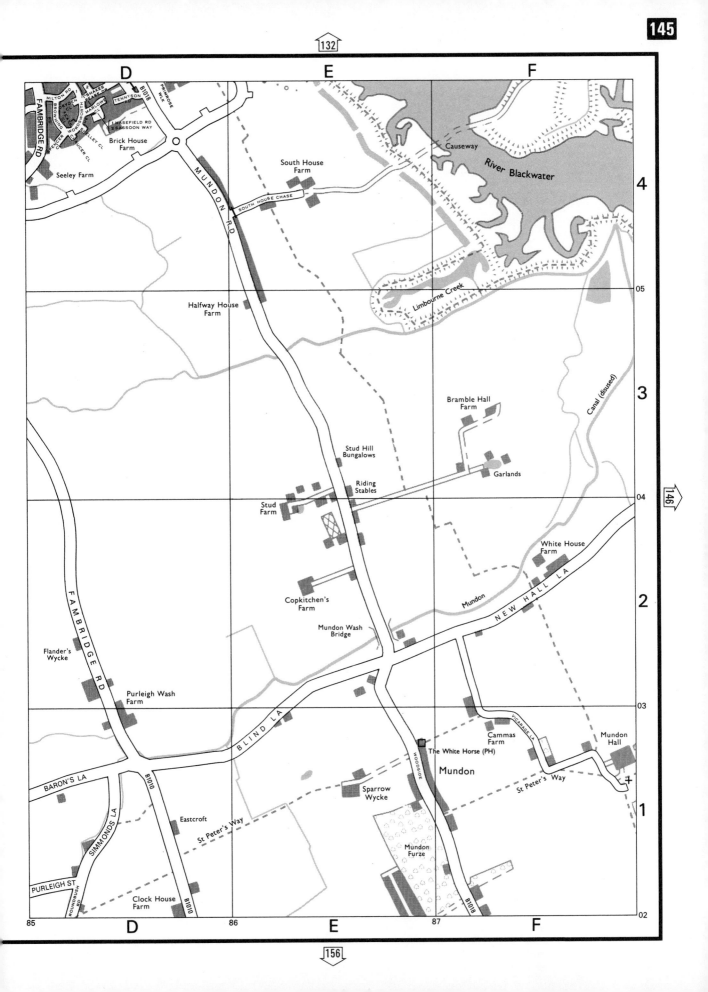

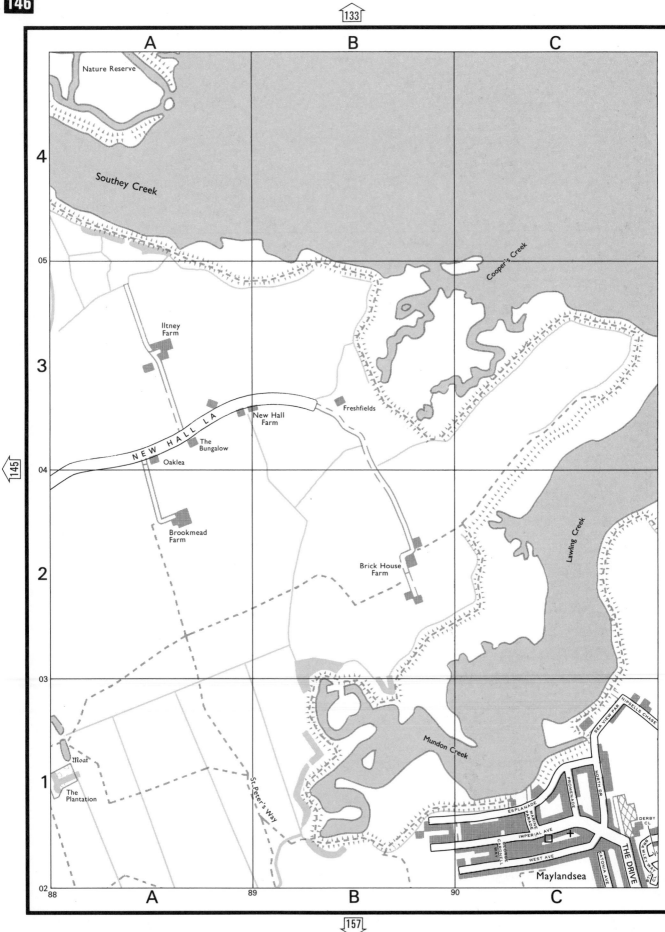

134

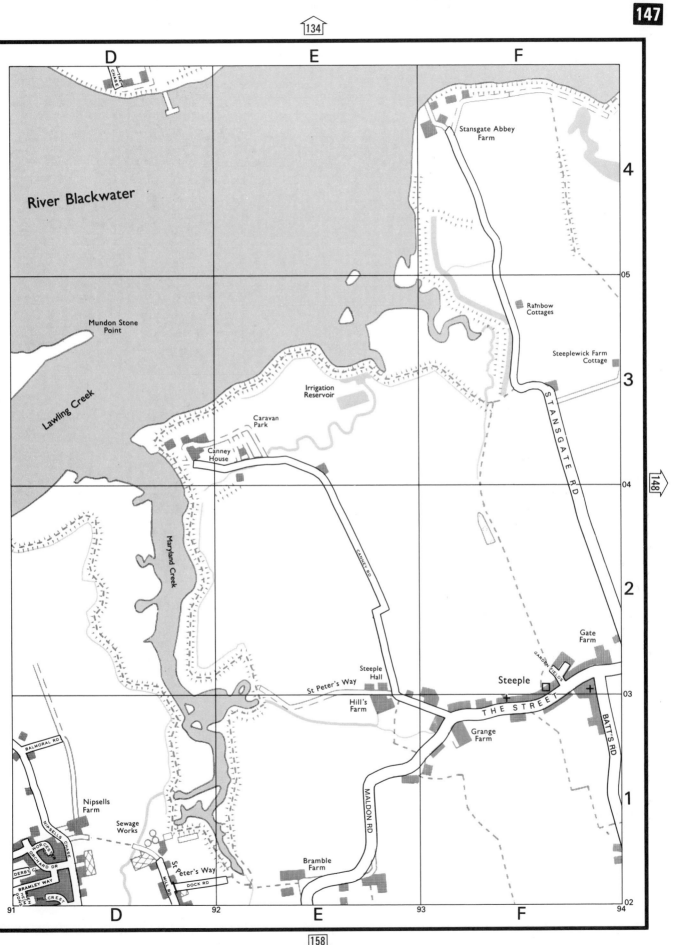

D   E   F

THE CHASE

River Blackwater

Stansgate Abbey Farm

4

05

Rainbow Cottages

Mundon Stone Point

Steeplewick Farm Cottage

Lawling Creek

Irrigation Reservoir

STANSGATE RD

3

148

Caravan Park

Canney House

04

Maryland Creek

CANNEY RD

2

Gate Farm

GARDEN FIELDS

Steeple

Steeple Hall

St Peter's Way

Hill's Farm

THE STREET

03

BATTS RD

Grange Farm

BALMORAL RD

Nipsells Farm

NIPSELLS CHASE

WORCESTER

Sewage Works

MALDON RD

ORCHARD DR

DERBY CL

1

St Peter's Way

BRAMLEY WAY

Bramble Farm

HILL CREST

MILL RD

DOCK RD

91   D   92   E   93   F   94

02

135

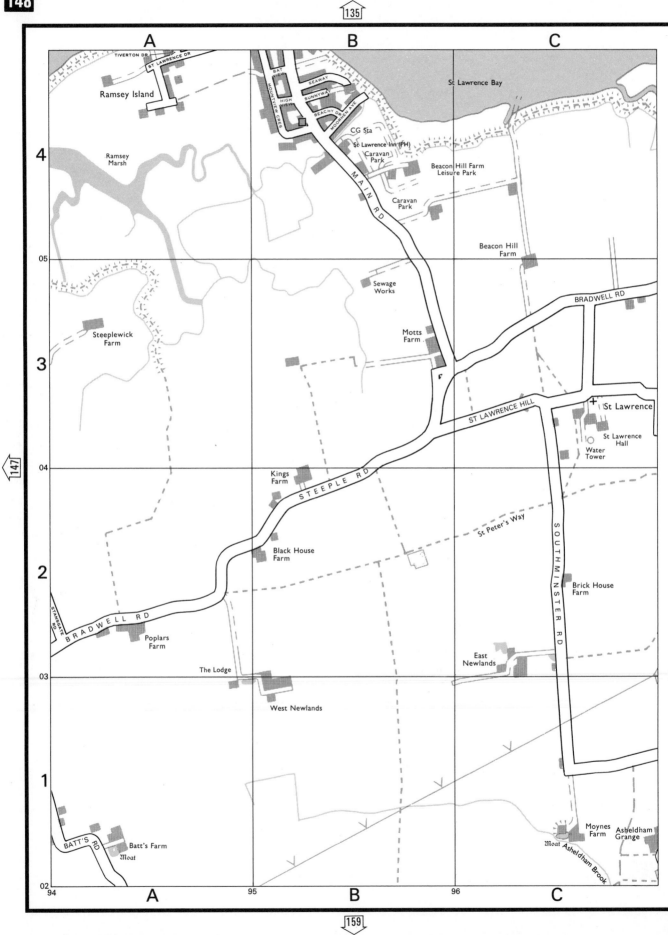

147

A   B   C

TIVERTON DR
ST LAWRENCE DR

Ramsey Island

BAT VIEW
MOUNTVIEW CRES
HIGH VIEW
SEAWAY
SUNNYWAY
BEACHY DR
MOORHEN AVE

St Lawrence Bay

CG Sta
St Lawrence Inn (PH)
Caravan Park

Beacon Hill Farm
Leisure Park

4

Ramsey Marsh

MAIN RD

Caravan Park

Beacon Hill Farm

05

BRADWELL RD

Sewage Works

Steeplewick Farm

Motts Farm

3

ST LAWRENCE HILL

St Lawrence

St Lawrence Hall
Water Tower

04

Kings Farm

STEEPLE RD

St Peter's Way

SOUTHMINSTER RD

2

Black House Farm

Brick House Farm

STANSGATE RD

BRADWELL RD

Poplars Farm

East Newlands

The Lodge

03

West Newlands

1

BATT'S RD

Batt's Farm

Moat

Moynes Farm
Asheldham Grange

Moat Asheldham Brook

02
94   A   95   B   96   C

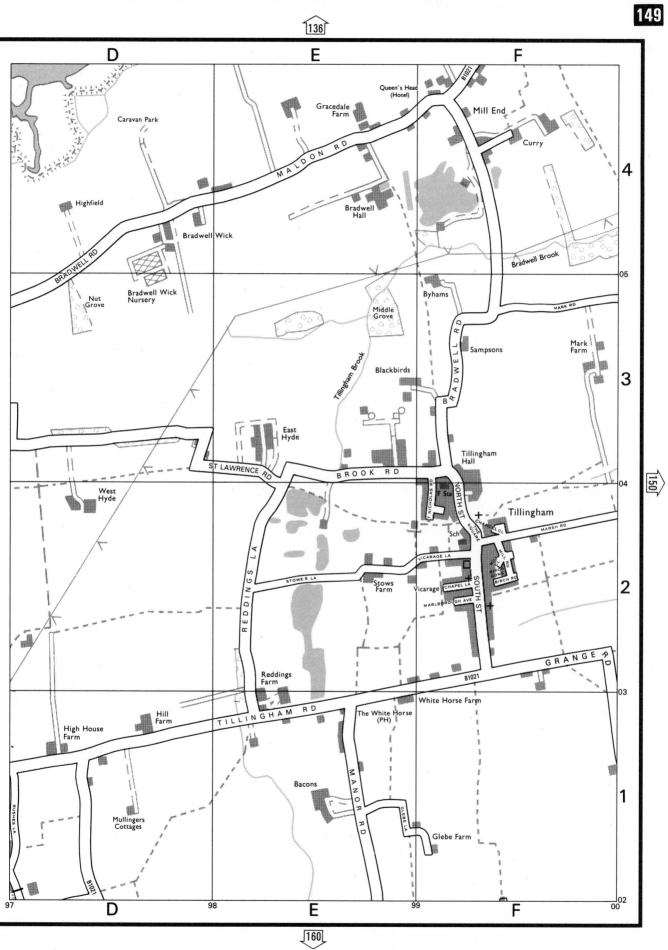

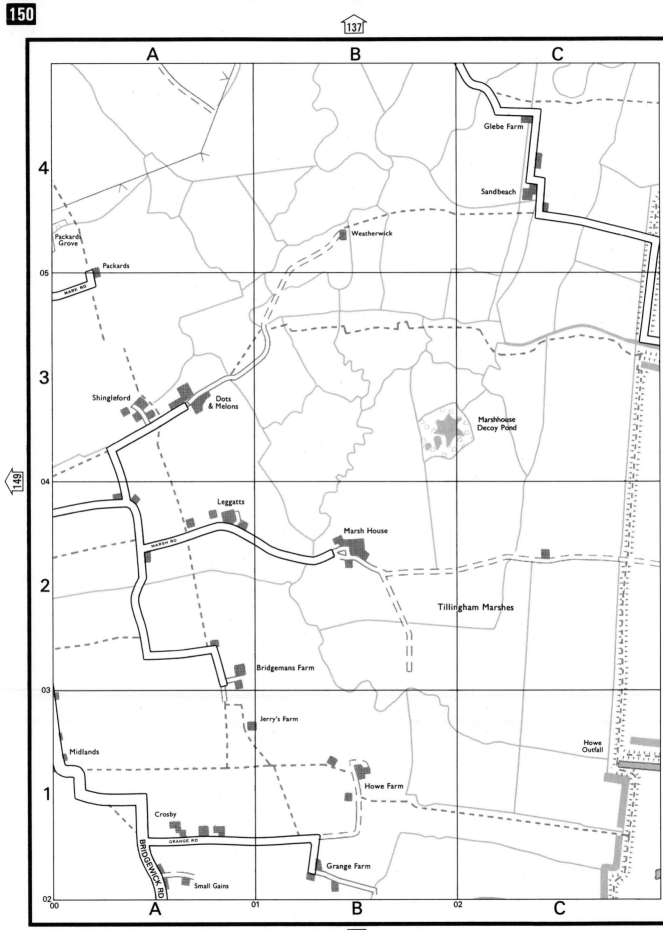

A

B

C

4

Packards
Grove

Packards

MARK RD

05

Glebe Farm

Sandbeach

Weatherwick

3

Shingleford

Dots
& Melons

Marshhouse
Decoy Pond

04

Leggatts

Marsh House

2

MARSH RD

Tillingham Marshes

Bridgemans Farm

03

Jerry's Farm

Midlands

Howe
Outfall

1

Howe Farm

Crosby

GRANGE RD

BRIDGEWICK RD

Grange Farm

Small Gains

02   00

A

01

B

02

C

138

D E F

4

05

Glebe
Outfall

Sandbeach
Outfall

Marshhouse
Outfall

Dengie Flat

3

04

2

03

1

03 D 04 E 05 F 02

141

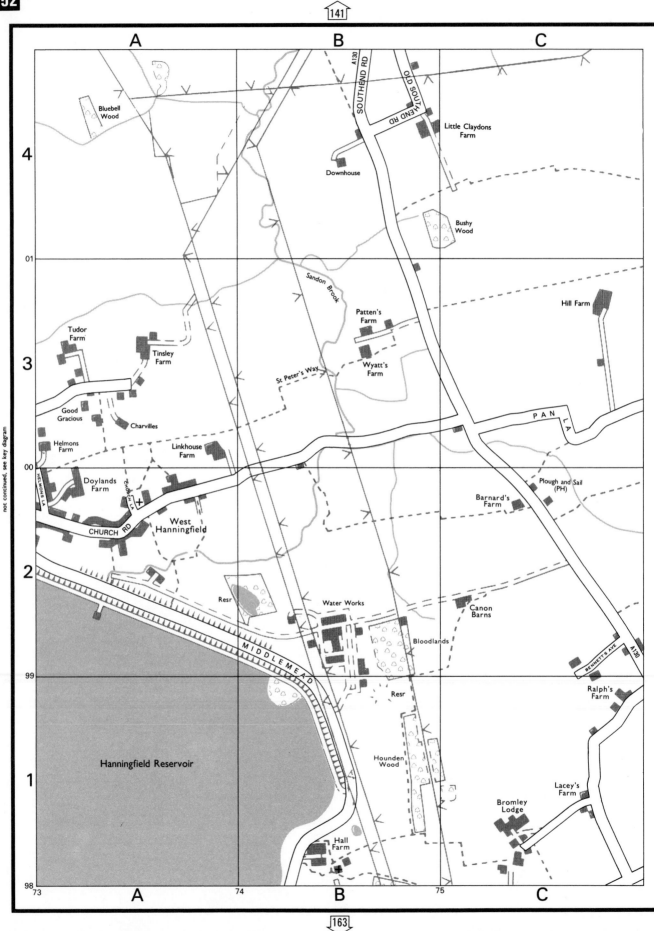

A   B   C

4

Bluebell
Wood

SOUTHEND RD
A130

OLD SOUTH

Little Claydons
Farm

Downhouse

Bushy
Wood

01

Sandon Brook

Hill Farm

Patten's
Farm

Tudor
Farm

3

Tinsley
Farm

St Peter's Way

Wyatt's
Farm

PAN   LA

Good
Gracious

Charvilles

Plough and Sail
(PH)

Helmons
Farm

Linkhouse
Farm

Barnard's
Farm

00

Doylands
Farm

West
Hanningfield

CHURCH RD

CHURCH LA

HELMONS LA

not continued, see key diagram

Resr

Water Works

Canon
Barns

2

Bloodlands

Ralph's
Farm

MIDDLEMEAD

BENNETT'S AVE

A130

99

Resr

Hounden
Wood

Lacey's
Farm

Hanningfield Reservoir

1

Bromley
Lodge

98
73   A   74   B   75   C

Hall
Farm

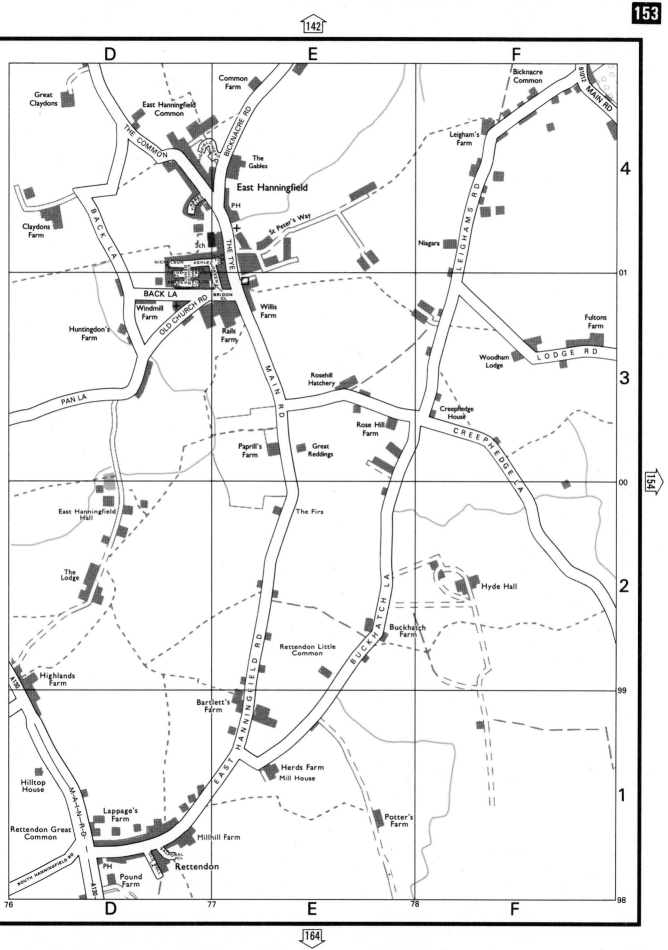

D

E

F

Great
Claydons

East Hanningfield
Common

THE COMMON

BICKNACRE RD

Common
Farm

Bicknacre
Common

B1012 MAIN RD

Leigham's
Farm

4

The Gables

East Hanningfield

St Peter's Way

Niagara

LEIGHAMS RD

BACK LA

Claydons
Farm

PH

Sch

+

NICHOLSON ASHLEY
AV
ACNE

EBEN-EZER
CL
PEASE CL
HILL HILL

THE TYE

YOUNG
GREEN

Fultons
Farm

01

BACK LA

BRIDON
CL

Willis
Farm

Woodham
Lodge

LODGE RD

Windmill
Farm

OLD CHURCH RD

Huntingdon's
Farm

Rails
Farm

Creephedge
House

3

PAN LA

MAIN RD

Rosehill
Hatchery

CREEPHEDGE LA

Rose Hill
Farm

1154

Paprill's
Farm

Great
Reddings

East Hanningfield
Hall

The Firs

00

The
Lodge

Hyde Hall

2

BUCKHATCH LA

Buckhatch
Farm

Rettendon Little
Common

A130

Highlands
Farm

EAST HANNINGFIELD RD

Bartlett's
Farm

99

Herds Farm
Mill House

Hilltop
House

MAIN RD

Potter's
Farm

1

Lappage's
Farm

Rettendon Great
Common

Millhill Farm

BALMORAL
JCL

OUTBELT

SOUTH HANNINGFIELD RD

A130

PH

Rettendon

Pound
Farm

76

D

77

E

78

F

98

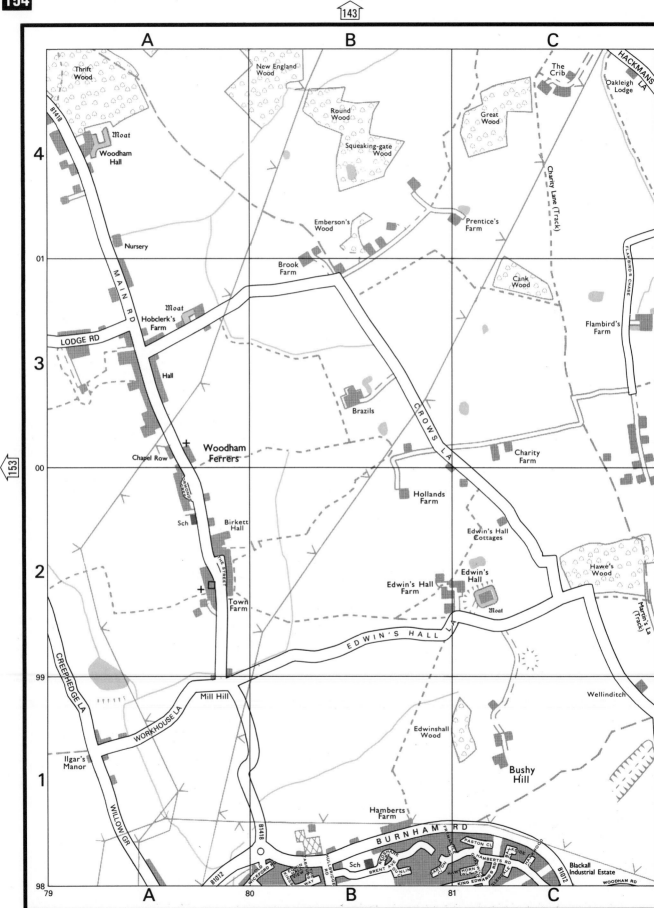

A B C

Thrift
Wood

New England
Wood

Round
Wood

The
Crib

Oakleigh
Lodge

HACKMANS LA

B1418

Moat

Woodham
Hall

Squeaking-gate
Wood

Great
Wood

Charity Lane (Track)

4

Nursery

Emberson's
Wood

Prentice's
Farm

FLAMBIRD'S CHASE

01

Brook
Farm

Cank
Wood

MAIN RD

Moat

Hobclerk's
Farm

Flambird's
Farm

LODGE RD

3

Hall

Brazils

CROW'S LA

Charity
Farm

Chapel Row

Woodham
Ferrers

00

Hollands
Farm

Edwin's Hall
Cottages

Sch

Birkett
Hall

Hawe's
Wood

THE STREET

Edwin's Hall
Farm

Edwin's
Hall

2

Town
Farm

Moat

Martin's La (Track)

EDWIN'S HALL LA

CREEPHEDGE LA

99

Mill Hill

Wellinditch

WORKHOUSE LA

Edwinshall
Wood

Ilgar's
Manor

Bushy
Hill

1

WILLOW GR

Hamberts
Farm

BURNHAM RD

B1418

Sch

Blackall
Industrial Estate

B1012

FREDA
PASTON CL

HAMBERTS RD

KING EDWARD'S RD

WOODHAM RD

B1012

98

79 A 80 B 81 C

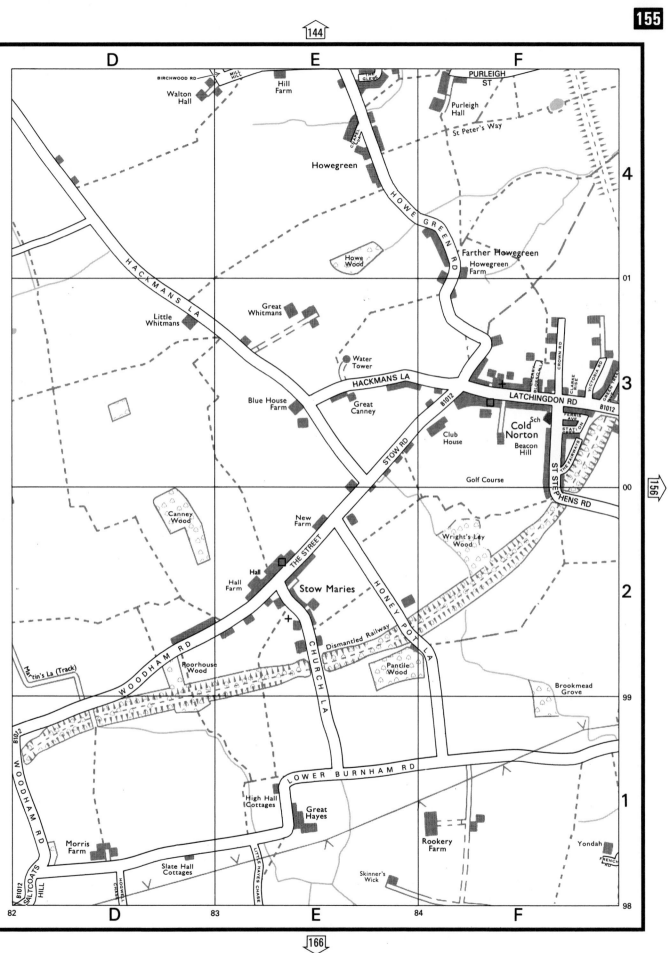

144

D E F

BIRCHWOOD RD
MILL HILL
Walton Hall
Hill Farm
THE GLEBE
PURLEIGH ST
Purleigh Hall
CHAPEL
St Peter's Way

4

Howegreen

HOWE GREEN RD

HACKMANS LA

Howe Wood

Farther Howegreen
Howegreen Farm

01

Little Whitmans

Great Whitmans

Water Tower

HACKMANS LA

Blue House Farm

Great Canney

STOW RD

B1012

LATCHINGDON RD

CROWN RD
BLACKBERRY
CLARKE RISE
VICTORIA RD
GREEN MAN

Cold Norton

Sch
FERRIS AVE
STATION

B1012

3

Club House

Beacon Hill

Golf Course

ST STEPHENS RD

THE FAIRWAYS

ST STEPHENS RD

00

Canney Wood

New Farm

THE STREET

Wright's Ley Wood

156

2

Hall

Hall Farm

Stow Maries

CHURCH LA

HONEY POT LA

Dismantled Railway

Pantile Wood

Brookmead Grove

WOODHAM RD

Martin's La (Track)

Poorhouse Wood

99

B1012

LOWER BURNHAM RD

1

WOODHAM RD

High Hall Cottages

Great Hayes

Rookery Farm

Yondah

Morris Farm

HOGWELL

CRAYS

LITTLE HAYES CHASE

Slate Hall Cottages

Skinner's Wick

FRENCH RD

B1012
SALTCOATS HILL

98

82 D 83 E 84 F 98

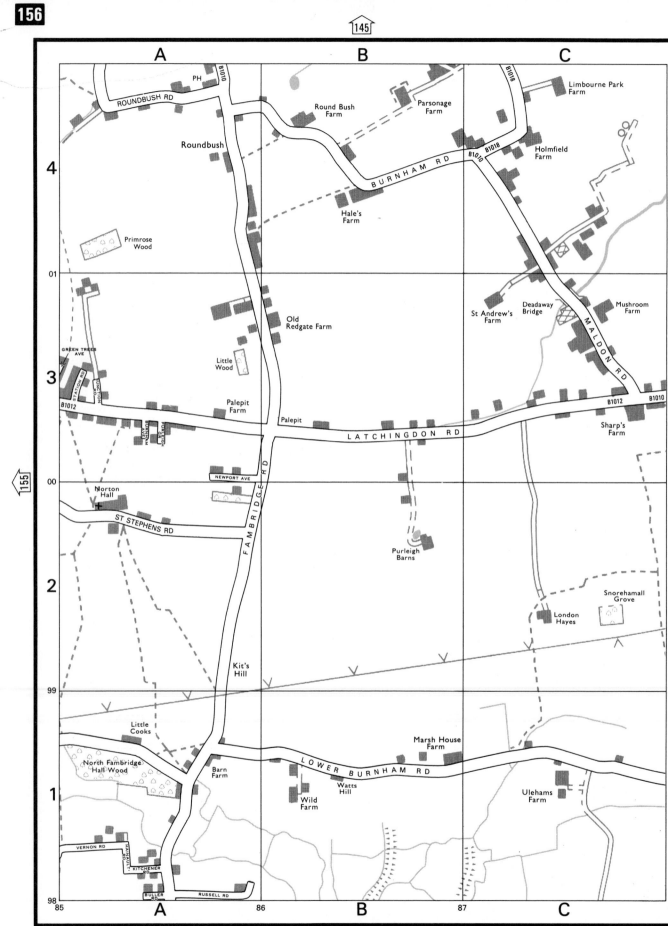

A   B   C

ROUNDBUSH RD
PH
B1010
Round Bush Farm
Parsonage Farm
Limbourne Park Farm
B1018
Roundbush
Holmfield Farm
B1018
B1010
4

BURNHAM RD

Primrose Wood
Hale's Farm

01

Old Redgate Farm
St Andrew's Farm
Deadaway Bridge
Mushroom Farm

GREEN TREES AVE
STATION RD
JUNCTION RD
Little Wood
MALDON RD

3
Palepit Farm
Palepit
B1012
B1010
B1012
BURNHAM AVE
PURLEIGH RD
Sharp's Farm

LATCHINGDON RD

NEWPORT AVE
00
Norton Hall
155
FAMBRIDGE RD
Purleigh Barns
ST STEPHENS RD

Snorehamall Grove

2
London Hayes

Kit's Hill

99
Little Cooks
Marsh House Farm

North Fambridge Hall Wood
Barn Farm
LOWER BURNHAM RD
Ulehams Farm

1
Watts Hill
Wild Farm

VERNON RD
HAINAULT RD
KITCHENER RD
BULLER RD
RUSSELL RD

98
85   A   86   B   87   C

D

E

F

THE DRIVE

KATONIA AVE

4

Lawling
Hall

Butterfields

01

STEEPLE RD

Brook
Hall

Tideway
Farm

Lawling
Cottages

Greenlane
Farm

Bridgeman's
Farm

School

3

BRIDGEMANS
GREEN

MEADOW WAY

CHASE
LUDGROVE

B1010

Good
Hares

The Huntsman & Hounds
(PH)

Moat

Warden's
Farm

Latchingdon

BUCHANAN

ST MICHAELS

SNOREHAM GDNS

WAY

Hall

Arley
Grange

BURNHAM RD

B1010

00

PH

MAIN RD

SOUTH
MINSTER
RD

GARDEN
CL

B1020

Red Lyons
Farm

LOWER CHASE

B1010 SUMMERHILL

Snoreham
Hall

The
Beeches

2

RECTORY LA

Surridges

Rosedale
Farm

Barnes
Farm

UPPER
CHASE

99

FAMBRIDGE RD

Latchingdon
Hall

Tyle
Hall

Grange
Farm

CHESTNUT FARM DR

Althorne
Hall

RIVER VIEW
TERR

STATION RD

1

Stamfords Hill
Cottages

River View
Park

Stamfords
Farm

Viking
Cottage

98

88

D

89

E

90

F

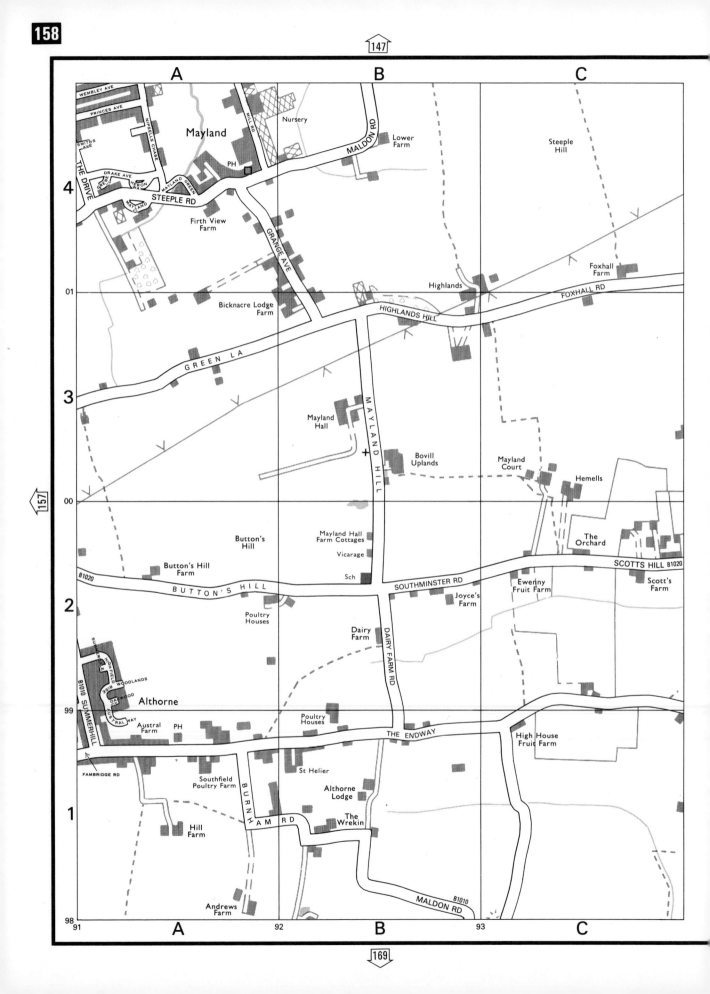

157

D E F

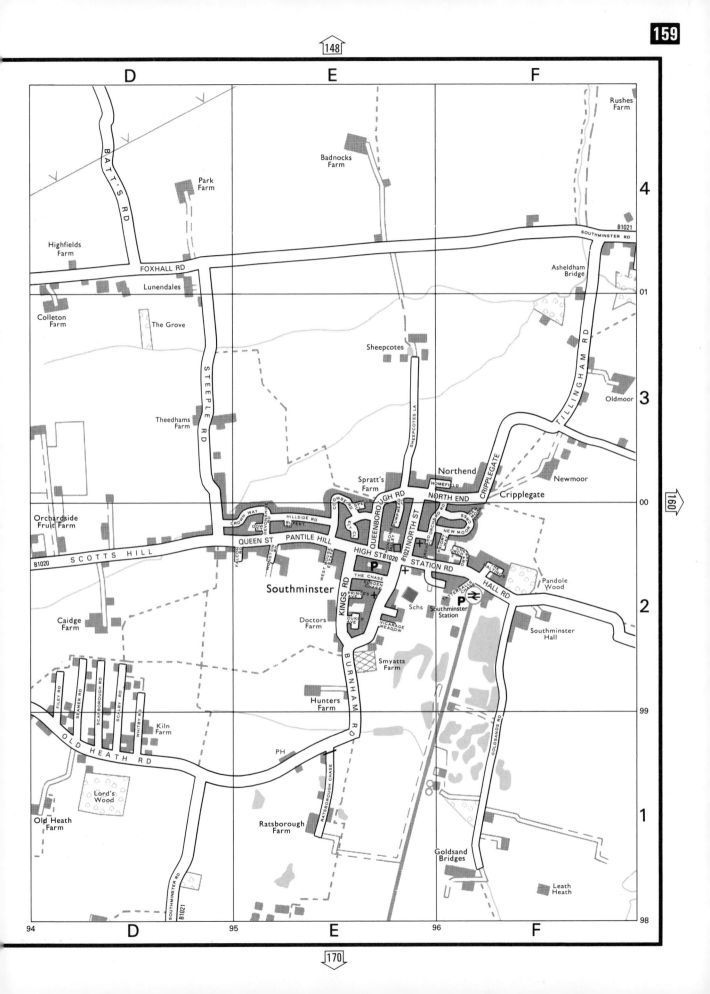

4

B1021

SOUTHMINSTER RD

Rushes Farm

Badnocks Farm

Park Farm

BATT'S RD

Highfields Farm

FOXHALL RD

Lunendales

Asheldham Bridge

01

Colleton Farm

The Grove

Sheepcotes

TILLINGHAM RD

Oldmoor

3

STEEPLE RD

Theedhams Farm

SHEEPCOTES LA

Northend

Newmoor

Spratt's Farm

NORTH END

HOMEFIELD

CRIPPLEGATE

Cripplegate

00

160

Orchardside Fruit Farm

CROWN WAY

HILLSIDE RD

QUEENBOROUGH RD

NORTH ST

NEW MOOR

PANTILE HILL

QUEEN ST

HIGH ST B1020

STATION RD

B1020 SCOTTS HILL

SCOTTS HILL

Southminster

KINGS RD

THE CHASE

P

Pandole Wood

2

Caidge Farm

Doctors Farm

BURNHAM RD

Schs

Southminster Station

P

HALL RD

Southminster Hall

VICARAGE MEADOW

Smyatts Farm

FILEY RD

SEAMER RD

SCARBOROUGH RD

SCALBY RD

WHITBY RD

Kiln Farm

Hunters Farm

99

OLD HEATH RD

PH

RATSBOROUGH CHASE

GOLDSANDS RD

Lord's Wood

1

Old Heath Farm

Ratsborough Farm

Goldsand Bridges

Leath Heath

SOUTHMINSTER RD

B1021

98

94 D 95 E 96 F

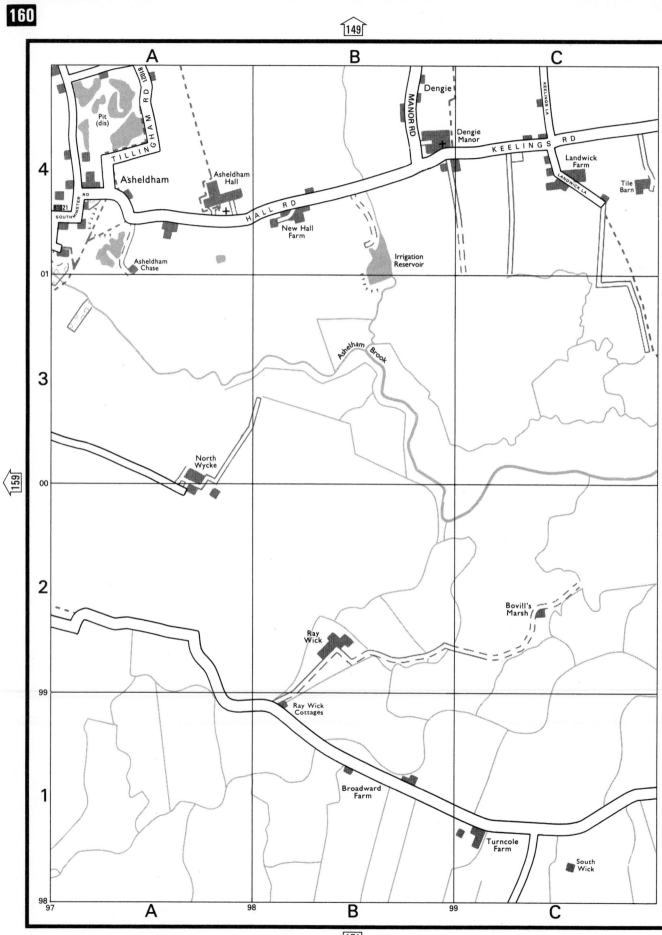

A   **B**   **C**

TILLINGHAM RD (2018)

Pit
(dis)

Asheldham

SOUTHMINSTER RD

B1021

Asheldham
Hall

HALL RD

MANOR RD

Dengie

Dengie
Manor

KEELINGS RD

KEELINGS LA

Landwick
Farm

LANDWICK LA

Tile
Barn

New Hall
Farm

Asheldham
Chase

Irrigation
Reservoir

Ashelham Brook

North
Wycke

Bovill's
Marsh

Ray
Wick

Ray Wick
Cottages

Broadward
Farm

Turncole
Farm

South
Wick

4

3

2

1

01

00

99

98

97   98   99

A   **B**   **C**

150

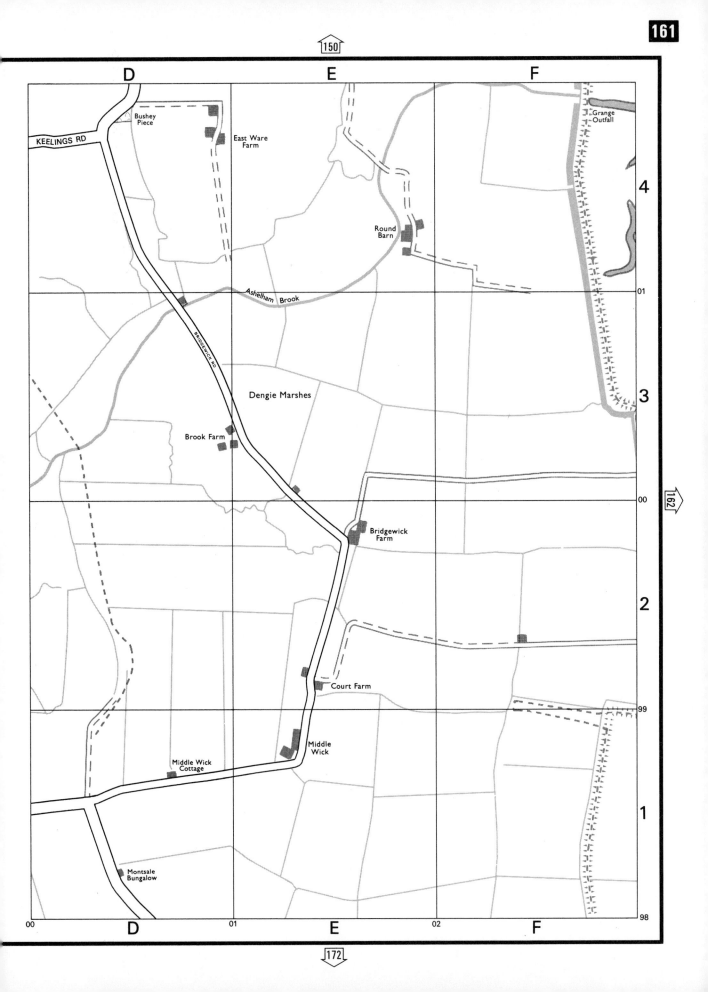

D

KEELINGS RD

Bushey
Piece

East Ware
Farm

Grange
Outfall

Round
Barn

Ashelham Brook

BRIDGEWICK RD

Dengie Marshes

Brook Farm

Bridgewick
Farm

Court Farm

Middle Wick

Middle Wick
Cottage

Montsale
Bungalow

162

D   E   F

4

3

2

1

01

00

99

98

00   01   02

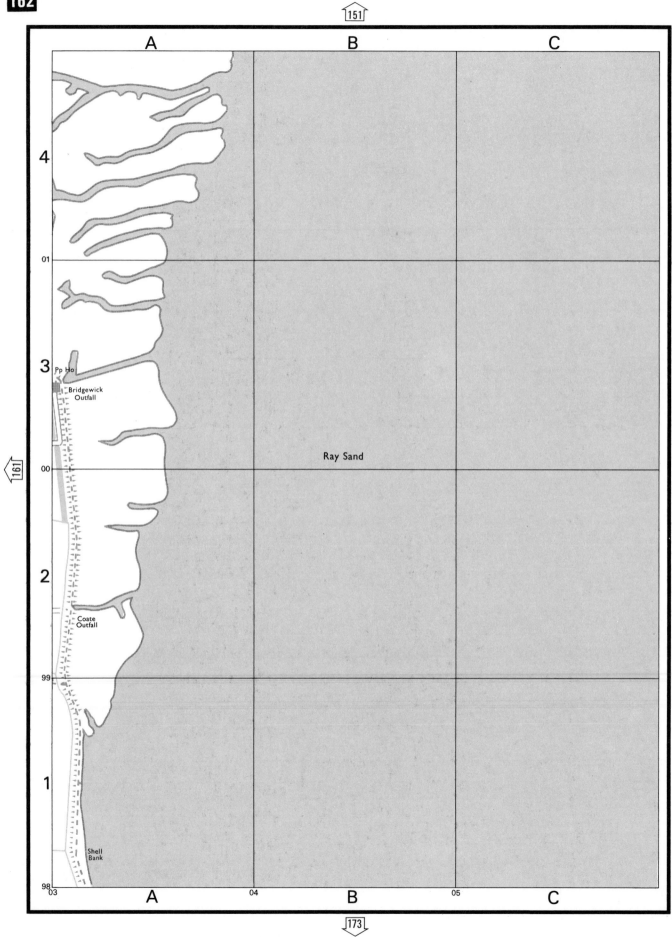

A

B

C

4

01

3

Pp Ho

Bridgewick
Outfall

Ray Sand

00

161

2

Coate
Outfall

99

1

Shell
Bank

98

03

A

04

B

05

C

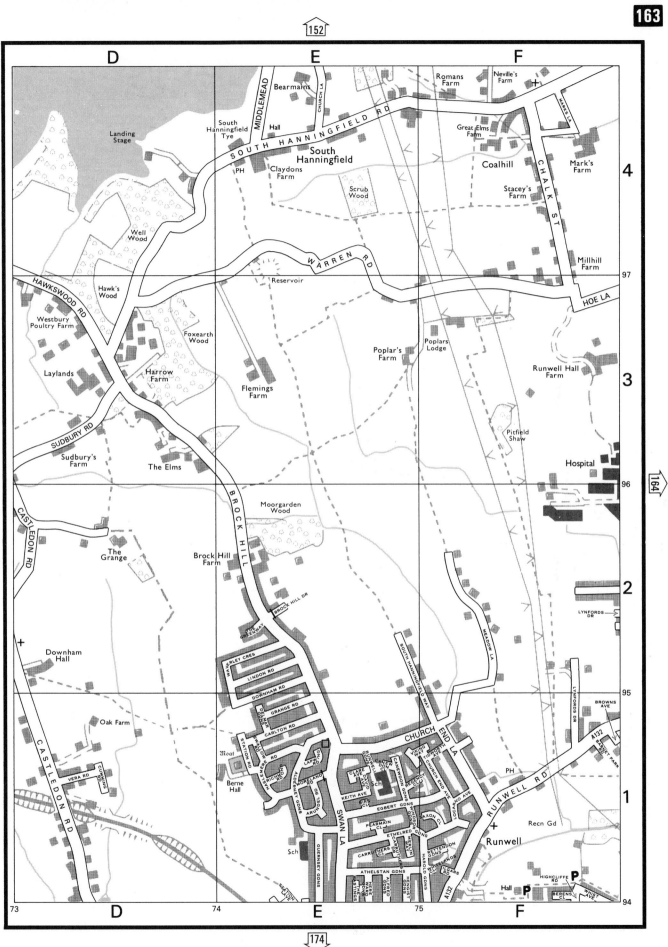

164

D E F

4

3

2

1

97

96

95

94

73 74 75

Landing
Stage

Well
Wood

MIDDLEMEAD

South
Hanningfield
Tye

Bearmains

Hall

CHURCH LA

SOUTH HANNINGFIELD RD

South
Hanningfield

PH

Claydons
Farm

Scrub
Wood

Romans
Farm

Neville's
Farm

Great Elms
Farm

Coalhill

Stacey's
Farm

MARKS LA

CHALK ST

Mark's
Farm

Millhill
Farm

HOE LA

WARREN RD

Reservoir

HAWKSWOOD RD

Hawk's
Wood

Westbury
Poultry Farm

Foxearth
Wood

Laylands

Harrow
Farm

Flemings
Farm

Poplar's
Farm

Poplars
Lodge

Runwell Hall
Farm

Pitfield
Shaw

SUDBURY RD

Sudbury's
Farm

The Elms

CASTLEDON RD

BROCK HILL

Moorgarden
Wood

Hospital

The
Grange

Brock Hill
Farm

BROCK HILL DR

LYNFORDS
DR

Downham
Hall

THE GREENWAY

MAWSLEY CRES

LINDON RD

DOWNHAM RD

GRANGE RD

CARLTON RD

SOUTH HANNINGFIELD WAY

MEADOW LA

BROWNS
AVE

LYNFORDS DR

A132

Oak Farm

VERA RD

CUMMING RD

CASTLEDON RD

Moat

Berne
Hall

STATION RD

SWAN LA

GUERNSEY GDNS

STATION LA

Sch

Sch

CHURCH END LA

RUNWELL RD

PH

Runwell

Recn Gd

Hall

P
P

HIGHCLIFFE
RD

BERENS
CL

WHIST
AVE

CHURCH END AVE

A132

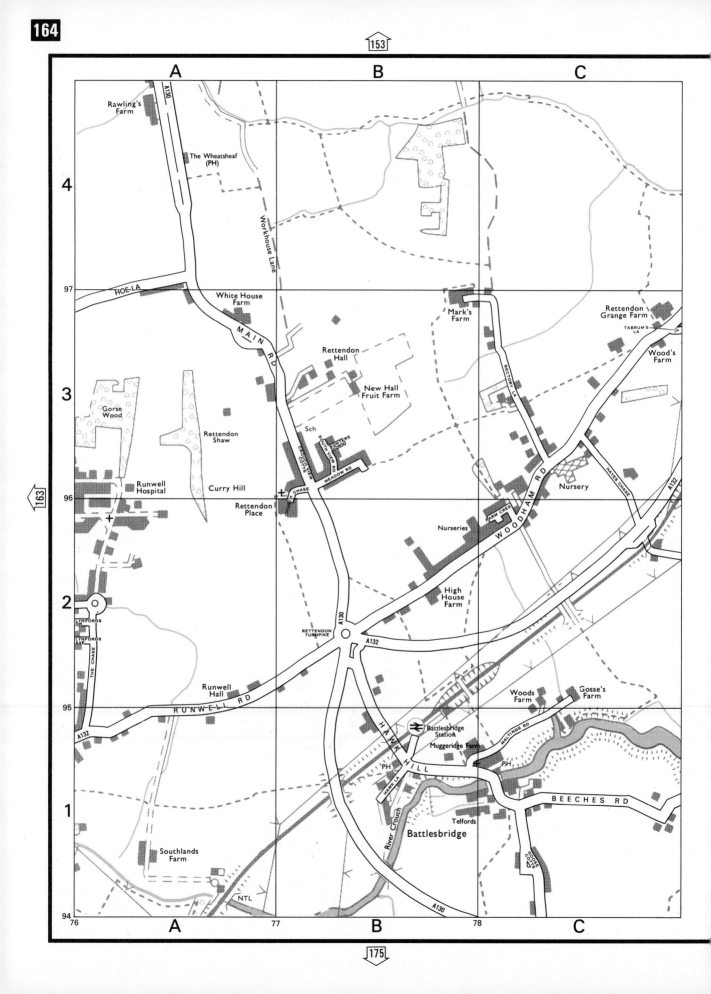

163

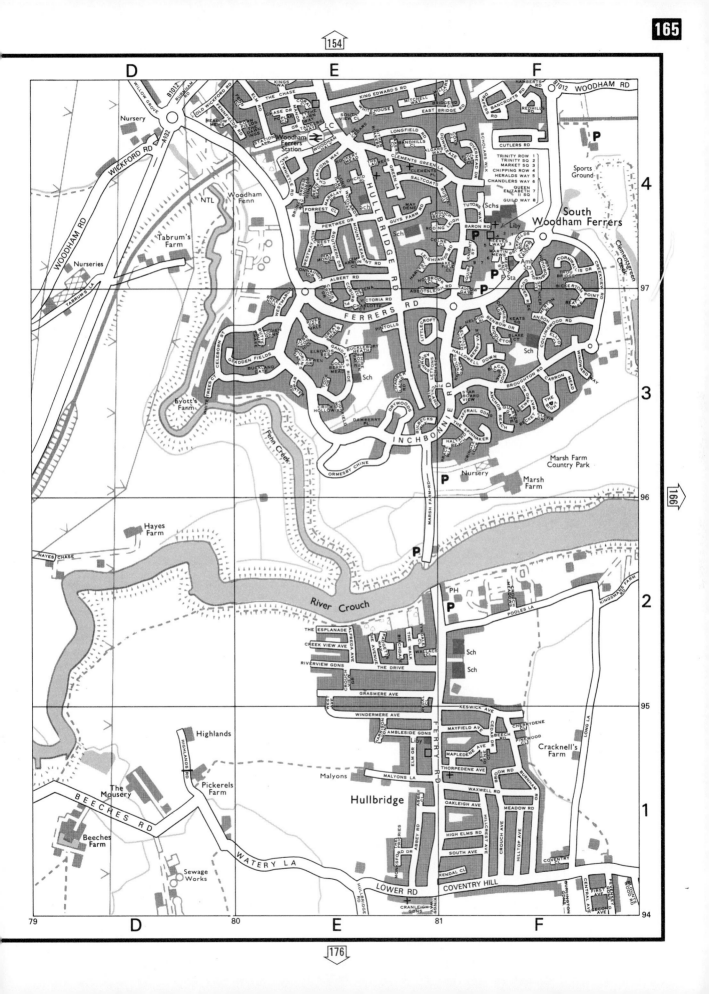

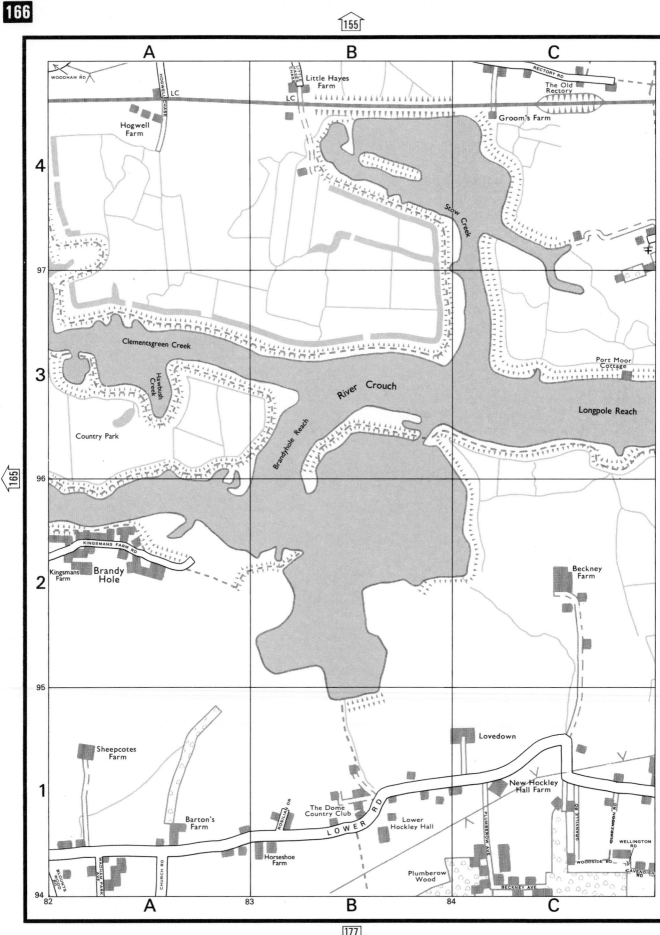

A   B   C

WOODHAM RD

Hogwell Farm
LC
HOGWELL CHASE

Little Hayes Farm
LC
LITTLE HAYES CHASE

RECTORY RD
The Old Rectory
Groom's Farm

4

Stow Creek

97

Clementsgreen Creek

Port Moor Cottage

Hawbush Creek

River Crouch

3

Longpole Reach

Country Park

Brandyhole Reach

165

96

Kingsmans Farm
KINGSMANS FARM RD
Brandy Hole

Beckney Farm

2

95

Sheepcotes Farm

Lovedown

New Hockley Hall Farm

1

Barton's Farm

ROSILIA DR
The Dome Country Club
LOWER RD
Lower Hockley Hall

PLUMBEROW AVE
GRANVILLE RD
CLARENDON RD
WELLINGTON RD

Horseshoe Farm

Plumberow Wood

WOODSIDE RD
CAVENDISH RD

BLOUNTS WOOD
WADHAM PARK AVE
CHURCH RD

BECKNEY AVE

94   82   A   83   B   84   C

156

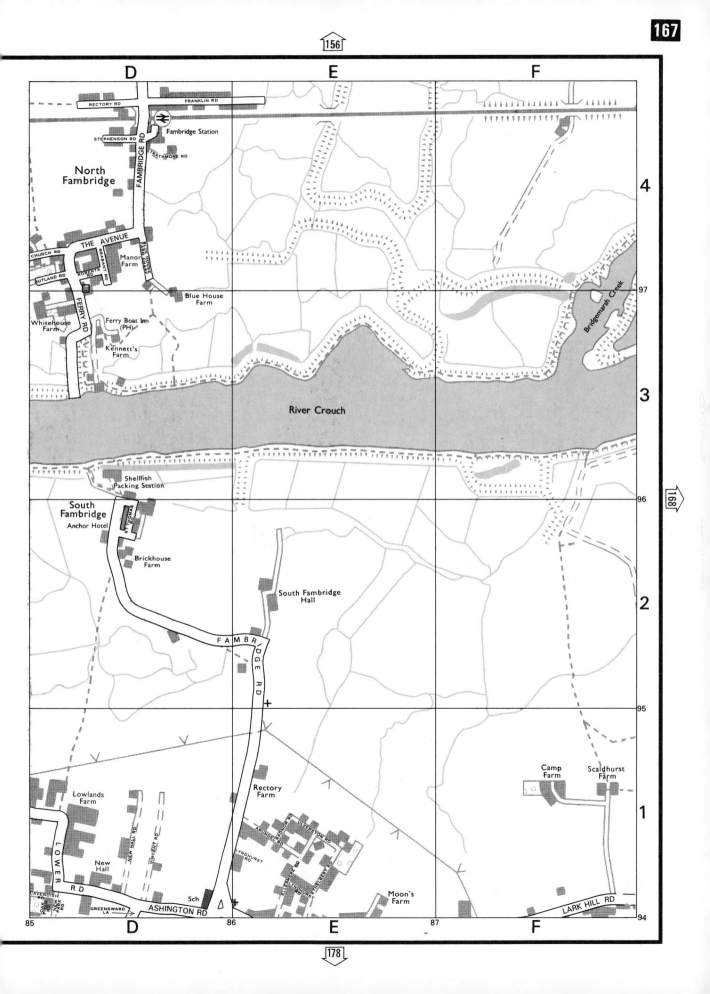

D   E   F

RECTORY RD

FRANKLIN RD

Fambridge Station

STEPHENSON RD

STRATHMORE RD

North
Fambridge

FAMBRIDGE RD

THE AVENUE

CHURCH RD

BRABANT RD

ROBERTS RD

RUTLAND RD

PARK HOUSE PARK CHASE

Manor
Farm

Blue House
Farm

FERRY RD

Whitehouse
Farm

Ferry Boat Inn
(PH)

Kennett's
Farm

4

Bridgemarsh Creek

97

River Crouch

3

Shellfish
Packing Station

96

South
Fambridge

Anchor Hotel

ST THOMAS

Brickhouse
Farm

South Fambridge
Hall

FAMBRIDGE RD

2

Camp
Farm

Scaldhurst
Farm

95

Lowlands
Farm

LOWER RD

NEW HALL RD

VINCENT RD

New
Hall

Rectory
Farm

ARUNDEL RD

MANOR RD

ULVERSTON RD

LYNDHURST RD

ELLESMERE RD

LYNDHURST

EYEBERRY ST

Moon's
Farm

1

CAVENDISH RD

GREENSWARD LA

Sch

ASHINGTON RD

LARK HILL RD

94

85   D   86   E   87   F

168

178

157

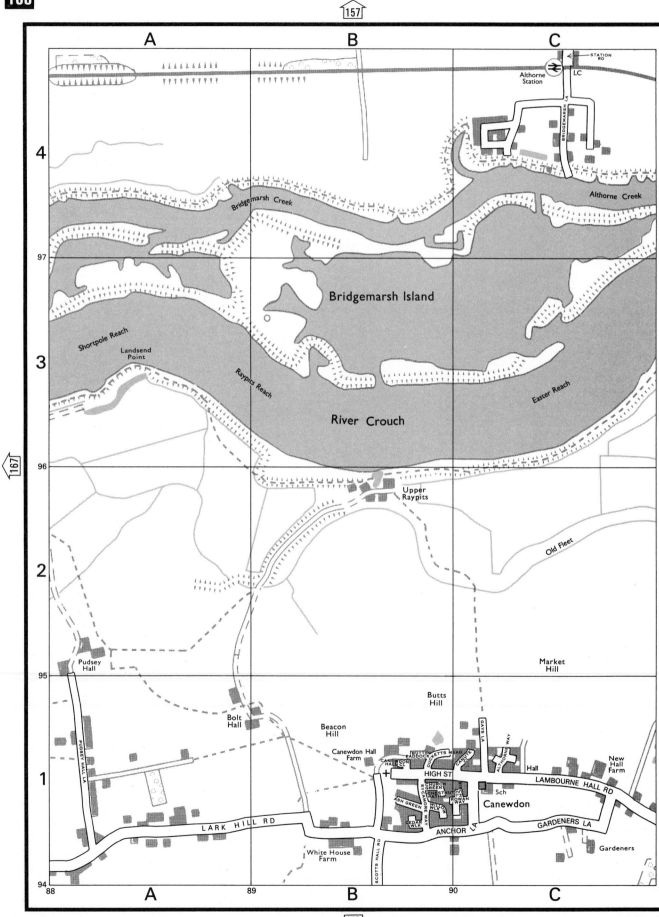

167

179

A B C

STATION RD

Althorne Station

LC

Bridgemarsh Creek

Althorne Creek

4

97

Bridgemarsh Island

Shortpole Reach

Landsend Point

3

Raypits Reach

Easter Reach

River Crouch

96

Upper Raypits

Old Fleet

2

95

Pudsey Hall

Market Hill

Butts Hill

Bolt Hall

Beacon Hill

New Hall Farm

Canewdon Hall Farm

CANEWDON HALL CL

BUTTS

PADDOCK

KETTS MEAD

DUCK

GAYS LA

ALTHORNE WAY

Hall

HIGH ST

CHURCH GREEN

CHESTNUT

CANUTE

Sch

LAMBOURNE HALL RD

1

CHURCH PATH

CONSTITUTION

ASH GREEN

SYCAMORE WAY

WILLOW WLK

ROWAN WAY

Canewdon

GARDENERS LA

PUDSEY HALL LA

CEDAR WLK

ANCHOR LA

Gardeners

LARK HILL RD

SCOTTS HALL RD

White House Farm

94

88 A 89 B 90 C

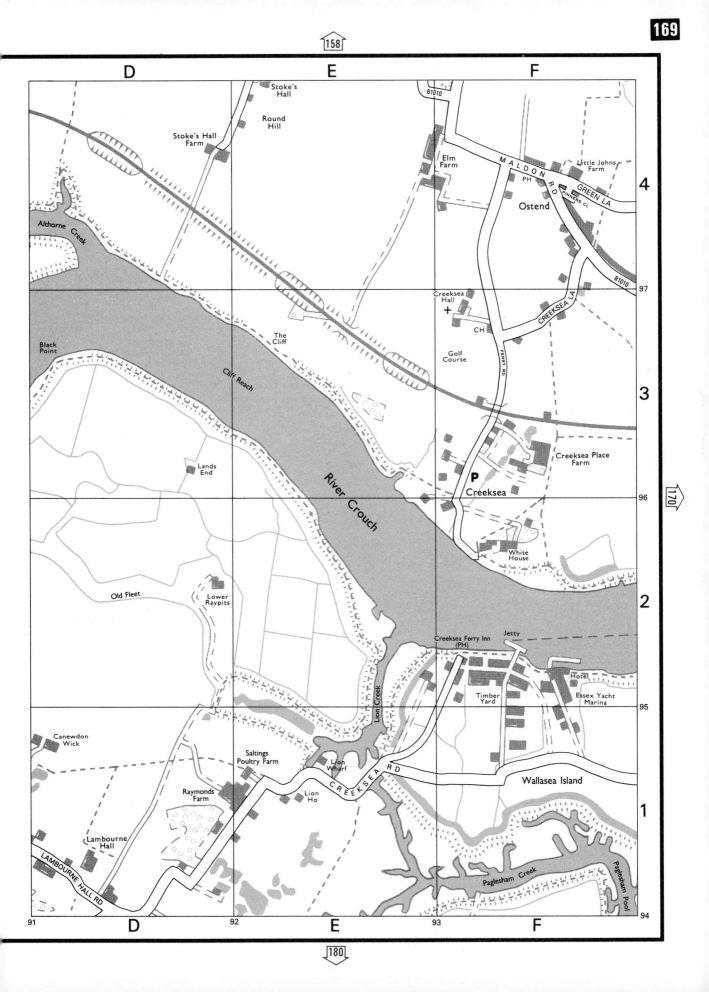

158

D
E
F

Stoke's
Hall

Round
Hill

Stoke's Hall
Farm

B1010

MALDON RD

Elm
Farm

Little Johns
Farm

GREEN LA

PH

PINNERS CL

Ostend

4

Althorne Creek

Creeksea
Hall

B1010

97

CREEKSEA LA

CH

The
Cliff

Golf
Course

Black
Point

FERRY RD

3

Cliff Reach

Creeksea Place
Farm

Lands
End

P

River Crouch

Creeksea

96

White
House

Old Fleet

Lower
Raypits

2

Creeksea Ferry Inn
(PH)

Jetty

Hotel

Lion Creek

Timber
Yard

Essex Yacht
Marina

95

Canewdon
Wick

Saltings
Poultry Farm

Lion
Wharf

CREEKSEA RD

Wallasea Island

Raymonds
Farm

Lion
Ho

1

Lambourne
Hall

LAMBOURNE HALL RD

Paglesham Creek

Paglesham Pool

91
D
92
E
93
F
94

170

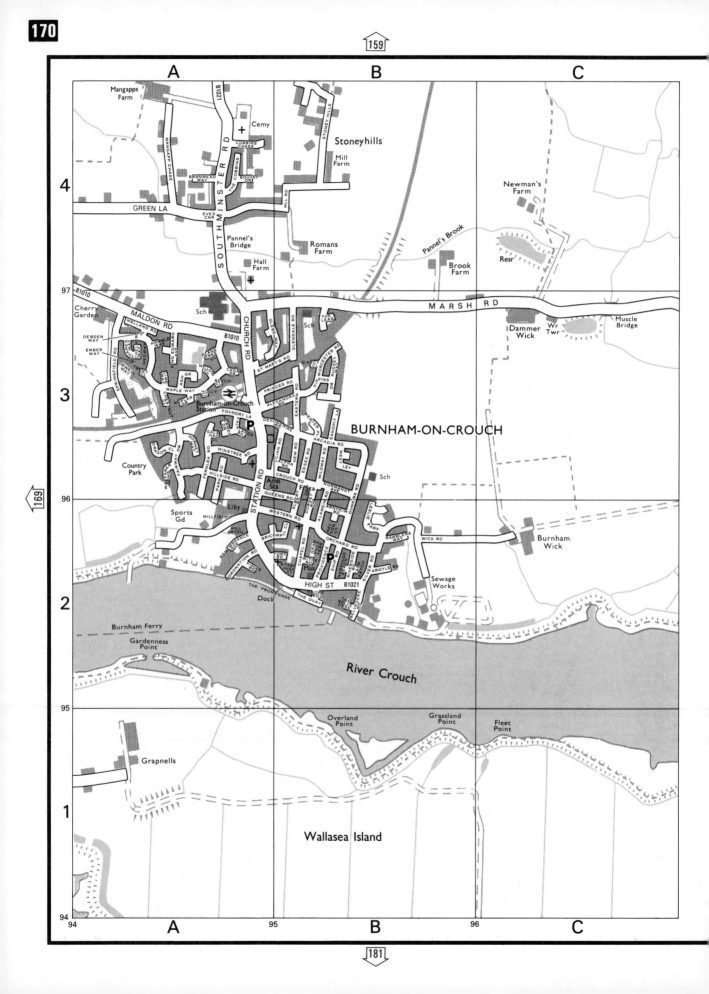

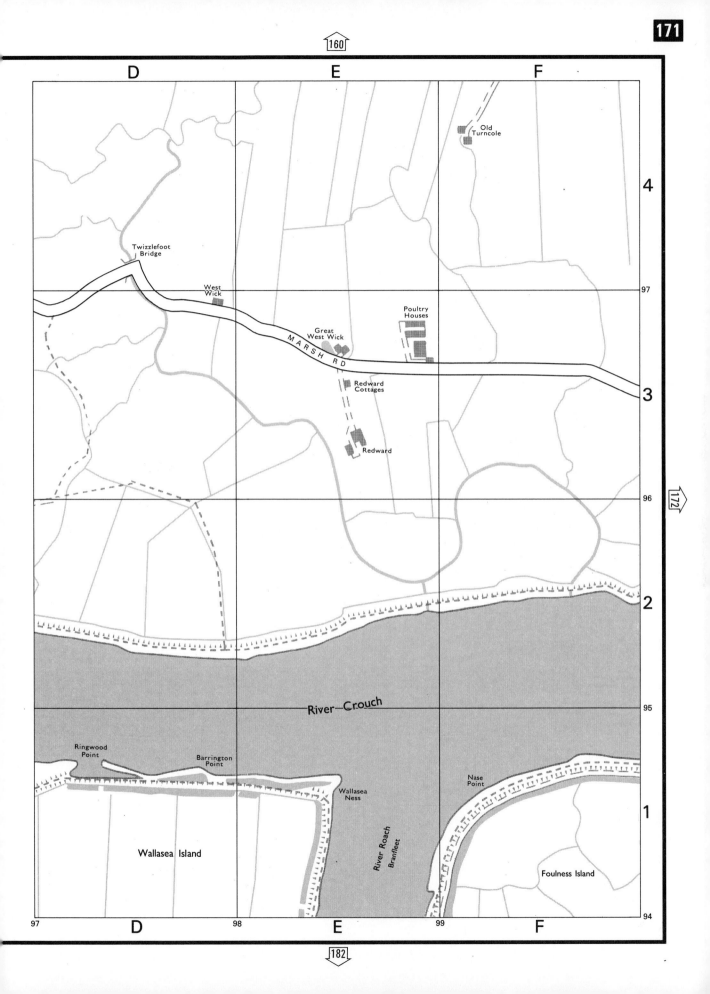

160

D E F

4

Old
Turncole

Twizzlefoot
Bridge

West
Wick

97

Poultry
Houses

MARSH RD

Great
West Wick

Redward
Cottages

3

172

Redward

96

2

95

River Crouch

Ringwood
Point

Barrington
Point

Nase
Point

Wallasea
Ness

1

Wallasea Island

River Roach
Branfleet

Foulness Island

97 98 99 94

D E F

182

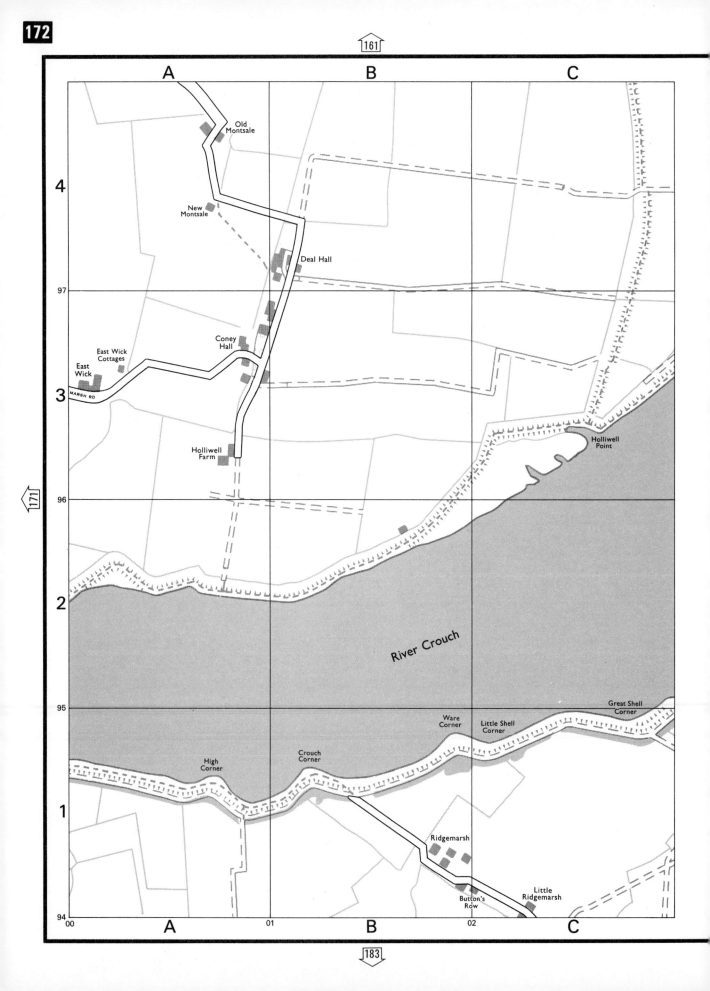

161

A   B   C

Old
Montsale

4

New
Montsale

Deal Hall

97

Coney
Hall

East Wick
Cottages

East
Wick

3

MARSH RD

Holliwell
Farm

Holliwell
Point

96

171

2

River Crouch

95

Great Shell
Corner

Ware
Corner

Little Shell
Corner

High
Corner

Crouch
Corner

1

Ridgemarsh

Button's
Row

Little
Ridgemarsh

94

00   A   01   B   02   C

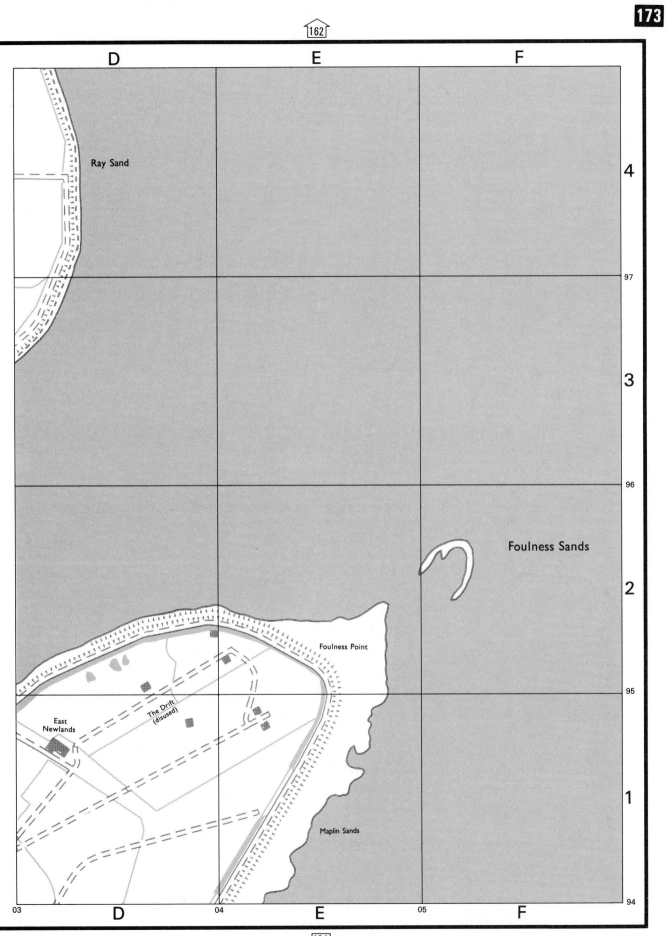

D

E

F

Ray Sand

4

97

3

96

Foulness Sands

2

95

Foulness Point

East
Newlands

The Drift
(disused)

Maplin Sands

1

94

03

D

04

E

05

F

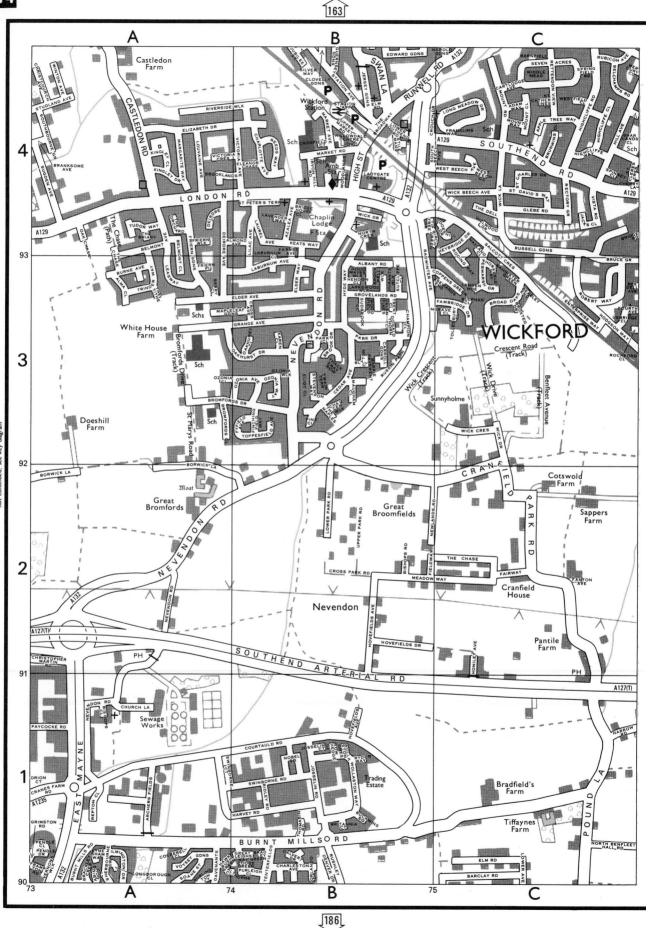

164

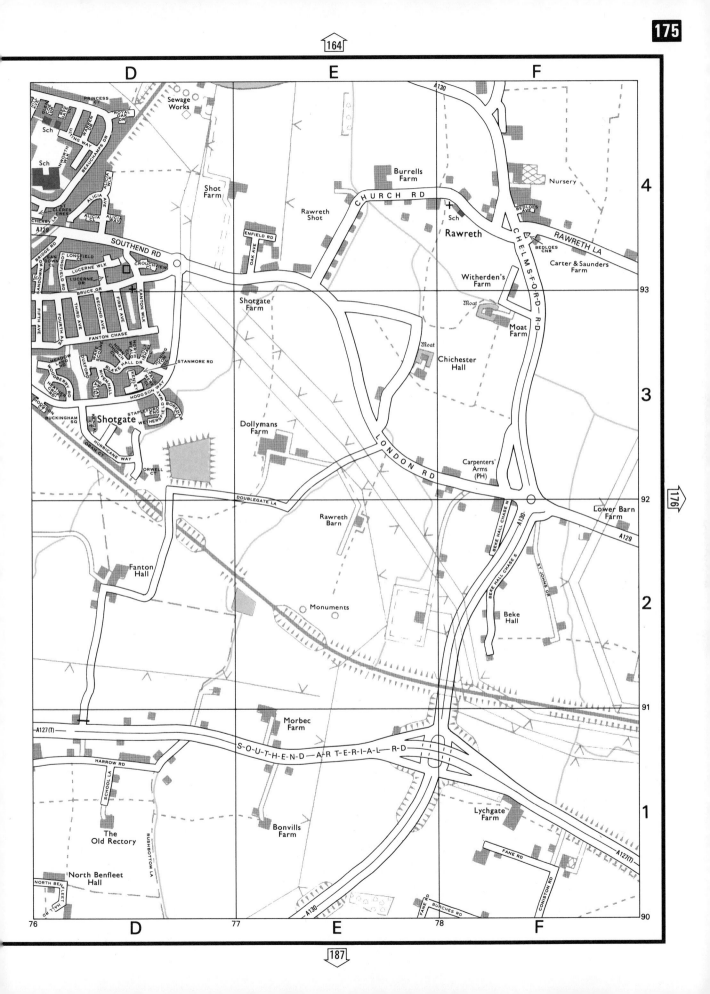

165

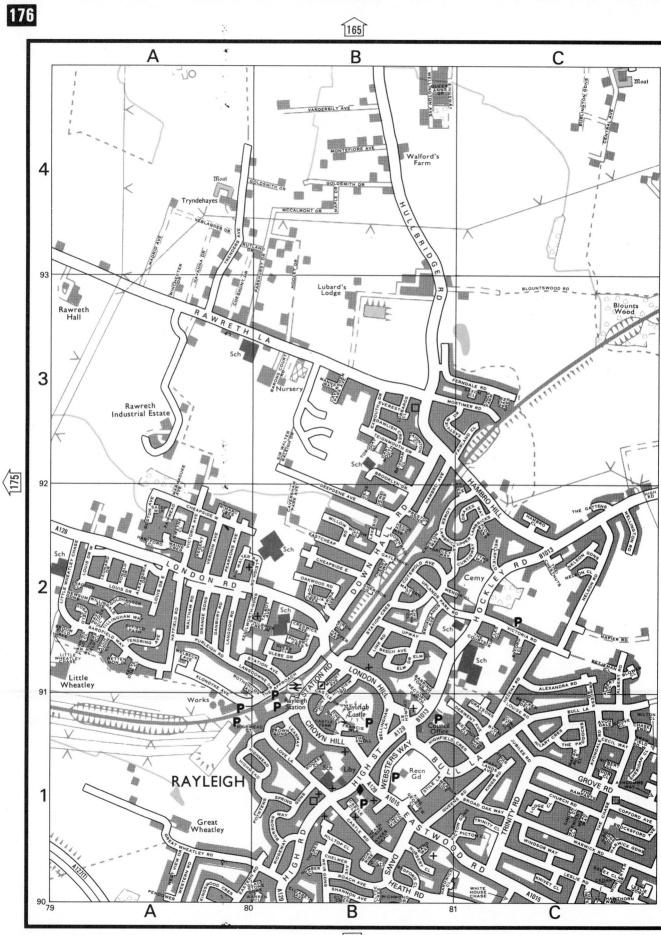

175

188

166

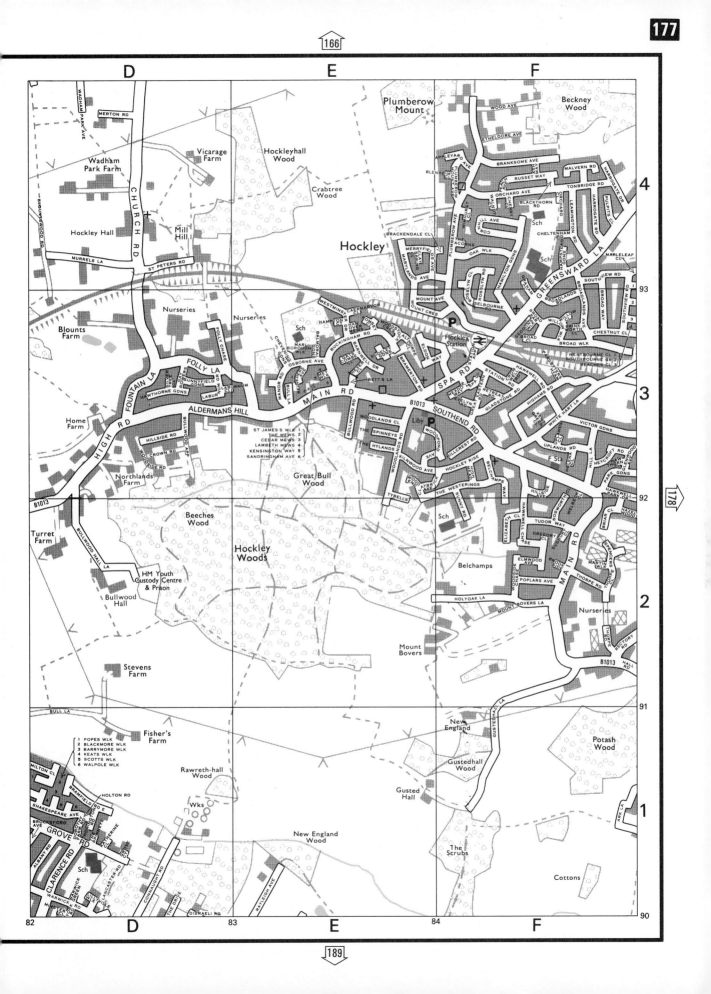

D

E

F

178
189

Beckney Wood

Plumberow Mount

Wadham Park Farm

Merton Rd

Vicarage Farm

Hockleyhall Wood

Crabtree Wood

Mill Hill

Hockley Hall

Hockley

Etheldore Ave

Branksome Ave

Malvern Rd

Russet Way

Tonbridge Rd

Orchard Ave

Blackthorn Rd

Cheltenham Ave

Harrogate Rd

Murrels La

St Peters Rd

Brackendale Cl

Sch

Marleleaf Cl

Merryfields Ave

Oak Wlk

South View Rd

Mount Ave

Broadlands

93

Nurseries

Blounts Farm

Nurseries

Folly Chase

Sch

Westminster

Caernarvon

Hampton

Selbourne Rd

Broadway

Southview Rd

Broad Wlk

Hockley Station

Chestnut Cl

Folly La

Balmoral

Betts La

SPA RD

Station Rd

Hawkwell Rd

Higham

Broad Wlk

Westbourne Cl

Southbourne Gr

Beeches Cl

3

Home Farm

HIGH RD

FOUNTAIN LA

ALDERMANS HILL

MAIN RD

SOUTHEND RD

White Hart La

Victor Gdns

Uplands Rd

Hill La

Park Gdns

Hawkwell Park Dr

Hillside Rd

Crown Rd

Woodside Rd

ST JAMES S WLK 1
THE MEWS 2
CEDAR MEWS 3
LAMBETH MEWS 4
KENSINGTON WAY 5
SANDRINGHAM AVE 6

Liby

Woodlands Cl

The Spinneys

The Hylands

Hillcrest Rd

Hockley Rise

F Sta

Hillside Ave

Northlands Farm

Great Bull Wood

The Westerings

Sch

Hawkwell Chase

Tudor Way

Hazel Wood

92

B1013

Beeches Wood

Hockley Woods

Tyrells

Elizabeth

Gregory Cl

Briar Cl

Martin Wlk

Turret Farm

BULLWOOD HALL LA

HM Youth Custody Centre & Prison

Belchamps

Elmwood Ave

Poplars Ave

MAIN RD

Thorpe Rd

Bullwood Hall

Holyoak La

Mount Bovers La

Nurseries

2

Mount Bovers

B1013

HALL RD

Stevens Farm

91

BULL LA

New England

Potash Wood

Fisher's Farm

1 POPES WLK
2 BLACKMORE WLK
3 BARRYMORE WLK
4 KEATS WLK
5 SCOTTS WLK
6 WALPOLE WLK

Rawreth-hall Wood

Gustedhall Wood

MILTON CL

Bramfield Rd E

Holton Rd

Wks

Gusted Hall

1

Shakespeare Ave

GROVE RD

Catherine Rd

New England Wood

The Scrubs

Ark La

Brocksford Ave

Albany Rd

Lancaster Rd

Connaught Rd

Cottons

CLARENCE RD

Sch

THE DRIVE

Bayleigh Ave

Disraeli Rd

90

82

D

83

E

84

F

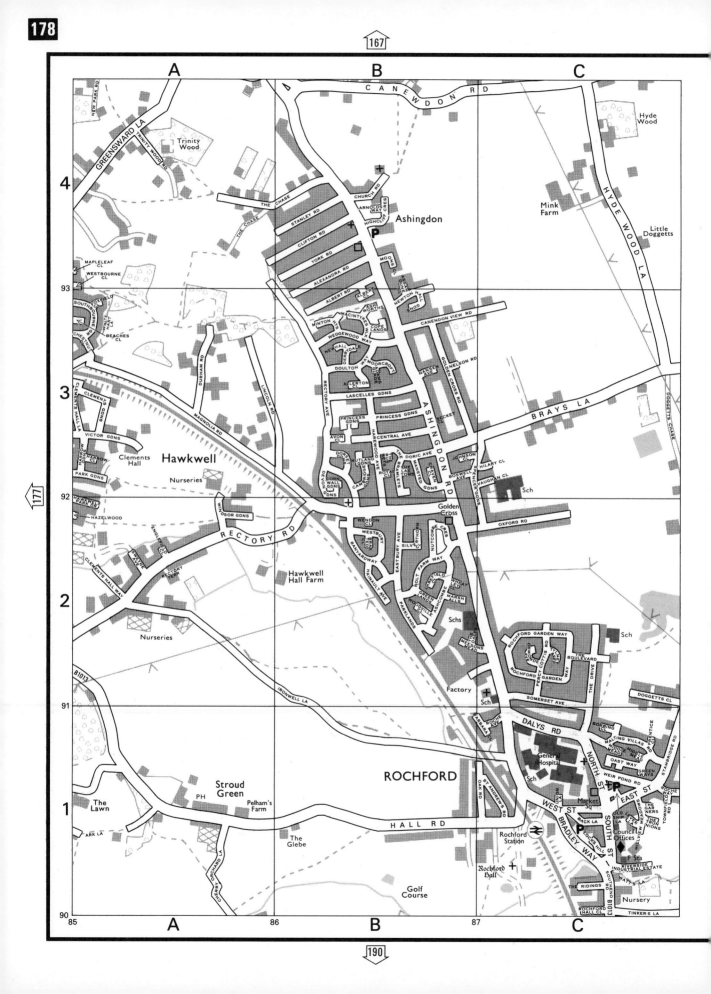

D E F

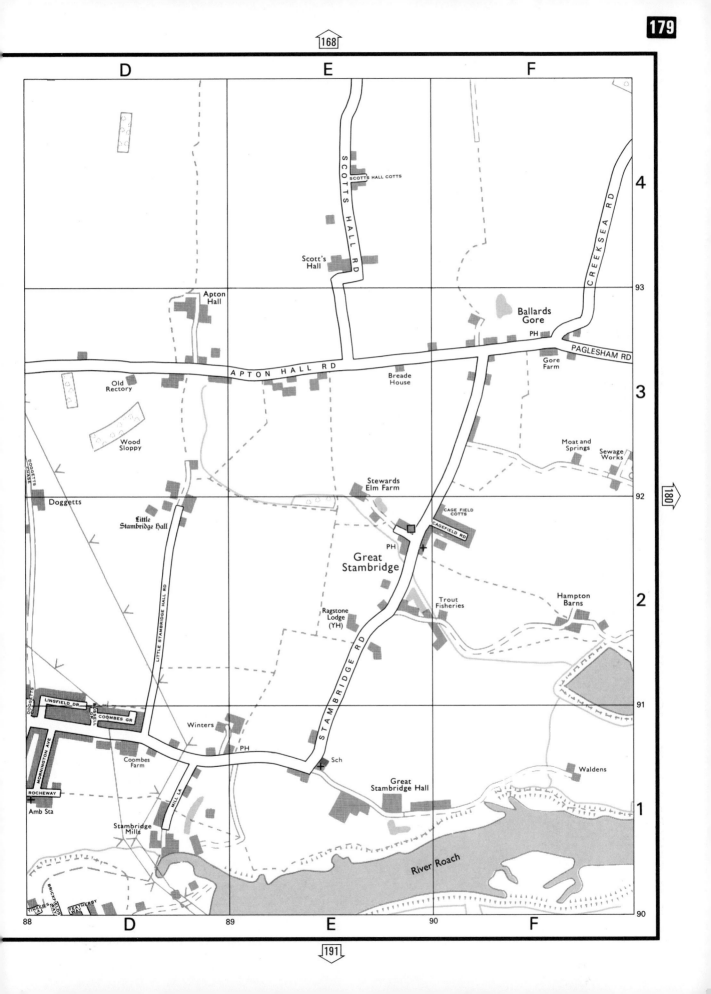

4

SCOTTS HALL RD

SCOTTS HALL COTTS

Scott's
Hall

93

Apton
Hall

Ballards
Gore

PH

PAGLESHAM RD

CREEKSEA RD

Old
Rectory

APTON HALL RD

Breade
House

Gore
Farm

3

Wood
Sloppy

Moat and
Springs

Sewage
Works

Doggetts

DOGGETTS CHASE

Stewards
Elm Farm

92

CAGE FIELD
COTTS

Little
Stambridge Hall

CAGEFIELD RD

PH

Great
Stambridge

Hampton
Barns

2

Ragstone
Lodge
(YH)

Trout
Fisheries

LITTLE STAMBRIDGE HALL RD

STAMBRIDGE RD

91

LINGFIELD DR

COOMBES GR

Winters

MORNINGTON AVE

RUSSELL CL

DOGGETTS CL

Coombes
Farm

PH

Sch

Waldens

ROCHEWAY

+
Amb Sta

MILL LA

Great
Stambridge Hall

1

Stambridge
Mills

River Roach

BRICKFIELD RD

TINKERS LA

FEATHERBY WAY

88 D 89 E 90 F 90

180

169

179

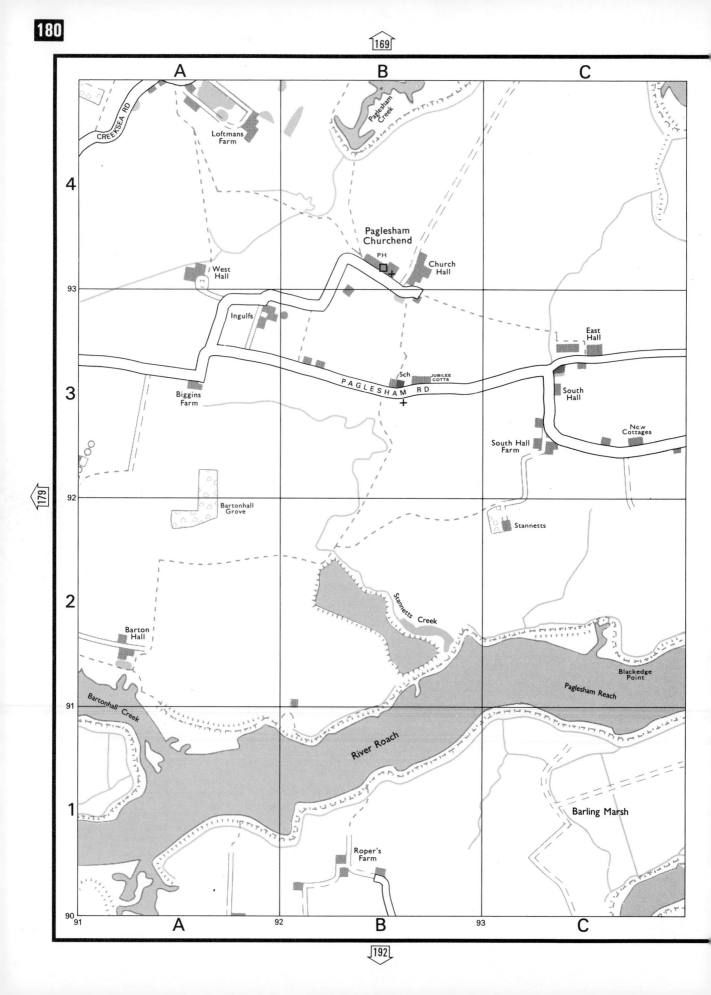

A B C

4

CREEKSEA RD

Loftmans
Farm

Paglesham
Creek

Paglesham
Churchend

93

PH

West
Hall

Church
Hall

Ingulfs

East
Hall

Sch JUBILEE
COTTS

PAGLESHAM RD

South
Hall

3

Biggins
Farm

South Hall
Farm

New
Cottages

92

Bartonhall
Grove

Stannetts

2

Stannetts Creek

Barton
Hall

Blackedge
Point

Paglesham Reach

91

Bartonhall Creek

River Roach

1

Barling Marsh

Roper's
Farm

90

91 92 93

A B C

192

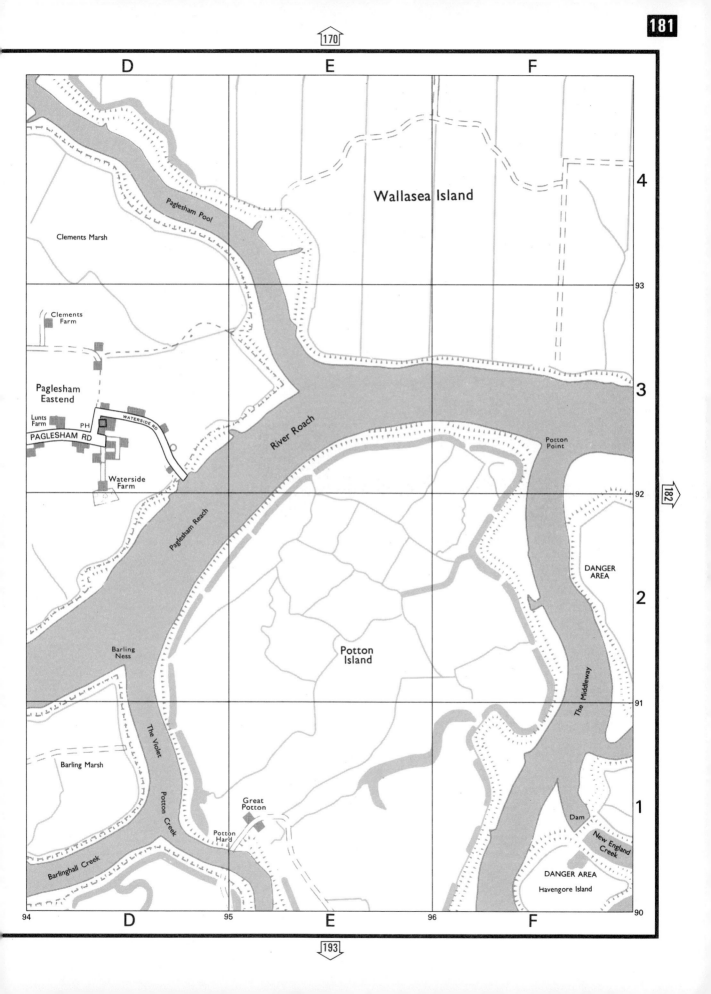

D E F

4 Wallasea Island

Paglesham Pool

Clements Marsh

93

Clements
Farm

3

Paglesham
Eastend

Lunts
Farm

PH

WATERSIDE RD

River Roach

Potton
Point

PAGLESHAM RD

Waterside
Farm

Paglesham Reach

92

DANGER
AREA

2

Barling
Ness

Potton
Island

The Middleway

91

The Violet

Barling Marsh

Potton Creek

Great
Potton

1

Dam

Potton Hard

New England
Creek

Barlinghall Creek

DANGER AREA
Havengore Island

94 D 95 E 96 F 90

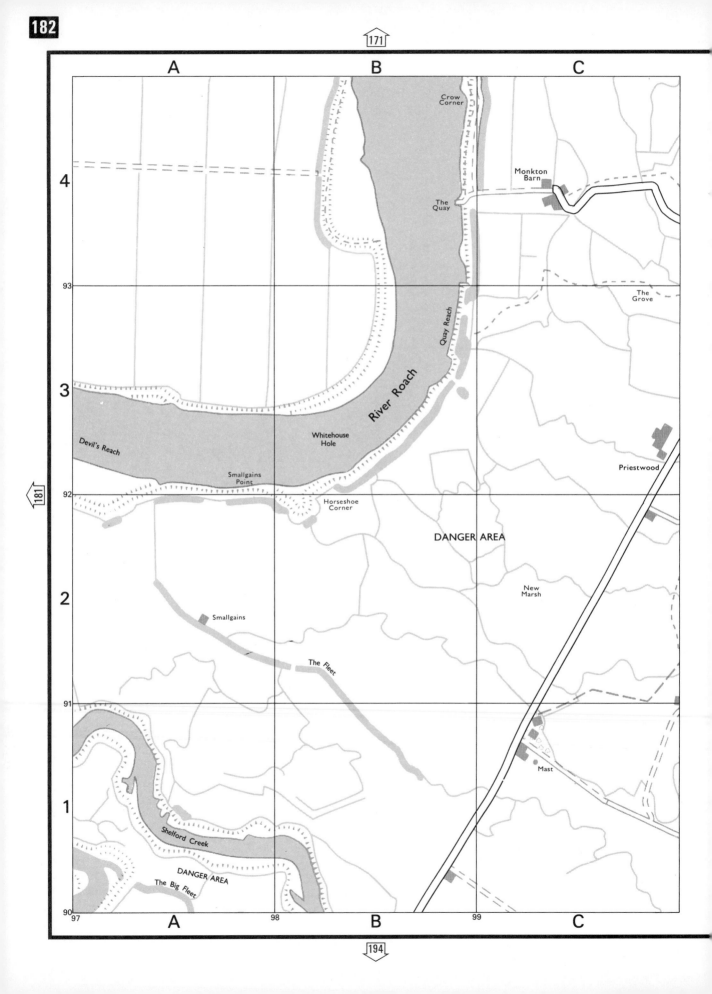

171

A   B   C

Crow
Corner

Monkton
Barn

The Quay

4

The
Grove

93

Quay Reach

River Roach

3

Devil's Reach

Whitehouse
Hole

Priestwood

Smallgains
Point

92

Horseshoe
Corner

DANGER AREA

New
Marsh

2

Smallgains

The Fleet

91

Mast

1

Shelford Creek

DANGER AREA

The Big Fleet

90

A   98   B   99   C

181

194

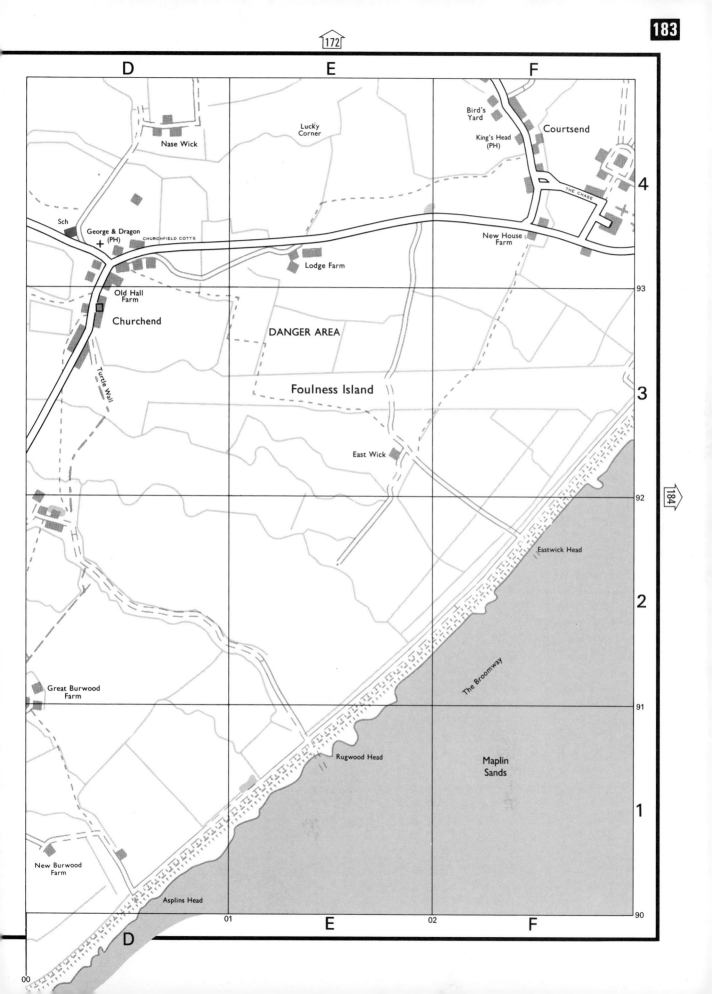

172

D   E   F

Bird's
Yard

Lucky
Corner

King's Head
(PH)

Courtsend

Nase Wick

THE CHASE

4

Sch

George & Dragon
(PH)

CHURCHFIELD COTTS

Lodge Farm

New House
Farm

93

Old Hall
Farm

Churchend

DANGER AREA

Turtle Wall

Foulness Island

3

East Wick

92

184

Eastwick Head

2

The Broomway

Great Burwood
Farm

91

Rugwood Head

Maplin
Sands

1

New Burwood
Farm

Asplins Head

01   E   02   F

90

D

00

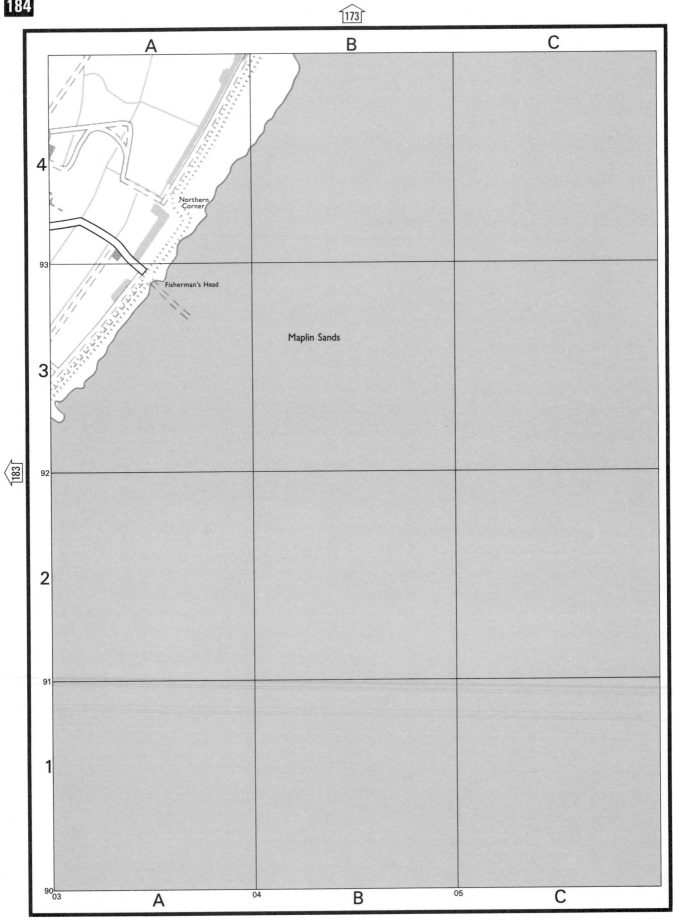

A B C

4

Northern
Corner

93

Fisherman's Head

Maplin Sands

3

92

2

91

1

90

A B C

BASILDON

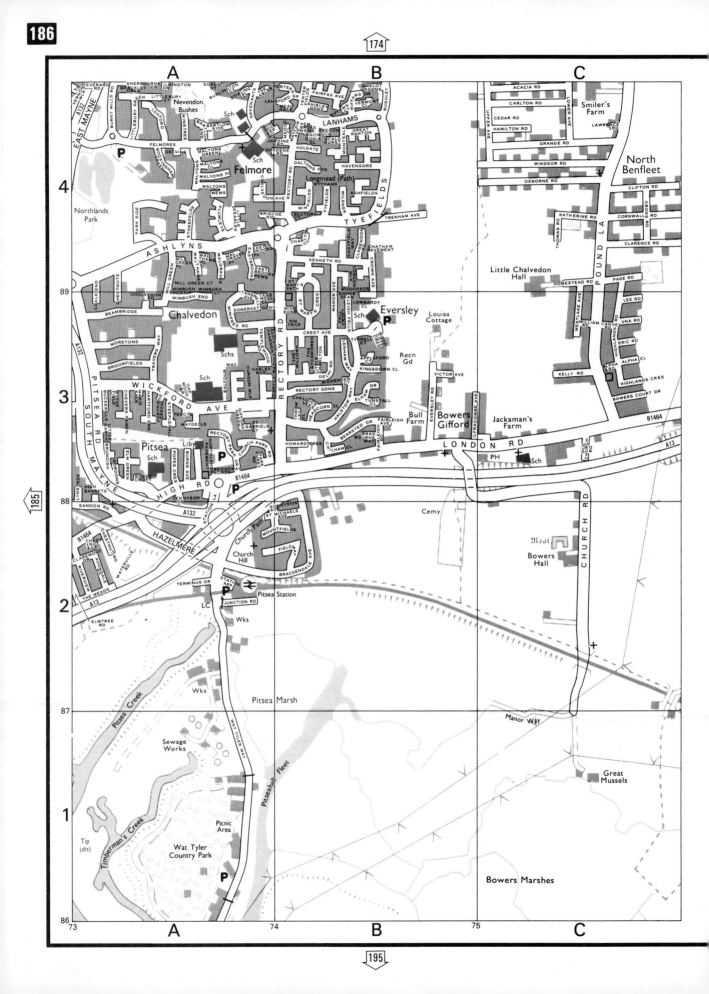

185

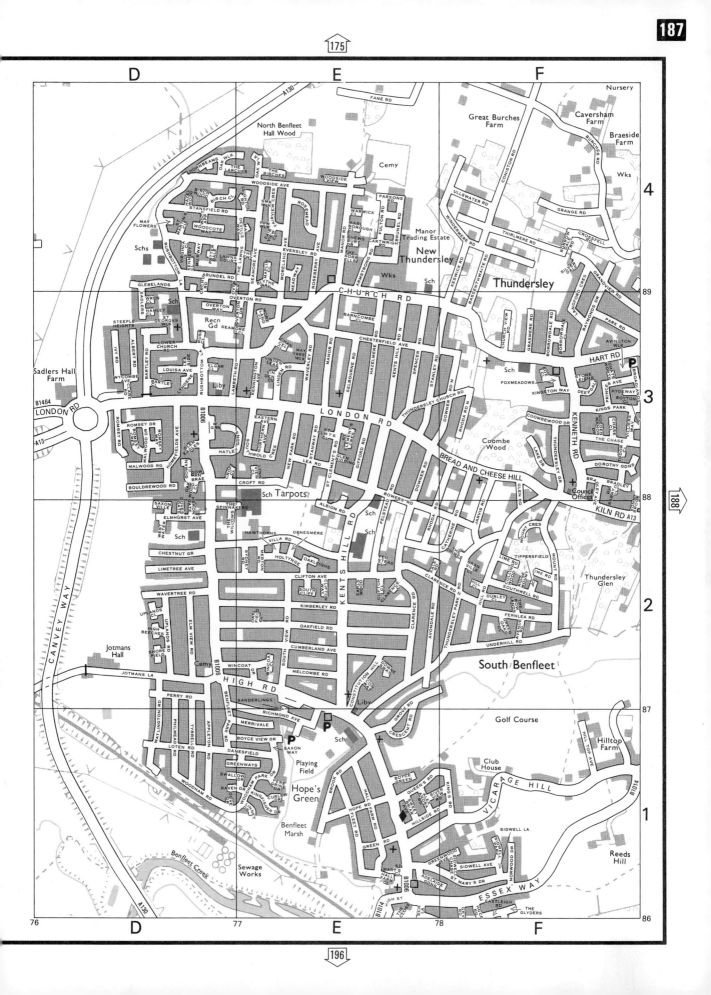

188

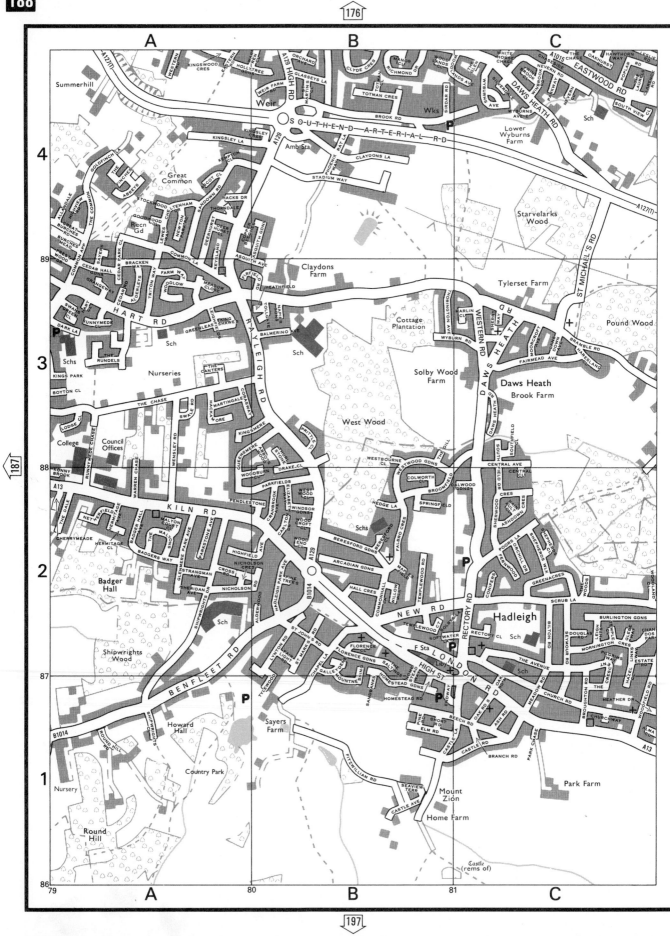

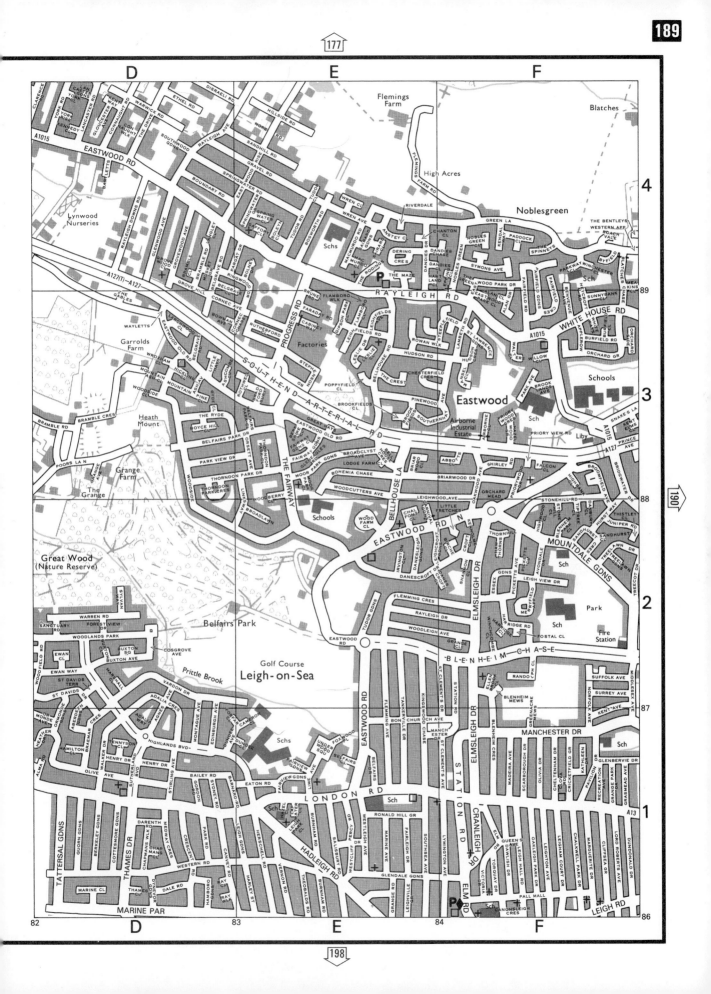

178

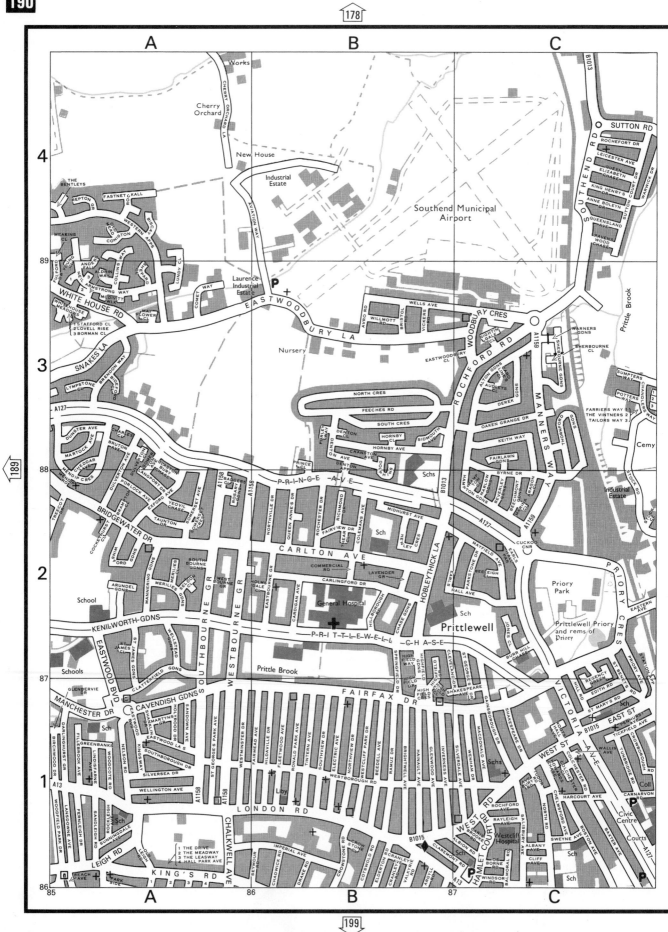

189

199

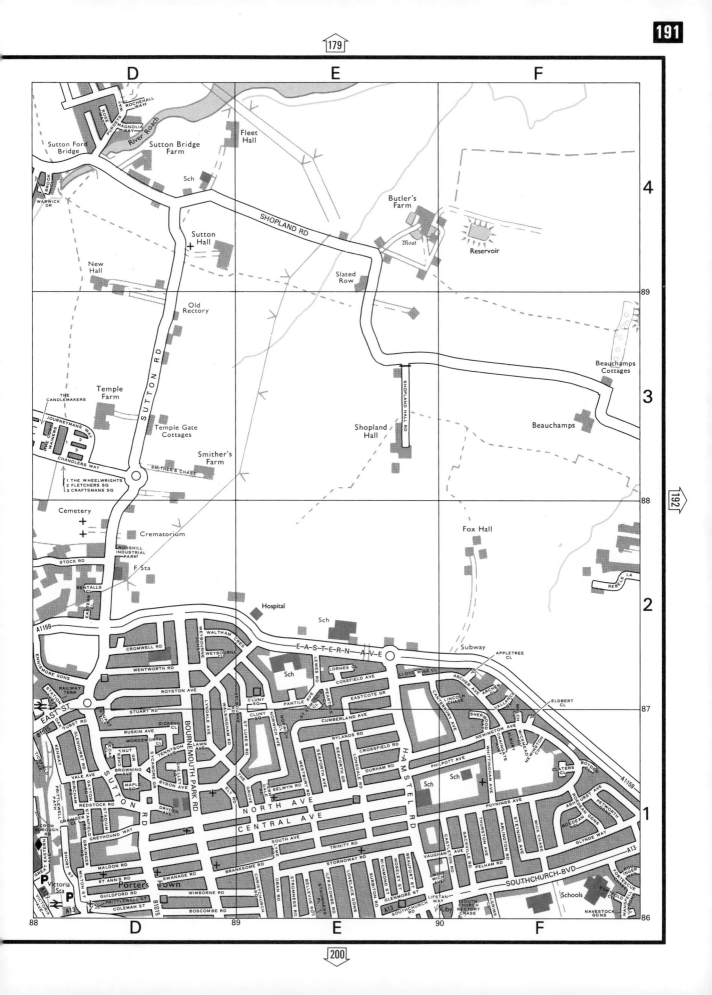

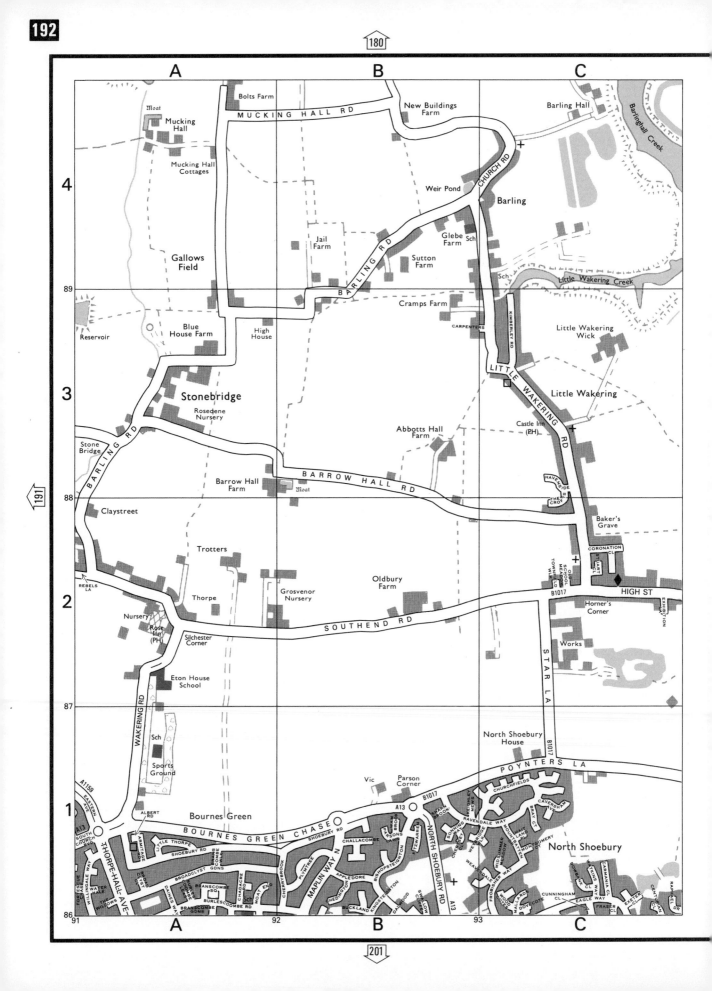

1191

A | **B** | **C**

4

Bolts Farm

New Buildings Farm

Barling Hall

Moat

Mucking Hall

MUCKING HALL RD

Barlinghall Creek

Mucking Hall Cottages

CHURCH RD

Weir Pond

Barling

Gallows Field

Jail Farm

BARLING RD

Glebe Farm

Sch

Sutton Farm

Sch

89

Little Wakering Creek

Cramps Farm

CARPENTERS

Reservoir

Blue House Farm

High House

KIMBERLEY RD

Little Wakering Wick

3

Stonebridge

Rosedene Nursery

LITTLE WAKERING RD

Little Wakering

Stone Bridge

BARLING RD

Abbotts Hall Farm

Castle Inn (PH)

Barrow Hall Farm

Moat

BARROW HALL RD

HAVENSIDE

THE CRO

88

Claystreet

Baker's Grave

CORONATION CL

Trotters

STUART CL

Oldbury Farm

TOWNFIELD WK

OLD SCHOOL MEAD

B1017

2

REBELS LA

Thorpe

Grosvenor Nursery

EXHIBITION

HIGH ST

Nursery

Horner's Corner

Rose Inn (PH)

SOUTHEND RD

Works

Silchester Corner

STAR LA

Eton House School

87

WAKERING RD

North Shoebury House

B1017

Sch

POYNTERS LA

Sports Ground

Vic

Parson Corner

CHURCHFIELDS

KEIGHLEY MEWS

CAVESHAM AVE

BRAY CT

A115Q

EASTERN

1

ALBERT RD

Bournes Green

B1017

A13

North Shoebury

SOUTH CHURCH RD

A13

BOURNES GREEN CHASE

SHOEBURY RD

CHALLACOMBE

NORTH SHOEBURY RD

THORPE-HALL-AVE

ARMITAGE

LITTLE THORPE

SHOEBURY RD

MAPLIN WAY N

A13

86

91 | **A** | **92** | **B** | **93** | **C**

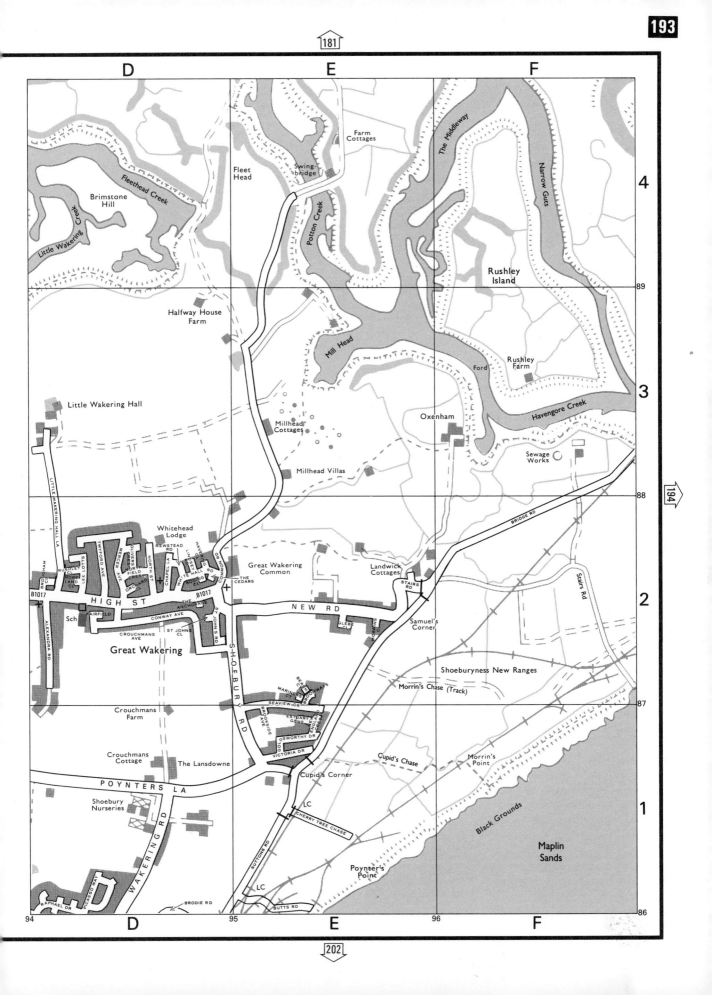

D E F

4

Brimstone
Hill

Fleethead Creek

Fleet
Head

Farm
Cottages

Swing-
bridge

The Middleway

Narrow Guts

Little Wakering Creek

Potton Creek

89

Halfway House
Farm

Mill Head

Rushley
Island

Little Wakering Hall

Millhead
Cottages

Oxenham

Ford

Rushley
Farm

3

Havengore Creek

Millhead Villas

Sewage
Works

88

194

Whitehead
Lodge

Newstead
Rd

Great Wakering
Common

Landwick
Cottages

STAIRS
RD

BRIDGE RD

Stairs Rd

2

LITTLE WAKERING HALL LA

RUSHLEY CL

MORELAND AV

LEE LOTTS

TWYFORD AVE

MERCER AVE

OLIVERS DR

QUERYS DR

ORCHARD

NORTH ST

CHAPEL LA

WHITE HALL RD

RODING

LINDSELL

HAVENGORE DR

CROMWELL DR

THE CEDARS

B1017

HIGH ST

B1017

NEW RD

Samuel's
Corner

Sch

FAIRFIELD

CONWAY AVE

THE
ANCHORAGE

ST JOHNS RD

GLEBE CL

RICHMOND

ALEXANDRA RD

CROUCHMANS
AVE

ST JOHNS
CL

Great Wakering

SHOEBURY RD

Shoeburyness New Ranges

Morrin's Chase (Track)

87

Crouchmans
Farm

MARINE
CT

BEACH
ROW

BROADWAY

SEAVIEW DR

BROOKSIDE AVE

ESTUARY
GDNS

OSWORTHY DR

VICTORIA DR

Cupid's Chase

Morrin's
Point

Crouchmans
Cottage

The Lansdowne

Cupid's Corner

POYNTERS LA

WAKERING RD

Shoebury
Nurseries

LC

CHERRY TREE CHASE

Black Grounds

1

SUTTONS RD

Maplin
Sands

RAPHAEL DR

PICASSO WAY

BRODIE RD

LC

Poynter's
Point

BUTTS RD

94 D 95 E 96 F

86

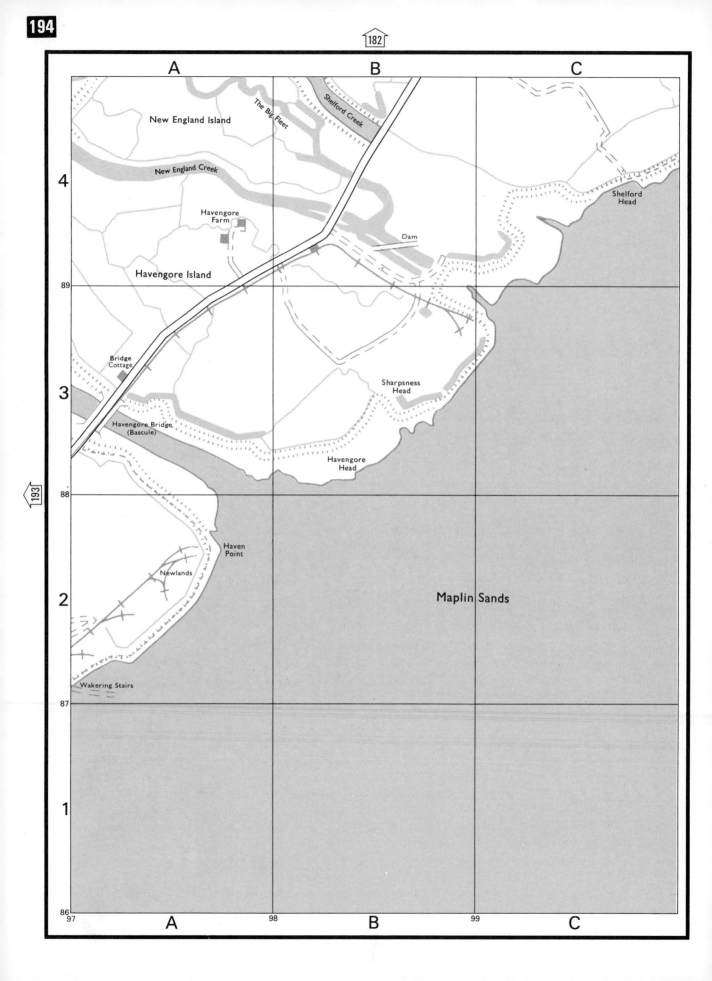

193

A
B
C

New England Island

The Big Fleet

Shelford Creek

New England Creek

Shelford Head

Havengore Farm

Dam

4

Havengore Island

89

Bridge Cottage

Sharpsness Head

3

Havengore Bridge (Bascule)

Havengore Head

88

Haven Point

Newlands

2

Maplin Sands

87

Wakering Stairs

1

86
97
98
99

A
B
C

186

D   E   F

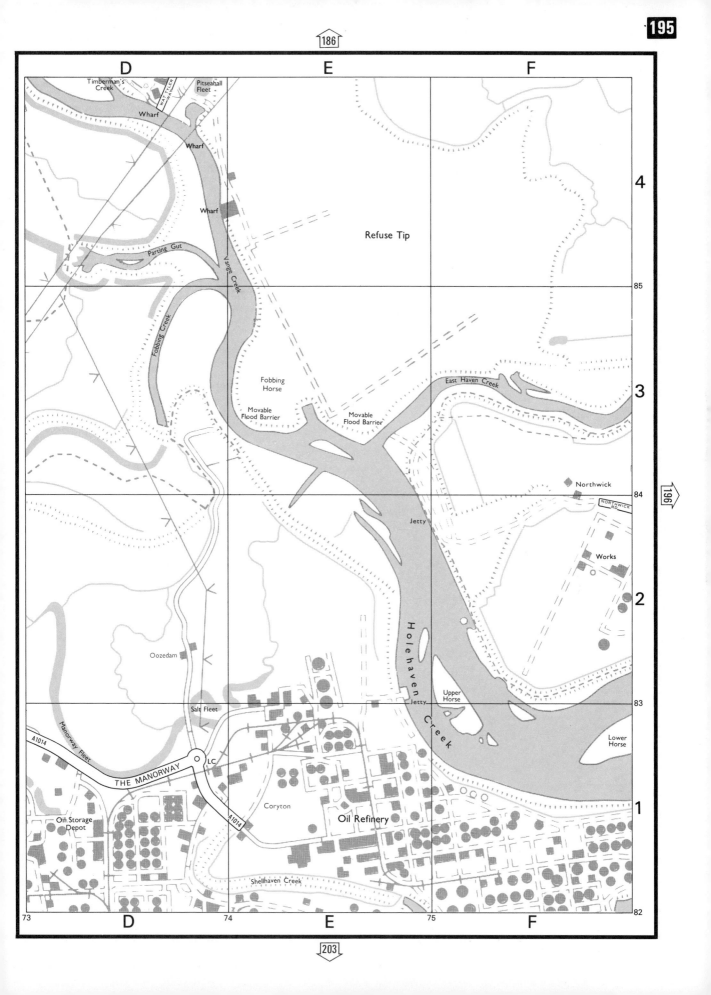

Timberman's
Creek

Pitseahall
Fleet

Wharf

Wharf

4

Wharf

Refuse Tip

Parting Gut

Vange Creek

85

Fobbing Creek

Fobbing
Horse

East Haven Creek

3

Movable
Flood Barrier

Movable
Flood Barrier

Northwick

84

196

Jetty

NORTHWICK
RD

Works

2

Oozedam

Holehaven Creek

Salt Fleet

Upper
Horse

83

A1014

Manorway Fleet

THE MANORWAY

LC

Jetty

Lower
Horse

1

A1014

Coryton

Oil Refinery

Oil Storage
Depot

Shellhaven Creek

82

73   D   74   E   75   F

203

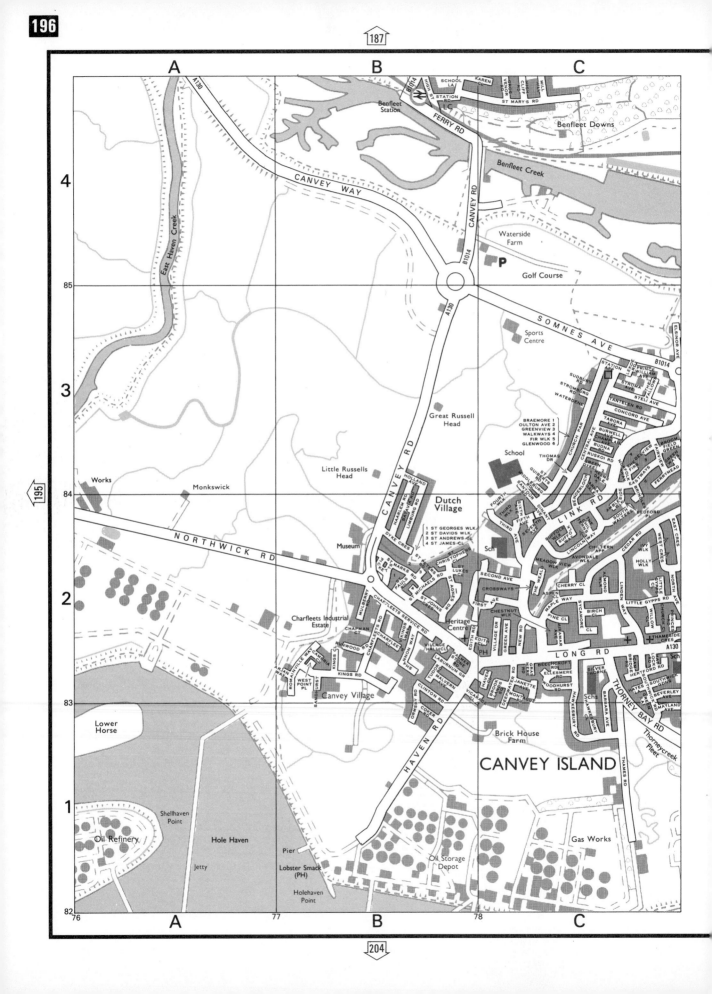

195

CANVEY ISLAND

A130

CANVEY WAY

FERRY RD

Benfleet Station

Benfleet Downs

Benfleet Creek

CANVEY RD

B1014

Waterside Farm

P

Golf Course

SOMNES AVE

Sports Centre

HIGH ST

SCHOOL LA

STATION RD

LC

KAREN CL

ST MARYS RD

MILL HILL

ELSINOR AVE

B1014

STATION RD

Great Russell Head

Little Russells Head

East Haven Creek

Works

Monkswick

NORTHWICK RD

CANVEY RD

Dutch Village

Museum

1 ST GEORGES WLK.
2 ST DAVIDS WLK.
3 ST ANDREWS CL
4 ST JAMES CL

BRAEMORE 1
OULTON AVE 2
GREENVIEW 3
WALKWAYS 4
FIR WLK 5
GLENWOOD 6

School

LINK RD

School

Sch

HOLLAND RD

HAAREM RD

LIMBURG RD

DYKE CRES

ST MARKS RD

ST PETERS CL

ST CHRISTOPHERS RD

ST LUKES CL

SECOND AVE

CROSSWAYS

FIRST AVE

ST MICHAELS RD

ST JOHNS CRES

ST AGNES CL

MEADOW VIEW

THE WEAL

AVONDALE WLK

CHILTERN WLK

ALMOND WLK

LINDEN WAY

WILLOW WLK

NORTH AVE

CHURCH RD

EAST CRES

WEST CRES

HOLLY WLK

CHERRY CL

CEDAR RD

BEDFORD

IVY WLK

SILVER HORN

LONG RD

A130

Sch

Charfleets Industrial Estate

CHAPMAN CT

CHARFLEETS SERVICE RD

CHARFLEETS RD

RUNWOOD RD

ROMAINVILLE WAY

KINGS CL

KINGS RD

WEST POINT PL

CAMBRIA CL

Canvey Village

SANDHURST

VILLAGE HALL CL

LABURNUM GR

TUDOR

ST ANNE RD

MALVERN

CLINTON RD

COKER RD

ORMSBY RD

HAVEN RD

VICARAGE CL

EDITH RD

EDITH CL

PH

Heritage Centre

Village Dr

Green Ave

New Rd

CHESTNUT WLK

PINE CL

MAPLE WAY

SYCAMORE CL

BIRCH CL

CHERRY CL

Brick House Farm

Oil Storage Depot

Gas Works

Lower Horse

Shellhaven Point

Oil Refinery

Hole Haven

Jetty

Pier

Lobster Smack (PH)

Holehaven Point

THORNEY BAY RD

Thorneycreek Fleet

THAMES RD

BEVERLEY RD

BARBARA AVE

HERTFORD RD

MAYLAND RD

76 **77** **78**

82 83 84 85

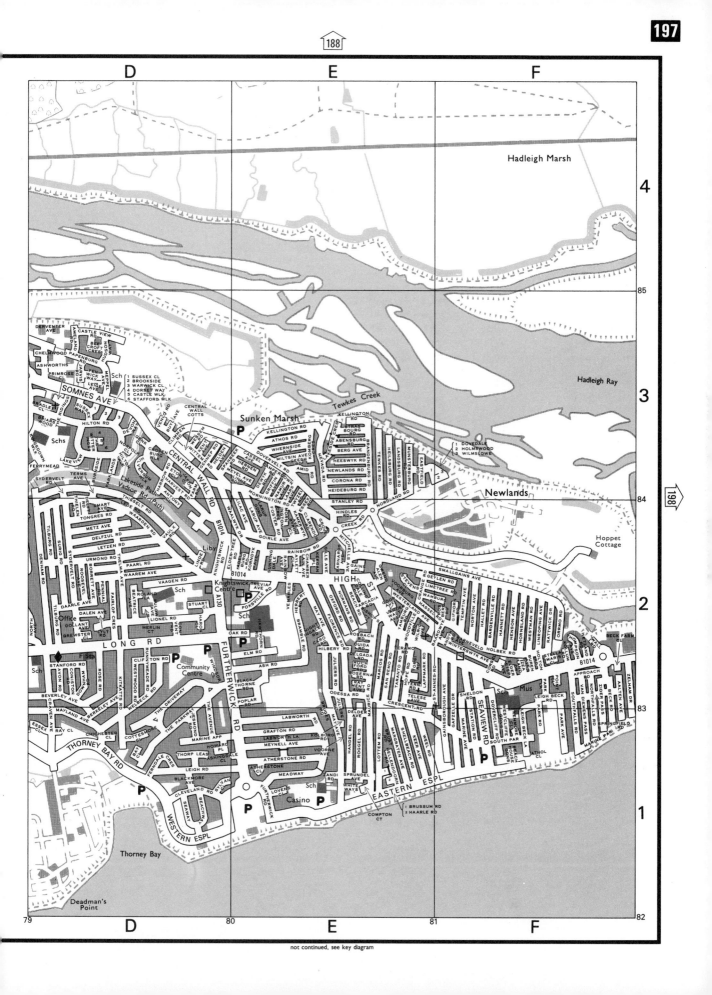

D　　　　　　E　　　　　　F

4

85

Hadleigh Marsh

Hadleigh Ray

3

Tewkes Creek

Sunken Marsh

1 SUSSEX CL
2 BROOKSIDE
3 WARWICK CL
4 DORSET WAY
5 CASTLE WLK
6 STAFFORD WLK

SOMNES AVE

CENTRAL WALL COTTS

Kellington Rd

1 DOVEDALE
2 HOLMSWOOD
3 WILMSLOWE

Newlands

84

Hoppet Cottage

CENTRAL WALL RD

B1014

Libv

B1014

HIGH ST

SMALLGAINS AVE

2

Knightswick Centre

Beck Farm Cl

B1014

Mus

LONG RD

FURTHERWICK RD

Office

Community Centre

SEAVIEW RD

83

THORNEY BAY RD

WESTERN ESPL

EASTERN ESPL

Casino

1 BRUSSUM RD
2 HAARLE RD

COMPTON CT

1

Thorney Bay

Deadman's Point

79　　　　　　80　　　　　　81　　　　　　82

D　　　　　　E　　　　　　F

189

197

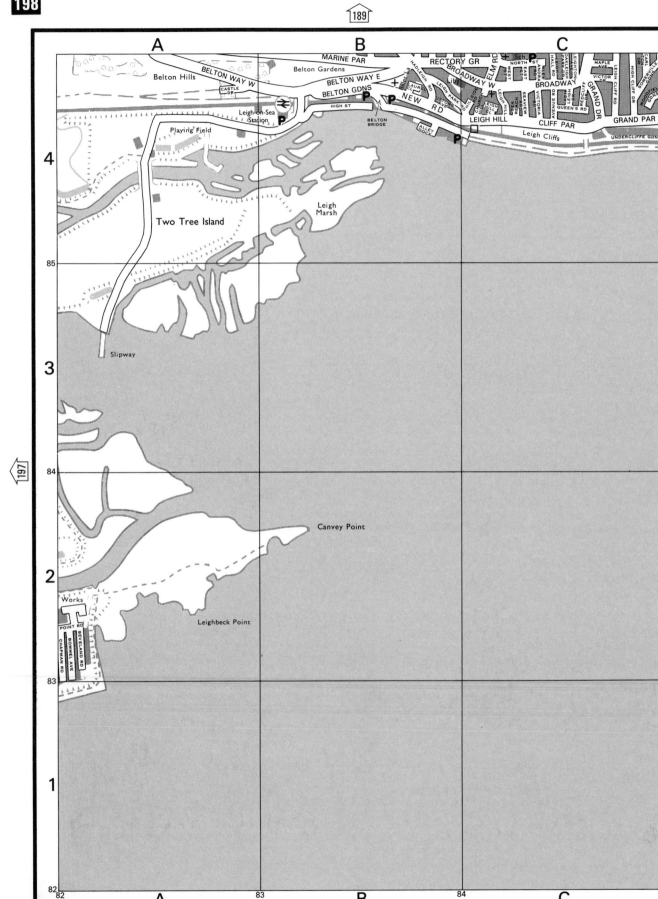

A

B

C

4

85

3

84

2

83

1

82

82 · 83 · 84

A · B · C

MARINE PAR

BELTON WAY W

Belton Gardens

Belton Hills

CASTLE DR

BELTON WAY E

BELTON GDNS

Leigh-on-Sea Station

HIGH ST

Playing Field

Two Tree Island

Leigh Marsh

Slipway

Canvey Point

Works

Leighbeck Point

POINT RD

CHAPMAN RD

BOMMEL AVE

BEVELAND RD

RECTORY GR

BROADWAY W

ELM RD

Sch

BROADWAY

GRAND DR

MAPLE AVE

HIGH CLIFF DR

VICTOR DR

CARL DR

SOMERVILLE GDNS

WOODFIELD GDNS

NEW RD

BELTON BRIDGE

ALLEY DOCK

LEIGH HILL

CLIFF PAR

Leigh Cliffs

GRAND PAR

UNDERCLIFFE GDNS

HADLEIGH RD

LEIGH PARK RD

NORTH

EAST

WEST

SEAVIEW

AVE

VICTORIA

QUEEN'S RD

HALL RD

LEIGH HILL

ST ANDREWS

LEIGHTON AVE

OAKLEIGH PARK DR

REDCLIFF DR

HAVEN

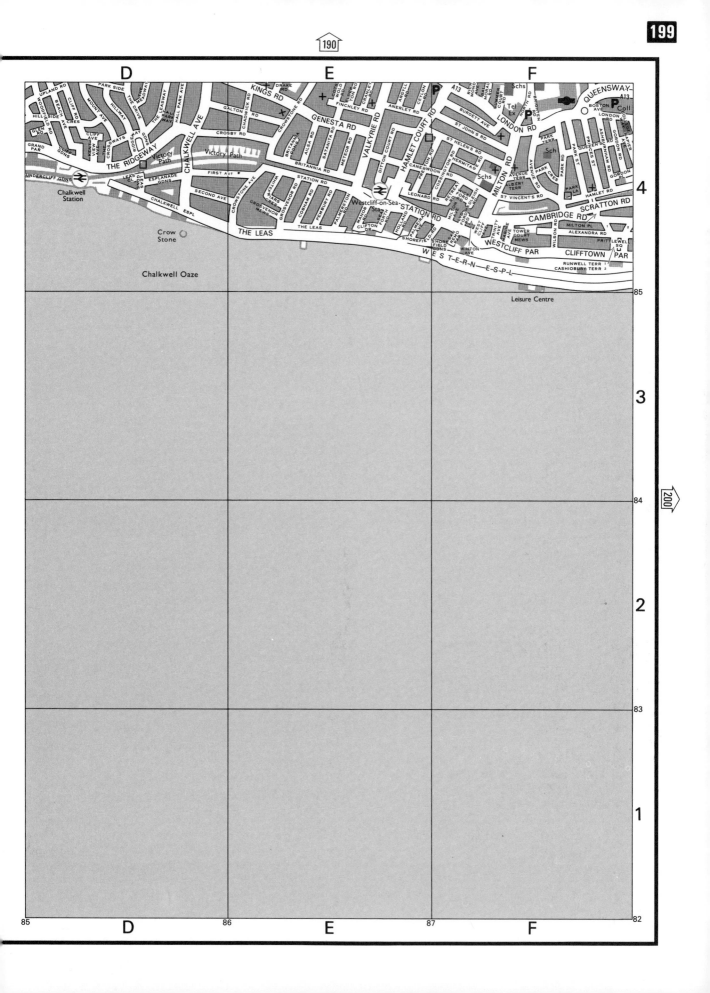

Chalkwell Oaze

Crow Stone

Chalkwell Station

Leisure Centre

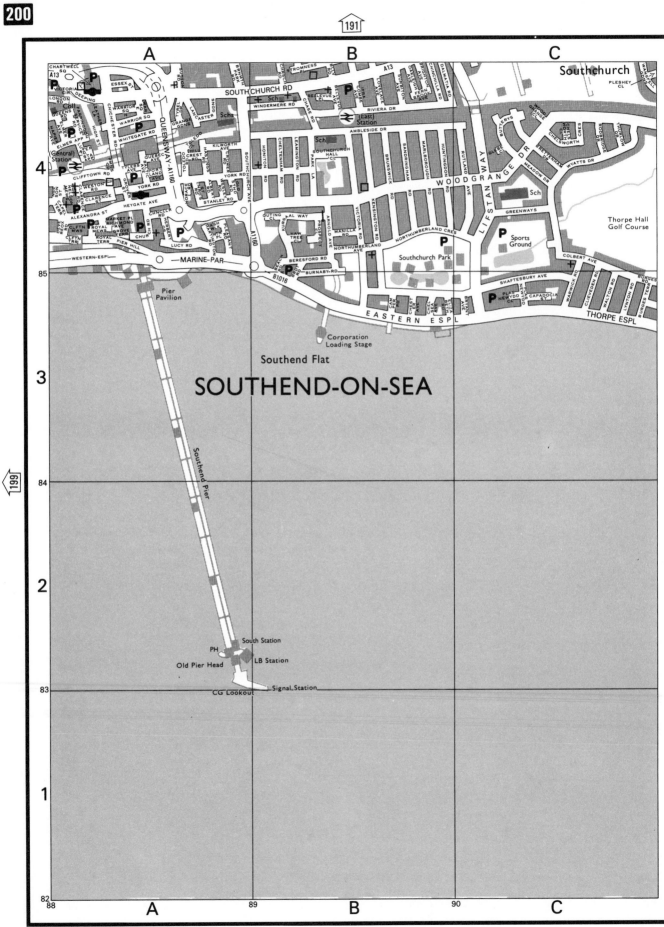

SOUTHEND-ON-SEA

Southchurch

Southend Flat

Southend Pier

Pier Pavilion

Corporation
Loading Stage

South Station
PH
LB Station
Old Pier Head
CG Lookout   Signal Station

Thorpe Hall
Golf Course

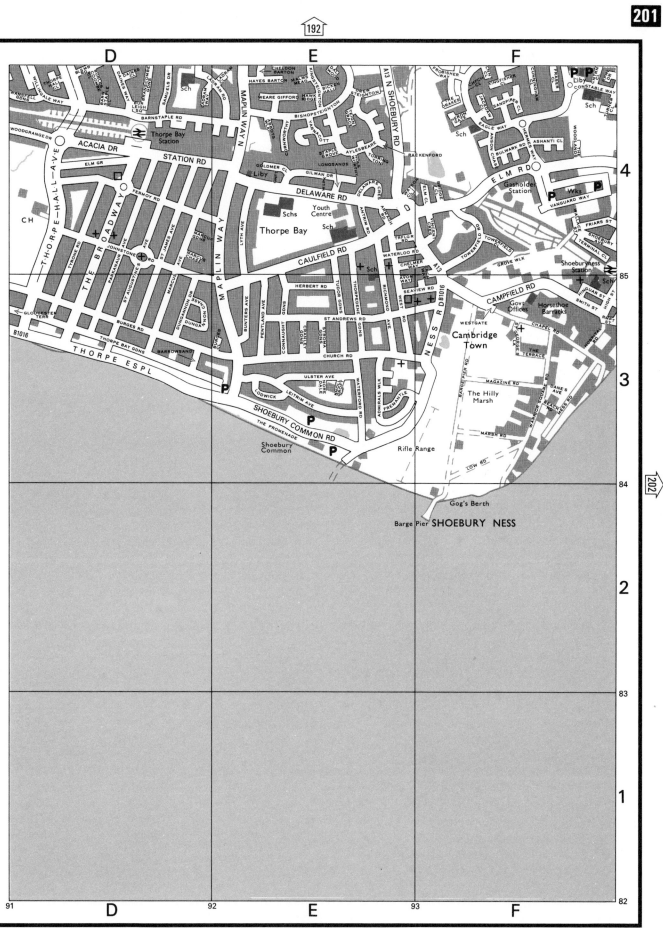

202

SHOEBURY NESS

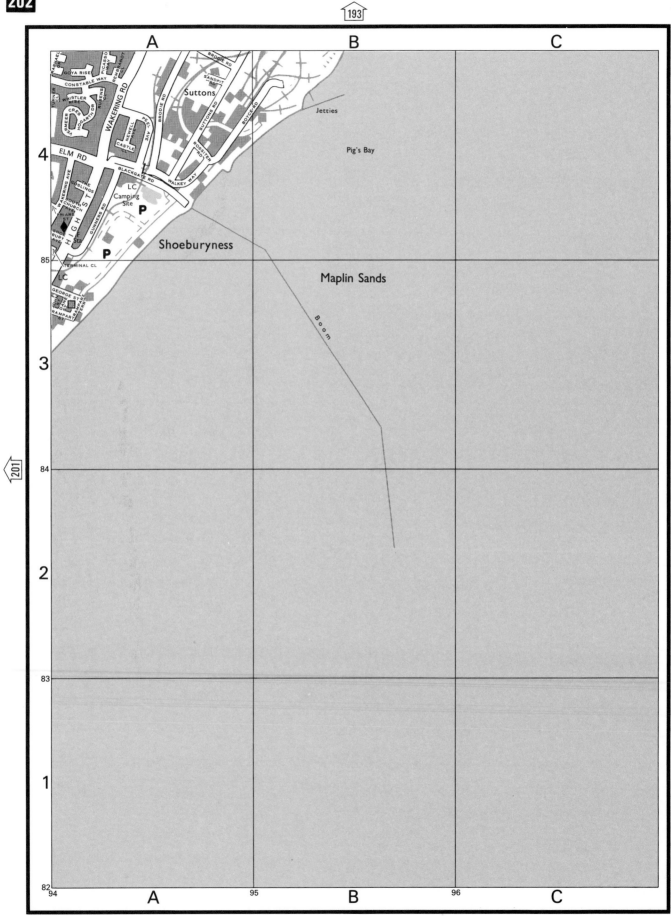

A   B   C

201

RAPHAEL
GOYA RISE
CONSTABLE WAY
PICASSO
REMBRANDT
BRODIE RD
SANDPIT RD
Suttons
TURNER CL
WHISTLER RISE
VERMEER CRES
HOGARTH DR
RUBENS CL
WAKERING RD
BRODIE RD
SUTTONS RD
BOYCE RD
Jetties
PEEL AVE
CASTLE CL
NEWELL APPR
FORSTER ROAD
Pig's Bay
ELM RD
WALKEY WAY
BLACKGATE RD
WAKERING AVE
THE GOSLINGS
SOUTH CHURCH
HIGH ST
CASTLE CL
GUNNERS RD
LC
Camping
Site
P
FRIARS
SHOE
BURY
AVE
P
Shoeburyness
Maplin Sands
TERMINAL CL
LC
GEORGE ST
RAMPART ST
ST
FERRY
Boom

85

84

83

82
94   95   96

4

3

2

1

A   B   C

195
204

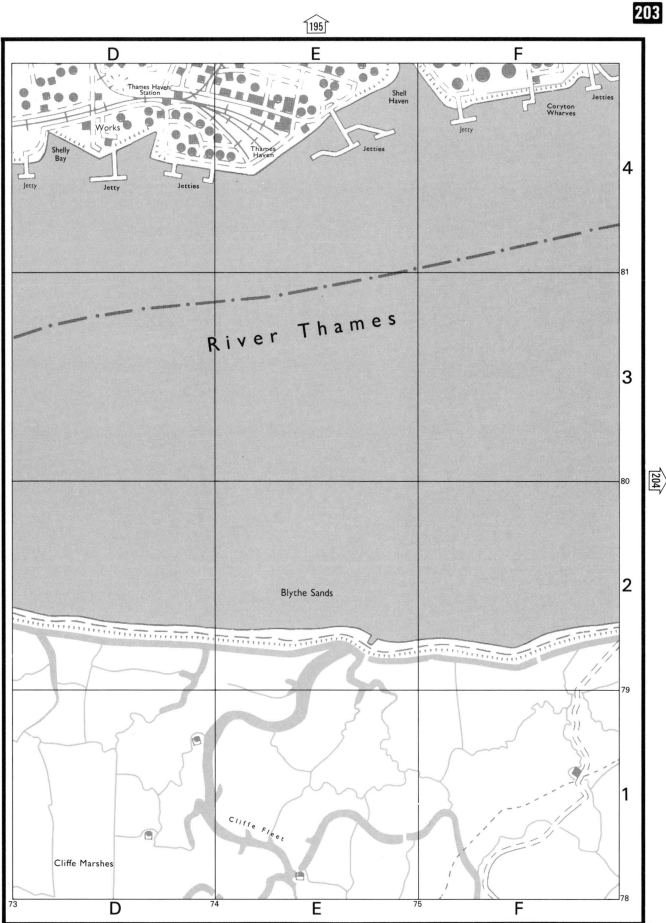

D   E   F

Thames Haven Station

Shell Haven

Coryton Wharves

Jetties

Works

Jetty

Shelly Bay

Thames Haven

Jetties

Jetty

Jetty

Jetty

Jetties

4

81

River Thames

3

80

2

Blythe Sands

79

Cliffe Fleet

1

Cliffe Marshes

78

73   D   74   E   75   F

not continued, see key diagram

196

203

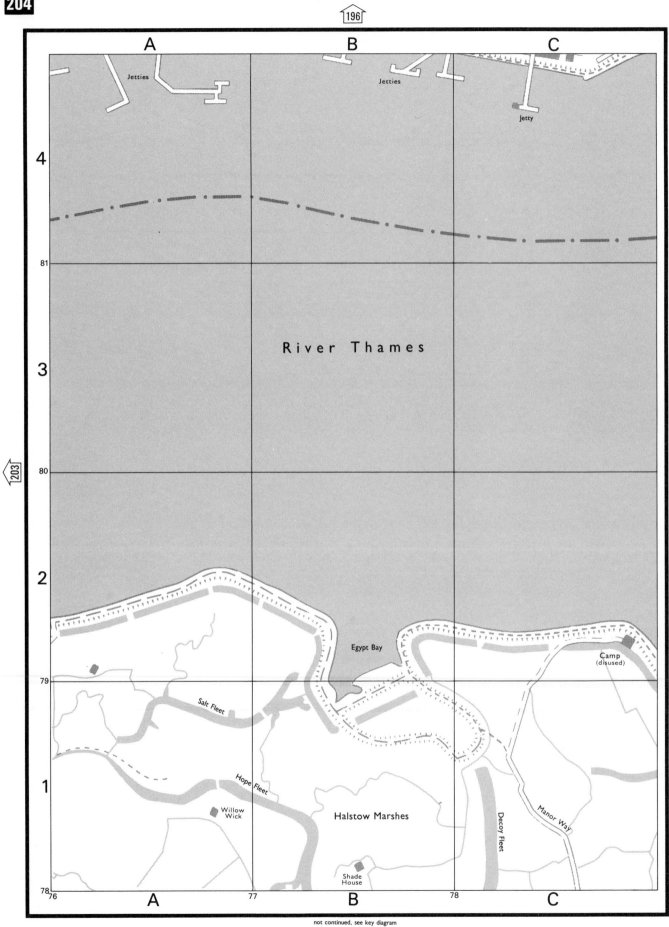

A · B · C

Jetties

Jetties

Jetty

4

81

River Thames

3

80

2

Egypt Bay

Camp
(disused)

79

Salt Fleet

Hope Fleet

1

Willow
Wick

Halstow Marshes

Decoy Fleet

Manor Way

Shade
House

78 76 · 77 · 78

A · B · C

not continued, see key diagram

USER'S NOTES

EXPLANATION OF THE STREET INDEX REFERENCE SYSTEM

Street names are listed alphabetically and show the locality, the map page number and a reference to the square in which the name falls on the map page.

Example: Cedar Way.   Gt Ben...*89* F4

Cedar Way	This is the full street name, which may have been abbreviated on the map.
Gt Ben	This is the abbreviation for the town, village or locality in which the street falls.
89	This is the page number of the map on which the street name appears.
F4	The letter and figure indicate the square on the map in which the centre of the street falls. The square can be found at the junction of the vertical column carrying the appropriate letter and the horizontal row carrying the appropriate figure.

ABBREVIATIONS USED IN THE INDEX
Road Names

Approach	App		North	N
Avenue	Ave		Orchard	Orch
Broadway	Bwy		Parade	Par
By-Pass	By-Ps		Passage	Pas
Causeway	Cswy		Place	Pl
Common	Comm		Pleasant	Plea
Corner	Cnr		Precinct	Prec
Cottages	Cotts		Promenade	Prom
Court	Ct		Road	Rd
Crescent	Cres		South	S
Drive	Dri		Square	Sq
Drove	Dro		Street, Saint	St
East	E		Terrace	Terr
Gardens	Gdns		Walk	Wlk
Grove	Gr		West	W
Heights	Hts		Yard	Yd
Lane	La			

Towns, Villages and Rural Localities

Aldham	Ald	65	D4
Alphamstone	Alph	18	C2
Alresford	Alres	88	A4
Althorne	Alth	158	A2
Ardleigh	Ard	51	F4
Asheldham	Ashel	160	A4
Ashen	Ashe	3	E1
Ashingdon	Ashi	178	B4
Barling	Barl	192	C4
Basildon	Basil	185	E2
Beaumont	Beau	73	F4
Belchamp Otten	Bel O	10	B4
Belchamp St Paul	Bel S P	5	D1
Belchamp Walter	Bel W	11	D3
Birch	Birch	84	A2
Black Notley	Bl Not	78	A3
Boreham	Bore	128	C4
Boxted	Box	31	F4
Bradfield	Brad	36	C1
Bradwell	Bradw	61	E1
Bradwell-on-Sea	Brad O S	137	D1
Braintree	Brain	59	E2
Brightlingsea	Brigh	106	B3
Broomfield	Broom	127	D4
Bulmer	Bul	11	F3
Bures	Bures	28	C4
Burnham-On-Crouch	Burn	170	B3
Canewdon	Cane	168	C1
Canvey Island	Canv	196	C1
Castle Hedingham	Ca Hed	15	F2
Cattawade	Catt	35	E4
Cavendish	Cav	1	B1
Chelmsford	Chelm	127	D2
Churchend	Church	183	D3
Clacton-on-Sea	Clact	110	A1
Clare	Cla	4	B4
Coggeshall	Cogg	63	D2
Colchester	Colch	67	E4
Cold Norton	Col N	155	F3
Colne Engaine	Col En	27	D1
Copford	Copf	65	E2
Corringham	Corr	185	D1
Danbury	Dan	142	C4
Dedham	Ded	33	F3
Dengie	Deng	160	B4
Earls Colne	Ea Col	45	E3
East Hanningfield	E Han	153	E4
East Mersea	E Mers	105	E1
Eight Ash Green	E A Gr	66	A4
Elmstead Market	Elmst M	70	A3
Fairstead	Fair	96	A3
Faulkbourne	Faulk	97	D4
Feering	Fee	81	F3
Fingringhoe	Fing	86	C3
Fordham	Ford	47	E3
Foxearth	Fox	6	B3
Frating	Frat	70	C1
Frinton-on-Sea	Frin	96	A3
Gestingthorpe	Gest	10	B1
Glemsford	Glems	2	B2
Goldhanger	Gold	133	F4
Gosfield	Gos	42	C4
Great Baddow	Gt Bad	140	C4
Great Bentley	Gt Ben	89	F4
Great Braxted	Gt Brx	99	E1
Great Bromley	Gt Bro	52	C1
Great Henny	Gt H	18	B4
Great Horkesley	Gt Hor	31	D1
Great Leighs	Gt Le	95	D4
Great Maplestead	Gt Map	16	B1
Great Oakley	Gt Oak	56	B2
Great Stambridge	Gt Stam	179	E2
Great Tey	Gt T	64	B4
Great Totham	Gt Tot	116	B3
Great Wakering	Gt Wak	193	D2
Great Wigborough	Gt Wig	102	C2
Great Yeldham	Gt Y	9	D1
Hadleigh	Hadl	188	C2
Halstead	Hals	25	F1
Harwich	Harw	40	B2
Hatfield Peverel	Hat Pev	114	A2
Hawkwell	Hawk	178	A3
Hazeleigh	Haze	144	A2
Higham	High	22	A2
Hockley	Hock	177	E4
Hullbridge	Hull	165	E1
Kelvedon	Kelv	81	E1
Lamarsh	Lam	19	E2
Langenhoe	Lang	86	A1
Langford	Langf	131	E4
Langham	Langh	32	C2
Latchingdon	Latch	157	D3
Lawford	Lawf	35	D2
Layer Breton	Lay Br	84	A1
Layer Marney	Lay M	101	E4
Layer-de-la-Haye	Lay H	84	C3
Little Baddow	Lit Bad	129	E2
Little Bentley	Lit Ben	71	F4
Little Braxted	Lit Brx	98	B1
Little Bromley	Lit Bro	53	D3
Little Clacton	Lit Cla	91	E2
Little Horkesley	Lit Hor	30	C2
Little Maplestead	Lit Map	17	D1
Little Oakley	Lit Oak	57	D4
Little Totham	Lit Tot	117	D2
Little Waltham	Lit Wal	112	A4
Little Yeldham	Lit Y	9	F2
Long Melford	L Mel	7	E4
Maldon	Mald	131	F1
Manningtree	Mann	35	E3
Margaretting	Marg	139	D1
Marks Tey	Mks T	65	D2
Mayland	May	158	A4
Messing	Mess	82	B1
Middleton	Midd	12	C2
Mistley	Mist	36	A2
Mount Bures	M Bure	28	C3
Mundon	Mund	145	F1
Nayland	Nay	20	A1
North Fambridge	N Fam	167	D4
Ovington	Ovi	4	A1
Paglesham Churchend	Pag Ch	180	B4
Panfield	Pan	59	D4
Pebmarsh	Peb	27	D4
Peldon	Peld	103	E3
Pentlow	Pent	5	F3
Purleigh	Purl	144	B1
Ramsey	Rams	39	D1
Rayleigh	Rayl	176	A1
Rayne	Ray	59	D1
Rettendon	Rett	153	D1
Ridgewell	Ridge	8	A3
Rivenhall	Rive	98	A4
Rochford	Roch	178	B1
Rowhedge	Rowh	86	C4
Runwell	Runw	163	F1
Sandon	Sand	141	E3
Shotley Gate	Sho G	40	A4
Sible Hedingham	Si Hed	15	F1
Silver End	Silv E	79	F2
South Benfleet	S Ben	187	F2
South Hanningfield	S Han	163	E4
South Woodham Ferrers	S Woo F	165	F4
Southend-On-Sea	South	200	B3
Southminster	Soum	159	E2
Springfield	Sprin	127	F3
St Lawrence	St L	148	C3
St Osyth	St O	108	A2
Stanway	Stanw	66	B3
Steeple	Steep	147	F2
Stisted	Stis	61	E3
Stonebridge	Stobr	192	A3
Stow Maries	Stow M	155	E2
Stratford St Mary	Str S M	22	B1
Sudbury	Sud	12	B4
Tendring	Tend	12	C3
Terling	Terl	96	B2
Thorpe-le-Soken	Th L S	74	A1
Thorrington	Thor	89	D3
Thundersley	Thund	187	F4
Tillingham	Till	149	F2
Tiptree	Tipt	100	A3
Tollesbury	Tolle	119	E1
Tolleshunt D'Arcy	Toll D	118	B2
Tolleshunt Knights	Toll K	101	D2
Tolleshunt Major	Toll M	117	C2
Toppesfield	Topp	14	B4
Twinstead	Twin	18	B3
Tye Green	T Gr	78	C3
Ulting	Ult	130	B4
Virley	Virl	119	D4
Wakes Colne	Wa Col	46	B3
Walton on the Naze	Walt	94	B4
Weeley	Weel	72	C1
West Bergholt	W Berg	48	C2
West Hanningfield	W Han	152	A2
West Mersea	W Mers	121	E3
Wethersfield	Weth	23	D1
White Notley	Wh Not	78	C1
Wickford	Wick	174	C3
Wickham Bishops	Wic Bis	115	E3
Wickham St Paul	Wic S P	17	D1
Witham	With	97	F2
Wivenhoe	Wiv	69	E1
Wix	Wix	55	E3
Woodham Mortimer	Woo Mor	143	E3
Woodham Walter	Woo Wa	130	B1
Wormingford	Worm	29	F3
Wrabness	Wrab	37	F2
Writtle	Writ	126	B1

Aalten Ave. Canv 197 F2
Abbas Wlk. Sud 13 E3
Abberton Rd. Fing 86 C2
Abberton Rd. Lay H 85 D3
Abbess Cl. Chelm 126 C1
Abbey Cl. Hull 165 E1
Abbey Cres. Th L S 74 A1
Abbey Fields. E Han 153 D4
Abbey La. Cogg 63 D1
Abbey Rd. Hull 165 E1
Abbey Rd. Sud 7 F1
Abbey St. Th L S 74 A1
Abbey Turning. Mald 131 E2
Abbeygate St. Colch 67 F3
Abbots Cl. Clact 109 F3
Abbots Gdns. St O 108 B2
Abbots La. E A Gr 66 A4
Abbot's Rd. Colch 68 A2
Abbots Wlk. South 201 E4
Abbotsleigh Rd. S Woo F 165 F3
Abbotswood. Thund 188 B3
Abbott Rd. Harw 39 F1
Abbotts Cl. Chelm 127 E2
Abbotts Cl. South 189 F3
Abdy Ave. Harw 39 F1
Abels Rd. Hals 43 E4
Abensburg Rd. Canv 197 E3
Abercorn Way. With 98 A1
Aberdeen Gdns. Hadl 189 D1
Abingdon Ct. Basil 174 A1
Abinger Cl. Clact 109 E3
Abraham Dr. Silv E 79 F2
Abreys. Thund 188 A4
Acacia Ave. Colch 68 C4
Acacia Dr. Mald 131 F1
Acacia Dr. South 201 D4
Acacia Gdns. With 98 A2
Acacia Rd. Basil 186 C4
Accomodation Rd. Box 49 E4
Achilles Way. Brain 60 A3
Achnacone Dr. Colch 49 E2
Ackland Ave. Colch 67 D4
Acorn Ave. Brain 59 E1
Acorn Ave. Hals 25 E1
Acorn Cl. Colch 50 B2
Acorn Cl. Harw 40 A1
Acorn Wlk. Thor 89 D3
Acorns The. Hock 177 F4
Acres End. Chelm 126 C2
Acton Cl. Sud 12 C4
Acton Green. Sud 12 C4
Acton La. Sud 7 F1
Adalia Cres. Hadl 189 D2
Adalia Way. Hadl 189 D1
Adam Way. Wick 174 C4
Adams Glade. Hawk 178 B3
Addison Pavement. Basil 186 A3
Addison Rd. Sud 13 D4
Adelaide Dr. Colch 68 A1
Adelaide Gdns. S Ben 187 E1
Adelaide St. Rams 39 F3
Adelsburg Rd. Canv 197 E2
Admirals Wlk. Chelm 126 C2
Admirals Wlk. South 201 E3
Aetheric Rd. Brain 59 F2
Affleck Rd. Colch 68 C4
Agar Rd. App. Walt 94 B4
Agate Rd. Clact 109 F1
Agincourt Rd. Clact 109 E2
Agnes Ave. Hadl 189 D2
Ailsa Rd. South 199 E4
Ainger Rd. Harw 39 F1
Aingers Green Rd. Gt Ben 90 A3
Airborne Cl. South 189 F3
Aire Wlk. With 97 F1
Aisne Rd. Colch 67 E2
Ajax Cl. Brain 60 A3
Akenfield Cl. S Woo F 165 F4
Alamein Rd. Burn 170 B2
Alamein Rd. Chelm 126 C3
Alamein Rd. Colch 67 E1
Alan Cl. South 189 F3
Alan Dr. Lit Cla 91 E1
Alan Grove. South 189 F3
Alan Rd. With 97 F1
Alan Way. Colch 66 C2
Alanbrooke Rd. Colch 68 B1
Albany Ave. South 190 C1
Albany Cl. Chelm 126 C3
Albany Cl. W Berg 48 C2
Albany Gdns E. Clact 110 A2
Albany Gdns W. Clact 110 A2
Albany Rd. Rayl 177 D1
Albany Rd. W Berg 48 C2
Albany Rd. Wick 174 B3
Albemarle Gdns. Brain 60 B3
Albermarle St. Harw 40 B3
Albert Cl. Ashi 178 B3
Albert Cl. Rayl 176 C2
Albert Gdns. Clact 110 A2
Albert Gdns. Cogg 63 D1
Albert Pl. Cogg 63 D1
Albert Rd. Ashi 178 B3
Albert Rd. Brain 60 A2
Albert Rd. Brigh 107 D3
Albert Rd. Burn 170 B2
Albert Rd. Rayl 176 C2
Albert Rd. S Woo F 165 E4
Albert Rd. South 192 A1
Albert Rd. South 200 A4
Albert Rd. Thund 187 D3
Albert Rd. With 98 A2
Albert St. Colch 67 F4
Albert St. Harw 40 B3
Albert Terr. South 199 F4
Albertine Cl. Stanw 66 B3
Albion Gr. Colch 68 A3
Albion Rd. S Ben 187 E2
Albion Rd. South 190 C1
Albion St. Rowh 87 D4
Albrighton Croft. Colch 50 B2
Albury. South 191 F1
Alcotes. Basil 185 F3
Aldeburgh Cl. Clact 109 D2
Aldeburgh Way. Sprin 127 E3
Alder Dr. Chelm 140 A3
Alder Wlk. With 98 A2
Alderbury Lea. S Woo F 142 C1
Aldercar Rd. Copf 65 F1
Alderford Maltings. Si Hed 24 C4
Alderford St. Si Hed 24 C4
Alderleys. Thund 188 A3
Aldermans Hill. Hock 177 D3
Alderney Gdns. Runw 163 E1
Alderton Rd. Colch 68 B4
Alderwood Way. S Ben 188 B2
Aldon Cl. Harw 39 E1
Aldridge Cl. Sprin 128 A2
Aldrin Way. South 190 A3
Alefounder Cl. Colch 68 C3
Alexander Ct. Sprin 127 F4
Alexander Mews. Sand 141 E1
Alexander Rd. Brain 59 F2
Alexandra Ave. W Mers 121 F3
Alexandra Dr. Wiv 69 E2
Alexandra Rd. Ashi 178 B4
Alexandra Rd. Burn 170 B3
Alexandra Rd. Clact 109 F2
Alexandra Rd. Colch 67 F3
Alexandra Rd. Gt Wak 193 D2
Alexandra Rd. Harw 40 B3
Alexandra Rd. Rayl 176 C2
Alexandra Rd. S Ben 187 E1
Alexandra Rd. Si Hed 15 E1
Alexandra Rd. South 198 C4
Alexandra Rd. South 199 F4
Alexandra Rd. Sud 13 D4
Alexandra Rd. Weel 72 C1
Alexandra St. Harw 40 B3
Alexandra St. South 200 A4
Alexandra Terr. Colch 67 F3
Alexandria Dr. Rayl 176 A2
Alfells Rd. Elmst M 69 F3
Alfred Gdns. Runw 163 E1
Alfred Terr. Walt 94 B4
Alfreda Ave. Hull 165 E2
Alfreg Rd. With 114 B4
Algars Way. S Woo F 165 E4
Alicia Ave. Wick 175 D4
Alicia Cl. Wick 175 D4
Alicia Way. Wick 175 D4
Alicia Wlk. Wick 175 D4
All Saints Ave. Colch 67 D2
All Saints Cl. Sprin 127 F2
Allandale. Thund 188 A4
Allectus Way. With 114 B4
Allen Way. St O 107 D2
Allendale Dr. Copf 65 E2
Allens Cl. Bore 112 C1
Allerton Cl. Hawk 178 B3
Alley Dock. South 198 B4
Alleyne Way. Clact 125 D4
Alma Cl. Hadl 189 E1
Alma Cl. Wick 174 A3
Alma Dr. Chelm 127 D1
Alma Rd. Hadl 189 D1
Alma Sq. Mann 35 E2
Alma St. Wiv 87 D4
Almond Ave. Wick 174 B4
Almond Cl. Clact 109 E2
Almond Cl. Tipt 100 B3
Almond Cl. Wiv 69 E1
Almond Way. Colch 68 C4
Almond Wlk. Canv 196 C2
Alpha Cl. Basil 186 C3
Alpha Cl. Brain 60 A1
Alpha Rd. Basil 186 C3
Alpha Rd. Burn 170 B3
Alpha Rd. St O 107 D2
Alphamstone Rd. Lam 19 D2
Alport Ave. Colch 67 E2
Alresford Rd. Elmst M 87 F4
Altbarn Cl. Colch 50 B3
Althorne Cl. Basil 174 A1
Althorne Way. Cane 168 C1
Althorpe Cl. Hock 177 E3
Alton Dr. Colch 67 D3
Alton Gdns. South 190 C3
Alton Park La. Clact 109 D1
Alton Park Rd. Clact 109 E1
Alton Rd. Clact 109 F1
Aluf Cl. With 114 C4
Alvis Ave. Clact 124 C3
Alyssum Cl. Bore 128 A3
Alyssum Wlk. Colch 68 B4
Amarells Rd. Lit Cla 91 E2
Amberley Cl. Elmst M 69 E1
Ambleside Dr. South 200 B4
Ambleside Gdns. Hull 165 E1
Ambleside Wlk. Canv 196 C2
Ambridge Rd. Cogg 62 C2
Ambrose Ave. Colch 66 C2
Ameland Rd. Canv 197 D3
America Rd. Ea Col 45 E1
America St. Mald 132 A1
Amid Rd. Canv 197 E3
Amos Hill. Gt H 18 A4
Amoss Rd. Gt Bad 140 C4
Ampers End. Basil 185 E3
Anchor End. Mist 36 A2
Anchor Hill. Wiv 87 D4
Anchor La. Cane 168 B1
Anchor La. Mald 132 A3
Anchor La. Mist 36 A2
Anchor Rd. Clact 109 F2
Anchor Rd. Tipt 100 B2
Anchor Reach. S Woo F 165 F3
Anchor St. Chelm 127 D1
Anchorage The. Gt Wak 193 D2
Anders Fall. South 190 A3
Anderson Ave. Chelm 126 C3
Andover Cl. Clact 110 A3
Andrew Cl. Brain 59 F3
Andrews Pl. Chelm 126 C2
Andyk Rd. Canv 197 F2
Anerley Rd. South 199 E4
Angel Cl. Basil 185 E2
Angel La. Glems 2 A2
Angle Side. Brain 60 A1
Anglefield. Clact 109 F1
Anglesea Rd. Wiv 87 E4
Anglia Cl. Colch 67 D2
Anglia Way. Brain 60 A1
Anne Boleyn Dr. Roch 190 C4
Anne Cl. Brigh 106 C3
Anson Chase. South 201 F4
Anson Cl. S Woo F 165 F3
Anson Way. Brain 60 B2
Anstey Cl. South 189 E4
Anthony Cl. Colch 50 B1
Antonio Wlk. Colch 68 C4
Antony Cl. Canv 197 D3
Antrim Rd. South 201 E4
Anzio Cres. Colch 67 E2
Apple Tree Way. Wick 174 C4
Appledore. South 192 B1
Appleford Ct. Basil 186 B3
Applerow. South 189 F3
Appleton Rd. S Ben 187 D1
Appletree Cl. South 191 F2
Appletree Cl. T Gr 78 C3
Appletree Wlk. Brain 60 A1
Appleyard Ave. Hock 177 F4
Approach Rd. Canv 197 F2
Approach The. Clact 125 D4
Approach The. Rayl 176 B2
Apton Hall Rd. Gt Stam 179 E3
Apton Hall Rd. Roch 179 E3
Aragon Cl. Clact 124 C4
Aragon Cl. South 190 C2
Arakan Cl. Colch 67 D1
Arboub La. Wic Bis 115 F3
Arbour La. Sprin 127 E2
Arbour Way. Colch 50 B2
Arbutus Cl. Chelm 140 A3
Arcadia Rd. Burn 170 B3
Arcadia Rd. Canv 197 E2
Arcadian Gdns. Hadl 188 B2
Archer Ave. South 191 F2
Archer Cl. South 191 F2
Archers Fields. Basil 174 A1
Archers Way. Chelm 140 B1
Arden Cl. Colch 50 B2
Arderne Cl. Harw 39 F1
Ardleigh Ct. Ard 51 F4
Ardleigh Rd. Ded 33 E2
Ardleigh Rd. Gt Bro 52 A2
Ardleigh Rd. Lit Bro 52 C3
Ardleyway. Rayl 176 B2
Argyle Ct. Kelv 81 E1
Argyle Rd. Burn 170 B2
Argyle Rd. Th L S 73 F1
Argyll Rd. Bore 128 A3
Argyll Rd. South 199 E4
Ariel Cl. Colch 68 C4
Arjan Way. Canv 196 B2
Ark La. Roch 178 A1
Arlington Rd. South 191 F1
Armadale. Canv 196 C3
Armagh Rd. South 201 E4
Armidale Wlk. Colch 68 A1
Armiger Way. With 98 A1
Armitage Rd. South 192 A1
Armond Rd. With 97 F2
Armoury Rd. W Berg 48 C2
Armstrong Cl. Dan 142 C4
Armstrong Rd. Thund 187 E4
Armstrong Way. Gt Y 9 D1
Arnheim Rd. Burn 170 B2
Arnhem Gr. Brain 59 F2
Arnhem Rd. Chelm 126 C3
Arnold Ave. South 200 B4
Arnold Dr. Colch 68 C3
Arnold Rd. Clact 109 E1
Arnold Villas. Tipt 100 B3
Arnold Way. Chelm 140 B2
Arnolds Way. Ashi 178 B4
Arnstones Cl. Colch 68 B4
Arras Rd. Colch 67 E2
Arrow Rd. Colch 68 C4
Arthur Ct. Chelm 126 C3
Arthur St. Colch 67 F3
Arthy Cl. Hat Pev 114 A2
Artillery Barracks Folley. Colch 67 F3
Artillery St. Colch 68 A3
Arun Cl. Sprin 127 E3
Arundel Gdns. South 190 A2
Arundel Rd. Ashi 167 E1
Arundel Rd. Runw 163 E1
Arundel Rd. Thund 187 D4
Arwen Gr. S Woo F 165 E3
Asbury Cl. Colch 68 B4
Ascot Cl. Thund 188 A4
Ash Bungalows. Brain 59 F2
Ash Cl. Brigh 106 C4
Ash Cl. Clact 109 E2
Ash Fall. With 97 F3
Ash Gr. Burn 170 A3
Ash Gr. Chelm 140 B4
Ash Gr. Mald 132 B3
Ash Gr. Sud 13 E3
Ash Gr. Wiv 69 E2
Ash Green. Cane 168 B1
Ash Ground Cl. Catt 35 E4
Ash Grove. Colch 86 A4
Ash Rd. Alres 88 A4
Ash Rd. Canv 197 E2
Ash Rd. Hadl 188 C1
Ash Tree Cl. Chelm 126 C1
Ash Tree Cres. Chelm 126 C1
Ash Tree Wlk. Basil 185 F3
Ash Way. Hock 177 F4
Ash Wlk. South 200 A4
Ashanti Cl. South 201 F4
Ashburnham Rd. South 199 F4
Ashbury Dri. Mks T 64 C2
Ashby Rd. With 115 D4
Ashcombe. Hawk 178 B2
Ashcombe Cl. South 189 D3
Ashcombe Way. Rayl 176 C1
Ashdene Cl. Hull 165 F1
Ashdown Cres. Hadl 188 C2
Ashdown Way. Colch 68 B4
Ashen Cl. Ashe 3 E1
Ashen Hill. Ashe 3 E1
Ashen La. Cla 3 E2
Ashen Rd. Ashe 8 A4
Ashen Rd. Bel S P 4 A3
Ashen Rd. Ovi 4 A1
Ashes Cl. Walt 93 F4
Ashes Rd. T Gr 78 C4
Ashfield Farm Rd. Ult 130 B4
Ashfields. Basil 186 B4
Ashford Rd. Chelm 126 C1
Ashingdale Cl. Canv 197 E1
Ashingdon Rd. Ashi 178 B3
Ashingdon Rd. Roch 178 B3
Ashleigh Dr. South 198 C4
Ashley Gdns. Colch 67 E4
Ashley Green. E Han 153 D4
Ashley Rd. Harw 40 A2
Ashlong Gr. Hals 25 F2
Ashlyns. Basil 186 A4
Ashlyn's Rd. Frin 93 F2
Ashmans Row. S Woo F 165 E3
Ashmere Rise. Sud 13 D4
Ashmole Dr. Walt 93 F3
Ashpole Rd. Brain 42 A1
Ashstead Cl. Clact 109 D3
Ashton Pl. Sprin 128 A2
Ashurst Ave. South 191 F1
Ashurst Cl. Rowh 86 C4
Ashurst Dr. Sprin 127 E4
Ashwells Meadow. Ea Col 45 D3
Ashwin Ave. Copf 65 E2
Ashworths. Canv 197 D3
Ashworths. Hawk 178 B3
Aspen Cl. Canv 196 C2
Aspen Way. Colch 68 B4
Asquith Ave. Thund 188 B3
Asquith Gdns. Thund 188 B4
Assandune Cl. Ashi 178 B4
Astell Ct. Frin 93 F2
Aster Cl. Clact 109 E2
Aster Ct. Sprin 127 F3
Astley Rd. Clact 109 E2
Athelstan Gdns. Runw 163 E1
Athelstan Rd. Colch 67 E3
Atherstone Cl. Canv 197 E1
Atherstone Rd. Canv 197 E1
Athol Cl. Canv 197 F1
Atholl Rd. Sprin 127 F3
Athos Rd. Canv 197 E3
Atlas Ct. Ea Col 45 D4
Atlas Rd. Ea Col 44 C4
Attlee Gdns. Colch 68 A3
Attwoods Cl. Chelm 140 B2
Aubrey Cl. Chelm 127 D4
Auckland Cl. Chelm 126 C3
Audley Rd. Colch 67 E3
Audley Way. Basil 185 D3
Audley Way. Frin 94 A3
Audleys Cl. South 190 C3
Audries Estate. Walt 94 A4
Augustine Way. S Woo F 142 C1
Augustus Way. With 114 C4
Austen Cl. Brain 78 A4
Austin Ave. Clact 124 C3
Autoway. Colch 50 B3
Autumn Cl. Clact 109 E3
Avebury Rd. South 190 C1
Aveline Rd. Ard 51 F4
Avenue Rd. Corr 185 D1
Avenue Rd. Gt Bad 140 B4
Avenue Rd. S Ben 187 F2
Avenue Rd. South 198 C4
Avenue Rd. South 199 F4
Avenue Rd. With 98 A2
Avenue Terr. South 199 F4
Avenue The. Brain 59 F2
Avenue The. Canv 197 D1
Avenue The. Clact 110 A4
Avenue The. Colch 67 E3
Avenue The. Gt Oak 56 A2
Avenue The. Hadl 188 C2
Avenue The. Hull 165 E2
Avenue The. N Fam 167 D4
Avenue The. W Berg 48 B2
Avenue The. With 98 A1
Avenue The. Wiv 69 D1
Aviation Way. Roch 190 B4
Avila Chase. Chelm 140 A1
Avington Wlk. Thund 187 F3
Avocet Cl. Kelv 81 E1
Avocet Way. Mald 132 B3
Avon Cl. Hawk 178 B3
Avon Rd. Canv 197 D2
Avon Rd. Chelm 126 B3
Avon Way. Colch 68 C3
Avon Way. South 201 E4
Avon Wlk. With 97 F2
Avondale Cl. Rayl 176 C1
Avondale Dr. South 189 F2
Avondale Rd. Basil 186 A2
Avondale Rd. Clact 110 A2
Avondale Rd. Rayl 176 C1
Avondale Rd. S Ben 187 E2
Avondale Wlk. Canv 196 C2
Avro Rd. South 190 B3
Aylesbeare. South 201 E4
Aylesbury Dr. Clact 110 C3
Aylett Cl. Canv 197 E2
Ayletts. Basil 185 F3
Ayloffe Rd. Colch 50 B1
Azalea Ave. Wick 174 B4
Azalea Way. Clact 109 E2

Baardwyk Ave. Canv 197 F2
Back La. Colch 66 C4
Back La. E Han 153 D4
Back La. Gt Oak 56 B2
Back La. Gt Tot 115 F2
Back La. Rams 39 D1
Back La. Roch 178 C1
Back La. Stis 61 E3
Back La E. Gt Bro 71 D3
Back La W. Gt Bro 70 C4
Back Rd. Ard 52 A3
Back Rd. Tolle 119 E2
Back Rd. Writ 126 A1
Back Waterside La. Brigh 106 C3
Bacon's La. Wa Col 46 B2
Baddow Hall Ave. Gt Bad 141 D4
Baddow Hall Cres. Gt Bad 141 D4
Baddow Place Ave. Gt Bad 141 D3
Baddow Rd. Chelm 140 C4
Baddow Rd. Chelm 127 E1
Baddow Rd. Gt Bad 140 C4
Baden Powell Dr. Colch 67 D2
Badger Hall Ave. S Ben 188 A2
Badgers Cl. South 190 A2
Badgers Green. Mks T 64 C2
Badgers Way. S Ben 188 A2
Badley Hall Rd. Gt Bro 52 C1
Badminton Rd. Clact 125 D4
Bailey Bridge Rd. Brain 59 F3
Bailey Dale. Stanw 66 B2
Bailey La. Cla 4 B4
Bailey Rd. Hadl 189 D1
Bailey The. Rayl 176 B1
Baines Cl. Colch 66 C3
Baker Ave. Hat Pev 114 A2
Baker Mews. Mald 132 A1
Baker Rd. Sho G 40 A4
Baker St. Chelm 127 D1
Bakers Cl. S Woo F 165 E4
Baker's La. Bl Not 77 E3
Baker's La. Colch 49 D1
Baker's La. Dan 142 C4
Baker's La. Toll M 117 E2
Baker's Rd. Bel S P 4 C1
Baldwin's La. Gt T 63 D4
Bale Cl. Colch 66 C2
Balfe Ct. Colch 68 C3
Balfour Way. Basil 186 A3
Balkerne Cl. Colch 67 F4
Balkerne Hill. Colch 67 F4
Balkerne Pass. Colch 67 F4
Ball Alley. Colch 67 F4
Ball La. Rowh 86 A3
Ballast Quay Rd. Elmst M 69 E1
Ballast Quay Rd. Elmst M 87 E4
Ballast Quay Rd. Fing 87 D3
Ballingdon Hill. Sudd 12 B3
Ballingdon St. Sud 12 B3
Ball's Chace. M Bure 28 C1
Ball's Chase. Hals 25 F1
Balmerino Ave. Thund 188 B3
Balmoral Ave. Clact 109 E2
Balmoral Gdns. Hock 177 E3
Balmoral Rd. South 190 C1
Balmoral Rd. Steep 147 D1
Baltic Ave. South 200 A4
Balton Way. Harw 39 F1
Bancrofts Rd. S Woo F 165 F4
Bandhills Cl. S Woo F 165 E4
Banister Cl. Clact 109 E3
Bank Pass. Colch 67 F4
Bank St. Brain 59 F2
Bankart La. Sprin 127 F2
Bankside Cl. S Woo F 154 C1
Bannister Green. Wick 174 C3
Banters La. Gt Le 77 D1
Banyardway. Hawk 178 B2
Barbara Ave. Canv 196 C1
Barbara Cl. Hawk 178 C1
Barbel Rd. Colch 50 C1
Barbrook La. Tipt 100 B3
Barbrook Way. S Woo F 142 C1
Barclay Cl. Gt Bad 141 D3
Barclay Rd. Basil 174 C1
Bardenville Rd. Canv 197 F2
Bardfield. Basil 185 F3
Bardfield Rd. Colch 68 A1
Bardfield Way. Rayl 176 A2
Bardfield Way. Walt 93 F3
Barfield. Mann 35 E2
Barfield Rd. W Mers 121 E3
Bargate La. Ded 34 A2
Barge Pier Rd. South 201 F3
Barker Cl. Lawf 35 D2
Barkis Cl. Chelm 126 B4
Barkstead Rd. Colch 50 B1
Barley Mead. Dan 143 D3
Barley Way. Colch 66 C3
Barling Rd. Barl 192 B4
Barling Rd. Stobr 192 A3
Barlon Rd. Lit Bro 52 C2
Barlow's Reach. Sprin 128 A2
Barn Green. Sprin 127 F4
Barn Hall Ave. Colch 68 B2
Barn La. Lawf 52 C4
Barnaby Rudge. Chelm 126 C4
Barnard Cl. Basil 185 F1
Barnard Rd. Chelm 140 B1

Barnard Rd. Hadl 189 E1
Barnardiston Rd. Colch 50 B1
Barnardiston Way. With 97 F2
Barnards Ave. Canv 197 E2
Barncombe Cl. Thund 187 E3
Barncroft Cl. Colch 50 A2
Barnes Mill Rd. Sprin 127 F1
Barnet Park Rd. Runw 163 F1
Barneveld Ave. Canv 197 F2
Barnfield. Fee 81 E2
Barnfield. Mann 35 E2
Barnfield. Wick 174 C4
Barnfield Cotts. Mald 132 A3
Barnfield Mews. Chelm 127 D3
Barnfield Rd. Gt Hor 49 E3
Barnhall Rd. Toll K 101 E1
Barnmead Way. Burn 170 A4
Barnstaple Cl. South 201 D4
Barnstaple Rd. South 201 D4
Barnwell Dr. Hock 177 E3
Baron Rd. S Woo F 165 F4
Baronia Croft. Colch 50 B2
Barons Court Rd. Rayl 176 B3
Baron's La. Purl 144 C1
Baronswood Way. Colch 67 E1
Barpack St. Brad 54 B4
Barr Cl. Wiv 69 E1
Barrack La. Harw 40 C2
Barrack Sq. Chelm 127 D1
Barrack St. Colch 68 A3
Barrie Pavement. Wick 174 B3
Barrington Cl. Basil 185 F4
Barrington Cl. Gt Bad 141 D3
Barrington Cl. Lit Cla 91 E1
Barrington Gdns. Basil 185 F4
Barrington Gdns. Clact 110 B3
Barrington Rd. Colch 68 A3
Barringtons Cl. Rayl 176 B2
Barrow Hall Rd. Barl 192 B3
Barrow Hall Rd. Stobr 192 B3
Barrowsand. South 201 D3
Barrymore Wlk. Rayl 177 D1
Bartlett Cl. May 146 C1
Bartletts. Rayl 189 D4
Bartley Cl. Thund 187 D3
Bartley Rd. Thund 187 D3
Bartlow End. Basil 186 A4
Bartlow Side. Basil 186 A4
Barton Cl. S Woo F 154 B1
Bartram Ave. Brain 60 B2
Barwell Way. With 98 A1
Basin Rd. Mald 132 C2
Bassenthwaite Rd. Thund 187 F4
Bassetts La. Lit Bad 130 A2
Bat Hall. Bul 12 A3
Bat View. St L 148 B4
Batavia Rd. Canv 196 B2
Bate-Dudley Dr. Brad o s 137 D2
Bateman Rd. Brigh 106 C4
Bateman's Rd. Clact 109 D2
Bath St. Wiv 87 D4
Bathurst Cl. Colch 68 A1
Battery La. Sho G 40 A4
Battisford Dr. Clact 109 D2
Battlesbrook Rd. Colch 68 B1
Batt's Rd. Steep 148 A1
Bawn Cl. Brain 60 A2
Bawtree Way. Colch 67 D3
Baxter Ave. South 190 C1
Bay Cl. Canv 197 D1
Bay Rd. Harw 40 B2
Bay View Cres. Lit Oak 57 E4
Bayard Ave. Brigh 106 C4
Bayley St. Ca Hed 15 F2
Baynards Cres. Walt 93 F3
Beach Ave. South 199 D4
Beach Cres. Clact 124 C3
Beach Ct. Gt Wak 193 E2
Beach House Gdns. Canv 197 F1
Beach Rd. Canv 197 E2
Beach Rd. Clact 109 F1
Beach Rd. Harw 40 B1
Beach Rd. South 200 B4
Beach Rd. South 201 F3
Beach Rd. St O 108 A1
Beach Rd. St O 123 E4
Beach Rd. W Mers 121 E3
Beach Way. Clact 124 C3
Beachcroft Ave. Walt 93 E3
Beaches Cl. Hock 178 A3
Beach's Dr. Chelm 126 B2
Beachway. Canv 197 D1
Beachy Dr. St L 148 B4
Beacon Cl. Brigh 106 C3
Beacon Heights. St O 107 D1
Beacon Hill. Gt Tot 116 A3
Beacon Hill. Mald 131 F1
Beacon Hill Ave. Harw 40 C2
Beacon Way. St O 107 D1
Beacon Way. Stanw 66 B3
Beaconsfield Ave. Colch 67 F3
Beaconsfield Cl. Sud 12 C4
Beaconsfield Rd. Clact 109 F2
Beaconsfield Rd. Sud 12 C4
Beadle Way. Gt Le 95 D3
Beadon Dr. Brain 60 A1
Beambridge. Basil 186 A3
Bear St. Nay 20 A1
Beardsley Dr. Sprin 127 F4
Bearsted Dr. Basil 186 B3
Beatrice Ave. Canv 197 D2
Beatrice Rd. Clact 109 F1
Beatrice Rd. Walt 76 C1
Beatty Gdns. Brain 60 B2
Beatty La. Basil 185 F3
Beatty Rise. S Woo F 165 F3
Beauchamps Dr. Wick 175 D4
Beaufort Gdns. Brain 60 A2
Beaufort Rd. Sprin 128 A2
Beaufort St. South 191 E1
Beaumont Ave. Brigh 107 D4
Beaumont Ave. Clact 109 E2
Beaumont Cl. Walt 93 F4
Beaumont Park. Dan 142 B3
Beaumont Pl. Brain 60 A2
Beaumont Rd. Gt Oak 56 B1
Beaumont Wlk. Chelm 126 B3
Beaver Cl. Colch 66 C4
Beazley End. Wick 174 C3
Beche Rd. Colch 68 A3
Beck Farm Cl. Canv 197 F2
Beck Rd. Canv 197 F2
Becker Rd. Colch 66 C2
Beckers Green Rd. Brain 60 B1
Becket Cl. Ashi 178 B3
Becket Way. S Woo F 165 F3
Becketts La. High 21 F4
Beckford Rd. Mist 36 A2
Beckingham Rd. Gt Tot 116 B3
Beckingham Rd. Toll D 118 B2
Beckingham St. Toll M 117 E2
Beckney Ave. Hock 166 C1
Becontree Cl. Clact 109 F4
Bedells Ave. Bl Not 78 A3
Bedford Cl. Brain 60 A2
Bedford Cl. Rayl 176 B1
Bedford Cl. Tipt 100 B3
Bedford Pl. Canv 196 C2
Bedford Rd. Clact 110 B3
Bedford Rd. Colch 49 F3
Bedloes Ave. Rayl 175 F4
Bedloes Cnr. Rayl 175 F4
Beech Ave. Brain 59 F3
Beech Ave. Rayl 176 B2
Beech Ave. Wiv 69 D1
Beech Cl. Burn 170 A3
Beech Ct. Basil 185 F3
Beech Gr. Si Hed 15 E1
Beech Green. Lit Brx 115 F3
Beech Hill. Colch 67 D3
Beech Rd. Basil 185 F3
Beech Rd. Hadl 188 C1
Beech Rd. Hull 165 F1
Beech Rd. Sud 13 D3
Beech Rd. With 98 A4
Beech Rise. Hat Pev 114 A2
Beechcroft Rd. Canv 196 C2
Beeches Cl. Chelm 126 C1
Beeches Ct. Chelm 126 C1
Beeches Rd. Chelm 126 C1
Beeches Rd. Mald 131 F3
Beeches Rd. Rayl 164 C1
Beechmont Gdns. South 190 C2
Beechwood Cl. Colch 67 E1
Beecroft Cres. Canv 197 D3
Beedell Ave. South 190 B1
Beedell Ave. Wick 174 C3
Beehive La. Basil 185 D3
Beehive La. Chelm 140 B3
Beehive La. Gt Bad 140 B3
Beeleigh Chase. Mald 131 E2
Beeleigh Cl. Colch 68 A1
Beeleigh Cl. South 190 C2
Beeleigh Cross. Basil 185 F4
Beeleigh East. Basil 185 F4
Beeleigh Link. Sprin 127 F2
Beeleigh Rd. Mald 131 F2
Beeleigh West. Basil 185 E4
Begonia Cl. Sprin 127 F3
Begonia Pl. Clact 109 E2
Beke Hall Chase N. Rayl 175 F2
Beke Hall Chase S. Rayl 175 F2
Bekeswell La. Chelm 139 F1
Bel-Air Estate. St O 124 A3
Belchamps Rd. Wick 174 C4
Belchamps Way. Hawk 177 F3
Beldams Cl. Th L S 74 A1
Beldowes. Basil 185 E3
Belfairs Cl. Hadl 189 E1
Belfairs Dr. South 189 E1
Belfairs Park Cl. Hadl 189 E3
Belfairs Park Dr. Hadl 189 D3
Belgrave Cl. Gt Bad 140 B4
Belgrave Cl. Rayl 189 D4
Belgrave Rd. Rayl 189 D4
Bell Cl. Colch 68 B1
Bell Hill. Dan 142 B4
Bell Hill. Lam 19 E2
Bell La. Pan 59 D4
Bell St. Gt Bad 140 C3
Bellamy Cl. Walt 93 E3
Belle Vue. Chelm 127 D1
Belle Vue Rd. Colch 49 F1
Belle Vue Rd. Sud 12 C4
Belle Vue Rd. Wiv 69 E1
Bellevue Ave. South 200 B4
Bellevue Pl. South 200 B4
Bellevue Rd. South 191 E1
Bellevue Terr. Hals 25 F1
Bellfield. Basil 185 F2
Bellfield Ave. Brigh 107 D4
Bellfield Cl. Brigh 107 D4
Bellhouse Cres. South 189 E3
Bellhouse La. South 189 E3
Bellhouse Rd. South 189 E3
Bellingham La. Rayl 176 B1
Bellmead. Chelm 127 D1
Bells Chase. Gt Bad 140 C3
Bells Hill. M Bure 29 D2
Bells Hill Rd. Basil 185 D1
Bells La. Glems 2 B3
Bells Rd. Bel W 10 C3
Belmonde Dr. Sprin 127 F4
Belmont Ave. Wick 174 A4
Belmont Cl. Sprin 127 F4
Belmont Cl. Wick 174 A4
Belmont Cres. Colch 50 B2
Belsize Ave. Clact 124 B3
Belton Bridge. Hadl 198 B4
Belton Gdns. Hadl 198 B4
Belton Way E. Hadl 198 B4
Belton Way W. Hadl 198 A4
Belvawney Cl. Chelm 126 C3
Belvedere Ave. Hock 177 E3
Belvedere Cl. Dan 142 C4
Belvedere Rd. Burn 170 B2
Belvedere Rd. Dan 142 C4
Belvedere The. Burn 170 B2
Bembridge Cl. Clact 109 F4
Bemerton Gdns. Walt 93 E3
Benbow Dr. S Woo F 165 F3
Bendalls Ct. Lawf 35 E2
Benderloch. Canv 196 C3
Benedict Dr. Chelm 126 C1
Benfield Way. Brain 60 A1
Benfleet Park Rd. S Ben 187 D1
Benfleet Rd. S Ben 188 A2
Bennett Cl. Brain 78 A4
Bennett Cl. Walt 94 A4
Bennett Ct. Colch 68 C3
Bennett Way. Hat Pev 114 A2
Bennett's Ave. E Han 152 C2
Bentalls Cl. South 191 D2
Bentley Ave. Clact 124 C3
Bentley Rd. Lit Bro 53 E2
Bentley Rd. St O 90 B3
Bentley Rd. Weel 90 B3
Bentley Rd. With 97 F2
Bentleys The. South 190 A4
Benton Cl. T Gr 78 C3
Benvenue Ave. South 189 F3
Berdens. Basil 185 E3
Berechurch Hall Rd. Colch 85 F4
Berechurch Rd. Colch 67 F1
Berens Cl. Runw 163 F1
Beresford Cl. Hadl 188 B2
Beresford Gdns. Hadl 188 B2
Beresford Rd. South 200 B4
Berg Ave. Canv 197 E3
Bergen Ct. Mald 144 C4
Bergholt Rd. Colch 49 E1
Bergholt Rd. Str S M 35 D4
Beridge Rd. Hals 25 E1
Berkeley Ave. Canv 197 D2
Berkeley Gdns. Hadl 189 D1
Berkeley Rd. Clact 109 F3
Berkley Cl. Colch 50 B2
Berkshire Cl. South 189 E3
Bernard Cl. Walt 93 F3
Berners Wlk. Basil 185 E4
Bernside. Brain 59 F1
Berrimans Cl. Colch 68 B3
Berry Cl. Wick 174 A3
Berry Vale. S Woo F 165 F3
Bertram Ave. Lit Cla 91 E1
Berwick Ave. Chelm 127 D4
Beryl Rd. Harw 39 E1
Bethany St. Wiv 87 D4
Betjeman Cl. Brain 78 A4
Betjeman Cl. Rayl 176 C2
Betts Green Rd. Lit Cla 91 E3
Bett's La. Hock 177 E3
Beveland Rd. South 198 A2
Beverley Ave. Canv 197 D2
Beverley Ave. W Mers 121 F4
Beverley Dr. Walt 93 F4
Beverley Gdns. South 190 C2
Beverley Rd. Colch 67 E3
Bevington Mews. With 98 A1
Bickenhall. South 201 E4
Bickerton Point. S Woo F 165 F3
Bicknacre Rd. Dan 142 C2
Bicknacre Rd. E Han 153 E4
Bicknacre Rd. S Woo F 142 C2
Biddenden Ct. Basil 186 B3
Bideford Cl. South 190 A3
Bight The. S Woo F 165 F3
Bignalls Croft. Colch 50 B2
Bijou Cl. Tipt 100 B3
Billy's La. Str S M 22 B1
Bilsdale Cl. Colch 50 B2
Bilton Rd. Chelm 126 C1
Bilton Rd. Hadl 188 C2
Birch Ave. Gt Ben 89 F4
Birch Ave. Harw 40 A2
Birch Cl. Brain 59 E1
Birch Cl. Brigh 106 C3
Birch Cl. Cane 168 C1
Birch Cl. Canv 196 C2
Birch Cl. Clact 109 E2
Birch Cl. Rayl 176 B2
Birch Cl. Thund 187 D4
Birch Cl. With 98 A2
Birch Gdns. Till 149 F2
Birch Green. Wick 174 B4
Birch Rd. Lay H 84 C3
Birch Rd. Till 149 F2
Birch Rise. Lit Brx 115 F3
Birch St. Birch 84 A2
Birch St. Nay 20 A1
Bircham Rd. South 191 D1
Birchdale. Hull 165 E2
Birche Cl. South 189 F2
Birches The. Thund 187 E4
Birches The. Walt 93 F3
Birches Wlk. Chelm 140 A1
Birchway. Birch 84 A1
Birchwood. Thund 187 D4
Birchwood Cl. Tipt 100 C3
Birchwood Cl. W Mers 121 E3
Birchwood Dr. South 190 A1
Birchwood Rd. Ded 33 D2
Birchwood Rd. Purl 144 A1
Birchwood Way. Tipt 100 C3
Bird La. Mess 100 C2
Birkdale Rise. Hat Pev 114 A2
Birkin Cl. Tipt 100 A2
Birs Cl. Runw 163 E1
Biscay. South 190 A4
Bishop Hall La. Chelm 127 D2
Bishop Rd. Chelm 127 D2
Bishop Rd. Colch 67 D2
Bishops Ave. Brain 60 A2
Bishops Cl. Basil 174 A1
Bishop's Ct. Canv 197 E2
Bishops La. Tipt 100 B4
Bishop's La. Twin 18 B2
Bishops Rd. Wick 174 B2
Bishopscourt Gdns. Sprin 127 F2
Bishopsteignton. South 192 B1
Bisley Cl. Clact 109 D3
Bittern Cl. Kelv 81 E1
Black Boy La. Wrab 38 A2
Blackberry Rd. Stanw 66 B2
Blackbrook Hill. Langh 33 D3
Blackbrook Rd. Gt Hor 49 E4
Blackfriars. Sud 12 B3
Blackgate Rd. South 202 A4
Blackheath. Colch 86 A4
Blackhouse La. Sud 13 E2
Blackley La. Gt Le 77 D2
Blacklock. Sprin 128 A2
Blackman Way. With 98 A1
Blackmore Ave. Canv 197 D1
Blackmore Wlk. Rayl 177 D1
Blacksmiths Hill. Cla 3 D2
Blacksmiths La. Bul 11 F1
Blacksmiths La. Wic Bis 115 F3
Blackthorn Cl. Writ 126 A1
Blackthorn Rd. Harw 39 F1
Blackthorn Rd. Hock 177 F4
Blackthorn Rd. With 97 F2
Blackthorne Ave. Colch 68 C4
Blackthorne Rd. Canv 197 E2
Blackwater Ave. Colch 50 C1
Blackwater Cl. Mald 132 C2
Blackwater Cl. Sprin 127 E3
Blackwater Dr. W Mer 121 D3
Blackwater La. With 115 D4
Blackwater Way. Brain 60 A2
Blackwood Chine. S Woo F 165 F3
Bladon Cl. Brain 59 F4
Bladon Cl. Tipt 100 C3
Blake Cl. Lawf 35 D2
Blake Ct. S Woo F 165 F3
Blake Dr. Brain 60 B2
Blake Dr. Clact 109 E3
Blake Hall Dr. Wick 175 D3
Blake Rd. With 97 F3
Blamsters Cres. Hals 43 E4
Blanchard Cl. Walt 93 D4
Blatches Chase. South 189 F4
Blenheim Chase. South 189 F2
Blenheim Cl. S Woo F 142 C1
Blenheim Cres. South 189 F1
Blenheim Dr. Colch 86 A4
Blenheim Gdns. Steep 147 D1
Blenheim Mews. South 189 F2
Blenheim Park Cl. South 189 F2
Blenheim Rd. Clact 109 E1
Blenheim Way. Tipt 100 C3
Blenneim Cl. Brain 59 F4
Blind La. Birch 83 D2
Blind La. Brigh 106 C4
Blind La. Gold 133 E4
Blind La. Purl 145 E1
Blind La. Sand 141 F2
Blind La. Toll K 101 D1
Bloomfield Ave. Walt 93 F4
Blooms Hall La. Glems 2 C4
Blott Rise. With 114 C4
Blountswood Rd. Hull 177 D4
Blower Cl. Rayl 176 C2
Blue Bridge Cotts. Hals 26 A1
Blue House Ave. Clact 109 D2
Blue House Farm Chase. N Fam 167 D4
Blue Mill La. Woo Wa 130 C2
Blue Mills Hill. With 115 E4
Blue Rd. Tipt 100 B3
Bluebell Ave. Clact 109 E2
Bluebell Cl. With 97 F2
Bluebell Green. Sprin 127 F4
Bluebell Way. Colch 49 E1
Bluehouse. Basil 185 D3
Blundens The. Nay 20 B3
Blunt's Hall Dr. With 97 E1
Blunts Hall Rd. With 97 E1
Blyford Rd. Clact 109 D2
Blythe Way. Thund 187 E4
Blyth's Meadow. Brain 59 F2
Blyton Cl. Wick 174 B3
Boadicea Way. Colch 67 E2
Boars Tye Rd. Silv E 79 E3
Bobbing Cl. Roch 178 C1
Bobbits Way. Wiv 87 E4
Bober Ct. Rowh 86 A4
Bocking End. Brain 59 F2
Bockingham Green. Basil 186 A4
Bocking's Gr. Clact 109 D3
Bodmin Rd. Sprin 127 F3
Bohemia Chase. South 189 E3
Bois Field Terr. Hals 25 F1
Bois Hall Gdns. Hals 25 F2
Boley Dr. Clact 110 A2
Boley Rd. Wa Col 46 A4
Boleyn Cl. Rayl 189 E4
Boleyn Way. Bore 112 C1
Boleyn Way. Clact 124 C4
Boleyns Ave. Brain 59 F3
Bolls La. Lay H 84 C3
Bolney Dr. Rayl 189 E4
Bommel Ave. South 198 A2
Bonchurch Ave. South 189 E1
Bond St. Chelm 127 E1
Bonham Cl. Clact 110 A3
Bonington Chase. Sprin 127 F3
Bonnygate. Basil 185 E4
Boone Pl. With 98 A1
Booth Ave. Colch 68 B4
Borda Cl. Chelm 127 D3
Boreham Cl. Wick 175 D3
Boreham Rd. Gt Le 95 D2
Borman Cl. South 190 A3
Borrett Ave. Canv 197 D2
Borrowdale Cl. Thund 187 F3
Borrowdale Rd. Thund 187 F3
Boscawen Gdns. Brain 60 B2
Boscombe Rd. South 191 D1
Boston Ave. Rayl 176 A2
Boston Ave. South 190 C1
Boswell Ave. Roch 178 B3
Boswells Dr. Chelm 127 E1
Bosworth Cl. Hawk 177 F2
Bosworth Rd. Rayl 189 E4
Botanical Way. St O 108 A3
Botany La. Weel 91 E3
Bouchers Mead. Sprin 127 F4
Bouldrewood Rd. S Ben 187 D3
Boulevard The. Roch 178 C2
Boulton Cotts. Mald 132 A3
Boundary Rd. Colch 68 C2
Boundary Rd. Rayl 189 D4
Bounderby Gr. Chelm 126 C3
Bounstead Hill. Lay H 85 E3
Bounstead Rd. Colch 85 E4
Bourchier Way. Hals 43 E4
Bourne Cl. Hals 43 E4
Bourne Rd. Colch 68 A2
Bourne Rd. W Berg 48 C1
Bournebridge Hill. Hals 43 D3
Bournemouth Park Rd. South 191 D1
Bournemouth Rd. Clact 110 C3
Bournes Green Chase. South 192 A1
Bouvel Dr. Burn 170 A4
Bouverie Rd. Chelm 140 A4
Bovingdon Rd. Brain 41 E1
Bovinger Way. South 191 F1
Bowbank Cl. South 192 C1
Bowdens La. Worm 29 F4
Bower Gdns. Mald 131 F2
Bower Hall La. W Mers 104 C1
Bower La. Basil 185 F4
Bowers Cl. Silv E 79 F2
Bowers Court Dr. Basil 186 C3
Bowers Rd. S Ben 187 E3
Bowes Rd. Elmst M 69 E1
Bowman Ave. Rayl 189 D3
Bowman's Park. Ca Hed 15 F2
Box Mill La. Hals 25 F2
Boxhouse La. Ded 33 E3
Boxted Church Rd. Gt Hor 31 E2
Boxted Rd. Colch 49 F3
Boxted Rd. Gt Hor 31 E2
Boyce Green. S Ben 187 E1
Boyce Hill Cl. Hadl 189 D3
Boyce Rd. South 202 A4
Boyce View Dr. S Ben 187 E1
Boyden Cl. South 191 F1
Boydin Cl. With 114 C4
Boyles Ct. Rowh 86 A4
Boyne Dr. Sprin 127 E3
Boyton Cl. Thund 187 F3
Brabant Rd. N Fam 167 D4
Brace Wlk. S Woo F 165 F3
Bracken Dell. Rayl 176 C1
Bracken The. Colch 50 A2
Bracken Way. Lang 86 A1
Bracken Way. Thund 188 A3
Brackendale Ave. Basil 186 B2
Brackendale Cl. Hock 177 F4
Brackenden Dr. Sprin 127 E4
Brackley Cres. Basil 174 A1
Bradbourne Way. Basil 186 B3
Bradbrook Cotts. W Berg 48 C2
Bradbury Dr. Brain 59 E2
Bradfield Rd. Wix 55 D4
Bradford St. Brain 60 A3
Bradford St. Chelm 127 D1
Bradfordbury. Hadl 189 E3
Brading Ave. Clact 110 A4
Bradley Ave. Thund 187 F3
Bradley Cl. Canv 197 D3
Bradley Cl. Thund 187 F3
Bradley Green. Basil 174 B1
Bradley Hill. Ovi 4 A3
Bradley Way. Roch 178 C1
Bradleyhall La. Th L S 73 E2
Bradwell Ct. Brain 78 B4
Bradwell Rd. Brad O S 149 D4
Bradwell Rd. St L 148 C3
Bradwell Rd. Steep 148 A2
Bradwell Rd. Till 149 F3
Braemar Ave. Chelm 140 A4
Braemar Cres. Hadl 189 D1
Braemore. Canv 196 C3
Braemore Cl. Colch 50 B2
Braggon's Hill. Glems 2 A4
Brain Rd. With 97 F2
Brain Valley Ave. Bl Not 78 A3
Braintree Rd. Gos 42 C3
Braintree Rd. T Gr 78 C4
Braintree Rd. Terl 96 A2
Braintree Rd. With 97 F2
Braiswick. Colch 49 D1
Braiswick La. Colch 49 E2
Bramble Cl. Rayl 189 D4
Bramble Cres. Hadl 189 D3
Bramble Rd. Canv 197 E2
Bramble Rd. Hadl 188 C3
Bramble Rd. Rayl 189 D4
Bramble Rd. With 97 F2
Brambles. Walt 94 A4
Brambles The. Colch 66 C2
Bramerton Rd. Hock 177 E3
Bramfield Rd E. Rayl 177 D1

Bramfield Rd W. Rayl 176 C1
Bramley Cl. Alres 88 A4
Bramley Cl. Brain 60 A1
Bramley Cl. Colch 67 D4
Bramley Way. May 146 C1
Bramleys The. Cogg 63 D2
Bramleys The. Hawk 178 B3
Brampton Cl. South 190 A2
Bramston Green. With 97 F2
Bramstone Cl. Gt Bad 140 C4
Bramwoods Rd. Gt Bad 140 C4
Branch Rd. Hadl 188 C1
Brandenburg Rd. Canv 197 E3
Brandon Rd. Brain 59 E1
Brands Cl. Sud 13 E3
Branksome Ave. Hock 177 F4
Branksome Rd. South 191 E1
Branscombe Cl. Frin 93 F3
Branscombe Gdns. South 201 D4
Branscombe Sq. South 192 A1
Branscombe Wlk. South 192 A1
Branston Rd. Clact 109 E2
Brantham Hill. Catt 35 E4
Braxted Cl. Hawk 178 B2
Braxted La. Gt Tot 116 B4
Braxted Rd. Gt Brx 99 E1
Braxted Rd. Lit Brx 116 A3
Bray Ct. South 192 C1
Braybrooke. Basil 185 D3
Brays La. Roch 178 C3
Braziers Cl. Chelm 140 B2
Breachfield Rd. Colch 67 E1
Bread and Cheese Hill. Thund 187 F3
Bream Ct. Colch 50 C1
Brecon Cl. Basil 186 B4
Bree Ave. Mks T 64 C2
Bree Hill. S Woo F 165 E3
Brempsons. Basil 185 D4
Brendon Pl. Chelm 126 C1
Brendon Way. South 190 A3
Brent Cl. With 97 F1
Brentwood Rd. Clact 110 B3
Bressingham Gdns. S Woo F 165 E4
Brettenham Dr. South 200 C4
Bretts Bldgs. Colch 68 A3
Brewster Cl. Canv 197 D2
Brian Bishop Cl. Walt 76 B2
Brian Cl. Chelm 140 A3
Briar Cl. Hawk 177 F2
Briar Rd. Gt Bro 52 A2
Briardale Ave. Harw 39 F2
Briarfields. Walt 93 E4
Briarswood. Canv 197 D3
Briarswood. Sprin 127 E4
Briarwood Ave. Clact 110 C3
Briarwood Cl. South 189 E3
Briarwood Dr. South 189 F3
Briarwood End. Colch 50 A2
Briary The. Wick 174 A4
Brices Way. Glems 2 A3
Brick House La. Bore 112 C1
Brick House Rd. Toll M 117 D4
Brick Kiln Cl. Cogg 63 D2
Brick Kiln La. Alres 88 C3
Brick Kiln La. Gt Hor 49 E4
Brick Kiln Rd. Colch 49 F1
Brick Kiln Rd. Sand 141 E4
Brick St. E A Gr 48 A1
Brickfield Rd. Basil 185 E1
Brickfields Rd. S Woo F 165 F4
Brickfields Way. Roch 179 D1
Brickhouse Cl. W Mers 121 D4
Brickhouse Rd. Col En 27 D2
Brickman's Hill. Brad 36 B2
Brickspring La. Gt Tot 116 B4
Brickwall Cl. Burn 170 A2
Bridewell St. Cla 4 A4
Bridge Cl. South 201 F4
Bridge Hall Rd. Bradw 61 E2
Bridge Hill. Ford 47 E4
Bridge House Cl. Wick 174 B4
Bridge Rd. Wick 175 D4
Bridge St. Bures 19 F1
Bridge St. Cogg 62 C1
Bridge St. Gt Y 9 D1
Bridge St. Hals 25 F1
Bridge St. With 97 F1
Bridge St. Writ 126 B1
Bridgebrook Cl. Colch 50 B1
Bridgefield Cl. Colch 68 B4
Bridgemans Green. Latch 157 D3
Bridgemarsh La. Alth 168 C4
Bridgend Cl. S Woo F 165 F4
Bridgewater Dr. South 190 A2
Bridgewick Rd. Deng 161 D3
Bridon Cl. E Han 153 D3
Bridport Rd. Sprin 127 E3
Brierley Ave. W Mers 121 F4
Bright Cl. Clact 109 E3
Brighten Rd. South 199 F4
Brightlingsea Rd. Thor 88 C2
Brightlingsea Rd. Wiv 69 E2
Brighton Ave. South 200 B4
Brighton Rd. Clact 110 C3
Brightside. Walt 93 F4
Brightwell Ave. South 190 B1
Brindles. Canv 196 C3
Brindley Rd. Clact 110 A4
Bringey The. Gt Bad 141 D3
Brinkley Cres. Colch 50 B1
Brinkley La. Colch 50 B3
Brinkworth Cl. Hock 177 F3
Brisbane Way. Colch 68 A1
Briscoe Rd. Basil 186 A4
Brise Cl. Brain 60 A1
Bristol Ct. Silv E 79 F2
Bristol Hill. Sho G 40 A4
Bristol Rd. Colch 68 A4
Bristol Rd. South 190 B3
Bristowe Ave. Gt Bad 141 D3
Britannia Cr. Wiv 69 D1
Britannia Ct. Basil 174 B1
Britannia Gdns. South 199 E4
Britannia Rd. South 199 E4
Brittany Way. Colch 68 A2
Britten Cl. Colch 68 C3
Britten Cres. Gt Bad 140 C4
Brixham Cl. Rayl 176 B3
Broad Cl. Hock 177 F3
Broad Green. Basil 185 E4
Broad La. Gt Hor 31 D1
Broad Oak Way. Rayl 176 C1
Broad Oaks. Wick 174 C3
Broad Oaks Park. Colch 50 C1
Broad Par. Hock 177 F3
Broad Rd. Brain 60 A4
Broad Rd. Wic S P 17 D4
Broad Street Green Rd. Gt Tot 116 A1
Broad Street Green Rd. Mald 132 B4
Broad Way. Hock 177 F3
Broad Wlk. Hock 177 F3
Broadclyst Ave. South 189 E3
Broadclyst Cl. South 192 A1
Broadclyst Gdns. South 192 A1
Broadfields. Wiv 69 E2
Broadlands. Thund 187 F3
Broadlands Ave. Hock 177 F3
Broadlands Ave. Rayl 176 B2
Broadlands Rd. Hock 177 F3
Broadlands Way. Colch 50 A1
Broadlawn. Hadl 189 D2
Broadmayne. Basil 185 E3
Broadmead Rd. Colch 50 C1
Broadmere Cl. Clact 110 C4
Broadstrood. St O 108 A3
Broadwater Gdns. Sho G 40 A4
Broadway. Clact 125 D4
Broadway. Glems 2 A3
Broadway. Silv E 79 E2
Broadway. South 198 B4
Broadway Ct. Silv E 79 E3
Broadway North. Basil 186 A3
Broadway The. Runw 174 B4
Broadway The. South 201 D4
Broadway W. South 198 B4
Brock Cl. With 114 C4
Brock Hill. Runw 163 E2
Brock Hill Dr. Runw 163 E2
Brockenhurst Way. S Woo F 142 C1
Brockham Cl. Clact 109 D3
Brockley Rd. Chelm 127 E1
Brocksford Ave. Rayl 176 C1
Brockwell La. Kelv 81 E1
Brockwell Wlk. Wick 174 B3
Brodie Rd. South 202 A4
Brograve Cl. Chelm 140 B2
Broman's La. E Mers 106 A1
Bromfords Cl. Wick 174 A3
Bromfords Dr. Wick 174 B3
Bromley Rd. Ard 51 E2
Bromley Rd. Colch 50 C1
Bromley Rd. Elmst M 70 A3
Bromley Rd. Frat 71 D2
Bromley Rd. Lawf 35 D1
Bronte Cl. Brain 78 A4
Bronte Rd. With 97 F3
Brook Cl. Brain 59 E1
Brook Cl. Gt Tot 116 A2
Brook Cl. Roch 191 D4
Brook Cl. Woo Wa 130 B1
Brook Dr. Basil 185 E1
Brook Dr. Wick 174 B3
Brook End Rd. Sprin 128 A2
Brook Farm Cl. Hals 26 A1
Brook Hall Rd. Fing 87 D3
Brook La. Chelm 140 C2
Brook La. Sprin 128 A1
Brook La. W Han 140 C2
Brook Meadow. Si Hed 15 E1
Brook Pl. Hals 25 F1
Brook Rd. Aldh 65 D4
Brook Rd. Gt T 64 B4
Brook Rd. Rayl 188 B4
Brook Rd. S Ben 187 E1
Brook Rd. Till 149 E3
Brook Rd. Toll K 101 D1
Brook St. Col En 26 C1
Brook St. Colch 68 A4
Brook St. Ded 33 F4
Brook St. Glems 2 A3
Brook St. Gt Bro 52 C1
Brook St. Mann 35 E2
Brook St. Wiv 87 D4
Brook Terr. Si Hed 15 F1
Brook View. Sand 141 E3
Brook Wlk. With 114 C4
Brooke Sq. Mald 132 A1
Brookfields. South 189 E3
Brookfields Cl. South 189 E3
Brookhouse Rd. Gt T 64 A4
Brookhurst Cl. Sprin 127 E2
Brookland. Tipt 100 B2
Brooklands. Clact 124 C3
Brooklands. Wick 174 A4
Brooklands Ave. South 189 F3
Brooklands Gdns. Clact 124 C3
Brooklands Rd. Catt 35 E4
Brooklands Rise. Catt 35 E4
Brooklands Sq. Canv 196 C2
Brooklands Wlk. Chelm 140 A4
Brooklyn Dr. Rayl 176 B3
Brooklyn Rd. Harw 40 B2
Brookside. Canv 197 D3
Brookside. Hawk 177 F2
Brookside Ave. Gt Wak 193 E1
Brookside Cl. Colch 68 A2
Broom Hill. Hals 25 F1
Broom Rd. Hull 165 F1
Broom St. Sud 13 D3
Broom Way. Lang 86 A1
Broome Gr. Wiv 69 D1
Broomfield. Hadl 188 B2
Broomfield. Silv E 79 E3
Broomfield Ave. Rayl 176 A2
Broomfield Ave. South 189 F3
Broomfield Cres. Wiv 69 D1
Broomfield Green. Canv 196 C3
Broomfield Rd. Chelm 127 D3
Broomfields. Basil 186 A3
Broomhills Industrial Estate. Brain 59 E1
Broomhills Rd. W Mers 121 E3
Broomways. Gt Wak 193 E2
Broton Dr. Hals 25 F1
Brougham Cl. Gt Wak 193 D2
Brougham Glades. Stanw 66 B3
Broughton Cl. Colch 67 E2
Broughton Rd. Hadl 188 C1
Broughton Rd. S Woo F 165 F3
Browning Ave. South 191 D1
Browning Cl. Colch 66 C3
Browning Rd. Brain 78 A4
Browning Rd. Mald 145 D4
Brownings Ave. Chelm 127 D3
Brownlow Bend. Basil 185 E3
Brownlow Cross. Basil 185 E3
Brownlow Green. Basil 185 E3
Browns Ave. Runw 163 F1
Brownsea Way. Colch 67 D2
Broxted Dr. Wick 174 C3
Bruce Gr. Chelm 140 A4
Bruce Gr. Wick 175 D4
Bruce Rd. Writ 126 A1
Bruff Dr. Walt 94 A4
Bruges Rd. Canv 197 E1
Brundells Rd. Gt Bro 71 D3
Brundish. Basil 186 A3
Brundon La. Sud 12 B4
Brunel Rd. Brain 60 A1
Brunel Rd. Clact 110 A4
Brunel Rd. South 189 E3
Brunel Rd. Thund 187 E4
Brunel Way. Colch 50 B3
Brunel Way. S Woo F 165 E4
Brunswick House Cut. Mist 36 A2
Brunswick Rd. South 200 B4
Brunwins Cl. Wick 174 C4
Brussum Rd. Canv 197 E1
Brust Rd. Canv 197 E1
Bruton Ave. South 190 A3
Bryanstone Mews. Colch 66 C3
Bryant Ave. South 200 C3
Bryant's La. Woo Mor 143 E4
Bryce Way. Basil 186 B3
Buchan Cl. Brain 78 A4
Buchanan Way. Latch 157 D3
Buck Hill. Bl Not 77 F3
Buckeridge Way. Brad O S 137 D2
Buckerills. Basil 186 A3
Buckfast Ave. Walt 93 E3
Buckhatch La. Rett 153 E2
Buckingham Dr. Colch 68 C4
Buckingham Rd. Hock 177 E3
Buckingham Sq. Wick 175 D3
Buckland. South 192 B1
Buckland Gate. S Woo F 165 E3
Bucklebury Heath. S Woo F 165 E3
Buckleys. Gt Bad 140 C4
Buckleys Cl. Wic Bis 115 F3
Buckley's La. Gt T 63 E3
Buckwins Sq. Basil 174 B1
Buckwoods Rd. Brain 60 A1
Buddleia Ct. Wiv 69 D1
Budna Rd. Canv 196 C3
Buffett Way. Colch 68 C3
Buick Ave. Clact 124 B3
Bulbecks Wlk. S Woo F 165 E3
Bulford La. Bl Not 78 B3
Bulford Mill La. T Gr 78 B3
Bull Hill Rd. Clact 109 F3
Bull La. Hock 177 E3
Bull La. L Mel 7 E4
Bull La. Mald 132 A2
Bull La. Rayl 176 C1
Bull La. Tipt 100 B2
Bullen Wlk. Chelm 140 B2
Buller Rd. N Fam 156 A1
Bullfinch Cl. Colch 68 C4
Bullock Wood Cl. Colch 50 B2
Bullocks La. Sud 12 C3
Bull's Hill. Ca Hed 15 F2
Bullwood App. Hock 177 D3
Bullwood Hall La. Rayl 177 D2
Bullwood Rd. Hock 177 E3
Bulmer Rd. Sud 12 B3
Bulmer St. Bul 11 E2
Bulow Ave. Canv 197 D2
Bulphan Cl. Wick 174 C3
Bulwark Rd. South 201 F4
Bumfords La. Hat Per 130 A4
Bumfords La. Ult 130 A4
Bundick's Hill. Chelm 126 C2
Bung Row. Gt Brx 99 E1
Bunters Ave. South 201 E3
Bunting Cl. Chelm 140 A3
Bunyan Rd. Brain 59 F2
Burches Mead. Thund 188 A4
Burches Rd. Thund 187 F4
Burdett Ave. South 199 F4
Burdett Rd. South 200 B4
Burdun Cl. With 114 B4
Bure Dr. With 97 E2
Buren Ave. Canv 197 F2
Bures Rd. Bures 30 A4
Bures Rd. Sud 13 D2
Burfield Cl. South 189 F3
Burfield Rd. South 189 F3
Burgate Cl. Clact 109 D2
Burges Cl. South 201 E3
Burges Rd. South 201 D3
Burges Terr. South 200 C3
Burgess Field. Sprin 127 F2
Burgundy Gdns. Basil 186 A4
Burkitts La. Sud 12 C4
Burleigh Sq. South 201 D4
Burlescoombe Cl. South 201 D4
Burlescoombe Leas. South 192 A1
Burlescoombe Rd. South 192 A1
Burlington Ct. Basil 174 A1
Burlington Gdns. Hadl 188 C2
Burlington Gdns. Hull 176 C4
Burlington Rd. Colch 67 F3
Burmanny Cl. Clact 109 E2
Burnaby Rd. South 200 B4
Burne Ave. Wick 174 A3
Burnham Ave. Col N 156 A3
Burnham Cl. Walt 94 A4
Burnham Rd. Alth 158 A1
Burnham Rd. Hull 165 F1
Burnham Rd. Latch 157 E3
Burnham Rd. Mund 156 B4
Burnham Rd. S Woo F 154 B1
Burnham Rd. Soum 159 E1
Burnham Rd. South 189 E1
Burnham Rd. Sprin 127 E3
Burnham Rd. Woo Mor 143 F3
Burns Ave. Basil 186 A3
Burns Ave. Colch 66 C3
Burns Cl. Mald 132 A1
Burns Cres. Chelm 140 B4
Burns Green. Gt Tot 116 A2
Burnside. Canv 197 D3
Burnside Cres. Chelm 127 D4
Burnt Dick Hill. Box 31 F4
Burnt Mills Rd. Basil 174 B1
Burnthouse Rd. Ea Col 45 F1
Burr Cl. Lit Oak 39 E1
Burr Hill Chase. South 190 C2
Burroughs Piece Rd. Sud 12 C4
Burrows Cl. Clact 109 E3
Burrows Cl. Lawf 35 D2
Burrow's Rd. Ea Col 45 D4
Burrows Way. Rayl 176 B1
Burrs Rd. Clact 110 A4
Burrswood Pl. Mald 132 C2
Burstall Cl. Clact 109 D2
Burton Pl. Sprin 127 F2
Burton's Green Rd. Hals 44 A2
Burwell Ave. Canv 196 C3
Bury Cl. Colch 68 A4
Bury Cl. Mks T 64 C2
Bury La. Hat Pev 113 F2
Bury The. St O 108 A2
Burywoods. Colch 49 D2
Bush Gr. Sud 12 B3
Bushell Way. Walt 93 F3
Bushey Cl. S Woo F 165 F4
Butchers La. Walt 94 A4
Butler Rd. Hals 25 E1
Butler's La. Wrab 37 F1
Butlers Way. Gt Y 9 D1
Butneys. Basil 185 D4
Butt La. Mald 132 A2
Butt Rd. Colch 67 F3
Butt Rd. Nay 20 B3
Butt Rd. Sud 13 D3
Butterbur Chase. S Woo F 165 E3
Buttercup Wlk. With 97 F2
Butterfield Rd. Bore 128 C4
Buttermere. Bl Not 77 E4
Butterys. South 200 C4
Button's Hill. Alth 158 A2
Butt's Green Rd. Dan 142 A2
Butt's Green Rd. Sand 141 F2
Butts La. Dan 142 C4
Butts Paddock. Cane 168 B1
Butts Rd. South 193 E1
Butts Way. Chelm 139 F2
Buxey Cl. W Mers 121 D4
Buxton Ave. Hadl 189 D2
Buxton Cl. Hadl 189 D2
Buxton Rd. Cogg 62 C2
Buxton Rd. Colch 68 A2
Buxton Sq. Hadl 189 D2
Buyl Ave. Canv 197 D3
Byfield. South 189 F4
Byfleets. Basil 185 F2
Byford Cl. Rayl 176 C2
Byng Cres. Th L S 74 A1
Byng Gdns. Brain 60 B2
Bypass Rd. St O 108 A3
Byrne Dr. South 190 C2
Byron Ave. Colch 66 C4
Byron Ave. South 191 D1
Byron Cl. Brain 78 A4
Byron Cl. Canv 197 E2
Byron Dr. Wic Bis 115 F3
Byron Rd. Chelm 127 E1
Byrony Cl. With 97 E2
Bywater Rd. S Woo F 165 E3
Cabinet Way. South 189 E3
Cadenhouse Mews. Colch 66 C4
Caernarvon Cl. Hock 177 E3
Cage Field Cotts. Gt Stam 179 F2
Cage La. Box 32 A3
Cagefield Rd. Gt Stam 179 F2
Cairns Rd. Colch 68 A1
Calamint Rd. With 97 E2
Caldbeck Way. Bl Not 77 E3
Caledonia Rd. Sho G 40 A4
California Cl. Colch 50 A2
California Rd. Mist 36 A2
Callis St. Cla 4 A4
Calm Patch. Burn 170 B2
Calvert Dr. Basil 174 B1
Calves La. Nay 20 A4
Cam Way. With 97 E1
Camberton Rd. Brain 59 F3
Camborne Cl. Sprin 127 F3
Cambrai Rd. Colch 67 E2
Cambria Cl. Canv 196 B2
Cambria Cl. Mist 36 A2
Cambridge Gdns. Hawk 178 B3
Cambridge Rd. Canv 196 C2
Cambridge Rd. Clact 109 F2
Cambridge Rd. Colch 67 E3
Cambridge Rd. Frin 94 A3
Cambridge Rd. South 199 F4
Cambridge Way. Bures 28 C4
Cambridge Wlk. Colch 67 E3
Camellia Ave. Clact 109 E2
Camellia Cl. Sprin 127 F3
Camellia Cres. Clact 109 E2
Camelot Gdns. Basil 186 B4
Cameron Cl. Hadl 189 E1
Camoise Cl. Topp 14 A4
Camomile Way. Colch 49 E1
Camp Folley N. Colch 68 A3
Camp Folley S. Colch 68 A3
Camp Rd. Gt Bro 71 D4
Campbell Cl. Chelm 140 A4
Campbell Dr. Colch 50 C1
Campbell Rd. With 97 F3
Camper Rd. South 200 B3
Camperdown Rd. Canv 197 E3
Campfield Rd. South 201 F3
Campion Rd. Colch 68 A3
Campion Way. With 97 F2
Campions Hill. Bures 30 B4
Camulodunum Way. Colch 67 E1
Canberra Cl. Chelm 126 C3
Canberra Cl. Colch 68 A1
Candlemakers The. South 191 D3
Candytuft Rd. Sprin 127 F3
Canendon View Rd. Ashi 178 B3
Canewdon Cl. Runw 163 E1
Canewdon Gdns. Runw 163 E1
Canewdon Hall Cl. Cane 168 B1
Canewdon Rd. Ashi 178 B4
Canewdon Rd. South 199 F4
Canford Cl. Gt Bad 140 C4
Canhams Rd. Sud 13 E3
Canney Rd. Steep 147 E2
Canning St. Harw 40 B3
Cannon Leys. Chelm 140 B2
Cannon Rd. Colch 68 A3
Cannon St. Colch 68 A3
Cannons Cl. Colch 67 E2
Canons Cl. S Woo F 142 C1
Canonsleigh Cres. South 189 F1
Cansey La. Brad 54 C3
Canterbury Ave. South 191 F2
Canterbury Cl. Basil 185 F4
Canterbury Rd. Clact 110 C3
Canterbury Rd. Colch 68 A3
Canterbury Rd. Sud 7 E1
Canterbury Way. Chelm 126 C2
Canters The. Thund 188 A3
Canuden Rd. Chelm 126 C1
Canute Cl. Cane 168 C1
Canvey Rd. Basil 186 C3
Canvey Rd. Canv 196 B2
Canvey Rd. Hadl 189 D1
Canvey Way. S Ben 187 D2
Canvey Wlk. Sprin 127 F3
Canwick Gr. Colch 68 B2
Cap Pillar Cl. Wiv 69 D1
Capadocia St. South 200 C3
Cape Cl. Colch 66 C3
Capel Cl. Chelm 127 D4
Capel Park. Walt 93 F4
Capel Rd. Colch 67 E3
Capel Terr. South 200 A4
Caper La. Birch 83 F2
Capons La. Dan 143 D3
Captains Rd. W Mers 121 D3
Captains Wood Rd. Gt Tot 116 A2
Cardigan Ave. South 190 B2
Cardinal Cl. Colch 69 D4
Card's Rd. Sand 141 E3
Carisbrooke Ave. Clact 110 A4
Carisbrooke Dr. S Woo F 165 E3
Carisbrooke Rd. South 190 C1
Carlingford Dr. South 190 B2
Carlisle Cl. Colch 68 A4
Carlton Ave. South 190 B2
Carlton Cl. Gt Y 9 D1
Carlton Dr. South 198 C4
Carlton Dr. Thund 188 B2
Carlton Rd. Basil 186 C4
Carlton Rd. Clact 110 A3
Carlton Rd. Runw 163 E1
Carmania Cl. South 192 C1
Carnarvon Rd. Clact 109 F2
Carnarvon Rd. South 190 C1
Carnation Cl. Sprin 127 F3
Carnival Gdns. South 189 E2
Caro Rd. Canv 197 E2
Carolina Way. Tipt 100 B3
Caroline Cl. Wiv 69 E2
Caroline's Cl. South 190 C3
Carpenters. Barl 192 C3
Carriage Dr. Sprin 127 F4
Carrington Ct. W Mers 121 E4
Carrington Way. Brain 59 F4
Carringtons Rd. Gt Bro 52 B2
Carroll Gdns. Wick 174 B3
Carron Mead. S Woo F 165 F3
Carrs Rd. Clact 109 E2
Carruthers Cl. Runw 163 E1
Carruthers Dr. Runw 163 E1
Carsons Dr. Sud 13 E3
Cartbridge Cl. Walt 94 A4
Carters Cl. Clact 109 D2
Carters Hill. Box 32 A3

Carters La. Lit Brx 115 F3
Cartlodge Ave. Wick 174 C4
Cartwright Rd. Thund 187 E4
Cartwright Wlk. Sprin 127 F1
Cashiobury Terr. South 199 F4
Cashmere Way. Basil 185 E1
Cassel Ave. Canv 197 E3
Cassino Rd. Chelm 126 C3
Cassino Rd. Colch 67 E2
Castle Ave. Hadl 188 B1
Castle Bailey. Colch 67 F4
Castle Cl. Ca Hed 15 F2
Castle Cl. Rayl 176 B1
Castle Cl. South 202 A4
Castle Dr. Hadl 198 A4
Castle Dr. Rayl 176 B2
Castle Hill. Ded 33 F3
Castle La. Ca Hed 15 F2
Castle La. Hadl 188 C1
Castle Rd. Clact 109 F2
Castle Rd. Colch 68 A4
Castle Rd. Hadl 188 C1
Castle Rd. Rayl 176 B1
Castle Terr. Rayl 176 B1
Castle View Rd. Canv 197 D3
Castle Way. St O 108 A2
Castle Wlk. Canv 197 D3
Castlegate St. Harw 40 B3
Castleton Rd. South 191 F1
Castleward Cl. Elmst M 87 E4
Caswell Mews. Sprin 127 F1
Catchpole La. Gt Tot 116 A2
Catchpool Rd. Colch 67 F4
Caterham Cl. Clact 109 E3
Catherine Cl. Clact 110 A3
Catherine Cl. E Han 153 D3
Catherine Hunt Way. Colch 67 E1
Catherine Rd. S Ben 187 F2
Catherines Cl. Gt Le 95 D3
Cat's La. Sud 13 D4
Cattawade End. Basil 185 E4
Cattawade Link. Basil 185 E4
Cattawade St. Catt 35 E4
Caulfield Rd. South 201 E4
Causeway Cl. Glems 2 B3
Causeway The. Brain 59 F2
Causeway The. Colch 50 B1
Causeway The. Gt Bad 140 C4
Causeway The. Gt Hor 31 D1
Causeway The. Hals 25 F1
Causeway The. Mald 132 A2
Causeway The. Ridge 8 A4
Causeway The. Topp 14 A4
Causeway The. Ult 130 B3
Causewayend. Lawf 35 D3
Causton Rd. Colch 67 F4
Caustones Cl. Sud 13 E3
Caustonway. Rayl 176 B2
Cavendish Ave. Colch 68 B2
Cavendish Dr. Clact 109 D2
Cavendish Dr. Lawf 35 D2
Cavendish Gdns. Brain 60 B3
Cavendish Gdns. South 190 A1
Cavendish La. Cav 1 C2
Cavendish La. Glems 2 A3
Cavendish Rd. Ashi 166 C1
Cavendish Rd. Cla 4 B4
Cavendish Way. Sud 12 C4
Caversham Ave. South 192 C1
Caversham Park Ave. Rayl 176 B3
Cawkwell Cl. Sprin 128 A2
Cecil Way. Rayl 176 C1
Cedar Ave. Brigh 106 C4
Cedar Ave. Chelm 127 D2
Cedar Ave. Tipt 100 B4
Cedar Ave. Wick 174 B3
Cedar Avenue West. Chelm 127 D2
Cedar Chase. Mald 132 B3
Cedar Cl. Rayl 188 C4
Cedar Cl. South 191 D1
Cedar Cl. Walt 94 A4
Cedar Cres. Lawf 35 E2
Cedar Dr. Hull 165 F1
Cedar Dr. With 98 A3
Cedar Gr. Burn 170 A3
Cedar Hall Gdns. Thund 188 A3
Cedar Mews. Hock 177 E3
Cedar Park Cl. Thund 188 A4
Cedar Rd. Basil 186 C4
Cedar Rd. Canv 196 C2
Cedar Rd. Thund 188 A3
Cedar Way. Gt Ben 89 F4
Cedar Wlk. Cane 168 B1
Cedars Rd. Colch 67 F3
Cedars The. Gt Wak 193 D2
Cedars The. S Woo F 165 E4
Celeborn St. S Woo F 165 D3
Centaury Cl. Stanw 66 B4
Central Ave. Canv 196 C3
Central Ave. Frin 94 A3
Central Ave. Hadl 188 C3
Central Ave. Hawk 178 B3
Central Ave. Hull 176 C4
Central Ave. South 191 E1
Central Ave. Walt 94 A3
Central Cl. Hadl 188 C2
Central Sq. Chelm 127 D1
Central Wall. Canv 197 D3
Central Wall Cotts. Canv 197 D3
Central Wall Rd. Canv 197 D3
Centre The. Hals 25 F1
Centurion Cl. South 201 F4
Ceylon Rd. South 199 E4
Chadacre Rd. South 192 A1
Chadburn Rd. L Mel 7 E4
Chadwick Rd. S Woo F 154 C1
Chadwick Rd. South 199 E4
Chaffinch Cl. South 201 F4
Chaffinch Gdns. Colch 68 C4
Chaingate Ave. South 191 F1
Chalfont Cl. South 189 E2
Chalfont Rd. Colch 50 B2
Chalk End. Basil 186 A3
Chalk St. Rett 163 F4
Chalklands. Sand 141 E2
Chalkwell Ave. South 199 D4
Chalkwell Espl. South 199 D4
Chalkwell Park Dr. South 189 F1
Challacombe. South 192 B1
Challenge Way. Colch 68 A3
Challis La. Brain 78 A4
Challis La. Brain 59 F1
Challock Lees. Basil 186 B3
Chalvedon Ave. Basil 186 A4
Chamberlain Ave. Canv 197 E2
Chamberlain Ave. Walt 94 A4
Chamberlains Rd. S Woo F 165 E3
Champion Cl. Wick 174 B3
Champions Way. S Woo F 165 E4
Champlain Ave. Canv 196 C3
Chancel Cl. Thund 187 E3
Chancel Cl. Till 149 F2
Chancellor Rd. South 200 A4
Chancery Grove. Colch 86 A4
Chancery Pl. Writ 126 A1
Chandlers Cl. Clact 109 D2
Chandlers Cl. W Mers 121 E4
Chandlers Ct. W Mers 121 E4
Chandlers Row. Colch 68 B3
Chandlers Way. S Woo F 165 F4
Chandlers Way. South 191 D3
Chandos Par. Hadl 188 C2
Chaney Rd. Wiv 69 D1
Chanterelle. Colch 50 A2
Chanton Cl. South 189 E4
Chantry La. Bore 113 D2
Chantry The. Colch 67 E4
Chapel Ct. Ard 51 F4
Chapel Cut. Mist 36 A2
Chapel Hill. Bel W 10 B2
Chapel Hill. Brain 60 A1
Chapel Hill. Hals 25 E1
Chapel La. Ard 51 D1
Chapel La. Box 32 A2
Chapel La. Elmst M 70 A3
Chapel La. Gt Bro 71 D3
Chapel La. Gt Wak 193 D2
Chapel La. High 21 E3
Chapel La. Lit Bad 129 D2
Chapel La. Mald 132 C1
Chapel La. Purl 155 E4
Chapel La. S Ben 188 B2
Chapel La. St O 108 A2
Chapel La. Sud 13 E1
Chapel La. Tend 72 C4
Chapel La. Thor 89 D3
Chapel La. Till 149 F2
Chapel La. W Berg 48 C2
Chapel La. Walt 93 D3
Chapel Rd. Beau 73 F4
Chapel Rd. Box 32 A2
Chapel Rd. Brigh 107 D4
Chapel Rd. Burn 170 B2
Chapel Rd. Gt Tot 116 B3
Chapel Rd. Langh 32 B2
Chapel Rd. Ridge 8 A4
Chapel Rd. South 201 F3
Chapel Rd. Stanw 66 B3
Chapel Rd. Tipt 100 C2
Chapel Rd. Toll D 118 C2
Chapel Rd. Tolle 118 C2
Chapel Rd. W Berg 48 C2
Chapel Rd. Wiv 87 D4
Chapel St. Cla 3 D2
Chapel St. Hals 25 F1
Chapel St. Wiv 87 D4
Chapel St N. Colch 67 F3
Chapel St S. Colch 67 F3
Chapelfields. Walt 93 F3
Chaplin Cl. Chelm 140 A1
Chaplin Dr. Colch 50 B1
Chaplins. Walt 93 F4
Chapman Ct. Canv 196 B2
Chapman Rd. Clact 109 F2
Chapman Rd. South 198 A2
Chapmans Cl. Hadl 189 D1
Chapmans La. W Mers 121 E4
Chapmans Wlk. Hadl 189 D1
Chappel Hill. Wa Col 46 B3
Chappel Rd. Ford 47 E4
Chappel Rd. Gt T 46 B1
Chappel Rd. M Bure 28 C2
Charfleets Cl. Canv 196 B2
Charfleets Rd. Canv 196 B2
Charfleets Service Rd. Canv 196 B2
Charles Cl. South 190 A3
Charles Ct. Wiv 69 E2
Charles Pell Rd. Colch 68 C4
Charles Rd. Brigh 106 C3
Charles St. Colch 68 A3
Charleston Ave. Basil 174 B1
Charlotte Ave. Wick 174 B4
Charlotte Ct. S Woo F 165 E3
Charlotte Dr. Walt 93 F3
Charlotte Way. With 98 A1
Charlton Cl. Basil 186 B4
Charnock Cl. Walt 93 F3
Charnwood Ave. Chelm 126 C1
Charterhouse. Basil 185 E3
Chartfield Dr. Walt 93 E4
Chartwell Cl. Brain 59 F4
Chartwell Sq. South 200 A4
Chase Cl. Thund 187 F3
Chase Ct. Colch 68 C4
Chase Dr. S Woo F 165 E4
Chase End. Rayl 176 C1
Chase Gdns. South 190 B2
Chase La. Harw 39 F1
Chase Rd. South 200 B4
Chase Rd E. Gt Bro 71 E4
Chase Rd W. Gt Bro 71 D3
Chase The. Aldh 65 D4
Chase The. Ashi 178 B4
Chase The. Bl Not 77 E3
Chase The. Bore 128 C4
Chase The. Brain 59 F4
Chase The. Church 183 F4
Chase The. Clact 110 C3
Chase The. Colch 68 A4
Chase The. Colch 68 B4
Chase The. Colch 68 C4
Chase The. Ded 34 A2
Chase The. Elmst M 70 A3
Chase The. Gold 134 A1
Chase The. Gt Bad 140 C3
Chase The. Kelv 81 E1
Chase The. Rayl 176 C1
Chase The. Runw 164 A2
Chase The. S Woo F 165 E4
Chase The. Soum 159 E2
Chase The. Thund 188 A3
Chase The. Toll D 118 A2
Chase The. Tolle 119 E1
Chase The. W Mers 121 E3
Chase The. Wick 174 A3
Chase The. Wick 174 C2
Chase Way The. Colch 49 E1
Chaseside. Rayl 188 C4
Chaseway. Basil 185 F2
Chatfield Way. Basil 186 B4
Chatham Pavement. Basil 186 B4
Chatsworth. Thund 187 F3
Chatsworth Gdns. Clact 109 E1
Chaucer Cl. Clact 109 D1
Chaucer Cl. Mald 145 D4
Chaucer Cres. Brain 78 A4
Chaucer Rd. Chelm 127 E1
Chaucer Rd. Sud 7 E1
Chaucer Way. Colch 66 C3
Chaucer Wlk. Wick 174 B3
Cheapside E. Rayl 176 B2
Cheapside W. Rayl 176 A2
Cheddar Ave. South 190 A3
Chedington. South 192 B1
Cheldon Barton. South 201 E4
Chelmer Ave. Rayl 176 B1
Chelmer Cl. Lit Tot 117 D2
Chelmer Cl. Walt 93 F4
Chelmer Lea. Gt Bad 140 C4
Chelmer Pl. Chelm 127 E2
Chelmer Rd. Brain 60 B1
Chelmer Rd. Sprin 127 F2
Chelmer Rd. With 97 F1
Chelmer Terr. Mald 132 A1
Chelmer Valley Rd. Chelm 127 D3
Chelmer Village Way. Sprin 128 A2
Chelmer Way. Burn 170 A3
Chelmer Way. South 201 E4
Chelmerton Ave. Gt Bad 140 C4
Chelmesford Rd. Purl 144 B2
Chelmsford Ave. South 190 C1
Chelmsford Rd. Chelm 126 B1
Chelmsford Rd. Clact 110 B3
Chelmsford Rd. Rayl 164 C1
Chelmsford Rd. Rayl 175 F4
Chelmsford Rd. Woo Mor 143 E3
Chelmwood. Canv 197 D3
Chelsea Ave. South 200 B3
Chelsea Rd. Sud 12 C4
Chelsworth Ave. Sud 13 D4
Chelsworth Cl. South 200 C4
Chelsworth Cres. South 200 C4
Cheltenham Dr. South 189 F1
Cheltenham dr. Thund 188 A4
Cheltenham Rd. Hock 177 F4
Cheltenham Rd. South 200 B4
Chelwater. Gt Bad 140 B4
Chequers La. Glems 2 B3
Chequers La. Mald 132 A1
Chequers Rd. Lit Bro 53 E4
Chequers The. Alres 88 A4
Cheriton Rd. Brain 60 B1
Cherry Blossom La. Col N 155 F3
Cherry Chase. Tipt 100 B2
Cherry Cl. Canv 196 C2
Cherry Cl. Hock 177 F4
Cherry Garden La. Dan 143 D4
Cherry Garden Rd. Mald 131 F1
Cherry La. Gt Y 15 D4
Cherry La. Wick 175 D4
Cherry Orchard. Soum 159 F2
Cherry Orchard La. Roch 178 A1
Cherry Row. Colch 66 C3
Cherry Tree Ave. Clact 109 E1
Cherry Tree Chase. Gt Wak 193 E1
Cherry Tree Cl. Lit Oak 57 D4
Cherry Tree La. Colch 86 A4
Cherrybrook. South 192 B1
Cherrydene Cl. Hull 165 F1
Cherrydown. Rayl 176 B2
Cherrydown East. Basil 185 D3
Cherrydown West. Basil 185 D3
Cherrygarden La. Chelm 140 A4
Cherrymeade. S Ben 188 A2
Cherrytree Rd. Sud 13 D4
Cherrytree Rise. With 98 A3
Cherrywood Dr. Colch 66 C3
Chertsey Cl. South 192 B1
Chervil Cl. Tipt 100 B2
Cherwell Dr. Chelm 126 B3
Cheshunt Dr. Rayl 176 A3
Chess La. With 98 A1
Chester Ave. South 200 B3
Chester Pl. Chelm 127 D3
Chester Way. Basil 185 F4
Chesterfield Ave. Thund 187 E3
Chesterfield Cres. South 189 E3
Chesterford Gdns. Basil 185 F4
Chesterford Green. Basil 185 F4
Chestnut Ave. Clact 109 E2
Chestnut Ave. Colch 86 A4
Chestnut Ave. Gos 42 C4
Chestnut Ave. Hat Pev 114 A2
Chestnut Ave. Mald 132 B3
Chestnut Ave. Walt 93 E3
Chestnut Cl. Burn 170 A3
Chestnut Cl. Hock 177 F3
Chestnut Ct. Basil 186 A2
Chestnut Farm Dr. Alth 157 F1
Chestnut Gr. Brain 59 F1
Chestnut Gr. S Ben 187 D2
Chestnut Gr. South 191 D1
Chestnut Path. Cane 168 B1
Chestnut Rd. Alres 88 A4
Chestnut Rd. Basil 186 A2
Chestnut Rd. Glems 2 A3
Chestnut Way. Brigh 106 C4
Chestnut Way. Tipt 100 B4
Chestnut Wlk. Canv 196 C2
Chestnut Wlk. Chelm 127 D3
Chestnut Wlk. Lit Bad 129 F1
Chestnuts. Basil 186 A4
Chestnuts The. Rayl 176 C2
Cheveling Rd. Colch 68 B1
Chevening Gdns. Hock 177 E3
Chevers Pawen. Basil 186 A3
Cheviot Dr. Chelm 126 B3
Chevy Ct. Harw 39 E1
Cheyne Ct. Sud 12 C3
Chichester Cl. Basil 185 F4
Chichester Cl. Canv 197 D1
Chichester Dr. Sprin 127 E2
Chichester Rd. South 200 A4
Chigborough Rd. Gt Tot 132 C3
Chignall Rd. Chelm 126 B3
Chilburn Rd. Clact 110 A4
Childwell Alley. Colch 68 A4
Chilham Cl. Basil 186 B3
Chiltern App. Canv 196 C2
Chiltern Cl. Colch 49 F1
Chiltern Cl. Rayl 176 B2
Chilterns The. Canv 196 C2
Chilton Cl. Gt Bad 140 B4
Chilton Cl. Gt Hor 49 D4
Chilton Cotts. Worm 29 F2
Chilton Ct. Sud 13 D4
Chimes The. S Ben 187 F2
Chimney Pot La. Purl 143 F2
Chinchilla Rd. South 200 B4
Chingford Ave. Clact 109 F4
Chinook. Colch 50 B2
Chipping Hill. Hals 25 F1
Chipping Hill. With 97 F2
Chipping Row. S Woo F 165 F4
Chippingdell. With 97 F2
Chipstead Wlk. Clact 109 E3
Chittock Gate. Basil 185 F3
Chittock Mead. Basil 185 F3
Chitts Hill. E A Gr 48 B1
Chitts Hill. Stanw 66 B4
Cholvedon Sq. Basil 186 A3
Chrismund Way. Gt T 46 B1
Christ Church Ct. Colch 67 E3
Christchurch Ave. Wick 174 A4
Christchurch Rd. South 191 E1
Christina Rd. With 114 C4
Christine Chase. Colch 66 C3
Christmas Field. Si Hed 15 E1
Christopher Ct. Sud 12 C4
Christopher Dr. Lit Cla 91 E1
Christopher La. Sud 12 C4
Christy Ave. Chelm 126 C2
Church Chase. Gt Brx 99 D2
Church Chase. Rett 164 B3
Church Cl. Canv 196 C2
Church Cl. Cav 1 B1
Church Cl. W Berg 48 C2
Church Cl. Wic Bis 115 E3
Church Cres. Clact 109 F1
Church End. Pan 59 D4
Church End Ave. Runw 163 F1
Church End La. Runw 163 F1
Church Farm Way. Colch 49 F2
Church Fields. Gt Y 8 C1
Church Gate. Glems 2 B3
Church Gr. Aldh 65 D4
Church Green. Cane 168 B1
Church Green. Cogg 63 D2
Church Green. Lit Y 9 E2
Church Green. Wic Bis 115 E3
Church Hill. Ea Col 45 E3
Church Hill. Lawf 34 C2
Church Hill. Purl 144 C1
Church Hill. Rams 39 D1
Church Hill. Rowh 86 C4
Church Hill. South 198 C4
Church Hill. Wh Not 78 C1
Church Hill. Woo Wa 130 B1
Church La. Alah 64 B2
Church La. Basil 174 A1
Church La. Beau 74 A3
Church La. Brain 59 F3
Church La. Ca Hed 15 F2
Church La. Chelm 127 D1
Church La. Cla 4 A4
Church La. Colch 67 F4
Church La. E Mers 105 F1
Church La. Frin 93 D2
Church La. Gt Wig 102 C2
Church La. Harw 40 C3
Church La. Lit Tot 117 D1
Church La. Mist 35 F2
Church La. Mks T 64 B2
Church La. Mks T 65 D2
Church La. Nay 20 A1
Church La. Ridge 8 A3
Church La. S Han 163 E4
Church La. Sprin 127 E2
Church La. Stanw 66 A2
Church La. Stow M 155 E2
Church La. Topp 14 A4
Church La. W Han 152 A2
Church La. Weel 91 D4
Church La. Writ 126 A1
Church Mead. Wh Not 78 C1
Church Meadow. Bul 11 F2
Church Par. Canv 196 C3
Church Park. Cla 3 E2
Church Park Rd. Basil 186 A3
Church Rd. Alres 88 A4
Church Rd. Ashi 178 B4
Church Rd. Barl 192 C4
Church Rd. Basil 186 C2
Church Rd. Basil 185 E3
Church Rd. Bl Not 78 A3
Church Rd. Bore 129 D3
Church Rd. Box 31 F3
Church Rd. Bradw 61 E1
Church Rd. Bradw 61 F3
Church Rd. Brigh 106 C4
Church Rd. Bul 11 F2
Church Rd. Burn 170 A3
Church Rd. Clact 110 A2
Church Rd. Copf 65 F1
Church Rd. Elmst M 70 A4
Church Rd. Ford 47 E3
Church Rd. Frat 70 B1
Church Rd. Gos 42 C4
Church Rd. Gt Tot 116 B1
Church Rd. Gt Y 8 C1
Church Rd. Hadl 188 C1
Church Rd. Hat Pev 114 A2
Church Rd. Hock 177 D4
Church Rd. Kelv 81 E1
Church Rd. Lay H 84 C2
Church Rd. Lit Bad 129 D3
Church Rd. Lit Bro 53 D2
Church Rd. N Fam 167 D4
Church Rd. Peld 103 E3
Church Rd. Rayl 176 C1
Church Rd. Rayl 175 E4
Church Rd. South 200 A4
Church Rd. South 201 E3
Church Rd. Sud 13 D3
Church Rd. T Gr 79 D3
Church Rd. Tend 72 A3
Church Rd. Terl 96 B1
Church Rd. Thor 89 D3
Church Rd. Thund 187 E3
Church Rd. Tipt 100 B3
Church Rd. Toll M 117 F1
Church Rd. Twin 18 B3
Church Rd. Ult 130 B3
Church Rd. W Berg 48 C2
Church Rd. W Han 152 A2
Church Rd. W Mers 121 D3
Church Rd. Walt 94 B4
Church Rd. Wic Bis 115 F3
Church Rd. Wic S P 17 D3
Church Rd. With 80 A1
Church Rd. Worm 29 F3
Church Rd. Wrab 37 F2
Church Sq. Bures 19 F1
Church Sq. St O 108 A2
Church St. Bel S P 5 D2
Church St. Box 32 A4
Church St. Chelm 127 D1
Church St. Cla 4 A4
Church St. Cogg 63 D1
Church St. Col En 27 D1
Church St. Colch 67 F4
Church St. Fee 81 D1
Church St. Gest 10 C1
Church St. Gold 133 F4
Church St. Gt Bad 141 D3
Church St. Gt Map 16 B1
Church St. Harw 40 C3
Church St. Mald 132 A1
Church St. Nay 20 B3
Church St. Pan 59 F4
Church St. Rayl 176 B1
Church St. Rowh 87 D4
Church St. Si Hed 15 E1
Church St. Sud 12 B3
Church St. Toll D 118 B2
Church St. Tolle 119 E1
Church St. With 97 F2
Church View. Ard 51 F4
Church View Rd. Thund 187 F3
Church Wlk. Colch 67 F4
Church Wlk. Mald 131 F2
Church Wlk. Sud 12 C4
Churchfield Cotts. Church 183 D4
Churchfield Rd. Cogg 63 D2
Churchfield Rd. Walt 94 B4
Churchfields. South 192 C1
Churchfields. W Mers 121 D3
Churchill Ave. Hals 26 A2
Churchill Cl. Brigh 106 C4
Churchill Dr. Sud 7 F1
Churchill Rd. Brain 59 F4
Churchill Rd. Tipt 100 C3
Churchill Rise. Sprin 127 F4
Churchill Way. South 200 A4
Churchill Way. Colch 68 A2
Churchponds. Ca Hed 15 F2
Churchway. Hadl 188 C1
Churchwell Ave. Copf 83 D4
Churnwood Rd. Colch 50 B1
Chuzzlewit Dr. Chelm 126 C4
Cimarron Cl. S Woo F 165 E4
Cinque Port Rd. Brigh 106 C4
Circular Rd. N. Colch 67 F3
Circular Rd E. Colch 67 F3
Circular Rd S. Colch 67 F2

Cistern Yd. Colch 67 F4
City Rd. W Mers 121 D3
Clachar Cl. Sprin 128 A2
Clacton Rd. Elmst M 70 B2
Clacton Rd. Frin 93 D1
Clacton Rd. Gt Oak 55 E1
Clacton Rd. Lit Oak 57 D3
Clacton Rd. Mist 54 A3
Clacton Rd. St O 108 A2
Clacton Rd. Thor 89 E2
Clacton Rd. Weel 91 D3
Clacton Rd. Wiv 69 E3
Clacton Rd. Wix 55 E3
Claire Cotts. Birch 83 F3
Claire Rd. Walt 93 D3
Clairmont Cl. Brain 59 F1
Clairmont Rd. Colch 66 C3
Clapgate Dr. Lit Cla 91 E1
Clara Reeve Cl. Colch 66 C2
Clare Ave. Runw 163 E1
Clare Cl. Hals 43 E4
Clare Rd. Brain 59 F1
Clare Rd. Thund 187 D3
Clare Way. Clact 109 D3
Claremont Dr. Basil 186 A2
Claremont Rd. Elmst M 87 E4
Claremont Rd. South 190 C1
Clarence Cl. S Ben 187 E2
Clarence Cl. Sprin 128 A2
Clarence Rd. Basil 186 C4
Clarence Rd. Cla 4 A4
Clarence Rd. Rayl 177 D1
Clarence Rd. S Ben 187 E2
Clarence Rd. South 200 A4
Clarence Rd. Sud 7 F1
Clarence Rd N. S Ben 187 F2
Clarence St. South 200 A4
Clarendon Park. Clact 110 A3
Clarendon Rd. Ashi 166 C1
Clarendon Rd. Basil 186 B4
Clarendon Rd. Canv 197 E2
Clarendon Way. Colch 49 F1
Clarke Rise. Col N 155 F3
Clarke's Rd. Harw 39 F2
Claters Cl. South 191 F1
Clatterfield Gdns. South 190 A1
Claud Ince Ave. T Gr 78 C3
Claudius Rd. Colch 68 A3
Claudius Way. With 114 C4
Clavering. Basil 185 F2
Clavering Rd. Brain 59 F3
Clay Hill Rd. Basil 185 E3
Clay La. St O 108 B4
Clay Lane Gr. Colch 50 B2
Claybrick Ave. Hawk 177 E3
Clayburn Circ. Basil 185 E3
Clayburn End. Basil 185 E3
Clayburn Side. Basil 185 E3
Claydon Cres. Basil 185 E4
Claydons La. Hadl 188 B4
Clayhall Rd. Clact 110 A3
Claypits Ave. Bures 29 D4
Claypits La. Fox 6 B3
Claypits Rd. Bore 112 C1
Clays Rd. Walt 94 A4
Clayspring Cl. Hock 177 E4
Clayton Rd. Harw 39 E1
Clearwater. Colch 68 A2
Clematis Tye. Sprin 127 F4
Clematis Way. Colch 68 C4
Clements Gdns. Hawk 178 A3
Clements Green La. S Woo F 165 E4
Clements Hall La. Hawk 178 A3
Clements Hall Way. Hawk 178 A2
Clements Pl. S Woo F 165 E4
Cleveland Cl. Colch 50 B2
Cleveland Dr. South 190 B2
Cleveland Rd. Basil 185 E3
Cleveland Rd. Canv 197 D1
Cleves Ct. Bore 112 C1
Clevis Dr. S Woo F 165 F3
Clickett End. Basil 185 E3
Clickett Hill. Basil 185 E3
Clickett Side. Basil 185 E3
Clieveden Rd. South 200 C3
Cliff Ave. South 190 C1
Cliff Ave. South 199 D4
Cliff Gdns. South 199 D4
Cliff Par. South 198 B4
Cliff Par. Walt 76 C1
Cliff Rd. Clact 110 C3
Cliff Rd. Harw 40 B2
Cliff Rd. South 199 D4
Cliff Way. Frin 94 A3
Cliffsea Gr. South 189 F1
Clifftown Par. South 199 F4
Clifftown Rd. South 200 A4
Clifton Ave. S Ben 187 E2
Clifton Cl. S Ben 187 E2
Clifton Dr. South 199 E4
Clifton Mews. South 200 A4
Clifton Rd. Ashi 178 B4
Clifton Rd. Basil 186 C4
Clifton Rd. Canv 197 D2
Clifton Terr. South 200 A4
Clifton Terr. Wiv 87 D4
Clifton Way. S Ben 187 E2
Climmen Rd. Canv 197 D3
Clinton Cl. E Han 153 E4
Clinton Rd. Canv 196 B2
Clive Rd. Colch 68 A3
Cliveden Cl. Chelm 126 C2
Clobbs Yd. Chelm 127 D4
Clockhouse Way. Brain 60 B1
Cloes La. Clact 109 D2
Cloisters The. Brain 60 A3
Clopton Dr. L Mel 7 E3
Clopton Green. Basil 185 D4
Close The. Clact 125 D4
Close The. Frin 93 D2
Close The. Frin 93 F3
Close The. Harw 40 A2
Close The. S Ben 187 E1
Close The. Sud 12 C4
Close The. T Gr 78 C3
Clough Rd. Colch 50 B3
Clova Rd. South 189 F1
Clovelly Gdns. Runw 174 B4
Clover Cl. Basil 185 F2
Clover Ct. Sud 13 E3
Clover Dr. Thor 89 D3
Clover Way. Ard 51 D3
Clover Way. Basil 185 F2
Cloverlands. Colch 50 B1
Cluanie Orch. Cav 1 C1
Cluny Sq. South 191 E2
Clyde Cres. Chelm 126 B2
Clyde Cres. Rayl 188 B4
Clydesdale Rd. Brain 59 F1
Coach La. Mald 131 F2
Coach Rd. Alres 88 A4
Coach Rd. Gt Hor 49 D4
Coan Ave. Clact 109 E1
Coast Rd. W Mers 121 D3
Coats Hutton Rd. Colch 67 D2
Cobbins Chase. Burn 170 A4
Cobbins The. Burn 170 A4
Cobbs Pl. Sprin 127 E2
Cobden Wlk. Basil 186 B4
Cobham Rd. South 199 E4
Coburb Pl. S Woo F 165 E3
Cock and Bell La. L Mel 7 E4
Cock Rd. Lit Map 17 D1
Cockaynes La. Alres 88 A4
Cockerell Cl. Basil 174 A1
Cockethurst Cl. South 190 A2
Cockett Wick La. St O 108 B1
Cockrell's Rd. Worm 30 A2
Codenham Green. Basil 185 D2
Codenham Straight. Basil 185 D2
Codham Little Park Dr. Weth 41 E3
Coggeshall Rd. Ard 33 F1
Coggeshall Rd. Bradw 61 E2
Coggeshall Rd. Brain 60 B2
Coggeshall Rd. Cogg 62 A1
Coggeshall Rd. Ea Col 45 D2
Coggeshall Rd. (Feering). Fee 81 E4
Coggeshall Rd. Gt T 64 A4
Coggeshall Rd. Kelv 81 D3
Coggeshall Rd. Mks T 64 B2
Coggeshall Rd. Stis 60 B2
Coggeshall Rd (Feering). Fee 81 F2
Coggeshall Way. Hals 26 A1
Coke St. Harw 40 B3
Cokefield Ave. South 191 E2
Coker Rd. Canv 196 B1
Cokers Cl. Bl Not 78 B3
Colam La. Lit Bad 129 E2
Colbert Ave. South 200 C4
Colchester Cl. South 190 C1
Colchester Rd. Ard 51 D2
Colchester Rd. Ard 51 F4
Colchester Rd. Bore 128 A3
Colchester Rd. Bures 28 C4
Colchester Rd. Clact 110 B3
Colchester Rd. Cogg 63 E1
Colchester Rd. Ded 33 F3
Colchester Rd. Ea Col 45 F3
Colchester Rd. Elmst M 69 F3
Colchester Rd. Gt Ben 71 E2
Colchester Rd. Gt Bro 52 A2
Colchester Rd. Gt Oak 55 D1
Colchester Rd. Gt Tot 116 B3
Colchester Rd. Hals 26 A1
Colchester Rd. Lang 104 A3
Colchester Rd. Lawf 35 D2
Colchester Rd. M Bure 29 D3
Colchester Rd. Mald 132 A3
Colchester Rd. South 190 C1
Colchester Rd. St O 108 A3
Colchester Rd. Tend 72 B1
Colchester Rd. Th L S 73 E1
Colchester Rd. Tipt 100 B4
Colchester Rd. Tolle 119 D3
Colchester Rd. Virl 102 A1
Colchester Rd. W Berg 30 A1
Colchester Rd. W Berg 48 C2
Colchester Rd. W Mers 121 E4
Colchester Rd. Wa Col 46 C3
Colchester Rd. Weel 72 B1
Colchester Rd. With 98 B2
Colchester Rd. Wiv 69 E2
Colchester Rd. Wix 55 D3
Cold Hall Chase. Gt Bro 70 C3
Coldnailhurst Ave. Brain 59 F3
Cole Green. Bel S P 5 D1
Cole Hill. Gt Le 95 D3
Coleman St. South 191 D1
Colemans Ave. South 190 B2
Colemans La. Dan 142 B4
Coleridge Rd. Mald 132 A1
Coles Brook Rd. Gt Ben 89 F2
Coles La. Walt 76 A1
Coles Oak La. Ded 33 E3
College Ct. Lawf 35 E2
College Rd. Brain 59 F1
College Rd. Clact 110 A2
College Way. South 199 F4
Coller Rd. Rams 39 D1
Colletts Chase. Worm 29 F3
Colley Rd. Gt Bad 141 D3
Colliers The. Mald 132 C2
Collindale Gdns. Clact 110 B3
Collingdale Cl. Canv 197 E2
Collingwood. S Ben 187 F2
Collingwood Cl. Brain 60 B3
Collingwood Rd. Basil 185 E2
Collingwood Rd. Clact 109 E1
Collingwood Rd. Colch 66 C3
Collingwood Rd. S Woo F 165 F3
Collingwood Rd. With 98 A1
Collingwood Terr. Basil 185 E3
Collingwood Wlk. Basil 185 E3
Collins Cl. Brain 59 F1
Collins Rd. Lit Map 17 E1
Collins Way. South 190 A3
Colne Bank Ave. Colch 67 E4
Colne Bank Ave. Colch 49 F1
Colne Chase. With 97 F1
Colne Cl. S Woo F 165 F4
Colne Park Rd. Ea Col 45 E4
Colne Pl. Basil 185 E2
Colne Rd. Bures 28 C4
Colne Rd. Clact 109 F1
Colne Rd. Cogg 63 D3
Colne Rd. Hals 26 A1
Colne Rd. Si Hed 24 C4
Colne Rise. Rowh 86 C4
Colne Springs. Ridge 8 A3
Colne St. Brigh 106 C3
Colne Valley Cl. Hals 25 E1
Colne View. St O 107 D1
Colne Way. St O 106 C2
Colneford Hill. Ea Col 45 E4
Colneys Cl. Sud 7 E1
Colthorpe Rd. Clact 109 F4
Coltishall Cl. Wick 175 D3
Columbine Gdns. Walt 94 A4
Columbine Mews. Stanw 66 B4
Columbines The. Cav 1 C1
Colvin Chase. Chelm 140 A1
Colvin Cl. Colch 66 C4
Colworth Cl. Hadl 188 B2
Colyers Reach. Sprin 128 A1
Comet Way. South 190 A3
Commerce Park. Colch 68 B2
Commerce Way. Colch 68 B2
Commercial Rd. South 190 B2
Common App. Thund 188 A4
Common La. Lit Bad 129 F1
Common La. Thund 188 A4
Common La. Woo Wa 130 A2
Common Rd. Gt Wak 193 D2
Common St. Cla 4 A4
Common The. Dan 142 C3
Common The. E Han 153 D4
Common The. Thund 188 A4
Commonhall La. Hadl 188 B2
Commons The. Colch 67 D3
Compasses Rd. Bradw 61 F3
Compton Ct. Canv 197 E1
Compton Rd. Colch 68 B4
Comyns Pl. Writ 126 A1
Con Way. S Ben 187 E2
Conan Doyle Cl. Brain 78 A4
Concord Ave. Canv 196 C3
Conder Way. Colch 68 B2
Conduit La. Woo Mor 143 F3
Conduit St. Chelm 127 D1
Conies Rd. Hals 43 E4
Conifer Cl. Colch 68 B4
Conifers. Hadl 188 C2
Coniston. South 190 A4
Coniston Cl. Bl. Not 77 E3
Coniston Cl. Rayl 176 C1
Coniston Rd. Canv 197 D2
Coniston Rd. Thund 187 F4
Connaught Ave. Frin 93 F2
Connaught Cl. Clact 110 A2
Connaught Dr. S Woo F 165 E4
Connaught Gdns. Brain 60 A2
Connaught Gdns. South 201 E3
Connaught Gdns E. Clact 110 A2
Connaught Gdns W. Clact 110 A2
Connaught Rd. Lit Cla 91 E3
Connaught Rd. Rayl 189 D4
Connaught Wlk. Rayl 189 D4
Conrad Rd. With 97 F3
Constable Ave. Clact 109 E3
Constable Cl. Colch 49 F2
Constable Cl. Lawf 35 D2
Constable Cl. W Mers 121 E4
Constable Rd. Sud 12 C4
Constable View. Sprin 127 F3
Constable Way. South 202 A4
Constance Cl. With 115 D4
Constantine Rd. Colch 67 E3
Constantine Rd. With 114 C4
Constitution Hill. S Ben 187 E2
Constitution Hill. Sud 12 C4
Convent Hill. Brain 60 A3
Convent La. Brain 60 A3
Convent Rd. Canv 197 D2
Conway Ave. Gt Wak 193 D2
Conway Cl. Elmst M 87 E4
Conway Cl. Hals 43 E4
Cook Cl. Harw 39 F1
Cook Cres. Colch 68 C4
Cook Pl. Sprin 127 F2
Cooks Green. Basil 174 B1
Cook's Hall Rd. W Berg 48 B2
Cooks Hill. Box 32 A3
Cook's La. Colch 66 C4
Coolyne Way. Clact 110 A4
Coombe Rd. Soum 159 E2
Coombe Rise. Chelm 127 D4
Coombes Gr. Roch 179 D1
Coombewood Dr. Thund 187 F3
Cooper Wlk. Colch 68 B4
Coopers Ave. Mald 132 B3
Coopers La. Clact 109 E2
Cooper's La. Ded 33 F3
Cooper's Row. Chelm 127 D3
Copdoek. Basil 185 E4
Copelands. Hawk 178 B3
Copford Ave. Rayl 176 C1
Copland Cl. Gt Bad 140 C4
Coppens Green. Wick 174 C3
Copper Beeches. Stanw 66 B3
Copper Beeches. Thund 188 A4
Copperas Rd. Brigh 106 C3
Copperfield Rd. Chelm 126 C4
Coppice End. Colch 50 A2
Coppice Rd. Alres 88 A4
Coppins Cl. Sprin 127 F2
Coppins Rd. Clact 109 E2
Copt Hall La. Gt Wig 103 E2
Copt Hill. Dan 142 C3
Coptfold Cl. South 191 F1
Coral Cl. S Woo F 165 E4
Coralin Wlk. Stanw 66 B3
Corasway. Thund 188 A3
Cordelia Cres. Rayl 176 B2
Cordell Pl. L Mel 7 E4
Cordell Rd. L Mel 7 E4
Cordwainers The. South 191 D3
Coriander Rd. Tipt 100 B2
Cormorant Wlk. Chelm 140 B3
Cornard Rd. Sud 12 C4
Cornec Ave. Rayl 189 D3
Cornec Chase. Rayl 189 E3
Cornel Cl. With 97 E2
Cornerth Cres. Sud 13 D3
Cornfields. S Woo F 165 E4
Cornflower Cl. Stanw 66 B4
Cornflower Dr. Sprin 127 F3
Cornflower Rd. Clact 125 D4
Cornford Way. Lawf 35 D2
Cornhill. Chelm 127 D1
Cornhill Ave. Hock 177 F4
Cornish Gr. S Woo F 165 F3
Cornwall Cl. Lawf 35 D2
Cornwall Cres. Chelm 127 D4
Cornwall Gdns. Brain 60 A2
Cornwall Gdns. Hawk 178 B3
Cornwall Rd. Basil 186 C4
Cornwallis Dr. S Woo F 165 F4
Cornwalls Dri. Mks T 64 C2
Cornworthy. South 201 E4
Coronation Ave. Brain 59 F1
Coronation Ave. Colch 68 A1
Coronation Cl. Gt Wak 192 C2
Coronation Rd. Burn 170 A2
Coronation Rd. Clact 109 E2
Coronation Way. T Gr 78 B3
Corporation Rd. Chelm 127 D2
Corsel Rd. Canv 197 F2
Cosgrove Ave. Hadl 189 D2
Cossington Rd. South 199 F4
Cotelands. Basil 185 F2
Cotman Ave. Lawf 35 D3
Cotman Rd. Clact 109 E3
Cotman Rd. Colch 67 D3
Cotswold Ave. Rayl 176 B2
Cotswold Cres. Chelm 126 B3
Cotswold Ct. Colch 50 B2
Cotswold Dr. L Mel 7 E3
Cotswold Rd. Clact 109 F3
Cotswold Rd. South 190 B1
Cottage Dr. Colch 68 B2
Cottage Gr. Clact 109 E3
Cottage Green. Clact 109 E3
Cottage Pl. Chelm 127 D2
Cottage Wlk. Clact 109 E3
Cottesmore Cl. Canv 197 D1
Cottesmore Gdns. Hadl 189 D1
Cottonwood Cl. Colch 67 E1
Coulde Dennis. E Han 153 D4
Coulsdon Cl. Clact 109 E3
Court St. Nay 20 A1
Courtauld Cl. Hals 25 F1
Courtauld Homes. Hals 25 F2
Courtauld Rd. Basil 174 B1
Courtauld Rd. Brain 60 A2
Courtenay Cl. Sud 7 E1
Courtlands. Chelm 127 D3
Courts The. Rayl 176 C2
Coval Ave. Chelm 127 D2
Coval La. Chelm 127 D2
Coventry Cl. Colch 68 A4
Coventry Cl. Hull 165 F1
Coventry Hill. Hull 165 F1
Coverts The. W Mers 121 E3
Coverts The. Writ 126 A1
Cow La. St O 107 E2
Cowdray Ave. Colch 50 A1
Cowdray Cres. Colch 67 F4
Cowell Ave. Chelm 126 C3
Cowpar Mews. Brain 78 A4
Cowslip Ct. Stanw 66 B4
Cowslip Mead. Basil 185 D3
Cox Rd. Alres 88 A4
Coxs Cl. S Woo F 165 F4
Cox's Hill. Lawf 35 D2
Crabb's Hill. Hat Pev 113 F2
Crabtree. Walt 93 E4
Crabtree La. Lit Hor 30 B1
Cracknell Cl. Wiv 69 D1
Craftsmans Sq. South 191 D3
Craigfield Ave. Clact 110 A3
Craig's Hill. Bures 28 C3
Craigs La. M Bure 28 C3
Craiston Way. Gt Bad 140 C3
Cramphorn Wlk. Chelm 126 C2
Cranbrook Ave. Thund 188 B2
Cranes Ct. Basil 185 E4
Cranes Farm Rd. Basil 185 D4
Cranes La. Basil 185 E4
Crane's La. Kelv 99 D4
Cranfield Ct. Runw 174 B4
Cranfield Park Rd. Wick 174 C2
Cranford Cl. Frin 93 F3
Cranleigh Cl. Clact 109 D3
Cranleigh Dr. South 189 F1
Cranleigh Gdns. Hull 165 E1
Cranley Ave. South 190 B1
Cranley Gdns. South 201 E3
Cranley Rd. South 190 B1
Cranmoregreen La. Glems 2 C2
Cranston Ave. South 190 B3
Craven Ave. Canv 197 D2
Craven Cl. Hawk 178 B3
Craven Dr. Colch 50 B2
Craylands. Basil 185 F4
Credon Cl. Clact 109 F4
Credon Dr. Clact 109 F4
Creek Rd. Canv 197 E2
Creek View. Basil 185 F2
Creek View Ave. Hull 165 E2
Creekhurst Cl. Brigh 107 D3
Creeksea La. Burn 169 F3
Creeksea Rd. Cane 169 E1
Creekview Rd. S Woo F 165 F4
Creephedge La. S Woo F 153 F2
Creffield Rd. Colch 67 E3
Crescent Rd. Canv 197 E2
Crescent Rd. Gt Bad 141 D4
Crescent Rd. Hadl 189 D1
Crescent Rd. Mald 131 F3
Crescent Rd. S Ben 187 E1
Crescent Rd. Tolle 119 F1
Crescent Rd. Walt 94 B4
Crescent The. Clact 110 A4
Crescent The. Frin 93 D2
Crescent The. Frin 93 F2
Crescent The. Gt Hor 31 D1
Crescent The. Hadl 188 C2
Crescent The. Mks T 65 D2
Crescent The. Th L S 73 F1
Crescent The. W Berg 48 B3
Cress Croft. Brain 60 B1
Cressing Rd. Brain 60 B1
Cressing Rd. With 97 F3
Crest Ave. Basil 186 B3
Crest The. South 189 E3
Crestlands. Alres 88 B4
Creswick Ave. Rayl 176 B2
Cricketers Cl. Sud 12 C3
Cricketfield Gr. South 189 F1
Crickhollow. S Woo F 165 E3
Crina Wlk. Basil 185 F3
Cringle Lock. S Woo F 165 F3
Cripplegate. Soum 159 F3
Crispin Ct. Colch 67 F4
Crittall Dr. Brain 59 E2
Crittall Rd. With 98 A2
Crocklands. Hals 44 A3
Crockleford Hill. Ard 51 D1
Crockleford Rd. Elmst M 69 F3
Crocus Cl. Clact 109 E2
Crocus Way. Sprin 127 F4
Croft Cl. Brain 60 A2
Croft Cl. S Ben 187 D3
Croft Cl. South 189 F2
Croft Ct. Sprin 127 F4
Croft Rd. Clact 109 E2
Croft Rd. Kelv 81 D1
Croft Rd. S Ben 187 E3
Croft Rd. Sud 12 C4
Croft The. Bures 19 F1
Croft The. Ea Col 45 D3
Croft The. Glems 2 B2
Croft The. Gt Y 9 D1
Crofts The. Barl 192 C2
Crome Cl. Colch 67 D3
Crome Rd. Clact 109 E3
Cromer Rd. South 200 A4
Crompton St. Chelm 126 C1
Cromwell Hill. Mald 131 F2
Cromwell La. Mald 131 F2
Cromwell Rd. Colch 67 F3
Cromwell Rd. Hock 177 F3
Cromwell Rd. South 191 D2
Cromwell Way. With 97 F1
Cropenburg Wlk. Canv 197 D3
Crosby Rd. South 199 E4
Cross Ave. Wick 174 B3
Cross Hill. Gt Oak 56 B1
Cross La. W Mers 121 F4
Cross Park Rd. Wick 174 B2
Cross Rd. Basil 186 C4
Cross Rd. Mald 132 A1
Cross Rd. S Ben 188 A2
Cross Rd. With 97 F3
Cross St. Sud 12 B4
Cross Way. W Mers 121 F4
Crossfell Rd. Thund 187 F4
Crossfield Rd. Clact 109 F2
Crossfield Rd. South 191 E1
Crossfield Way. Walt 93 D3
Crossfields. Nay 20 B3
Crossley Ave. Clact 124 C4
Crosstree Wlk. Colch 68 A2
Crossways. Canv 196 C2
Crossways. Chelm 140 B4
Crossways. Clact 125 D4
Crossways. Col En 26 C1
Crossways Hill. Woo Wa 130 A2
Crossways The. South 199 D4
Crouch Ave. Hull 165 F1
Crouch Beck. S Woo F 165 F4
Crouch Dr. Wick 174 B4
Crouch Dr. With 97 F1
Crouch Meadows. Hull 165 F2
Crouch Rd. Burn 170 B3
Crouch St. Colch 67 F3
Crouch View Cotts. Rett 164 B3
Crouch View Gr. Hull 165 E2
Crouch Way. South 201 F4
Crouchmans Ave. Gt Wak 193 D2
Crouchman's Farm Rd. Ult 130 B4
Crouchview Cl. Wick 175 D4
Crow La. Tend 73 D2
Crow Pond Rd. Terl 96 B2
Crowborough Rd. South 190 C1

Crowhall La. Brad 36 C2
Crowhurst Ct. Colch 67 F4
Crowhurst Rd. Colch 67 F4
Crown Ave. Basil 186 B4
Crown Bay Rd. Colch 68 B4
Crown Gdns. Rayl 176 B1
Crown Hill. Rayl 176 B1
Crown La. Tend 72 B2
Crown La N. Ard 50 C4
Crown La S. Ard 51 D2
Crown Rd. Clact 109 E1
Crown Rd. Col N 155 F3
Crown Rd. Hock 177 D3
Crown St. Ca Hed 15 F2
Crown St. Ded 33 F3
Crown Way. Soum 159 E2
Crownfield Rd. Glems 2 A3
Crows La. S Woo F 154 B3
Crowstone Ave. South 199 E4
Crowstone Cl. South 190 B1
Crowstone Rd. South 199 E4
Cruce Way. St O 106 C2
Crummock Cl. Bl Not 77 E3
Cuckoo Cnr. South 190 C2
Cuckoo Hill. Bures 19 F1
Cuckoo Hill. Si Hed 24 A4
Culver Par. Colch 67 F4
Culver Rise. S Woo F 165 F4
Culver Sq. Colch 67 F4
Culver St E. Colch 67 F4
Culver St N. Colch 67 F4
Culver Wlk. Colch 67 F4
Culverdown. Basil 185 D3
Culvert Cl. Cogg 62 C1
Cumberland Ave. Mald 131 F1
Cumberland Ave. S Ben 187 E2
Cumberland Ave. South 191 E1
Cumberland Cl. Brain 60 A2
Cumberland Cres. Chelm 127 D4
Cumming Rd. S Han 163 D1
Cunningham Cl. South 201 F4
Cunnington Rd. Brain 60 B2
Cuppers Cl. With 97 F1
Curds Rd. Ea Col 45 D2
Curlew Cl. Clact 109 F3
Curlew Cl. Kelv 81 E1
Curlew Cl. Mald 132 B3
Curlew Cres. Basil 185 D2
Curlew Dr. S Ben 187 E1
Curling Tye. Basil 185 E4
Curling Tye La. Woo Wa 131 D2
Curling Wlk. Basil 185 E4
Currants Farm Rd. Brain 59 F3
Current's La. Harw 40 C3
Curtisway. Rayl 176 C2
Curzon Rd. Sud 13 D4
Curzon Way. Sprin 128 A1
Curzon Wlk. Basil 186 A3
Custom House La. Harw 40 B3
Cut The. Tipt 100 B3
Cut Throat La. With 98 A2
Cut-a-thwart La. Mald 131 E2
Cuthedge La. Cogg 80 B4
Cutlers Rd. S Woo F 165 F4
Cutmore Pl. Chelm 139 F4
Cuton Hall La. Bore 128 A3
Cutting Dr. Hals 25 F1
Cymbeline Way. Colch 67 D4
Cypress Cl. Clact 109 F4
Cypress Dr. Chelm 140 B3
Cypress Gr. Colch 68 C4
Cypress Mews. W Mers 121 D4
Cypress Rd. With 98 A2
Cyril Child Cl. Colch 68 C4

Daarle Ave. Canv 197 D2
Daen Ingas. Dan 142 B4
Daffodil Way. Sprin 127 F4
Dagnets La. Gt Le 77 E1
Dahlia Cl. Clact 109 E2
Dahlia Cl. Sprin 127 F3
Dahlia Wlk. Colch 68 B4
Daimler Ave. Clact 124 B3
Daines Cl. South 201 D4
Daines Way. South 201 D4
Dairy Farm Rd. May 158 B2
Dairy Rd. Sprin 127 F2
Dairyhouse La. Brad 54 C4
Daisleys La. Gt Le 95 D1
Daisy Ct. Bore 128 A3
Dale Rd. Hadl 189 D1
Dale The. S Ben 188 A2
Dale The. Wiv 87 E4
Dalen Ave. Canv 197 D2
Dales The. Harw 39 F1
Dales The. Hawk 178 B2
Daleview Ave. Wix 55 E3
Dallwood Way. Brain 60 A2
Dalmatia Rd. South 200 B4
Dalrymple Cl. Sprin 127 E2
Daltes La. St O 108 B2
Daltons Fen. Basil 186 B4
Dalwood. South 192 B1
Dalwood Gdns. Hadl 188 C2
Dalys Rd. Roch 178 C1
Damant's Farm La. Th L S 74 B1
Damases La. Bone 113 D1
Damask Rd. Stanw 66 B4
Dampier Rd. Cogg 62 C2
Danbury Cl. Mks T 64 C2
Danbury Cl. South 189 F2
Danbury Down. Basil 185 F4
Danbury Rd. Rayl 176 A2
Danbury Vale. Dan 143 D3
Dancing Dick's La. With 97 D1
Dandies Chase. South 189 F4
Dandies Cl. South 189 E4
Dandies Dr. South 189 E4
Dane Rd. Chelm 126 C1
Dane St. South 202 A3
Dane's Ave. South 201 F3
Danes Ct. Sud 13 D2
Danescroft Cl. South 189 F2
Danescroft Dr. South 189 E2
Danesfield. S' Ben 187 E1
Danesleigh Gdns. South 189 E2
Daneum Holt. Cla 4 A3
Daniel Cole Rd. Colch 67 F2
Daniel Dr. Colch 67 D1
Daniel Way. Silv E 79 F2
Daniell Cl. Clact 109 E3
D'Archy Rd. Tipt 100 C1
D'arcy Ave. Mald 132 A1
D'Arcy Cl. Burn 170 B3
D'arcy Cl. Walt 93 F3
D'ARCY Rd. Colch 68 B2
D'arcy Rd. St O 108 A3
Darcy Rise. Lit Bad 129 F1
D'arcy Way. Brigh 106 C4
D'Arcy Way. Toll D 118 C2
Darenth Rd. Hadl 189 D1
Dark La. Thund 188 A3
Darkhouse La. Rowh 87 D4
Darlinghurst Gr. South 190 A1
Darnay Rise. Chelm 126 B3
Darnel Way. Stanw 66 A4
Darnet Rd. Tolle 119 F1
Darrell Cl. Chelm 127 D3
Dart Cl. With 97 E1
Dartmouth Cl. Rayl 176 B3
Dartmouth Rd. Sprin 127 F3
Darwin Cl. Brain 59 F1
Darwin Cl. Colch 68 A1
Davenants. Basil 174 A1
Davey Cl. Colch 68 B3
David Ave. Runw 163 E1
Davidson Cl. Sud 13 E2
Dawberry Pl. S Woo F 165 E3
Dawes La. W Mers 121 F4
Dawlish Cres. Rayl 176 B3
Dawlish Dr. South 189 F1
Dawnford Cl. Stanw 66 B4
Dawnings The. S Woo F 165 E4
Daws Heath Rd. Hadl 188 C3
Daws Heath Rd. Rayl 188 C4
Days Cl. Chelm 127 D4
Dazeley's La. Str S M 34 C4
De Burgh Rd. Colch 66 C3
De Greys Cl. Sud 13 E3
De Staunton Cl. Alres 88 A4
De Vere Ave. Mald 132 A1
De Vere Cl. Hat Pev 114 A2
De Vere Cl. Wiv 87 D4
De Vere Estate. Gt Ben 89 E4
De Vere La. Wiv 87 D4
De Vere Rd. Colch 67 D3
De Vere Rd. Ea Col 44 C4
De Vere Way. Harw 39 F1
De Veres Rd. Hals 25 E1
Dead La. Ard 51 E4
Dead La. Gt Ben 89 F1
Dead La. Lawf 35 E1
Dead La. Lit Cla 91 D1
Deadman's La. Gt Bad 140 B2
Deal Cl. Brain 59 F3
Deal Way. Brigh 106 C4
Dean Rogers Pl. Brain 59 F4
Dean St. Brigh 106 C4
Dean Way. Chelm 126 C1
Deanery Gdns. Brain 59 F4
Deanery Hill. Brain 59 F4
Deane's Cl. Harw 40 A1
Deanhill Ave. Clact 110 A3
Debden Way. Burn 170 A3
Deben Cl. With 97 F1
Deben Dr. Sud 13 D4
Deben Rd. Colch 50 C1
Dedham Ave. Clact 109 D3
Dedham Meade. Ded 33 F2
Dedham Rd. Ard 33 E1
Dedham Rd. Box 32 A3
Dedham Rd. Lawf 34 C2
Dedham Rd. Str S M 22 C1
Deepdale. Thund 187 F3
Deepdale Rd. Harw 40 A2
Deepdene. Basil 185 D3
Deepdene Ave. Rayl 176 B2
Deeping. South 200 A4
Deeping Wlk. St O 108 A3
Deepwater Rd. Canv 196 C2
Deer Park Cl. Ca Hed 15 F2
Deerhurst. Thund 188 A4
Deerhurst Chase. S Woo F 142 C1
Deerhurst Cl. Thund 188 A4
Defoe Cres. Colch 49 F2
Deford Rd. With 114 B4
Deirdre Ave. Wick 174 A4
Deirdre Cl. Wick 174 A4
Delamere Rd. Chelm 126 C1
Delamere Rd. Colch 50 B2
Delaware Cres. South 201 E4
Delaware Rd. South 201 E4
Delder Ave. Canv 197 E1
Delft Rd. Canv 197 D2
Delfzul Rd. Canv 197 D2
Delgada Rd. Canv 197 E2
Delhi Rd. Basil 186 B3
Dell The. Basil 185 D2
Dell The. Gt Bad 140 C3
Dell The. Sud 13 D3
Dell The. Wick 174 C4
Delmar Gdns. Runw 163 E1
Delview. Canv 196 C3
Delvins. Basil 186 A4
Delvyn's La. Gest 16 B4
Dencourt Cres. Basil 185 F3
Dene Cl. Rayl 176 B2
Dene Ct. Chelm 126 B3
Dene Gdns. Rayl 176 B2
Denesmere. S Ben 187 E2
Deneway. Basil 185 E1
Dengayne. Basil 185 E3
Dengie Cl. With 114 C4
Denham Cl. Elmst M 87 E4
Denham Rd. Canv 197 D2
Denmark St. Colch 67 F3
Denten Cl. With 115 D4
Denton App. South 190 B3
Denton Ave. South 190 B3
Denton Cl. South 190 B3
Denver Dr. Basil 174 B1
Derby Cl. May 146 C1
Derby Cl. Steep 147 D1
Derbydale. Hawk 178 B3
Derek Gdns. South 190 C3
Dering Cres. South 189 E4
Derventer Ave. Canv 197 D3
Derwent Ave. Rayl 176 C1
Derwent Gdns. Clact 110 B3
Derwent Rd. Colch 50 B2
Derwent Way. Bl Not 77 E4
Derwent Way. Chelm 126 B2
Devereaux Cl. Walt 93 F4
Devereox Rd. South 200 A4
Devon Gdns. Hawk 178 B3
Devon Rd. Colch 67 D2
Devon Way. Canv 197 D3
Devon Way. Clact 110 C4
Devon Way. Harw 39 E1
Devonshire Gdns. Brain 60 A2
Devonshire Rd. Burn 170 B3
Devonshire Rd. Soum 159 E2
Dewlands. Basil 185 D4
Dewsgreen. Basil 185 F2
Dewyk Rd. Canv 197 E3
Dial Rd. Gt Ben 89 F2
Diana Way. Clact 109 E1
Dickens Cl. Brain 78 A4
Dickens Cl. South 191 D1
Dickens Pl. Chelm 126 B4
Dickett's Hill. Gt Y 15 D3
Digby Mews. W Mers 121 E3
Dilbridge Rd. Colch 68 B4
Dilston. Dan 143 D3
Dinant Ave. Canv 196 C2
Dinants Cres. Mks T 64 C2
Dinsdale Cl. Colch 68 B4
Dismals The. Terl 96 A1
Disraeli Rd. Rayl 189 D4
Distillery La. Colch 68 B2
Ditton Court Rd. South 199 E4
Dixon Ave. Chelm 126 C2
Dixon Ave. Clact 109 E3
Dixon Cl. Lawf 35 D2
Dixon Way. Wiv 69 D1
Dobbies La. Mks T 64 C2
Dock La. Gt Oak 57 D2
Dock Rd. May 147 D1
Dockfield Ave. Harw 39 F2
Dockwra La. Dan 143 D4
Doctor's La. Ashe 3 E1
Docwra Rd. Kelv 81 E1
Doeshill Dr. Wick 174 C4
Doggetts Chase. Roch 178 C3
Doggetts Cl. Roch 178 C2
Doghouse Rd. Bradw 61 F2
Dollant Ave. Canv 197 D2
Dolphins. South 190 B2
Dombey Cl. Chelm 126 C4
Doms La. Terl 96 A1
Domsey Bank. Mks T 64 C2
Domsey Chase. Fee 82 B4
Don Ct. With 97 E1
Donald Thorn Cl. Wick 174 B3
Donald Way. Chelm 140 B4
Donard Dr. W Berg 48 B2
Doney Chase. Lit Brx 115 F3
Donkey La. Str S M 22 C1
Donne Dr. Clact 125 D4
Donyland Way. Rowh 86 C4
Dooley Rd. Hals 25 E1
Dorewards Ave. Brain 59 F4
Doric Ave. Hawk 178 B3
Dorking Cres. Clact 109 E3
Dorothy Curtice Ct. Copf 65 F3
Dorothy Farm Rd. Rayl 177 D1
Dorothy Gdns. Thund 187 F3
Dorothy Sayers Dr. With 98 A3
Dorset Ave. Gt Bad 140 C3
Dorset Cl. Clact 110 C3
Dorset Cl. Gt Bad 140 C3
Dorset Gdns. Hawk 178 B3
Dorset Rd. Burn 170 B2
Dorset Rd. Mald 144 C4
Dorset Way. Canv 197 D3
Douglas Cl. Chelm 140 B2
Douglas Gr. With 97 E1
Douglas Rd. Clact 109 E2
Douglas Rd. Hadl 188 C2
Douglas Rd. Harw 40 A2
Douglas Wlk. Chelm 140 A4
Doulton Way. Hawk 178 B3
Dove Cres. Harw 39 E1
Dove Dr. S Ben 187 D1
Dove La. Chelm 140 A3
Dovecote. South 192 C1
Dovedale. Canv 197 E3
Dovedale Gdns. Clact 110 B3
Dover Cl. Brain 59 F3
Dover Cl. Clact 125 E4
Dover Rd. Brigh 106 C4
Dovercliff Rd. Canv 197 F1
Dovervelt Rd. Canv 197 E3
Dovesgate. S Ben 187 D2
Dow Ct. Soum 159 E2
Dowches Dr. Kelv 81 E2
Dowches Gdns. Kelv 81 E2
Dowling Rd. M Bure 28 C2
Down Hall Rd. Rayl 176 B2
Downer Rd. S Ben 187 E3
Downer Rd N. Thund 187 F3
Downesway. S Ben 187 E2
Downey Cl. Basil 185 E4
Downhall Cl. Rayl 176 B2
Downham Rd. Canv 197 D2
Downham Rd. Runw 163 E2
Downleaze. S Woo F 165 F4
Downs Rd. Mald 132 A2
Downs The. Nay 20 B3
Downsway. Sprin 127 E3
Downton Wlk. Tipt 100 B3
Dragon Cl. Burn 170 A3
Drake Ave. May 158 A4
Drake Cl. Thund 188 B3
Drake Gdns. Brain 60 B2
Drake Rd. South 190 B1
Drakes App. Clact 109 D1
Drakes La. Lit Wal 112 A4
Drakes The. South 201 F4
Drakes Way. Rayl 176 C2
Drapers Chase. Mald 132 B2
Drapers Rd. S Woo F 165 F4
Drapery Common. Glems 2 A2
Drayton Cl. Mald 132 A1
Drewsteignton. South 201 E4
Driberg Way. Brain 60 A1
Driffield Cl. Fee 81 E2
Drift The. Sud 13 E3
Driftway. Basil 185 F2
Drive The. Chelm 127 D3
Drive The. Clact 110 A4
Drive The. Harw 40 A1
Drive The. Hull 165 E2
Drive The. May 157 F4
Drive The. Rayl 189 D4
Drive The. Roch 178 C2
Drive The. South 199 D4
Driveway The. Canv 197 D2
Droitwich Ave. South 191 E1
Drood Cl. Chelm 126 C4
Drum Field. Str S M 22 B1
Drury La. Brain 59 F2
Drury La. Ridge 8 A3
Drury Rd. Colch 67 E3
Dryden Ave. South 191 D1
Dryden Cl. Mald 145 D4
Drywoods. S Woo F 165 E3
Du Cane Pl. With 98 A1
Dubarry Cl. Thund 187 F3
Duck La. Ded 33 F2
Ducketts Mead. Cane 168 B1
Dudley Cl. Colch 68 A2
Dudley Rd. Clact 109 E2
Dudley Rd. Ea Col 44 C4
Dudley Rd. Fing 86 C2
Duffield Dr. Colch 68 C4
Duffield Rd. Gt Bad 140 B3
Duffs Hill. Glems 2 A3
Dugard Ave. Colch 66 C2
Duggers La. Brain 60 A1
Dugmore Ave. Walt 93 E4
Duke St. Brigh 106 C3
Duke St. Chelm 127 D2
Dukes Ave. Soum 159 E2
Dukes La. Sprin 127 F2
Dukes Park Industrial Estate.
Sprin 127 F2
Dukes Rd. Brain 59 F3
Dulverton Ave. South 190 A2
Dulverton Cl. South 190 A3
Dulwich Rd. Clact 110 B3
Dumont Ave. St O 107 D1
Duncan Rd. Colch 67 D2
Duncan Rise. Gt Y 8 C1
Dundee Ave. Hadl 189 D1
Dundee Cl. Hadl 189 E1
Dundonald Dr. South 189 F1
Dungannon Chase. South 201 D3
Dungannon Dr. South 201 D3
Dunkirk Rd. Burn 170 B3
Dunlin Cl. Mald 132 B3
Dunlin Cl. S Woo F 154 B1
Dunlin Ct. Kelv 81 E1
Dunmore Rd. Sprin 128 A2
Dunnock Way. Colch 69 D4
Dunster Ave. South 190 A3
Dunthorne Rd. Colch 50 C1
Dunthorpe Rd. Clact 109 E3
Dupont Cl. Clact 109 E3
Durants Wlk. Wick 174 B3
Durham Rd. Hawk 178 A3
Durham Rd. South 191 E1
Durham Sq. Colch 68 A4
Durley Cl. S Ben 187 F2
Durrington Cl. Basil 185 E3
Duxford. Wick 175 D3
Dyer's Rd. Mald 132 A1
Dyer's Rd. Stanw 66 B2
Dyke Cres. Canv 196 B2
Dykes Chase. Mald 131 F2
Dyne's Hall Rd. Gt Map 25 E4
Dynevor Gdns. Hadl 189 D1

Eagle Ave. Walt 76 B1
Eagle La. Brain 59 F3
Eagle Way. South 201 F4
Earlhams Cl. Harw 39 F1
Earls Colne Rd. Gt T 46 A1
Earls Hall Ave. South 190 C2
Earls Hall Dr. Clact 108 C3
Earls Hall Par. South 190 C2
Earlsmead. With 97 F2
Earlswood. S Ben 187 E2
Earlswood Way. Colch 67 E1
East Bay. Colch 68 A4
East Bridge Rd. S Woo F 165 F4
East Cres. Canv 196 C2
East Dock Rd. Rams 39 F3
East Gores Rd. Gt T 63 F3
East Hanningfield Rd. Re 153 E1
East Hanningfield Rd. Sand 142 A1
East Hill. Colch 68 A4
East La. Ded 34 A3
East Mayne. Basil 174 A1
East Mersea Rd. W Mers 104 C1
East Mill. Hals 25 F1
East Rd. E Mers 105 F1
East Rd. W Mers 121 F4
East Sq. Basil 185 D3
East St. Brain 60 A2
East St. Cogg 63 D1
East St. Colch 68 A4
East St. Gold 134 A1
East St. Harw 40 B2
East St. Roch 178 C1
East St. South 190 C1
East St. South 198 C4
East St. Sud 12 C4
East St. Tolle 119 E1
East St. Wiv 87 D4
East Stockwell St. Colch 67 F4
East Terr. Walt 76 B1
East Thorpe. Basil 185 E3
East Wlk. Basil 185 D3
Eastbourne Gr. South 190 B2
Eastbrooks. Basil 186 A4
Eastbrooks Mews. Basil 186 A4
Eastbrooks Pl. Basil 186 A4
Eastbury Ave. Hawk 178 B2
Eastcheap. Rayl 176 B2
Eastcliff Ave. Clact 110 A2
Eastcote Gr. South 191 E2
Eastend Rd. Brad O S 137 E2
Easterford Rd. Kelv 81 E1
Easterling Cl. Harw 40 A2
Eastern App. Sprin 127 F3
Eastern Ave. S Ben 187 E3
Eastern Ave. South 191 E2
Eastern Cl. South 191 D2
Eastern Cres. Chelm 126 C3
Eastern Espl. Canv 197 E1
Eastern Espl. South 200 B3
Eastern Prom. St O 106 C2
Eastern Rd. Brigh 106 C3
Eastern Rd. Burn 170 B3
Eastern Rd. Rayl 176 A1
Eastfield Rd. Canv 197 E3
Eastgate. Basil 185 D3
Eastgate St. Harw 40 B3
Easthorpe Rd. Copf 82 B4
Eastleigh Rd. S Ben 187 F1
Easton Rd. With 98 A2
Easton Way. Frin 94 A3
Eastview Dr. Rayl 176 B3
Eastways. Canv 196 C3
Eastways. With 98 A2
Eastwood Bvd. South 190 A2
Eastwood Dr. Colch 50 A2
Eastwood La S. South 190 A1
Eastwood Old Rd. Hadl 189 D3
Eastwood Old Rd. South 189 D3
Eastwood Park Cl. South 189 F3
Eastwood Park Dr. South 189 F4
Eastwood Rd. Rayl 188 C4
Eastwood Rd. South 189 E1
Eastwood Rd N. South 189 F2
Eastwood Rise. Rayl 189 E4
Eastwoodbury Cl. South 190 C3
Eastwoodbury La. South 190 B3
Eaton Rd. Hadl 189 E1
Eaton Way. Gt Tot 116 C4
Ebenezer Cl. With 97 F3
Ebony Cl. Colch 67 E1
Eckersley Rd. Chelm 127 E2
Eden Cl. With 97 F2
Eden Way. Chelm 126 B3
Edenside. Walt 93 F4
Edgefield Ave. Lawf 35 D2
Edgware Rd. Clact 109 E3
Edgworth Rd. Sud 12 C4
Edinburgh Ave. Hadl 189 D1
Edinburgh Cl. With 115 D4
Edinburgh Gdns. Brain 60 B2
Edison Cl. Brain 59 F1
Edison Gdns. Colch 50 B1
Edison Rd. Clact 110 C3
Edith Cl. Canv 196 C2
Edith Rd. Canv 196 B2
Edith Rd. Clact 109 F1
Edith Rd. South 190 C1
Edith Rd. Walt 93 E4
Edmund Rd. With 114 C4
Edward Ave. Brigh 106 C4
Edward Cl. Lit Cla 91 F3
Edward Dr. Chelm 140 B4
Edward Gdns. Runw 174 B4
Edward Rd. Th L S 91 F4
Edward St. Rams 39 F3
Edwin Hall View. S Woo F 154 B1
Edwin's Hall La. S Woo F 154 B2
EENWOOD Gr. Colch 50 B2
Egbert Gdns. Runw 163 E1
Egerton-Green Rd. Colch 67 D2
Egremont St. Glems 2 A2
Egremont Way. Stanw 66 B2
Egret Cres. Colch 69 D4
Eight Acre La. Colch 67 E1
Eld La. Colch 67 F4
Eldbert Cl. South 191 F1
Elder Ave. Wick 174 B3
Elder Tree Rd. Canv 197 E2
Elder Way. Wick 174 B3
Elderberry Gdns. With 98 A2
Elderstep Ave. Canv 197 F2
Elderton Rd. South 190 B1

Eldon Cl. Colch 50 C1
Eldon Way. Hock 177 F3
Eldred Ave. Colch 67 D2
Eldred Dr. Sud 13 E2
Eleanor Chase. Wick 174 B4
Eleanor Cl. Tipt 100 B3
Eleanor Wlk. Tipt 100 B3
Electric Ave. South 190 B1
Elgar Cl. Thund 187 D3
Elgin Ave. Chelm 127 D1
Elham Dr. Basil 186 B3
Elianore Rd. Colch 67 D4
Eliot Cl. Wick 174 B3
Eliot Way. Mald 132 A1
Elizabeth Ave. Rayl 176 B1
Elizabeth Ave. With 115 D4
Elizabeth Cl. Hawk 177 F2
Elizabeth Dr. Wick 174 A4
Elizabeth Rd. Harw 40 A2
Elizabeth Rd. South 200 B3
Elizabeth Way. Brigh 106 C3
Elizabeth Way. Hals 25 F1
Elizabeth Way. Hat Pev 114 A2
Elizabeth Way. Mald 132 A3
Elizabeth Way. Sud 12 B3
Elizabeth Way. Thund 188 B2
Elizabeth Way. Wiv 69 E2
Ellen Way. Bl Not 77 E4
Ellenbrook Cl. South 189 F2
Ellesmere Rd. Ashi 167 E1
Ellesmere Rd. Canv 196 C2
Elliot Cl. S Woo F 165 F3
Elliots Dr. Walt 94 A4
Ellis Rd. Box 31 F2
Ellis Rd. Brad 54 B4
Ellis Rd. Clact 109 F1
Ellistons Yd. Sud 12 B3
Elm Ave. Mald 132 B3
Elm Bungalows. Brain 59 E2
Elm Cl. Alres 88 A4
Elm Cl. Broom 127 D4
Elm Cl. Gt Bad 140 C3
Elm Cl. Rayl 176 B2
Elm Cl. Si Hed 15 E1
Elm Cl. South 201 F4
Elm Cl. Tipt 100 B4
Elm Cres. Colch 68 B4
Elm Dr. Hals 25 F1
Elm Dr. Rayl 176 B2
Elm Drive. Brigh 106 B4
Elm Gr. Clact 109 F3
Elm Gr. Hull 165 E1
Elm Gr. South 201 D4
Elm Gr. Walt 93 E3
Elm Gr. Wiv 69 D1
Elm Green. Basil 186 A3
Elm Green La. Dan 142 B4
Elm La. Fee 64 A1
Elm Rd. Basil 174 C1
Elm Rd. Canv 197 E2
Elm Rd. Chelm 140 A4
Elm Rd. Hadl 188 B1
Elm Rd. Lit Cla 91 E2
Elm Rd. Runw 174 B4
Elm Rd. S Woo F 165 E4
Elm Rd. South 189 F1
Elm Rd. South 201 F4
Elm Rd. Sud 13 D4
Elm Rise. With 98 A3
Elm Tree Ave. Walt 93 F4
Elm Tree Cl. Walt 93 F4
Elm View Rd. S Ben 187 D2
Elm Way. Bore 112 C1
Elmden Ct. Clact 109 F3
Elmer App. South 200 A4
Elmer Ave. South 200 A4
Elmfield Cl. Clact 110 C4
Elmhurst Ave. S Ben 187 D2
Elmhurst Rd. Harw 40 B2
Elms Dr. Chelm 127 D2
Elms Hall Rd. Col En 44 C4
Elmsleigh Dr. South 189 F2
Elmstead Rd. Colch 68 C3
Elmstead Rd. Wiv 69 E2
Elmtree Rd. Basil 186 A2
Elmwood Ave. Colch 67 E1
Elmwood Ave. Hawk 177 F2
Elmwood Dr. W Mers 121 E4
Elronds Rest. S Woo F 165 E3
Elsden Chase. Soum 159 E2
Elsenham Cres. Basil 185 F3
Elsinor Ave. Canv 196 C3
Elton Wlk. Tipt 100 B3
Elwes Cl. Colch 50 B1
Elwin Rd. Tipt 100 B3
Ely Cl. Soum 159 E2
Ely Rd. South 191 D1
Elysian Gdns. Tolle 119 E1
Ember Way. Burn 170 A3
Emberson Ct. Sprin 127 F2
Empire Rd. Harw 40 B2
Empress Ave. W Mers 121 F3
Endean Ct. Wiv 69 D1
Endeavour Cl. Tolle 119 E1
Endsleigh Ct. Colch 67 E4
Endway. Hadl 188 C1
Endway The. May 158 B1
Enfield Rd. Wick 175 E4
Englefield Cl. Hawk 178 A2
Enid Way. Colch 49 E1
Ennerdale Ave. Bl Not 77 E3
Ennismore Gdns. South 191 D2
Enterprise Ct. Brain 60 A1
Enterprise Way. Wick 174 C3
Epping Cl. Chelm 126 C1
Epping Cl. Clact 109 F4
Epping Cl. South 189 F4
Epsom Cl. Clact 109 E3
Erbury Pl. Cla 4 A4
Eric Rd. Basil 186 C3
Erica Wlk. Colch 68 C4
Erick Ave. Chelm 127 D4
Eridge Cl. Sprin 127 E4
Erle Havard Rd. W Berg 48 C2
Ernalds Cl. Ea Col 45 D4
Ernest Rd. Wiv 69 E1
Ernulph Wlk. Colch 68 A4
Errington Rd. Colch 67 E3
Esplanade. Frin 93 F2
Esplanade. Harw 40 C3
Esplanade. May 146 C1
Esplanade Gdns. South 199 D4
Esplanade The. Clact 111 D3
Esplanade The. Hull 165 E2
Essex Ave. Chelm 127 D4
Essex Ave. Clact 124 C3
Essex Ave. Sud 7 F1
Essex Cl. Canv 197 D1
Essex Cl. Rayl 176 C1
Essex Gdns. South 189 F2
Essex Hall Rd. Colch 49 F1
Essex Knowle. Bures 19 F1
Essex Rd. Brain 60 A2
Essex Rd. Burn 170 B3
Essex Rd. Canv 197 E2
Essex Rd. Mald 131 F1
Essex St. South 200 A4
Essex Way. S Ben 187 F1
Estate Rd. Hadl 188 C2
Estella Mead. Chelm 126 C4
Estuary Cres. Sho G 40 A4
Estuary Gdns. Gt Wak 193 E1
Estuary Mews. Tolle 119 E1
Estuary Park Rd. W Mers 121 F3
Estuary Rd. Sho G 40 A4
Ethel Rd. Rayl 189 D4
Ethelbert Rd. Ashi 167 E1
Etheldore Ave. Hock 177 F4
Ethelred Gdns. Runw 163 E1
Eton Cl. Canv 197 D3
Eton Rd. Clact 109 F2
Eton Rd. Frin 94 A3
Eudo Rd. Colch 67 E2
Europa Way. Rams 39 F2
Evelyn Rd. Hock 177 F3
Evelyn Wood Rd. T Gr 78 C3
Everard Rd. Basil 186 A4
Everest. Rayl 176 B3
Everest Way. Mald 132 A3
Evergreen Dr. Colch 50 B2
Everitt Way. Si Hed 15 F1
Eversley Rd. Basil 186 B3
Eversley Rd. Thund 187 E4
Eves Cnr. Burn 170 A4
Eves Cres. Chelm 127 D3
Eves Ct. Harw 39 E1
Ewan Cl. Hadl 189 D2
Ewan Cl. Stanw 66 B3
Ewan Way. Hadl 189 D2
Ewan Way. Stanw 66 B4
Ewell Hall Chase. Kelv 81 E1
Exchange Way. Chelm 127 D1
Exeter Cl. Basil 185 F4
Exeter Cl. Brain 60 A3
Exeter Cl. Gt Hor 49 D4
Exeter Cl. South 192 C1
Exeter Dr. Colch 68 A4
Exeter Rd. Sprin 127 F3
Exford Ave. South 190 A2
Exhibition La. Gt Wak 192 C2
Exmoor Cl. Chelm 126 B1
Exmouth Dr. Rayl 176 B3
Eynesham Way. Basil 174 A1
Faber Rd. With 114 C4
Fabians Cl. Cogg 63 D2
Factory Hill. Tipt 100 C2
Factory La E. Hals 25 F1
Factory La W. Hals 25 F1
Factory Terr. Hals 25 F1
Faggots Yd. Brain 59 F3
Fair Cl. Brigh 107 D3
Fair Green. Glems 2 A3
Fair Mead. Basil 185 E4
Fairfax Ave. Basil 186 B4
Fairfax Dr. South 190 B1
Fairfax Mead. Sprin 127 F1
Fairfax Rd. Colch 67 F3
Fairfield. Gt Wak 193 D2
Fairfield Cres. South 189 F3
Fairfield Gdns. South 189 F3
Fairfield Rd. Brain 59 F1
Fairfield Rd. Chelm 127 D3
Fairfield Rd. Clact 109 F2
Fairfield Rd. South 189 F4
Fairhaven Ave. W Mers 121 F3
Fairhead Rd. Colch 68 B4
Fairhouse Ct. Basil 185 E3
Fairland Cl. Rayl 176 C3
Fairlawn Gdns. South 190 C3
Fairleads. Dan 142 C4
Fairleigh Ave. Basil 186 B3
Fairleigh Dr. South 189 E1
Fairleigh Rd. Basil 186 B3
Fairlight Rd. S Ben 188 B2
Fairlop Cl. Clact 109 F4
Fairlop Cres. Canv 197 D2
Fairlop Gdns. Basil 185 E3
Fairmead. Rayl 176 A2
Fairmead Ave. Hadl 188 C3
Fairmead Ave. South 190 B1
Fairstead. Basil 185 D3
Fairstead Hall Rd. Fair 96 A3
Fairstead Rd. Fair 96 B3
Fairstead Rd. Terl 96 B2
Fairview. Canv 196 C3
Fairview Cl. Thund 187 E4
Fairview Cres. Thund 187 E4
Fairview Dr. South 190 B2
Fairview Gdns. Hadl 189 E1
Fairview Rd. Basil 185 F3
Fairview Wlk. Thund 187 E4
Fairway. Gt Bad 140 B4
Fairway. Wick 174 B2
Fairway Dr. Burn 170 A3
Fairway Gdns. South 189 E3
Fairway Gdns Cl. South 189 E3
Fairway The. South 189 E3
Fairway The. Thund 187 E4
Fairways The. Col N 155 F3
Fairy Hall La. Ray 59 D1
Fal Dr. With 97 F1
Falbro Cres. Hadl 188 B2
Falcon Cl. South 189 F3
Falcon Cres. Colch 68 A3
Falcon Rd. Soum 159 E2
Falcon Sq. Ca Hed 15 F2
Falcon Way. Basil 185 E2
Falcon Way. Chelm 140 A3
Falcon Way. Clact 109 F3
Falcon Yd. Wiv 87 D4
Falkenham End. Basil 185 E4
Falkenham Path. Basil 185 E4
Falkenham Rise. Basil 185 E4
Falkenham Row. Basil 185 E4
Falkland Cl. Bore 128 C4
Falklands Dr. Mann 35 E2
Falklands Rd. Burn 170 A3
Fallowfield Cl. Harw 39 F2
Fallowfield Rd. Colch 67 E1
Fallows The. Canv 196 C3
Falmouth Rd. Sprin 127 F3
Fambridge Chase. Wh Not 78 C1
Fambridge Cl. Mald 132 A1
Fambridge Dr. Wick 174 C3
Fambridge Rd. Alth 157 F1
Fambridge Rd. Ashi 167 E2
Fambridge Rd. Col N 156 A2
Fambridge Rd. Mald 156 A2
Fambridge Rd. N Fam 156 A2
Fambridge Rd. Purl 156 A2
Fane Rd. Thund 187 E4
Fanny's La. St O 90 B1
Fanton Ave. Wick 174 C2
Fanton Chase. Wick 175 D3
Fanton Wlk. Wick 175 D3
Faraday Cl. Brain 59 F1
Faraday Rd. South 189 E3
Farford Field. Sud 13 E3
Farm Cres. Rett 164 C2
Farm Rd. Canv 197 D3
Farm Rd. Gt Oak 56 B2
Farm Way. Thund 188 A3
Farm Wlk. Brigh 106 C4
Farmers Way. Clact 109 D2
Farmfield Rd. Gt T 46 A1
Farmleigh Ave. Clact 109 F4
Farnes Ave. Wick 174 B4
Farriers End. Stanw 66 B3
Farriers Way. South 190 C3
Farrington Way. Lawf 35 D2
Farrow Rd. Chelm 139 F4
Farthing Centre The. Chelm 127 D1
Fastnet. South 190 A4
Faulkbourne Rd. Faulk 97 E2
Faulkbourne Rd. With 97 E2
Fauners. Basil 185 D3
Fawkner Cl. Sprin 127 F1
Featherby Way. Roch 179 D1
Feeches Rd. South 190 B3
Feedhams Cl. Wiv 69 E2
Feering Dr. Basil 185 F3
Feering Green. Basil 185 F3
Feering Hill. Fee 81 E2
Feering Rd. Fee 63 D1
Feering Row. Basil 185 F3
Felixstowe Cl. Clact 109 D2
Fellcroft. Basil 186 B3
Felmores. Basil 186 A4
Felstead Cl. Colch 86 A4
Felstead Cl. S Ben 187 E2
Felstead Rd. S Ben 187 E3
Fen La. Ard 33 E1
Fen St. Nay 20 A1
Fenn Cl. S Woo F 165 E4
Fenn Rd. Hals 26 A1
Fennell Cl. Tipt 100 B3
Fennes Rd. Brain 41 F1
Fennfields Rd. S Woo F 165 D4
Fennings Chase. Colch 68 A4
Fenno Cl. Colch 66 C2
Fenwick Way. Canv 197 D3
Ferdinand Wlk. Colch 68 C4
Fermoy Rd. South 201 D4
Fern Hill. Glems 2 A4
Fern Way. Clact 124 C4
Fernbrook Ave. South 200 B4
Ferndale Cres. Canv 197 D1
Ferndale Rd. Harw 40 B3
Ferndale Rd. Rayl 176 C3
Ferndale Rd. South 191 E1
Ferndown Rd. Frin 93 F3
Ferndown Way. Hat Pev 114 A2
Fernie Rd. Brain 59 E1
Fernlea. Colch 49 E1
Fernlea Rd. Burn 170 A3
Fernlea Rd. Harw 40 B3
Fernlea Rd. S Ben 187 F2
Fernleigh Dr. South 190 A1
Fernwood. Hadl 188 C2
Fernwood Ave. Clact 110 C3
Ferrers Rd. S Woo F 165 E3
Ferris Ave. Col N 155 F3
Ferry Rd. Burn 169 F3
Ferry Rd. Canv 196 B4
Ferry Rd. Fing 87 D3
Ferry Rd. Hull 165 E1
Ferry Rd. N Fam 167 D3
Ferrymead. Canv 196 C3
Festival Gdns. Toll D 118 B2
Feverills Rd. Lit Cla 91 E2
Fiat Ave. Clact 124 B3
Fiddlers Folly. E A Gr 47 F1
Fiddlers Hill. E A Gr 47 F1
Field Way. Wiv 69 E1
Field Wlk. Walt 94 A4
Fields Cl. Weel 90 C3
Fields Farm Rd. Lay H 85 D2
Fieldway. Basil 186 B2
Fieldway. Wick 174 B2
Fifth Ave. Canv 196 C2
Fifth Ave. Chelm 127 D3
Fifth Ave. Frin 93 F3
Fifth Ave. Wick 175 D3
Filey Rd. Soum 159 D2
Fillebrook Ave. South 190 A1
Filliol Cl. E Han 153 D3
Finch Dr. Gt Ben 71 E1
Finchdale. Clact 109 F3
Finches The. Thund 188 A4
Finchfield. Rayl 176 B1
Finchingfield Way. Colch 86 A4
Finchingfield Way. Wick 174 B3
Finchland View. S Woo F 165 E3
Finchley Ave. Chelm 140 A4
Finchley Rd. South 199 E4
Finch's. Lit Brx 115 F3
Finer Cl. Clact 109 E3
Fingringhoe Rd. Colch 68 B1
Fingringhoe Rd. Lang 86 A2
Finham Cl. Colch 68 C4
Fir Tree Cl. Colch 50 A2
Fir Tree La. Lit Bad 129 F1
Fir Tree Rise. Chelm 140 A3
Fir Tree Wlk. Mald 132 B3
Fir Way. Clact 125 D3
Fir Wlk. Canv 196 C3
Firecrest Rd. Chelm 140 B3
Firecrest Rd. Gt Bad 140 B3
Firfield Rd. Thund 188 B3
Firlie Wlk. Colch 68 A1
Firmins Ct. W Berg 48 B2
Firs Chase. W Mers 121 D3
Firs Dr. Writ 126 A1
Firs Hamlet. W Mers 121 D3
Firs Rd. Tipt 100 B2
Firs Rd. W Mers 121 D4
Firs The. Canv 196 C3
Firs The. Lay H 85 D3
First Ave. Canv 196 C2
First Ave. Chelm 127 D3
First Ave. Clact 110 A2
First Ave. Frin 93 F2
First Ave. Glems 2 B3
First Ave. Hals 26 A1
First Ave. Harw 40 B2
First Ave. Hull 165 F1
First Ave. South 199 D4
First Ave. Walt 76 B2
First Ave. Weel 72 C1
First Ave. Wick 175 D3
Firstore Dr. Colch 66 C4
Firwood's Rd. Hals 43 F4
Fish St. Gold 133 F3
Fisher Way. Brain 60 B2
Fishponds Hill. Lit Hor 30 C2
Fisin Wlk. Colch 66 C2
Fitch's Cres. Mald 132 A1
Fitzgerald Cl. Lawf 35 D2
Fitzgilbert Rd. Colch 67 E2
Fitzwalter La. Dan 142 B3
Fitzwalter Pl. Chelm 126 C2
Fitzwalter Rd. Bore 128 C4
Fitzwalter Rd. Colch 67 D3
Fitzwarren. South 192 B1
Fitzwilliam Rd. Colch 67 D4
Fitzwilliam Rd. Hadl 188 B1
Five Acres. S Woo F 142 C2
Five Acres. Walt 94 A4
Fiveash La. Bradw 61 F1
Flag Hill. St O 89 F1
Flagstaff Rd. Colch 67 F3
Flail Cl. Elmst M 69 F3
Flambird's Chase. Purl 154 C4
Flamboro Cl. South 189 E3
Flamboro Wlk. South 189 E3
Flanders Cl. Brain 59 F3
Flanders Field. Colch 68 A2
Flatford Dr. Clact 109 D3
Flatford Rd. Str S M 34 B4
Flax La. Glems 2 B2
Fleet Rd. S Ben 187 E1
Fleetway. Basil 185 F2
Fleetwood Ave. Clact 110 C4
Fleetwood Ave. South 190 B1
Fleetwood Cl. Clact 110 C4
Fleming Cl. Brain 59 F1
Flemings Farm Rd. Rayl 189 E4
Flemming Ave. South 189 E1
Flemming Cres. South 189 E2
Fletchers Sq. South 191 D3
Flintwich Manor. Chelm 126 C4
Flixton Cl. Clact 109 D2
Flood La. Colch 50 B3
Flora Rd. With 97 E2
Florence Cl. Hadl 188 B2
Florence Gdns. Hadl 188 B2
Florence Neale House. Canv 197 D2
Florence Rd. Canv 197 E2
Florence Rd. Walt 76 C1
Florie's Rd. Gt T 63 F4
Flowers Way. Clact 125 D4
Fobbing Farm Cl. Basil 185 D2
Fodderwick. Basil 185 D3
Foksville Rd. Canv 197 E2
Fold The. Basil 185 D3
Folkards La. Brigh 106 C4
Folley The. Lay H 85 D3
Folley The. Stanw 66 B3
Folly Chase. Hock 177 D3
Folly La. Hock 177 D3
Folly The. Toll K 100 C1
Folly The. Wiv 87 D4
Ford La. Alres 88 A3
Ford La. Colch 49 E3
Ford Rd. Clact 109 E2
Ford St. Alah 47 E1
Fordham Rd. Ford 29 F1
Fordham Rd. M Bure 28 C1
Fordham Rd. Worm 29 F1
Fordson Rd. Bore 128 A3
Fordstreet Hill. Aldh 47 E1
Fordwich Rd. Brigh 88 C1
Forefield Green. Sprin 127 F4
Foresight Rd. Colch 68 B1
Forest Dr. Chelm 126 C1
Forest Park Ave. Clact 109 F4
Forest Rd. Colch 68 B4
Forest Rd. With 98 A3
Forest View Dr. Hadl 189 D2
Forfar Cl. Hadl 189 E1
Forfields Way. T Gr 78 C3
Forge Cres. Bradw 61 E2
Forge St. Ded 34 A3
Forrest Cl. S Woo F 165 E4
Forsythia Cl. Sprin 127 F4
Fort William Rd. Basil 185 D1
Fortescue Chase. South 191 F1
Fortune Cl. Gt Le 95 D4
Fossetts La. Ford 47 F2
Fostal Cl. South 189 F2
Foster Rd. Canv 197 E2
Foster Rd. Gt Tot 116 A2
Foster Rd. Rams 39 F3
Foulgar Cl. S Woo F 165 F4
Foundry La. Burn 170 A3
Foundry La. Copf 65 E2
Foundry La. Ea Col 45 D3
Fountain La. Copf 83 F4
Fountain La. Hock 177 D3
Fourth Ave. Canv 196 C2
Fourth Ave. Chelm 127 D3
Fourth Ave. Clact 110 B2
Fourth Ave. Frin 93 F2
Fourth Ave. Glems 2 A3
Fourth Ave. Hals 26 A1
Fourth Ave. Wick 175 D3
Fox Burrows La. Writ 126 A1
Fox Cl. Thund 187 F3
Fox Cres. Chelm 126 C2
Foxden. With 98 B3
Foxes La. E A Gr 47 E1
Foxfield Cl. Hock 178 A3
Foxglove Cl. With 97 E2
Foxglove Way. Sprin 127 F3
Foxhall Rd. Steep 159 D4
Foxholes Rd. Gt Bad 140 C3
Foxmead. With 98 B3
Foxmeadows. Thund 187 F3
Fox's Rd. Ashe 3 F1
Foxwood Pl. Hadl 189 E1
Frampton Rd. Basil 174 A1
Frances Cl. Wiv 69 D1
Francis Cl. Tipt 100 B2
Francis Ct. Silv E 79 E3
Francis Rd. Brain 59 E1
Francis Rd. Sud 12 C4
Francis St. Brigh 106 C3
Francis Way. Colch 50 B1
Francis Way. Silv E 79 E2
Francis Wlk. Rayl 176 B1
Frank Clater Cl. Colch 68 A4
Franklin Rd. N Fam 167 D4
Franklins Way. Wick 174 C4
Fraser Cl. Chelm 140 B4
Fraser Cl. South 201 F4
Frating Hill. Frat 70 B2
Frating Rd. Ard 52 A2
Frating Rd. Frat 89 D4
Frating Rd. Gt Bro 70 C3
Fratting Abbey Farm Rd. Thor 89 E3
Freebournes Rd. With 98 A1
Freeland Rd. Clact 109 F1
Freelands. Brigh 107 D3
Fremantle. South 201 E3
Fremantle Cl. S Woo F 154 B1
Fremantle Rd. Colch 68 A1
Fremnells The. Basil 185 E4
French Rd. Stow M 155 F1
French's Sq. Chelm 127 E1
Frensham Cl. Stanw 66 B4
Frere Way. Fing 87 D3
Freshwater Dr. Basil 185 F2
Frettons. Basil 185 F3
Friars Cl. Clact 109 F3
Friars Cl. Colch 50 B1
Friars Cl. Elmst M 87 E4
Friars La. Brain 60 A2
Friars La. Mald 131 F1
Friars St. South 201 F4
Friars St. Sud 12 C4
Friars Wlk. Chelm 127 D1
Friends Field. Bures 19 F1
Friern Gdns. Wick 174 A4
Friern Pl. Wick 174 A3
Friern Wlk. Wick 174 A4
Frietuna Rd. Walt 93 F3
Frinton Rd. Clact 110 B3
Frinton Rd. Th L S 92 B4
Frinton Rd. Walt 93 E3
Frobisher Dr. Clact 108 C1
Frobisher Rd. Harw 39 F1
Frobisher Way. Brain 60 B2
Frobisher Way. South 192 C1
Frog Hall Cl. Fing 87 D3

Fronk's Ave. Harw 40 B1
Fronk's Rd. Harw 40 A1
Frowick La. St O 90 A1
Fryatt Ave. Harw 40 A2
Fryth The. Basil 185 F4
Fulford Dr. South 190 A3
Fullbridge. Mald 132 A2
Fuller's Cl. Kelv 81 D1
Fuller's Rd. Colch 68 B1
Fulmar Cl. Colch 69 D4
Fulton Rd. Thund 187 E4
Furlongs. Basil 185 E2
Furrow Cl. Colch 66 C3
Furrowfelde. Basil 185 D2
Further Meadow. Writ 139 D4
Furtherwick Rd. Canv 197 E2
Furze Cres. Alres 88 A4
Furze La. Gt Bro 71 D3
Fyfield Ave. Wick 174 B3
Fyfield Path. Rayl 176 A2
Fyfields. Basil 186 B4

Gablefields. Sand 141 E3
Gables The. Basil 186 A4
Gables The. Hadl 189 D3
Gadwall Reach. Kelv 81 E1
Gafzelle Dr. Canv 197 F1
Gager Dr. Tipt 100 C3
Gage's Rd. Bel S P 4 C1
Gaiger Cl. Sprin 127 E4
Gains Cl. Canv 197 E2
Gainsborough Ave. Canv 197 F2
Gainsborough Cl. Clact 109 D3
Gainsborough Cl. W Mers 121 E3
Gainsborough Cres. Sprin 127 F2
Gainsborough Dr. Lawf 35 D2
Gainsborough Dr. South 190 C1
Gainsborough Rd. Colch 67 D3
Gainsborough Rd. Sud 12 C4
Gainsborough St. Sud 12 C4
Gainsford Ave. Clact 110 A2
Gainsford End Rd. Topp 14 A3
Galahad Cl. Burn 170 A3
Galleydene. Hadl 188 B2
Galleydene Ave. Chelm 140 B2
Galleywood Rd. Chelm 140 A3
Galleywood Rd. Gt Bad 140 C3
Galliford Rd. Mald 132 A2
Galloway Dr. Lit Cla 91 E2
Galsworthy Cl. Brain 78 A4
Galton Rd. South 199 E4
Gambleside. Basil 185 F2
Gandalf's Ride. S Woo F 165 E3
Ganges Rd. Sho G 40 A4
Gaol La. Sud 12 C4
Gap The. Clact 111 D3
Garden Cl. Alth 157 F2
Garden Farm. W Mers 121 E4
Garden Field. Hat Pev 113 F2
Garden Fields. Gt T 64 B4
Garden Fields. Steep 147 F2
Garden Pl. Sud 12 B4
Garden Rd. Clact 125 D4
Garden Rd. Walt 94 A4
Gardeners. Gt Bad 140 B3
Gardeners La. Cane 168 C1
Gardeners Rd. Hals 25 F1
Gardenia Pl. Clact 109 D2
Gardenia Wlk. Colch 68 C4
Garland Rd. Rams 39 F3
Garners The. Roch 178 C1
Garnons Chase. Worm 30 A3
Garrettlands. Sand 141 F3
Garrod Ct. Rowh 86 A4
Gascoigne Rd. Colch 68 B4
Gate St. Mald 131 F2
Gatefield Cl. Walt 93 F4
Gateway. Basil 185 D3
Gatscombe Cl. Hock 177 E3
Gattens The. Rayl 176 C2
Gauden Rd. Brain 59 F4
Gay Bowers. Basil 185 E4
Gay Bowers. Hock 177 D3
Gay Bowers La. Dan 142 C3
Gay Bowers Rd. Dan 142 C2
Gay Bowers Way. With 115 D4
Gay Links. Basil 185 D4
Gayleighs. Rayl 176 B2
Gays La. Cane 168 C1
Gayton Rd. South 191 D1
Gazelle Ct. Colch 50 B2
Geesh Rd. Canv 197 E3
Generals La. Bore 112 A1
Genesta Cl. Tolle 119 E1
Genesta Rd. South 199 E4
Genk Cl. Canv 197 D3
Gennep Rd. Canv 197 D3
George Ave. Brigh 106 C4
George Cardnell Way. May 146 C1
George Cl. Clact 109 E1
George Cut. Brigh 106 C3
George La. Glems 2 A2
George Rd. Brain 59 E1
George St. Chelm 127 D1
George St. Colch 67 F4
George St. Harw 40 B3
George St. South 202 A3
George Yd. Brain 59 F2
Geranium Cl. Clact 109 E2
Geranium Wlk. Colch 68 B4
Gerard Rd. Clact 109 E3
Gernon Rd. Ard 51 F4
Gestingthorpe Rd. Bel W 10 C3
Geylen Rd. Canv 197 F2
Ghyllgrove. Basil 185 D4
Gibcracks. Basil 185 F3
Gibson Rd. Si Hed 24 B4
Giffins Cl. Brain 59 F1
Gifford Green. Basil 186 A3
Gifford Rd. S Ben 187 E3
Gifhorn Rd. Canv 197 F2
Gilberd Rd. Colch 68 A2
Gilbert Cl. Rayl 176 C1
Gilbert Rd. Cla 4 A4
Gilbert Way. Brain 60 B3
Gilchrist Way. Brain 59 F2
Gilda Terr. Brain 59 D1
Gilderdale Cl. Colch 50 B2
Gilders Way. Clact 109 E3
Gill The. Hadl 188 B3
Gills Ave. Canv 197 E2
Gilman Dr. South 201 E4
Gilmore Way. Gt Bad 141 D3
Gilpin Way. Bl Not 77 E4
Gilwell Park Cl. Colch 67 D2
Gimson Cl. With 97 F1
Gippeswyck. Basil 185 E4
Gipson Park Cl. South 189 E3
Girling St. Sud 12 B4
Gladden Fields. S Woo F 165 E3
Glade The. Basil 185 E2
Glade The. Colch 50 C1
Gladeview. Clact 109 F4
Gladstone Ct. Chelm 127 D1
Gladstone Gdns. Rayl 176 B1
Gladstone Rd. Colch 68 A3
Gladstone Rd. Hock 177 F3
Gladstone Rd. Tipt 100 B2
Gladwin Rd. Colch 67 E2
Glasseys La. Rayl 188 B4
Glastonbury Chase. South 190 A3
Glebe Ave. Brain 59 F3
Glebe Cl. Elmst M 70 A3
Glebe Cl. Gt Wak 193 E2
Glebe Cl. Rayl 176 B2
Glebe Cl. South 200 C4
Glebe Cl. Wix 55 E3
Glebe Cres. With 97 F2
Glebe Dr. Rayl 176 B2
Glebe Field. Basil 185 E4
Glebe Gdns. Fee 81 F3
Glebe La. Deng 149 E1
Glebe Rd. Chelm 127 D2
Glebe Rd. Colch 67 E1
Glebe Rd. Kelv 81 D1
Glebe Rd. Mald 132 B3
Glebe Rd. Tipt 100 B3
Glebe Rd. Wick 174 C4
Glebe The. Purl 144 B1
Glebe Way. Burn 170 B3
Glebe Way. Clact 125 D4
Glebe Way. Frin 93 F3
Glebe Way. Hadl 188 C2
Glebefield Rd. Hat Pev 114 A2
Glebelands. Thund 187 D4
Glen Ave. Colch 67 D4
Glen Rd. Basil 185 F2
Glen Rd. S Ben 187 F3
Glen Rd. South 199 D4
Glen The. Rayl 188 C4
Glenbervie Dr. South 189 F1
Glencoe Dr. Wick 175 D4
Glendale. S Woo F 154 C1
Glendale Gdns. South 189 E1
Glendale Gr. Colch 50 B2
Glendale Rd. Burn 170 B3
Gleneagles. S Ben 187 D3
Gleneagles Rd. South 189 E3
Gleneagles Way. Hat Pev 114 A2
Glenhurst Rd. South 191 D1
Glenmere. Basil 185 E1
Glenmere Park Ave. S Ben 188 A2
Glenmore St. South 191 E1
Glenridding. S Ben 187 E3
Glenside. Sud 13 D3
Glentress Cl. Colch 50 B2
Glenwood. Canv 196 C3
Glenwood Ave. Hawk 177 F3
Glenwood Ave. Rayl 189 D4
Glenwood Ave. South 190 B1
Glisson Sq. Colch 67 D2
Globe Cl. Tipt 100 B3
Globe Wlk. Tipt 100 B3
Gloucester Ave. Chelm 140 B3
Gloucester Ave. Colch 67 E2
Gloucester Ave. Mald 131 F1
Gloucester Ave. Rayl 189 D4
Gloucester Cres. Chelm 127 D3
Gloucester Gdns. Brain 60 A2
Gloucester Terr. South 201 D3
Gloucester Way. Sud 7 E1
Glyders The. S Ben 187 F1
Glynde Way. South 191 F1
Goat Hall La. Chelm 140 A2
Goat House La. Haze 143 F2
Goat House La. Purl 143 F2
Goat Lodge Rd. Gt Tot 116 A3
Gobions. Basil 185 D2
Goda Cl. With 114 C4
Goddard Way. Sprin 127 F1
Godfrey's Mews. Chelm 127 D1
Godlings Way. Brain 59 F1
Godmans La. Mks T 64 C2
Godric Rd. With 114 C4
Godwin Cl. Hals 25 E1
Godwit Ct. Kelv 81 E1
Goff's La. Beau 73 F4
Goings La. W Mers 121 E3
Goirle Ave. Canv 197 E2
Goldberry Mead. S Woo F 165 E3
Goldcrest Cl. Colch 69 D4
Golden Cross Rd. Ashi 178 B3
Golden Dawn Way. Colch 49 F1
Golden La. Th L S 73 F2
Golden Lion La. Harw 40 C3
Golden Manor Dr. Thund 187 F3
Golden Noble Hill. Colch 68 A3
Goldenacres. Sprin 127 F4
Goldenlond. Nay 20 B3
Goldfinch Cl. Colch 69 D4
Goldfinch La. Thund 188 A4
Goldhanger Cl. Rayl 176 A2
Goldhanger Cross. Basil 185 F4
Goldhanger Ct. Brain 78 B4
Goldhanger Rd. Gold 132 B2
Goldhanger Rd. Mald 132 B2
Golding Thoroughfare. Sprin 127 F2
Golding Way. St O 108 A3
Goldingham Dr. Brain 78 A4
Goldings Cres. Basil 185 F2
Goldlay Ave. Chelm 127 E1
Goldlay Gdns. Chelm 127 E1
Goldlay Rd. Chelm 127 E1
Goldmer Cl. South 201 E4
Goldsands Rd. Soum 159 F1
Goldsmith Dr. Rayl 176 B4
Goldsworthy Dr. Gt Wak 193 E1
Golf Green Rd. Clact 125 D4
Goodchild Way. Gt Y 9 D1
Goodey Cl. Colch 68 A3
Goodlake Cl. Harw 39 F1
Goodmayes Wlk. Wick 174 B3
Goodwood Cl. Thund 188 A4
Goojerat Rd. Colch 67 E3
Goor Ave. Canv 197 E2
Goose Cotts. Rayl 164 C1
Gordon Pl. South 199 F4
Gordon Rd. Basil 185 E3
Gordon Rd. Chelm 140 A3
Gordon Rd. Hadl 189 D1
Gordon Rd. Harw 40 A1
Gordon Rd. South 199 F4
Gordon Way. Harw 40 A1
Gordons. Basil 186 A3
Gore La. Brain 59 D1
Gore The. Basil 185 D4
Goring Rd. Colch 50 B1
Gorse La. Clact 110 A4
Gorse La. Tipt 100 B2
Gorse Way. Clact 124 C4
Gorse Way. Stanw 66 B2
Gorse Wlk. Colch 68 B4
Gosbecks Rd. Colch 67 D1
Gosfield Cl. Rayl 176 A2
Gosfield Hall Dr. Gos 42 B4
Gosfield Rd. Colch 86 A4
Gosfield Rd. Gos 42 B2
Goshawk Dr. Chelm 140 A3
Goslings The. Silv E 79 E3
Goslings The. South 202 A4
Gouldings Ave. Walt 94 A4
Goulds Rd. Alph 18 C1
Gowan Brae. S Ben 187 D3
Gowan Cl. S Ben 187 D3
Gowers Ave. Gt Bad 140 C3
Gowers End. Glems 2 B3
Goya Rise. South 202 A4
Graces Cl. With 115 D4
Graces La. Lit Bad 129 D1
Graces Wlk. Frin 94 A3
Grafton Pl. Sprin 128 A2
Grafton Rd. Canv 197 E1
Grafton Rd. Harw 40 B2
Graham Cl. Hock 177 F4
Grainger Cl. South 191 D1
Grainger Rd. South 191 D1
Grampian Gr. Chelm 126 B3
Granary Cl. Latch 157 D3
Grand Dr. South 198 C4
Grand Par. South 198 C4
Grandview Rd. Thund 187 F4
Grange Ave. Hadl 189 D3
Grange Ave. May 158 B4
Grange Ave. Wick 174 B3
Grange Cl. Hals 43 F4
Grange Cl. South 189 F2
Grange Cl. Walt 94 A4
Grange Farm Rd. Colch 68 B2
Grange Gdns. Rayl 176 A2
Grange Gdns. South 200 A4
Grange Hill. Cogg 62 C1
Grange Park Dr. South 189 F1
Grange Rd. Basil 186 C4
Grange Rd. Gt Hor 49 D4
Grange Rd. Harw 40 A2
Grange Rd. Lane 52 C4
Grange Rd. Runw 163 E1
Grange Rd. South 189 E1
Grange Rd. Thund 187 F4
Grange Rd. Till 150 A1
Grange Rd. Tipt 99 F2
Grange Rd. Wic Bis 115 F2
Grange Way. Colch 68 B2
Granger Ave. Mald 131 F1
Grangeway. Thund 188 A3
Grantham Ct. Colch 68 A4
Grantham Rd. Gt Hor 49 D4
Granville Cl. S Ben 187 F2
Granville Cl. W Berg 48 C2
Granville Rd. Ashi 166 C1
Granville Rd. Clact 109 F2
Granville Rd. Colch 68 A3
Granville Terr. Burn 170 B2
Grapnells. Basil 185 F2
Grasby Cl. Wiv 69 D1
Grasmead Ave. South 189 F1
Grasmere Ave. Hull 165 E2
Grasmere Cl. Bl Not 77 E3
Grasmere Gdns. Walt 93 F4
Grasmere Rd. Canv 196 C2
Grasmere Rd. Thund 187 F3
Grassfields. Walt 93 F3
Grassmere. Colch 50 A3
Gratmore Green. Basil 185 F2
Gravel Hill. Nay 20 A1
Gravel Hill Way. Harw 39 F1
Gravel Rd. Rayl 189 E4
Gravel The. Cogg 62 C1
Gray Rd. Colch 67 E3
Grayling Dr. Colch 50 C1
Grays Cl. W Mers 121 E3
Gray's Cotts. Colch 68 A4
Grays Mead. Si Hed 15 E1
Graysons Cl. Rayl 176 C1
Great Bentley Rd. Frat 71 D1
Great Burches Rd. Thund 188 A4
Great Cob. Sprin 127 F3
Great Eastern Ave. South 191 D1
Great Eastern Rd. Hock 177 F3
Great Eastern Rd. Sud 12 C4
Great Gibcracks Chase. Sand 142 A1
Great Harrods. Walt 94 A4
Great Hays. South 189 E3
Great Holland Common Rd. Clact 92 B1
Great Leighs Way. Basil 174 B1
Great Mistley. Basil 185 E3
Great Oaks. Basil 185 D3
Great Ranton. Basil 186 B4
Great Saling. Wick 175 D3
Great Smials. S Woo F 165 E3
Great Spenders. Basil 185 E4
Great Sq. Brain 59 F2
Great Tey Rd. Aldh 64 B2
Great Totham Rd. Lit Brx 115 F3
Great Wheatley Rd. Rayl 176 A1
Great Yd. Hals 43 F4
Great Yeldham Rd. Topp 14 B4
Greate House Farm Rd. Lay H 85 D3
Grebe Cl. May 158 A4
Green Acres Rd. Lay H 85 D3
Green Ave. Canv 196 C2
Green Cl. Sprin 127 E2
Green Cl. Writ 126 A1
Green End La. Frin 93 D3
Green Farm Rd. Col En 27 D1
Green La. Aldh 47 E1
Green La. Ard 51 E1
Green La. Ard 51 E4
Green La. Box 31 E3
Green La. Burn 170 A4
Green La. Canv 196 C2
Green La. Colch 50 B2
Green La. Gt Hor 49 E3
Green La. Gt Hor 31 E3
Green La. High 22 B2
Green La. Latch 158 A3
Green La. Lit Tot 117 E2
Green La. S Woo F 165 E4
Green La. South 189 F4
Green La. T Gr 78 A1
Green La. Tipt 100 B3
Green La. Walt 76 B1
Green La. Weel 91 D3
Green Man La. Lit Brx 115 F4
Green Mead. S Woo F 165 E4
Green Meadows. Dan 143 D3
Green Oaks Cl. S Ben 187 F2
Green Rd. S Ben 187 E1
Green The. Chelm 126 C2
Green The. Cla 3 E2
Green The. Clact 109 D1
Green The. Mist 35 F2
Green The. South 189 F4
Green The. Writ 126 A1
Green Trees Ave. Col N 155 F3
Green Way. Col En 27 D1
Greenacre Mews. South 189 E1
Greenacres. Clact 110 A3
Greenacres. Cogg 62 C1
Greenacres. Colch 49 F2
Greenacres. Hadl 188 C2
Greenbanks. South 190 A1
Greendyke. Canv 196 C3
Greenfield Dr. Gt T 46 B1
Greenfields. Gos 42 C4
Greenfinch End. Colch 68 C4
Greenford Rd. Clact 109 E2
Greenhurst Rd. Brigh 107 D3
Greenland Gr. St O 107 E2
Greenlands. Hawk 178 B2
Greenleas. Thund 188 A3
Green's Yd. Colch 67 F4
Greensmill. Lawf 35 E3
Greenstead Ct. Colch 68 B3
Greenstead Rd. Colch 68 B4
Greensted The. Basil 185 F3
Greensward La. Hock 177 F4
Greenview. Canv 196 C3
Greenway. Frin 93 F3
Greenway Cl. Clact 110 A4
Greenway Gdns. Bl Not 77 E4
Greenway The. Clact 110 A4
Greenway The. Runw 163 E2
Greenways. Canv 196 C3
Greenways. Chelm 127 D3
Greenways. Fee 81 E2
Greenways. Gos 42 C4
Greenways. Mald 131 F1
Greenways. Roch 178 C1
Greenways. S Ben 187 E1
Greenways. South 200 C4
Greenways The. Cogg 63 D2
Greenwood Ave. S Ben 187 F1
Gregory Cl. Hawk 177 F2
Gregory St. Sud 12 C4
Grendel Way. Clact 110 C3
Grenfell Ave. Clact 110 C3
Grenfell Cl. Colch 50 B1
Grenville Cl. Walt 76 C1
Grenville Rd. Brain 59 F1
Grey Ladys. Chelm 140 A1
Greyhound Hill. Langh 32 C3
Greyhound Rd. Glems 2 A2
Greyhound Way. South 191 D1
Greys Cl. Cav 1 B1
Greys Paddock. Kelv 81 E1
Greystones Cl. Colch 67 D2
Grieves Ct. Stanw 66 B2
Griffin Ave. Canv 197 E3
Grimston Rd. Colch 68 A2
Grimston Way. Walt 94 A4
Groom Pk. Clact 109 F2
Grooms La. Silv E 79 F2
Grosvenor Cl. Gt Bad 140 B4
Grosvenor Cl. Tipt 100 B3
Grosvenor Mews. South 199 E4
Grosvenor Rd. S Ben 196 C4
Grosvenor Rd. South 199 E4
Grove Ave. W Mers 121 E3
Grove Ave. Walt 94 A4
Grove Cl. Rayl 176 C1
Grove Ct. Rayl 177 D1
Grove Farm Rd. Toll D 117 D4
Grove Field. Brain 42 B1
Grove Hill. Ded 33 E2
Grove Hill. Langh 32 C3
Grove Hill. Rayl 189 D4
Grove Orch. Brain 42 B1
Grove Rd. Canv 197 E2
Grove Rd. Catt 35 E4
Grove Rd. Chelm 127 D1
Grove Rd. Lit Cla 91 E3
Grove Rd. Rayl 176 C1
Grove Rd. S Ben 187 E2
Grove Rd. Tipt 100 C3
Grove Terr. South 200 A4
Grove The. Clact 109 F1
Grove The. Ea Col 45 D3
Grove The. S Wood F 129 F2
Grove The. South 191 E1
Grove The. With 98 A1
Grove Wlk. South 201 F3
Grovelands Rd. Wick 174 B3
Grover St. South 200 A4
Grovewood Ave. Rayl 189 D4
Grovewood Cl. Rayl 189 D4
Gryme's Dyke Way. Stanw 66 C2
Guernsey Gdns. Runw 163 E1
Guild Way. S Woo F 165 F4
Guildford Rd. Colch 68 A4
Guildford Rd. South 191 D1
Guithavon Rd. With 97 F1
Guithavon Rise. With 97 F1
Guithavon St. With 97 F1
Guithavon Valley. With 97 F1
Gun Hill. Langh 33 D4
Gun Hill Pl. Basil 185 E3
Gunfleet. South 201 E4
Gunfleet Cl. W Mers 121 D4
Gunners Rd. South 202 A4
Gurdon Rd. Colch 67 F2
Gurney Benham Cl. Colch 67 D2
Gurton Rd. Cogg 63 D2
Gustedhall La. Roch 177 F2
Gutteridge Hall La. Weel 90 C4
Gutters La. Chelm 127 D4
Guy Cook Cl. Sud 13 E3
Guys Farm Rd. S Woo F 165 E4
Gwendalen Ave. Canv 197 E2
Gwyn Cl. Bore 112 C1
Gwynne Rd. Harw 40 B2
Gypsy La. Copf 82 B3

Haarle Rd. Canv 197 E1
Haarlem Rd. Canv 196 B2
Hackamore. Thund 188 A3
Hackmans La. Col N 155 D4
Hackmans La. Purl 155 D4
Hacks Dr. Thund 188 A4
Haddon Cl. Rayl 176 A2
Hadfelda Sq. Hat Pev 114 A2
Hadleigh Park Ave. S Ben 188 B2
Hadleigh Rd. Clact 109 D2
Hadleigh Rd. Frin 94 A3
Hadleigh Rd. High 22 A3
Hadleigh Rd. South 189 E1
Hadleigh Rd. South 199 F4
Hadley Cl. Brain 42 A1
Hadrians Cl. With 114 C4
Haggars La. Frat 70 C2
Haig Ct. Chelm 127 D1
Hainault Ave. Hawk 178 B2
Hainault Ave. South 190 B1
Hainault Cl. Hadl 188 C2
Hainault Gr. Chelm 126 C1
Hainault Rd. N Fam 156 A1
Halfacres. With 115 D4
Halks Rd. With 97 F2
Hall Chase. Mks T 65 D2
Hall Cl. Clact 110 C3
Hall Cl. Gt Bad 141 D3
Hall Cres. Hadl 188 B2
Hall Cut. Brigh 106 C3
Hall Estate. Gold 133 F4
Hall Farm Cl. Fee 81 F2
Hall Farm Cl. S Ben 187 E1
Hall Farm Rd. S Ben 187 E1
Hall La. Harw 40 A1
Hall La. Ridge 8 A3
Hall La. Sand 141 E3
Hall La. Th L S 74 A1
Hall La. Walt 76 B1
Hall Park Ave. South 199 D4
Hall Park Way. South 199 D4
Hall Rd. Ashel 160 B4
Hall Rd. Bel W 11 D3
Hall Rd. Copf 65 F2
Hall Rd. Deng 160 B4
Hall Rd. Ford 47 E3
Hall Rd. Fox 7 D2
Hall Rd. Gt Bro 52 B1
Hall Rd. Gt Tot 116 A2
Hall Rd. M Bure 28 C3
Hall Rd. Mald 132 A2
Hall Rd. Pan 59 D3

Hall Rd. Roch 178 B1
Hall Rd. Soum 159 F2
Hall Rd. Tipt 100 B2
Hall Rd. Tolle 119 E1
Hall Rd. W Berg 48 B3
Hall Rise. Sud 12 B3
Hall Rise. With 114 C4
Hall St. Chelm 127 D1
Hall St. L Mel 7 E4
Hall View Rd. Gt Ben 89 F4
Hallet Rd. Canv 197 F2
Hallowell Down. S Woo F 165 F3
Halstead Rd. E A Gr 47 F1
Halstead Rd. Ea Col 45 D3
Halstead Rd. Ford 47 D2
Halstead Rd. Gos 24 C1
Halstead Rd. Gos 42 C2
Halstead Rd. Si Hed 25 D3
Halstead Rd. Stanw 66 B4
Halstead Rd. Walt 93 D4
Halstow Way. Basil 186 B3
Haltwhistle Rd. S Woo F 165 E4
Halyard Reach. S Woo F 165 F3
Hamberts Rd. S Woo F 154 C1
Hamble Cl. With 97 F1
Hamble Way. Burn 170 A3
Hamboro Gdns. Hadl 189 D1
Hambro' Ave. Rayl 176 B2
Hambro Cl. Rayl 176 C2
Hambro Hill. Rayl 176 C2
Hamford Cl. Walt 76 B1
Hamford Dr. Gt Oak 56 B2
Hamilton Cl. Hadl 189 D1
Hamilton Gdns. Hock 177 F4
Hamilton Rd. Basil 186 C4
Hamilton Rd. Colch 67 E3
Hamilton Rd. Frin 93 D3
Hamilton Rd. Sud 12 C4
Hamilton Rd. Wiv 87 D4
Hamilton St. Rams 39 F3
Hamlet Court Rd. South 199 E4
Hamlet Ct. Bures 28 C4
Hamlet Dr. Colch 68 C4
Hamlet Rd. Chelm 127 D1
Hamlet Rd. South 199 F4
Hamley Cl. Thund 187 D3
Hammonds Rd. Lit Bad 128 C2
Hammonds Rd. Sand 128 C2
Hampstead Ave. Clact 109 E3
Hampstead Gdns. Hock 177 F4
Hampton Cl. South 190 C2
Hampton Ct. Hock 177 E3
Hampton Gdns. South 190 C2
Hampton Rd. Gt Bad 140 C3
Hamstel Rd. South 191 E1
Hanbury Gdns. Colch 50 A3
Hanbury Rd. Chelm 139 F4
Handel Rd. Canv 197 E1
Handley's La. Lit Brx 115 F3
Hankin Ave. Harw 39 E1
Hannett Rd. Canv 197 F2
Hanningfield Cl. Rayl 176 A2
Hanover Cl. Basil 185 F3
Hanover Ct. Walt 94 A4
Hanover Dr. Basil 185 F3
Hanover Mews. Hock 177 E3
Hanwell Cl. Clact 109 E3
Harborough Hall Rd. Mess 82 C1
Harbour Cres. Harw 40 C3
Harcourt Ave. Harw 40 A2
Harcourt Ave. South 190 C1
Hardings Reach. Burn 170 B2
Hardwick Cl. Rayl 176 B1
Hardy Cl. Brain 78 A4
Hardy Cl. Catt 35 E4
Harebell Cl. Colch 50 A2
Harebell Dr. With 97 F2
Haresland Cl. Hadl 188 C3
Harewood Ave. Hawk 178 B3
Harewood Rd. Chelm 126 C1
Harfred Ave. Mald 132 C2
Harley St. Hadl 189 E1
Harley Wlk. Basil 186 A3
Harlings Gr. Chelm 127 E2
Harman Wlk. Clact 109 E3
Harness Cl. Sprin 127 F4
Harold Gdns. Runw 163 F1
Harold Gr. Frin 93 F2
Harold Rd. Brain 59 F1
Harold Rd. Clact 109 F1
Harold Rd. Frin 93 F2
Harold Way. Frin 93 F2
Haron Cl. Canv 197 D2
Harpclose Rd. Sud 12 C4
Harper Way. Rayl 176 B2
Harpur's Rd. Glems 2 A2
Harridge Cl. South 189 F2
Harridge Rd. South 189 F2
Harrison Dr. Brain 60 A1
Harrison Gdns. Hull 165 E1
Harrison Rd. Colch 67 F2
Harrogate Dr. Hock 177 F4
Harrogate Rd. Hock 177 F4
Harrow Cl. Hawk 178 A3
Harrow Gdns. Hawk 178 A3
Harrow Rd. Basil 175 D1
Harrow Rd. Canv 197 D3
Harrow Rd. Clact 109 F2
Harrow Way. Gt Bad 141 D3
Harsnett Rd. Colch 68 A3
Hart Cl. Thund 188 A3
Hart Rd. Thund 188 A3
Hart St. Chelm 127 D1
Hartest Way. Sud 13 D3
Hartford Cl. Rayl 176 A2
Hartford End. Basil 186 A3
Hartington Pl. South 200 A4
Hartington Rd. South 200 A4
Hartland Cl. South 189 E4
Hartley Cl. Sprin 128 A2
Hart's La. Ard 33 D1
Harvard Ct. Colch 50 A2
Harvest Cl. S Woo F 165 E4
Harvest End. Stanw 66 B3
Harvest Rd. Canv 197 D3
Harvest Way. Elmst M 69 F3
Harvesters' Way. Gt T 64 A4
Harvey Cl. Lawf 35 E2
Harvey Cres. Stanw 66 B2
Harvey Rd. Basil 174 B1
Harvey Rd. Colch 67 D1
Harvey Rd. Gt Tot 116 A2
Harvey Rd. Wiv 69 E1
Harvey St. Hals 25 F1
Harwich Rd. Ard 51 E3
Harwich Rd. Ard 51 F4
Harwich Rd. Beau 74 A4
Harwich Rd. Brad 36 C1
Harwich Rd. Colch 68 B4
Harwich Rd. Gt Bro 70 C3
Harwich Rd. Gt Oak 56 B2
Harwich rd. Lawf 34 B1
Harwich Rd. Lit Ben 71 E4
Harwich Rd. Lit Ben 53 F2
Harwich Rd. Lit Cla 91 F3
Harwich Rd. Lit Oak 57 E4
Harwich Rd. Mist 36 A2
Harwich Rd. Rams 56 A4
Harwich Rd. Wix 37 E1
Harwich Rd. Wix 55 F3
Harwich Rd. Wrab 37 E1
Haselfoot Rd. Bore 128 C4
Haskell Mews. Brain 78 A4
Haslemere Gdns. Walt 93 F4
Haslemere Rd. Runw 163 E1
Hasler Rd. Tolle 119 E1
Hassel Rd. Canv 197 E2
Hastings Ave. Clact 125 E4
Hastings Pl. Brigh 106 C4
Hastings Rd. Colch 67 D2
Hastings Rd. South 200 A4
Hastings The. Runw 163 E1
Hatchcroft Gdns. Elmst M 70 A3
Hatfield Gr. Chelm 126 B1
Hatfield Rd. Hat Pev 114 C2
Hatfield Rd. Langf 131 D4
Hatfield Rd. Rayl 176 A2
Hatfield Rd. Terl 96 B1
Hatfield Rd. With 114 C4
Hatherley The. Basil 185 E4
Hatley Gdns. S Ben 187 E3
Havanna Dr. Rayl 176 A4
Haven Ave. Clact 111 D3
Haven Cl. Basil 185 F2
Haven Cl. Canv 196 C2
Haven Rd. Canv 196 B1
Haven Rd. Colch 68 B2
Haven The. Harw 39 F2
Havengore. Basil 186 B4
Havengore. Sprin 127 F3
Havenside. Barl 192 C3
Havering Cl. Clact 109 F4
Havering Cl. Colch 50 A1
Havering Cl. Gt Wak 193 D2
Havisham Way. Chelm 126 C4
Hawbush Green. T Gr 78 C3
Hawfinch Rd. Lay H 85 D3
Hawfinch Wlk. Chelm 140 A3
Hawk Hill. Rett 164 B1
Hawk La. Runw 164 B1
Hawkbush Green. Basil 174 A1
Hawkendon Rd. Clact 109 D2
Hawkes Rd. Cogg 62 C2
Hawkesbury Bush La. Basil 185 D1
Hawkesbury Cl. Canv 196 C1
Hawkesbury Rd. Canv 196 C1
Hawkesway. Clact 109 F3
Hawkhurst Cl. Chelm 126 C1
Hawkins Cl. Purl 143 F1
Hawkins Rd. Alres 88 A4
Hawkins Rd. Colch 68 B3
Hawkins Way. Brain 60 B2
Hawkridge. South 201 E4
Hawksway. Basil 185 D2
Hawkswood Rd. S Han 163 D3
Hawkwell Chase. Hawk 177 F2
Hawkwell Park Dr. Hawk 177 F3
Hawkwell Rd. Hock 177 F3
Hawkwood Cl. S Woo F 154 C1
Hawkwood Rd. Si Hed 24 B4
Hawlmark End. Mks T 64 C2
Hawthorn Ave. Colch 68 C4
Hawthorn Cl. Chelm 140 B3
Hawthorn Cl. Hawk 177 F3
Hawthorn Rd. Canv 197 E2
Hawthorn Rd. Clact 109 F3
Hawthorn Rd. Hat Pev 114 A3
Hawthorn Rd. Sud 13 D4
Hawthorn Rise. With 98 A3
Hawthorn Way. Rayl 176 C1
Hawthorn Wlk. S Woo F 154 C1
Hawthorne Gdns. Hock 177 D3
Hawthornes. Purl 144 B1
Hawthorns. S Ben 187 E2
Hawthorns. Si Hed 15 E1
Hawthorns. South 189 F2
Hawthorns. Walt 93 F4
Hawthorns The. Dan 143 D4
Hawtree Cl. South 200 B4
Hay Green. Dan 142 C4
Hay La. Brain 60 B2
Haycocks La. W Mers 104 C1
Haye La. Fing 86 B2
Hayes Barton. South 201 E4
Hayes Chase. Rett 164 C3
Hayes Cl. Chelm 127 D1
Hayes La. Canv 196 C2
Hayes Rd. Clact 109 F2
Hayhouse Rd. Ea Col 45 D3
Haynes Green Rd. Lay M 101 D4
Haytor Cl. Brain 60 B1
Haywain The. Stanw 66 B3
Hayward Ct. Colch 68 B4
Hazel Cl. Hadl 188 C2
Hazel Cl. South 189 E1
Hazel Cl. Thor 89 D3
Hazel Cl. With 98 A2
Hazel Gr. Brain 59 F1
Hazeleigh Hall La. Haze 144 B3
Hazell Ave. Colch 67 D1
Hazelmere. Basil 186 A2
Hazelmere Rd. Thund 187 E3
Hazelton Rd. Colch 50 B1
Hazelville Cl. Harw 39 F1
Hazelwood. Hawk 177 F2
Hazelwood. Thund 187 D4
Hazelwood Cres. Lit Cla 91 E1
Hazelwood Gr. South 189 F3
Hazlemere Rd. Clact 110 B2
Head La. Sud 13 D3
Head St. Gold 133 F3
Head St. Hals 25 F1
Head St. Rowh 86 C4
Headcorn Cl. Basil 186 B3
Headgate. Colch 67 F3
Headgate Ct. Colch 67 F4
Hearsall Ave. Chelm 127 D4
Heath Dr. Chelm 140 A3
Heath Rd. Alres 88 A4
Heath Rd. Brad 54 B4
Heath Rd. Colch 66 C3
Heath Rd. E A Gr 48 A1
Heath Rd. Mist 36 A1
Heath Rd. Rowh 86 C4
Heath Rd. St O 90 C1
Heath Rd. Stanw 66 B2
Heath Rd. Tend 54 B1
Heath Rd. Tend 72 C4
Heath Rd. Wiv 69 D1
Heath The. Ded 33 F2
Heath The. Lay H 85 D3
Heather Cl. Clact 110 A4
Heather Cl. Lay H 84 C3
Heather Ct. Sprin 127 F3
Heather Dr. Colch 66 C3
Heather Dr. Hadl 189 D1
Heathercroft Rd. Wick 175 D3
Heathfield. Rayl 176 B1
Heathfield. Thund 188 B3
Heathfield Rd. Chelm 127 D4
Heathfields. E A Gr 66 A4
Heathgate. Wic Bis 115 E3
Heathlands. Thor 89 D3
Heaton Way. Tipt 100 B3
Heckfords Rd. Gt Ben 71 F1
Hedge Dr. Colch 67 D2
Hedge La. Hadl 188 B2
Hedgehope Ave. Rayl 176 B2
Hedgerow The. Basil 185 F2
Hedingham Rd. Bul 11 E1
Hedingham Rd. Gos 24 C1
Hedingham Rd. Hals 25 F2
Hedingham Rd. Wic S P 17 D4
Heeswyk Rd. Canv 197 E3
Heideburg Rd. Canv 197 E3
Heights The. Dan 142 B4
Heilsburg Rd. Canv 197 E3
Helden Ave. Canv 197 D3
Helena Cl. Hawk 177 F3
Helena Ct. S Woo F 165 E3
Helena Rd. Rayl 176 C2
Helford Ct. With 97 E1
Hellendoorn Rd. Canv 197 E1
Helm Cl. Gt Hor 49 E4
Helmons La. W Han 152 A2
Helmsdale. Canv 196 C3
Helpeston. Basil 185 E3
Helston Rd. Sprin 127 F3
Hemingway Rd. With 97 F3
Hemlock Cl. With 98 A2
Hemmings Ct. Mald 144 C4
Hendon Cl. Clact 109 E3
Hendon Cl. Wick 174 B3
Hengist Gdns. Runw 163 E1
Henley Cres. South 190 B2
Henley Ct. Colch 66 C4
Henniker Gate. Sprin 128 A2
Henny Back Rd. Alph 18 C2
Henny Rd. Lam 19 D3
Henrietta Cl. Wiv 69 E2
Henry Dixon Rd. With 98 B3
Henry Dr. Hadl 189 D1
Henry Rd. Chelm 127 D2
Henson Ave. Canv 197 F2
Heralds Way. S Woo F 165 F4
Herbage Park Rd. Woo Wa 130 B1
Herbert Gr. South 200 A4
Herbert Rd. Canv 197 E2
Herbert Rd. Clact 109 F2
Herbert Rd. South 201 E3
Hereford Rd. Clact 110 C3
Hereford Rd. Colch 68 A4
Hereford Wlk. Basil 185 F4
Hereward Cl. Wiv 69 E2
Hereward Gdns. Runw 163 E1
Hermes Dr. Burn 170 A3
Hermes Way. South 201 F4
Hermitage Ave. S Ben 188 A2
Hermitage Cl. S Ben 188 A2
Hermitage Rd. South 199 F4
Hernen Rd. Canv 197 E3
Heron Dale. Basil 185 E3
Heron Glade. Clact 109 F4
Heron Rd. Kelv 81 E1
Heron Way. Mald 132 B3
Heron Way. May 158 A4
Herongate. S Ben 187 D2
Herongate. South 201 F4
Heronsgate. Walt 93 F3
Herrick Cl. Colch 67 D3
Herring's Way. Ford 47 E3
Herschell Rd. Hadl 189 E1
Hertford Dr. Basil 185 E1
Hertford Rd. Canv 196 C2
Hervilly Way. Walt 94 A4
Hester Pl. Burn 170 B3
Hetherington Cl. Colch 86 A4
Hetzand Rd. Canv 197 F2
Hever Cl. Hock 177 E3
Hewes Cl. Colch 68 C4
Hewitt Rd. Lit Oak 39 E1
Heybridge Dr. Wick 174 C4
Heybridge House Industrial Estate. Mald 132 A2
Heybridge St. Mald 132 A3
Heycroft Dr. T Gr 78 C3
Heycroft Rd. Hawk 177 F3
Heycroft Rd. South 189 F3
Heycroft Way. Gt Bad 140 C3
Heycroft Way. Tipt 100 B3
Heygate Ave. South 200 A4
Heythrop The. Sprin 127 E2
Heywood Way. Mald 132 A3
Hickford Hill. Bel S P 4 C3
Hickling Cl. South 189 D3
Hickory Ave. Colch 68 B4
High Barrets. Basil 186 A3
High Beeches. S Ben 187 D2
High Chelmer. Chelm 127 D1
High Cliff Dr. South 198 C4
High Croft. Col En 27 D1
High Elms Rd. Hull 165 F1
High Garrett. Brain 42 B1
High Lift Villas. Box 32 B4
High Mead. Hawk 177 F3
High Pasture. Lit Bad 129 E2
High Rd. Basil 186 A3
High Rd. Hock 177 D3
High Rd. Lay H 85 D3
High Rd. Rayl 176 B1
High Rd. S Ben 187 E2
High Ridge. Gt Brx 116 B4
High St. Brad O S 137 D1
High St. Brain 59 F1
High St. Brigh 106 C3
High St. Bures 19 F1
High St. Burn 170 B2
High St. Cane 168 B1
High St. Canv 197 E2
High St. Cav 1 B1
High St. Chelm 127 D1
High St. Cla 4 A4
High St. Clact 109 F1
High St. Colch 67 F4
High St. Ded 33 F4
High St. Ea Col 45 D3
High St. Gt Bad 140 C4
High St. Gt Oak 56 B2
High St. Gt Wak 193 D2
High St. Gt Y 9 D1
High St. Hadl 188 B2
High St. Hadl 198 B4
High St. Hals 25 F1
High St. harw 40 B2
High St. Kelv 81 E1
High St. Langh 32 B2
High St. Mald 132 A1
High St. Mann 35 E2
High St. Mist 35 F2
High St. Nay 20 A1
High St. Rayl 176 B1
High St. Rowh 87 D4
High St. S Ben 187 E1
High St. Soum 159 E2
High St. South 202 A4
High St. South 200 A4
High St. Th L S 73 F1
High St. Tolle 119 E1
High St. W Mers 121 D3
High St. Walt 94 B4
High St. Wick 174 B4
High St. Wiv 87 D4
High St N. W Mers 121 E4
High Tree La. Walt 76 B1
High View. St L 148 B4
High View Ave. Clact 109 F3
High View Cl. Clact 109 F3
Higham Hill. High 22 A4
Higham Rd. High 22 B2
Higham Rd. Str S M 22 B2
Highams Chase. Gold 134 A4
Highams Rd. Hock 177 F3
Highbank Cl. South 189 F3
Highbirch Rd. St O 90 B2
Highbury Terr. Hals 25 F1
Highbury Way. Sud 13 D3
Highclere Rd. Colch 50 A2
Highcliff Cres. Ashi 178 B4
Highcliff Rd. S Ben 196 C4
Highcliffe Cl. Wick 174 C4
Highcliffe Rd. Wick 174 C4
Highcliffe Way. Wick 174 C4
Highfield. Cla 4 B4
Highfield Ave. Harw 40 A2
Highfield Ave. S Ben 188 B2
Highfield Cl. Brain 60 A3
Highfield Cl. Dan 142 B3
Highfield Cl. South 190 B1
Highfield Cres. Rayl 176 B1
Highfield Cres. South 190 B1
Highfield Dr. Colch 67 E4
Highfield Dr. South 190 B1
Highfield Gdns. South 190 B2
Highfield Gr. South 190 B2
Highfield Mead. E Ham 153 D4
Highfield Rd. Chelm 126 C2
Highfield Rise. Alth 158 A2
Highfield Stile Rd. Brain 60 A3
Highfield Way. South 190 B2
Highfields. Gt Y 9 D1
Highfields. Hals 43 F4
Highfields La. Mess 99 F4
Highfields Rd. With 97 F1
Highland Rd. Corr 185 D1
Highlands. Gos 24 C1
Highlands Ave. Basil 185 E2
Highlands Bvd. Hadl 189 D1
Highlands Chalet Pk. Clact 110 A4
Highlands Cres. Basil 186 C3
Highlands Dr. Mald 131 F1
Highlands Hill. May 158 B3
Highlands Rd. Basil 186 C3
Highlands Rd. Rayl 165 D1
Highmead. Rayl 176 B1
Highmead Ct. Rayl 176 B1
Highview Cl. Sud 7 F1
Highview Rd. Thund 188 A4
Highwood Cl. South 189 F2
Highwoods App. Colch 50 B2
Highwoods Sq. Colch 50 A2
Hilary Cl. Roch 178 C3
Hilary Cres. Rayl 176 C1
Hilbery Rd. Canv 197 E2
Hildaville Dr. South 190 B1
Hill Ave. Wick 174 C4
Hill Cl. L Mel 7 E4
Hill Cl. S Ben 187 F2
Hill Cotts. Gt Ben 89 F1
Hill Cres. Chelm 127 E1
Hill Ct. Basil 185 E3
Hill La. Hawk 177 F3
Hill Rd. Chelm 127 E1
Hill Rd. Clact 109 F3
Hill Rd. Cogg 63 D1
Hill Rd. Harw 40 B2
Hill Rd. S Ben 187 F2
Hill Rd. South 190 C1
Hill Top Ave. S Ben 187 F1
Hill View. S Woo F 142 C1
Hill View Rd. Sprin 127 E2
Hillary Cl. Mald 132 A3
Hillary Cl. Sprin 127 E2
Hillborough Rd. South 190 B2
Hillcrest. Clact 110 A3
Hillcrest. Steep 147 D1
Hillcrest. Walt 93 E4
Hillcrest Cotts. Langh 32 C3
Hillcrest Rd. Hock 177 F3
Hillcrest Rd. S Woo F 165 E4
Hillcrest Rd. South 200 A4
Hillcrest Rd. Sud 7 F1
Hillcrest View. Basil 185 E2
Hillhouse La. Tend 73 D2
Hillhouse La. Th L S 73 D2
Hilliards Rd. Gt Bro 53 E1
Hillie Bunnies. Ea Col 45 D4
Hillman Ave. Clact 124 C3
Hills Cl. Brain 59 F2
Hills Cres. Colch 67 D3
Hills Rd. Si Hed 24 B4
Hillside. Frin 93 F2
Hillside Ave. Hawk 177 F3
Hillside Cres. Clact 110 B3
Hillside Cres. South 199 D4
Hillside Gdns. Brain 59 F1
Hillside Gr. Chelm 140 A4
Hillside Mews. Chelm 140 A4
Hillside Rd. Burn 170 A3
Hillside Rd. Hock 177 D3
Hillside Rd. Rayl 189 E4
Hillside Rd. S Ben 187 E1
Hillside Rd. Soum 159 E2
Hillside Rd. South 198 C4
Hillside Rd. Sud 13 D4
Hillston Cl. Colch 68 A1
Hilltop Ave. Hull 165 F1
Hilltop Cl. Rayl 176 B1
Hilltop Cres. Weel 72 C1
Hilltop Rise. Weel 72 C1
Hillview Cl. Rowh 86 C4
Hillview Rd. Rayl 176 B2
Hillway. South 199 D4
Hillwood Gr. Wick 174 C4
Hilton Cl. Mann 35 E2
Hilton Rd. Canv 197 D3
Hilton Way. Si Hed 24 C4
Hilton Wlk. Canv 197 D3
Hilton Wlk. Si Hed 24 C4
Hilversum Wlk. Canv 197 D3
Hindles Rd. Canv 197 E2
Hines Cl. Aldh 65 D4
Hinguar St. South 201 F3
Hitcham Rd. Cogg 62 C2
Hitchcock Pl. Sud 7 F1
Hitchin Mews. Brain 78 A4
Hither Blakers. S Woo F 165 E4
Hitherwood Rd. Colch 67 E1
Hobart Cl. Chelm 126 C3
Hobbiton Hill. S Woo F 165 E3
Hobbs Dr. Box 32 A3
Hobbs La. Glems 2 B1
Hobleythick La. South 190 B2
Hockley Cl. Basil 185 E3
Hockley Cl. Brad O S 137 E1
Hockley Green. Basil 185 F3
Hockley Rd. Basil 185 E3
Hockley Rd. Brad O S 137 E1
Hockley Rd. Rayl 176 C2
Hockley Rise. Hock 177 F3
Hodges Holt. With 115 D4
Hodgson Ct. Wick 175 D3
Hodgson Way. Wick 175 D3
Hoe Dr. Colch 67 D3
Hoe La. Pent 5 F4
Hoe La. Rett 164 A3

Hoe Mill Rd. Woo Wa 130 C2
Hogarth Dr. South 202 A4
Hogarth End. Walt 93 F4
Hog's La. Str S M 34 C4
Hogwell Chase. Stow M 166 A4
Holbech Rd. Basil 185 F4
Holbek Rd. Canv 197 F2
Holborough Cl. Colch 68 C4
Holbrook Cl. Clact 109 D2
Holbrook Cl. S Woo F 165 E4
Holdsworth Cl. Glems 2 A2
Holgate. Basil 186 B4
Holland Ave. Canv 196 B3
Holland Park. Clact 110 A2
Holland Rd. Clact 110 A2
Holland Rd. Frin 93 F2
Holland Rd. Lit Cla 91 F1
Holland Rd. South 199 E4
Holland Rd. Walt 93 D3
Hollands Wlk. Basil 185 E1
Holledge Cres. Walt 93 F3
Hollies Rd. Bradw 61 D1
Holliland Croft. Gt T 64 B4
Hollis Lock. Sprin 128 A2
Hollow La. Broom 126 C4
Hollow La. Bures 19 F2
Hollow Rd. Ashe 3 F2
Hollow Rd. Kelv 80 C1
Holloway Rd. Mald 132 A3
Holly Bank. With 97 F1
Holly Cl. Burn 170 A3
Holly Cl. Colch 67 E1
Holly La. Gt Hor 31 E2
Holly Oaks. Worm 29 F2
Holly Rd. Stanw 66 B3
Holly Way. Chelm 140 B4
Holly Way. Elmst M 70 A3
Holly Way. Tipt 100 B3
Holly Wlk. Canv 196 C2
Holly Wlk. With 98 A3
Hollybush Hill. Gt Ben 89 F1
Hollymead Cl. Colch 49 F2
Hollytree Gdns. Rayl 188 B4
Hollywood Cl. Gt Bad 140 C3
Holm Oak. Colch 68 A2
Holman Cres. Colch 67 D2
Holman Rd. Hals 43 F4
Holmbrook Way. Frin 93 F3
Holmes Rd Hals 43 F4
Holmsdale Cl. South 190 B2
Holmswood. Canv 197 F3
Holmwood Cl. Clact 109 D3
Holsworthy. South 201 E4
Holt Dr. Rowh 86 A4
Holt Dr. Wic Bis 115 F3
Holt Farm Way. Hawk 178 B2
Holton Rd. Canv 197 F2
Holton Rd. Rayl 177 D1
Holt's Rd. Lit Hor 30 A2
Holtynge. S Ben 187 E2
Holybread La. Lit Bad 129 E2
Holyoak La. Hawk 177 F2
Holyrood. Harw 39 F1
Holyrood Dr. South 190 A1
Home Farm La. Ard 52 A4
Home Mead. Writ 126 A1
Homefield. Soum 159 F3
Homefield Cl. Chelm 126 B3
Homefield Rd. Colch 67 E1
Homefield Rd. With 98 A2
Homefield Way. Ea Col 45 D4
Homefield Way. T Gr 78 B4
Homefields Ave. S Ben 187 D3
Homerton Cl. Clact 109 F4
Homestead Gdns. Hadl 188 B1
Homestead Rd. Basil 186 C4
Homestead Rd. Hadl 188 B1
Homestead Way. Hadl 188 B2
Homing Rd. Lit Cla 91 E2
Honey Bridge Rd. Nay 20 B4
Honey Cl. Gt Bad 140 B3
Honey Pot La. Stow M 155 E2
Honeypot La. Basil 185 D4
Honeypot La. St Os 91 D2
Honeypot La. Toll K 101 D1
Honeypot La. Wix 54 C2
Honeysuckle Way. Colch 68 C4
Honeysuckle Way. Thor 89 D3
Honeysuckle Way. With 97 E2
Honeywood Ave. Cogg 63 D2
Honeywood Rd. Hals 26 A2
Honiley Ave. Wick 174 B2
Honington Cl. Wick 175 D3
Honiton Rd. South 200 B4
Honywood Cl. Mks T 64 C2
Honywood Rd. Colch 67 E3
Hood Gdns. Brain 60 B2
Hooley Dr. Rayl 176 B4
Hop Gardens La. Woo Wa 130 C2
Hope Rd. Canv 197 E2
Hope Rd. S Ben 187 E1
Hopkins Cl. Walt 93 F3
Hopkin's La. Harw 40 B3
Hopkins Mead. Sprin 128 A1
Hopkirk Cl. Dan 142 C4
Hopper Wlk. Colch 68 B3
Hopping Jacks La. Dan 142 C4
Hoppit Mead. Brain 59 F1
Horace Rd. South 200 A4
Hordle Pl. Harw 40 B2
Hordle St. Harw 40 B2
Horkesley Hill. Gt Hor 31 D4
Horkesley Rd. Box 49 F4
Horkesley Way. Wick 174 C3
Horley Cl. Clact 109 E3
Horn La. Cogg 63 D1
Hornbeam Cl. Chelm 140 A3
Hornbeam Cl. Colch 67 E1
Hornbeam Wlk. With 98 A2
Hornbeams. Thund 187 D4
Hornbeams The. Lit Oak 57 D4
Hornby Ave. South 190 B3
Hornby Cl. South 190 B3
Hornchurch Cl. Wick 175 D3
Horne Row. Dan 142 B3
Horner Pl. With 98 A1
Hornet Way. Burn 170 A3
Hornsland Rd. Canv 197 F2
Horse and Groom La. Chelm 140 A2
Horsey Rd. Walt 93 E4
Horsley Cross. Basil 185 D4
Hospital La. Colch 67 E3
Hospital Rd. Colch 67 E3
Hospital Rd. South 201 F3
Houblon Dr. Chelm 140 B1
Houchin's La. Cogg 63 D2
Hovefields Ave. Wick 174 B2
Hovefields Dr. Wick 174 B2
Howard Ave. Harw 39 F1
Howard Chase. Basil 185 D4
Howard Cl. Brain 60 B2
Howard Cres. Basil 186 B3
Howard Dr. Sprin 128 A1
Howard Pl. Canv 197 D1
Howard Rd. Clact 110 B2
Howard Vyse Ct. Clact 109 F3
Howards Chase. South 190 C1
Howbridge Hall Rd. With 114 C4
Howbridge Rd. With 114 C4
Howe Chase. Hals 25 F2
Howe Cl. Colch 68 B4
Howe Green Rd. Purl 155 F4
Hoyners. Dan 143 D4
Hubbards Chase. Walt 94 A4
Hubert Rd. Colch 67 D4
Hucklesbury Ave. Clact 110 C4
Hudson Cl. Clact 109 E3
Hudson Cl. Harw 40 A1
Hudson Cres. South 189 F3
Hudson Rd. South 189 E3
Hudson Way. Canv 197 D3
Hudsons La. High 21 D3
Hugh Dickson Rd. Colch 49 F1
Hughes Stanton Way. Lawf 35 D2
Hull La. Terl 96 A1
Hullbridge Rd. Rayl 176 B4
Hullbridge Rd. S Woo F 154 B1
Hullbridge Rd. S Woo F 165 E4
Hull's La. Sand 141 F4
Hulton Cl. Bore 128 C4
Humber Ave. Clact 124 C3
Humber Cl. Rayl 176 B1
Humber Rd. Sprin 127 E3
Humber Rd. With 97 E1
Humphry Rd. Sud 12 C4
Hundred La. Box 32 B2
Hundred La. Langh 32 B2
Hungerdown La. Lawf 34 C1
Hunnable Rd. Brain 59 F1
Hunt Ave. Mald 132 A3
Hunt Cl. Fee 81 E2
Hunt Dr. Clact 109 E3
Hunt Rd. Ea Col 45 D3
Hunt Way. Walt 93 F3
Hunter Dr. Lawf 35 D2
Hunter Rd. Brain 60 B1
Hunter's Chase. Ard 33 F1
Hunters Ridge. Colch 50 A2
Hunters Way. Sprin 127 F4
Huntingdon Rd. South 200 B4
Huntingdon Way. Clact 109 F3
Hunt's Cl. Writ 139 D4
Hunt's Dr. Writ 139 D4
Hunts Farm Cl. Tolle 119 E1
Hunts Hill. Glems 2 A2
Hunwicke Rd. Colch 68 C4
Hurnard Dr. Colch 67 D4
Hurrell Down. Bore 112 C1
Hurrells La. Lit Bad 128 C2
Hurricane Way. Wick 175 D3
Hurst Cl. Brigh 107 D3
Hurst Way. South 189 F2
Hyacinth Cl. Clact 109 E2
Hyacinth Cl. Tolle 119 D1
Hyacinth Ct. Sprin 127 F4
Hyde Chase. Purl 143 E2
Hyde Farm Chase. Dan 143 D2
Hyde Green. Dan 143 D4
Hyde La. Dan 143 D3
Hyde Rd. Sud 12 C4
Hyde Way. Wick 174 B3
Hyde Wood La. Ashi 178 C4
Hydeway. Thund 187 F3
Hydewood Rd. Lit Y 9 D2
Hylands The. Hock 177 E3
Hythe Cl. Brain 59 F3
Hythe Cl. Clact 125 E4
Hythe Gr. Brigh 88 C1
Hythe Hill. Colch 68 B3
Hythe Quay. Colch 68 B3
Hythe Station Rd. Colch 68 B3
Hythe The. Mald 132 A1

Iceni Way. Colch 67 D2
Ilfracombe Ave. South 200 B4
Ilex Cl. Colch 67 E1
Ilfracombe Ave. Basil 186 B3
Ilfracombe Rd. South 191 E1
Ilgars Rd. Runw 163 F1
Ilmington Dr. Basil 174 A1
Imogen Cl. Colch 68 C4
Imperial Ave. May 146 C1
Imperial Ave. South 190 B1
Imphal Cl. Colch 67 E1
Inchbonnie Rd. S Woo F 165 F3
Ingarfield Rd. Clact 110 C3
Ingelrica Ave. Hat Pev 114 A2
Ingestre St. Harw 40 B3
Inglenook. Clact 110 A4
Inglis Rd. Colch 67 E3
Ingram Mews. Brain 78 A4
Ingram's Piece. Ard 51 F4
Ingram's Well Rd. Sud 12 C4
Ingrave Cl. Wick 174 C3
Inkerpole Pl. Sprin 127 F2
Inverness Ave. South 190 B1
Inverness Cl. Colch 68 A4
Inworth La. Wa Col 28 B1
Inworth Rd. Fee 81 F2
Inworth Wlk. Colch 68 A1
Inworth Wlk. Wick 175 D4
Ipswich Rd. Clact 110 B3
Ipswich Rd. Colch 50 B2
Ipswich Rd. Langh 32 C1
Ipswich Rd. Str S M 22 C2
Ireton Rd. Colch 67 E3
Iris Cl. Sprin 127 F3
Iron Latch La. E A Gr 66 B4
Iron Latch La. Stanw 66 B4
Ironwell La. Hawk 178 B2
Ironwell La. Roch 178 B2
Irvine Rd. Colch 67 E3
Irvington Cl. South 189 E2
Irvon Hill Rd. Wick 174 B4
Isbourne Rd. Colch 68 C4
Ishams Chase. With 115 E4
Island La. Walt 75 F1
Island Rd. Walt 75 F2
Ivy La. E Mers 106 A2
Ivy Lodge Rd. Gt Hor 49 E4
Ivy Rd. Thund 187 D3
Ivy Wlk. Canv 196 C2

Jacaranda Cl. Sprin 127 F3
Jack Hatch Way. Wiv 69 D2
Jackdaw Cl. South 201 F4
Jacks Cl. Wick 174 C4
Jackson Pl. Gt Bad 140 B3
Jackson Rd. Clact 109 F1
Jaggards Rd. Cogg 63 D2
James Carter Rd. Colch 66 C2
James Cl. Wiv 69 E2
James Gdns. St O 108 A3
James Rd. Clact 109 E1
James St. Brigh 106 C3
James St. Colch 68 A3
Jameson Pl. Sud 12 C4
Jameson Rd. Clact 109 E2
Jameson Rd. Sud 12 C4
Janette Ave. Canv 196 C2
Janmead. With 98 A2
Jaques Cl. Glems 2 B3
Jardine Rd. Basil 186 B4
Jarmin Rd. Colch 67 F4
Jarvis Field. Lit Bad 129 E3
Jarvis Rd. Canv 197 D3
Jarvis Rd. S Ben 187 F2
Jasmine Cl. Colch 68 C4
Jasmine Cl. Sprin 127 F4
Jasmine Way. Clact 125 D4
Jason Cl. Canv 197 D3
Jays La. Mks T 64 C2
Jaywick La. Clact 109 D1
Jefferson Cl. Colch 66 C3
Jeffery Rd. Gt Bad 141 F4
Jeffrey Cl. Colch 66 C3
Jeffrey's Rd. T Gr 78 C3
Jellicoe Way. Brain 60 B2
Jenkin's Hill. Brad 36 B2
Jenner Cl. Brain 59 F1
Jenner Mead. Sprin 128 A2
Jersey Gdns. Runw 174 B4
Jersey Rd. Mald 132 A1
Jesmond Rd. Canv 197 D1
Jessica Cl. Colch 68 C4
Joes Rd. Sud 13 F4
John Ball Wlk. Colch 67 F4
John English Ave. Brain 59 F2
John Harper St. Colch 67 F4
John Henry Keene Memorial Homes. Chelm 127 D2
John Kent Ave. Colch 67 D1
John Raven Ct. Fee 81 E2
John Ray Gdns. Bl Not 78 A3
John Ray St. Brain 60 A2
John St. Brigh 106 C3
John St. South 202 A3
Johnson Cl. Brain 78 A4
Johnson Cl. Roch 178 B3
Johnson Rd. Gt Bad 141 D3
Johnson Rd. St O 108 A2
Johnson's Dr. Elmst M 70 A3
Johnston Cl. Clact 110 C3
Johnston Cl. Hals 43 F4
Johnstone Rd. South 201 D4
Jones Cl. South 190 C2
Jonquil Way. Colch 49 E1
Joseph Gdns. Silv E 79 F2
Josselin Cl. Ea Col 45 D4
Josselin Ct. Basil 174 B1
Josselin Rd. Basil 174 B1
Jotmans La. S Ben 187 D2
Journeymans Way. South 191 D3
Joyce's Chase. Gold 134 A4
Jubilee Ave. Clact 109 F4
Jubilee Cl. Harw 39 F1
Jubilee Cotts. Pag Ch 180 B3
Jubilee Ct. Si Hed 24 C4
Jubilee Dr. Runw 174 B4
Jubilee End. Lawf 35 E3
Jubilee La. Ard 51 E2
Jubilee Rd. Rayl 176 C1
Jubilee Rd. Sud 12 C4
Jubilee Rise. Dan 143 D3
Jubilee Way. Walt 93 F3
Julien Court Rd. Brain 60 A2
Juliers Cl. Canv 197 E2
Juliers Rd. Canv 197 E2
Junction Rd. Basil 186 A2
Junction Rd. Col N 156 A3
Juniper Cres. With 98 A2
Juniper Dr. Chelm 140 A3
Juniper Rd. Bore 128 C4
Juniper Rd. South 189 F2
Juniper Rd. Stanw 66 B3
Juniper Way. Colch 68 B4
Jupes Hill. Ded 34 B2
Jupe's Hill. Wa Col 28 B1
Juvina Cl. With 114 C4

Kale Croft. Stanw 66 B3
Kale Rd. S Ben 187 F2
Kamerwyk Ave. Canv 197 E2
Karen Cl. S Ben 196 C4
Karen Cl. Wick 174 B3
Katherine Cl. Rayl 177 D1
Katherine Rd. Basil 186 C4
Kathleen Dr. South 189 F1
Katonia Ave. May 146 C1
Kay Cl. Gt Le 95 D4
Keable Rd. Mks T 64 C2
Keating Cl. Lawf 35 D2
Keats Ave. Brain 77 F4
Keats Cl. Mald 145 D4
Keats Rd. Colch 66 C3
Keats Sq. S Woo F 165 F3
Keats Way. Wick 174 B4
Keats Wlk. Rayl 177 D1
Keble Cl. Colch 67 E3
Keddington Hill. Sud 13 D1
Keeble Cl. Tipt 100 C3
Keegan Pl. Canv 197 E2
Keelars La. Elmst M 69 F1
Keelers Way. Gt Hor 49 D4
Keelings La. Deng 160 C4
Keelings Rd. Deng 160 C4
Keene Way. Chelm 140 A2
Keer Ave. Canv 197 E1
Keighley Mews. South 192 B1
Keith Ave. Runw 163 E1
Keith Cl. Clact 110 A4
Keith Way. South 190 C3
Kellington Rd. Canv 197 E3
Kelly Rd. Basil 186 C3
Kelredon Rd. Mess 82 B1
Kelso Cl. Gt Hor 49 E3
Kelvedon Cl. Chelm 127 D3
Kelvedon Cl. Rayl 176 A2
Kelvedon Hall La. Gt Brx 99 F2
Kelvedon Rd. Cogg 81 D4
Kelvedon Rd. Lit Brx 115 F3
Kelvedon Rd. Toll D 100 A4
Kelvedon Rd. Toll D 118 B3
Kembles. Rayl 176 C2
Kempson Dr. Sud 13 E3
Kempton Cl. Thund 188 A4
Kemsley Rd. Ea Col 45 D3
Ken Cooke Ct. Colch 67 F4
Kendal Cl. Hull 165 F1
Kendal Cl. Rayl 176 C1
Kendal Ct. Wick 175 D3
Kendal Rd. Colch 68 A3
Kendal Road Folley. Colch 68 A3
Kendal Way. South 189 F4
Kenholme. South 189 F2
Kenilworth Gdns. Rayl 176 B2
Kenilworth Gdns. South 190 A2
Kenilworth Gr. Th L S 74 A1
Kenilworth Rd. Clact 110 C3
Kenley Cl. Wick 175 D3
Kenmore Cl. Canv 197 F1
Kennedy Cl. Rayl 189 D4
Kennedy Cl. Thund 187 D4
Kennedy Way. Clact 110 A3
Kennet Way. Chelm 126 B3
Kenneth Rd. Basil 186 B4
Kenneth Rd. Thund 187 F3
Kennington Ave. Thund 187 E3
Kensington Rd. South 200 B4
Kensington Way. Hock 177 E3
Kent Ave. Canv 197 D3
Kent Ave. South 189 F1
Kent Cl. Brigh 106 C4
Kent Elms Cl. South 189 F3
Kent Gdns. Brain 60 A2
Kent Green Cl. Hock 177 F3
Kent View Ave. South 199 D4
Kent View Rd. Basil 185 F2
Kent Way. Rayl 189 D4
Kentings The. Brain 59 F1
Kent's Ave. Clact 110 C3
Kents Grass. Tolle 119 E1
Kents Hill Rd. S Ben 187 E2
Kents Hill Rd N. Thund 187 E3
Kenway. South 191 D1
Kenworthy Rd. Brain 59 F1
Kenyon Cl. Str S M 22 B1
Kerby Rise. Sprin 127 F1
Kerridge's Cut. Mist 36 A2
Kersey Ave. Sud 13 D3
Kersey Dr. Clact 109 D3
Kestrel Way. Clact 109 F3
Kestrel Wlk. Chelm 140 A2
Keswick Ave. Clact 110 B3
Keswick Ave. Hull 165 F1
Keswick Cl. Rayl 176 C1
Keswick Cl. Walt 93 F4
Keswick Rd. Thund 187 F4
Ketleys. Chelm 140 B2
Ketleys View. Pan 59 D4
Kew La. Frin 93 D2
Key Rd. Clact 109 F2
Keyes Way. Brain 60 B2
Keymer Way. Colch 66 C2
Keynes Way. Harw 39 F1
Keysland. Thund 188 A3
Kilburn Gdns. Clact 109 E3
Kildermorie Cl. Colch 50 B2
Kilmaine Rd. Harw 39 F1
Kiln Barn Ave. Clact 109 F4
Kiln Dr. Sud 13 D3
Kiln Rd. Thund 188 A2
Kilns Hill. Cogg 62 C3
Kilnwood Ave. Hock 177 E3
Kilworth Ave. South 200 A4
Kimberley Rd. Barl 192 C3
Kimberley Rd. Colch 68 A3
Kimberley Rd. S Ben 187 E2
Kincaid Rd. St O 108 A2
King Charles Rd. W Mers 121 E3
King Coel Rd. Colch 66 B4
King Edward Ave. Burn 170 A3
King Edward Quay. Colch 68 B3
King Edward VII Dr. Sho 40 A4
King Edward VLL Dr. 40 A4
King Edward VII Dr. Sho G 40 A4
King Edward Way. Wth 114 C4
King Edward's Rd. S Woo F 165 E4
King George Rd. Colch 67 F2
King George's Ave. Harw 40 A2
King George's Cl. Rayl 176 B1
King Harold Rd. Colch 67 D2
King Henry's Dr. Roch 190 C4
King St. Brad 54 B4
King St. Ca Hed 15 F2
King St. Mald 132 A1
King St. Sud 12 C4
King Stephen Rd. Colch 68 A3
Kingfisher Cl. Colch 68 C4
Kingfisher Cl. Mald 132 B3
Kingfisher Cl. South 201 F4
Kingfisher Dr. S Ben 187 E1
Kingfisher Way. Kelv 81 E1
Kingfishers. Basil 185 E2
Kingfishers. Clact 109 F3
Kingley Cl. Wick 174 A4
Kingley Dr. Wick 174 A4
Kings Ave. Clact 110 B3
Kings Chase. With 98 A1
Kings Cl. Canv 196 B2
Kings Cl. Lawf 35 E2
Kings Cl. Rayl 176 C1
King's Cl. St O 108 A2
Kings Farm. Rayl 176 C3
Kings Head Ct. Colch 67 F4
King's Head St. Harw 40 C3
Kings Hill. Sud 13 D3
King's La. L Mel 7 F4
Kings La. Stis 60 C2
Kings Mead. Peb 27 D4
Kings Meadow. Sud 13 D3
Kings Meadow Rd. Colch 67 F4
Kings Mews. Wiv 69 E2
Kings Par. Clact 110 C3
Kings Park. Thund 187 F3
King's Quay St. Harw 40 C3
King's Rd. Brain 59 F3
King's Rd. Burn 170 A2
Kings Rd. Canv 196 B2
Kings Rd. Chelm 126 C2
King's Rd. Clact 109 E1
Kings Rd. Glems 2 B3
Kings Rd. Gt Tot 116 B4
Kings Rd. Hals 25 F1
King's Rd. Harw 40 A2
Kings Rd. Rayl 176 C1
King's Rd. S Ben 187 F1
Kings Rd. Soum 159 E2
King's Rd. South 190 A1
Kings Way. S Woo F 154 B1
Kings Wlk. Tolle 119 F1
Kingsbridge Cl. Brain 59 F4
Kingsbury Cl. Mks T 64 C2
Kingsbury Wlk. Sud 13 E3
Kingsdown Cl. Basil 186 B3
Kingsdown Wlk. Canv 197 D3
Kingshawes. Thund 188 A3
Kingsland Beach. W Mers 121 E3
Kingsland Cl. W Mers 121 E3
Kingsland Rd. W Mers 121 E3
Kingsley Cres. Thund 188 B4
Kingsley La. Thund 188 A4
Kingsman Dr. Clact 109 E3
Kingsmans Farm Rd. Hull 166 A2
Kingsmere. Thund 188 A3
Kingsmere Cl. W Mers 121 E4
Kingsteignton. South 201 E4
Kingston Ave. Sprin 127 F2
Kingston Cres. Sprin 127 F2
Kingston Way. Thund 187 F3
Kingsway. Colch 67 F4
Kingsway. Harw 40 B2
Kingsway. Hull 165 E1
Kingsway. South 190 A1
Kingsway. Tipt 100 B3
Kingswood Chase. South 189 E1
Kingswood Cres. Rayl 176 A1
Kingswood Ct. Basil 185 F3
Kingswood Rd. Basil 185 E3
Kingswood Rd. Colch 49 F2
Kingwell Ave. Clact 109 F3
Kinloch Chase. With 114 C4
Kino Rd. Walt 94 B4
Kipling Cl. Chelm 127 D3
Kipling Way. Brain 78 A4
Kirby Hall Rd. Ca Hed 15 E3
Kirby Rd. Basil 185 F3
Kirby Rd. Walt 94 A4
Kirk Pl. Sprin 127 F2
Kirkbaye. Walt 93 F3
Kirkby Rd. Frin 93 D3
Kirkhurst Cl. Brigh 107 D3
Kirklees. Chelm 127 D2
Kirkmans Rd. Chelm 140 B2
Kirkton Cl. Sho G 40 A4

Kitchen Hill. Bul 12 A3
Kitchener Rd. N Fam 156 A1
Kitchener Way. Sho G 40 A4
Kitkatts Rd. Canv 197 D2
Kittiwake Dr. Mald 132 B3
Klondyke Ave. Rayl 176 A2
Knapton Cl. Sprin 127 E4
Knight St. S Woo F 165 F4
Knights Cl. Lawf 35 E2
Knights Rd. Brain 60 B1
Knights Rd. Cogg 62 C1
Knightsbridge Cl. Colch 67 E2
Knightswick Rd. Canv 197 D2
Knivet Cl. Rayl 176 C1
Knoll The. Rayl 176 B1
Knollcroft. South 201 E3
Knowle The. Basil 185 E2
Knowles Cl. Hals 25 F1
Knox Gdns. Clact 109 F3
Knox Rd. Clact 109 F3
Kohima Rd. Colch 67 D1
Kolburg Rd. Canv 197 E1
Kollum Rd. Canv 197 F2
Komberg Cres. Canv 197 E3
Konnybrook. Thund 188 A2
Korndyk Ave. Canv 197 E2
Kreswell Gr. Harw 40 A1
Kursaal Way. South 200 B4
Kynaston Pl. With 98 A1
Kynaston Rd. Pan 59 D4

Laars Ave. Canv 197 E3
Laburnum Ave. Wick 174 B3
Laburnum Cl. Clact 109 E2
Laburnum Cl. Gt Ben 89 F4
Laburnum Cl. Hock 177 E3
Laburnum Cl. Wick 174 B4
Laburnum Cres. Walt 93 E3
Laburnum Dr. Chelm 140 B3
Laburnum Gr. Canv 196 B2
Laburnum Gr. Colch 68 C4
Laburnum Gr. Hock 177 D3
Laburnum Way. Hat Pev 114 A2
Laburnum Way. With 98 A3
Labworth La. Canv 197 E1
Labworth Rd. Canv 197 E1
Ladbrook Dr. Colch 68 A2
Ladbrooke Rd. Clact 109 E3
Ladell Cl. Colch 66 C2
Ladram Cl. South 201 E4
Ladram Rd. South 201 E4
Ladram Way. South 201 D4
Lady La. Chelm 140 B4
Ladygate Centre. Wick 174 B4
Ladysmith Ave. Brigh 106 C4
Laing Rd. Colch 68 C3
Lake Ave. Clact 109 E2
Lake Dri. Thund 187 F3
Lake Way. Clact 124 C3
Lake Wlk. Clact 109 E2
Lakeside. Rayl 176 B2
Lakeside Cres. Canv 197 E3
Lakeview. Canv 197 D3
Lakin Cl. Sprin 128 A2
Lamarsh Hill. Bures 19 F1
Lamarsh Hill. Gt H 19 D3
Lamarsh Rd. Alph 19 D2
Lamb La. Si Hed 24 B4
Lambert's Rd. Gt T 45 F1
Lambeth Mews. Hock 177 E3
Lambeth Rd. South 189 F3
Lambeth Rd. Thund 187 E3
Lambeth Wlk. Clact 109 F3
Lambourne Cl. Clact 109 F4
Lambourne Cl. Stanw 66 B2
Lambourne Cres. Basil 185 F3
Lambourne Gr. Mald 144 C4
Lambourne Hall Rd. 168 C1
Lammas Way. Wiv 69 E1
Lancaster Gdns. Rayl 189 D4
Lancaster Gdns. South 200 A4
Lancaster Gdns E. Clact 110 A2
Lancaster Gdns W. Clact 110 A2
Lancaster Rd. Rayl 189 D4
Lancaster Rd. Sud 7 E1
Lancaster Way. Brain 59 F2
Lancaster Way. Ea Col 44 C1
Lanchester Ave. Clact 124 B3
Lancia Ave. Clact 124 B3
Land Cl. Clact 109 E3
Land La. Colch 68 A4
Landermere. Basil 185 D4
Landermere Rd. Th L S 74 A3
Landsburg Rd. Canv 197 E3
Landsdown Rd. Sud 13 D4
Landseer Rd. Colch 67 D3
Landwick La. Deng 160 C4
Lane Rd. Wa Col 46 B4
Lane The. Clact 109 E2
Lane The. Mist 35 F2
Lane The. W Mers 121 D4
Langdale. Bl Not 77 E4
Langdale Gdns. Chelm 140 B4
Langdon Rd. Rayl 176 A2
Langenhoe. Wick 174 C3
Langenhoe Hall La. Lang 104 B4
Langford Cres. Thund 187 F3
Langford Gr. Basil 186 B4
Langford Rd. Mald 131 F3
Langford Rd. Wic Bis 115 E1
Langham Dr. Clact 109 D2
Langham La. Langh 32 B1
Langham Rd. Box 31 F1
Langley Cl. Rayl 189 D4
Langley Hill. Lam 19 E2
Langleys. Basil 185 D2
Langport Dr. South 190 A2
Langton Ave. Chelm 126 C3
Lanham Green Rd. T Gr 79 D4
Lanhams. Basil 186 B4
Lanisdale. Dan 143 D4
Lansdown Ave. Hadl 188 C3
Lansdowne Ave. South 190 A1
Lansdowne Cl. Tipt 100 B3
Lansdowne Dr. Rayl 176 B2
Lanvalley Rd. Colch 66 C3
Lappmark Rd. Canv 197 E2
Lapwater Cl. South 189 E1
Lapwing Dr. Kelv 81 E1
Lapwing Dr. Mald 132 B3
Lapwing Rd. Runw 163 E1
Larch Cl. Colch 68 B4
Larch Gr. Chelm 140 B3
Larch Gr. Nay 20 A1
Larch Gr. With 98 A3
Larch Wlk. Hat Pev 114 A3
Larch Wlk. Mald 132 B3
Larches The. Bore 128 C4
Larches The. Thund 187 E4
Larchwood Cl. Hadl 189 D3
Lark Hill Rd. Cane 168 A1
Lark Rise. Sud 12 B3
Larkfield Cl. Hawk 178 B2
Larkfield Rd. Gt Ben 71 E1
Larksfield Cres. Harw 40 A2
Larkswood Wlk. Wick 174 B3
Larkway. Walt 93 F4
Larneys The. Walt 93 F4
Larup Ave. Canv 197 E2
Larup Gdns. Canv 197 E2
Lascelles Gdns. Hawk 178 B3
Latchetts Shaw. Basil 185 D2
Latchingdon Cl. Rayl 176 A2
Latchingdon Rd. Col N 156 B3
Latchingdon Rd. Latch 156 B3
Latchingdon Rd. Purl 156 B3
Lathcoates Cres. Gt Bad 140 C4
Launceston Cl. Colch 68 A1
Laundry Gdns. Sud 12 B3
Laurel Ave. Harw 39 F1
Laurel Ave. Wick 174 B4
Laurel Cl. Clact 110 A4
Laurel Cl. South 198 B4
Laurel Dr. L Mel 7 E4
Laurel Gr. Chelm 140 A4
Laurels The. Rayl 188 C4
Laurels The. S Woo F 165 E4
Laurence Ave. With 115 D4
Laurence Cl. Elmst M 69 F3
Laurence Croft. Writ 126 A1
Lavender Cl. Tipt 100 B2
Lavender Ct. Sprin 127 F3
Lavender Gr. South 190 B2
Lavender Way. Colch 49 E1
Lavender Way. Wick 174 B4
Lavender Wlk. Clact 125 D4
Lavenham Cl. Clact 109 D2
Laver Ct. Colch 67 E2
Lawford La. Writ 126 B1
Lawling Ave. Mald 132 B3
Lawlinge Rd. Latch 157 D3
Lawn Ave. South 191 D1
Lawn Chase. With 97 F1
Lawn La. Sprin 127 E3
Lawns Cl. W Mers 121 E4
Lawns The. Sprin 127 E3
Lawns The. Thund 187 E4
Lawnscourt. Thund 187 D4
Lawrence Rd. Basil 186 C4
Lawshall's Hill. Wa Col 27 E1
Laxton Ct. Colch 67 D2
Laxton Gr. Frin 93 D2
Laxton Rd. Alres 88 A4
Laxtons The. Hawk 178 B3
Layer Breton Hill. Lay Br 84 A1
Layer Rd. Colch 67 E2
Layer Rd. Gt Wig 102 C3
Layer Rd. Lang 85 F2
Layer Rd. Lay H 85 D4
Layer Rd. Stanw 85 D4
Layzell Croft. Sud 13 E2
Le Cateau Rd. Colch 67 F3
Lea Cl. Brain 60 B1
Lea Gr. Hat Pev 114 C1
Lea La. Gt Brx 98 C1
Lea Rd. S Ben 187 E3
Leach Cl. Gt Bad 141 D4
Leam Cl. Colch 68 C4
Leamington Rd. Hock 177 F4
Leamington Rd. South 200 B4
Leapingwell Cl. Sprin 128 A2
Leas Cl. South 199 D4
Leas Gdns. South 199 D4
Leas Rd. Clact 109 E1
Leas Rd. Colch 67 E1
Leas The. Burn 170 B3
Leas The. Frin 94 A3
Leas The. South 199 E4
Leaside. Thund 187 D3
Leasway. Rayl 176 B1
Leasway. Wick 174 A3
Leasway The. South 199 D4
Leather La. Brain 59 F2
Leather La. Gt Y 9 D1
Leather La. South 200 A4
Lede Rd. Canv 197 D2
Lee Lotts. Gt Wak 193 D2
Lee Rd. Basil 186 C3
Lee Rd. Harw 40 B2
Lee Wick La. St O 107 E1
Lee Woottens La. Basil 185 D2
Leech's La. Colch 49 E2
Leeward Rd. S Woo F 165 F3
Leeway The. Dan 142 C4
Legerton Cotts. Wa Col 28 B1
Legg St. Chelm 127 D2
Leicester Ave. Roch 190 C4
Leicester Cl. Clact 108 C1
Leicester Cl. Colch 68 A4
Leicester Ct. Silv E 79 E2
Leige Ave. Canv 197 D3
Leigh Beck La. Canv 197 F1
Leigh Beck Rd. Canv 197 F2
Leigh Cliff Rd. South 198 C4
Leigh Dr. Wic Bis 115 E3
Leigh Fells. Basil 186 B3
Leigh Gdns. Hadl 189 E1
Leigh Hall Rd. South 189 F1
Leigh Hill. South 198 B4
Leigh Hill Cl. South 198 C4
Leigh Hts. Hadl 188 C2
Leigh Park Cl. South 189 E1
Leigh Park Rd. South 198 B4
Leigh Rd. Canv 197 D1
Leigh Rd. South 190 A1
Leigh View Dr. South 189 F2
Leigham Court Dr. South 189 F1
Leighams Rd. E Han 153 F4
Leighcroft Gdns. South 189 E2
Leighfields. Thund 188 A3
Leighfields Ave. South 189 E3
Leighfields Rd. South 189 E3
Leighlands Rd. S Woo F 165 E4
Leighton Ave. South 189 F1
Leighton Rd. Thund 187 E4
Leighville Gr. South 189 E1
Leighwood Ave. South 189 F3
Leitrim Ave. South 201 E3
Lekoe Rd. Canv 196 C3
Lenham Way. Basil 186 B3
Leon Dr. Basil 185 E2
Leonard Dr. Rayl 176 A2
Leonard Mews. Brain 78 A4
Leonard Rd. Basil 185 D1
Leonard Rd. South 199 E4
Les Bois. Lay H 85 D3
Leslie Cl. South 189 E3
Leslie Dr. South 189 E3
Leslie Gdns. Rayl 176 C1
Leslie Park. Burn 170 B2
Leslie Rd. Rayl 176 C1
Lethe Grove. Colch 85 F4
Lettons Chase. S Woo F 165 E3
Letzen Rd. Canv 197 D2
Levens Way. Bl Not 77 E3
Lever La. Roch 178 C1
Lewes Rd. South 191 E2
Lewes Way. Thund 188 A4
Lewis Dr. Chelm 140 A3
Lexden Ct. Colch 67 E4
Lexden Gr. Colch 66 C4
Lexden Rd. Colch 67 E3
Lexden Rd. W Berg 48 B2
Ley Field. Mks T 64 C2
Ley The. Brain 60 B1
Leybourne Dr. Sprin 127 F4
Leys Dr. Lit Cla 91 E1
Leys Rd. Wiv 69 E2
Leys The. Basil 185 E2
Leys The. Sprin 127 F3
Leyton Ct. Clact 109 F4
Leywood Cl. Brain 60 B1
Licac Ct. Wiv 69 D1
Lichfield Cl. Chelm 126 C2
Lichfield Cl. Colch 68 A4
Lichfields The. Basil 185 F4
Lifchild Cl. With 115 D4
Lifstan Way. South 200 C4
Lilac Ave. Canv 197 E2
Lilac Ave. Wick 174 B4
Lilac Cl. Chelm 140 B3
Lilian Rd. Burn 170 B3
Lilley's La. Gt Bro 52 B2
Lillies The. Brain 42 A1
Lillyville Wlk. Rayl 177 D1
Lily Cl. Sprin 127 F3
Limbourne Dr. Mald 132 B3
Limburg Rd. Canv 196 B2
Lime Ave. Colch 68 B4
Lime Ave. Hadl 189 E1
Lime Ave. Harw 40 A2
Lime Cl. Clact 109 E2
Lime Cl. With 98 A3
Lime Gr. Sud 12 B3
Lime Rd. S Ben 187 F2
Lime St. Brigh 106 C3
Lime Way. Burn 170 A3
Lime Wlk. Chelm 140 B3
Limes The. Chelm 140 A1
Limes The. Gos 42 C4
Limes The. L Mel 7 E4
Limes The. Rayl 176 C1
Limetree Ave. S Ben 187 D2
Limetree Rd. Canv 197 F2
Lincoln Ave. Clact 124 B3
Lincoln Chase. South 191 F2
Lincoln La. Gt Hor 31 E1
Lincoln Rd. Basil 185 F4
Lincoln Rd. Hawk 178 A3
Lincoln Way. Canv 196 C2
Lincoln Way. Colch 68 A4
Linde Rd. Canv 197 D2
Linden Cl. Chelm 140 B4
Linden Cl. Colch 50 C1
Linden Cl. Lawf 35 D2
Linden Cl. Rayl 176 C1
Linden Cl. Thund 187 E3
Linden Dr. Clact 109 F4
Linden Leas. Thund 187 E3
Linden Rd. Thund 187 E3
Linden Way. Canv 196 C2
Lindens The. Brain 60 A1
Lindford Dr. Basil 185 F3
Lindisfarne Ave. South 190 A1
Lindisfarne Ct. Mald 144 C4
Lindon Rd. Runw 163 E2
Lindsell Green. Basil 185 F3
Lindsell La. Basil 185 F3
Lindsey Ave. Sud 13 D3
Lindsey Rd. Gt Wak 193 D2
Lingcroft. Basil 185 D2
Lingfield Dr. Roch 179 D2
Lingwood Cl. Dan 142 C4
Link Cl. Colch 49 F2
Link Rd. Brigh 107 D3
Link Rd. Canv 196 C2
Link Rd. Clact 109 E1
Link Rd. Hals 43 E4
Link Rd. Rayl 176 B2
Links Dr. Chelm 139 F4
Links Rd. Bradw 79 E4
Links Way. Hadl 188 C2
Linksway. Hadl 189 E3
Linkway. Basil 185 D3
Linley Gdns. Clact 109 E1
Linne Rd. Canv 197 E3
Linnet Cl. South 201 F4
Linnet Dr. Chelm 140 A3
Linnet Dr. S Ben 187 E1
Linnet Way. Gt Ben 89 E4
Linnets. Basil 185 D2
Linnets. Clact 109 F3
Linroping Ave. Canv 197 F2
Linstead Cl. Clact 109 D2
Lion Rd. Glems 2 A3
Lion Wlk. Colch 67 F4
Lionel Hurst Cl. Sud 13 E3
Lionel Rd. Canv 197 D2
Lionfield Terr. Sprin 127 E2
Lisle Rd. Colch 68 A3
Lister Rd. Brain 77 F4
Liston La. Fox 7 D4
Listonhall Chase. Si Hed 24 A3
Litchfield. Harw 39 F1
Litchfield Cl. Clact 109 F3
Littell Tweed. Sprin 128 A2
Little and Great Sir Hughes La. W Han 141 D1
Little Baddow Rd. Dan 142 C4
Little Baddow Rd. Woo Wa 130 B2
Little Bakers. Walt 94 A4
Little Bentley. Basil 185 D4
Little Bentley Rd. Tend 54 A1
Little Braxted La. With 98 B2
Little Bromley Rd. Ard 52 A4
Little Bromley Rd. Gt Bro 52 C2
Little Bromley Rd. Lit Ben 53 F1
Little Charlton. Basil 186 B3
Little Chittock. Basil 185 F3
Little Church St. Harw 40 B3
Little Clacton Rd. Frin 92 C1
Little Clacton Rd. Lit Cla 109 D4
Little Dorrit. Chelm 126 C4
Little Fields. Dan 143 D4
Little Fretches. South 189 F2
Little Garth. Basil 186 A3
Little Gypps Cl. Canv 196 C2
Little Gypps Rd. Canv 196 C2
Little Harrods. Walt 94 A4
Little Hayes Chase. Stow 155 E1
Little Hays. South 189 D3
Little Horkesley Rd. Worm 30 A2
Little Hyde Cl. Gt Y 9 D1
Little Hyde Rd. Gt Y 9 D1
Little London La. Woo Wa 130 B2
Little Meadow. Writ 126 A1
Little Nell. Chelm 126 C4
Little Oaks. Basil 185 D3
Little Searles. Basil 186 A4
Little Spenders. Basil 185 E2
Little Sq. Brain 59 F2
Little St Mary's. L Mel 7 E4
Little Stambridge Hall Rd. Gt Stam 179 E2
Little Stile. Writ 139 D4
Little Tey Rd. Fee 81 F3
Little Thorpe. South 192 A1
Little Totham Rd. Gold 117 E1
Little Totham Rd. Lit Tot 117 E1
Little Wakering Hall La. Gt Wak 193 D2
Little Wakering Rd. Barl 192 C3
Little Wheatley Chase. Rayl 176 A2
Little Wood. Walt 93 F3
Little Yeldham Rd. Lit Y 9 E2
Littlebury Ct. Basil 186 A4
Littlebury Gdns. Colch 68 B2
Littlebury Green. Basil 186 A4
Littlecroft. S Woo F 165 E3
Littlefield Rd. Colch 67 E1
Littlethorpe. Basil 185 F2
Llewellyn Cl. Sprin 127 E2
Lloyd Rd. Sho G 40 A4
Lloyd Wise Cl. South 191 E2
LMINGTON Rd. Colch 50 B1
Loamy Hill Rd. Toll M 117 D4
Lobelia Cl. Bore 128 A3
Locarno Ave. Runw 163 F1
Lock Rd. Hals 43 F4
Lockhart Ave. Colch 67 E4
Lockram La. With 98 A1
Lockram La. With 97 F1
Locks Hill. Roch 178 C1
Lodge Ave. Gt Bad 140 C4
Lodge Cl. Clact 109 F2
Lodge Cl. Lit Oak 57 E4
Lodge Cl. Rayl 176 C1
Lodge Cl. Thund 188 A3
Lodge Cres. Bore 128 C4
Lodge Ct. W Berg 48 C2
Lodge Farm Cl. South 189 E3
Lodge Farm La. St O 108 B2
Lodge Farm Rd. Glems 2 B2
Lodge La. Ard 51 D3
Lodge La. Ard 51 E3
Lodge La. Brigh 106 C4
Lodge La. Lang 86 B1
Lodge La. Langh 50 B4
Lodge La. Peld 103 E4
Lodge La. Purl 144 B1
Lodge La. Tend 72 C3
Lodge Rd. Brain 59 F1
Lodge Rd. Haze 144 A3
Lodge Rd. Lit Cla 92 A2
Lodge Rd. Lit Oak 57 E4
Lodge Rd. Mald 131 F2
Lodge Rd. Mess 82 B2
Lodge Rd. S Woo F 153 F3
Lodge Rd. Writ 139 D4
Lodgelands Cl. Rayl 176 C1
Lodwick. South 201 E3
Loftin Way. Gt Bad 140 B4
Lombardy Cl. Basil 186 B3
Lombardy Pl. Chelm 127 D2
London Hill. Chelm 139 F1
London Hill. Rayl 176 B2
London Land Cotts. Worm 29 F2
London Rd. Basil 187 D3
London Rd. Basil 185 E2
London Rd. Bill 174 A4
London Rd. Bl Not 77 E3
London Rd. Brain 59 F1
London Rd. Chelm 139 F4
London Rd. Clact 109 F4
London Rd. Copf 65 E2
London Rd. Fee 81 F2
London Rd. Gt Hor 30 C2
London Rd. Gt Le 77 E3
London Rd. Hadl 189 E1
London Rd. Kelv 81 D1
London Rd. Mald 131 E2
London Rd. Mks T 64 C1
London Rd. Rayl 176 A2
London Rd. South 190 B1
London Rd. Stanw 66 C4
London Rd. Thund 187 D3
London Rd. Wick 174 A4
London Rd. Wick 175 E3
Long Acres. Fee 81 F3
Long Brandocks. Writ 126 A1
Long Gages. Basil 185 D4
Long Green. T Gr 78 C4
Long La. Frin 93 D2
Long La. Hull 165 F1
Long Meadow Dr. Wick 174 C4
Long Meadows. Harw 39 F1
Long Pastures. Glems 2 B2
Long Rd. Canv 196 C2
Long Rd. E. Ded 34 A2
Long Rd. Lawf 35 D2
Long Rd. Mist 35 D2
Long Rd W. Ded 33 F2
Long Riding. Basil 185 E3
Long Wyre St. Colch 67 F4
Longacre. Basil 185 E4
Longacre. Chelm 139 E4
Longacres. Brain 60 A1
Longacres Rd. T Gr 78 C3
Longbarn Hill. Brad 37 D1
Longborough Cl. Basil 174 A1
Longcroft Rd. Colch 68 B4
Longfellow Rd. Mald 132 A1
Longfield. With 97 F3
Longfield Cl. Wick 175 D4
Longfield Rd. Gt Bad 140 C4
Longfield Rd. S Woo F 165 E4
Longfield Rd. Wick 175 D4
Longfields. St O 108 A2
Longhams Dr. S Woo F 165 E4
Longleaf Dr. Brain 77 F4
Longleat Cl. Chelm 126 C4
Longmead Ave. Gt Bad 140 C4
Longmeads. Wic Bis 115 F3
Longmeads Cl. Writ 126 A1
Longmore Ave. Gt Bad 140 C4
Longridge. Colch 68 C4
Longsands. South 201 E4
Longship Way. Mald 144 C4
Longstomps Ave. Chelm 140 A4
Lonsdale Rd. South 191 E1
Lord Holland Rd. Colch 67 F2
Lord Roberts Ave. South 189 F1
Lordship Rd. Writ 126 A1
Lordswood Rd. Colch 67 E1
Lorien Gdns. S Woo F 165 E3
Lorkin's La. Twin 18 B2
Lornes Cl. South 191 E2
Loten Rd. S Ben 187 D1
Lottem Rd. Canv 197 E1
Lott's La. Brad 54 B4
Lott's Rd. Clact 91 D2
Lotts Yd. Colch 68 A3
Louis Dr. W. Rayl 176 A2
Louis Dr E. Rayl 176 A2
Louisa Ave. Thund 187 D3
Louise Rd. Rayl 176 C1
Louvaine Ave. Wick 174 A4
Love La. Brigh 106 C4
Love La. Rayl 176 B1
Love Way. Clact 109 E3
Lovelace Ave. South 200 B4
Lovelace Gdns. South 191 E1
Lovell Rise. South 190 A3
Lovens Cl. Canv 197 E1
Lover's La. Gt Ben 90 A4
Loves Wlk. Gt Bad 140 C4
Loves Wlk. Writ 139 D4
Lovibond Pl. Sprin 127 F2
Low Rd. Harw 39 F1
Low Rd. South 201 F3
Low St. Glems 2 B3
Lowe Chase. Walt 94 A4
Lowefields. Ea Col 45 E3
Lower Anchor St. Chelm 127 D1
Lower Ave. Basil 186 C4
Lower Chase. Alth 157 F2

Lower Church Rd. Thund 187 D3
Lower Farm Rd. Box 21 D1
Lower Green. Chelm 140 B1
Lower Green. Wa Col 28 B1
Lower Harlings. Sho G 40 A4
Lower Holt St. Ea Col 45 E3
Lower Lambricks. Rayl 176 B2
Lower Langley. Gt T 46 B1
Lower Marine Par. Harw 40 B1
Lower Park Rd. Brigh 106 C4
Lower Park Rd. Wick 174 B2
Lower Rd. Ashi 166 B1
Lower Rd. Ashi 167 D1
Lower Rd. Birch 84 A3
Lower Rd. Fox 7 D2
Lower Rd. Hull 166 B1
Lower Rd. Lay Br 102 A4
Lower Rd. M Bure 29 D3
Lower Rd. Peld 103 E3
Lower Southend Rd. Wick 174 B4
Lower St. Cav 1 B1
Lower St. Glems 2 C3
Lower St. Str S M 33 E4
Loxford. Basil 186 A4
Luard Way. Birch 84 A2
Luard Way. With 97 F1
Lubbards Cl. Rayl 176 B3
Lucas Ave. Chelm 140 B3
Lucas Ave. Ford 47 E3
Lucas Rd. Colch 67 F3
Lucas's La. Beau 73 E3
Lucerne Dr. Wick 175 D4
Lucerne Rd. Elmst M 70 A3
Lucerne Wlk. Wick 175 D4
Luces La. Ca Hed 15 F2
Lucksfield Way. Gt Bad 140 C3
Lucy Cl. Stanw 66 B3
Lucy La N. Stanw 66 A4
Lucy La S. Stanw 66 B4
Lucy Rd. South 200 A4
Ludgores La. Dan 142 B3
Ludgrove. Latch 157 D3
Ludham Hall La. Bl Not 77 E4
Luff Way. Walt 93 F4
Lufkin Rd. Colch 49 F2
Lugar Cl. Colch 68 C3
Luker Rd. South 200 A4
Lumber Leys. Walt 94 A4
Luncies Rd. Basil 185 F3
Lundy Cl. South 190 A3
Lunnish Hill. Rams 38 C1
Lupin Dr. Sprin 127 F3
Lupin Mews. Sprin 127 F3
Lupin Way. Clact 109 E2
Lushington Ave. Walt 93 F3
Lushington Rd. Lawf 35 E2
Lydford Rd. South 199 F4
Lydgate Cl. Lawf 35 D2
Lydia Dr. St O 107 D1
Lylt Rd. Canv 197 D2
Lyme Rd. South 191 E1
Lymington Ave. Clact 110 A4
Lymingon Ave. South 189 F1
Lympstone Cl. South 190 A3
Lyndale Ave. South 191 D1
Lyndene. Thund 187 D3
Lyndhurst Dr. S Woo F 142 C1
Lyndhurst Rd. Ashi 167 E1
Lyndhurst Rd. Clact 110 B2
Lynfords Ave. Runw 164 A2
Lynfords Dr. Runw 164 A2
Lynfords Dr. Runw 163 F1
Lynmouth Ave. Chelm 140 B4
Lynmouth Gdns. Chelm 127 E1
Lynn View Cl. S Ben 187 E3
Lynne Cl. Walt 93 E3
Lynstede. Basil 186 A3
Lynton Cl. Harw 40 A2
Lynton Dr. Sprin 127 F3
Lynton Rd. S Ben 188 B2
Lyon Cl. Chelm 140 A2
Lyons Hall Rd. Brain 60 B4
Lyster Ave. Gt Bad 141 D4
Lyth Ave. South 201 E4

Macbeth Cl. Colch 68 C4
Macdonald Ave. South 190 C1
Macintyres Wlk. Hawk 178 B3
Mackay Ct. Colch 68 A1
Maclarens. Gt Tot 116 A3
Macmurdo Cl. South 189 E4
Macmurdo Rd. South 189 E4
Madeira Ave. South 189 F1
Madeira Rd. Clact 110 B2
Madeline Pl. Chelm 126 C3
Madgements Rd. Stis 61 D4
Madrid Ave. Rayl 176 A4
Magazine Farm Way. Colch 67 D3
Magazine Rd. South 201 F3
Magdalen Cl. Clact 109 F2
Magdalen Rd. Clact 109 F2
Magdalen St. Colch 68 A3
Magdalene Cres. Silv E 79 E2
Magnolia Cl. Chelm 140 A3
Magnolia Cl. With 98 A4
Magnolia Dr. Colch 68 C4
Magnolia Rd. Hawk 178 A3
Magnolia Way. Roch 191 D4
Magwitch Cl. Chelm 126 C4
Maidenburgh St. Colch 67 F4
Maidment Cres. With 114 C4
Main Rd. Alth 157 F2
Main Rd. Bore 128 B4
Main Rd. Dun 142 B4
Main Rd. E Han 153 E3
Main Rd. Frat 70 C2
Main Rd. Frin 93 D2
Main Rd. Harw 40 A2
Main Rd. Harw 40 C3
Main Rd. Hawk 177 F2
Main Rd. Hock 177 E3
Main Rd. Rams 39 D1
Main Rd. Rett 164 A3
Main Rd. S Woo F 154 A3
Main Rd. St L 148 B4
Main Rd. Worm 29 F2
Maine Cres. Rayl 176 A2
Maitland Pl. South 192 C1
Makins Rd. Rams 39 F3
Malard Cl. Tolle 119 E1
Maldon Ct. Sud 13 D4
Maldon Rd. Birch 83 F2
Maldon Rd. Brad O S 149 E4
Maldon Rd. Burn 169 F4
Maldon Rd. Colch 67 E3
Maldon Rd. Dan 143 D3
Maldon Rd. Dan 143 D4
Maldon Rd. Gold 133 E3
Maldon Rd. Gt Bad 141 E4
Maldon Rd. Gt Brx 99 F1
Maldon Rd. Gt Tot 116 A2
Maldon Rd. Gt Wig 102 C1
Maldon Rd. Hat Pev 114 B1
Maldon Rd. Kelv 81 E1
Maldon Rd. Langf 131 E3
Maldon Rd. Latch 156 C3
Maldon Rd. Marg 139 E1
Maldon Rd. Sand 141 E4
Maldon Rd. South 191 D1
Maldon Rd. Stanw 66 B1
Maldon Rd. Steep 147 E1
Maldon Rd. Tipt 100 B2
Maldon Rd. Toll D 118 B1
Maldon Rd. Toll M 118 B1
Maldon Rd. With 115 D4
Maldon Rd. Woo Mor 144 A4
Malgraves. Basil 186 A4
Malgraves Pl. Basil 186 A4
Mallard Cl. Kelv 81 E2
Mallard Cl. Lay H 85 D3
Mallard Rd. Chelm 140 A3
Mallard Way. Sud 13 E3
Mallards. South 192 C1
Mallow Field. Hals 25 F1
Malmsmead. South 201 E4
Maltese Rd. Chelm 127 D2
Malthouse Rd. Mann 35 E2
Malting Farm La. Ard 33 E1
Malting Green Rd. Lay H 85 D3
Malting La. Cla 4 A4
Malting La. Walt 75 E1
Malting Rd. Colch 67 E1
Malting Rd. Peld 103 F3
Malting Villas Rd. Roch 178 C1
Malting Yd. Wiv 87 D4
Maltings Cl. Bures 19 F1
Maltings Ct. With 114 C4
Maltings La. With 114 C4
Maltings Rd. Brigh 88 C1
Maltings Rd. Gt Bad 141 D3
Maltings Rd. Rett 164 C1
Maltings The. Ray 59 D1
Maltings The. Soum 159 F2
Malvern Ave. Canv 196 B2
Malvern Cl. Chelm 126 B3
Malvern Cl. Rayl 176 B2
Malvern Rd. Hock 177 F4
Malvern Way. Gt Hor 49 D4
Malwood Dr. S Ben 187 D3
Malwood Rd. S Ben 187 D3
Malyon Court Cl. S Ben 188 A2
Malyon Rd. With 114 C4
Malyons. Basil 186 A4
Malyons Cl. Basil 186 A4
Malyons Green. Basil 186 A4
Malyons La. Hull 165 E1
Malyons Mews. Basil 186 A4
Malyons Pl. Basil 186 A4
Malyons The. S Ben 188 A2
Manchester Dr. South 189 E1
Manchester Dr. South 189 F1
Manchester Rd. Clact 110 C3
Mandeville Rd. Mks T 64 C2
Mandeville Way. Thund 187 E4
Mandeville Way. Walt 93 F3
Manfield. Hals 25 F1
Manfield Gdns. St O 108 A3
Mangapp Chase. Burn 170 A4
Manilla Rd. South 200 B4
Mannering Gdns. South 190 A2
Manners Way. South 190 C3
Manningtree Rd. Ded 34 A3
Manningtree Rd. Lit Ben 71 F4
Manningtree Rd. Str S M 35 D4
Manns Way. Rayl 176 B3
Manor Ave. Basil 186 B3
Manor Cl. Cav 1 B1
Manor Cl. Gt Hor 49 E4
Manor Cl. Rayl 188 B4
Manor Dr. Gt Bad 140 C4
Manor House Way. Brigh 106 C4
Manor La. Harw 40 A1
Manor Rd. Chelm 127 E1
Manor Rd. Colch 67 F4
Manor Rd. Deng 149 E1
Manor Rd. Frin 93 D2
Manor Rd. Harw 40 A2
Manor Rd. Hat Pev 114 B1
Manor Rd. Hock 177 E3
Manor Rd. S Woo F 165 E4
Manor Rd. South 199 E4
Manor Rd. Sud 7 F1
Manor Rd. Thund 187 E3
Manor Rd. W Berg 48 C3
Manor Rd. Wiv 69 E1
Manor Rd. Woo Wa 131 D2
Manor St. Brain 60 A2
Manor Way. Clact 111 D3
Manors Way. Silv E 79 E2
Manse Chase. Mald 132 A1
Mansel Cl. South 189 F3
Mansted Gdns. Hawk 178 B3
Maple Ave. Brain 59 E1
Maple Ave. Mald 132 B3
Maple Ave. South 198 C4
Maple Cl. Clact 109 E2
Maple Cl. Hals 26 A1
Maple Cl. Harw 40 A2
Maple Dr. Chelm 140 A3
Maple Dr. Rayl 176 B4
Maple Dr. Walt 93 E3
Maple Dr. With 98 A3
Maple Leaf. Tipt 100 B4
Maple Rd. Sud 13 D3
Maple Sq. South 191 D1
Maple Way. Burn 170 A3
Maple Way. Canv 196 C2
Maple Way. Colch 68 A2
Mapledene Ave. Hull 165 F1
Mapleford Sweep. Basil 185 E2
Mapleleaf Cl. Hock 177 F4
Mapleleaf Gdns. Wick 174 A3
Maples The. Wick 174 B3
Maplesfield. Hadl 188 B2
Maplestead. Basil 185 E4
Maplin Cl. Thund 187 E4
Maplin Gdns. Basil 185 F3
Maplin Way. South 201 E3
Maplin Way N. South 192 B1
Marasca End. Rowh 86 A4
Maraschino Cres. Rowh 86 A4
Marconi Rd. Chelm 127 D2
Marcos Rd. Canv 197 E2
Marcus Ave. South 201 D4
Marcus Chase. South 201 D4
Marcus Gdns. South 201 D4
Marennes Cres. Brigh 106 C4
Mareth Rd. Colch 67 E1
Margaret Cl. Brigh 106 C3
Margaret Rd. Colch 67 F4
Margaretting Rd. Chelm 139 F1
Margaretting Rd. Writ 139 D3
Margarite Way. Wick 174 A4
Margraten Ave. Canv 197 E1
Marguerite Dr. South 189 F1
Maria St. Harw 40 B3
Marigold Ave. Clact 109 E3
Marigold Cl. Colch 68 C4
Marigold Cl. Sprin 127 F3
Marina Ave. Rayl 176 B2
Marina Cl. South 190 C2
Marina Gdns. Clact 110 B3
Marina Mews. Walt 94 B4
Marina Rd. Hat Pev 114 A2
Marine App. Canv 197 D1
Marine Ave. Canv 197 F1
Marine Ave. South 189 E1
Marine Ave. South 199 F4
Marine Cl. Hadl 189 D1
Marine Par. Canv 197 F1
Marine Par. Hadl 198 B4
Marine Par. Harw 40 B2
Marine Par. May 146 C1
Marine Par. South 200 A4
Marine Par E. Clact 110 A2
Marine Par W. Clact 109 F1
Mariners Ct. Gt Wak 193 E2
Marion Ave. Clact 109 F3
Mariskals. Basil 186 A3
Mark Rd. Till 149 F3
Market Ave. Runw 174 B4
Market End. Cogg 62 C1
Market Hill. Cla 4 A4
Market Hill. Cogg 63 D2
Market Hill. Hals 25 F1
Market Hill. Mald 132 A2
Market Hill. Sud 12 C4
Market Pavement. Basil 185 D3
Market Pl. Brain 59 F2
Market Pl. Mald 131 F1
Market Pl. South 200 A4
Market Rd. Chelm 127 D1
Market Rd. Wick 174 B4
Market Sq. Basil 185 D3
Market Sq. S Woo F 165 F4
Market St. Brain 59 F2
Market St. Harw 40 C3
Markland Cl. Chelm 140 B2
Marklay Dr. S Woo F 165 E4
Marks Gdns. Brain 60 B1
Marks Hall Rd. Cogg 62 C3
Marks La. Rett 163 F4
Marland Dr. Mald 131 F1
Marlborough Ave. Till 149 F2
Marlborough Cl. Clact 109 E2
Marlborough Cl. Thund 187 E4
Marlborough Dr. Sud 12 C4
Marlborough Rd. Brain 60 A2
Marlborough Rd. Chelm 127 D1
Marlborough Rd. South 200 B4
Marlborough Wlk. Hock 177 E3
Marlin Cl. Hadl 188 C3
Marlow Gdns. South 190 C2
Marlowe Cl. Brain 78 A4
Marlowe Cl. Mald 145 D4
Marlowe Rd. Clact 109 D1
Marlowe Way. Colch 66 C3
Marlpits Rd. Purl 143 F2
Marmaduke Ave. Rayl 176 A2
Marne Rd. Colch 67 F2
Marney Cl. Gt Bad 140 C4
Marney Dr. Basil 185 F3
Marney Way. Frin 94 A3
Marram Cl. Colch 66 A3
Marsh Cres. Rown 87 D4
Marsh Farm La. Thor 89 E1
Marsh Farm Rd. S Woo F 165 E3
Marsh Rd. Burn 171 E3
Marsh Rd. High 21 F3
Marsh Rd. South 201 F3
Marsh Rd. Till 150 A2
Marsh Way. Brigh 106 C3
Marshall Cl. Fee 81 E2
Marshall Cl. Hadl 189 D2
Marshalls. Hawk 178 B2
Marshalls Cl. Rayl 176 C1
Marshalls Rd. Brain 59 F1
Marston Beck. Sprin 128 A1
Martello Rd. Walt 94 B4
Marten's La. Nay 20 C4
Martin End. Lay H 85 D3
Martin Mews. S Woo F 165 F4
Martin Wlk. Hawk 177 F2
Martingale. Thund 188 A3
Martingale Dr. Sprin 127 F4
Martin's Rd. Hals 25 F1
Martinsdale. Clact 109 F3
Martock Ave. South 190 A3
Martyns Gr. South 190 A1
Martyns Rise. L Mel 7 E3
Marvens. Chelm 140 B2
Mary La N. Gt Bro 71 D4
Mary La S. Gt Bro 71 D3
Mary Warner Rd. Ard 51 F4
Maryborough Gr. Colch 68 A1
Marylands Ave. Hock 177 E4
Mascalls The. Gt Bad 140 C4
Mascalls Way. Gt Bad 140 C4
Masefield Dr. Colch 66 C3
Masefield Rd. Brain 78 A4
Masefield Rd. Mald 145 D4
Mashey Rd. Lit Y 9 E3
Mason Cl. Colch 67 D2
Mason Rd. Clact 109 D2
Mason Rd. Colch 49 F1
Matching Green. Basil 185 E4
Matfield Cl. Sprin 127 E4
Mathews Cl. Str S M 22 B1
Matlock Rd. Canv 196 C2
Matthews Cl. Hals 26 A2
Maugham Cl. Wick 174 B3
Maurice Rd. Canv 197 E2
May Ave. Canv 197 E1
May Ave. Canv 197 E2
May Wlk. Chelm 140 B4
Mayberry Wlk. Colch 68 A2
Maybury Cl. Mks T 64 C2
Mayda Cl. Hals 25 E1
Maydells. Basil 186 A3
Maydene. S Woo F 165 E4
Mayes La. Dan 142 C4
Mayes La. Lit Oak 39 E1
Mayes La. Sand 141 F3
Mayfair Ave. Basil 186 B4
Mayfield Ave. Hull 165 F1
Mayfield Ave. South 190 C2
Mayfield Cl. Colch 50 B1
Mayfield Rd. Writ 126 A1
Mayflower Ave. Harw 40 C3
Mayflower Cl. South 190 A3
Mayflowers. Thund 187 D4
Mayford Way. Clact 109 D3
Mayland Ave. Canv 197 D1
Mayland Cl. Mald 132 B2
Mayland Cl. May 158 A4
Mayland Green. May 158 A4
Mayland Hill. May 158 B3
Mayland Rd. With 98 A1
Maylands Dr. Bl Not 77 E4
Mayling Rd. Brain 59 E1
Mayne Crest. Sprin 127 F3
Mayors Wlk. Colch 67 F4
Maypole Dr. St O 108 A2
Maypole Green Rd. Colch 67 E1
Maypole Rd. Gt Tot 131 F4
Maypole Rd. Tipt 100 B4
May's La. Ded 33 F2
Maysent Ave. Brain 59 F3
Maytree Wlk. Thund 187 E3
Maze The. South 189 E4
McCalmont Dr. Rayl 176 B4
McDivitt Wlk. South 190 A3
Mead Pastures. Woo Wa 130 B2
Mead Path. Chelm 139 F4
Mead The. Sud 13 D2
Meadgate. Basil 186 B4
Meadgate Ave. Gt Bad 140 C4
Meadow Cl. Clact 110 A4
Meadow Cl. Gt Bro 71 D3
Meadow Cl. Hals 43 F4
Meadow Cl. Pan 59 D4
Meadow Dr. South 200 C4
Meadow Grass Cl. Colch 66 A3
Meadow La. Runw 163 F2
Meadow La. Sud 12 C4
Meadow La. W Mers 121 E3
Meadow Mews. S Woo F 165 D4
Meadow Rd. Colch 67 E1
Meadow Rd. Hadl 188 C1
Meadow Rd. Hull 165 F1
Meadow Rd. Rett 164 B3
Meadow Side. Chelm 127 D2
Meadow View Cl. Colch 66 C3
Meadow View Rd. Sud 12 B3
Meadow View Wlk. Canv 196 C2
Meadow Way. Bl Not 78 B3
Meadow Way. Clact 125 D4
Meadow Way. Hock 177 F3
Meadow Way. Lang 86 A1
Meadow Way. Latch 157 D3
Meadow Way. Wick 174 B2
Meadowclose. Thund 188 A3
Meadowcroft Way. Walt 93 F4
Meadowland Rd. Wick 175 D3
Meadowside.C 127 E2
Meadowside. Brain 59 F3
Meadowside. Rayl 176 B1
Meads The. Basil 186 A2
Meadway. Canv 197 E1
Meadway. Gos 42 C4
Meadway. Lawf 35 D2
Meadway. Mald 132 A1
Meadway. Rayl 176 C1
Meadway. Thund 187 E4
Meadway The. South 199 D4
Meakins Cl. South 189 F4
Mearns Pl. Sprin 127 F2
Mede Way. Wiv 69 E2
Medlar Cl. With 98 A2
Medoc Cl. Basil 186 B4
Medway. Burn 170 A3
Medway Ave. With 97 E1
Medway Cl. Chelm 126 B2
Medway Cres. Hadl 189 D1
Meekings Rd. Sud 13 D4
Meers The. Walt 93 F3
Meesons Mead. Hawk 178 B2
Meeting Field. L Mel 7 E4
Meeting La. E Mers 105 E1
Meeting La. Ridge 8 A4
Melbourne Ave. Chelm 126 C3
Melbourne Chase. Colch 68 A1
Melbourne Rd. Clact 109 F2
Melcombe Rd. S Ben 187 E2
Melford Rd. Cav 1 C1
Melford Rd. Sud 7 E1
Mell Rd. Tolle 119 F1
Mellor Chase. Colch 66 C4
Melrose Gdns. Clact 110 B3
Melrose Rd. W Mers 121 E3
Melton Cl. Clact 109 D2
Melville Heath. S Woo F 165 F3
Mendip Cl. Rayl 176 C2
Mendip Cres. South 190 A2
Mendip Rd. Chelm 126 B3
Mendip Rd. South 190 A2
Mendlesham Cl. Clact 109 D2
Menin Rd. Colch 67 E2
Menish Way. Sprin 128 A2
Meon Cl. Sprin 127 E3
Meppel Ave. Canv 197 D3
Mercer Ave. Gt Wak 193 D2
Mercers Way. Colch 67 F4
Merchant St. S Woo F 165 F4
Mercia Cl. Gt Bad 141 D3
Mercury Cl. Wick 174 C4
Meredene. Basil 185 F3
Meredith Rd. Clact 109 F2
Merilies Cl. South 190 A2
Merilies Gdns. South 190 A2
Merivale Cl. Lawf 35 E2
Merivale Rd. Lawf 35 D2
Merlin Ct. Canv 197 D2
Merlin End. Colch 50 C1
Merlin Pl. Chelm 126 C3
Merlin Way. Runw 163 E1
Merriam Cl. Catt 35 E4
Merricks La. Basil 185 F1
Merrilees Cres. Clact 110 B3
Merrivale. S Ben 187 E1
Merryfield App. South 189 F2
Merryfields Ave. Hock 177 E4
Merrymount Gdns. Clact 110 A3
Mersea Ave. W Mers 121 D3
Mersea Rd. Colch 68 A2
Mersea Rd. Peld 103 F3
Mersea Rd. South 86 B3
Mersea View. St O 107 D2
Mersey Fleet Way. Brain 60 B1
Mersey Rd. With 97 F1
Mersey Way. Chelm 126 B3
Merstham Dr. Clact 109 E3
Merton Ct. Rowh 86 A4
Merton Pl. S Woo F 165 F3
Merton Rd. Hock 177 D4
Merton Rd. S Ben 187 E2
Mess Rd. South 201 F3
Messines Rd. Colch 67 E2
Meteor Rd. South 199 E4
Methersgate. Basil 185 E4
Metz Ave. Canv 197 D2
Mews Ct. Chelm 127 D1
Mews The. Frin 93 F2
Mews The. Hock 177 E3
Mey Wlk. Hock 177 E3
Meyel Ave. Canv 197 E3
Meynell Ave. Canv 197 E1
Meyrick Cres. Colch 67 F3
Micawber Way. Chelm 126 B4
Michaelstowe Cl. Harw 39 E1
Michaelstowe Dr. Harw 39 E1
Mid Colne. Basil 185 E2
Middle Crockerford. Basil 185 F2
Middle Green. Wa Col 28 B1
Middle King. Brain 60 B1
Middle Mead. Roch 178 C1
Middle Mead. Wick 174 C4
Middle Mill Rd. Colch 67 F4
Middle Way. L Mel 7 E4
Middleborough. Colch 67 F4
Middleburg Rd. Canv 196 C3
Middlefield. Hals 25 F1
Middlefield Rd. Mist 36 A2
Middlemead. S Han 152 B2
Middlemead. W Han 152 B2
Middlesex Ave. South 189 F2
Middleton Cl. Clact 109 E3
Middleton Rd. Sud 12 B3
Middleton Row. S Woo F 165 F3
Middlewick Cl. Colch 68 A1
Midguard Way. Mald 144 C4
Midhurst Ave. South 190 B2
Midland Cl. Colch 67 F2
Midsummer Meadow. South 192 C1
Midway. Clact 124 C3

Midway Rd. Colch 67 E1
Milburn Cres. Chelm 126 B1
Mildmay Rd. Burn 170 B3
Mildmay Rd. Chelm 127 D1
Mildmays. Dan 142 B4
Mile End Rd. Colch 49 F2
Miles Cl. Stanw 66 B3
Milford Cl. Elmst M 69 E1
Military Rd. Colch 68 A3
Mill Chase. Hals 25 F1
Mill Cl. Till 149 F2
Mill Cl. Tipt 100 B3
Mill Fields. Dan 143 D3
Mill Green. Basil 186 A4
Mill Green. Burn 170 A2
Mill Green Ct. Basil 186 A4
Mill Green Pl. Basil 186 A4
Mill Hill. Brain 60 A1
Mill Hill. Chelm 139 F1
Mill Hill. Lawf 34 B2
Mill Hill. Mann 35 E2
Mill Hill. Purl 144 B1
Mill Hill. S Ben 196 C4
Mill Hill. Sub 12 B4
Mill Hill. Worm 29 F3
Mill La. Ard 52 A2
Mill La. Birch 83 F2
Mill La. Brad 36 B1
Mill La. Cav 5 D4
Mill La. Col En 45 D4
Mill La. Dan 143 D3
Mill La. Ded 33 F4
Mill La. Frin 92 C2
Mill La. Gt Le 95 D4
Mill La. Gt Map 25 F4
Mill La. Gt Stam 179 D1
Mill La. Gt Y 9 D2
Mill La. Harw 40 B2
Mill La. Lay H 85 D3
Mill La. Lit Bad 129 F2
Mill La. Mald 132 A2
Mill La. Nay 20 B4
Mill La. Peb 27 D4
Mill La. Sud 12 B4
Mill La. T Gr 78 B3
Mill La. Terl 96 A1
Mill La. Th L S 73 F1
Mill La. Toll M 117 F2
Mill La. Virl 119 D4
Mill La. Walt 94 B4
Mill La. Weel 91 D3
Mill La. With 97 F1
Mill Lane Cl. Weel 91 D3
Mill Rd. Box 31 F2
Mill Rd. Burn 170 B4
Mill Rd. Cla 4 B4
Mill Rd. Colch 49 F3
Mill Rd. Ford 47 E2
Mill Rd. Fox 6 B3
Mill Rd. Gt Tot 116 B4
Mill Rd. Mald 132 A1
Mill Rd. May 158 A4
Mill Rd. Mks T 65 E2
Mill Rd. Ridge 8 A3
Mill Rd. Till 149 F2
Mill Rd. W Mers 121 E4
Mill St. Brigh 107 D3
Mill St. Colch 68 A3
Mill St. Nay 20 A1
Mill St. Nay 20 B4
Mill St. St O 107 F2
Mill Tye. Sud 13 D2
Mill Vue Rd. Sprin 127 F1
Mill Wlk. Tipt 100 B3
Millars Cl. S Woo F 165 F4
Millbridge Rd. With 97 F1
Miller's Barn Rd. Clact 109 D1
Millers Cl. Brain 60 A4
Millers Cl. Gt Hor 49 D4
Millers Cl. Stanw 66 B3
Millers Croft. Gt Bad 140 C3
Millers Gdns. Kelv 81 D1
Millers La. Stanw 66 B3
Millers Mead. Fee 81 F2
Millfield. Burn 170 A2
Millfields. Writ 126 A1
Milligans Chase. Chelm 140 A1
Millson Bank. Sprin 128 A2
Millview Meadows. Roch 178 C1
Millways. Gt Tot 116 A2
Millwrights. Tipt 100 B3
Milner Rd. Sud 13 D4
Milton Ave. Brain 78 A4
Milton Ave. South 199 F4
Milton Cl. Colch 66 C3
Milton Cl. Rayl 177 D1
Milton Pl. Chelm 127 D3
Milton Pl. South 199 F4
Milton Rd. Harw 40 B2
Milton Rd. Lawf 35 D1
Milton Rd. Mald 145 D4
Milton Rd. South 199 E4
Milton Rd. With 97 F3
Milton St. South 191 D1
Miltsin Ave. Canv 197 E3
Mimosa Cl. Sprin 127 F3
Minden Rd. Sud 12 C4
Minerva Cl. Harw 39 F1
Minsmere Way. Sud 13 E3
Minster Cl. Rayl 177 D1
Minton Hts. Hawk 178 B3
Miramar Ave. Canv 196 C2
Mistley End. Basil 185 E3
Mistley Path. Basil 185 E3
Mistley Side. Basil 185 E3
Mitchell Ave. Hals 25 F1
Mitchell Way. S Woo F 165 E4
Mitchells Ave. Canv 197 E2
Mitton Vale. Sprin 127 F1
Moat End. South 192 A1
Moat Farm Chase. With 97 F2
Moat Field. Basil 185 E4
Moat La. Alph 19 D2
Moat Rd. Ford 47 E3
Moat Rise. Rayl 176 B1
Modlen Rd. Walt 94 A4
Mollands. Basil 185 F2
Molrams La. Gt Bad 141 D3
Monkdowns Rd. Cogg 63 D2
Monklands Ct. Hals 25 E1
Monks Ct. With 97 F2
Monk's La. Ded 33 E3
Monks Lodge Rd. Gt Map 16 B2
Monks Mead. S Woo F 142 C1
Monks Rd. Ea Col 45 D4
Monksford Dr. Hull 165 E1
Monkside. Basil 185 E4
Monkwick Ave. Colch 67 F1
Mons Rd. Colch 67 E2
Montague Ave. Hadl 189 D1
Montague Pl. Canv 196 C2
Montbretia Cl. Stanw 66 B3
Montbretia Ct. Clact 109 E2
Montefiore Ave. Rayl 176 B4
Montgomery Cl. Colch 68 A2
Montgomery Cl. Sprin 127 F4
Montgomery Ct. South 192 C1
Montrose Rd. Sprin 127 F2
Montsale. Basil 186 B4
Moons Cl. Ashi 178 B4
Moor Hall La. S Woo F 142 C2
Moor Park Cl. South 189 E3
Moor Park Gdns. South 189 E3
Moor Rd. Gt T 64 A4
Moor Rd. Langh 32 B2
Moorcroft. Hawk 178 B3
Moorcroft Ave. Hadl 188 C3
Moores Ave. Basil 185 E1
Moorhen Ave. St L 148 B4
Moors Cl. Fee 81 F3
Moors Cl. Gt Ben 71 F1
Moor's Farm Chase. Lit Tot 117 D2
Moor's La. Gt Ben 71 F1
Moorsfield. Sud 13 D2
Moorside. Colch 68 A4
Mope La. Wic Bis 115 E3
Moran Ave. Chelm 127 D4
Morant Rd. Colch 68 A3
Morebarn Rd. Gt Bro 52 C1
Moreland Ave. Thund 187 E4
Moreland Cl. Gt Wak 193 D2
Moreland Cl. Thund 187 E3
Moreland Rd. Runw 163 E1
Morella Cl. Gt Ben 89 F4
Morello Ct. Rowh 86 A4
Moretons. Basil 186 A3
Moretons. Chelm 140 A1
Morley Rd. Hals 25 F1
Morley Rd. Tipt 100 B2
Morleys Rd. Ea Col 45 D3
Mornington Ave. Roch 179 D1
Mornington Cres. Canv 197 E2
Mornington Cres. Hadl 188 C2
Mornington Rd. Cres 197 E2
Morrins Cl. Gt Wak 193 E2
Morris Ave. Clact 124 C3
Morris Rd. Chelm 127 E1
Morrow La. Ard 52 A3
Mors End. Str S M 22 B1
Morses La. Brigh 88 C1
Morten Rd. Colch 67 F4
Mortimer Rd. Hat Pev 114 A2
Mortimer Rd. Rayl 176 C3
Morton Rd. Gt Tot 116 A2
Morton Way. Hals 26 A2
Moss Cl. Basil 185 F2
Moss Dr. Basil 185 F2
Moss Path. Chelm 140 B2
Moss Rd. Stanw 66 C2
Moss Rd. With 98 A2
Moss Way. W Berg 48 C2
Moss Wlk. Chelm 140 A3
Mossfield Cl. Colch 67 E3
Mott's La. Mks T 64 B2
Motts La. With 98 A2
Moulsham Chase. Chelm 140 B4
Moulsham Dr. Chelm 140 A4
Moulsham St. Chelm 127 D1
Moulsham Thrift. Chelm 140 A3
Mount Ave. Hock 177 F3
Mount Ave. Rayl 176 B2
Mount Ave. South 199 D4
Mount Bovers La. Hawk 177 F2
Mount Cl. Rayl 176 B1
Mount Cl. Wick 174 C4
Mount Cres. Hock 177 E3
Mount Cres. S Ben 187 F2
Mount Hill. Hals 25 E1
Mount Lodge Chase. Gt Tot 116 B3
Mount Pleasant. Hals 25 F1
Mount Pleasant. Mald 131 F1
Mount Pleasant Estate. Gt Tot 116 C3
Mount Pleasant Rd. S Woo F 165 E4
Mount Rd. Brain 60 A2
Mount Rd. Cogg 63 D1
Mount Rd. S Ben 187 F2
Mount Rd. Wick 174 C4
Mount Rise. Hals 25 E1
Mount The. Colch 66 C3
Mount The. Tolle 119 E1
Mount Way. Wick 174 C4
Mountain Ash Ave. South 189 D3
Mountain Ash Cl. South 189 D3
Mountains Rd. Gt Tot 116 B4
Mountbatten Cl. Sud 7 F1
Mountbatten Dr. Colch 68 A2
Mountbatten Dr. South 192 C1
Mountbatten Rd. Brain 60 B3
Mountbatten Rd. Sud 7 F1
Mountbatten Way. Sprin 127 F4
Mountdale Gdns. South 189 F2
Mountfields. Basil 186 B2
Mounthill Ave. Sprin 127 E2
Mountnessing. Hadl 188 B1
Mountview Cres. St L 148 B4
Mountview Rd. Clact 110 A3
Moverons La. Brigh 88 B1
Mowden Hall La. Hat Pev 113 F1
Moy Rd. Colch 68 A1
Mucking Hall Rd. Barl 192 B4
Muirway. Thund 187 D4
Mulberry Ave. Colch 68 A2
Mulberry Gdns. With 98 A2
Mulberry Rd. Canv 196 B2
Mulberry Way. Sprin 127 E3
Mullins Rd. Brain 59 F3
Mumford Cl. W Berg 48 C2
Mumford Rd. W Berg 48 B2
Mundon Rd. Brain 60 B1
Mundon Rd. Mald 145 E4
Munnings Dr. Clact 109 E3
Munnings Rd. Colch 67 D3
Munnings Way. Lawf 35 D3
Munro Rd. With 97 F3
Munsons Alley. Soum 159 E2
Munsterburg Rd. Canv 197 E3
Murchison Cl. Chelm 126 C3
Murray Cl. Brain 59 F3
Murrell Lock. Sprin 128 A2
Murrels La. Hock 177 D4
Muscade Cl. Tipt 100 B3
Museum St. Colch 67 F4
Musk Cl. Stanw 66 B4
Musket Gr. Rayl 189 D4
Muswell Wlk. Clact 109 E3
Mychett Cl. Clact 109 D3
Myland Hall Chase. Colch 50 B2
Myrtle Gr. Colch 68 A3

Nabbott Rd. Chelm 126 C1
Nalla Gdns. Chelm 127 D4
Namur Ave. Canv 197 E3
Nancy Smith Cl. Colch 67 F3
Nansen Ave. Ashi 178 B3
Nansen Rd. Clact 110 B3
Napier Ave. Clact 124 B3
Napier Ave. South 200 A4
Napier Ct. Chelm 126 C3
Napier Gdns. Thund 188 B3
Napier Rd. Colch 67 F3
Napier Rd. Rayl 176 C2
Narvik Cl. Mald 144 C4
Nash Cl. Colch 67 D3
Nash Cl. Lawf 35 D3
Nassau Rd. St O 108 A2
Navestock Cl. Rayl 176 B4
Navestock Gdns. South 191 F1
Navigation Rd. Chelm 127 E1
Nayland Cl. Wick 174 C4
Nayland Dr. Clact 109 D2
Nayland Rd. Bures 28 C4
Nayland Rd. Colch 49 E3
Nayland Rd. Gt Hor 31 D2
Nayland Rd. Gt Hor 49 E3
Nayland Rd. Lit Hor 30 C3
Nayland Rd. W Berg 48 B4
Nayling Rd. Brain 59 E1
Naze Park Rd. Walt 76 C2
Nazeing The. Basil 185 F3
Neale Rd. Hals 25 F1
Neasden Ave. Clact 109 E3
Neil Armstrong Way. South 190 A3
Nelson Cl. Rayl 176 C2
Nelson Ct. Burn 170 B2
Nelson Gdns. Brain 60 B2
Nelson Gdns. Rayl 176 C2
Nelson Mews. South 200 A4
Nelson Pl. S Woo F 165 F3
Nelson Rd. Ashi 178 B3
Nelson Rd. Basil 185 F3
Nelson Rd. Clact 109 F1
Nelson Rd. Colch 66 C3
Nelson Rd. Harw 40 B2
Nelson Rd. Rayl 176 C2
Nelson Rd. South 190 A1
Nelson St. Brigh 106 C3
Nelson St. South 200 A4
Ness Rd. South 201 F3
Ness Wlk. With 97 E1
Nether Ct. Hals 26 A1
Nether Hill. Gest 10 C2
Nether Mayne. Basil 185 D2
Nether Priors. Basil 185 E3
Nether Rd. Cav 1 B1
Netherfield. S Ben 188 A2
Nethergate St. Cla 4 A4
Nevada Rd. Canv 197 E3
Nevendon Rd. Basil 174 A1
Nevendon Rd. Wick 174 B3
Nevern Cl. Rayl 188 C4
Nevern Rd. Rayl 188 C4
Neville Shaw. Basil 185 D3
New Bowers Way. Sprin 127 F3
New Captains Rd. W Mers 121 D3
New Cut. Bures 28 C4
New Cut. Glems 2 A2
New Cut. Gt Ben 89 F4
New Cut. Lay H 84 C3
New Dukes Way. Sprin 127 F3
New England Cres. Gt Wak 193 E1
New Farm Rd. Stanw 66 B3
New Hall La. Mund 145 F2
New Hall Rd. Ashi 167 D1
New Kiln Rd. Colch 67 E4
New La. Fee 81 F3
New Lodge Chase. Lit Bad 129 D1
New London Rd. Chelm 127 D1
New Meadgate Terr. Gt Bad 140 B4
New Moor Cl. Soum 159 F2
New Moor Cres. Soum 159 F2
New Nabbots Way. Sprin 127 F4
New Park. Ca Hed 15 F2
New Park Rd. Ashi 167 D1
New Park Rd. S Ben 187 E3
New Park St. Colch 68 A3
New Pier St. Walt 94 B4
New Queens Rd. Sud 7 F1
New Rd. Aldh 47 D1
New Rd. Burn 170 B3
New Rd. Canv 196 C2
New Rd. Gos 42 C3
New Rd. Gt Bad 141 D3
New Rd. Gt Wak 193 E2
New Rd. Hadl 188 B2
New Rd. Hat Pev 114 A2
New Rd. Kelv 81 E1
New Rd. L Mel 7 D4
New Rd. Mann 35 E2
New Rd. Mess 82 B1
New Rd. Mist 35 F2
New Rd. Stanw 66 B3
New Rd. Terl 96 B2
New Rd. Tipt 100 B3
New Rd. Tolle 119 E1
New St. Brain 59 F1
New St. Brigh 106 C3
New St. Chelm 127 D2
New St. Glems 2 A3
New St. Hals 25 F1
New St. Mald 131 F1
New St. Sud 12 C4
New Thorpe Ave. Th L S 74 A1
New Town Rd. Colch 68 A3
New Town Rd. Th L S 73 F1
New Village. Catt 35 E4
New Way. St O 106 C2
New Writtle St. Chelm 127 D1
Newbarn Rd. Gt T 46 A1
Newbridge Hill. W Berg 48 B2
Newbridge Rd. Tipt 100 C3
Newcastle Ave. Colch 66 C2
Newcomen Way. Colch 50 B3
Newcourt Rd. Sprin 127 E2
Newell Ave. South 202 A4
Newgate St. Walt 94 B4
Newhall. Hawk 178 B3
Newhaven La. Harw 40 B3
Newhouse Rd. Ea Col 44 C2
Newington Ave. South 191 F1
Newington Cl. South 191 F1
Newington Gdns. Clact 109 F4
Newland Pl. With 98 A1
Newland Precinct. With 98 A1
Newland St. With 98 A1
Newlands Dr. With 98 A1
Newlands La. Nay 20 A1
Newlands Rd. Canv 197 E3
Newlands Rd. Wick 174 B2
Newman's Rd. Sud 12 C4
Newmill La. Catt 36 A4
Newnham Cl. Brain 59 F1
Newnham Green. Mald 131 F2
Newport Ave. Col N 156 A3
Newport Cl. Gt Bad 141 D3
Newport Cl. Harw 40 A1
Newport Dr. Clact 110 A4
Newport Way. Walt 94 A3
Newpots Cl. Peld 103 E3
Newpots La. Peld 103 F2
Newstead Rd. Gt Wak 193 D2
Newsum Gdns. Rayl 176 A2
Newton Cl. Brain 59 F1
Newton Croft. Sud 13 D4
Newton Hall Gdns. Ashi 178 B3
Newton Park Rd. Thund 188 A4
Newton Rd. Harw 40 A2
Newton Rd. Sud 13 D4
Newton Way. St O 108 A3
Nicholas Cl. Writ 126 A1
Nicholas Ct. Chelm 126 C3
Nicholas Ct. With 97 F1
Nichols Cl. Lawf 35 D2
Nicholson Cres. S Ben 188 A2
Nicholson Pl. E Han 153 D4
Nicholson Rd. S Ben 188 A2
Nickleby Rd. Chelm 126 B3
Nien - Oord. Clact 109 E2
Nightingale Cl. Clact 109 F3
Nightingale Cl. Colch 69 D4
Nightingale Cl. Harw 39 F1
Nightingale Cl. South 190 C3
Nightingale Hill. Langh 32 C3
Nightingale Rd. Canv 197 E2
Nightingale Way. Clact 109 F3
Nineacres. Brain 60 A1
Nipsells Chase. May 147 D1
Nipsells Chase. Steep 147 D1
Noakes Ave. Gt Bad 140 C3
Noaks Rd. High 22 B4
Nobel Sq. Basil 174 B1
Nobles Green Cl. South 189 F4
Nobles Green Rd. South 189 F4
Nook The. Wiv 87 E4
Norbury Cl. Mks T 64 C2
Nordland Rd. Canv 197 E2
Nore Rd. Rayl 189 E4
Noredale. South 201 E3
Norfolk Ave. Clact 110 C4
Norfolk Ave. South 189 F2
Norfolk Ave. W Mers 121 E4
Norfolk Cl. Canv 197 D3
Norfolk Cl. Mald 131 F1
Norfolk Cres. Colch 50 A1
Norfolk Dr. Chelm 127 D4
Norfolk Gdns. Brain 60 A2
Norfolk Rd. Mald 131 F1
Norfolk Way. Canv 196 C3
Norman Cl. Mks T 64 C2
Norman Cl. St O 108 A2
Norman Cres. Rayl 176 C3
Norman Hill. Terl 96 A1
Norman Rd. Clact 110 C3
Norman Rd. Mann 35 E2
Norman Way. Colch 67 D2
Norman Way. St O 106 C2
Normandie Way. Bures 28 C4
Normandy Ave. Burn 170 B3
Normandy Ave. Colch 68 A2
Normans Rd. Canv 197 E2
Norris Cl. Brain 60 B3
North Ave. Canv 196 C2
North Ave. Chelm 126 C3
North Ave. South 191 E1
North Benfleet Hall Rd. Wick 174 C1
North Colne. Basil 185 E2
North Cres. South 190 B3
North Cres. Wick 174 B4
North Crockerford. Basil 185 F2
North Dell. Sprin 127 F4
North Dr. Gt Bad 140 C4
North Dr. May 146 C1
North End. Soum 159 F3
North End Rd. Gest 10 B1
North End Rd. Lit Y 9 F2
North Gunnels. Basil 185 D3
North Hill. Colch 67 F4
North Hill. Lit Bad 129 E3
North La. Copf 65 D3
North Rd. Bel W 10 C3
North Rd. Brigh 106 C4
North Rd. Clact 109 F3
North Rd. Gt Y 9 D1
North Rd. South 190 C1
North Rise. Sud 13 D3
North Shoebury Rd. South 192 B1
North St. Gt Wak 193 D2
North St. Mald 132 A1
North St. Mann 35 E2
North St. Roch 178 C1
North St. Soum 159 E2
North St. South 198 C4
North St. Sud 12 C4
North St. Till 149 F2
North St. Toll D 118 C3
North St. Tolle 119 E1
North St. Walt 76 B1
North St. Walt 94 B4
North Station Rd. Colch 67 F4
North Weald Cl. Wick 175 D3
Northbourne Rd. Clact 109 F2
Northcroft. Sud 12 C4
Northern Ave. S Ben 187 E3
Northern Rd. Sud 13 D4
Northfield Cres. Gt Wak 193 D2
Northfield Gdns. Colch 50 A2
Northgate St. Colch 67 F4
Northlands Pavement. Basil 186 A3
Northumberland Ave. South 200 B4
Northumberland Cl. Brain 60 A2
Northumberland Cres. South 200 B4
Northumberland Ct. Sprin 127 F2
Northview Dr. South 190 B1
Northville Dr. South 190 B2
Northwick Rd. Canv 196 A2
Norton Ave. Canv 197 F2
Norton Rd. Chelm 127 D2
Norway Cres. Harw 39 F2
Norwich Ave. South 191 E1
Norwich Cl. Colch 68 A4
Norwich Cl. South 191 E1
Norwich Wlk. Basil 185 F4
Norwood Ave. Clact 110 A3
Norwood Dr. S Ben 187 F1
Norwood End. Basil 185 E4
Norwood Way. Walt 94 A4
Notley Rd. Brain 59 F1
Nottingham Rd. Clact 110 C3
Nounsley Rd. Hat Pev 114 A1
Nunnery St. Ca Hed 15 E2
Nunn's Rd. Colch 67 F4
Nuns Meadow. Gos 42 C4
Nunty's La. Cogg 44 A1
Nursery Cl. Rayl 176 B1
Nursery Cl. Stanw 66 B3
Nursery Dr. Brain 60 A3
Nursery La. Dan 142 C4
Nursery Rd. Chelm 140 A4
Nursery Rd. Sud 13 D3
Nutcombe Cres. Hawk 178 B2

Oak Ave. Wick 175 E4
Oak Bungalows. Brain 59 F2
Oak Chase. Wick 174 A4
Oak Cl. Th L S 74 A1
Oak Cl. W Berg 48 C2
Oak Fall. With 98 A3
Oak Farm Rd. Woo Wa 130 C1
Oak Hill. Weth 41 D4
Oak Lodge Tye. Bore 128 A3
Oak Rd. Canv 197 E2
Oak Rd. Hals 43 E4
Oak Rd. Lit Map 26 A4
Oak Rd. Mald 132 B3
Oak Rd. Peb 26 C4
Oak Rd. Roch 178 C1
Oak Rd. Sud 13 D3
Oak Rd. Tipt 100 B4
Oak Rd. Wa Col 46 A2
Oak Rd. With 98 B3
Oak Rd N. Hadl 188 C1
Oak Rd S. Hadl 188 C1
Oak Ridge. Lit Oak 57 D4
Oak Tree Rd. Alres 88 A4
Oak Wlk. Hock 177 F4
Oak Wlk. Si Hed 15 E1

Oak Wlk. Thund 187 D4
Oak Wlk. Thund 187 E4
Oak Wood Gr. Basil 186 A3
Oakapple Cl. Colch 67 E1
Oakdene Rd. Basil 186 B4
Oaken Grange Dr. South 190 C3
Oakfield Cl. S Ben 187 E2
Oakfield Rd. Ashi 167 D1
Oakfield Rd. S Ben 187 E2
Oakhurst Cl. Wick 174 B3
Oakhurst Dr. Wick 174 B3
Oakhurst Rd. Rayl 188 C4
Oakhurst Rd. South 191 D1
Oakland Rd. Harw 40 B2
Oakland Way. Lit Bad 129 F1
Oaklands Ave. Colch 66 C3
Oaklands Cl. Bl Not 77 E4
Oaklands Cres. Chelm 140 A4
Oaklea Ave. Sprin 127 F2
Oakleigh Ave. Hull 165 F1
Oakleigh Ave. South 200 B4
Oakleigh Park Dr. South 189 F1
Oakleigh Rd. Clact 109 F4
Oakleighs. S Ben 187 E2
Oakley Rd. Brain 59 F4
Oakley Rd. Harw 39 E1
Oakley Rd. Wix 55 F3
Oakmead Rd. St O 107 D2
Oaks Dr. Colch 67 E4
Oaks The. Walt 93 F3
Oakview. Harw 39 F1
Oakwood Ave. Clact 110 C4
Oakwood Ave. South 189 F3
Oakwood Ave. W Mers 121 E4
Oakwood Cl. S Ben 187 D3
Oakwood Cl. Walt 93 F3
Oakwood Ct. Alth 158 A2
Oakwood Dr. W Mers 121 E4
Oakwood Gdns. W Mers 121 E4
Oakwood Rd. Rayl 176 B2
Oast Way. Roch 178 C1
Oatfield Cl. Stanw 66 B3
Oatlands. Elmst M 69 F3
Oban Ct. Wick 175 D3
Oban Rd. South 191 E1
Oberon Cl. Colch 68 C4
Observer Way. Kelv 81 E2
Ockelford Ave. Chelm 126 C3
Ockendon Way. Walt 94 A4
Octavia Dr. With 114 C4
Oddcroft. Col En 26 C1
Odessa Rd. Canv 197 E2
Office La. Lit Tot 117 D2
Old Barn Rd. M Bure 29 D3
Old Bell La. Rett 153 D1
Old Church La. Bul 11 F1
Old Church La. W Berg 48 B3
Old Church Rd. Basil 186 C3
Old Church Rd. E Han 153 D3
Old Coach Rd. Colch 68 A4
Old Court. L Mel 7 E4
Old Court Rd. Chelm 127 E2
Old Forge Rd. Bore 128 C4
Old Forge Rd. Lay H 85 D3
Old Hall La. Tolle 119 E3
Old Hall La. Walt 76 B2
Old Heath Rd. Colch 68 B2
Old Heath Rd. Soum 159 D1
Old House La. Box 32 A1
Old House Rd. Gt Hor 49 D4
Old La. Bradw 61 E3
Old Leigh Rd. South 190 A1
Old London Rd. Woo Wa 130 C1
Old Market Pl. Sud 12 C4
Old Mead. South 190 A4
Old Mill La. Cogg 81 E4
Old Parsonage Way. Frin 93 F3
Old Pier St. Walt 94 B4
Old Rd. Bradw 61 E3
Old Rd. Clact 109 F2
Old Rd. Cogg 63 E1
Old Rd. Fee 81 F4
Old Rd. Frin 93 F2
Old Rd. Wic S P 17 E3
Old Rose Gdn. Colch 49 E2
Old School La. Elmst M 70 A3
Old School Meadow. Gt Wak 192 C2
Old Ship La. Roch 178 C1
Old Southend Rd. Sand 152 B4
Old Southend Rd. South 200 A4
Old Vicarage Rd. Harw 40 A2
Old Way. Frin 93 F2
Old Wickford Rd. S Woo F 165 D4
Oldbury Ave. Gt Bad 140 C4
Olde Forge. Brigh 88 C1
Oldwyk. Basil 185 F2
Olive Ave. Hadl 189 D1
Olive Gr. Colch 67 E1
Oliver Pl. With 98 A1
Oliver Way. Chelm 126 C4
Olivers Cl. Clact 109 F2
Olivers Cl. L Mel 7 E4
Olivers Cres. Gt Wak 193 D2
Olivers Dr. With 115 D4
Olivers La. Colch 67 D1
Olivers Rd. Clact 109 F2
Olivia Dr. South 189 F1
Onslow Cres. Colch 68 A1
Ophir Rd. Brigh 106 C3
Orange Rd. Canv 197 E2
Orange Tree Cl. Chelm 140 B3
Orchard Ave. Hals 25 E1
Orchard Ave. Hock 177 F4
Orchard Ave. Rayl 188 B4
Orchard Cl. Clact 109 E3
Orchard Cl. Copf 65 E1
Orchard Cl. Gt Bad 140 B3
Orchard Cl. Gt Oak 56 B2
Orchard Cl. Gt Wak 193 D2
Orchard Cl. Hat Pev 114 A2
Orchard Cl. Hock 177 F4
Orchard Cl. Mald 131 F1
Orchard Cl. Rams 39 D1
Orchard Cl. Ridge 8 A3
Orchard Cl. Soum 159 E2
Orchard Cl. Tolle 119 F1
Orchard Cl. Writ 126 A1
Orchard Dr. Brain 60 A1
Orchard Dr. Frin 93 D2
Orchard Dr. Steep 147 D1
Orchard Gdns. Colch 68 A4
Orchard Gr. South 189 F3
Orchard Mead. South 189 F3
Orchard Rd. Alres 88 A4
Orchard Rd. Burn 170 B2
Orchard Rd. Colch 67 F4
Orchard Rd. Kelv 81 E2
Orchard Rd. Mald 131 F1
Orchard Rd. Soum 159 E2
Orchard Rd. Thund 187 D4
Orchard Side. South 189 F3
Orchard St. Chelm 127 D1
Orchard The. Wick 174 A4
Orchard Way. Glems 2 A2
Orchards. With 97 F1
Orchid Pl. S Woo F 165 E4
Orchill Dr. Hadl 188 C2
Orford Cres. Sprin 127 E3
Oriel Cl. Sud 13 D3
Orion Ct. Basil 174 A1
Orion Way. Brain 60 A2
Orlando Ct. Walt 94 B4
Orlando Dr. Basil 174 B1
Ormesby Chine. S Woo F 165 E3
Ormonde Ave. Hadl 189 D1
Ormonde Ave. Roch 178 C2
Ormonde Gdns. Hadl 189 D1
Ormonds Cres. S Woo F 154 A2
Ormsby Rd. Canv 196 B2
Orpen Cl. W Berg 48 B2
Orpen's Hill. Birch 84 A3
Orrmo Rd. Canv 197 F2
Orsett Ave. Hadl 189 E3
Orsett End. Basil 185 E4
Orsino Wlk. Colch 68 C4
Orvis La. Str S M 34 C4
Orwell Cl. Colch 50 C1
Orwell Ct. Wick 175 D3
Orwell Rd. Clact 109 F1
Orwell Rd. Harw 40 B2
Orwell Way. Burn 170 A3
Orwell Wlk. With 97 F2
Osbert Rd. With 114 C4
Osborne Ave. Hock 177 E3
Osborne Cl. Clact 110 A4
Osborne Rd. Basil 186 C4
Osborne Rd. Basil 185 E3
Osborne Rd. South 190 C1
Osborne Rd. W Mers 121 F3
Osborne St. Colch 67 F3
Osea Rd. Gold 133 D2
Osea Way. Sprin 127 F3
Osprey Way. Chelm 140 A3
Ospreys. Clact 109 F3
Othello Cl. Colch 68 C4
Otten Rd. Bel S P 5 D1
Ottershaw Way. Clact 109 D3
Ouida Rd. Canv 197 E2
Oulton Ave. Canv 196 C3
Oulton Cl. Harw 39 F2
Ouse Chase. With 97 E1
Outing Cl. South 200 B4
Outpart Eastward. Harw 40 C3
Overhall Hill. Col En 27 E1
Overmead Dr. S Woo F 165 F4
Overton Cl. Thund 187 E3
Overton Dr. Thund 187 E3
Overton Rd. Thund 187 D3
Overton Way. Thund 187 D3
Owen Ward Cl. Colch 67 D2
Owl's Hill. Terl 96 A2
Owls Retreat. Colch 68 C4
Oxenford Cl. Harw 39 F1
Oxford Cl. Sud 13 D3
Oxford Cres. Clact 109 F2
Oxford Ct. Ea Col 45 D3
Oxford Ct. Sprin 127 F3
Oxford Meadow. Si Hed 15 E1
Oxford Rd. Canv 197 E2
Oxford Rd. Clact 109 F2
Oxford Rd. Colch 67 E3
Oxford Rd. Frin 94 A3
Oxford Rd. Hals 25 E1
Oxford Rd. Mann 35 E2
Oxford Rd. Roch 178 C2
Oxley Hill. Lang 85 F2
Oxley Hill. Toll D 118 A4
Oxlip Rd. With 97 F2
Oyster Pl. Sprin 127 F2
Oyster Tank Rd. Brigh 106 C3
Ozonia Ave. Wick 174 B3
Ozonia Cl. Wick 174 A3
Ozonia Way. Wick 174 B3
Ozonia Wlk. Wick 174 B3

Paarl Rd. Canv 197 D2
Packards La. Ford 29 F1
Packe Cl. Fee 81 E2
Paddock Cl. Harw 40 B2
Paddock Cl. South 189 F4
Paddock Dr. Sprin 127 F4
Paddock Way. Wiv 69 E2
Paddocks The. Bures 28 C4
Paddocks The. Gt Ben 89 F3
Paddocks The. Gt Tot 116 A2
Paddocks The. Rayl 176 C1
Paddocks The. With 98 A1
Padgetts Way. Hull 165 E2
Page Cl. With 114 B4
Page Rd. Basil 186 C4
Page Rd. Clact 109 F2
Pagel Mead. Basil 185 D3
Pages La. Toll D 118 C1
Paget Rd. Rowh 86 C4
Paget Rd. Wiv 87 E4
Paglesham Rd. Pag Ch 180 B3
Paignton Ave. Sprin 127 E3
Paignton Cl. Rayl 176 B3
Palfrey Hts. Catt 35 E4
Pall Mall. South 189 F1
Pallister Rd. Clact 109 F1
Palm Cl. Chelm 140 B3
Palm Cl. With 98 A4
Palm Rd. Corr 185 D1
Palmeira Ave. South 199 E4
Palmers Croft. Sprin 128 A1
Palmerston Rd. South 199 E4
Palmerston Rd. Th L S 74 A1
Palmerstone Rd. Canv 196 B2
Pampas Cl. Colch 50 A2
Pan La. E Han 152 C3
Pan La. E Han 153 D3
Pan Wlk. Chelm 126 B3
Panfield La. Brain 59 F3
Pannels Cl. Glems 2 A2
Pantile Ave. South 191 E2
Pantile Hill. Soum 159 E2
Pantling's La. Kelv 81 D3
Panton Cres. Colch 68 C4
Panton Mews. Brain 78 A4
Papenburg Rd. Canv 197 D3
Papillon Rd. Colch 67 F4
Parade The. Walt 94 B4
Paradise Rd. Writ 139 D4
Pargat Dr. Rayl 189 E4
Pargetters Hyam. Hock 177 F3
Park Ave. Canv 197 F1
Park Ave. Chelm 126 C2
Park Ave. South 189 F3
Park Boulevard. Clact 110 C3
Park Chase. Hadl 188 C1
Park Chase. St O 108 B3
Park Cl. Sud 13 D4
Park Cl. Wick 174 B3
Park Cotts. Gos 42 C4
Park Dr. Brain 78 A4
Park Dr. Brigh 106 C4
Park Dr. Hals 25 F1
Park Dr. Mald 132 A1
Park Dr. Wick 174 B3
Park Drive Par. Brigh 106 C4
Park Gdns. Hawk 177 F3
Park La. Bul 11 F1
Park La. Canv 197 F2
Park La. Ea Col 45 D3
Park La. Glems 2 B2
Park La. Gos 42 C4
Park La. Langh 32 C2
Park La. South 200 B4
Park La. South 199 F4
Park La. Toll K 101 D2
Park La. Topp 14 A4
Park Lane Cl. Ea Col 45 D3
Park Rd. Ard 51 F2
Park Rd. Burn 170 A3
Park Rd. Canv 197 F1
Park Rd. Chelm 127 D1
Park Rd. Clact 109 E1
Park Rd. Colch 69 D2
Park Rd. Colch 67 E3
Park Rd. Gt Bro 71 E4
Park Rd. Gt Hor 31 D4
Park Rd. Hadl 189 D1
Park Rd. Harw 40 B2
Park Rd. Mald 131 F1
Park Rd. Nay 20 C2
Park Rd. Silv E 80 A1
Park Rd. South 199 F4
Park Rd. Sud 13 D4
Park Rd. Thund 187 F3
Park Rd. Wiv 87 E4
Park Side. Basil 186 A4
Park Side. South 190 A1
Park Sq E. Clact 125 D4
Park Sq W. Clact 124 C4
Park St. Nay 20 B3
Park St. South 199 F4
Park Terr. South 199 F4
Park The. Mann 35 E2
Park Vale Cl. Ca Hed 15 F2
Park View Cres. Gt Bad 140 C3
Park View Dr. Hadl 189 D3
Park Way. Clact 109 E1
Park Wood La. Lit Tot 117 D2
Parkanaur Ave. South 201 D4
Parkdale. Dan 142 B4
Parker Ct. Brad o S 136 C2
Parker Rd. Chelm 127 E1
Parker Way. Hals 43 F4
Parker's Way. Nay 20 A1
Parkeston Rd. Harw 40 A2
Parkeston Rd. Rams 39 F3
Parkfield St. Rowh 86 C4
Parkfields. Si Hed 15 E1
Parkfields. Thund 188 B2
Parkgate Rd. Silv E 80 A2
Parkhall Rd. Gos 41 F4
Parkhurst Dr. Rayl 176 B4
Parkhurst Rd. Basil 186 A3
Parklands. Brain 78 A4
Parklands. Canv 197 D3
Parklands. Hawk 178 B2
Parklands Ave. Rayl 176 C1
Parklands Cl. Glems 2 B3
Parklands Dr. Sprin 127 E2
Parklards Way. Chelm 140 B1
Parkstone Ave. S Ben 188 A2
Parkstone Dr. South 190 C2
Parkway. Chelm 127 D1
Parkway. Rayl 188 C4
Parkway Cl. South 189 F4
Parkway The. Canv 197 D1
Parkwood Ave. Wiv 69 D1
Parkwood Dr. Sud 7 F1
Parmenter Dr. Sud 13 E3
Parnell Cl. Colch 68 A1
Parr Dr. Colch 66 C2
Parry Dr. Clact 109 E3
Parsonage La. Lit Bad 129 E1
Parsonage La. Rams 38 A1
Parsonage La. Tend 72 C4
Parsonage St. Hals 25 F1
Parson's Field. Ded 34 A3
Parson's Heath Rd. Colch 50 C1
Parson's Hill. Colch 67 D3
Parsons Hill. Gt Bro 70 C4
Parsons La. Colch 68 B3
Parsons Lawn. South 192 B1
Parsons Rd. Thund 187 E4
Parsonson Wlk. Colch 68 C3
Partridge Ave. Chelm 126 C3
Partridge Cl. Gt Oak 56 B2
Partridge Dr. Ford 47 E3
Partridge Green. Basil 186 A3
Paschal Way. Gt Bad 140 C4
Paslowes. Basil 185 F2
Paston Cl. S Woo F 154 C1
Patching Hall La. Chelm 127 D4
Paternoster Row. Walt 94 B4
Path The. Gt Ben 89 F4
Pathfields Rd. Clact 109 E2
Pathway The. Walt 93 F3
Pathways. Basil 185 F3
Patmore Rd. Colch 50 B1
Patten Cl. Mks T 64 C2
Patterdale. Thund 187 D4
Pattern Bush Cl. Catt 35 E4
Pattison Cl. With 115 D4
Pattiswick Cnr. Basil 185 F4
Pattiswick Sq. Basil 185 F4
Pattocks. Basil 185 F3
Pattock's La. Gt T 46 B1
Pattrick's La. Harw 40 B2
Pauline Cl. Clact 110 A3
Pauls Cres. Elmst M 69 F3
Pauls Way. Clact 109 D1
Pavilion Dr. South 189 F1
Pawle Cl. Gt Bad 141 D4
Paxman Ave. Colch 67 D2
Paxton Rd. Clact 110 A4
Paycocke Way. Cogg 63 D2
Payne Pl. E Han 153 D3
Payne's La. Lit Bro 53 E2
Paynters Hill. Basil 185 F2
Paynters Mead. Basil 185 F2
Peace Rd. Stanw 66 B4
Peach Ave. Hock 177 F4
Peacocks Cl. Cav 1 B1
Peacocks Rd. Cav 1 B1
Peakes Cl. Tipt 100 A2
Pearce Manor. Chelm 139 F4
Pearmain Cl. Runw 163 E1
Pearmain Way. Stanw 66 B2
Pearsons Ave. Rayl 176 A2
Peartree Business Centre. Stanw 66 C2
Peartree Cl.. Brain 60 A1
Peartree Cl. South 191 E2
Peartree Hill. M Bure 29 D3
Peartree La. S Woo F 142 C2
Peartree Rd. Stanw 66 C2
Peartree Way. Lit Cla 91 E1
Pease Pl. E Han 153 D3
Pebmarsh Cl. Colch 86 A4
Pebmarsh Dr. Wick 174 C3
Pebmarsh Rd. Alph 18 C1
Pebmarsh Rd. Col En 26 C1
Pebmarsh Rd. Peb 18 C1
Pecockes Cl. Sud 13 E3
Pedder's Cl. Colch 66 C2
Pedlars Cl. Dan 143 D3
Pedlars Path. Dan 143 D3
Peel Ave. South 202 A4
Peel Cres. Brain 59 F2
Peel Rd. Sprin 127 F2
Peerswood Rd. Colch 67 E1
Peg Millar's La. Fair 96 C3
Peg Millar's La. Terl 96 C3
Pegasus Way. Brain 59 F3
Pegasus Way. Colch 50 B1
Peggotty Cl. Chelm 126 C3
Peldon Pavement. Basil 185 E4
Peldon Rd. Gt Wig 103 D2
Peldon Rd. Lang 86 A1
Peldon Rd. Peld 103 F4
Pelham Cl. Harw 39 F1
Pelham Rd. South 191 F1
Pelham's La. Colch 67 F4
Pelly Ave. With 115 D4
Pembroke Ave. Mald 131 F1
Pembroke Cl. Colch 68 B2
Pembroke Gdns. Clact 110 C3
Pembroke Mews. Basil 186 B4
Pembroke Pl. Chelm 127 D4
Pembury Rd. South 199 E4
Pendle Cl. Basil 174 A1
Pendlestone. Thund 188 B2
Pendower. Rayl 176 A1
Penfold Rd. Clact 109 F1
Penhurst Ave. South 190 C1
Penlan Hall La. Ford 47 D3
Penn Mews. Brain 78 A4
Pennial Rd. Canv 197 D2
Pennine Rd. Chelm 126 B3
Pennsylvania La. Tipt 100 B3
Penny Royal Rd. Dan 142 C3
Pennyroyal Cres. With 97 F2
Penrice Cl. Colch 68 C3
Penticton Rd. Brain 59 E1
Pentland Ave. Chelm 127 D3
Pentland Ave. South 201 E3
Pentlow Dr. Cav 1 C1
Pentlow Hill. Pent 6 A4
Pentlow La. Cav 1 C1
Penzance Cl. Sprin 127 F3
Pepper's Rd. Box 31 F1
Pepys St. Harw 40 B3
Percival Rd. Walt 76 B1
Percival Rd. Walt 75 E1
Percy Cottis Rd. Roch 178 C2
Percy Rd. South 189 E1
Percys. Basil 186 A3
Peregrine Cl. Basil 185 D2
Peregrine Cl. Clact 109 F4
Peregrine Ct. Colch 68 C4
Peregrine Dr. Chelm 140 A2
Peregrine Dr. S Ben 187 E1
Perriclose. Sprin 127 E4
Perrin Pl. Chelm 127 D1
Perry Green. Basil 185 D4
Perry Hill. Sprin 127 E2
Perry La. Langh 33 D2
Perry Rd. S Ben 187 D2
Perry Rd. Tipt 100 B3
Perry Rd. With 98 A1
Perry Spring. Basil 185 E3
Perry Way. With 98 A1
Perryfield. Sud 13 D2
Persardi Ct. Rowh 86 A4
Pershore End. Colch 66 C3
Perth Cl. Colch 68 A1
Pertwee Cl. Brigh 106 C4
Pertwee Dr. Gt Bad 140 C3
Pertwee Dr. S Woo F 165 E4
Pesthouse La. Gt Oak 56 B2
Peter Bruff Ave. Clact 109 E3
Peterborough Way. Basil 185 F4
Peterfield's La. Gos 42 C3
Petersfield. Chelm 127 D4
Petrebrook. Sprin 128 A2
Petrel Way. Chelm 140 B3
Pettit La. T Gr 79 D2
Petunia Cres. Sprin 127 F3
Petworth Cl. Elmst M 87 E4
Petworth Gdns. South 191 F1
Pevensey Gdns. Hull 165 F1
Peverel Ave. Hat Pev 114 B1
Pharos La. W Mers 121 E3
Philbrick Cres E. Rayl 176 B2
Philbrick Cres W. Rayl 176 B2
Philip Cl. Walt 94 A4
Philip Rd. With 114 C4
Phillip Rd. Wiv 87 D4
Phillips Chase. Brain 60 A3
Phillips Field Rd. Sud 13 D3
Philmead Rd. S Ben 187 D1
Philpott Ave. South 191 F1
Phoenix Gr. Chelm 140 A4
Phoenix Way. Hadl 188 B4
Picasso Way. South 193 D1
Pickers Way. Clact 110 C4
Picketts. Canv 196 B2
Picketts Ave. South 189 F2
Picketts Cl. South 189 F2
Pickford Wlk. Colch 68 C3
Pickwick Ave. Chelm 126 B3
Picton Cl. Rayl 176 C1
Picton Gdns. Rayl 176 C1
Pier App. Walt 94 B4
Pier Ave. Clact 109 F1
Pier Gap. Clact 109 F1
Pier Hill. South 200 A4
Pierce Glade. Tipt 100 B3
Pierrefitte Way. Brain 59 F2
Pightle Way. Walt 94 A4
Pilborough Way. Colch 66 C2
Pilcox Hall La. Tend 72 B4
Pilgrims Cl. South 191 F1
Pilgrims Way. Hadl 188 C2
Pinch Hill. Bul 12 A4
Pine Cl. Canv 196 C2
Pine Cl. Catt 35 E4
Pine Cl. Gt Ben 89 F4
Pine Cl. Hadl 189 D3
Pine Cl. Wick 174 B3
Pine Gr. W Mers 121 D4
Pine Gr. With 98 A3
Pine Rd. Hadl 188 B1
Pinecroft Gdns. Colch 50 A2
Pinecroft Rise. Sud 12 B3
Pines Rd. Chelm 126 B3
Pines The. Hat Pev 114 A3
Pinetrees. S Ben 188 B2
Pinewood Ave. South 189 E3
Pinewood Cl. Clact 109 F4
Pinewood Cl. Hull 165 F1
Pinewood Cl. Walt 93 E3
Pinkham Dr. With 114 C4
Pinmill. Basil 185 E3
Pinners Cl. Burn 169 F4
Pintails. Basil 186 B3
Pintolls. S Woo F 165 E3
Pipchin Rd. Chelm 126 C3
Piper Rd. Colch 67 D4
Piper's Tye. Chelm 140 B2
Pippins Rd. Burn 170 B3
Pippins The. Glems 2 B3
Pirie Rd. W Berg 48 C2
Pit La. Tipt 100 B3
Pitmans Cl. South 200 A4
Pitmire La. Lam 19 D3
Pitsea Rd. Basil 186 A3
Pitseaville Gr. Basil 185 F3
Pitt Ave. With 115 D4
Pitt Chase. Gt Bad 140 C3
Pitt Green. With 115 D4

Plains Farm Cl. Colch 50 B3
Plains Field. Brain 60 B1
Plains Rd. Gt Tot 116 C3
Plains Rd. Lit Tot 116 C3
Plaistow Green Rd. Hals 43 E3
Plane Tree Cl. Burn 170 A3
Plane Tree Cl. Chelm 140 A3
Plantation Rd. Bore 112 C1
Planton Way. Brigh 106 B4
Plas Newydd. South 200 C3
Plas Newydd Cl. South 200 C3
Plashetts. Basil 185 E4
Playle Chase. Gt Tot 116 A2
Pleasant Rd. South 200 A4
Pleshey Cl. South 200 C4
Plough Dr. Colch 67 D3
Plough Green. Bul 11 F1
Plough La. Sud 12 B4
Plough Rd. Gt Ben 89 F3
Ploughmans Headland. Stanw 66 B3
Plover Wlk. Chelm 140 A2
Plowmans. Rayl 176 C2
Plum St. Glems 2 A3
Plumberow Ave. Hock 177 F4
Plumberow Mount Ave. Hock 177 F4
Plume Ave. Colch 67 D2
Plume Ave. Mald 131 F1
Plumleys. Basil 186 A4
Plummers Rd. Ford 47 F4
Plumptre La. Dan 142 B3
Plumtree Ave. Gt Bad 140 C3
Plymouth Rd. Clact 125 E4
Plymouth Rd. Sprin 127 F3
Plymtree. South 192 B1
Pocklington Cl. Sprin 128 A2
Point Cl. Canv 197 F2
Point Clear Rd. St O 107 E2
Point Rd. Canv 197 F2
Pointer Pl. Walt 93 F4
Pointwell La. Cogg 81 D4
Pole Barn La. Frin 94 A3
Pole La. Wh Not 78 B2
Polecat Rd. T Gr 79 D3
Pollard Wlk. Clact 109 E3
Pollards Green. Sprin 127 F1
Polley Cl. Walt 93 F4
Polstead St. Nay 20 B3
Polstead Way. Clact 109 D2
Polsteads. Basil 185 F2
Pomfret Mead. Basil 185 D3
Pond Chase. Colch 67 D2
Ponders Rd. Ford 47 E2
Pondfield Rd. Colch 50 B1
Pondholton Dr. With 115 D4
Ponds Rd. Chelm 140 A1
Poole St. Cav 1 B1
Poole St. Gt Y 15 D4
Pooles La. S Woo F 165 F2
Poors La. Hadl 188 C2
Poors La N. Hadl 189 D3
Poperinghe Rd. Colch 67 F2
Popes Cres. Basil 186 A3
Pope's La. Colch 67 F4
Pope's Rd. Wa Col 46 B2
Popes Wlk. Rayl 177 D1
Poplar Cl. Chelm 140 B3
Poplar Cl. Clact 109 D1
Poplar Cl. Gt Y 9 D1
Poplar Cl. Hals 43 F4
Poplar Cl. S Woo F 165 E4
Poplar Cl. With 98 A4
Poplar Ct. Sud 13 D4
Poplar Gr. Burn 170 A3
Poplar Rd. Canv 197 E2
Poplar Rd. Rayl 188 C4
Poplar Rd. Sud 13 D4
Poplar Way. Walt 93 E3
Poplars Ave. Hawk 177 F2
Poplars Cl. Alres 88 A4
Poppy Gdns. Colch 68 B2
Poppy Green. Bore 128 A3
Poppyfield Cl. South 189 E3
Pork Hall La. Gt Le 95 D3
Pork La. Frin 92 C3
Porlock Ave. South 190 A2
Port La. Colch 68 A3
Porter Way. Clact 109 D2
Porters. Basil 186 B4
Porters Cl. E A Gr 47 F1
Porters Cotts. E A Gr 47 F1
Porter's La. E A Gr 47 F1
Porters Pk. Bone 113 D1
Portland Ave. Harw 40 B2
Portland Ave. South 200 A4
Portland Cl. Brain 60 A2
Portland Cres. Harw 40 B2
Portland Rd. Colch 67 F3
Portlight Cl. Mist 36 A2
Portobello Rd. Walt 94 B4
Portreath Pl. Chelm 127 D4
Portsmouth Rd. Clact 125 E4
Portway Ct. Hals 25 F2
Post Office La. Glems 2 A3
Post Office La. Lit Tot 117 D2
Post Office Rd. Chelm 127 D4
Post Office Rd. Woo Mor 143 F3
Postman's La. Lit Bad 129 F1
Pot Kiln Chase. Gest 10 C1
Pot Kiln Rd. Sud 13 D3
Pot Kilns The. Sud 13 E3
Potter St. Si Hed 24 C4
Potters Way. South 190 C3
Pottery La. Ca Hed 15 F2
Pottery La. Chelm 127 D3
Pound Farm Dr. Harw 40 A2
Pound Fields. Writ 139 D4
Pound La. Basil 186 C4
Powers Hall End. With 97 F2
Pownall Cres. Colch 67 F2
Poynings Ave. South 191 F1
Poyntens. Rayl 176 B1
Poynters La. Gt Wak 192 C1
Poynters La. South 192 C1
Prentice Cl. Roch 178 C1
Prentice Hall La. Tolle 119 D1
Prentice Hall La. Tolle 135 D4
President Rd. Colch 66 C3
Preston Gdns. Rayl 176 B2
Preston Rd. Clact 110 B3
Preston Rd. South 199 E4
Prestwood Cl. Thund 188 A4
Prestwood Dr. Thund 188 A3
Pretoria Rd. Hals 25 F1
Prettygate Rd. Colch 67 D2
Prettygate Rd. Colch 67 D3
Pricries The. Hull 165 E1
Primrose Cl. Canv 197 D3
Primrose Hill. Chelm 126 C2
Primrose La. Rams 56 A4
Primrose La. Tipt 100 B3
Primrose Pl. With 97 F2
Primrose Rd. Clact 110 C3
Primrose Wlk. Colch 68 C4
Primrose Wlk. Mald 132 A1
Primula Cl. Clact 109 E2
Primula Way. Bore 128 A3
Prince Albert Rd. W Mers 121 E3
Prince Ave. South 190 B2
Prince Charles Cl. Clact 109 E1
Prince Charles Cl. Sud 12 C4
Prince Charles Rd. Colch 68 A1
Prince Cl. South 190 B3
Prince of Wales Rd. Gt Tot 116 A2
Prince Philip Ave. Clact 109 E1
Prince Philip Rd. Colch 68 A1
Prince St. Sud 12 C4
Prince William Ave. Canv 196 C3
Princel La. Ded 33 F4
Princes Ave. May 158 A4
Princes Ave. Soum 159 E2
Princes Ave. Thund 187 F3
Prince's Espl. Walt 76 B1
Princes Rd. Burn 170 B3
Princes Rd. Canv 196 C2
Princes Rd. Chelm 140 A4
Princes Rd. Clact 110 B3
Princes Rd. Harw 40 A2
Princes Rd. Mald 132 A1
Princes St. Mald 131 F2
Princes St. South 199 F4
Princess Anne Cl. Clact 109 E1
Princess Ct. Wick 175 D4
Princess Gdns. Hawk 178 B3
Princess Rd. Rayl 176 C1
Princess St. Rams 39 F3
Princeton Mews. Colch 50 A2
Prior Cl. Hals 43 E4
Prior Way. Colch 49 F1
Priors Cl. Basil 185 E3
Priors East. Basil 185 E3
Prior's Green. Stis 61 E4
Priory Ave. South 190 C2
Priory Cl. Chelm 126 C1
Priory Cl. Hat Pev 114 A1
Priory Cotts. Birch 83 F3
Priory Cres. South 190 C2
Priory Ct. Hat Pev 114 A2
Priory Farm Rd. Hat Pev 114 A1
Priory La. S Woo F 142 C1
Priory Rd. Clact 109 F2
Priory Rd. Sud 7 F1
Priory Rd. Tipt 99 F1
Priory Rd. Wa Col 46 A2
Priory St. Colch 68 A4
Priory St. Ea Col 45 D4
Priory The. Writ 126 A1
Priory View Rd. South 189 F3
Priory Way. Soum 159 F2
Priory Wlk. Sud 12 C3
Priory Wood Cres. South 189 F3
Priorywood Dr. South 189 F3
Prittle Cl. Thund 188 B3
Prittlewell Chase. South 190 B2
Prittlewell Sq. South 199 F4
Prittlewell St. South 191 D1
Proctor Way. Mks T 64 C2
Progress Ct. Brain 59 F2
Progress Rd. South 189 E3
Promenade. Harw 40 B2
Promenade. May 146 C1
Promenade. Walt 76 C1
Promenade The. Burn 170 B2
Promenade The. South 201 E3
Promenade Way. Brigh 106 C3
Prospect Cl. Hat Pev 114 A2
Prospect Cl. South 200 B4
Prospect Park. Frin 93 D3
Prospero Cl. Colch 68 C4
Provence Cl. Stanw 66 B4
Providence. Burn 170 B2
Provident Sq. Chelm 127 E1
Prunus Ct. Rowh 86 A4
Prykes Dr. Chelm 127 D1
Pryor Cl. With 98 A1
Pryors Rd. Chelm 140 B1
Pudding La. Birch 84 A2
Pudsey Hall La. Cane 168 A1
Puffinsdale. Clact 109 F3
Pulpitfield Cl. Walt 94 A4
Pulpits Cl. Hock 177 F4
Pump Hill. Gt Bad 140 C4
Pump Hill. St O 108 B2
Pump La. Dan 142 B3
Pump La. Sprin 127 F3
Pump Mead Cl. Soum 159 E2
Pump Rd. Purl 144 B1
Purbeck Ct. Gt Bad 140 C3
Purcell Cl. Colch 68 C3
Purcell Cole. Writ 126 A1
Purdeys Way. Roch 191 D4
Purleigh Cl. Basil 174 B1
Purleigh Gr. Col N 156 A3
Purleigh Rd. Rayl 176 A2
Purleigh St. Purl 144 C1
Purley Way. Clact 109 D3
Purley Way. South 190 B3
Pye Cnr. Ca Hed 15 F2
Pyefleet Cl. Brigh 106 C4
Pyefleet Cl. Fing 87 E3
Pyefleet View. Lang 86 A2
Pyesand. Walt 93 E4
Pygot Pl. Brain 59 F2
Pyms Rd. Chelm 140 A2
Pyne Gate. Chelm 140 A1

Quakers' Alley. Colch 67 F4
Quarter Gate. S Woo F 165 F3
Quay La. Beau 74 A3
Quay La. Sud 12 C3
Quay La. Walt 75 E1
Quay St. Mann 35 E2
Quay The. Burn 170 B2
Quay The. Harw 40 C3
Quebec Ave. South 200 A4
Queech La. Catt 36 A4
Queen Anne Dr. W Mers 121 E3
Queen Anne Gdns. W Mers 121 E3
Queen Anne Rd. W Mers 121 E3
Queen Anne's Dr. South 190 B2
Queen Anns Gr. Hull 176 B4
Queen Elizabeth Ave. Clact 109 E1
Queen Elizabeth Chase. Roch 190 C4
Queen Elizabeth II Sq. S Woo F 165 F4
Queen Elizabeth Way. Colch 68 A1
Queen Mary Ave. Colch 67 F2
Queen St. Brigh 106 C3
Queen St. Ca Hed 15 F2
Queen St. Chelm 127 D1
Queen St. Cogg 63 D2
Queen St. Colch 67 F4
Queen St. Gt Oak 56 B2
Queen St. Mald 132 A1
Queen St. Si Hed 24 C3
Queen St. Soum 159 E2
Queen Victoria Dr. Sho G 40 A4
Queenborough La. Brain 77 E4
Queenborough Rd. Soum 159 E2
Queenbury Cl. W Mers 121 F3
Queen's Ave. Mald 132 A1
Queen's Ave. South 189 F1
Queens Cl. Sud 12 C4
Queen's Cnr. W Mers 121 E4
Queen's Gdns. Pan 59 D4
Queen's Head Rd. Box 31 F2
Queens Mews. W Mers 121 D3
Queens Rd. Brain 59 F3
Queens Rd. Burn 170 B3
Queen's Rd. Chelm 127 E1
Queen's Rd. Clact 109 E1
Queen's Rd. Colch 67 E3
Queen's Rd. Ea Col 45 D4
Queen's Rd. Frin 93 F2
Queen's Rd. Harw 40 A1
Queens Rd. Rayl 176 B1
Queen's Rd. S Ben 187 E1
Queen's Rd. South 198 C4
Queen's Rd. South 199 F4
Queens Rd. Sud 12 C4
Queen's Rd. W Berg 48 B2
Queen's Rd. Wiv 87 E4
Queensland Ave. Roch 190 C4
Queensland Cres. Chelm 126 C3
Queensland Dr. Colch 68 A1
Queensmere. Thund 188 A3
Queensway. Clact 110 B3
Queensway. Lawf 35 E2
Queensway. South 200 A4
Queensway. Sud 13 D3
Queensway. Tipt 100 B3
Quendon Rd. Basil 185 F4
Quendon Way. Frin 94 A3
Quilp Dr. Chelm 126 C4
Quilters Cl. Basil 185 E4
Quilters Cl. Clact 110 C3
Quilters Straight. Basil 185 E4
Quinion Cl. Chelm 126 B4
Quorn Gdns. Hadl 189 D1

Rachael Gdns. Silv E 79 F2
Rackenford. South 201 E4
Radiator Rd. Sud 13 D3
Radnor Rd. Ashi 167 E1
Radwinter Ave. Wick 174 B3
Raglan Rd. Frin 94 A3
Raile Wlk. L Mel 7 E4
Railway Sq. Chelm 127 D2
Railway St. Chelm 127 D2
Railway St. Mann 35 E2
Railway St..Brain 60 A2
Railway Terr. Clact 109 F2
Railway Terr. South 191 D2
Rainbow Ave. Canv 197 E2
Rainbow Mead. Hat Pev 114 A3
Rainbow Rd. Canv 197 E2
Rainbow Rd. W Mers 121 E3
Rainbow Way. Col En 26 C1
Rainham Way. Frin 94 A3
Rainsborowe Rd. Colch 67 E2
Rainsford Ave. Chelm 126 C2
Rainsford La. Chelm 126 C1
Rainsford Rd. Chelm 126 C2
Rambler Cl. Stanw 66 B4
Ramblers Way. Burn 170 B2
Rampart St. South 202 A3
Rampart Terr. South 202 A3
Ramparts Cl. Gt Hor 49 D4
Ramparts The. Rayl 176 C1
Ramplings Ave. Clact 109 F3
Ramsay Dr. Basil 185 F2
Ramsey Chase. Latch 157 D3
Ramsey Cl. Mald 132 B2
Ramsey Rd. Hals 43 E4
Ramsey Rd. Harw 39 E1
Ramuz Dr. South 190 B1
Rana Ct. Brain 59 F2
Rana Dr. Brain 59 F2
Randolph Cl. South 189 F2
Randulph Terr. Sprin 127 E2
Randway. Rayl 176 B1
Rangoon Cl. Colch 67 D1
Ransom Rd. Tipt 100 B3
Ranulph Way. Hat Pev 114 A2
Raphael Dr. South 193 D1
Raphael Dr. Sprin 127 F4
Rat La. Hadl 188 B4
Ratcliffe Rd. Colch 66 C3
Ratsborough Chase. Soum 159 E1
Rattwick Dr. Canv 197 F2
Raven Dr. S Ben 187 E1
Raven Way. Colch 49 F2
Ravendale Way. South 192 B1
Ravens Ave. Hals 43 F4
Ravensbourne Dr. Chelm 126 C1
Ravenscourt Dr. Basil 185 F3
Ravensdale. Basil 185 D2
Ravensdale. Clact 109 F3
Ravensfield. Basil 185 F3
Ravenswood Chase. Roch 190 C4
Rawden Cl. Harw 40 A2
Rawreth La. Rayl 176 A3
Rawstorn Rd. Colch 67 F4
Ray Ave. Harw 40 A2
Ray Cl. Canv 197 D1
Ray Cl. Hadl 189 D1
Ray La. Rams 39 D2
Ray The. Sprin 127 F3
Ray Wlk. Hadl 189 D1
Raydon Way. Sud 13 E3
Rayleigh Ave. Rayl 189 E4
Rayleigh Ave. South 190 C1
Rayleigh Cl. Brain 60 B2
Rayleigh Cl. Colch 50 A1
Rayleigh Downs Rd. Ray 189 D4
Rayleigh Dr. South 189 E2
Rayleigh Rd. Rayl 189 E3
Rayleigh Rd. South 189 E3
Rayleigh Rd. Thund 188 A3
Rayment Ave. Canv 197 E2
Raymonds Cl. S Woo F 165 E4
Raymonds Dr. Thund 187 F3
Rayne Rd. Brain 59 E2
Rayner Rd. Colch 67 D2
Rayner Way. Hals 25 F1
Rayside. Basil 185 E3
Readers Ct. Gt Bad 140 C3
Reaper Rd. Colch 67 D3
Rebecca Gdns. Silv E 79 F2
Rebels La. Barl 191 F2
Rebow Rd. Harw 40 A1
Rebow Rd. Wiv 87 D4
Rebow St. Colch 68 A3
Recreation Ave. South 189 F1
Recreation Rd. Clact 109 F2
Recreation Rd. Colch 68 A3
Recreation Rd. Si Hed 24 B4
Recreation Way. Brigh 106 C4
Recreation Wlk. Sud 13 D3
Rectory Ave. Hawk 178 B3
Rectory Cl. Colch 49 F1
Rectory Cl. Glems 2 A3
Rectory Cl. Hadl 188 C2
Rectory Ct. Basil 186 B4
Rectory Garth. Rayl 176 B1
Rectory Gdns. Basil 186 B3
Rectory Gr. South 198 B4
Rectory Gr. Wick 174 C4
Rectory Hill. Nay 20 B4
Rectory Hill. Wiv 69 E1
Rectory La. Chelm 127 D2
Rectory La. Lang 86 A2
Rectory La. Latch 157 D2
Rectory La. Rams 39 D1
Rectory La. Rett 164 C3
Rectory La. Wic S P 17 E3
Rectory La. With 98 A4
Rectory La. Woo Mor 143 F3
Rectory Meadow. Bradw 61 E1
Rectory Park Dr. Basil 186 A3
Rectory Rd. Alah 64 C4
Rectory Rd. Basil 186 B3
Rectory Rd. Copf 65 E1
Rectory Rd. Frat 70 C1
Rectory Rd. Frin 93 D2
Rectory Rd. Hadl 188 C2
Rectory Rd. Hawk 178 A2
Rectory Rd. Langh 32 C4
Rectory Rd. Lit Ben 71 F4
Rectory Rd. Midd 12 C2
Rectory Rd. N Fam 166 C4
Rectory Rd. Rams 56 C3
Rectory Rd. Rowh 86 C4
Rectory Rd. Si Hed 15 E1
Rectory Rd. St O 90 C2
Rectory Rd. Stis 61 D4
Rectory Rd. Tipt 100 B3
Rectory Rd. Toll K 101 E1
Rectory Rd. Weel 91 D3
Rectory Rd. Wiv 69 E1
Rectory Rd. Woo Wa 130 B2
Rectory Rd. Wrab 38 A2
Rectory Rd. Writ 139 D4
Rectory Terr. Hawk 178 A2
Red Barn La. Gt Oak 56 A1
Red Barn Rd. Brigh 106 C4
Red House La. Sud 13 D2
Red Lion Yd. Colch 67 F4
Redbridge Rd. Clact 109 F4
Redcliff Dr. South 198 C4
Redcliff Rd. Chelm 127 D1
Reddings La. Till 149 E2
Rede Way. Sud 13 E3
Redgate Cl. Wick 175 D4
Redgates Pl. Sprin 127 F2
Redgrave Rd. Basil 185 F2
Redhills Rd. S Woo F 165 F4
Redhouse La. Box 31 E1
Redmaynes Dr. Chelm 139 F4
Redmill. Colch 67 D2
Redrose Wlk. Clact 109 E2
Redruth Cl. Sprin 127 F3
Redshank Cres. S Woo F 154 B1
Redshank Dr. Mald 132 B3
Redstock Rd. South 191 D1
Redwood Cl. Colch 68 C4
Redwood Cl. With 98 A4
Reed Cl. Clact 109 E3
Reed Hall Ave. Colch 67 E2
Reeds Way. Wick 174 B4
Reeves Way. S Woo F 165 F4
Refinery Rd. Rams 39 F3
Regency Cl. Runw 163 E1
Regency Cl. Sprin 127 E2
Regency Green. South 190 C2
Regent Cl. Brigh 106 C4
Regent Cl. Rayl 176 A2
Regent Rd. Brigh 106 C4
Regent St. Mann 35 E2
Regent St. Rowh 87 D4
Regina Rd. Chelm 127 E2
Reigate Ave. Clact 109 E3
Rembrandt Cl. South 202 A4
Rembrandt Gr. Sprin 127 F3
Rembrandt Way. Colch 67 D3
Remembrance Ave. Burn 170 A2
Remembrance Ave. Hat Pev 114 A2
Remercie Rd. Mist 36 A2
Remus Cl. Colch 49 F3
Rennie Rd. Chelm 127 E1
Renoir Pl. Sprin 127 F4
Repton Cl. Basil 174 A1
Repton Gr. South 190 A4
Retreat Rd. Hock 177 F3
Retreat Rd. South 199 F4
Retreat The. With 98 A1
Rettendon Cl. Rayl 176 A2
Rettendon Gdns. Runw 163 F1
Rettendon Turnpike. Rett 164 B2
Rettendon View. Wick 174 C4
Reymead Cl. W Mers 121 E4
Reynard Ct. Gt Bad 140 C3
Reynards Cl. Walt 93 E3
Reynolds Ave. Colch 67 D3
Reynolds Gate. S Woo F 165 F3
Rhoda Rd. S Ben 187 F2
Rhoda Rd N. Thund 187 F3
Richard Ave. Brigh 106 C3
Richard Ave. Wiv 69 E2
Richards Wlk. Clact 109 F3
Richardson Wlk. Colch 66 C3
Richmond Ave. S Ben 187 E1
Richmond Ave. South 200 A4
Richmond Ave. South 201 E3
Richmond Ave. South 199 F4
Richmond Cres. Harw 40 A1
Richmond Dr. Clact 109 D1
Richmond Dr. Rayl 188 B4
Richmond Dr. South 190 B2
Richmond Rd. Runw 163 E1
Richmond Rd. Sprin 128 A2
Richmond Rd. W Mers 121 E3
Richmond St. South 191 E1
Rickling. Basil 185 F2
Rickstones Rd. With 98 A3
Ridge The. Lit Bad 129 F1
Ridge The. Walt 94 A4
Ridgemount. S Ben 187 F2
Ridgeway. Rayl 176 B1
Ridgeway Gdns. South 199 D4
Ridgeway The. Brain 60 A1
Ridgeway The. Harw 40 A2
Ridgeway The. South 199 D4
Ridgewell Rd. Gt Y 8 C2
Ridgewell Way. Colch 67 F1
Ridings The. Canv 197 D3
Ridings The. Gt Bad 140 B4
Ridings The. Roch 178 C1
Ridlands Cl. T Gr 78 C3
Ridley Rd. Basil 174 B1
Ridley Rd. Chelm 127 D4
Riffams Ct. Basil 186 B4
Riffams Dr. Basil 186 B4
Riffhams Chase. Lit Bad 129 E1
Riffhams Dr. Gt Bad 141 D4
Riffhams La. Dan 142 B4
Rifle Hill. Brain 59 F1
Rigby Ave. Mist 36 A2
Rigby Rd. Mist 36 A2
Rignals La. Chelm 140 B2
Riley Ave. Clact 124 C3
Rimini Cl. Colch 67 E2
Ringwood Dr. Rayl 189 E4
Ripley Cl. Clact 109 D3
Ripple Way. Colch 50 A1
Rippleside. Basil 185 F3
Risby Cl. Clact 109 D2
Rise The. E A Gr 66 A4
Rivendell Vale. S Woo F 165 E3
Rivenhall. Wick 175 D3
River Cl. Hals 25 F1
River Cotts. Bore 128 C4
River Hill. Terl 96 A2
River View. Brain 59 F1
River View. With 115 D4
River View Rd. S Ben 187 F1
River View Terr. Alth 157 F1

Riverdale. South 189 E4
Rivermead. Chelm 127 D2
Riverside. Bradw 61 E2
Riverside Ave E. Lawf 35 E2
Riverside Ave W. Lawf 35 E3
Riverside Industrial Estate. Roch 178 C1
Riverside Rd. Burn 170 B2
Riverside Way. Kelv 81 E1
Riverside Wlk. Colch 67 F4
Riverside Wlk. Wick 174 A4
Riverton Dr. St L 135 D1
Rivertons. Basil 185 F2
Riverview. Basil 186 A2
Riverview. Lawf 35 E2
Riverview Ct. Basil 185 F2
Riverview Gdns. Hull 165 E2
Riviera Dr. South 200 B4
Rivish La. L Mel 7 E4
Roach Ave. Rayl 176 B1
Roach Vale. Colch 50 C1
Roach Vale. South 189 F4
Robert Way. Wick 174 C3
Robert Way. Wiv 69 E2
Robert's Hill. M Bure 28 C2
Roberts Rd. Colch 68 A3
Roberts Rd. N Fam 167 D4
Robin Cl. Gt Ben 89 E4
Robin Way. Chelm 140 A3
Robin Way. Sud 12 B3
Robinsbridge Rd. Cogg 62 C1
Robinsdale. Clact 109 F3
Robinson Rd. Brigh 107 D4
Robjohns Rd. Chelm 139 F4
Robletts Way. Worm 29 F2
Rochdale Way. Colch 68 C3
Roche Ave. Hawk 178 C1
Rochefort Dr. Roch 190 C4
Rochehall Way. Roch 191 D4
Rochester Dr. South 190 B2
Rochester Way. Basil 185 F4
Rochester Way. Sud 7 E1
Rocheway. Roch 179 D1
Rochford Ave. South 190 C1
Rochford Cl. Wick 174 C3
Rochford Garden Way. Roch 178 C2
Rochford Hall Cl. Roch 178 C1
Rochford Rd. Canv 197 E2
Rochford Rd. Chelm 127 E1
Rochford Rd. South 190 B3
Rochford Rd. St O 108 A2
Rochford Way. Walt 94 A4
Rockall. South 190 A4
Rockingham Cl. Colch 50 B2
Rockleigh Ave. South 190 A1
Rodbridge Dr. South 200 C4
Rodbridge Hill. L Mel 7 D3
Roddam Cl. Colch 67 E3
Roding Cl. Gt Wak 193 D2
Roding Leigh. S Woo F 165 F4
Roding Way. Wick 174 C3
Rodings The. South 189 E4
Rodney Gdns. Brain 60 B2
Rodney Pl. Sud 7 F1
Rodney Way. Chelm 139 F4
Roedean Cl. South 191 F1
Roedean Gdns. South 191 F1
Rogation Cl. Stanw 66 B3
Roggel Rd. Canv 197 E1
Rokell Way. Walt 93 F3
Rokells. Basil 185 D4
Rokescroft. Basil 186 A3
Roland La. Canv 197 D2
Rolands Cl. Chelm 127 D4
Rolley La. Kelv 81 E1
Rolph Cl. Th L S 74 A1
Romainville Way. Canv 196 B2
Roman Hill. Rowh 86 A4
Roman Rd. Chelm 127 D1
Roman Rd. Colch 68 A4
Roman Way. L Mel 7 E3
Roman Way. St O 107 D2
Romans Pl. Writ 126 A1
Romans Way. Writ 126 A1
Romford Cl. Colch 68 A4
Romney Cl. Brain 59 F3
Romney Cl. Brigh 88 C1
Romney Cl. Clact 109 E3
Romney Cl. Walt 93 F4
Romsey Cl. Hock 177 E3
Romsey Cres. S Ben 187 D3
Romsey Dr. S Ben 187 D3
Romsey Rd. S Ben 187 D3
Romsey Way. S Ben 187 D3
Romulus Cl. Colch 49 F3
Ronald Dr. Rayl 176 A2
Ronald Hill Gr. South 189 E1
Ronald Park Ave. South 190 B1
Ronald Rd. Hals 43 F4
Roodegate. Basil 185 D3
Rookeries The. Mks T 65 D2
Rookery Chase. Ard 33 F1
Rookery Cl. Hat Pev 114 A3
Rookery Cl. Rayl 176 B1
Rookery La. Gt Tot 116 C4
Rookery La. Tipt 100 B4
Rookery Mead. S Woo F 165 E4
Rookery The. Lawf 35 E2
Rookyards. Basil 185 F3
Roosevel Ave. Canv 197 D2
Roosevelt Way. Colch 68 A2
Roothings The. Mald 132 A3
Roots Hall Ave. South 190 C1
Roots La. Wic Bis 115 F3
Rope Wlk. Brigh 107 D3
Rope Wlk. Mald 132 A1
Roper's Chase. Writ 139 D4
Rosabelle Ave. Wiv 69 D1
Rosalind Cl. Colch 68 C4
Rosary Gdns. South 190 A2
Rosbach Rd. Canv 197 E2
Rosberg Rd. Canv 197 F2
Rose Acre. Basil 185 F3
Rose Acre. High 22 C3
Rose Ave. Stanw 66 B2
Rose Cres. Colch 49 E1
Rose Glen. Chelm 140 B4
Rose Hill. Brain 60 A1
Rose La. Virl 119 D4
Rose La. Wiv 87 D4
Rose Rd. Canv 197 D2
Rose Way. Roch 191 D4
Rosebank. Harw 40 A2
Rosebank Rd. W Mers 121 D3
Rosebay Cl. With 97 E2
Roseberry Ave. Thund 187 E4
Rosebery Ave. Colch 68 A4
Rosebery Rd. Chelm 140 A4
Rosecroft Cl. Clact 109 F3
Roselaine. Basil 185 D4
Rosemary Ave. Brain 59 F2
Rosemary Cres. Clact 109 F1
Rosemary Cres. Tipt 100 B3
Rosemary La. Ca Hed 16 A3
Rosemary La. Hals 25 F1
Rosemary La. Thor 89 D3
Rosemary Rd. Clact 109 F1
Rosemary Rd W. Clact 109 F1
Rosemary Way. Clact 125 D4
Rosemead. Thund 187 E4
Roserna Rd. Canv 197 E2
Rosewood Cl. Colch 50 A2
Rosilian Dr. Hull 166 B1
Roslings Cl. Chelm 126 B3
Rossendale. Chelm 126 C1
Rossendale Cl. Colch 50 B2
Rossetta Cl. Wiv 69 D1
Rosshill Industrial Park. Stobr 191 D2
Rossiter Rd. South 202 A4
Rosslyn Cl. Hock 177 F4
Rosslyn Rd. Hock 177 F4
Rothbury Rd. Chelm 126 B1
Rothchilds Ave. Rayl 176 B2
Rothesay Ave. Chelm 140 A4
Rothmans Ave. Gt Bad 140 C3
Rothwell Cl. Hadl 189 E3
Roughtons. Chelm 140 B2
Round Cl. Colch 67 D4
Round Hill Rd. S Ben 188 A1
Roundacre. Basil 185 D3
RoundBush Corner. Birch 83 E2
Roundbush Rd. Lay M 83 E1
Roundbush Rd. Purl 156 A4
Rous Chase. Chelm 140 A1
Rouses La. Clact 108 C2
Rover Ave. Clact 124 C4
Row The. Str S M 22 B1
Rowallan Cl. Colch 67 D2
Rowan Cl. Clact 109 E2
Rowan Cl. Gt Ben 89 F4
Rowan Cl. Harw 40 A2
Rowan Cl. Stanw 66 B2
Rowan Dr. Mald 132 B3
Rowan Way. Cane 168 C1
Rowan Way. Hat Pev 114 A2
Rowan Way. With 98 A3
Rowan Wlk. South 189 E3
Rowhedge Cl. Basil 174 B1
Rowhedge Ferry Rd. Wiv 87 D4
Rowhedge Rd. Colch 68 C1
Rowherns La. Lit Ben 71 F2
Rowlands The. S Ben 187 F2
Rowland's Yd. Harw 39 F1
Rowley Cl. Catt 35 E4
Roxburghe Rd. Weel 90 C3
Roxwell Ave. Chelm 126 B2
Roxwell Rd. Chelm 126 B2
Roxwell Rd. Writ 126 B2
Royal Cl. Hawk 178 B3
Royal Mews. South 200 A4
Royal Oak Dr. Wick 175 D4
Royal Sq. Ded 33 F4
Royal Terr. South 200 A4
Roydon Bridge. Basil 185 E4
Roydon Way. Walt 93 F3
Royston Ave. South 191 D2
RTERS Brook Wlk. Colch 50 B1
Ruaton Dr. Clact 109 E2
Rubens Cl. South 202 A4
Rubens Gate. Sprin 127 F4
Rubicon Ave. Wick 174 C4
Rudd Ct. Colch 50 C1
Rudkin Rd. Colch 49 F3
Rudsdale Way. Colch 66 C3
Ruffles Cl. Rayl 176 C2
Rugby Rd. Sud 13 D2
Rugosa Cl. Stanw 66 B4
Rumseys Fields. Dan 142 C4
Rundells Wlk. Basil 185 F4
Rundels The. Thund 188 A3
Runnacles St. Silv E 79 E3
Running Mare La. Chelm 140 A2
Runnymeade Rd. Canv 197 D2
Runnymede Chase. Thund 188 A3
Runsell La. Dan 143 D4
Runsell View. Dan 143 D4
Runwell Gdns. Runw 163 E1
Runwell Rd. Runw 164 A2
Runwell Rd. Runw 163 F1
Runwell Terr. South 199 F4
Runwood Rd. Canv 196 B2
Rupert Rd. Soum 159 E2
Rurik Ct. Mald 144 C4
Rush Cl. Thund 187 D3
Rush Green Rd. Clact 109 D2
Rushbottom La. Basil 175 D1
Rushes La. Ashel 149 D1
Rushley. Basil 174 B1
Rushley Cl. Gt Wak 193 D2
Rushleydale. Sprin 127 F3
Rushmere Cl. W Mers 121 E3
Ruskin Ave. South 191 D1
Ruskin Cl. Walt 93 F4
Ruskin Path. Wick 174 B3
Ruskin Rd. Chelm 127 F1
Ruskoi Rd. Canv 196 C3
Russell Gdns. Chelm 140 A2
Russell Gdns. Wick 174 C4
Russell Gr. Roch 179 D1
Russell Rd. Clact 110 A2
Russell Rd. N Fam 156 A1
Russell Way. Chelm 139 F4
Russell's Rd. Hals 43 D4
Russet Cl. Brain 60 A1
Russet Way. Burn 170 B3
Russet Way. Hock 177 F4
Russets The. Hawk 178 B3
Rutherford Cl. Rayl 189 E3
Rutland Ave. Colch 67 D2
Rutland Ave. South 200 C4
Rutland Dr. Rayl 176 A4
Rutland Gdns. Brain 60 A2
Rutland Gdns. Hawk 178 B3
Rutland Rd. Chelm 127 D4
Rutland Rd. N Fam 167 D4
Rydal Cl. Hull 165 E2
Rydal Cl. Rayl 176 C1
Rydal Way. Bl Not 77 E3
Ryde Ave. Clact 110 A4
Ryde Cl. Hadl 189 D3
Ryde The. Hadl 189 D3
Ryder Way. Basil 174 B1
Rye Cl. Brigh 88 C1
Rye Cl. Colch 66 C3
Rye Cl. Hat Pev 114 A2
Rye Field The. Lit Bad 129 E2
Rye La. Lay H 85 D2
Rye Mill La. Fee 81 F2
Ryedene. Basil 185 F2
Ryedene Cl. Basil 185 F2
Ryedene Pl. Basil 185 F2
Ryegate Rd. Colch 67 F4
Ryes La. Bul 12 A1
Rylands Rd. South 191 E1
Ryle The. Writ 139 D4
Rysley. Lit Bad 129 E2

Sackville Cl. Chelm 126 C2
Sackville Rd. South 191 F1
Sackville Way. W Berg 48 B2
Saddle Rise. Sprin 127 F4
Sadler Cl. Colch 68 A2
Sadlers. Thund 187 D3
Sadlers Cl. Walt 93 E3
Saffory Cl. Rayl 189 E4
Saffron Way. Tipt 100 B2
Sage Rd. Colch 68 A1
Sage Wlk. Tipt 100 B2
St Agnes Dr. Canv 196 B2
St Alban's Rd. Clact 110 A2
St Alban's Rd. Colch 67 E4
St Andrew's Ave. Colch 68 B3
St Andrews Cl. Alres 88 A4
St Andrews Cl. Canv 196 B2
St Andrew's Gdns. Colch 68 B4
St Andrews Pl. Brigh 88 C1
St Andrews Rd. Bore 112 C1
St Andrew's Rd. Clact 109 F2
St Andrews Rd. Hals 25 F1
St Andrew's Rd. Hat Pev 114 A2
St Andrew's Rd. Roch 178 C1
St Andrews Rd. South 201 E3
St Andrews Rd. Sud 13 D3
St Andrew's Rd. Weel 72 C1
St Andrew's Rise. Bul 11 F3
St Agnes Cl. Cogg 63 D1
St Annes Rd. Canv 197 F2
St Anne's Rd. Colch 68 B4
St Anns Rd. Clact 109 F2
St Ann's Rd. South 191 D1
St Anthony's Dr. Chelm 140 B4
St Augustine's Ave. South 201 D3
St Austell Rd. Colch 50 B1
St Austin's La. Harw 40 C3
St Barbara's Rd. Colch 67 E2
St Bartholomew Cl. Colch 50 B2
St Bartholomews La. Sud 7 E1
St Benet's Rd. South 190 C1
St Bernard Rd. Colch 50 B1
St Botolphs Church Wlk. Colch 67 F3
St Botolph's Circus. Colch 67 F3
St Botolph's St. Colch 67 F3
St Botolph's Terr. Walt 94 B4
St Bridge Ct. Colch 50 B1
St Catharines Cl. Colch 67 E1
St Catherine Rd. L Mel 7 E4
St Catherines Cl. Wick 174 C4
St Catherine's Rd. Chelm 126 C1
St Charles Dr. Wick 174 C4
St Christopher Rd. Colch 50 B1
St Christophers Cl. Canv 196 B2
St Christophers Way. Clact 125 D4
St Clair Cl. Clact 109 F4
St Clair's Dr. St O 108 A3
St Clair's Rd. St O 108 A3
St Clare Dr. Colch 67 D4
St Clare Rd. Colch 67 D3
St Clement Rd. Colch 50 B1
St Clement's Ave. South 189 F1
St Clement's Cl. S Ben 187 E3
St Clement's Cres. S Ben 187 E3
St Clement's Dr. South 189 F2
St Clement's Rd. S Ben 187 E3
St Cleres Cres. Wick 174 C4
St Clere's Hall La. St O 108 A2
St Cleres Way. Dan 142 B4
St Columb Ct. Colch 50 B1
St Cyrus Rd. Colch 50 B2
St David's Cl. Colch 68 B4
St Davids Dr. Hadl 189 D2
St Davids Terr. Hadl 189 D2
St David's Way. Wick 174 C4
St Davids Wlk. Canv 196 B2
St Dominic Rd. Colch 50 B1
St Edmund's Cl. South 191 E2
St Edmund's Ct. Colch 68 B4
St Edmund's Hill. Bures 19 E3
St Edmund's Hill. Sud 19 E3
St Edmunds La. Bures 19 F1
St Fabian's Dr. Chelm 126 C2
St Faith Rd. Colch 50 B1
St Fillan Rd. Colch 50 B1
St Gabriels Ct. Basil 186 A3
St George's Ave. Harw 40 B1
St Georges Cl. Gt Bro 52 C1
St George's Dr. South 190 C2
St George's La. South 201 F3
St George's Park Ave. South 190 A1
St Georges Wlk. Canv 196 B2
St Georges Wlk. Thund 187 D3
St Giles Cl. Mald 131 F1
St Giles Cres. Mald 131 F1
St Gregory's Ct. Sud 12 B4
St Guiberts Rd. Canv 196 C3
St Helena Rd. Colch 67 E3
St Helens Ave. Clact 110 A4
St Helen's Green. Harw 40 C3
St Helen's La. Colch 67 F4
St Helen's Rd. South 199 F4
St Ives Cl. Clact 109 D2
St Ives Rd. Peld 103 F3
St James Ave. South. South 201 D4
St James Cl. Canv 196 B2
St James Cl. South 190 A2
St James Gdns. South 190 A2
St James Park. Chelm 126 B2
St James Rd. Basil 185 E3
St James Rd. Brain 59 F3
St Jame's St. Ca Hed 15 F2
St James's Wlk. Hock 177 E3
St Jean Wlk. Tipt 100 B3
St John Ave. Brain 59 F1
St John's Ave. Chelm 140 A4
St John's Ave. Colch 67 F3
St Johns Cl. Gt Wak 193 D2
St Johns Cres. Canv 196 B2
St John's Cres. Gt Hor 49 D4
St John's Ct. Tolle 119 E1
St Johns Dr. Rayl 175 F2
St John's Green. Colch 67 F3
St John's Green. Writ 126 A1
St John's Rd. Chelm 140 A4
St John's Rd. Clact 109 D3
St John's Rd. Colch 50 B2
St John's Rd. Gt Wak 193 D2
St John's Rd. S Ben 188 B2
St John's Rd. South 199 F4
St John's Rd. Wiv 87 E4
St John's Rd. Writ 126 A1
St John's St. Colch 67 F3
St Joseph Rd. Colch 50 B2
St Jude Gdns. Colch 50 B1
St Judes Cl. Colch 50 B1
St Julian Gr. Colch 68 A3
St Lawrence Dr. St L 135 D1
St Lawrence Gdns. South 189 F3
St Lawrence Hill. St L 148 C3
St Lawrence Rd. Colch 50 B1
St Lawrence Rd. Till 149 E3
St Leonards Rd. Colch 68 B3
St Leonard's Rd. South 200 A4
St Luke's Chase. Tipt 100 B3
St Lukes Cl. Canv 196 B2
St Luke's Cl. Colch 50 B1
St Luke's Rd. South 191 E1
St Margaret's Rd. Sprin 127 F2
St Mark Dr. Colch 50 B1
St Marks Rd. Canv 196 B2
St Marks Rd. Clact 109 F2
St Mark's Rd. S Ben 188 B2
St Martins Cl. Clact 109 F2
St Martin's Cl. Rayl 188 B4
St Martin's Cl. Thund 187 D4
St Mary's Cl. Gt Bad 140 C3
St Mary's Cl. Pan 59 D4
St Mary's Cl. S Ben 187 E1
St Mary's Cres. Basil 186 B3
St Mary's Dr. S Ben 187 F1
St Mary's La. Mald 132 A1
St Mary's Path. Basil 186 B4
St Mary's Rd. Brain 60 A2
St Mary's Rd. Burn 170 B3
St Mary's Rd. Clact 109 F2
St Mary's Rd. Frin 94 A3
St Mary's Rd. Gt Ben 89 F3
St Mary's Rd. Kelv 81 E1
St Mary's Rd. S Ben 196 C4
St Mary's Rd. South 190 C1
St Mary's Rd. With 98 A4
St Michaels Ave. Basil 186 B2
St Michaels Cl. Latch 157 D3
St Michaels Ct. Mann 35 E2
St Michael's La. Brain 59 F1
St Michael's Rd. Brain 59 F1
St Michaels Rd. Canv 196 B2
St Michael's Rd. Chelm 140 A4
St Michaels Rd. Colch 67 E1
St Michael's Rd. Harw 40 A1
St Michael's Rd. Rayl 188 C4
St Michael's Rd. Th L S 73 F1
St Michaels Wlk. Chelm 140 B1
St Mildreds Rd. Chelm 140 A4
St Monance Way. Colch 50 B1
St Nazaire Rd. Chelm 126 C3
St Neots Cl. Colch 50 B1
St Nicholas Cl. With 97 F2
St Nicholas Pass. Colch 67 F4
St Nicholas Rd. Till 149 F2
St Nicholas Rd. With 97 F2
St Nicholas St. Colch 67 F4
St Nicholas Way. Cogg 63 D2
St Osyth Rd. Alres 88 B4
St Osyth Rd. Clact 109 E2
St Osyth Rd. Lit Cla 91 E1
St Pauls Rd. Canv 196 B2
St Paul's Rd. Clact 110 A2
St Paul's Rd. Colch 67 F4
St Peter's Ave. Mald 131 F1
St Peter's Cl. Brain 59 F2
St Peter's Cogg 63 D1
St Peters Ct. Sud 12 C4
St Peter's Rd. Brain 59 F2
St Peters Rd. Canv 196 B2
St Peter's Rd. Chelm 126 C1
St Peters Rd. Hock 177 D4
St Peter's Rd. W Mers 121 D3
St Peter's St. Colch 67 F4
St Peter's Terr. Wick 174 B4
St Peter's Wlk. Brain 59 F2
St Peters's-in-the-Fields. Brain 59 F2
St Runwald St. Colch 67 F4
St Saviour Cl. Colch 50 B1
St Stephens Rd. Col N 156 A2
St Thomas Cl. Colch 50 C1
St Thomas Rd. Ashi 167 D2
St Vincent Chase. Brain 60 A3
St Vincent Rd. Clact 109 E1
St Vincents Rd. Chelm 140 A4
St Vincent's Rd. South 199 F4
Sairard Cl. South 189 E4
Sairard Gdns. South 189 E4
Salary Cl. Colch 50 C1
Salcombe Rd. Brain 60 B1
Salcott Cres. Wick 174 C4
Salem Wlk. Rayl 176 A2
Salerno Cres. Colch 67 E1
Salerno Way. Chelm 126 C3
Salforal Cl. Rett 153 D1
Salisbury Ave. Colch 67 F3
Salisbury Ave. South 190 C1
Salisbury Rd. Clact 110 B3
Salisbury Rd. South 189 E1
Salmon Cl. Colch 66 C2
Salmon's La. Gt T 64 A2
Saltcoats. S Woo F 165 E4
Saltcoats Hill. Stow M 155 D1
Salter Pl. Sprin 127 F1
Salter's Meadow. Toll D 118 B2
Saltings The. Hadl 188 B2
Salvia Cl. Clact 109 E2
Samphire Cl. With 97 E2
Sampson's La. Peld 103 F2
Samsons Cl. Brigh 106 C4
Samson's Rd. Brigh 88 C1
Samuel Manor. Sprin 127 F2
Samuels Dr. South 201 D4
San Remo Par. South 199 F4
San Remo Rd. Canv 197 E2
Sanctuary Rd. Hadl 189 D2
Sandbanks. Hadl 188 B1
Sanderling Gdns. Mald 132 B3
Sanderlings. S Ben 187 E1
Sanders Dr. Colch 67 D4
Sandford Cl. Wiv 87 E4
Sandford Mill Rd. Sprin 128 A1
Sandford Mill Rd. Sprin 127 F1
Sandford Rd. Chelm 127 F2
Sandhill Rd. Rayl 189 E4
Sandhurst. Canv 196 B2
Sandhurst Cl. South 189 F2
Sandhurst Cres. South 189 F2
Sandleigh Rd. South 190 A1
Sandon Cl. Gt Hor 49 E4
Sandon Hall Bridleway. Sand 141 E2
Sandon Rd. Basil 185 F3
Sandown Ave. South 190 A1
Sandown Cl. Clact 110 A4
Sandown Cl. Wick 175 D4
Sandown Rd. Thund 188 A4
Sandown Rd. Wick 175 D4
Sandpiper Cl. Colch 69 D4
Sandpiper Cl. Mald 132 B3
Sandpiper Cl. South 201 F4
Sandpiper Wlk. Chelm 140 B3
Sandpit La. Burn 170 B3
Sandpit Rd. Brain 59 F2
Sandpit Rd. South 202 A4
Sandringham Ave. Hock 177 E3
Sandringham Ct. Sud 13 D4
Sandringham Rd. South 200 B4
Sandwich Cl. Brain 59 F3
Sandwich Rd. Brigh 106 C4
Sandwich Rd. Clact 125 E4
Sandy Hill. M Bure 29 E3
Sandy La. Bul 12 A3
Sandy La. Sud 12 A3
Santour Rd. Canv 196 C3
Saran Ct. Wiv 69 D1
Sarcel. Stis 61 E3
Sargeant Cl. Colch 68 A2
Sarre Way. Brigh 106 C4
Sassoon Way. Mald 145 D4
Satanita Rd. South 199 E4
Saul's Ave. With 115 D4
Sauls Bridge Cl. With 115 D4
Saunders Ave. Brain 59 F2
Savill Rd. Colch 68 B1
Saville St. Walt 76 B1
Sawkins Ave. Gt Bad 140 B3
Sawkins Cl. Gt Bad 140 B3
Sawkins Gdns. Gt Bad 140 B3
Sawney Brook. Writ 126 A1
Sawyer's Rd. Toll D 117 E3
Saxmunden Way. Clact 109 D2
Saxon Cl. Colch 66 C2
Saxon Cl. Rayl 176 C3

Saxon Cl. Runw 163 F1
Saxon Dr. With 97 F2
Saxon Way. Chelm 127 D4
Saxon Way. Clact 110 C3
Saxon Way. Mald 132 A1
Saxon Way. S Ben 187 E1
Saxonville. S Ben 187 D2
Saxted Dr. Clact 109 D2
Sayers. Thund 188 A3
Saywell Brook. Sprin 128 A1
Scalby Rd. Soum 159 D2
Scaldhurst. Basil 186 B4
Scarboroug Dr. South 189 F1
Scarborough Rd. Soum 159 D2
Scarfe Way. Colch 68 C3
Scarletts. Basil 185 E4
Scarletts Cl. With 115 D4
Scarletts Rd. Colch 68 B3
Sceptre Rd. Tolle 119 E1
School Chase. Hals 43 F4
School Hill. Birch 84 A2
School La. Basil 175 D1
School La. Birch 84 A2
School La. Ded 33 F4
School La. Frat 71 D1
School La. Gt Hor 31 D1
School La. Gt Wig 102 C2
School La. Lawf 35 D1
School La. Lit Hor 30 B3
School La. Mist 35 F2
School La. S Ben 196 B4
School La. Str S M 22 B1
School La. W Berg 48 C2
School Rd. Colch 68 A1
School Rd. Copf 65 E2
School Rd. Elmst M 70 A2
School Rd. Frin 93 F3
School Rd. Gt Oak 56 B2
School Rd. Gt Tot 116 A2
School Rd. Langh 32 C2
School Rd. Lit Hor 30 B2
School Rd. Lit Map 26 A4
School Rd. Lit Tot 117 D2
School Rd. Lit Y 9 E2
School Rd. Mess 82 B1
School Rd. Pent 5 F3
School Rd. Sho G 40 A4
School Rd. Si Hed 24 B4
School Rd. Silv E 79 F2
School Rd. Tend 72 C3
School Rd. Wic Bis 115 F3
School Rd. Wic S P 17 E3
School St. Nay 20 B3
School St. Sud 12 C4
School View Rd. Chelm 126 C2
School Wlk. Brain 59 F2
Schoolfield. Glems 2 A3
Scofield Ct. Sud 13 D3
Scotland St. Nay 20 C3
Scott Cl. Brain 78 A4
Scott Dr. Colch 66 C3
Scotts Hall Cotts. Cane 179 E4
Scotts Hall Rd. Cane 179 E4
Scotts Hill. Soum 159 D2
Scotts Wlk. Chelm 126 B3
Scotts Wlk. Rayl 177 D1
Scraley Rd. Gt Tot 132 B3
Scraley Rd. Mald 132 B3
Scratton Rd. South 199 F4
Screens Ct. Chelm 126 B2
Scrip's Rd. Cogg 81 D4
Scrub La. Hadl 188 C2
Scylla Cl. Mald 132 B3
Scythe Way. Colch 67 D2
Sea Cornflower Way. Clact 125 D4
Sea Cres. Clact 124 C3
Sea Flowers Way. Clact 125 D4
Sea Glebe Way. Clact 125 D4
Sea Holly Way. Clact 125 D3
Sea King Cres. Colch 50 A2
Sea Lavender Way. Clact 125 D4
Sea Pink Way. Clact 125 D3
Sea Reach. South 198 C4
Sea Rosemary Way. Clact 125 D4
Sea Shell Way. Clact 125 D3
Sea Thistle Way. Clact 125 D4
Sea View Par. May 146 C1
Sea View Par. St L 135 E1
Sea View Prom. Tolle 135 D1
Sea Way. Clact 124 C3
Seabrook Gdns. Bore 112 C1
Seabrook Rd. Gt Bad 141 D3
Seaden Ct. Clact 110 A4
Seafield Ave. Mist 36 A2
Seafield Rd. Harw 40 A1
Seafields Gdns. Clact 110 B3
Seafields Rd. Clact 110 B3
Seaforth Ave. South 191 E1
Seaforth Gr. South 191 E1
Seaforth Rd. South 199 E4
Seagers. Gt Tot 116 A2
Seamer Rd. Soum 159 D2
Seamore Ave. Thund 187 E4
Seamore Cl. Thund 187 E3
Seamore Wlk. Thund 187 E4
Seaton Cl. Lawf 35 D2
Seaview Ave. Basil 185 E2
Seaview Ave. Lit Oak 57 E4
Seaview Ave. W Mers 121 F3
Seaview Dr. Gt Wak 193 E2
Seaview Rd. Brigh 106 C4
Seaview Rd. Canv 197 F1
Seaview Rd. South 198 C4
Seaview Rd. South 201 F3
Seaview Rd. St O 124 A4
Seaview Terr. Hadl 188 B1
Seaview Terr. St O 107 D2
Seaway. Canv 197 D1
Seaway. St L 148 B4
Seawick Rd. St O 124 A3
Sebastian Cl. Colch 68 C4
Second Ave. Canv 196 C2
Second Ave. Chelm 127 D3
Second Ave. Clact 110 A2
Second Ave. Frin 93 F2
Second Ave. Glems 2 B3
Second Ave. Hals 26 A1
Second Ave. Harw 40 B2
Second Ave. Hull 165 F1
Second Ave. South 199 D4
Second Ave. Sud 7 F1
Second Ave. Walt 76 B2
Second Ave. Weel 90 C4
Second Ave. Wick 175 D3
Seddons Wlk. Hock 177 F3
Selbourne Rd. Hock 177 F3
Selbourne Rd. South 191 E2
Selbourne Rd. Thund 187 E3
Seldon Cl. South 190 A2
Seldon Rd. Tipt 100 B3
Selwyn Rd. South 191 E1
Serpentine Wlk. Colch 49 F1
Seven Acres. Wick 174 C4
Seven Ash Green. Sprin 127 E3
Seventh Ave. Canv 196 C2
Seventh Ave. Chelm 127 D3
Severalls La. Colch 50 B3
Severn Rd. Clact 109 F3
Sewards End. Wick 174 C3
Sewell's La. Bel S P 5 D1
Sexton Cl. Rowh 86 A4
Seymour Rd. Clact 108 C1
Seymour Rd. Hadl 188 C2
Seymour Rd. South 190 B1
Seymour St. Chelm 127 D1
Shackleton Cl. Harw 39 F1
Shaftesbury Ave. Harw 40 A2
Shaftesbury Ave. South 200 C3
Shair La. Tend 72 A1
Shakespeare Ave. Rayl 177 D1
Shakespeare Ave. South 190 C1
Shakespeare Cl. Brain 78 A4
Shakespeare Dr. Mald 132 A1
Shakespeare Dr. South 190 C1
Shakespeare Rd. Colch 66 C3
Shakeston Cl. Writ 139 D4
Shamrock Cl. Tolle 119 E1
Shanklin Cl. Clact 110 A4
Shanklin Dr. South 190 A1
Shannon Ave. Rayl 176 B1
Shannon Cl. South 189 F2
Shannon Way. Canv 196 B2
Sharlands Cl. Wick 174 C4
Sharnbrook. South 192 B1
Sharpington Cl. Chelm 140 B2
Shatters Rd. Lay Br 84 A1
Shaw Cl. Walt 93 F4
Shaw Rd. L Mel 7 E4
Shaw Rd. With 97 F3
Shearers Way. Bore 112 C1
Shears Cres. W Mers 121 E3
Sheepcoates La. Gt Tot 116 C1
Sheepcot Rd. Ca Hed 15 F2
Sheepcotes La. Silv E 79 F3
Sheepcotes La. Soum 159 E3
Sheepen Pl. Colch 67 F4
Sheepen Rd. Colch 67 E4
Sheepgate La. Cla 4 A4
Sheepshead Hill. Sud 13 E3
Sheering Wlk. Colch 67 F1
Sheerwater Mews. Colch 69 D4
Sheldon Rd. Canv 197 F2
Shellbeach Rd. Canv 197 E1
Shellcroft. Col En 26 C1
Shelley Ave. Sud 13 D3
Shelley Cl. Mald 145 D4
Shelley Rd. Chelm 127 E1
Shelley Rd. Colch 66 C3
Shelley Sq. South 191 D1
Shelley Wlk. Brain 78 A4
Shelleys La. T Gr 78 C4
Shepard Cl. South 190 A3
Shepherds Cl. Hadl 188 C2
Shepherds Croft. Stanw 66 B3
Shepherds La. Glems 2 A3
Shepherds Wlk. Hadl 188 C2
Sheppard Cl. Clact 109 E3
Sheppard Dr. Sprin 128 A2
Sherborne Rd. Sprin 127 E3
Sherbourne Cl. Roch 190 C3
Sherbourne Cl. Walt 93 F4
Sherbourne Dr. Basil 174 A1
Sherbourne Gdns. Roch 190 C3
Sherbourne Rd. Colch 68 C4
Sheridan Ave. S Ben 188 A2
Sheridan Cl. Rayl 176 C1
Sheridan Wlk. Colch 66 C3
Sheriffs Way. Clact 109 F4
Sheriton Sq. Rayl 176 B2
Sherry Way. Hadl 188 C3
Sherwood Cl. Colch 68 B4
Sherwood Cres. Hadl 188 C2
Sherwood Dr. Chelm 126 B1
Sherwood Dr. Clact 109 F3
Sherwood Way. Fee 81 E2
Sherwood Way. South 191 F1
Shewell Wlk. Colch 67 F4
Shewsbury Dri. Thund 187 E4
Shillito Cl. Colch 66 C2
Ship Hill. Brad 36 C2
Ship Rd. Burn 170 B2
Shipwrights Cl. S Ben 188 A1
Shipwrights Dr. S Ben 188 A2
Shire Cl. Sprin 127 F4
Shirebourn Vale. S Woo F 165 E3
Shirley Ct. Clact 109 D1
Shirley Gdns. Basil 186 B4
Shirley Rd. South 189 F3
Shoebridge's Hill. Ded 33 F3
Shoebury Ave. South 201 F4
Shoebury Common Rd. South 201 F4
Shoebury Rd. Gt Wak 193 E2
Shoebury Rd. South 192 A1
Shop La. E Mers 105 F2
Shop Rd. Lit Bro 53 D3
Shopland Hall Rd. Stobr 191 E3
Shopland Rd. Stobr 191 E4
Shore La. Brad 36 C2
Shore Rd. Burn 170 B2
Shorefield. S Ben 187 D2
Shorefield Gdns. South 199 F4
Shorefield Rd. South 199 E4
Short Cut Rd. Colch 67 F4
Short Cut Rd. Colch 67 F4
Short Rd. Hadl 188 B1
Short St. South 191 D1
Short Wyre St. Colch 67 F4
Shortacre. Basil 185 E3
Shortlands. Basil 185 D3
Shortridge Ct. With 114 C4
Shrub End Rd. Colch 67 D2
Shrubland Ct. Clact 110 A3
Shrubland Rd. Colch 68 A3
Shrubland Rd. Mist 36 A2
Shrublands Cl. Chelm 127 E1
Shums Hill. Walt 93 E4
Shut La. Ea Col 45 D3
Siam Pl. Sud 12 C4
Sidmouth Ave. South 190 B3
Sidmouth Rd. Sprin 127 F3
Sidwell Ave. S Ben 187 F1
Sidwell Chase. S Ben 187 F1
Sidwell La. S Ben 187 F1
Sidwell Park. S Ben 187 F1
Silcock Cl. Colch 50 B1
Silcott St. Brigh 106 C3
Sillett Cl. Clact 109 E3
Silvanus Cl. Colch 67 E3
Silver Rd. Burn 170 B2
Silver St. Mald 131 F2
Silver St. Silv E 79 E2
Silver Way. Runw 174 B4
Silverdale. Rayl 188 C4
Silverdale. Thund 187 F4
Silverdale Ave. South 190 C1
Silversea Dr. South 190 A1
Silverthorn Cl. Hawk 178 B2
Silverthorne. Canv 196 C2
Silverthorne Cl. Colch 68 A2
Silvertree Cl. Hock 177 D3
Simmonds La. Purl 145 D1
Simmonds Way. Dan 142 C4
Simons La. Colch 68 A3
Simpsons La. Tipt 100 A2
Sims Cl. Ea Col 45 D4
Singer Ave. Clact 124 C4
Singleton Ct. Sud 13 D3
Sinnington End. Colch 50 B2
Sioux Cl. Colch 50 B2
Sir Isaac's Wlk. Colch 67 F4
Sir Walter Raleigh Dr. Rayl 176 B2
Sir Walter Raleigh Dr. Rayl 176 B3
Sirdar Rd. Rayl 188 B4
Siskin Cl. Colch 68 C4
Sittang Cl. Colch 67 E1
Sitwell Cl. Lawf 35 D2
Siward Rd. With 114 B4
Six Bells Ct. Brain 59 F3
Sixth Ave. Canv 196 C2
Sixth Ave. Chelm 127 D3
Skate's Hill. Glems 2 A1
Skelmersdale Rd. Clact 109 F2
Skerry Rise. Chelm 127 D4
Skiddaw Cl. Bl Not 77 E4
Skinner's La. Chelm 140 A2
Skitts Hill. Brain 60 A1
Sky Hall Hill. Box 32 B4
Skylark Wlk. Chelm 140 A3
Skyrmans Fee. Walt 93 F3
Sladbury's La. Clact 110 B4
Slade Rd. Clact 110 B3
Slades Cl. Glems 2 B3
Slade's La. Chelm 140 A2
Slades The. Basil 185 F2
Sloe Hill. Hals 25 E1
Slough La. Ard 51 E3
Slough La. Purl 143 E2
Slough La. Wiv 69 D3
Slough Rd. Dan 143 E2
Smaley La. L Mel 7 E4
Smallbridge Entry. Bures 29 E4
Smallgains Ave. Canv 197 F2
Smallwood Rd. Colch 67 D2
Smart Ave. Canv 197 D2
Smeaton Cl. Colch 50 B3
Smeetham Hall La. Bul 11 F4
Smith St. South 201 F3
Smither's Chase. Stobr 191 D3
Smithers Dr. Gt Bad 141 D3
Smiths Ave. May 158 A4
Smythe Cl. Clact 109 E3
Smythies Ave. Colch 68 A4
Snakes La. South 190 A3
Snape Cl. Clact 109 D2
Sneating Hall La. Th L S 92 C4
Snelling Gr. Gt Bad 140 C3
Sniveller's La. Kelv 80 B2
Snoreham Gdns. Latch 157 D3
Snowberry Gr. Colch 68 A2
Snowdonia Cl. Basil 186 B4
Snowdrop Cl. Sprin 127 F4
Snowdrop Cl. With 97 F2
Soane St. Basil 174 A1
Soft Rd. Bel W 10 C3
Softwater La. Hadl 188 C2
Soils The. Rams 56 C3
Solbys La. Hadl 188 C2
Somerdean. Basil 186 B3
Somers Rd. Colch 67 D2
Somerset Ave. Roch 178 C2
Somerset Ave. South 190 A2
Somerset Cl. Colch 67 D2
Somerset Cres. South 190 A2
Somerset Gdns. Basil 186 A3
Somerset Pl. Chelm 127 D4
Somerset Way. Clact 108 C1
Somerton Ave. South 190 A3
Somerville Gdns. South 198 C4
Somme Rd. Colch 67 E2
Somnes Ave. Canv 196 C3
Sonell Ct. Wiv 69 D1
Sonning Way. South 192 B1
Sonters Down. Rett 164 B3
Sorrel Cl. Colch 49 E1
Sorrell The. Thund 187 E4
South Ave. Hull 165 F1
South Ave. South 191 E1
South Beech Ave. Wick 174 B4
South Cl. Hals 43 F4
South Cl. St O 108 A2
South Colne. Basil 185 E2
South Cres. South 190 B3
South Crockerford. Basil 185 F2
South Green Rd. Fing 86 C2
South Gunnels. Basil 185 D3
South Hanningfield Rd. Rett 153 D1
South Hanningfield Way. Runw 163 E2
South Heath Rd. Gt Ben 89 F2
South Hill Cl. Dan 142 B3
South House Chase. Mald 145 E4
South Mayne. Basil 186 A3
South Par. Canv 197 F1
South Primrose Hill. Chelm 126 C2
South Riding. Basil 185 F3
South St. Brad O S 137 D1
South St. Brain 59 F1
South St. Colch 67 F3
South St. Mann 35 E2
South St. Roch 178 C1
South St. Till 149 F2
South St. Toll D 118 B2
South Strand. Lawf 35 E3
South View Cl. Rayl 188 C4
South View Rd. Rett 164 B3
South View Rd. S Ben 187 E2
South Wlk. Basil 185 D3
Southborough Dr. South 190 A1
Southborough Rd. Chelm 140 A4
Southbourne Gdns. South 190 A2
Southbourne Gr. Hock 178 A3
Southbourne Gr. South 190 A2
Southbourne Gr. Wick 174 A4
Southchurch Ave. South 202 A4
Southchurch Ave. South 200 A4
Southchurch Bvd. Sou 191 F1
Southchurch Hall Cl. South 200 B4
Southchurch Rd. South 200 B4
Southchurch Rectory Chase. South 191 F1
Southcliff. S Ben 187 E2
Southcliff. Walt 94 B4
Southcliff Park. Clact 110 A2
Southcote Cres. Basil 185 F4
Southcote Rd. With 97 F2
Southcote Row. Basil 185 F4
Southcote Sq. Basil 185 F4
Southcroft Cl. Walt 93 E3
Southend Arterial Rd. Rayl 188 B4
Southend Arterial Rd. South 189 E3
Southend Arterial Rd. Thund 188 B4
Southend Rd. Barl 192 B2
Southend Rd. Gt Bad 141 E2
Southend Rd. Hock 177 F3
Southend Rd. Roch 190 C4
Southend Rd. Sand 141 E2
Southend Rd. W Han 141 E2
Southend Rd. Wick 175 D4
Southend Rd. Woo Mor 143 E3
Southern Dr. S Woo F 165 E4
Southernhay. Basil 185 D3
Southernhay. South 189 E3
Southey Cl. Mald 132 B2
Southfalls Rd. Canv 197 F2
Southfield Cl. Hadl 188 C3
Southfield Dr. Hadl 188 C2
Southfields. Ded 33 F3
Southgate St. L Mel 7 E3
Southgreen Gdns. Clact 109 E2
Southland Cl. Colch 50 B1
Southlands Chase. Sand 141 F1
Southminster Rd. Ashel 160 A4
Southminster Rd. Burn 170 A4
Southminster Rd. May 158 B2
Southminster Rd. St L 148 C2
Southsea Ave. South 189 E1
Southview Cl. S Woo F 165 E4
Southview Dr. Clact 110 C3
Southview Dr. South 190 B1
Southview Dr. Walt 94 B4
Southview Rd. Basil 185 F3
Southview Rd. Dan 142 B3
Southview Rd. Hock 177 F4
Southwalters. Canv 196 C2
Southwark Path. Basil 185 F4
Southway. Brigh 106 C4
Southway. Colch 67 F3
Southwell Rd. S Ben 187 F2
Southwick Gdns. Canv 196 C2
Southwick Rd. Canv 196 C2
Southwold Cres. S Ben 187 E3
Southwold Way. Clact 109 D3
Southwood Chase. Dan 143 D2
Southwood Gdns. Rayl 189 D4
Sowerberry Cl. Chelm 126 C4
Spa Cl. Hock 177 F3
Spa Dr. St L 135 D1
Spa Rd. Fee 81 F2
Spa Rd. Hock 177 F3
Spa Rd. With 97 F1
Spains Hall Pl. Basil 185 E3
Spalding Ave. Chelm 126 C3
Spalding Way. Gt Bad 140 C4
Spanbeek Rd. Canv 197 D3
Spanbies Rd. Str S M 22 B1
Spansey Ct. Hals 25 E1
Sparkey Cl. With 115 D4
Sparks La. Ridge 8 A3
Sparling Cl. Colch 67 E1
Sparlings The. Walt 93 E4
Sparrow Cl. Si Hed 24 B4
Sparrow Rd. Sud 13 D3
Sparrows Herne. Basil 185 D2
Sparrows Herne. Clact 109 F3
Speedwell Cl. With 97 E2
Speedwell Rd. Colch 68 B1
Spells Cl. Soum 159 E2
Spencer Cl. Mald 145 D4
Spencer Ct. S Woo F 165 F4
Spencer Gdns. Roch 178 B3
Spencer Rd. Th L S 74 A1
Spencer Rd. Thund 187 E3
Spencer Sq. Brain 59 F4
Spencers. Hawk 177 F2
Spendells Cl. Walt 76 B1
Spenders Cl. Basil 185 E4
Spenlow Dr. Chelm 126 B4
Spennells The. Th L S 74 A1
Spenser Way. Clact 108 C1
Spicers La. L Mel 7 E4
Spindle Wood. Colch 50 A2
Spinks La. With 97 F1
Spinnaker The. S Woo F 165 F3
Spinnakers The. S Ben 187 D2
Spinnel's Hill. Wix 37 D1
Spinnel's La. Wix 55 E4
Spinney Cl. Wick 174 C4
Spinney The. Brain 60 B1
Spinneys The. Hock 177 E3
Spinneys The. Rayl 177 D1
Spinneys The. South 189 F4
Spires The. Gt Bad 140 C3
Spital Rd. Mald 131 F1
Sporehams La. Dan 142 B2
Sportsmans La. Hat Pev 114 A1
Sportsway. Colch 67 F4
Spots Wlk. Chelm 140 B2
Spout La. Sud 19 E4
Spratts La. Lit Bro 53 D2
Spring Chase. Brigh 106 C4
Spring Chase. Wiv 69 D1
Spring Cl. Clact 109 E3
Spring Cl. Lit Bad 129 E3
Spring Elms La. Lit Bad 129 F2
Spring Gardens Rd. Wa Col 46 C3
Spring Gdns. Rayl 176 B1
Spring La. Colch 67 D4
Spring La. E A Gr 66 A4
Spring La. Gt Tot 116 B4
Spring La. Hat Pev 114 C1
Spring La. W Berg 48 C2
Spring La. Wiv 69 D1
Spring Meadow. Glems 2 A3
Spring Pond Cl. Gt Bad 140 C4
Spring Rd. Brigh 106 C4
Spring Rd. St O 108 A2
Spring Rd. Tipt 100 B2
Spring Rise. Chelm 140 B1
Spring Sedge Cl. Stanw 66 B4
Spring Way. Si Hed 15 F1
Springbank Ave. Lawf 35 D2
Springett's Hill. Lam 19 E1
Springfield. Hadl 188 B2
Springfield Cotts. Mald 132 A3
Springfield Dr. South 190 B2
Springfield Green. Sprin 127 F2
Springfield Park Ave. Chelm 127 E1
Springfield Park Hill. Chelm 127 E1
Springfield Park La. Chelm 127 F1
Springfield Park Par. Chelm 127 E1
Springfield Park Rd. Chelm 127 E1
Springfield Pl. Sprin 127 E3
Springfield Rd. Burn 170 A3
Springfield Rd. Canv 197 F2
Springfield Rd. Chelm 127 E2
Springfield Rd. Sprin 127 E2
Springfield Rd. Sud 7 F1
Springfield Rd. Wick 174 C4
Springfields. Basil 185 F2
Springfields. Brigh 106 C3
Springhill Cl. Gt Hor 70 C4
Springlands Way. Sud 7 F1
Springmead. Bl Not 77 E4
Springvalley La. Ard 51 E2
Springwater Cl. Rayl 189 E4
Springwater Gr. Rayl 189 E4
Springwater Rd. Rayl 189 E4
Springwood Ct. Brain 59 E2
Springwood Dr. Brain 59 E2
Spruce Ave. Colch 68 C4
Spruce Cl. W Mers 121 D4
Spruce Cl. With 98 A2
Sprundel Ave. Canv 197 E1
Spurgeon Cl. Si Hed 15 F1
Spurgeon Pl. Kelv 81 E1
Spurgeon St. Colch 68 B3
Square The. Colch 67 D2
Square The. Mald 132 A3
Square The. Till 149 F2
Squire St. S Woo F 165 F4
Squirrells Ct. Chelm 126 C3
Stabbings Ct. Burn 170 B2
Stable Cl. Colch 66 C3
Stable Ct. W Mers 121 F4
Stablecroft. Sprin 127 F4
Stablefield Rd. Walt 94 A4

Stadium Rd. South 191 D1
Stadium Way. Hadl 188 B4
Stafford Cl. South 190 A3
Stafford Cl. Walt 93 F3
Stafford Wlk. Canv 197 D3
Stagden Cross. Basil 185 F3
Stairs Rd. Gt Wak 193 F2
Stalin Rd. Colch 68 A2
Stallards Cres. Walt 93 F3
Stambourne Rd. Gt Y 8 B2
Stambourne Rd. Topp 14 A4
Stambridge Rd. Clact 109 E2
Stambridge Rd. Gt Stam 179 E1
Stammers Rd. Colch 49 F2
Standard Ave. Clact 124 B3
Standard Rd. Colch 68 B3
Standley Rd. Walt 76 B1
Stane Field. Mks T 64 C2
Stanes Rd. Brain 59 F3
Stanfield Cl. Stanw 66 C2
Stanfield Rd. South 191 D1
Stanford Rd. Canv 197 D2
Stanley Ave. Brigh 107 D4
Stanley Rd. Ashi 178 B4
Stanley Rd. Canv 197 E2
Stanley Rd. Clact 109 E1
Stanley Rd. Hals 25 E1
Stanley Rd. South 200 A4
Stanley Rd. Sud 12 C4
Stanley Rd. Thund 187 E3
Stanley Rd. Wiv 69 E1
Stanley Rise. Sprin 127 F2
Stanley Wood Ave. Sud 7 F1
Stanley Wooster Way. Colch 68 C4
Stanmore Cl. Clact 109 E3
Stanmore Rd. Wick 175 D3
Stanmore Way. St O 108 A2
Stannard Way. Sud 13 D3
Stansfield Rd. Thund 187 D4
Stansgate Rd. Steep 147 F3
Stanstead Rd. Hals 43 F4
Stansted Cl. Chelm 126 C1
Stansted Rd. Colch 68 A1
Stansted Way. Walt 94 A3
Stanway Cl. Glems 2 B3
Stanway Rd. S Ben 187 E3
Stanwell St. Colch 67 F3
Stanwyn Ave. Clact 109 F2
Stapleford End. Wick 175 D3
Staplegrove. South 201 E4
Staplers Heath. Gt Tot 116 A2
Star La. Gt Wak 192 C2
Starboard View. S Woo F 165 F3
Starling's Hill. Si Hed 24 C2
Station App. Basil 186 A2
Station App. Brain 60 A1
Station App. Canv 196 B3
Station App. Frin 93 F3
Station App. Hock 177 F3
Station App. Runw 174 B4
Station App. S Woo F 165 E4
Station App. South 200 A4
Station App. South 190 C2
Station Ave. Rayl 176 B2
Station Ave. Runw 174 B4
Station Ave. South 191 D2
Station Cres. Col N 155 F3
Station Cres. Rayl 176 B2
Station Hill. Bures 19 F1
Station La. Basil 186 A2
Station La. Harw 40 B2
Station Rd. Alres 88 A4
Station Rd. Alth 157 F1
Station Rd. Ard 51 F4
Station Rd. Brad 36 C1
Station Rd. Brain 59 F1
Station Rd. Brigh 106 C3
Station Rd. Burn 170 A2
Station Rd. Canv 197 F1
Station Rd. Cla 4 B4
Station Rd. Clact 109 F1
Station Rd. Col En 26 C1
Station Rd. Col N 156 A3
Station Rd. Ea Col 45 D4
Station Rd. Frat 89 D4
Station Rd. Gt Ben 89 F4
Station Rd. Harw 40 B2
Station Rd. Harw 40 C3
Station Rd. Hat Pev 113 F3
Station Rd. Hock 177 F3
Station Rd. Kelv 81 E2
Station Rd. L Mel 7 E3
Station Rd. Lawf 35 E3
Station Rd. Mald 132 A2
Station Rd. Mks T 65 D2
Station Rd. Rams 39 F3
Station Rd. Rayl 176 B2
Station Rd. Runw 163 E1
Station Rd. S Ben 196 B4
Station Rd. Si Hed 15 F1
Station Rd. Soum 159 E2
Station Rd. South 201 D4
Station Rd. South 199 E4
Station Rd. South 189 F1
Station Rd. South 189 F2
Station Rd. Sud 12 C4
Station Rd. Sud 12 C4
Station Rd. Th L S 91 F4
Station Rd. Thor 89 D3
Station Rd. Tipt 100 B2
Station Rd. Toll D 118 C3
Station Rd. Tolle 119 E1
Station Rd. Wa Col 46 B3
Station Rd. Wa Col 45 F4
Station Rd. Walt 93 D3
Station Rd. Wh Not 78 C1
Station Rd. Wic Bis 115 D2
Station Rd. With 98 A2
Station Rd. Wiv 87 D4
Station Rd. Wrab 37 F2
Station St. Walt 94 B4
Station Way. Basil 185 D3
Steam Mill Rd. Brad 54 A4
Steele Cl. Mks T 64 C2
Steeple Cl. Mald 132 B3
Steeple Heights. Thund 187 D3
Steeple Rd. Latch 157 E3
Steeple Rd. Soum 159 D3
Steeple Rd. St L 148 B2
Steeplefield. South 189 F3
Steeplehall. Basil 186 A3
Steerforth Cl. Chelm 126 B4
Steli Ave. Canv 196 C3
Stella Maris Cl. Canv 197 F2
Stepfield. With 98 A1
Stephan Cranfield Cl. Rowh 87 D4
Stephenson Rd. Brain 60 A1
Stephenson Rd. Clact 110 A4
Stephenson Rd. Colch 50 B3
Stephenson Rd. N Fam 167 D4
Stephenson Rd. South 189 E3
Stephenson Rd W. Clact 92 A1
Sterling Cl. Colch 66 C3
Stevens Cl. Canv 197 E2
Stevens Rd. With 97 F1
Stevens Wlk. Colch 68 C4
Stevenson Way. Wick 174 B3
Stewards Cl. Walt 93 F4
Stewart Rd. Chelm 140 A4
Steyning Ave. South 191 F1
Stile La. Rayl 176 B1
Stilemans. Wick 174 B4
Stiles The. Mald 132 C2
Stirling Ave. Hadl 189 D1
Stirling Pl. Basil 186 A4
Stirrup Cl. Sprin 127 F4
Stivvy's Rd. Woo Wa 130 B2
Stock Chase. Mald 132 A3
Stock Cl. South 190 C2
Stock Rd. South 190 C2
Stock Terr. Mald 132 A3
Stockhouse Cl. Toll K 101 D1
Stockhouse Rd. Lay M 101 D4
Stockwell. Colch 67 F4
Stockwood. Thund 188 A4
Stoke Ash Cl. Clact 109 D2
Stoke Rd. Cla 4 A3
Stoke Rd. Nay 20 A1
Stokefelde. Basil 186 A4
Stokes The. Walt 94 A4
Stone Green Rd. Gt Oak 55 F1
Stone La. Wrab 37 F3
Stone Path Dr. Hat Pev 113 F2
Stone Rd. Gt Bro 53 D1
Stonebridge Hill. Col En 44 C4
Stonebridge Wlk. Chelm 127 D1
Stonecrop. Colch 49 E1
Stonehall Dr. Lit Cla 91 E1
Stonehall La. Gt Oak 55 D1
Stoneham Ave. Clact 109 D2
Stoneham St. Cogg 62 C1
Stonehill Cl. South 189 F2
Stonehill Rd. South 189 F3
Stonehill Way. W Mers 121 D3
Stoneleighs. Thund 187 F3
Stoney Hills. Burn 170 B4
Stoney La. Brigh 107 D4
Stores La. Tipt 100 B3
Stornoway Rd. South 191 E1
Stour Cl. Glems 2 B1
Stour Cl. Harw 39 E1
Stour Gdns. Sud 13 D2
Stour Green. Cla 4 A3
Stour Rd. Harw 40 B3
Stour St. Cav 5 E4
Stour St. Mann 35 E2
Stour St. Sud 12 C4
Stour Vale. Cla 4 A3
Stourdale Cl. Lawf 35 D2
Stourside. Sho G 40 A4
Stourton Rd. With 97 F2
Stourview Ave. Mist 36 A2
Stourview Cl. Mist 36 A2
Stow Rd. Col N 155 E3
Stowe's La. Till 149 E2
Straight Rd. Box 31 F1
Straight Rd. Brad 36 B1
Straight Rd. Colch 66 C3
Straight Rd. Gt Ben 90 A2
Straight Way. Birch 84 A1
Stranger's Chr. Brigh 88 C1
Strangman Ave. S Ben 188 A2
Strasbourg Rd. Canv 197 E3
Stratford Pl. Walt 94 B4
Stratford Rd. Clact 110 B3
Stratford Rd. Ded 33 E3
Strathmore Rd. N Fam 167 D4
Straw La. Sud 12 C4
Strawberry Cl. Brain 60 A1
Strawberry La. Tipt 100 C2
Street The. Ard 51 F4
Street The. Ashe 3 E1
Street The. Brad 36 C1
Street The. Bradw 61 E2
Street The. Bul 11 F3
Street The. Chelm 140 A1
Street The. Cla 3 E2
Street The. Fee 81 F3
Street The. Gos 42 C4
Street The. Gt T 64 A4
Street The. Hat Pev 114 A2
Street The. Latch 157 D3
Street The. Lit Cla 91 E2
Street The. Mess 82 B1
Street The. Midd 12 C2
Street The. Peb 27 D4
Street The. Rams 39 D1
Street The. S Woo F 154 A2
Štreet The. Steep 147 F1
Street The. Stis 61 D3
Street The. Stow M 155 E2
Street The. T Gr 79 D3
Street The. Tend 72 C3
Street The. Terl 96 B2
Street The. Toll M 117 D3
Street The. Topp 14 A4
Street The. Virl 119 D4
Street The. Wa Col 46 B3
Street The. Walt 75 D1
Street The. Weel 72 C1
Street The. Wh Not 78 C1
Street The. Wic Bis 115 F3
Street The. Woo Wa 130 B1
Stretford Ct. Silv E 79 E2
Strickmere. Str S M 22 B1
Stroma Ave. Canv 196 C3
Stroma Gdns. South 201 E3
Stromburg Rd. Canv 196 C3
Stromness Pl. South 191 E1
Stromness Rd. South 191 E1
Strood Cl. W Mers 121 D4
Strood The. W Mers 104 B2
Strudwick Cl. Brain 59 F1
Strutt Cl. Hat Pev 114 A2
Stuart Cl. Canv 197 D2
Stuart Cl. Gt Bad 141 D4
Stuart Cl. Gt Wak 192 C2
Stuart Cl. South 191 D1
Stuart Rd. South 191 D1
Stuarts Way. Brain 60 A1
Stubbs Cl. Lawf 35 D2
Stubbs Cl. Walt 93 F4
Stubbs La. Brain 60 B1
Stublands. Basil 185 F3
Studd's La. Colch 49 E2
Stump La. Sprin 127 E2
Sturrick La. Gt Ben 89 E4
Sturrocks. Basil 185 F2
Sudbourne Ave. Clact 109 D2
Sudbrook Cl. Wick 174 B3
Sudbury Cl. Hawk 177 F2
Sudbury Hill. Ca Hed 15 F2
Sudbury Rd. Bul 11 F3
Sudbury Rd. Bures 19 F1
Sudbury Rd. Ca Hed 16 A2
Sudbury Rd. Canv 196 C3
Sudbury Rd. Gest 10 C1
Sudbury Rd. Hals 25 F2
Sudbury Rd. L Mel 7 E2
Sudbury Rd. Lit Map 17 E1
Sudbury Rd. Nay 20 B3
Sudbury Rd. S Han 163 D3
Sudeley Gdns. Hock 177 E3
Suffolk Ave. South 189 F2
Suffolk Ave. W Mers 121 E4
Suffolk Cl. Clact 110 C4
Suffolk Cl. Colch 50 A1
Suffolk Dr. Sprin 128 A2
Suffolk Knowle. Bures 19 F1
Suffolk Rd. Mald 131 F1
Suffolk Rd. Sud 12 C4
Suffolk Sq. Sud 12 C4
Suffolk St. Walt 94 B4
Suffolk Way. Canv 196 C2
Suffolk Wlk. Canv 196 C2
Sugar La. Si Hed 23 F4
Sugden Ave. Wick 174 A4
Sulleys Hill. High 22 A4
Sullivan Cl. Colch 68 C3
Summercourt Rd. South 199 F4
Summerdale. Alth 158 A2
Summerfields. Si Hed 15 F1
Summerhill. Alth 157 F2
Sumpters Way. South 190 C3
Sunbeam Ave. Clact 124 C3
Sundale Cl. Clact 110 C3
Sunflower Cl. Sprin 127 F3
Sunnedon. Basil 185 E3
Sunningdale. Canv 197 E2
Sunningdale Ave. South 190 A1
Sunningdale Fall. Hat Pev 114 A2
Sunningdale Rd. Chelm 126 C2
Sunningdale Way. Walt 93 F4
Sunny Point. Walt 76 B2
Sunny Rd. Hawk 177 F3
Sunnybank Cl. South 189 F3
Sunnyfield Gdns. Hock 177 D3
Sunnyfields Rd. Brain 42 B1
Sunnymede Cl. Thund 188 A3
Sunnyside. Brain 59 F2
Sunnyside Ave. Basil 186 B2
Sunnyside Rd. Ford 47 E3
Sunnyside Way. Lit Cla 91 E1
Sunnyway. St L 148 B4
Sunrise Ave. Chelm 127 D3
Surbiton Ave. South 200 B4
Surbiton Rd. South 191 E1
Surig Rd. Canv 197 D2
Surrey Ave. South 189 F2
Surrey La. Tipt 100 B2
Sussex Cl. Bore 128 C4
Sussex Cl. Canv 197 D3
Sussex Gdns. Clact 110 C3
Sussex Rd. Colch 67 E4
Sussex Way. Canv 197 D3
Sutcliffe Cl. Wick 174 B3
Sutherland Bvd. Hadl 189 D1
Sutor Cl. With 97 F1
Sutton Court Dr. Roch 190 C4
Sutton Mead. Sprin 128 A2
Sutton Park Ave. Colch 67 D2
Sutton Rd. Roch 190 C4
Sutton Rd. South 191 D1
Sutton Rd. Stobr 191 D3
Suttons Rd. Gt Wak 193 E1
Swale Rd. Thund 188 A3
Swallow Cl. Lay H 85 D3
Swallow Dale. Basil 185 E2
Swallow Dr. S Ben 187 E1
Swallow Field. Ea Col 45 D3
Swallow Path. Chelm 140 A2
Swallow Rd. Runw 163 E1
Swallowcliffe. South 192 B1
Swallowdale. Clact 109 F4
Swallowdale. Colch 68 B2
Swallow's Row. Gt Ben 72 A1
Swan Chase. Si Hed 24 C4
Swan Cl. Hat Pev 114 A2
Swan Dale. Clact 109 F4
Swan Gr. Wa Col 46 B3
Swan La. Runw 163 E1
Swan Mead. Basil 185 E2
Swan Pass. Colch 67 F4
Swan Rd. Beau 73 E3
Swan Side. Brain 59 F2
Swan St. Kelv 81 E2
Swan St. Si Hed 15 F1
Swan St. Wa Col 46 B2
Swan Yd. Cogg 63 D1
Swanage Rd. South 191 D1
Swanfield. L Mel 7 E4
Swans Green Cl. Thund 188 A3
Swanscomb Rd. Wa Col 45 F2
Swanstead. Basil 185 F2
Swaynes. Str S M 22 B1
Sweden Cl. Harw 39 F2
Sweet Briar Ave. S Ben 187 E1
Sweet Briar Rd. Stanw 66 B4
Sweetbriar Lodge. Canv 196 C2
Sweyne Ave. Hawk 178 A2
Sweyne Ave. South 190 C1
Sweyne Cl. Rayl 176 A2
Swift Ave. Clact 124 C3
Swift Cl. Brain 78 A4
Swinborne Ct. Basil 174 A1
Swinborne Rd. Basil 174 B1
Swinbourne Dr. Brain 59 E2
Swiss Ave. Chelm 127 D2
Sycamore Cl. Canv 196 C2
Sycamore Cl. With 98 A4
Sycamore Gr. Brain 59 E1
Sycamore Gr. South 191 D1
Sycamore Pl. Gt Ben 89 F4
Sycamore Rd. Colch 68 B4
Sycamore Rd. Mald 132 B3
Sycamore Rd. Sud 13 D4
Sycamore Way. Cane 168 B1
Sycamore Way. Catt 35 E4
Sycamore Way. Chelm 140 B3
Sycamore Way. Clact 109 E2
Sycamore Way. Walt 93 E3
Sycamores The. Basil 186 B3
Sydervelt Rd. Canv 197 D2
Sydner Cl. Gt Bad 141 D3
Sydney Rd. Hadl 189 D1
Sydney Rd. S Ben 187 E2
Sydney St. Brigh 106 C3
Sydney St. Colch 68 A1
Syers Field. Weth 23 D1
Sykes Mead. Rayl 176 B1
Sylvan Cl. Canv 197 D1
Sylvan Cl. Chelm 140 A3
Sylvan Way. Hadl 189 D2
Symons Ave. South 189 F4

Tabor Ave. Brain 59 F2
Tabor Cl. Brigh 106 C4
Tabor Rd. Colch 68 B4
Tabora Ave. Canv 196 C3
Tabors Ave. Gt Bad 140 C4
Tabor's Hill. Gt Bad 140 C4
Tabrum's La. Rett 165 D3
Tabrums The. 154 B1
Taffrail Gdns. S Woo F 165 F3
Tailors Way. South 190 C3
Takely End. Basil 185 D3
Takely Ride. Basil 185 D3
Talbot Ave. Clact 124 C3
Talbot Ave. Rayl 176 B2
Talbot Rd. Lit Cla 91 E2
Talbot Rd. Sud 7 F1
Talbot St. Harw 40 B3
Talcott Rd. Colch 68 A1
Talisman Cl. Tipt 100 B3
Talisman Wlk. Tipt 100 B3
Tall Trees. Colch 49 F2
Tallow Gate. S Woo F 165 F3
Tally Ho. Colch 50 A2
Tallyho Corner. Str S M 22 B1
Tamar Ave. With 97 F1
Tamar Rise. Sprin 127 E3
Tamarisk Way. Clact 124 C3
Tamarisk Way. Colch 68 C4
Tambour Cl. Gt T 64 B4
Tamworth Cha. Colch 68 A1
Tan La. Lit Cla 91 F2
Tangerine Cl. Colch 68 B3
Tangmere Cl. Wick 175 D3
Tankerville Dr. South 189 E1
Tanner Cl. Clact 109 D2
Tanners Way. S Woo F 165 E4
Tanswell Ave. Basil 186 A3
Tanswell Cl. Basil 186 A3
Tantelen Rd. Canv 196 C3
Tapley Rd. Chelm 126 C4
Tapsworth Cl. Clact 109 E3
Tapwoods. Colch 67 D4
Tara Cl. Colch 50 B1
Taranto Rd. Canv 197 E2
Tarragon Cl. Tipt 100 B2
Tasman Ct. Chelm 126 C3
Tattersal Gdns. Hadl 189 D1
Tattersall Way. Chelm 139 F4
Tattersalls Chase. Soum 159 F2
Taunton Dr. South 190 A2
Taunton Rd. Sprin 127 F3
Tavistock Rd. Sprin 127 F3
Tawney's Ride. Bures 29 D4
Taylor Ave. Chelm 126 C3
Taylor Ct. Colch 67 F4
Taylor Dr. Mann 35 E2
Taylor's Rd. Rowh 86 C4
Teak Wlk. With 98 A2
Teal Way. Kelv 81 E1
Tees Cl. With 97 F1
Tees Rd. Sprin 127 E3
Teign Dr. With 97 E1
Teigngrace. South 201 E4
Teignmouth Dr. Rayl 176 B3
Telese Ave. Canv 197 E2
Telford Rd. Brain 60 A1
Telford Rd. Clact 110 B4
Telford Way. Colch 50 B3
Temperance Yd. Ea Col 45 D3
Templars Cl. With 97 F2
Temple Cl. Hadl 188 C2
Temple Cl. Walt 94 A3
Temple Ct. Colch 50 B1
Temple La. Silv E 79 E2
Temple La. T Gr 79 E2
Temple Pattle. Catt 35 E4
Templewood Ct. Hadl 188 B2
Templewood Rd. Basil 186 A3
Templewood Rd. Colch 50 C1
Templewood Rd. Hadl 188 B2
Temptin Ave. Canv 197 F2
Tendring Ave. Rayl 176 A2
Tendring Rd. Tend 72 A4
Tendring Rd. Tend 54 C1
Tendring Rd. Th L S 73 E2
Tennyson Ave. South 191 D1
Tennyson Cl. Brain 77 F4
Tennyson Cl. Hadl 189 D1
Tennyson Dr. Basil 186 A3
Tennyson Rd. Chelm 126 C3
Tennyson Rd. Mald 145 D4
Tenpenny Hill. Alres 88 C3
Tenter Field. Str S M 22 B1
Tenterfield Rd. Mald 132 A1
Tenterfields. Basil 186 B4
Teramo Rd. Canv 197 E2
Terling. Basil 185 D3
Terling Cl. Colch 68 A1
Terling Hall Rd. Hat Pev 113 E3
Terling Rd. Hat Pev 113 F3
Terling Rd. With 97 E2
Terminal Cl. South 201 F4
Terminus Dr. Basil 186 A2
Termitts Chase. Hat Pev 113 F4
Terms Ave. Canv 197 D3
Tern Cl. Kelv 81 E2
Terndale. Clact 109 F3
Terni Rd. Canv 197 E2
Terrace Hall Chase. Gt Hor 49 E3
Terrace The. South 201 F3
Terra-Cotta Pl. Glems 2 C4
Tewkes Rd. Canv 197 E3
Tewkesbury Rd. Clact 109 F2
Tey Rd. Alah 64 C4
Tey Rd. Aldh 65 D4
Tey Rd. Cogg 63 D3
Tey Rd. Ea Col 45 E2
Tey Rd Cl. Ea Col 45 E3
Thackeray Cl. Brain 78 A4
Thackeray Row. Wick 174 B3
Thames Ave. Chelm 126 B2
Thames Cl. Brain 60 B1
Thames Cl. Hadl 189 D1
Thames Cl. Rayl 176 B1
Thames Dr. Hadl 189 D1
Thames Rd. Canv 196 C2
Thames Way. Burn 170 A3
Thameside Cres. Canv 196 C2
Thatchers Dr. Elmst M 69 F3
Thaxted Wlk. Colch 86 A4
Thear Cl. South 190 B2
Thelma Ave. Canv 197 D2
Thelsford Wlk. Colch 68 C4
Theobalds Rd. Hadl 189 E1
Thielen Rd. Canv 197 D2
Third Ave. Canv 196 C2
Third Ave. Chelm 127 D3
Third Ave. Clact 110 B2
Third Ave. Frin 93 F2
Third Ave. Glems 2 B3
Third Ave. Hals 26 A1
Third Ave. Harw 40 B2
Third Ave. Walt 76 B2
Third Ave. Wick 175 D3
Third Wlk. Canv 196 C2
Thirlmere Cl. Bl Not 77 E4
Thirlmere Rd. Thund 187 F4
Thirslet Dr. Mald 132 B2
Thirtle Cl. Clact 109 E3
Thisselt Rd. Canv 197 D2
Thistledown. Basil 185 E3
Thistledown. Pan 59 D4
Thistledown Ct. Basil 185 E3
Thistley Cl. Gold 133 F3
Thistley Cl. South 189 F2
Thistley Green Rd. Brain 60 A4
Thomas Bell Rd. Ea Col 45 D3
Thomas Dr. Canv 196 C3
Thomas Rd. Basil 186 C4
Thomas Rd. Clact 109 E2
Thomas St. Brigh 106 C3
Thomas Wakley Cl. Colch 49 F3
Thomasin Rd. Basil 174 B1
Thompson Ave. Canv 197 F2
Thompson Ave. Colch 66 C3
Thorington Ave. Hadl 188 B3
Thorington Rd. Rayl 177 D1
Thorin's Gate. S Woo F 165 E3
Thornberry Ave. Weel 72 C1
Thornborough Ave. S Woo F 165 F4

Thornbury Rd. Clact....109 F2
Thorndale. Thund....188 A4
Thorndon Cl. Clact....109 D2
Thorndon Park Cl. Hadl....189 E3
Thorndon Park Cres. Hadl....189 D3
Thorndon Park Dr. Hadl....189 D3
Thorne Rd. Kelv....81 D1
Thorney Bay Rd. Canv....197 D1
Thornford Gdns. South....190 C3
Thornhill. Purl....144 B1
Thornhill. South....189 F2
Thornhill Cl. Walt....93 F4
Thorns Way. Walt....94 A4
Thornwood. Colch....49 F2
Thornwood Cl. W Mers....121 E3
Thorolds. Basil....185 F2
Thoroughgood Rd. Clact....109 F2
Thorp Leas. Canv....197 D1
Thorpe Bay Gdns. South....201 D3
Thorpe Cl. Hawk....177 F2
Thorpe Espl. South....201 D3
Thorpe Hall Ave. South....201 D4
Thorpe Hall Cl. South....201 D4
Thorpe Park La. Th L S....92 B4
Thorpe Rd. Beau....74 A3
Thorpe Rd. Clact....109 F4
Thorpe Rd. Hawk....177 F2
Thorpe Rd. Th L S....92 C4
Thorpe Rd. Walt....92 C4
Thorpe Rd. Weel....73 D1
Thorpedene Ave. Hull....165 F1
Thorpedene Gdns. South....201 E3
Thorrington Cross. Basil....185 E3
Thorrington Rd. Gt Ben....89 E4
Thorrington Rd. Lit Cla....91 E2
Threadneedle St. Ded....33 F4
Three Crowns Rd. Colch....49 F1
Three Gates Cl. Hals....43 E4
Three Mile Hill. Chelm....139 E1
Thrift Wood. S Woo F....142 C1
Throwley Cl. Basil....186 B3
Thrushdale. Clact....109 F3
Thundersley Church Rd. Thund....187 F3
Thundersley Gr. Thund....187 F3
Thundersley Park Rd. S Ben....187 F2
Thurlow Dr. South....200 C4
Thurlston Cl. Colch....50 B1
Thurlstone. Thund....188 B3
Thurstable Cl. Tolle....119 F1
Thurstable Rd. Tolle....119 E1
Thurstable Way. Tolle....119 F1
Thurston Ave. South....191 F1
Thyme Mews. With....97 F2
Thyme Rd. Tipt....100 B3
Tiberius Gdns. With....114 C4
Tickfield Ave. South....190 C1
Tidings Hill. Hals....43 F4
Tidworth Ave. Runw....163 F1
Tighfield Wlk. S Woo F....165 E3
Tilburg Rd. Canv....197 D2
Tilbury Rd. Gt Y....9 D2
Tilbury Rd. Ridge....8 B4
Tile Barn La. Lawf....34 B1
Tile House Rd. Gt Hor....49 D4
Tilkey Rd. Cogg....62 C2
Tillingham Rd. Ashel....160 A4
Tillingham Rd. Soum....159 F3
Tillingham Rd. Till....149 E1
Tillingham Way. Rayl....176 A2
Tillwicks Cl. Ea Col....45 D4
Tilney Turn. Basil....185 F2
Timberlog Cl. Basil....185 F3
Timberlog La. Basil....185 F3
Timbermans View. Basil....185 F2
Timpsons La. Sprin....127 F2
Tindal Sq. Chelm....127 D1
Tindal St. Chelm....127 D1
Tinker St. Rams....56 B4
Tinker's La. Roch....178 C1
Tinkler Side. Basil....185 D3
Tinnocks La. St L....135 D1
Tintern Ave. South....190 B1
Tippersfield. S Ben....187 F2
Tippett Cl. Colch....68 C3
Tiptree Cl. South....189 F2
Tiptree Gr. Wick....174 B4
Tiptree Hall La. Tipt....100 A1
Tiptree Rd. Gt Brx....99 E1
Tiptree Rd. Lit Brx....115 F3
Titania Cl. Colch....68 C4
Tithe Cl. With....97 F2
Tithe The. Wick....174 A3
Tobruk Rd. Chelm....126 C3
Tobruk Rd. Colch....67 E2
Tofts Chase. Lit Bad....129 F3
Tog La. Gt Hor....31 D2
Toledo Cl. South....200 A4
Toledo Rd. South....200 A4
Tollesbury Cl. Wick....174 C3
Tollesbury Rd. Toll D....118 C1
Tollesbury Rd. Tolle....118 C1
Tolleshunt D'arcy Rd. Toll M....117 F2
Tollgate. Thund....188 B3
Tollgate Dr. Stanw....66 B4
Tollgate East. Stanw....66 B3
Tollgate Rd. Stanw....66 B3
Tollgate W. Stanw....66 B3
Tolliday Cl. Wiv....69 D1
Tom Tit La. Woo Mor....143 F4
Tonbridge Rd. Hock....177 F4
Tongres Rd. Canv....197 D2
Tony Webb Cl. Colch....50 B2
Took Dr. S Woo F....165 E3
Top Rd. Toll K....101 D1
Top Rd. Woo Wa....130 B1
Toppesfield Ave. Wick....174 B3
Toppesfield Rd. Gt Y....14 C4
Toppesfield Rd. Gt Y....15 D4
Torquay Cl. Rayl....176 B3
Torquay Dr. South....189 F1
Torquay Rd. Sprin....127 E3
Torrington. South....201 E4
Torrington Cl. Sprin....127 F3
Torsi Rd. Canv....197 E2
Torver Cl. Bl Not....77 E3
Totham Hill Green. Gt Tot....116 C3
Totlands Dr. Clact....110 A4
Totman Cl. Rayl....188 B4
Totman Cres. Rayl....188 B4
Totnes Wlk. Sprin....127 F3
Totteridge Cl. Clact....109 E3
Toucan Way. Basil....185 D2
Toucan Way. Clact....109 F3
Toulmin Rd. Hat Pev....114 A2
Tower Ave. Chelm....126 C2
Tower Court Mews. South....199 F4
Tower Cut. Brigh....106 C3
Tower Rd. Clact....109 F1
Tower Rd. Wiv....69 D1
Tower St. Brigh....106 C3
Towerfield Cl. South....201 F4
Towerfield Rd. South....201 F4
Towers Rd. Mald....132 B3
Town Croft. Chelm....127 D3
Town End Field. With....114 C4
Town Sq. Basil....185 D3
Townfield Rd. Roch....178 C1
Townfield St. Chelm....127 D2
Townfield Wlk. Gt Wak....192 C2
Towngate. Basil....185 D3
Townsend Rd. Tipt....100 B4
Towse Cl. Clact....109 E3
Traddles Ct. Chelm....126 C3
Trafalgar Rd. Clact....109 F1
Trafalgar Rd. Colch....66 C3
Trafalgar Rd. South....201 E4
Trafalgar Way. Brain....60 A2
Travers Way. Basil....186 A3
Tree Cl. Clact....109 F4
Treecot Dr. South....190 A2
Treelawn Dr. South....189 F2
Treelawn Gdns. South....189 F2
Trenchard Cres. Sprin....127 E4
Trenders Ave. Rayl....176 A4
Trenham Ave. Basil....186 B4
Trent Cl. Burn....170 A3
Trent Cl. Wick....174 B3
Trent Rd. Chelm....126 B3
Trent Rd. With....97 F1
Trevia Ave. Canv....197 E2
Trews Gdns. Kelv....81 E2
Trimley Cl. Basil....185 E4
Trimley Cl. Clact....109 D2
Trinder Way. Wick....174 A3
Trinity Ave. South....199 F4
Trinity Cl. Chelm....127 E2
Trinity Cl. Elmst M....69 E1
Trinity Cl. Mann....35 E2
Trinity Cl. Rayl....176 C1
Trinity Rd. Chelm....127 E1
Trinity Rd. Hals....25 E1
Trinity Rd. Mann....35 E2
Trinity Rd. Rayl....176 C1
Trinity Rd. South....191 E1
Trinity Row. S Woo F....165 F4
Trinity Sq. Colch....67 F4
Trinity Sq. S Woo F....165 F4
Trinity St. Colch....67 F4
Trinity St. Hals....25 F1
Trinity Wood Rd. Hock....178 A4
Triton Way. Thund....188 A3
Triumph Ave. Clact....124 C4
Trotters Field. Brain....60 A2
Trotwood Cl. Chelm....126 C4
Troubridge Cl. S Woo F....165 F4
Trunette Rd. Clact....109 E2
Trunnions The. Roch....178 C1
Trusses Rd. Brad o S....136 C2
Tryon Ct. Hals....25 E1
Tudor Cl. Brigh....106 C4
Tudor Cl. Clact....109 D1
Tudor Cl. Rayl....176 C1
Tudor Cl. Rayl....189 E4
Tudor Cl. Sud....7 F1
Tudor Cl. Thund....187 F3
Tudor Cl. Walt....76 B1
Tudor Cl. With....97 F1
Tudor Gdns. South....189 E2
Tudor Gdns. South....201 E3
Tudor Green. Clact....124 C4
Tudor Green. Sud....7 F1
Tudor Rd. Canv....196 B2
Tudor Rd. Rayl....189 E4
Tudor Rd. South....190 C1
Tudor Rd. Sud....7 F1
Tudor Way. Hawk....177 F2
Tudor Way. Wick....174 A4
Tudwick Rd. Tipt....100 C1
Tudwick Rd. Toll D....117 F3
Tudwick Rd. Toll M....117 F3
Tufnell Way. Colch....49 E1
Tugby Pl. Chelm....126 C3
Tulip Cl. Sprin....127 F4
Tulip Way. Clact....109 E2
Tulip Wlk. Colch....68 B4
Tumbler's Green. Stis....61 E4
Tunbridge Rd. South....190 C1
Tunstall Cl. Basil....186 B3
Tunstall Cl. St O....108 A3
Tupman Cl. Chelm....126 B3
Turkentine. Sud....13 E3
Turkey Cock La. E A Gr....65 F4
Turkey Oaks. Chelm....127 E2
Turner Ave. Lawf....35 D3
Turner Cl. South....201 F4
Turner Cl. Wiv....69 E1
Turner Rd. Colch....49 F2
Turnstone End. Colch....68 C4
Turpins Ave. Clact....110 B3
Turpins Cl. Clact....110 B3
Turpins La. Walt....93 F3
Turpins The. Basil....185 E4
Turstan Rd. With....114 C4
Tusser Cl. With....98 A4
Tusser Ct. Gt Bad....140 B4
Tusset Mews. Colch....66 C4
Tutors Way. S Woo F....165 F4
Twain Terr. Wick....174 B3
Tweed Cl. Hals....43 E4
Twining Rd. Colch....66 C2
Twitten La. Chelm....140 A1
Twitty Fee. Dan....143 D4
Twyford Ave.Gt Wak....193 D2
Twyzel Rd. Canv....197 E3
Tyburn Hill. Wa Col....46 A3
Tydeman Cl. Stanw....66 B2
Tye Green. Glems....2 A3
Tye Hill. Lawf....34 C2
Tye La. Elmst M....69 F2
Tye Rd. Elmst M....69 F4
Tye Rd The. Gt Ben....90 A4
Tye The. E Han....153 E4
Tyefields. Basil....186 B4
Tyehurst Cres. Colch....50 B1
Tyler Ave. Clact....109 D2
Tyler St. Rams....39 F3
Tylers Ave. South....200 A4
Tylers Cl. Chelm....140 A3
Tylers Ride. S Woo F....165 F4
Tylewood. S Ben....188 B1
Tylney Ave. Roch....178 C2
Tylneys Rd. Hals....26 A2
Tyms Way. Rayl....176 C2
Tyndale Cl. Hull....165 E2
Tyndale Dr. Clact....109 D1
Tyndales La. Dan....143 D3
Tyne Way. Chelm....126 B3
Tynedale Ct. Colch....50 A2
Tynedale Sq. Colch....50 A2
Tyrel Dr. South....200 A4
Tyrells. Hawk....177 E3
Tyrells Cl. Sprin....127 F2
Tyrells Way. Gt Bad....140 C4
Tyrone Rd. South....201 D4
Tyrrell Ct. Basil....186 B3
Tyrrell Rd. S Ben....187 D1
Tythe Barn Way. S Woo F....165 E4
Tythe Cl. Sprin....127 F4
Tythings The. Hals....43 E4

Ullswater Cl. Bl Not....77 E3
Ullswater Rd. Thund....187 F4
Ulster Ave. South....201 E3
Ulting Hall Rd. Ult....130 C4
Ulting La. Langf....130 C3
Ulting La. Ult....130 C3
Ulting Rd. Hat Pev....114 B1
Ulting Way. Wick....175 D4
Ulverston Rd. Ashi....167 E1
Una Rd. Basil....186 C3
Una Rd. Rams....39 F3
Undercliffe Gdns. South....198 C4
Underhill Rd. S Ben....187 F2
Underwood Squ. Hadl....189 E1
Union La. Roch....178 C1
Union Rd. Clact....125 D4
Unity Cl. Colch....68 A2
UNTAIN Ash Cl. Colch....50 B1
Upland Cres. W Mers....121 E4
Upland Dr. Colch....50 B1
Upland Rd. South....199 D4
Upland Rd. W Mers....121 E4
Uplands Cl. Hawk....177 F3
Uplands Cl. S Ben....187 D2
Uplands Cres. Sud....7 F1
Uplands Ct. Clact....109 E1
Uplands Dr. Sprin....127 E4
Uplands Park Rd. Rayl....176 B2
Uplands Rd. Clact....109 E1
Uplands Rd. Hawk....177 F3
Uplands Rd. S Ben....187 D2
Uplands Rd. Sud....7 F1
Upp Hall La. Gt T....64 B3
Upper Ave. Basil....186 C4
Upper Branston Rd. Clact....109 E2
Upper Bridge Rd. Chelm....127 D1
Upper Chapel St. Hals....25 F1
Upper Chase. Alth....157 F2
Upper Chase. Chelm....140 A4
Upper East St. Sud....12 C4
Upper Farm Rd. Ashe....8 B4
Upper Fenn Rd. Hals....26 A1
Upper Fourth Ave. Frin....93 F3
Upper Holt St. Ea Col....45 E3
Upper Lambricks. Rayl....176 C2
Upper Market Rd. Runw....174 B4
Upper Park Rd. Brigh....106 C4
Upper Park Rd. Clact....109 E2
Upper Park Rd. Wick....174 B2
Upper Rd. Sud....19 F4
Upper Roman Rd. Chelm....127 D1
Upper Second Ave. Frin....93 F3
Upper St. Glems....2 C4
Upper St. Str S M....22 B1
Upper Third Ave. Frin....93 F3
Upper Trinity Rd. Hals....25 F1
Upton Cl. W Berg....48 B2
Upway. Rayl....176 B2
Upway The. Basil....185 E4
Urmond Rd. Canv....197 D2
Uttons Ave. South....198 B4
Uxbridge Cl. Wick....174 C3

Vaagen Rd. Canv....197 D2
Vale Ave. South....191 D1
Vale Cl. Colch....50 C1
Vale End. Chelm....140 B2
Vale The. Basil....185 E2
Valentine Way. Silv E....79 E2
Valentines. Wick....174 B3
Valentines Dr. Colch....50 B1
Valfreda Way. Wiv....69 D1
Valkyrie Cl. Tolle....119 E1
Valkyrie Rd. South....199 E4
Vallance Cl. South....191 F2
Valletta Cl. Chelm....127 D2
Valley Bridge. Chelm....127 D3
Valley Cl. Stanw....66 C2
Valley Cres. W Berg....48 C2
Valley Rd. Brain....60 A2
Valley Rd. Clact....110 A3
Valley Rd. Colch....68 C2
Valley Rd. Harw....39 E1
Valley Rd. Sud....13 F4
Valley Rd. Wiv....87 E4
Valley View. Glems....2 C4
Valleybridge Rd. Clact....110 A3
Van Dieman's La. Chelm....140 B4
Van Dieman's Rd. Chelm....140 B4
Van Diemens Pass. Canv....197 F2
Van Dyck Rd. Colch....67 D3
Vanderbilt Ave. Rayl....176 B4
Vanderwalt Ave. Canv....197 E2
Vane La. Cogg....63 D1
Vanessa Dr. Wiv....69 D1
Vange Corner Dr. Corr....185 D1
Vange Hill Dr. Basil....185 F2
Vange Park Rd. Basil....185 D1
Vanguard Way. Brain....60 A2
Vanguard Way. South....201 F4
Vansittart St. Harw....40 B3
Varden Cl. Chelm....126 C3
Vardon Dr. Hadl....189 D2
Vaughan Ave. South....191 F1
Vaughan Cl. Roch....178 C3
Vaulx Rd. Canv....197 D2
Vauxhall Ave. Clact....124 C3
Vauxhall Dr. Brain....59 E1
Vellacotts. Chelm....127 D4
Venables Cl. Canv....197 E2
Venlo Rd. Canv....197 D3
Ventnor Dr. Clact....110 A4
Vera Rd. S Han....163 D1
Verlander Dr. Rayl....176 A4
Vermeer Cres. South....202 A4
Vermeer Ride. Sprin....127 F4
Vermont Cl. Basil....186 B4
Vermont Cl. Clact....110 A2
Vernon Ave. Rayl....176 A2
Vernon Rd. Hadl....189 E1
Vernon Rd. N Fam....156 A1
Vernon Way. Brain....60 B3
Vernons Rd. Wa Col....46 C3
Vernons Wlk. Basil....174 A1
Veronica Wlk. Colch....68 C4
Vesta Cl. Cogg....62 C1
Veyses End. Str S M....22 B1
Viaduct Rd. Chelm....127 D1
Viborg Gdns. Mald....144 C4
Vicarage Ave. Wh Not....78 C1
Vicarage Cl. Canv....196 B2
Vicarage Cres. Hat Pev....114 A2
Vicarage Gdns. Clact....109 F1
Vicarage Hill. S Ben....187 F1
Vicarage La. Gt Bad....140 C3
Vicarage La. Mund....145 F1
Vicarage La. Th L S....73 F1
Vicarage La. Till....149 F2
Vicarage La. Walt....94 B4
Vicarage Meadow. Hals....25 F1
Vicarage Meadow. Soum....159 E2
Vicarage Mews. Gt Bad....140 C3
Vicarage Rd. Bel S P....5 D1
Vicarage Rd. Chelm....140 A4
Vicars Orchard. Bul....11 F3
Viceroy Cl. Colch....68 A2
Vickers Rd. South....190 B3
Victor Ave. Basil....186 B3
Victor Dri. South....198 C4
Victor Gdns. Hawk....177 F3
Victor Rd. Colch....68 A3
Victoria Ave. Rayl....176 A2
Victoria Ave. South....190 C1
Victoria Ave. Walt....93 E4
Victoria Ave. Wick....174 B4
Victoria Chase. Colch....67 F4
Victoria Circus. South....200 A4
Victoria Cl. Wiv....69 D1
Victoria Cres. Chelm....127 D2
Victoria Cres. Lawf....35 E2
Victoria Cres. Wick....174 A4
Victoria Dr. Gt Wak....193 E1
Victoria Dr. South....189 F1
Victoria Espl. W Mers....121 F3
Victoria Pl. Brigh....106 C3
Victoria Pl. Colch....68 A3
Victoria Pl. Colch....67 F4
Victoria Rd. Basil....185 E1
Victoria Rd. Chelm....127 E2
Victoria Rd. Clact....110 A2
Victoria Rd. Col N....155 F3
Victoria Rd. Colch....67 E3
Victoria Rd. Mald....132 A1
Victoria Rd. Rayl....176 C2
Victoria Rd. S Woo F....165 E3
Victoria Rd. South....200 B4
Victoria Rd. South....198 C4
Victoria Rd. Walt....94 B4
Victoria Rd. Weel....91 D3
Victoria Rd S. Chelm....127 D1
Victoria St. Brain....60 A1
Victoria St. Harw....40 B2
Victory Rd. Clact....109 E2
Victory Rd. W Mers....121 D3
Viking Rd. Mald....131 F1
Viking Way. Clact....110 C3
Viking Way. Runw....163 E1
Vikings Way. Canv....196 B2
Villa Rd. S Ben....187 E2
Villa Rd. Stanw....66 B3
Village Cl. Walt....93 E4
Village Dr. Canv....196 C2
Village Gate. Sprin....128 A2
Village Hall Cl. Canv....196 B2
Village Way. Walt....93 E3
Villiers Pl. Bore....112 C1
Villiers Way. Thund....187 F3
Vince Cl. W Mers....121 E3
Vincent Cres. South....201 F4
Vincent Rd. Ashi....167 D1
Vine Dr. Wiv....69 E2
Vine Farm Rd. Wiv....69 E2
Vine Rd. Tipt....100 B3
Vinesse Rd. Lit Hor....30 B2
Vineway The. Harw....40 A2
Vineyard Gate. Colch....67 F3
Vineyard St. Colch....67 F3
Vineyards The. Gt Bad....140 C4
Vint Cres. Colch....67 E3
Vintners The. South....190 C3
Viola Wlk. Colch....68 C4
Violet Cl. Sprin....127 F4
Virgil Rd. With....97 F3
Virginia Cl. Clact....109 D1
Virginia Cl. Thund....187 D4
Virley Cl. Mald....132 B2
Vista Ave. Walt....75 E1
Vista Rd. Clact....110 A2
Vista Rd. Wick....174 C4
Vivian Ct. Walt....94 B4
Volwycke Ave. Mald....144 C4
Voorburg Ave. Canv....197 E2
Voorne Ave. Canv....197 E1
Voysey Gdns. Basil....174 A1

Waalwyk Dr. Canv....197 E2
Waarden Rd. Canv....197 D2
Waarem Ave. Canv....197 D2
Waddesdon Rd. Harw....40 B2
Wade Rd. Clact....110 A4
Wade Reach. Walt....94 A4
Wadham Park Ave. Hock....177 D4
Wagtail Dr. Mald....132 B3
Wakefield Cl. Colch....68 A4
Wakelin Way. With....98 A1
Wakering Ave. South....202 A4
Wakering Rd. Gt Wak....193 D1
Wakering Rd. South....192 A1
Wakes St. Wa Col....46 B3
Wakescolne. Wick....175 D3
Wakeshall La. Bel S P....9 E4
Waldegrave. Basil....185 D2
Waldegrave Cl. Lawf....35 D2
Waldegrave Way. Lawf....35 E2
Waldegraves La. W Mers....122 A4
Walden Cl. Gt Tot....116 A2
Walden House Rd. Gt Tot....116 A2
Walden Way. Walt....94 A3
Waldingfield Rd. Sud....12 C4
Waldringfield. Basil....185 D4
Walford Cl. Cogg....63 D2
Walford Pl. Sprin....127 F1
Walford Way. Cogg....63 D2
Walk The. E A Gr....66 A4
Walk The. Hull....165 E2
Walker Dr. Hadl....189 D1
Walkers Cl. Sprin....127 E4
Walkey Way. South....202 A4
Walkways. Canv....196 C3
Wall La. Wrab....37 F3
Wall Rd. Canv....197 F2
Wall St. St O....123 E3
Wallace Cl. Hull....165 E2
Wallace Cres. Chelm....140 B4
Wallace St. South....201 F4
Wallace's La. Bore....112 C2
Wallasea Gdns. Sprin....127 F3
Wallflower Ct. Sprin....127 F3
Wallis Ave. South....190 C1
Wallis Ct. Colch....66 C2
Walls The. Mist....35 F3
Walnut Ct. Hock....177 F4
Walnut Dr. With....98 A2
Walnut Gr. Brain....59 F1
Walnut Tree La. Sud....12 B4
Walnut Tree Way. Colch....67 D2
Walnut Tree Way. Tipt....100 B4
Walnut Way. Brigh....106 C4
Walnut Way. Clact....109 E1
Walpole Wlk. Rayl....177 D1
Walsingham Cl. Sud....13 E3
Walsingham Rd. Colch....67 F3
Walsingham Rd. South....191 D1
Walter Way. Silv E....79 E2
Walters Cl. Chelm....140 B2
Walters Cl. South....189 F3
Walters Yd. Colch....67 F4
Waltham Cres. South....191 D2
Waltham Glen. Chelm....140 B4
Waltham Rd. Bore....112 C3
Waltham Rd. Rayl....176 A2
Waltham Rd. Terl....95 F1
Waltham Way. Frin....94 A3
Walthams. Basil....186 A4
Walthams Pl. Basil....186 A4
Walton Rd. Clact....110 A2
Walton Rd. South....200 C3
Walton Rd. Th L S....74 B1
Walton Rd. Walt....94 A4
Walton Rd. Walt....93 E4
Wambrook. South....192 B1
Wamburg Rd. Canv....197 F2
Wansfell Gdns. South....200 C4
Wantz Chase. Mald....132 A1
Wantz Haven. Mald....132 A1

Wantz Rd. Mald 132 A1
Warburton Ave. Si Hed 24 B4
Warde Chase. Walt 94 A4
Wargrave Rd. Clact 109 E2
Warham Rd. Harw 39 F1
Warley Way. Frin 94 A3
Warner Dr. Brain 59 E2
Warners Gdns. South 190 C3
Warnham Cl. Clact 109 D3
Warren Chase. Thund 188 A2
Warren Cl. Rayl 188 B4
Warren Dr. Wick 175 D4
Warren La. Stanw 66 B2
Warren La. Writ 126 B2
Warren Rd. Brain 60 B1
Warren Rd. Hadl 189 D2
Warren Rd. Hals 25 E1
Warren Rd. S Han 163 E4
Warrens The. Walt 93 F3
Warrenside. Brain 78 A4
Warrior Sq E. South 200 A4
Warrior Sq N. South 200 A4
Warrior Square Rd. South 201 F3
Warwick Cl. Canv 197 D3
Warwick Cl. Mald 132 A1
Warwick Cl. Rayl 176 C1
Warwick Cl. Thund 187 E4
Warwick Cres. Clact 109 F2
Warwick Cres. Mald 132 A1
Warwick Dr. Mald 132 A1
Warwick Dr. Roch 190 C4
Warwick Gdns. Rayl 176 C1
Warwick Green. Rayl 177 D1
Warwick Rd. Clact 109 F2
Warwick Rd. Rayl 176 C1
Warwick Rd. Rayl 189 D4
Warwick Rd. South 200 C3
Warwick Sq. Chelm 126 C2
Wash La. Clact 109 E1
Wash La. Gold 133 D4
Wash La. Lit Tot 133 D4
Washford Gdns. Clact 109 E1
Washington Cl. Mald 131 F1
Washington Rd. Mald 131 F1
Wat Tyler Way. Basil 186 A1
Wat Tyler Wlk. Colch 67 F4
Watchouse Rd. Chelm 140 B2
Water La. Bures 19 F1
Water La. Cav 1 B1
Water La. Colch 67 E4
Water La. Lit Hor 30 C4
Water La. Nay 20 C4
Water La. Peb 27 D4
Water La. Stis 61 E3
Waterdene. Canv 196 C3
Waterford Rd. South 201 E3
Waterhale. South 192 A1
Waterhouse La. Ard 52 B3
Waterhouse La. Chelm 126 C1
Waterhouse St. Chelm 126 C1
Waterloo La. Chelm 127 E1
Waterloo Rd. South 201 E4
Watermill Rd. Fee 81 F2
Waterside. Brigh 106 C3
Waterside Rd. Brad o S 136 C2
Waterside Rd. Pag Ch 181 D3
Waterville Rd. Basil 186 A2
Waterworks Dr. Clact 109 D3
Waterworks Rd. Tolle 119 E1
Watery La. Bradw 62 A1
Watery La. Rayl 165 E1
Watkins Way. South 192 C1
Watlington Rd. S Ben 187 D1
Watson Cl. South 201 E4
Watson Rd. Clact 109 F2
Watt's La. Roch 178 C1
Watts Rd. Colch 67 D1
Wavell Ave. Colch 67 E2
Wavell Cl. Sprin 127 E4
Waveney Dr. Sprin 127 E3
Waverley Cres. Runw 163 E2
Waverley Rd. Thund 187 E3
Wavertree Rd. S Ben 187 D2
Wavring Ave. Walt 93 F4
Waxwell Rd. Hull 165 F1
Wayfarer Gdns. Burn 170 A3
Wayletts. Hadl 189 D3
Wayside. Dan 142 C4
Weald The. Canv 196 C2
Wear Dr. Sprin 127 E3
Weare Gifford. South 201 E4
Weaverdale. South 192 C1
Weavers. Basil 185 F2
Weavers Cl. Colch 66 C3
Weaver's Ct. Sud 12 C4
Weavers Dr. Glems 2 A2
Weavers La. Sud 12 C4
Weavers Row. Hals 25 F1
Weaversfield. Silv E 79 E3
Webster Cl. Si Hed 24 B4
Websters Way. Rayl 176 B1
Wedgewood Way. Hawk 178 B3
Weel Rd. Canv 197 E1
Weeley BY-PASS Rd. Weel 72 C1
Weeley Rd. Gt Ben 89 F4
Weeley Rd. Lit Cla 91 E2
Weggs Willow. Colch 68 B4
Weight Rd. Chelm 127 E1
Weir Farm Rd. Rayl 188 B4
Weir Gdns. Rayl 176 B1
Weir La. Rowh 86 B4
Weir Pond Rd. Roch 178 C1
Welbeck Ave. Rayl 176 A2
Welbeck Cl. Hawk 177 F3
Welbeck Rd. Canv 197 D2
Welch Cl. South 191 F1
Well Field. Writ 126 A1
Well La. Birch 83 D3
Well La. Chelm 140 A1
Well La. Cla 4 A4
Well La. Copf 83 D3
Well La. Dan 142 B4
Well Side. Mks T 64 C2
Well St. Brigh 106 C4
Well Terr. Mald 132 A3
Welland Ave. Chelm 126 B3
Welland Rd. Burn 170 A3
Wellands. Wic Bis 115 F3
Wellands Cl. Wic Bis 115 E3
Weller Gr. Chelm 126 C4
Wellesley Rd. Clact 109 F2
Wellesley Rd. Colch 67 F3
Wellfield Way. Walt 93 E3
Wellington Ave. Hull 176 B4
Wellington Ave. South 190 A1
Wellington Cl. Brain 60 B2
Wellington Cl. Chelm 126 B3
Wellington Rd. Ashi 166 C1
Wellington Rd. Harw 40 C3
Wellington Rd. Mald 131 F1
Wellington Rd. Rayl 176 C2
Wellington St. Brigh 106 C3
Wellington St. Colch 67 F3
Wellmeads. Chelm 140 A4
Wells Ave. South 190 B3
Wells Ct. Sprin 127 E3
Wells Gdns. Basil 185 F4
Wells Hall Rd. Sud 13 E2
Wells Rd. Colch 68 A4
Well's St. Chelm 127 D2
Wellsfield. Rayl 176 C2
Wellstead Gdns. South 190 A2
Wellstye Green. Basil 185 F4
Welshwood Park Rd. Colch 50 C1
Wembley Ave. May 158 A4
Wendene. Basil 185 F2
Wendon Cl. Hawk 178 B2
Wenham Dr. South 190 C1
Wenlock Rd. Weel 90 C3
Wensley Rd. Thund 188 A3
Wents Cl. Gt Ben 71 F1
Wentworth Cl. Hat Pev 114 A2
Wentworth Cres. Brain 59 F3
Wentworth Meadows. Mald 131 F1
Wentworth Rd. South 191 D2
Wesley Ave. Colch 68 B4
Wesley Rd. South 200 A4
Wessem Rd. Canv 197 D3
West Ave. Chelm 126 C3
West Ave. Clact 109 F1
West Ave. Hull 165 E2
West Ave. May 146 C1
West Beech Ave. Wick 174 C4
West Beech Cl. Wick 174 C4
West Belvedere. Dan 142 C4
West Bowers Rd. Woo Wa 130 B2
West Chase. 131 F2
West Cres. Canv 196 C2
West Dock Rd. Rams 39 F3
West End Rd. Tipt 100 A2
West Green. S Ben 187 D3
West Hanningfield Rd. Sand 140 C1
West Hanningfield Rd. W Han 140 C1
West House Estate. Soum 159 E2
West Lawn. Chelm 140 B1
West Ley. Burn 170 B3
West Lodge Rd. Colch 67 E3
West Point Pl. Canv 196 B2
West Rd. Clact 125 E4
West Rd. Hals 25 F1
West Rd. South 190 C1
West Rd. South 201 E3
West Sq. Chelm 127 D1
West Sq. Mald 131 F2
West St. Cogg 62 C1
West St. Colch 67 F3
West St. Harw 40 C3
West St. Roch 178 C1
West St. Rowh 86 C4
West St. South 190 C1
West St. South 198 C4
West St. Tolle 119 E1
West St. Walt 94 B4
West St. Wiv 87 D4
West Station Yd. Mald 131 F1
West Stockwell St. Colch 67 F4
West Thorpe. Basil 185 E3
West View Cl. Colch 50 A2
West View Dr. Rayl 176 A1
West Wood Cl. Thund 188 B2
Westborough Rd. South 190 B1
Westbourne Cl. Hadl 188 B3
Westbourne Cl. Hock 178 A4
Westbourne Gr. Gt Bad 140 B4
Westbourne Gr. South 190 A2
Westbourne Gr. South 190 A2
Westbury. Hawk 178 B2
Westbury Rd. Frin 93 D3
Westbury Rd. South 191 E1
Westcliff Ave. South 199 F4
Westcliff Dr. South 189 E1
Westcliff Par. South 199 F4
Westcliff Park Dr. South 190 B1
Westcliffe Gdns. Canv 197 F1
Westerdale. Sprin 127 E4
Westergreen Meadow. Brain 59 F1
Westerings. Purl 144 B1
Westerings. S Woo F 142 C1
Westerings The. Gt Bad 140 C3
Westerings The. Hawk 177 F3
Westerland Ave. Canv 197 E2
Westerlings The. T Gr 78 C3
Western Apps. South 190 A4
Western Cl. Silv E 79 F2
Western Espl. Canv 197 D1
Western Espl. South 199 F4
Western La. Silv E 79 F2
Western Prom. Brigh 106 B3
Western Prom. St O 106 C2
Western Rd. Brigh 106 C3
Western Rd. Burn 170 B2
Western Rd. Hadl 188 C3
Western Rd. Hadl 189 D1
Western Rd. Rayl 176 A1
Western Rd. Silv E 79 F2
Western's End. Catt 35 E4
Westfield. Cla 4 A3
Westfield Ave. Chelm 127 D2
Westfield Cl. Wick 174 C4
Westfield Dri. Cogg 63 D2
Westgate. South 201 F3
Westlake Ave. Basil 186 C3
Westlake Cres. Wiv 69 D1
Westleigh Ave. South 189 E1
Westman Rd. Canv 197 F2
Westmarch. S Woo F 165 E3
Westminster Dr. Hock 177 E3
Westminster Dr. South 190 A1
Westminster Gdns. Brain 60 A2
Westmorland Cl. Mist 36 A2
Weston Rd. Colch 68 A2
Weston Rd. South 200 A4
Westridge Rd. Clact 110 A3
Westropps. L Mel 7 E3
Westwater. S Ben 187 D2
Westway. Chelm 139 F4
Westway. Colch 67 F4
Westway. S Woo F 165 E4
Westwood Dr. W Mers 121 F3
Westwood Gdns. Hadl 188 B3
Westwood Rd. Canv 197 D2
Wet La. Box 31 F3
Wethersfield Cl. Rayl 176 A2
Wethersfield Rd. Colch 86 A4
Wethersfield Rd. Si Hed 15 E1
Wethersfield Way. Wick 175 D3
Weybourne Cl. South 191 D2
Weybourne Gdns. South 191 D2
Weybridge Wlk. South 192 C1
Weymouth Cl. Clact 125 E4
Weymouth Rd. Sprin 127 F3
Whaley Rd. Colch 68 B4
Wharf La. Bures 28 C4
Wharf Rd. Chelm 127 E1
Wharf Rd. Mald 132 C2
Wharfe Cl. With 97 F1
Wheatfield Rd. Stanw 66 B3
Wheatfield Way. Chelm 126 C2
Wheatlands. Elmst M 69 F3
Wheatley Ave. Brain 60 B2
Wheatley Cl. Hawk 178 B2
Wheaton Rd. With 98 A1
Wheatsheaf Cl. Wrab 37 F3
Wheatsheaf La. Wrab 37 E2
Wheeler Cl. Colch 68 C3
Wheelwrights The. South 191 D3
Whernside Ave. Canv 197 E3
Whist Ave. Runw 163 F1
Whistler Rise. South 202 A4
Whitby Rd. Soum 159 D2
White Cotts. Fair 95 E2
White Elm Rd. S Woo F 143 D1
White Hall Rd. Gt Wak 193 D2
White Hart La. Hock 177 F3
White Hart La. Sprin 127 F4
White Hart La. W Berg 48 C3
White Horse Ave. Hals 43 E4
White Horse La. Mald 131 F1
White Horse La. With 97 F2
White House Chase. Rayl 176 C1
White House Rd. South 189 F3
White Lodge Cres. Th L S 74 B1
White Trees Ct. S Woo F 165 D3
Whitefriars Cres. South 199 E4
Whitefriars Way. Colch 67 D3
Whitegate Rd. Brigh 107 D3
Whitegate Rd. South 200 A4
Whitehall Cl. Colch 68 B2
Whitehall Ct. With 98 A1
Whitehall La. Th L S 73 E1
Whitehall Rd. Colch 68 B2
Whitehouse Cres. Gt Bad 140 B4
Whitehouse Hill. Virl 119 D4
Whitehouse La. Bel S P 5 D1
Whitehouse La. W Berg 48 B2
Whitehouse Meadows. South 190 A3
Whitehouse Rd. S Woo F 165 E4
Whitelands Cl. Runw 163 F1
Whiteshott. Basil 185 D2
Whitethorn Gdns. Chelm 140 B4
Whiteways. Canv 197 E1
Whiteways. South 189 F3
Whiteways Ct. With 97 F2
Whitewell Rd. Colch 67 F3
Whitlands. Glems 2 A3
Whitmore Ct. Basil 185 F4
Whitmore Way. Basil 185 E4
Whittaker Way. W Mers 121 D4
Whittingham Ave. South 191 F1
Whytewaters. Basil 185 F2
Whyverne Cl. Sprin 127 F3
Wick Beech Ave. Wick 174 C4
Wick Chase. South 191 F1
Wick Cres. Wick 174 C3
Wick Dr. Wick 174 B4
Wick Dr. Wick 174 C3
Wick La. Ard 51 D4
Wick La. Fing 87 E2
Wick La. Harw 40 A1
Wick La. St O 90 B2
Wick La. Wick 174 C4
Wick Rd. Burn 170 B2
Wick Rd. Colch 68 B1
Wick Rd. Gt Ben 90 A3
Wick Rd. High 21 E1
Wick Rd. Langh 32 C2
Wickfield Ash. Chelm 126 B3
Wickford Ave. Basil 186 A3
Wickford Rd. S Woo F 165 D4
Wickford Rd. South 199 F4
Wickham Hall La. Wic Bis 115 E2
Wickham Pl. Basil 185 E3
Wickham Rd. Colch 67 E3
Wickham Rd. With 114 C4
Wickham's Chase. S Woo F 143 E1
Wicklow Ave. Chelm 126 B3
Wickmead Cl. South 191 F1
Wicks Cl. Brain 59 E2
Widford Chase. Chelm 139 F4
Widford Cl. Chelm 139 F4
Widford Gr. Chelm 139 F4
Widford Park Pl. Chelm 139 F4
Widford Rd. Chelm 139 F4
Widgeon Pl. Kelv 81 E1
Widgeons. Basil 186 B3
Wigboro Wick La. St O 107 F1
Wigborough Rd. Lay H 84 C1
Wigborough Rd. Peld 103 E2
Wignall St. Lawf 34 C2
Wilbye Cl. Colch 67 D2
Wilkin Ct. Colch 67 D2
Wilkinsons Mead. Sprin 128 A2
Willett Rd. Colch 67 D2
William Boys Cl. Colch 68 B4
William Cl. Wiv 69 E2
William Dr. Clact 109 E1
William Rd. Basil 186 C3
William's Wlk. Colch 67 F4
Willingale Ave. Rayl 176 A2
Willingale Way. South 192 A1
Willingham Way. Colch 68 C4
Willmott Rd. South 190 B3
Willoughby Ave. W Mers 121 E3
Willoughby Dr. Sprin 127 F1
Willoughby's La. Brain 60 B4
Willow Ave. Walt 93 E3
Willow Cl. Brigh 106 B3
Willow Cl. Burn 170 A3
Willow Cl. Canv 196 C2
Willow Cl. Hock 177 F3
Willow Cl. Rayl 176 B2
Willow Cl. South 189 F3
Willow Cres. Hat Pev 114 A2
Willow Dene. Si Hed 15 E1
Willow Dr. Rayl 176 B2
Willow Gr. S Woo F 154 A1
Willow Hall La. Wix 55 E4
Willow Meadows. Si Hed 24 C4
Willow Rise. With 98 A3
Willow Tree Way. Ea Col 45 D3
Willow Way. Clact 125 D4
Willow Way. Harw 39 F1
Willow Wlk. Cane 168 B1
Willow Wlk. Hadl 188 B2
Willow Wlk. Hock 177 F3
Willow Wlk. Tipt 100 B4
Willow Wlk. Weel 90 C4
Willowbank. Chelm 140 A2
Willowdale Centre. Runw 174 B4
Willows The. Basil 186 B3
Willows The. Bore 128 C4
Willows The. Colch 68 A2
Willows The. S Ben 187 D2
Willows The. South 192 A1
Wilmslowe. Canv 197 F3
Wilrich Ave. Canv 197 E2
Wilsner. Basil 186 B4
Wilson Cl. Wiv 69 D1
Wilson Marriage Rd. Colch 50 B1
Wilson Rd. South 199 F4
Wilson's La. Mks T 64 C2
Wimarc Cres. Rayl 176 A2
Wimborne Rd. South 191 D1
Wimbourne Gdns. Walt 93 F4
Wimbush Ct. Basil 186 A4
Wimbush End. Basil 186 A3
Wimbush Mews. Basil 186 A4
Wimhurst Cl. Hock 177 F4
Wimpole Rd. Colch 68 A3
Winbrook Cl. Rayl 188 C4
Winbrook Rd. Rayl 188 C4
Winchcombe Cl. South 189 F2
Winchelsea Dr. Gt Bad 140 C4
Winchelsea Pl. Brigh 106 C4
Winchester Cl. South 189 F4
Winchester Dr. Rayl 176 A3
Winchester Rd. Colch 68 A3
Winchester Rd. Frin 94 A3
Wincoat Cl. S Ben 187 E2
Wincoat Dr. S Ben 187 E2
Windermere Ave. Hull 165 E1
Windermere Dr. Bl Not 77 E3
Windermere Rd. Clact 110 B3
Windermere Rd. South 200 B4
Windermere Rd. Sud 13 D4
Windermere Rd. Thund 187 F4
Windham Rd. Sud 13 D4
Windmill Fields. Cogg 62 C2
Windmill Gdns. Brain 60 A4
Windmill Park. Clact 109 F3
Windmill Rd. Brad 36 B1
Windmill Rd. Hals 25 E1
Windmill Row. Glems 2 B3
Windmill View. Tipt 100 B3
Windrush Dr. Sprin 127 E3
Windsor Ave. Clact 109 E2
Windsor Cl. Canv 197 D2
Windsor Cl. Colch 68 A1
Windsor Ct. Brigh 106 C3
Windsor Gdns. Brain 60 A2
Windsor Gdns. Hawk 178 A2
Windsor Gdns. Runw 163 E1
Windsor Gdns. Thund 188 B2
Windsor Pl. Sud 13 D4
Windsor Rd. Basil 186 C4
Windsor Rd. South 190 C1
Windsor Rd. W Mers 121 E4
Windsor Way. Chelm 126 C1
Windsor Way. Rayl 176 C1
Windward Way. S Woo F 165 F3
Winfields. Basil 186 B4
Wingate Cl. Brain 59 F2
Winifred Rd. Basil 186 A3
Winnock Rd. Colch 68 A3
Winsford Gdns. South 190 A2
Winsley Rd. Colch 68 A3
Winsley Sq. Colch 68 A2
Winston Ave. Colch 67 D2
Winston Ave. Tipt 100 C3
Winston Way. Hals 26 A2
Winstree. Basil 186 A4
Winstree Cl. Lay H 84 C3
Winstree Rd. Burn 170 A3
Winstree Rd. Stanw 66 B3
Winterbournes. Walt 94 A4
Winter's Hill. Lay B 83 F1
Winter's Rd. Lay B 83 F1
Winterswyk Ave. Canv 197 F2
Winton Ave. South 199 F4
Winton Ave. Wick 174 A4
Wisdoms Green. Cogg 63 D2
Wistaria Pl. Clact 109 E3
Wiston Rd. Bures 30 B4
Witch Elm. Harw 39 F1
Witch La. Cogg 63 D4
Witchards. Basil 185 D3
Witham Lodge. With 114 C4
Witham Rd. Bl Not 78 A3
Witham Rd. Langf 131 E4
Witham Rd. Lit Brx 115 F3
Witham Rd. T Gr 79 D2
Witham Rd. Terl 96 C1
Witham Rd. Toll M 117 E3
Witham Rd. Wh Not 78 A3
Withrick Wlk. St O 108 A3
Witney Rd. Burn 170 B2
Wittem Rd. Canv 197 D3
Witterings The. Canv 197 D3
Witting Cl. Clact 109 E3
Witton Wood Rd. Frin 93 F3
Wivenhoe Cross. Wiv 69 E1
Wivenhoe Park Cnr. Colch 69 D3
Wivenhoe Rd. Alres 88 A4
Wivenhoe Rd. Ard 51 E1
Wix By-Pass. Lit Ben 53 F1
Wix Rd. Brad 36 C1
Wix Rd. Gt Oak 56 A2
Wix Rd. Gt Oak 55 E2
Wix Rd. Rams 38 C1
Woburn Ave. Walt 93 E4
Wolfe Ave. Colch 68 A3
Wollards Gdns. L Mel 7 E4
Wollaston Cres. Basil 174 B1
Wollaston Way. Basil 174 B1
Wolseley Ave. Clact 124 C3
Wolseley Rd. Chelm 127 D1
Wolton Rd. Colch 67 D1
Wolves Hall La. Tend 54 C1
Wonston Rd. Soum 159 E2
Wood Ave. Hock 177 F4
Wood Dale. Gt Bad 140 C3
Wood End. Hawk 177 E3
Wood Farm Cl. South 189 E2
Wood Field End. Lay H 85 D3
Wood La. E A Gr 47 F1
Wood La. Mald 132 A3
Wood Rd. Mald 132 A3
Wood St. Chelm 140 A4
Woodberry Cl. Hadl 189 E3
Woodberry Rd. Wick 175 D3
Woodberry Way. Walt 94 A4
Woodbridge Gr. Clact 109 D2
Woodburn Cl. Thund 188 A2
Woodbury Cres. South 190 C3
Woodcock Cl. Colch 68 C3
Woodcote Cres. Basil 186 B3
Woodcote Rd. South 190 A1
Woodcote Way. Thund 187 D4
Woodcotes. South 192 C1
Woodcroft Cl. Thund 188 B2
Woodcutters Ave. South 189 E3
Woodend Cl. Thund 188 B2
Woodfield. Wick 174 B3
Woodfield Cl. Walt 94 A4
Woodfield Cotts. Mald 132 B3
Woodfield Dr. W Mers 121 D4
Woodfield Gdns. South 198 C4
Woodfield Park Dr. South 190 A1
Woodfield Rd. Brain 60 A2
Woodfield Rd. Hadl 189 D2
Woodfield Rd. South 199 D4
Woodfield Way. Hat Pev 114 A2
Woodford Cl. Clact 109 F4
Woodgrange Cl. South 200 C4
Woodhall Cl. Sud 7 F1
Woodhall Rd. Chelm 127 D4
Woodhall Rd. Sud 7 F1
Woodham Dr. Hat Pev 114 A2
Woodham Halt. S Woo F 165 E4
Woodham Mortimer Rd. Woo Wa 143 F4
Woodham Park Dr. S Ben 187 E1
Woodham Rd. Rett 164 C3
Woodham Rd. S Ben 187 D1
Woodham Rd. S Woo F 155 D2
Woodham Rd. Stow M 155 D2
Woodhays. Basil 186 B4
Woodhill Rd. Dan 142 A3
Woodhill Rd. Sand 142 A3
Woodhurst Rd. Canv 196 C2
Woodland Cl. Hadl 188 C2
Woodland Cl. Hat Pev 114 A3
Woodland Rd. Chelm 127 D2
Woodland Rise. Weel 72 C1
Woodland Way. Gos 42 C4
Woodland Way. Wiv 69 D1

Woodlands. Alth	158 A2	Woodside. Lit Bad	129 F1
Woodlands. Brain	60 B2	Woodside. Mund	145 E1
Woodlands. Colch	50 C1	Woodside. Walt	94 A3
Woodlands. Gt Oak	56 A1	Woodside Ave. Thund	187 E4
Woodlands Ave. Rayl	188 C4	Woodside Chase. Hawk	177 F2
Woodlands Cl. Basil	185 F2	Woodside Cl. Colch	50 C1
Woodlands Cl. Clact	110 A4	Woodside Cl. South	189 D3
Woodlands Cl. Hock	177 E3	Woodside Rd. Ashi	198 C3
Woodlands Cl. Rayl	188 B4	Woodside Rd. Hock	177 D3
Woodlands Dr. Basil	185 E1	Woodside View. Thund	187 E4
Woodlands Park. Hadl	189 D2	Woodstock. W Mers	121 E4
Woodlands Rd. Hock	177 E3	Woodstock Cres. Hock	177 E3
Woodlands Rd. Wick	174 B4	Woodview Cl. Colch	50 B2
Woodlands The. Brigh	106 C4	Woodview Dr. Gt Le	95 D4
Woodlands The. South	201 F4	Woodville Cl. Hawk	178 B2
Woodleigh Ave. South	189 E2	Woodville Rd. Canv	197 E2
Woodlow. Thund	188 A3	Woodyards. Brad o S	136 C2
Woodpecker Cl. Colch	68 C4	Woolards Way. S Woo F	165 E4
Woodpond Ave. Hock	177 F3	Woolner Rd. Clact	109 E3
Woodroffe Cl. Sprin	128 A2	Woolpack. South	201 E4
Woodrolfe Farm La. Tolle	119 F1	Woolpack La. Brain	59 F3
Woodrolfe Park. Tolle	119 F1	Woolwich Rd. Clact	109 E3
Woodrolfe Rd. Tolle	119 F1	Worcester Cl. Brain	60 A1
Woodrow Way. Colch	68 C4	Worcester Cl. Colch	68 A4
Woodrows La. Clact	109 D3	Worcester Cl. Steep	147 D1
Woodrush End. Colch	66 A3	Worcester Cres. Alres	88 A4
Woods The. Hadl	188 C2	Worcester Ct. Gt Bad	141 D3
Woodside. Hadl	189 D3	Worcester Dr. Rayl	176 C1

Worcester Rd. Burn	170 B3	Wyburns Ave. Rayl	188 C4
Wordsworth Ave. Mald	145 D4	Wyburns Ave E. Rayl	188 C4
Wordsworth Cl. South	191 D1	Wych Elm. Colch	68 A2
Wordsworth Ct. Chelm	127 D3	Wycke Hill. Mald	144 B4
Wordsworth Rd. Brain	59 F4	Wycke La. Tolle	119 F1
Wordsworth Rd. Colch	66 C3	Wycliffe Cl. Colch	49 F1
Workhouse Hill. Box	31 F2	Wycombe Ave. Thund	187 D3
Workhouse La. S Woo F	154 A1	Wyedale Dr. Colch	66 C3
Workhouse Rd. Lit Hor	30 B1	Wykeham Rd. Writ	126 A1
Worlds End La. Fee	81 E2	Wykes Green. Basil	185 E4
Worthington Way. Colch	66 C2	Wyncolls Rd. Colch	50 B3
Wrabness Rd. Rams	38 B2	Wyndham Cl. Colch	86 A4
Wrabness Rd. Rams	39 D1	Wyndham Cres. Clact	110 A3
Wren Ave. Rayl	189 E4	Wynters. Basil	185 D2
Wren Ave. South	189 E4	Wythams. Basil	186 B4
Wren Cl. Gt Ben	71 E1	Wythefield. Basil	186 A3
Wren Cl. South	189 E4		
Wren Cl. Thund	187 D3	Yale Mews. Colch	50 A2
Wrendale. Clact	109 F3	Yamburg Rd. Canv	197 E2
Wright's Ave. T Gr	78 C3	Yare Ave. With	97 E1
Writtle Rd. Chelm	139 F4	Yarnacott. South	201 E4
Writtle Wlk. Basil	185 F4	Yarwood Rd. Chelm	127 F1
Wroxham Cl. Colch	67 D3	Yeldham Lock. Sprin	128 A1
Wroxham Cl. South	189 D3	Yeldham Rd. Ca Hed	15 E2
Wulvesford. With	114 B4	Yeldham Rd. Si Hed	15 E2
Wyatts Dr. South	200 C4	Yeovil Chase. South	190 A2
Wyatts La. Sud	19 E4	Yew Cl. With	98 A3
Wyburn Rd. Hadl	188 C3	Yew Tree Cl. Colch	68 C4

Yew Tree Cl. Hat Pev	114 A3		
Yew Tree Gdns. Chelm	140 B3		
Yew Way. Clact	124 C3		
Yorick Ave. W Mers	121 E3		
Yorick Rd. W Mers	121 E3		
York Cl. Rayl	189 D4		
York Cl. Sud	12 C4		
York Gdns. Brain	60 A2		
York Pl. Colch	68 A4		
York Rd. Ashi	178 B4		
York Rd. Brigh	106 C3		
York Rd. Burn	170 B2		
York Rd. Chelm	140 A4		
York Rd. Clact	110 C3		
York Rd. Ea Col	45 D3		
York Rd. Rayl	189 D4		
York Rd. South	200 A4		
York Rd. Sud	12 C4		
York Rise. Rayl	189 D4		
York St. Mann	35 E2		
Young Cl. Clact	109 E3		
Young Cl. South	190 A4		
Ypres Rd. Colch	67 F2		
Zandi Rd. Canv	197 E1		
Zealand Dr. Canv	197 F2		
Zelham Dr. Canv	197 F2		
Zider Pass. Canv	197 F2		